Years of Renewal
European History
1470–1600

Edited by
JOHN LOTHERINGTON

Contributors
KATHERINE BRICE, DAVID GROSSEL,
JOHN LOTHERINGTON, ADRIAN ROBERTS,
CAROLINE STEINSBERG

Hodder & Stoughton
A MEMBER OF THE HODDER HEADLINE GROUP

Orders: please contact Bookpoint Ltd, 39 Milton Park, Abingdon, Oxon OX14 4TD.
Telephone: (+44) 01235 400414, Fax: (+44) 01235 400454. Lines are open from 9.00–6.00,
Monday to Saturday, with a 24-hour message answering service. Email address:
orders@bookpoint.co.uk

British Library Cataloguing in Publication Data
A catalogue record for this title is available from The British Library

ISBN 0 340 72128 6

First published 1999
Impression number   10 9 8 7 6 5 4 3 2 1
Year   2004 2003 2002 2001 2000 1999

The front cover shows *Pope Leo X* by Raphael, reproduced courtesy of AKG, London.

Produced by Gray Publishing, Tunbridge Wells, Kent.
Printed in Great Britain for Hodder & Stoughton Educational, a division of Hodder
Headline Plc, 338 Euston Road, London NW1 3BH by J.W. Arrowsmith Ltd, Bristol.

Contents

↬ LIST OF TABLES ↫

⤙ LIST OF MAPS ⤚

⤙ LIST OF DIAGRAMS ⤚

⇜ LIST OF ILLUSTRATIONS ⇝

∾ LIST OF PROFILES ∾

⤳ LIST OF ANALYSES ⤶

⤳ ACKNOWLEDGEMENTS ⤳

The Publisher would like to thank the following for permission to reproduce material in this book:

Edward Arnold, for extracts from *The Invocavit Sermons* by Martin Luther, transl. E.G. Rupp and B. Drewery (1970) used on page 162 and 'The Ecclesiastical Ordinances', 'The Institutes of the Christian Religion' and 'A letter to Gaspard de Coligny' by John Calvin in *John Calvin* by G.R. Potter and M. Greengrass (1983) used on pages 347, 349, 350 and 351 Batsford, for extracts from *The Sack of Rome* by E.R. Chamberin (1979) used on page 248; Ernest Benn, for an extract from *The Revolt of the Netherlands* (2nd edition) by P. Geyl (1958) used on page 432; Basil Blackwell, for an extract from *Spain under the Hapsburgs*, vol. 1 (2nd edition) by John Lynch (1981) used on page 405; Boston, for extracts from *The Character of Philip II. The Problem of Moral Judgements in History*, edited by J.C. Rule and J.J. TePaske (1983) used on pages 417 and 419; European Studies Review, for extracts from *A New Governor for the Netherlands: the Appointment of Don Luis de Requesens* by A.W. Lovett used on page 433 and an extract from *The Governorship of Requesens. A Spanish View* by A.W. Lovett used on page 434; Cambridge University Press, for extracts from *Renaissance Warrior and Patron: The Reign of Francis I* by R.J. Knecht (1994) used on page 285 and 'The Consilium de Emendenda Ecclesia' and the 'Draft Charter of the Society of Jesus' in *Renaissance and Reformation 1300–1648*, edited by G.R. Elton (1968) used on pages 360 and 389; Cape, for an extract from *The Age of Catherine de Medici* by Sir John Neale (1943) used on page 492; Hambledon, for an extract from *Princes, Politics and Religion* by N.M. Sutherland (1984) used on page 494; Harper, for an extract from *The Autobiography of St Ignatius Loyola* transl. J.F. O'Callaghan (1974) used on pages 387 and 388; Harvester Press, for extracts from *The Emperor Charles V* by K. Brandi (1939) used on pages 241 and 251; Michael Joseph, for an extract from *Catherine de Medici* by H.R. Williamson (1973) used on page 494; Longman, for extracts from 'The Peace of Madrid repudiated' in *French Renaissance Monarchy: Francis I and Henry II* by Charles de Lannoy, transl. R.J. Knecht (1984) used on pages 274 and 275, *The Commentaries of Blaise de Monluc*, edited by Ian Roy (1971) used on pages 464 and 465; Macmillan, for extracts from *The Golden Century of Spain 1501–1621* by R.T. Davies (1937) used on pages 419 and 420, *Philip II* by G. Parker (1998) used on page 419 and *A History of France, 1460–1560: The Emergence of a Nation State* by David Potter (1995) used on page 285; North Missouri State University Press, for extracts from *Politics, Religion and Diplomacy in Early Modern Europe: Essays in Honour of Lamar Jensen*, edited by M.R. Thorp and A.J. Slavin (1994) used on pages 396 and 397; Oxford University Press, for an extract from *The European Dynastic States* by R. Bonney (1991) used on pages 455 and 456; Princeton, for extracts from *The Sack of Rome 1527* by Andre Chastel (1983) used on pages 247 and 248; Penguin, for extracts from *The Prince* by Machiavelli, transl. George Bull (1961) used on pages 127 and 128, *The Courtier* by Castiglione, transl. George Bull (1967) used on page 133, and *Praise of Folly* by Erasmus, transl. Betty Radice (1971) used on page 136; Routledge & Kegan Paul, for an extract from *The Night Battles* by Carlo Ginzburg, transl. John and Anne Tedeschi (1983) used on pages 203 and 204; Charles Scribner & Sons, for an extract from 'Oratio de dignitate hominis' by Pico della Mirandola in *Latin Writings of the Italian Humanists*, edited by F.A. Gragg (1927) used on page 124; Thames and Hudson, for an extract from *Philip II of Spain* by Peter Pierson (1975) used on page 392; University of Wisconsin, for an extract from *Representative Institutions in France, 1421–1559* by J. Russell Major (1960) used on page 285; Allen Unwin, for an extract from *Catherine de Medici* by J. Heritier, transl. Charlotte Haldane (1963) used on page 492; Variorum, for an extract from *War and Society in Hapsburg Spain* by I.A.A. Thompson (1992) used on page 454; W.W. Norton & Company, for an extract from *The Spanish Armada* by C. Martin and G. Parker (1988) used on page 453.

The publishers would like to thank the following for permission to reproduce copyright illustrations from this book:

Accademia Venice/Arlinari Art resources, New York page 21; AKG pages 2, 141, 142, 144, 183, 186, 196, 208, 217, 264, 278, 331, 397, 451, 462, 466; BBC Hulton picture library page 246; Bibliothéque de Protentantisme, Paris page 478; Bibliothéque Publique et Universitaire, Geneva page 330; Biblioteca Publica Episcopal, Barcelona/Bridgeman Art Gallery page 386; Bridgeman Art Gallery pages 29, 143, 252; British Museum, London page 182; Cornaro Chapel, S. Maria della vittoria, Rome/Scala page 375; Germanischen

Nationalmuseum, Nuremberg page 69; Graphischen Sammlung, Albertina, Wien page 497; Hereford Cathedral, Hereford page 2; Hispanic Society of America, New York pages 420, 428; Hospital Tavera, Toledo page 397; Koninklijk Museum voor Schöne Kunsten, Antwerp page 213; Kupferstichkabinett, Staatliche Museen Preußischer Kulturesitz, Berlin page 184; Kunsthistoriches Museum, Vienna page 196, 217, 466; Musée Conde/Giraudon Art Resource page 29; Musée de Louvre pages 278, 302, 303; National Gallery of Ireland, Dublin page 439; National Gallery, London pages 74, 140; National Maritime Museum, Greenwich pages 444; Palazzo Barberini, Rome page 143; Palazzo Medici-Riccardi, Florence page 141; Prado, Madrid pages 144, 393; Science Museum, London page 90; Stadt- und Universitätsbibliothek, Berne page 185; Uffizi, Scala page 252; the Vatican, Rome page 142; Victoria and Albert museum, London page 502; Wittenberg, Lutherhalle page 186.

Preface: How to use this book

1 ↜ GENERAL

This book has been fully revised to incorporate recent research and to meet the latest demands of the examiners. It is designed to give those starting out on the study of sixteenth-century Europe an accessible and thought-provoking introduction to the subject. It is also a workbook containing documents and exercises. As well as providing information, it is structured to help students acquire an awareness and a method for putting the limited time they have for further researches to the best use.

2 ↜ KEY ISSUES

The key issues you will find in the margins are intended to test understanding and to stimulate debate. Written answers to the questions would be an effective way of taking structured notes.

3 ↜ DOCUMENTS

In some chapters you will find documents interspersed within the narrative, along with questions in the margin. These are not just illustrations or separate exercises, but an important part of the narrative. They fill a gap in the text; by answering the questions on the documents you will in effect be writing that part of the text for yourself. It is important to note down the facts and quotations you draw from these documents to ensure that your notes are complete.

4 ↜ BIBLIOGRAPHIES

At the end of each chapter there is a short bibliography, one of general use for the whole period being found at the end of Chapter 1. The books included are those most suitable for students, rather than the more daunting specialist works, and they should be readily available in libraries or paperback editions. There is a brief comment on the usefulness of each book and a starring system:

** Consult if at all possible
* Recommended.

One problem with any reading list is that it becomes almost instantly out of date. One way to keep up with the latest views is to read a journal regularly, keeping an eye on the reviews section. History Today and History Review are the most accessible and attract contributions from leading historians. For the more adventurous, Past and Present has a record of publishing articles with stimulating new approaches.

5 ↪ STRUCTURED AND ESSAY QUESTIONS

There are a number of structured and essay questions at the end of each chapter, to show the type of approach possible. It is a good idea to read through these questions before you work on the chapter, to help you to pick out what is most important in the text.

6 ↪ EXERCISES

There are a variety of exercises following each chapter to help in developing your ideas and in organising the material. Two types of exercise recur frequently:

● Advice on answering structured questions and essays, which will help you to develop the skills necessary to avoid just 'telling the story' and to construct a clear and convincing argument instead.
● Documentary exercises which go further than the use of documents in the text. Several sources will be used and, as well as comprehension and the detection of bias, comparisons will be made and conclusions compiled to give an overall picture. This should at least give a taste of the creativity and the problems of the practising historian.

Introduction: Renaissance Europe

1

To understand ourselves, we have to understand our past. Only those hooked on a superficial idea of 'relevance' can believe that the identity of Europe may be explained merely through the history of the last few decades. The fifteenth and sixteenth centuries saw some of the key developments that were to shape not only modern Europe, but, through European exploration and colonialism, the rest of the world. Rulers (generally called princes) fought ever more expensive wars which had to be organised and paid for, so the state developed in fits and starts as bureaucracies grew and tax officials multiplied. Established European ideas were shaken by cultural change – the Renaissance – and by religious struggle – the Reformation, movements that still reverberate today. These challenging new ideas circulated through Europe at unprecedented speed, the invention of printing in the 1450s being the greatest technological breakthrough in communications until telecommunications and the internet. Meanwhile, beneath all this, slower and less obvious but equally vital changes were underway in economies and societies; for instance, there was population growth, which meant less land and food to go round but stimulated economic growth. We have to be careful when looking for the origins of today's Europe not to see simple similarities to ourselves, or steady 'progress' towards the modern age. Much of the sixteenth century was a strange and remote world; it was, after all, the century that first saw the appearance of witch hunts, which were to recur until the 1700s. In looking at the fifteenth and sixteenth centuries we are exploring our own identity but also looking at a 'world we have lost'.

1 ⌐ THE SHAPE OF EUROPE AROUND 1500

Erasmus, the most revered scholar of the early sixteenth century, anticipated a golden age of peace and unity in Europe. He hoped that all Christians would join in a crusade to retake Jerusalem, still thought of as the centre of the world, as in the mediaeval *Mappa mundi* (Picture 1). He was also a leading figure in what we now call the Renaissance – the revival of the eloquence and the knowledge of the great cultures of ancient Rome and Greece, which he saw as essential to the renewal of

PICTURE 1
Mappa mundi

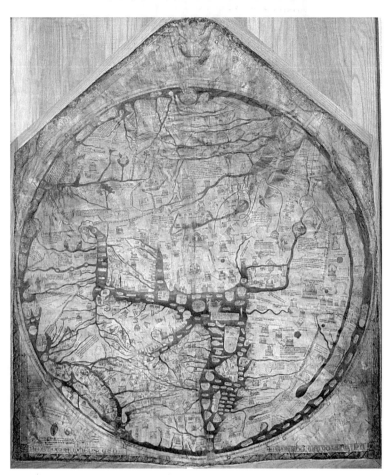

schism division in the
Church

heretics Christians who
deviated from what
were thought to be the
essential beliefs of the
Church

European civilisation. In harmony with this renewal he wanted to see the Church reformed, but saw no threat to its unity under the leadership of the Popes. Indeed, the Church seemed at its most stable in centuries. For sixty years, from the 1370s to the 1430s, the Church had been split in a 'Great **Schism**' between two Popes, one in Avignon and one in Rome, and even a third at one unlucky stage. Also, the Church had been threatened by various groups of **heretics** who had rebelled against its teaching and authority, such as the Hussites in Bohemia (now the Czech Republic) and the Lollards in England. In the early 1500s all that was in the past and the Church appeared at its most secure, if in need of an overhaul. To reform the Church, Erasmus hoped that a unifying lead would be taken by one of the princes of Europe, most suitably the Holy Roman Emperor, whose power base was confined at first to south-eastern Germany (not in Rome), but who nevertheless held the highest status in Europe by virtue of his imperial title. All these hopes for peaceful renewal were to crash during the course of the sixteenth century, as European princes chose to fight each other more intensively than ever before and as religious struggles

MAP 1
Europe in 1490

following the Reformation turned into savage international and civil wars. A divided Europe emerged, which set a pattern lasting until at least the late twentieth century.

Looking at the map of the states of Europe in the sixteenth century, Portugal and France seem very close to their modern borders, although this can be misleading as the lines on the map should indicate fuzzy border zones rather than the clearly marked frontiers familiar to us. These were not the clearly delineated, united **nation states** looked for by nineteenth-century historians when they studied the period. (Such historians thought that nation states were the highest point of political evolution and that they originated around 1500.) *Spain*, for instance, was unified by 1479 as a result of the marriage ten years earlier between Ferdinand of Aragon and Isabella of Castile, but this had by no means been inevitable. The chances of war and dynastic politics almost united Castile with *Portugal* instead. In any case, Castile and the three regions of Aragon retained completely separate domestic governments; only

nation state a state incorporating one nation or ethnic group

See Chapter 2 and map on page 32

their foreign policy was united. *France* had expanded towards its present borders under Louis XI (1461–83) but this was not an inevitable move towards the 'natural frontiers' of a nation state – his successor Charles VIII quite happily gave away the annexed French provinces of Roussillon and Cerdagne to buy off Ferdinand of Aragon before he invaded Italy in 1494 to pursue his dynastic claim on Naples. **Dynastic rights** mattered much more than national borders. Across the channel, *England* and *Scotland* were looking very much like separate nation states, but two centuries later they were to merge into the United Kingdom – how far that can be seen as a British nation state or a state embracing several nations is again a matter for debate.

dynastic rights a prince's inherited claim on a territory

Italy was a mosaic of small states. In the south there was the feudal kingdom of *Naples* with *the Papal states* in the centre. To the north were city states, the major ones being *Florence, Milan* and *Venice*. As the focus of much of Europe's trade and wealth, the cultural leader of Europe in the Renaissance, the centre of the Church in Rome, and criss-crossed throughout by unresolved dynastic disputes, Italy was irresistible to foreign princes yearning for glory, territory and intent on staying one step ahead of any rivals. First the French invaded in 1494 and then the Spanish – the Italian Wars were to bring chaos to the peninsula for over sixty years. The consequence was domination first by the Spanish and then by other foreign powers up until the nineteenth century. Machiavelli had laid as much stress on the need for Italian patriotic unity to combat the foreign invader as on his well-known advice to princes to cultivate cunning and ruthlessness; but no one took his words to heart.

See Chapters 2, 3 and 8

Across the Alps lay the *Holy Roman Empire*, which included modern Germany, the Czech Republic (then Bohemia) and Switzerland. Switzerland, however, a loose federation of German, French and Italian-speaking cantons, had long since established its independence under medieval leaders such as William Tell, and it maintained its independence and financial viability by hiring out its fighting men as mercenaries to surrounding powers. The Empire was almost synonymous with Germany during our period. There was growing consciousness of a German nation, pioneered around 1500 by writers in Alsace – a region now firmly part of France, more as a result of the fortunes of war than of national destiny. But like Machiavelli, these writers were not much heeded. Germany was even more fragmented into principalities than Italy, its city states known as the imperial cities, and its tiny lordships ruled over by imperial knights who sometimes supplemented the revenues of their micro-states by becoming the robber barons beloved of legend. Despite his status as first in rank in Europe, the Emperor was elected, the Electors being three leading German archbishops and four **secular** princes of whom he had to take notice. He commanded no central government, being able to raise taxes only by agreement, and it took a truly dire emergency for that to happen. There was a German parliament, the Imperial Diet, but it was more likely to list its grievances against the Emperor, and even more so the Pope, than to initiate any decisive action. There had been attempts

secular of the world rather than religious

at reform. In 1495 an Imperial Supreme Court, the *Reichskammerger-icht*, was established, followed in 1500 by an Imperial Governing Council, the *Reichsregiment*. However, there was a conflict between the desire for greater imperial unity and the fear of increasing the power of the Emperor, so the reforms failed.

It was the Habsburg dynasty that controlled the largest territories in the Holy Roman Empire from its main base in Austria. This impressed the Electors sufficiently to for them to elect a Habsburg as Emperor at each election from 1440 until the abolition of the Empire in 1806. In 1519, when Charles V became Emperor, he had at his disposal the inherited territories of the Netherlands, Spain and part of Italy, as well as his German lands. But the more power that Charles had, the more fear and enmity he inspired from all sides. He failed to crush the Lutheran Reformation in Germany, which further divided the Holy Roman Empire, and the larger imperial dream of leading a united Europe faded. As a consequence, Germany's identity and its role in Europe continued to be a source of conflict and uncertainty until recent times.

Other countries, such as the Netherlands or Savoy, which was sandwiched between France and Italy, were dominated by neighbouring powers. The Netherlands had been at the core of the Duchy of Burgundy which had been a great power in its own right, but following the death of the last duke, Charles the Bold, at a battle near Nancy in 1477, it had been dismembered. The Netherlands passed by marriage to the Habsburgs, while France took the province of ducal Burgundy to the south. The Burgundian inheritance remained a point of contention between the French kings and the Habsburgs for much of the period. The Revolt of the Netherlands against Philip II, who had inherited them from his father Charles V along with Spain, was at the centre of European conflict in the later sixteenth century.

To the north, the ruler with the greatest authority was the king of Denmark who, since the Union of Kalmar in 1397, had ruled *Norway* and *Sweden* as well. However, the Swedes in practice handled their own affairs and Gustavus Vasa founded an independent dynasty there in 1523. The new king of Sweden built up his authority steadily, culminating at the Diet of Västerås in 1544, where the Crown was declared hereditary in the Vasa family.

Countries to the north and east of Europe seem remote at this time from the mainstream of history. There is some justification for this view, for instance in a much lower population density. Even in 1600, at the end of our period, a population density of forty-four per square kilometre in Italy or thirty-four in France compares with fourteen in Poland and just 1.5 in Sweden and its neighbours. Given the slow communications – villages could be several days' journey from one another – there was little chance for advanced economic or political organisation. Indeed, large stretches of this region of Europe were in what might be described as a prehistoric stage. Many of the forests, mountains and river systems were only just being explored and

See Chapter 8

KEY ISSUE

What limited the powers of the Holy Roman Empire?

See Chapter 14

TABLE 1
European population estimates (in millions)

	1500	1600
European total	60	85
Holy Roman Empire	12	20
France	10	15
Italy	10	13
Spain	7.5	10
England	3.5	5.5

Q

Where in Europe was the fastest population growth?

colonised by small groups moving amidst the vast but silent drift of population from Germany towards Siberia.

The lands around the Baltic were colonial in the economic sense as well as in terms of the movement of populations. They could provide the raw materials that the more developed economies of the south needed. Becoming an economic colony was particularly the fate of *Poland–Lithuania*, the largest country to border on the Baltic, with its reserves of timber and grain. The **constitution** of that kingdom was much like that of the Holy Roman Empire – the king was elected and any attempt at centralised power could be defeated in the Sejm, the Polish parliament. With the king often preoccupied by his far-off borders with Muscovy (which became Russia) and the Ottoman Empire (the heartland of which was Turkey), Polish nobles were in effect answerable only to themselves.

constitution the fundamental law of a state determining who has authority

However, historians have been far too ready to write off central and east European history, as Norman Davies has powerfully argued in his *Europe: A History*. There was a view earlier this century that these were countries of which we knew little and that seemed to be confirmed by the descent of the Iron Curtain following the Second World War. Since 1989 Europe has defined itself anew, and central and eastern European history no longer seems so remote. More notice is taken, for instance, of the fact that when the Renaissance spread north from Italy in the late 1400s, scholars, texts and the printing press were assembled in Cracow in Poland faster than in London. Further to the south, Buda was home to the flourishing court of King Mathias Corvinus of *Hungary* (1458–90), who assembled one of the great libraries of Europe and was a renowned patron of the arts. He was a great soldier and consolidated what he had won in battle with careful administration and attention to justice. Following his death the kingdom was to collapse under pressure from the Turks (Buda fell after the Battle of Mohacs in 1526), but Hungary was not suddenly to become cut off from the rest of Europe. It was still one of the first countries outside Germany where the Reformation took root. Meanwhile the Habsburgs took over the rump of the kingdom, along with Bohemia (now the Czech Republic).

Far more genuinely remote, with virtually no trade or other links with the countries of western Europe, was *Muscovy* and its grand dukes. Russia had been carved up in the thirteenth century by the Tatar hordes invading from the east. Their leaders, the Khans, exacted tribute – protection money – from Russian cities and principalities, but in 1480 Ivan III of Muscovy refused to pay, got away with it and made conquests of his own, known as 'the gathering of Russia'. The Tatars were in decline and they left a power vacuum that Ivan was eager to fill. His imperial pretensions expanded beyond his conquests. He claimed to be the heir of the **Byzantine Empire** of Constantinople, lost to the Turks in 1453, and so assumed the title of Tsar, meaning Caesar. He certainly acted in an imperial way, assuming more **absolute power** over his subjects than any other European ruler. Muscovy would have been a highly centralised state if its administration, over-stretched and corrupt, had matched its political thought. Only through brute force

Byzantine Empire the continuation of the eastern half of the Roman Empire; survived more or less until 1453, when conquered by the Ottoman Turks

absolute power unrestricted power

were the difficulties of communicating power over such vast areas occasionally overcome.

Its remoteness from the rest of Europe was also religious. Muscovy was the stronghold of orthodox Christians, who had become separated from the Latin Christianity of Rome in the eleventh century. They jealously guarded the purity of their **liturgy**, and so gave a distinct character to the culture of much of eastern Europe. That culture was very resilient. In the Balkans, it was to endure five centuries of rule by the **Ottoman** Turks, and still remain intact.

By the end of the fifteenth century, it looked as though the Sultans of the *Ottoman Empire* might redraw the map of Europe. Having seized Constantinople from the last Byzantine Emperor in 1453, the Turks renamed it Istanbul and made it the centre of a magnificent phase of Islamic civilization and political power. The Sultans could draw on subject populations from south-east Europe through most of the Middle East. They had no need to fear rebellious noblemen, as leading Turks did not have a secure base in inherited land, only holding estates in return for service to their ruler. The grand vizier, the head of government, was technically a slave. Selim I, 'the Grim', (1512–20) emphasised this by executing eight of them. With such a concentration of power in his hands, the Sultan could tap resources as he chose.

It was not just neighbouring south-east Europe which was under threat from such a well-organised and determined power. Their navy gave the Ottomans striking power across the eastern Mediterranean as far as Italy. They gained a foothold there, seizing Otranto for a year (1480–81), and their power was to be carried into the western Mediterranean by supporting the so-called Barbary pirates who worked from North African bases, preying on Christian shipping and raiding the coasts of Spain and Italy. But the Ottomans' most solid advances were in the Balkans. They did face powerful resistance – for instance, there was the freedom fighter (or terrorist from the Turkish point of view) named Vlad Dracul, in the mountains of what is now Romania. He rallied his countrymen and terrified his enemy by building up a reputation for extreme cruelty. One **woodcut** shows him eating a meal while gazing contentedly on the Turks impaled on stakes around him. (His bloodthirsty tactics won him fame as a national hero in his home country and he passed into legend as the model for Count Dracula.) The Turks were held up by the likes of Vlad the Impaler, but they were not stopped, and were to threaten central Europe for two centuries to come. Their last siege of Vienna took place as late as 1683.

2 ↪ GOVERNMENT BY PRINCES

There were independent cities and small republics in the Early Modern period but government was largely in the hands of princes (the term used to describe all those with **sovereign** powers, not just the sons of kings). They were once seen as the creators of 'new monarchies',

---

See Chapter 16

liturgy the 'script' of religious services

Ottoman the name given to the Turkish Empire

See Chapter 10

woodcut cheap, printed drawing; often like a cartoon

KEY ISSUE

What was distinctive about central and eastern Europe?

sovereign entitled to make laws without having to recognise a superior authority

gentry the rank of
landowners below
nobility

exercising centralised authority through administrators who were
lawyers or **gentry**, in contrast to their predecessors who had been much
more dependent on the nobility. Although administrators were used –
for instance, lawyers known as *letrados* in Spain or *maîtres* in France –
their use was not new, stretching back into the Middle Ages in France,
Spain and England. And centralisation could be reversed, as I.A.A.
Thompson has shown in the case of Spain. There, the pressures of war
were so great by the end of the sixteenth century that the raising and
supply of troops had to be handed over to nobles, towns and private
enterprise because the central government which had been built up
over the previous hundred years could not cope.

Even where a prince and his central government maintained their
grip, there was no simple chain of command. For all his prestige a
prince's authority was just part of a system of interlocking rights and
obligations. He had to respect his subjects' liberties – not yet universal
liberty but rather the numerous individual privileges of all the
corporations, the towns, the Church and, of course, the nobility. Very
often, the main loyalty was to the province and its privileges rather than
to the realm – this is known as particularism. In France at the time, the
word 'nation' itself referred to the province and not to the country as a
whole. Many of the political problems of the Early Modern period
resulted from the prince attempting to impose his will on a province
and being fiercely resisted. The alternative to what was often futile
confrontation with particularism was to win the support of the local
nobility.

A prince had various ways of securing the co-operation of his
nobility and the realm in general. He was usually on the move, bringing
his direct personal influence to bear on as many of his **vassals** as
possible. (As a consequence of this constant movement capital cities
had not yet fully developed, and the prince took many government
officials with him as he travelled. Mules carried the government
records, and if there were too many they might just be dumped
wherever the royal court happened to be.) The prince's authority was
supported by the view that he was appointed by God. And some
monarchs were thought to have special sacred powers – in England and
France for instance, it was thought that the king's touch could cure
scrofula, a skin disease. The prince was at the centre of great rituals,
such as ceremonial wearing of the crown, which enhanced his prestige.
If he was an effective commander in battle he won the allegiance of that
warrior caste, the nobility, with their strong sense of man-to-man
loyalty.

Prestige, however, was not always effective in bending the nobility to
the prince's will. It was **patronage** that oiled the wheels of the
government machine. The prince was the 'fount of honour' and had at
his disposal prestigious and profitable government jobs (known as
offices) as well as titles, pensions and lands. Whenever there were not
enough offices to go around, the solution seemed to be to create new
ones in order to give them away. When a prince was insufficiently

vassal someone who is
bound to serve a lord in
return for favour and
protection

patronage benefits
given by a superior,
often professional
advancement or gifts of
money

generous or gave benefits only to less important royal favourites, then opposition to the point of rebellion could result.

The demands of financing wars and of supplying patronage led to the expansion of bureaucracy in Early Modern Europe. In its most crude form, known as **venality**, offices were not just given away but sold. The prince would gain what was often desperately needed ready cash, and the buyer of the office could then enjoy the status and the perks that went with it – for instance, a judge might pocket the fines he imposed. Such a bureaucracy was scarcely that of a centralised 'new monarchy' and it was a long way from a modern professional civil service, given that office-holders tended to regard their offices as personal property – today we would simply call it corruption. But the creation of offices itself represented a new royal interference at various levels of society, and one of the features of Early Modern politics was the attempt by princes to use further patronage or royal agents to control the administrators they had created. This was the modern state in its infancy.

> **venality** the sale of offices – government jobs – for cash

In many realms taxes were supposed to be raised only in an emergency and had to be granted by the equivalent of parliament, usually called the *Estates* but known as the *Cortes* in Spain and the *Diet* in Germany. They were not elected in our sense, but usually brought together the nobility with representatives of the towns and country districts and sometimes clergy. The king of France could collect some taxation on his own authority and bypass the Estates General, but up to half the provinces of France had Provincial Estates with which he had to bargain. However, even where the prince had to take notice of the Estates, it did not necessarily damage his authority. With careful management he could persuade the Estates to support him, and that could help to secure acceptance for royal policies in the country as a whole.

Some historians have seen a movement in the period towards absolutism, royal authority freed from any restraints. Admittedly there were lawyers and political thinkers who argued the case for absolutism, and there were institutional developments in the form of reformed treasuries, administrative councils or the despatch to provinces of royal agents. However, these were as likely to disappear as to be created, and had not yet replaced the medieval institutions of government by the end of the sixteenth century. Monarchs still had to grapple with the complexities of those rights and obligations which they and their subjects shared. In any case, government at home often took second place to the other main duty of the prince, which was to go to war in defence of his realm and his rights; it was usually the latter that provoked conflict. Warfare was to grow in scale and expense during the Early Modern period and the gathering of men and money for it was to strain loyalties and the machinery of government to the utmost.

> **KEY ISSUE**
>
> *What were the usual limits to a prince's authority and how did he overcome them?*

3 ∾ WARFARE AND INTERNATIONAL RELATIONS

When Erasmus anticipated peace and unity he was going right against the grain of contemporary assumptions. War was regarded as the natural state of affairs, in Martin Luther's words, 'as necessary as eating, drinking or any other business'. The Christian view was that war was a punishment for sin, therefore inevitable amongst sinful mankind. Princes regarded glory in battle as the highest fulfilment in their role as leaders, and far more attention was paid to taking an advantage in warfare than on how to avoid it.

Medieval warfare is characterised, or perhaps caricatured, by the picture of a great charge of chivalric knights. Every man would fight for himself, concerned about his own honour and the potential ransom for any enemy he managed to capture. While there were more organised tactics than this on some medieval battlefields, there was a general lack of discipline and too great a reliance on the social rank of the combatants. That is why the Swiss were able to inflict such dreadful slaughter on the chivalry of Burgundy at Nancy in 1477. The Swiss were common mountain men but they had learnt to fight with pikes in close ranks and had also learnt discipline. In turn, by the middle of the sixteenth century the Swiss pikemen were to prove vulnerable to the other new development on the battlefield – the use of firearms.

Artillery was to become of particular use in siege warfare and it was the arquebus, the primitive gun held to the shoulder, shortly to develop into the musket, which was to be the most devastating on the battlefield. At first, more or less random firing by the gunners, known as arquebusiers, was used to harass the enemy before the pikemen went in to do the main job. Then, during the Italian Wars, the well-trained Spanish infantry went over to the use of the pike like the Swiss, with the variation that arquebusiers were promoted to a vital defensive role. The pikemen were still responsible for the main thrust in an attack but the arquebusiers aimed to prevent enemy cavalry or infantry getting close enough in their assaults to break up the pikemen's formation. These formations of pikemen and arquebusiers were the *tercios* of the Spanish army, which were to dominate the battlefields of Europe for most of the sixteenth century. The chivalry despised this use of the arquebus rather than the sword and seemed to regard it as cheating. The flower of the French chivalry, Chevalier Bayard, executed any arquebusiers he captured – until he himself was felled by a bullet.

See Chapter 3

In any case, wars were rarely won by decisive battles, but far more often by **attrition** or relentless siege warfare. Frank Tallett stresses the continuity of these strategies from the Middle Ages throughout the sixteenth century and beyond. However, new technology did make a difference to the methods used. In 1494 it took the latest artillery at the disposal of King Charles VIII of France just eight hours to demolish the fortifications of Monte San Giovanni which, before cannon, had withstood a siege of seven years. (Cannon became very prestigious

attrition the gradual wearing down of the enemy

objects – they were often named, Pope Pius II even calling one after his mother, and they could be the most ostentatious of wedding presents from one prince to another.) The answer to the threat of cannon was to build lower walls. The *trace italienne* was developed – low, broad walls protected by extensive earthworks, with bastions which were diamond-shaped projections of masonry, making it very difficult to approach the main wall. All this meant that sieges tended to be long and very expensive.

Artillery also had some effect on naval warfare. The aim in battles at sea had long been to grapple with the enemy, board his vessels and fight what was almost a land battle at sea. This form of warfare was slow to change in the Mediterranean. The great Battle of Lepanto in 1571 saw 100 000 men join battle in the traditional way. However, in the Atlantic, the sixteenth century saw more and more ships being fitted with cannon, and the broadside thus became a possibility. All the same, at sea there were other factors that could intervene before the artillery became of any use. Too many cannon on board could make a ship top-heavy and sink it. The Spanish Armada was defeated not by broadsides but by English fireships and the weather.

The development of gunpowder technology was important, but in battles the tactical response and the deployment of infantry seemed even more important. If they were to continue to be successful in war, the nobility had to become rather more like professional soldiers than uncontrollable feudal warriors. As to cannon specifically, J.R. Hale has stressed that big guns were not a royal monopoly – aristocrats and fortified towns often owned them – but it was still the case that the expense of full artillery trains was so great that only princes, and the greater princes at that, could regularly afford them, usually by exploiting national resources. The gap between princes and nobility was growing greater. Princes also tried to bring to an end to private wars amongst the nobility, although the limited success of that policy could be seen in the great religious civil wars of the late sixteenth century.

> ### KEY ISSUE
>
> *In what ways did gunpowder technology change the face of warfare?*

> See Chapters 14 and 15

If a prince wished to pursue an energetic foreign policy, there was one way of avoiding the costs of war or making wars more cost effective; this was through careful use of diplomacy. Diplomacy was also the all-important art of international public relations. As Philip II commented, 'The dignity and reputation of princes is of no less importance to them than their states.' A diplomatic system was just starting to develop in the fifteenth century, and became known as Renaissance diplomacy.

'An ambassador is an honest man sent to lie abroad for the good of his country.' These words of Sir Henry Wotton, English ambassador in Venice in the early 1600s, give us a caricature of what diplomacy had become by the end of our period. It would not have been seen that way in the late Middle Ages. Ambassadors did not lie (in the sense of stay) abroad. They travelled, often in great pomp, but only to deliver messages – perhaps a marriage proposal or a threat of war – quickly returning home without having negotiated or got to know their host country. They would not joke about lying, in the sense of misleading, as that would be to break the code of chivalry governing diplomatic practice. They might also not represent a prince or country, as it was quite normal for great noblemen and cities to despatch ambassadors on their own account. It was Renaissance diplomacy, developed by the advanced states of Italy in the fifteenth century, which was to transform all this into a system resembling our own.

The instability of Italy made its politicians more creative. Many were insecure dictators, and few had dependable allies or borders unthreatened by expanding neighbours. They relied on cunning as an alternative to expensive military strength, and that called for diplomats who could argue with brilliance and haggle with tenacity, knowing all the strengths and weaknesses of their potential enemies or allies. To perfect that knowledge, it was necessary for the ambassador to live in the country of the potential enemy or ally. The use of resident ambassadors with powers to negotiate may seem obvious to us but it was an innovation in the Early Modern period.

The states of Italy did not, however, compete with each other chaotically. Renaissance diplomacy showed itself to be creative, with the emergence of a balance of power for the first time in Italy after the Peace of Lodi in 1454. The various rulers and diplomats recognised that it was in their own interests to join together to restrict any one state which appeared to be getting too powerful, and therefore a threat to everybody else. This balance of power did not survive the French invasion of 1494, but by this time, there was a most willing student who was to carry some aspects of Renaissance diplomacy into the rest of Europe – Ferdinand of Aragon, who ruled jointly over Spain with Isabella of Castile.

Despite an absence of orderly records (in 1508 not one copy of an important Spanish treaty with England could be found) and a marked reluctance to pay the necessary costs, Ferdinand sent skilled and loyal resident ambassadors to the royal courts and leading cities of Europe. He also inspired the secular objectives of the state to be given the highest value. Fonseca, one of his diplomats and a bishop, said of breaching a treaty oath, 'I place this object of His Highness higher than the safety of my immortal soul.' As Garrett Mattingly put it in his pioneering work on Renaissance diplomacy, 'the state, by the law of its being, could think only of itself'.

Ferdinand used diplomacy to try and encircle France with a series of Spanish alliances with her neighbours, but no balance of power emerged. The great states of western Europe were too secure and too unwieldy – only one state had to change sides to completely wreck any chance of a balance. Renaissance Europe became Reformation Europe. By the mid-sixteenth century, religion had once again become the dominant theme in international relations and was to remain so for a century. Power and profit could be placed in a balance but the claim that God was on your side overturned the scales altogether. A century later John Locke identified religious divisions as 'the perpetual foundations of war and contention, all those flames that have made such havoc and desolation in Europe, and have not been quenched with the blood of so many millions'.

4 ⌐ THE CHURCH, BELIEFS AND COMMUNICATIONS

For most of us today, the state regulates the way we live our lives. For people at the end of the Middle Ages, the Church shared that dominant role. There was no sense of religion as a matter of private conscience, and atheism was almost inconceivable in the sixteenth century. The parish priest had a more direct effect on an ordinary person's life than any government official. The beliefs that mattered most were not those of a political ideology but the teachings of the Church. And in 1500, apart from some surviving pockets of heresy and the orthodox Church in the easternmost part of Europe, 'the Church' meant the Church of Rome.

A *Structure*

The Pope, as Head of the Church, was the supreme legislator and judge, issuing instructions called papal bulls. But power over this greatest of European institutions could not be completely concentrated in one man. Cardinals were appointed by the Pope but they were not merely servants; they had increasing influence in the Curia, the papal civil service in Rome, and it was they who elected a new Pope as soon as the old one had died.

With regard to other important ecclesiastical appointments, princes demanded influence and the Popes were regularly forced into compromises with them. Church and state could never be disentangled. Bishops were, after all, amongst the most powerful landowners in any kingdom and no prince could allow an entirely free choice of who should be appointed.

While a bishop had powers over the ordinary parish priests, the so-called secular clergy, he had no direct power over monks, known as the regular clergy. They were organised in various monastic orders, which were international and subject only to the Pope. The larger monastic houses were ruled over by abbots, who might control extensive estates and be as powerful and as independent as any bishop or lord. There were also the friars, mainly the orders of the Franciscans and Dominicans. They had started to settle down in one place like monks although some kept to their original task as wandering preachers, thereby much annoying the secular clergy, who saw them as competitors and trespassers in their parishes. The Dominicans had also taken on a special role as inquisitors, rooting out heresy; that could lead as much to quarrels over jurisdiction – who could judge whom – as to the preservation of the Faith.

Ordinary laymen had no say in running the Church, but they did form their own religious clubs called confraternities. Some cities had several dozen of them and John Bossy estimates that at least ten per cent of all adults from the thirteenth century onwards were members of one or more confraternities. Members would worship together, feast together and support each other in sickness or provide for burial. Some confraternities had special duties, such as those who organised the procession on the Feast of Corpus Christi and put on the Mystery Plays, dramatised stories from the Bible. These confraternities posed no threat to the Church but there could be anxiety that they were independent of clerical control.

The Church was organised as a hierarchy but there was no simple chain of command. Bishops, abbots, chapters (the governing bodies of cathedrals) and confraternities all had a clear sense of their privileges and the independence which went with them. That considerably restricted the power of the Pope to interfere in the day-to-day working of the Church.

B *The condition of the Church*

abuses immorality or corruption

simony the sale of Church offices; ecclesiastical venality

pluralism the holding of more than one post in the Church at a time

When surveying the late medieval Church, historians have often highlighted its **abuses**, the ways in which it had been diverted from its spiritual mission by the corruption of the world. There was **simony** – Pope Leo X (1513–21) raised half a million ducats by selling 2000 Church offices. Not surprisingly, this led to **pluralism** and to absenteeism, when a clergyman acquired offices solely for their income, rather than because he was going to perform any of their duties. The absence of some clergy from their posts, though, was not necessarily their own choice. They might have been called away on government service or have found it necessary to spend some time at a university. Cardinal Jean of Lorraine could hardly have been blamed for failing to perform his duties as Coadjutor of Metz, given that his family had him appointed in 1501 at the age of three. Apportionment of blame aside, the Church was being exploited by many of its officials, rather than being served by them.

There had been attempts to keep the Church separate from the world through the rule of celibacy. Priests without wives, it was hoped, would be more dedicated to the Church and would stand apart from worldly society, having no descendants to whom to bequeath Church property. But priests were as much prey as modern politicians to the lusts of the flesh, and there was no effective discipline to keep them to their vows if they chose to wander. A cardinal or bishop might have his courtesan, as a high-class prostitute was known, an ordinary priest his concubine, a wife in all but name. Where a bishop got to know about a priest and his concubine, the routine was to exact a fine rather than to split them up. It seemed to be the case that, in some respects, the rules of the Church were there to be broken so that money could be made.

This was borne out by the activities of Church courts. Religious matters and many we would regard as secular, such as the regulation of wills, came within the jurisdiction of Church courts. Although they may have offered justice more often than many Protestant historians have allowed, Church courts could be put to corrupt uses. As one papal official is quoted as saying, 'The Lord desireth not the death of a sinner but rather that he should pay and live.' It is certainly the case that these ecclesiastical courts looked after their own. Any criminal who could claim 'benefit of clergy', and simple literacy was regarded as pretty good evidence, would be tried before a Church court and guaranteed a light penalty, even for such a serious crime as murder. Such abuses bred resentment amongst many of the laity, the mass of people without benefit of clergy.

Church taxation provoked laymen more than anything else. The tithe, ten per cent of all produce, had to be paid over to support the Church and there were other taxes as well, such as Peter's Pence, a tax on hearths paid to the Pope. Demands were voiced in Estates (parliaments) throughout Europe that the jurisdiction and financial exploitation by the Church should be cut. However, this did not inevitably lead to that rebellion against the Church that became the Reformation.

The Church seemed secure in that it was, on the whole, serving the needs of the world. Its very abuses made it valued. Powerful families could add Church offices to their other acquisitions. Convents might be scandalously lax but that was because they were useful as dumping grounds for the daughters of well-to-do families who could not be married off. Relics of saints, which pilgrims travelled to see and touch, and to pay for the privilege, were often frauds. The venerated forearm of Saint Andrew might just be a pig's bone; sceptical travellers noted enough wood from the Cross to make a forest of crosses and enough of the Virgin's milk to launch ships. But, where the fraud was successful, the people were content with what the Church provided.

Most abuses were not new. Some gave rise to objection and there were movements for reform, but many abuses were generally accepted as part of the natural order of things. It was only when beliefs changed in the Reformation that they were seen as really destructive of the Church.

> **KEY ISSUE**
>
> *Given widespread criticism of the abuses of the Church, how had they continued for so long?*

C *Religious rituals and beliefs*

Social and religious boundaries were often the same; the community was generally a parish. Apart from perhaps a manor house or castle, the church was the most substantial building in the village and more than likely to be the most permanent structure, being built of stone. Outside the church would be the graveyard where the dead, the ancestors of the parish, could lie still gathered in community. In processions around the church and within it there took place the ceremonies that marked the stages of the individual's life and gave the community its identity.

The Church's religious calendar followed the seasons, all-important in a rural society. Easter, the celebration of life coming forth from death, could take on extra meaning, being also the time to celebrate the renewal of fertility in Spring. Christmas, the celebration of birth amidst darkness, is near to the winter solstice and still carries with it many of the traditions associated with ancient Roman ceremonies and the pagan festival of Yule. Saints' feast days marked other stages in the agricultural cycle and, where appropriate, the saint's image could be carried in procession to bring blessings and fertility to the fields. Spiritual life and making a living from the soil went hand in hand.

Saints, increasing in number at the end of the Middle Ages, both official and locally invented, could be prayed to for specific assistance. For instance, before a journey was undertaken, St Christopher could be called upon for his protection. Sometimes the statue of a saint came to be thought of as having magical powers but, if it had been prayed to and had failed to deliver the goods, it might be mutilated or tossed into a river. A more official approach to saints was to seek their services in interceding with Christ to forgive sins. Cults grew up around those saints thought to be most effective; the most widespread cult was that of the Virgin Mary. It seemed in some cases as though she was being worshipped almost as a mother goddess.

Saints and the services of the Church in general were in greatest demand when calamity threatened. When the plague was nearby, St Roch, the saint thought to guard against it, would receive more votive offerings (gifts dedicated to the saint in return for help). In fear of hail which might destroy the crops, special prayers would be said to ward off the evil spirits which stirred up such tempests, and when a storm began, the church bells would be rung in an attempt to quell it – a practice that Protestant reformers, try as they might, never managed to stamp out.

There is much in the above religious practices which seems more pagan than Christian. The historian Jean Delumeau sees the people of medieval Europe as effectively pagan while paying lip service to official Christianity. (His views will be considered in more detail in relation to the Counter-Reformation.) John Bossy has argued differently, suggesting that there was an authentic Christianity that treated spiritual and social needs as one. This can be seen most clearly in the seven sacraments, the most important ceremonies of the Church.

The seven sacraments were seen as the special channels of Christ's grace, through which humankind could be redeemed from sin. There was ordination, the service when a man is set apart as a priest for the service of Christ. There were the four sacraments which introduced the individual to the Church soon after birth (baptism), brought him or her into full adult membership (confirmation), sanctified union with a fellow Christian (marriage) and prepared for the passage into the after-life (the last rites, known as Extreme Unction). The religious function of these four sacraments merged with a social function. Baptism introduced the new individual to the community and established social bonds with people of different families who acted as godparents.

Confirmation varied in age but it often marked the onset of puberty and the adult responsibilities that go with it. Marriage could actually be contracted outside church simply by the oaths of the couple in front of witnesses but, more and more, the blessing of the priest was taken to be an essential addition to the sacrament. Only a ceremony in church was properly public and could unite two families as well as two individuals. The anointing with oil at the last rites mirrored the use of water at baptism, separating the individual from the living community just as baptism had brought him or her into it.

Ever since Adam and Eve's original disobedience to God, people had been doomed to inherit this original sin as part of their humanity, and the penalty for sin was eternal torment. All the sacraments were intended to qualify the effects of sin. The sacrament of penance dealt with the individual's specific sins. The individual would confess his or her faults to the priest, undertake a suitable penalty and then receive absolution, i.e. release from the consequence of his sin. Penance served any number of social purposes; specific sins were in need of control lest they disrupted the community. Pride, for instance, provoked resentment and conflict; adultery might destroy a family. But sin itself could not be eradicated through individual human efforts. The penalty for sin could only be paid by Christ's sacrifice on the Cross and it was the Eucharist that celebrated His sacrifice.

The **Eucharist** was a sacrament and a miracle. The priest at the altar would consecrate bread and wine and they would then become the Body and Blood of Christ, His sacrifice on the Cross thus being brought into the physical experience of the priest and, unless it was a private mass, the congregation. There was the problem that the bread and wine continued to look like bread and wine, but doubters could be told of the miracle at Viterbo when the consecrated bread supposedly bled, and men of learning could grapple with the doctrine of **transubstantiation**. Academic philosophers of the time saw a difference between the appearance of something (its 'accidents') and its inner nature (its 'substance'). So the 'accidents' of the bread and wine could remain the same while its 'substance' could be transformed – 'transubstantiated' – into the Body and Blood of Christ. For the ordinary parishioner, however, what mattered was the occurrence of the miracle and not its technicalities.

Only the priest was allowed to drink the consecrated wine, owing to his superior spiritual status. Parishioners received communion in one kind only – the consecrated bread – and some did so only once a year at Easter, but that served to emphasise the special holiness of the ceremony. The community was brought together at the Eucharist to be relieved of its sin. A vital part of the ceremony was the Peace, usually symbolised by a kiss. It was the purging of the community from anxiety and conflict, the restoration of charity. Charity meant much more than our giving to good causes. It meant that which gives life to a community, and the Eucharist was an essential part of it. This social importance of the Eucharist explains, paradoxically, why men would

Eucharist the ceremony derived from the Last Supper, with the consecration of bread and wine

transubstantiation the Catholic belief that in the Eucharist the bread and wine are physically transformed into the Body and Blood of Christ

KEY ISSUE

Why was the Church so central to European society in 1500?

scholasticism the dominant philosophy of the Middle Ages

See Chapters 5 and 6

fight to the death over differing interpretations of it once the Reformation had begun.

D *Thought and the printing press*

The Church dominated intellectual pursuits in the Middle Ages. Intellectuals were churchmen and, although other subjects such as law and medicine were studied, the 'Queen of the Sciences' was theology. There had, however, been influences from outside the Christian tradition, principally Aristotle, one of the greatest philosophers of classical Greece, whose ideas had become known in western Europe during the thirteenth century through the writings of Arab scholars. Aristotelianism was at the heart of medieval philosophy, which was known as **scholasticism**. It was scholasticism that came up with the distinction between 'accidents' and 'substance' discussed above. The philosopher who did most to reconcile Christianity with Aristotelianism was St Thomas Aquinas (*c.* 1225–74). His work had been an immense stimulus, but by the 1400s there was a tendency to debate the most minute details of acknowledged authorities rather than to think afresh.

It was not until the Early Modern period that there were serious challenges to Aristotelianism. The men of the Renaissance attacked it on aesthetic and ethical grounds – they asserted that the logic-chopping of the scholastics was barbaric in style and entirely useless in pursuit of the good life. The leaders of the Reformation attacked scholastic thinking as the basis for the theological errors of the medieval Church. But it was the development of printing which, more than anything else, helped to break the monopoly over thought held by Aristotelianism and the medieval Church.

In 1454 or thereabouts in the German city of Mainz, Johann Gutenberg produced what became known as the Gutenberg Bible. It looked like other bibles of the period with the same style of lettering and painstakingly hand-painted illuminations. The difference was that it was the first to have been printed with movable type – there were 300 Gutenberg Bibles, rather than just one copied out by scribes. Gutenberg tried to keep his invention to himself in order to sell his books in the same market and at the same price as handwritten volumes. That was why hand-painted illuminations were added. But one of the most revolutionary developments in European history could not be kept secret for long.

In 1483 a Florentine scholar had to pay three times as much for the preparation of his text by a printer as he would have paid to a scribe. The printer, though, was to provide not one copy but over a thousand, so that access to knowledge was increased immensely. Those of the literate élite who had always read books could now obtain more; those with money, but not enough to pay scribes, could now afford to buy books.

Historians who play down printing's importance point out that literacy rates were very low – Bernd Moeller estimates for instance that only three to four per cent of Germany's population could read by 1500. Also, while printing helped to spread knowledge, the books being printed were entirely traditional, at least until the early 1500s. The new technique did not seem to be giving rise to new ideas. Elizabeth Eisenstein has challenged this view with her account of scholars being confronted for the first time with the anomalies and contradictions of the traditional academic authorities of the Middle Ages through the variety of printed texts. For Eisenstein, printing is a crucial element in the intellectual ferment of the Early Modern period, whether in culture, religion or science.

The Renaissance and the Reformation will be examined later but some points can be made about them jointly with regard to printing. There had been 'renaissances' of classical ideas in the earlier Middle Ages, just as there had been attempted 'reformations' by those whom the Church labelled as heretics. But such efforts, whether in culture or religion, had been localised and temporary. Printing certainly had a part to play in making the Renaissance and the Reformation international and permanent in their effects, in contrast to their medieval forerunners.

The business of science was also driven forward. Copernicus (1473–1543) suggested that the earth orbits the sun. This contradicted the **Ptolemaic** model of the universe upheld by the Church, which had the sun orbiting the earth. Copernicus could contradict this most fundamental assumption about the universe not because of 'modern scientific observation' but because he was able to cite the discrepancies in calculations presented to him in printed texts. Tycho Brahe (1546–1601), another great astronomer, was to concentrate much more on direct observation of the stars but he also employed up to fifty printers in order to publish the accumulated data. It must be noted that this did not guarantee immediate advancement for science. The printing presses rolled off far more works by alchemists and other pseudo-scientists, and the presses also made it easier for the authorities, mainly the Church, to declare what was orthodox, in opposition to new ideas such as those of the astronomers. But another feature of printing is that it makes knowledge much more difficult to control. Censorship was attempted by governments and by the Church, but there were always printers somewhere in Europe who could ignore it and guarantee that the new ideas, such as those in science, stayed in circulation.

This ambiguity in the effects of printing can be seen in affairs of state as well as of the mind. A prince could now have a decree printed, guaranteeing that all copies would be identical and so enabling him to demand much more precise obedience. On the other hand, the publication of definite texts of laws gave the subject a defence against an **arbitrary government** trying to claim that the law was on its side when it was not.

Printing does not 'explain' the Early Modern period but, as Eisenstein notes, it greatly affected the pattern of continuity and

Ptolemaic referring to Ptolemy's map of the heavens

arbitrary government government not controlled by law, custom or precedent

KEY ISSUE

What was the significance of technological and scientific advance in this period?

change. Francis Bacon thought that printing, gunpowder and the compass were the three inventions which had 'changed the appearance and state of the whole world'. He might also have noted that the armourer needed printed treatises on weapons in order to make good use of gunpowder, and that the navigator needed reliable printed maps as much as he needed the compass. The invention of printing had multiple effects.

5 ↪ SOCIETY

It is easy to assume that new technology, such as printing then and the internet now, will revolutionise all of society, but underlying social structures may still change with only glacial slowness. For instance, the family, particularly in southern Europe, was not the nuclear family of parents and children, but remained the extended family of several generations, cousins and servants gathered under one roof. The place of women within the family and within society in general was changing in the sixteenth century, but not in the direction of greater emancipation. As widows controlling estates and as members of guilds, they had had some economic influence in the Middle Ages, but in the Early Modern period they were increasingly deprived of their economic freedom and subordinated to men even more, despite those eminent examples of powerful women such as Elizabeth I.

See pages 200–2

The people of Renaissance Europe did not think in terms of classes but of social 'orders' determined by rank and function rather than economic status. In theory there were three orders – those who fought (the nobility), those who prayed (the monks and the priests) and those who worked (the townsmen and the peasants). In practice it was more complicated, with much variation in relationships between and within each order.

The nobility was distinguished by symbols such as coats of arms and liveries (uniforms) for its servants. It was not noted not for production but for consumption – conspicuous consumption of luxuries that indicated rank. Members of the nobility enjoyed a wide range of privileges, an important one being exemption from **direct taxation** in most countries on the (increasingly spurious) grounds that they served as feudal warriors. Hereditary rank automatically endowed them with status but real power depended on their control of the land. They had **seigneurial** rights over the peasantry, which meant that they not only acted as landlords but had independent powers as judges. Where a nobleman controlled large estates he could often act as a prince in his own right, paying homage to his king but in practice virtually ignoring him. The nobility, however, were not all magnates (great aristocrats). Alongside *les grands* in France or the *grandees* of Spain, there were also the poor noblemen whose rank remained but whose fortunes had declined so that they pushed a plough and were indistinguishable from the peasants, except by the gloves they wore and the sword they hung

direct tax an income or wealth tax, rather than a sales tax

seigneurial describes the rights of a feudal lord to administer justice on his lands

PICTURE 2

Procession in the Piazza San Marco *by Gentile Bellini. A visual demonstration of religious and social rank.*

above the fireplace to symbolise their noble heritage. At a lesser extreme were the gentry, not such powerful landowners as the magnates but of great importance in that any nobleman with political aspirations relied on support from amongst them. The ambitious nobleman supplied his supporters with favours or bribes – it was patronage that fuelled rank with power.

Churchmen could be the social equals of the nobility. Indeed, in the Middle Ages there was a claim that the lowliest priest, by virtue of his spiritual vocation, was superior to the greatest nobleman. In practice, it was the bishops and abbots who did wield power because they were often as much landowners and *seigneurs* as the leading noblemen. Although it was common for a bishop to be a younger son of a noble family, the Church was still the main career open to talent. With an education and a command of Latin – the language of the Church – an ambitious clergyman could go far within the Church or in government service. This was social mobility but it was limited, especially as the clergy were not permitted (legitimately) to father families to whom they could pass their honours and lands. Also, like the poor nobility, many of the poorer priests were indistinguishable from the peasants they served.

The peasants were the workers on the land. During the Middle Ages most had been serfs, not quite slaves, as they were permitted their own plots of land, but bound to work on their lords' estates and to pay **feudal dues** such as heriot, which was a death duty. By the fifteenth century, as a result of the post-Black Death labour shortage, when

feudal dues labour time or payments owed to a lord other than rent

peasants could demand a better deal, serfdom had largely died out in western Europe. However, this did not mean that the lot of the peasants permanently improved. In eastern Europe there was to be a 'second serfdom' established during the Early Modern period by nobility eager to make profits out of the expanding grain trade. Even in Western Europe, by 1500 the population was starting to increase again and there was a growing shortage of land. Some peasants profited from economic changes, with inflation outstripping customary rents, and they became well-to-do farmers – yeomen in England, *laboureurs* in France – but many were reduced to being landless labourers, dependent on the chances of employment to avoid starvation. Occasionally the more articulate peasants would protest or even rebel but, for the most part, the peasants laboured silently and were exploited, regarded by their superiors as being little better than brutes.

Townsmen did not fit easily into the scheme of three social orders. Some were poor wage-labourers, but the **burghers** who governed the towns often had a lifestyle akin to that of the nobility, living off the rents on land they had bought or the interest on government bonds. Indeed, the aim of many wealthy merchants was to commit 'class treachery' as it has been called, and acquire titles of nobility through purchase or government office. Between the extremes of wage-labourer and powerful office-holder or merchant, there were many gradations of social status. So much depended on which craft guild or religious confraternity the townsman belonged to – the group counted for far more than the individual.

In several areas, cities had been largely independent, the most dynamic force in historical developments during the Middle Ages. During the Early Modern period they were gradually brought under control by the princes of Europe. They were to come into their own again with the onset of the Industrial Revolution and large-scale urbanisation, but before then, the nobility remained the most important element in society, as princes were continually forced to recognise in their attempts to secure or extend the powers of royal government.

burgher citizen of a town

KEY ISSUE

How far was rank more important than wealth in European society in 1500?

6 ⤳ THE ECONOMY

It is important to know something about the material basis of life in the sixteenth century but there are difficulties in discussing 'the economy' of Early Modern Europe in general terms. It is a technical and controversial subject and, while some massive studies have been made, the evidence is scattered and incomplete. It is also the case that the European economy scarcely existed for many of the continent's inhabitants, who were far away from the main trade routes and were farming little above subsistence level; that is, aiming to grow just enough to live on and to pay their share in supporting lords and priests. There was often precious little of a surplus for trading purposes. For them it was the local economy which mattered, focused on a town unlikely to be further than fifteen miles away.

Towns might be thought of as centres of change, and they certainly contained a greater variety of livelihoods, but they do need to be viewed very differently from towns today. The bloated population of Naples touched 200 000 by 1500 but a respectably-sized central European city might number only 2000 inhabitants – scarcely more than a village in our view. Such cities or towns defined themselves physically by their city walls and legally by the charters which had established their corporations and guilds, the bodies which controlled local government and industry. The guilds were associations of those engaged in a particular trade that laid down regulations for the price, size and quality of their products and generally discouraged disruptive change as much as possible. They also protected their trade from being flooded by rural labourers.

There was a clear distinction between town and country for people in and around 1500. For us, if we were to walk around such a town, that distinction might seem less clear. We would see no factories but small workshops instead, which we would be tempted to define as cottage industries. We might see the carpenter or cloth-worker farming part-time on a plot of land inside the city walls – countryside within the city. Our main impression would be of the small scale of the urban economy and how closely it was integrated with the traditional needs of a rural economy.

While we need to be aware of the enormous difference in scale and rate of innovation between the modern economy and that of sixteenth-century Europe, it would be a mistake to think of the latter as being simply undeveloped. There had always been some international trade, and since the eleventh century it had been growing as merchants, particularly from Italy, took goods from the Mediterranean and the East into northern Europe. High finance was developing, along with the trade routes. By 1500 in a city such as Antwerp, which had become the leading centre of trade between north and south in Europe, bills of exchange were used, through which, for example, a Florentine merchant could pay for goods in Antwerp by drawing on funds owed to him in that city rather than having to physically take the money there from Florence. The bill of exchange is thus the ancestor of the modern cheque. Another business innovation was double-entry book-keeping; more rational accounting enabled the merchant to establish whether he was actually making a profit.

Despite such innovations, there were some brakes on commercial development. It was not so easy to raise a loan given that the Church saw lending money at interest as a sin, which it called usury. It used to be thought that the Protestants were the first to ignore this restriction, but Catholics had already seen ways of getting round it. In 1515 Johannes Eck, a Catholic spokesman who was to be a leading opponent of the Protestants, argued that it was not sinful to charge up to five per cent interest a year on a loan as that only covered the risk, the potential loss to the lender. Eck was arguing on behalf of the Fuggers, an

Augsburg family who were bankers and traders on an international scale.

In the later Middle Ages there had been an increasing number of banking families to exploit the new financial techniques and provide the finance for trading expeditions and for princes whose warlike ambitions outstripped their income. Some of these families attained considerable power – the Medici, for instance, were to move on from lending to the government of Florence to taking it over – but it was the Fuggers who had the most diverse interests. They traded in spices, wool and silk throughout Europe. They were the biggest mine-owners, with interests in silver in the Tyrol and copper in Hungary. They 'farmed', that is, leased the right to collect the revenue from the huge estates of Spain's three military orders of crusading knights; they had won such concessions from the Habsburgs, the rising dynasty of Europe, whose finances they virtually ran until the middle of the sixteenth century. Even then, before concerted attempts by governments to direct the overall economy, the requirements of politicians had a great impact on the shape of the economy.

monopolies exclusive rights to manufacture or sell something

Governments sometimes directed trade through **monopolies**. For instance, the kings of Castile had granted the city of Burgos a monopoly in the marketing of wool, which was to be the foundation of its prosperity. Such monopolies were used by governments to reward the favoured with privileges or to bring trade under closer control so that it could be more easily taxed. There was no sign yet of consistent national trading policies. Customs duties had to be paid when travelling within a country, not just on its borders; for example, between Paris and Rouen a merchant would have to pay fifteen tolls. But princes, with an eye to attracting gold and silver away from rivals, did pass laws, known in England as Navigation Acts, to confine trade to their own subjects' shipping. All this amounts to 'state intervention', but it consisted of regulation and not the large-scale financial intervention which modern governments have regarded as normal until recently.

debasement reducing the content of the valuable metal in a coin

The government's impact on the economy was not confined to intentional intervention, however. When short of ready cash a prince might **debase** the coinage, replacing some of the silver content with copper. That could lead to a sharp burst of inflation, ruining some or making fortunes for more astute speculators. But the most regular spin-off of government policy came from the amount that was spent on war. The men of an army needed food, clothing and other supplies. By 1500 more faith and more cash were being placed in artillery which created an armaments industry, metal foundries becoming amongst the biggest of industrial operations at the time. Armies were more obviously agents of destruction – cities were looted and trade routes cut – but they could also act as stimulants to economic activity.

There was certainly economic growth and change in the sixteenth century but its significance should not be exaggerated. There were some examples of what might look like modern industrial capitalism – the Fugger's copper and silver mines for instance where there was heavy investment and a large, wage-paid workforce – but most industry was still craft work, with limited investment in those small workshops governed by conservative guilds.

If we were to track down capitalists around 1500, we would find them engaged in commerce, as the greater profits were to be made in the transfer of goods and not in their production. But, although those profits enabled some merchants to live like aristocrats, there were limits to the development of commercial capitalism in the later Middle Ages. This was partly because most merchants were likely to abandon trade to live an aristocratic life of leisure when they could afford it; it has been estimated that a merchant family which grew in wealth through three generations would then become *rentiers*, living off rents or government bonds. The Medici, a fine example of capitalist success, depended not so much on their bank by the middle of the fifteenth century, as on what they could siphon off from governing Florence. There was a spirit of enterprise but it was not particularly strong, or regarded as being especially good.

rentier someone who lives off rents or government bonds, rather than producing any wealth

Although merchants had moved towards capitalism's 'rational control of resources', through book-keeping for instance, they did not organise themselves into the equivalent of the modern company. Firms of merchants were often of the same family which, like family businesses today, can founder when the talent runs out. There were *compagnies*, but these were more like clubs and, although they did foster economic co-operation, the merchants did not share the long-term investments and profits, the risks and the tasks, as in a modern company.

Merchants' attitudes and organisation perhaps reflected the main restriction to the development of capitalism in Europe around 1500, namely a slow-changing, narrow, agricultural base. As the sixteenth century progressed there were two new developments which made this less of a determining factor – the opening of sea routes to the Indian and Pacific Oceans and general, almost continuous inflation.

While the creative error of Christopher Columbus in finding the New World in 1492 may be seen as more momentous in the long term, the sea route to India found by the Portuguese Vasco da Gama in 1497 was to have far more immediate economic impact. New sources of supply were opened up for the spice trade, costs were brought down and the monopoly hold of Mediterranean merchants on the eastern trade was broken. Trading posts were set up along the coasts of Africa, India and into the East Indies. The Portuguese tried to keep these new trade routes to themselves, but later on in the sixteenth century they were to be invaded by the Dutch and the English. Those two nationalities of north-western Europe were to seize the new opportunities, developing a more expansive, aggressive commercial capitalism than had been known before. A world economy was emerging and the expansion of Europe had begun.

See Chapter 4

The economy within Europe had been sluggish for most of the fifteenth century but from 1470, for the next hundred years or so, it was to grow. Along with that growth came inflation, the great Price Rise of the sixteenth century. In explanation of it, Earl J. Hamilton, writing in

KEY ISSUE

How developed was capitalism around 1500?

bullion gold and silver

the 1930s, pointed to **bullion** arriving in Europe from the New World, which meant an increased amount of money in Europe chasing the same amount of goods, thus allowing for prices to rise. However, the Hamilton thesis, although still represented as standard in some textbooks, has been regularly attacked by a succeeding generation of scholars on the grounds of its theoretical inadequacies and the general

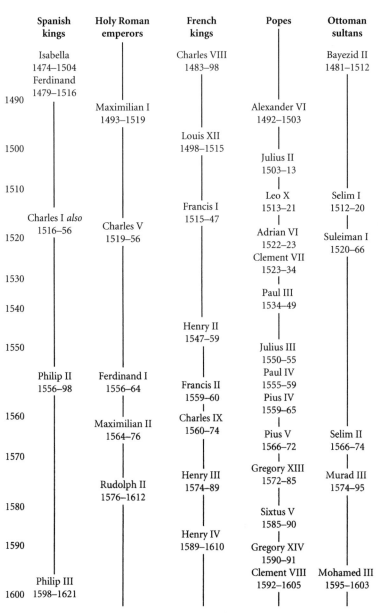

	Spanish kings	Holy Roman emperors	French kings	Popes	Ottoman sultans
	Isabella 1474–1504		Charles VIII 1483–98		Bayezid II 1481–1512
	Ferdinand 1479–1516				
1490		Maximilian I 1493–1519		Alexander VI 1492–1503	
1500			Louis XII 1498–1515	Julius II 1503–13	
1510				Leo X 1513–21	Selim I 1512–20
	Charles I *also* 1516–56	Charles V 1519–56	Francis I 1515–47		
1520				Adrian VI 1522–23	Suleiman I 1520–66
				Clement VII 1523–34	
1530				Paul III 1534–49	
1540			Henry II 1547–59		
1550				Julius III 1550–55	
	Philip II 1556–98	Ferdinand I 1556–64	Francis II 1559–60	Paul IV 1555–59	
				Pius IV 1559–65	
1560		Maximilian II 1564–76	Charles IX 1560–74		
1570				Pius V 1566–72	Selim II 1566–74
		Rudolph II 1576–1612	Henry III 1574–89	Gregory XIII 1572–85	Murad III 1574–95
1580				Sixtus V 1585–90	
1590			Henry IV 1589–1610	Gregory XIV 1590–91	
				Clement VIII 1592–1605	Mohamed III 1595–1603
1600	Philip III 1598–1621				

TABLE 2
Sixteenth-century rulers

Ruler listed where reign lasted longer than one year

lack of evidence. The arrival of the bullion (even when that mined in Europe is included) does not correlate in time or place with the greater part of the inflation. In place of Hamilton's theory, there are many that compete. Although no agreed view has emerged, it is recognised that an increase in the volume of commercial transactions and a growth in the European population after its late medieval downswing could have contributed to a pressure on prices through a greater demand for goods. Certainly the population growth correlates much more closely with the Price Rise than does the influx of bullion.

Inflation averaged about two per cent a year. That may not seem much to modern eyes but it made a relentless impact over a century on the more primitive economy of sixteenth-century Europe. It helped to stimulate industrial growth as wages lagged behind prices, and so profits were greater and more money was available for investment. By 1560, 'real' wages (in terms of purchasing power) were down between twenty per cent and fifty per cent from the latter half of the fifteenth century. It is a great irony that, for the economy in general, the Price Rise was part of its health and development, while for countless numbers of individuals it meant poverty or destitution.

7 ᔆ BIBLIOGRAPHY

**R. Bonney, *The European Dynastic States 1494–1660* (OUP, 1991). *P. Zagorin, *Rebels and Rulers 1500–1660, Vol I* (CUP, 1982) includes a general survey of state and society. **M. Howard, *War in European History* (OUP, 1976) is the best and the briefest on the subject. *F. Tallett, *War and Society in Early Modern Europe* (Routledge, 1992) is more focused on the seventeenth century, but has a useful final section on the impact of war. *M.S. Anderson, *The Rise of Modern Diplomacy 1450–1919* (Longman, 1993) especially the first chapter. *H. Kamen, *European Society 1500–1700* (Hutchinson, 1984). **J. Bossy, *Christianity in the West 1400–1700* (OUP, 1985) is quite difficult but brilliant. **E. Eisenstein, *The Printing Revolution in Early Modern Europe* (CUP, 1983), see page 19. *F. Braudel *Civilisation and Capitalism* (Fontana, 1985) consists of three volumes, all well worth browsing through.

KEY ISSUE

What were the causes of the price rise of the sixteenth century, and what were its consequences?

TABLE 3

Index of real wages in Spain: an example of how wages, adjusted to take inflation into account, fluctuated in the sixteenth century

1510	100
1520	Figures not available
1530	71
1540	Figures not available
1550	76
1560	86
1570	82
1580	80
1590	82
1600	71

2

Ferdinand and Isabella

OVERVIEW

In the middle of the fifteenth century Iberia was made up of a number of Christian kingdoms and, in the south, the Moorish (Muslim) emirate of Granada. The marriage of Prince Ferdinand of Aragon and Princess Isabella of Castile in 1469 at first seemed unlikely to bring any degree of unity to the two kingdoms, which were the two main competitors for power in the peninsula. After Ferdinand became King of Aragon and after they had won a civil war for control of Castile, the two set about consolidating the control of their kingdoms. This was to be a long and complex process, attempting to limit the influence of the powerful nobility and towns in Castile, improving the state of royal finances and making the government more efficient. After a prolonged struggle Granada fell to Ferdinand and Isabella in 1492, an event which was perhaps the high point of their reign. Thereafter Ferdinand and Isabella worked to bring religious unity to their possessions by removing the liberty of the Jews and the Muslims to follow their religion. They also sought to increase Spanish power abroad by opposing the ambitions of France in the Italian peninsula (and acquiring a dominant position in southern Italy as a result) and by seizing ports on the North African coast. During their reigns the first steps were taken towards the creation of a Spanish Empire in the Americas. The death of Isabella in 1504 provoked a succession crisis in Castile which saw Ferdinand temporarily ousted from that kingdom, but by 1507 he was back in effective control of both Aragon and Castile until his own death in 1516. The extent to which Ferdinand and Isabella succeeded in creating a united Spain out of their very different kingdoms is still a point of debate amongst historians. Most would now conclude that they were able to bring a degree of unity through their shared ambitions and actions, but that Aragon and Castile remained separate in their governments, their economies and, in some cases, in their national interests.

1 ᔐ SPAIN IN 1469

In October 1469 Isabella, the eighteen-year-old half-sister of the King of Castile, married Ferdinand, the seventeen-year-old son of the King of Aragon. Undoubtedly the most politically effective marital partnership

PICTURE 3
*Ferdinand of Aragon and
Isabella of Castile, c. 1482
(Spanish manuscript)*

of this, or perhaps any other period, they faced huge problems at the start of their married life. It was by no means sure that Isabella would take the throne of Castile; in the event it was necessary for Ferdinand and Isabella to defeat internal opponents and foreign invasion to enforce her claim after the death of her half-brother in 1474. Ferdinand became King of Aragon in 1479. They then had to govern the very different kingdoms of Aragon and Castile, taking into account the traditional hostility between their subjects. However, their royal marriage had established a dynastic union which, apart from some periods of crisis, was to hold the realms of Spain together permanently.

At the time of the marriage of Ferdinand and Isabella, Iberia was divided into five main political entities – Castile, Aragon, Portugal, Navarre and Granada.

A *Castile*

CASTILIAN SOCIETY

The kingdom of Castile sprawled across most of central Spain, being by far the largest state in the peninsula. It was four times greater in area

PROFILE

FERDINAND OF ARAGON AND ISABELLA OF CASTILE (1474–1516)

The marriage was an arranged one and the two made an unlikely couple. Ferdinand had been born in 1452, the son of King John II of Aragon, whom he succeeded as king in 1479. He was well educated and grew up with a liking for the arts and music. Ferdinand gained early military experience in wars in Catalonia, experience which proved invaluable when he had to support his wife's claim to the Castilian throne in the years after 1474. Contemporaries regarded Ferdinand as a supremely able monarch: a cunning negotiator, a capable soldier and a ruthless statesman. The Italian writer Guicciardini compared him to the great Holy Roman Emperor Charlemagne. Machiavelli summed him up superbly by saying that he 'kept his subjects' minds uncertain and astonished and left no time for men to settle down and act against him' and declared that 'from being a weak king he has risen to being, for fame and glory, the first king of Christendom'. Ferdinand had a reputation for lechery and fathered a number of children outside marriage, but this did not prevent him being genuinely fond of his wife. In the will he made shortly before his death in 1516 he instructed that he should be buried beside her in the cathedral of Granada.

Isabella was born in 1451, her father being King John II of Castile; her half-brother became King Henry IV three years later. Noble opposition to Henry grew in the second half of the 1460s but Isabella refused to become a focus for plotting, and was rewarded by being recognised as heiress to the throne in 1468. Her marriage to Ferdinand took place without Henry IV's approval (he would have preferred her to marry the much older Alfonso V of Portugal). From the outbreak of civil war in Castile against Joanna, a rival claimant to the throne on Henry IV's death, Isabella showed herself to be a shrewd and energetic ruler, fully capable of governing successfully in the dangerous world of fifteenth-century Iberia. She was intensely pious and took a particular interest in the religious affairs of her realm, as well as being a patron of Spanish and Flemish artists. On her death in 1504 the Archbishop of Toledo mourned, 'A queen has disappeared who has no equal on earth for her greatness of spirit, purity of heart, Christian piety, equal justice to all.'

than the Spanish territories of Aragon and, with about five million people, accounted for seventy to eighty per cent of the population of Iberia. During the early Middle Ages much of southern Castile had been occupied by invading Moors from North Africa. The long struggle to regain this lost territory (known as the 'Reconquest') did much to determine the nature of Castilian society. The warrior nobility, or *hidalgo* class, had taken the lead in the Reconquest and their values of military prowess and conquest became the dominant ones in Castile. The most important aristocratic families carved out massive domains, which gave them considerable political and economic power in relation to the Crown. Below the nobility in the social scale, the middle class in the towns of Castile was only small, and almost non-existent in the rural parts of the kingdom. The mass of the population was made up of poor, often landless, peasants who had little prospect of escaping a life of grinding poverty but who were to provide the armies of Spain with a constant flow of hardy recruits. Economically, Castile depended heavily on the revenue from wool exports provided by the huge flocks that grazed on the grasslands of the Castilian interior.

THE PROBLEM OF THE SUCCESSION IN CASTILE

In the mid-fifteenth century the most notable feature of the political scene in Castile was the weakness of the Crown. King Henry IV, who came to the throne in 1454, lacked personal authority and the institutions to impose his will on the country. He was not, however, the complete catastrophe as a king that some older historians have portrayed and recent writers have given him credit for initiating some of the methods of government taken over by Isabella. It was strongly rumoured that Henry was unable to produce an heir (he was nicknamed 'the Impotent') and when a daughter was born to him and his queen it was believed by many that the baby was the product of the liaison between the queen and one of the king's noble favourites, Beltràn de la Cueva. The young Princess Joanna became widely known as 'la Beltraneja' and her right to succeed to the throne was disputed by many nobles who looked to Henry's half-sister, Isabella, as the rightful heir. Henry had proved totally unable to control his warlike nobility, anarchy reigned in many parts of the kingdom and a contested succession seemed the best recipe for continued instability. Castile did, however, possess one great political advantage: it was a unitary state with one language, one system of taxation, one *Cortes* (parliament) and one system of law.

B *Aragon*

Turning to Aragon, there too political disorder had been prevalent. King John II at least possessed a clear male heir in the person of Ferdinand, but he was faced by civil war in the period 1462–72. Unlike Castile, Aragon was split into a number of states – Aragon itself, Catalonia and Valencia. Each of these jealously guarded its own **Cortes**, language, laws and privileges (*fueros*). The power of the Aragonese Crown was thus restricted by particularism (assertion of local independence) in a manner that the Castilian monarchy was not. In the Mediterranean, the Crown of Aragon also ruled Sardinia and Sicily.

TIMELINE

1469 Ferdinand of Aragon and Isabella of Castile marry
1474 Isabella becomes Queen of Castile: outbreak of civil war
1476 *Santa Hermandad* set up
Portuguese invasion of Castile halted at the Battle of Toro
1479 Ferdinand becomes King of Aragon
Treaty of Alcacovas between Castile and Portugal
Castilian civil war ends in victory for Isabella

Cortes a representative assembly in each of the Spanish kingdoms

The population of Aragon in Spain was about one million and the kingdom was sparsely peopled.

Catalonia had traditionally enjoyed a thriving commercial position in the Mediterranean, based on the export of textiles, and the prosperity of the coastal areas had provided benefits for the whole of Aragon, but by the mid-fifteenth century the trading pre-eminence of Catalonia was in decay. This was partly due to serious visitations of the plague, partly to the challenge of Castilian merchants and sailors who were beginning to penetrate into the western Mediterranean and partly to the activities of the Genoese, who took over much of the Catalan trade. However, Valencia was enjoying an economic boom during the fifteenth century, with exports of pottery, rice and fruit and high-quality gold coinage in circulation.

The potential of Aragon seemed to be much less than that of Castile, but David Abulafia has recently argued that the eventual superiority of Castile was by no means a foregone conclusion. Aragon already had a more developed economy than Castile, it possessed overseas possessions and the political instability of Castile threatened to tear it apart.

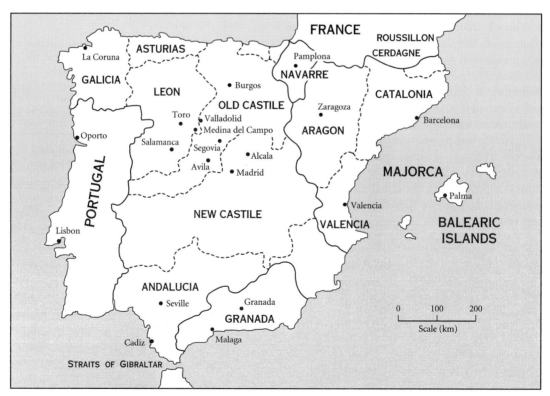

MAP 2
The kingdoms of Spain in 1474

C *The other Iberian states*

The three other states in the Iberian peninsula were Portugal, Navarre and Granada. Portugal had won her struggle to avoid Castilian domination in the late fourteenth century and by the middle of the next century was becoming increasingly preoccupied with exploration of the African coast. However, this did not stop her interfering in the affairs of Castile when the opportunity arose. Navarre was a small kingdom, but it straddled the Pyrenees and was therefore important in the rivalry between France and Spain. Granada was the last Moorish bastion in Spain, although an annual tribute was paid to Castile. It will be considered at length in a later section.

See Chapter 4

KEY ISSUE

What were the major differences between Aragon and Castile at the time of Ferdinand and Isabella's marriage?

2 ⤳ THE CIVIL WAR IN CASTILE

A *The outbreak of war, 1474*

The death of Henry IV in December 1474 plunged Castile into civil war. Within twenty-four hours of the passing of her brother, Isabella had secured the royal treasury at Segovia and had been proclaimed queen. She could not, however, feel secure while her rival, Joanna, remained at liberty. La Beltraneja, who was only thirteen years old, was held in Madrid under the protection of the powerful Marquis of Villena, who rejected attempts by Ferdinand and Isabella to bribe him into handing her over. Joanna soon became a figurehead for those who genuinely believed in her right to the throne and for those who merely wished to prolong the state of near anarchy in Castile for their own advantage. Across Castile, noble families ranged themselves behind one or other of the princesses, often because they could use the dynastic dispute to settle local scores.

B *Portuguese intervention against Isabella*

Joanna's prospects of success were increased considerably by the support of Alfonso V of Portugal, who sensed that intervention in Castile might bring the kingdom under Portuguese control if he married Joanna. Faced with imminent invasion, Ferdinand and Isabella reacted with an energy that was to typify their political and personal partnership. They confirmed the privileges of loyal nobles and attempted to buy the support of waverers; they cultivated the support of Castilian cities, vilified Alfonso in a stream of propaganda, fortified strategic points, concluded a truce with the Moors of Granada in order to guard their southern flank and even made a somewhat spurious claim to the Portuguese throne.

C *Isabella's victory*

In early summer 1475, Alfonso invaded Castile. Ferdinand, who supplied Isabella with military experts, challenged Alfonso to a duel to settle the matter – an offer which the ageing King of Portugal, hardly surprisingly, refused – and then led an army to counter the invasion. Several months of inconclusive sparring followed but at the Battle of Toro in March 1476 Ferdinand halted Alfonso and his Castilian supporters. Alfonso withdrew, ending the threat from the west. After Toro, other events helped to turn the war in favour of Isabella. Alfonso's ally, Louis XI of France, more interested in conquering Burgundy than helping Alfonso, made peace with Castile. In 1478, Isabella gave birth to a son, thus providing a clear line of succession and attracting the support of many of those nobles who had been uncommitted. The accession of Ferdinand to the throne of Aragon following the death of John II in 1479 increased his military resources and his prestige in Castile.

By September 1479, Alfonso was glad to make peace in the Treaty of Alcaçovas. Alfonso gave up all claims to Castile and in return Isabella renounced Castilian claims to Portugal's possessions in the Atlantic and Africa. Joanna lived as a nun until her death in 1530.

Victory in the Castilian civil war was Ferdinand and Isabella's first great achievement and it must be stressed that it was achieved jointly. The bulk of their army was Castilian but Ferdinand brought in siege and artillery experts from Aragon and the Aragonese navy played an important part in the war at sea. Ferdinand also negotiated support from a number of the Castilian nobles, including the powerful families of Alva, Mendoza and Enriquez. The defeat of Joanna and her adherents did not, however, mean an immediate restoration of political stability. The monarchs now faced the task of halting the disorder that had plagued Castile for decades.

See map on page 32

KEY ISSUE

Why did Isabella emerge victorious from the Castilian civil war?

3 ↜ THE PACIFICATION OF CASTILE

The traditional view of Ferdinand and Isabella's actions following the civil war is that they ruthlessly suppressed any potential sources of opposition and extended the scope of royal power in Spain. There is some truth in this assessment. Certainly the monarchs were determined that there should be no repeat of the chaos which Castile had endured before their victory, but the degree of their success in destroying the forces which made for instability is questionable.

A *Peripatetic kingship*

The first method by which the monarchs attempted to impose their authority was by travelling through Castile, meeting leading nobles and citizens and dealing with potential problems at first hand. For example, when revolt broke out in Galicia in 1485–86 both Ferdinand and Isabella travelled to this remote area to deal with the trouble. This 'peripatetic' style of **kingship** was medieval in origin and survived well into the sixteenth century. It was not until the reign of Philip II that Madrid was designated as the capital of Spain. Constant movement about Castile to some extent offset the difficulties of having only a small standing army available for internal security, very little bureaucracy in the provinces and an inadequate revenue.

> **peripatetic kingship** a style of government in which the monarch(s) tours the country in an attempt to ensure sound government and justice

B *The nobility*

Perhaps the most serious threat to the stability of Castile came from the nobility. The most powerful families of **grandees** collectively controlled economic and military resources far in excess of anything Ferdinand and Isabella could hope to muster. Moreover, the monarchs owed Isabella's throne to those nobles who had helped them in the civil war and were obliged to look to their nobles to supply them with troops for foreign wars and to deal with internal rebellion. The aggressive instincts of the Castilian aristocracy were held in check by a subtle mixture of threats, pressure and bribery. As early as 1480, the monarchs attempted to buy support when, at the Cortes of Toledo, nobles were confirmed in possession of any royal land which they had managed to acquire before 1464 whilst the monarchs resumed ownership of Crown lands alienated after that date. There was no attempt to remove the nobility's exemption from taxation, nobles who remained loyal were not disarmed and privileges, honours and titles were granted as inducements to good behaviour. However, if Ferdinand and Isabella felt their interests to be prejudiced they acted decisively. The strategic port of Cadiz was confiscated from the Duke of Cadiz in 1492 and the Duke of Medina Sidonia was obliged to surrender Gibraltar in 1502. Nevertheless, in both these cases the aggrieved aristocrat was compensated with territories elsewhere. Henry Kamen has claimed that 'the taming of the Castilian aristocracy was an outstanding achievement of the Catholic kings. The great lords were taken into partnership with the Crown and confirmed in their estates and private armies.' It is true that many Castilian nobles served the Crown faithfully both in Spain and abroad, but it must not be forgotten that, after the death of Isabella in 1504, considerable numbers rejected the authority of Ferdinand and supported the claim to the throne of the monarchs' daughter Joanna and her husband Philip of Burgundy. Moreover, effective power at the local level lay with the nobles, some of whom controlled whole regions, one such being the Count of Lemos in Galicia.

> **grandees** the most powerful of the aristocracy

> **KEY ISSUE**
>
> *How successful was Ferdinand and Isabella's policy towards the Castilian nobility?*

C *The towns*

THE SANTA HERMANDAD

To increase their military potential, Ferdinand and Isabella revived and extended the system of mounted militia provided by the *Hermandad*

> *Hermandad* brotherhood of Castilian towns

or association of Castilian towns. This institution dated from 1190 when four towns had agreed to patrol the roads and deter banditry, as well as resolving trading disputes. Such associations became common during periods of instability in the Middle Ages and at the Cortes of Madrigal in 1476, the monarchs regularised them into the *Santa Hermandad* or 'Holy Brotherhood'. A council of the *Hermandad*, supervised by the Crown, was established to administer it and the *Hermandad* provided substantial numbers of troops for the campaigns against Granada. In 1490, for example, it provided 10 000 men, approximately one-quarter of the total. The towns represented in the Hermandad met together in a *Junta* or assembly and this provided Ferdinand and Isabella with a useful method of consulting the cities and an even more useful method of levying taxation. In 1491–92, for example, the Crown received sixty-four million *maravadís* from the Junta of the *Hermandad*, equivalent to a quarter of annual revenue. This used to be seen as evidence of royal centralisation but, with the end of the war against Granada, the *Santa Hermandad* declined in importance and after 1498 reverted to its original role of rural police force.

THE CORREGIDORES

The towns of Castile were a potential source of opposition, and Ferdinand and Isabella followed a tradition of royal intervention in their affairs. In the fourteenth century royal officials known as *corregidores* had been appointed in some Castilian towns to help decide local disputes and to ensure that the interests of the Crown were upheld. In 1480, the Cortes of Toledo agreed that *corregidores* could be despatched to towns where they did not already exist and by 1494 there were fifty-four towns in Castile with a *corregidor* in residence. They dealt with public order and administrative matters and have traditionally been regarded as agents of government centralisation. However, although the *corregidores* were appointed by the Crown they were paid locally and were certainly subject to local pressures. There were constant complaints from the towns that they were inefficient or favoured the nobility. The policies of Ferdinand and Isabella cannot be seen as a total success in this area for it was the towns which revolted against their successor, Charles, in the Revolt of the *Comuneros*.

corregidores officials appointed by the crown to supervise the affairs of Castilian towns

D *The military orders*

Ferdinand and Isabella also brought under royal control the military orders of Santiago, Alcantara and Calatrava. These were medieval crusading corporations that had acquired massive landholdings during the Reconquest. They controlled considerable military might (providing one-tenth of the infantry and one-sixth of the cavalry for the war against Granada) and the masterships of the orders were highly prized by the *grandee* families. Isabella wanted Ferdinand to be elected grand master of each order but he turned down the first offer, which had been made under pressure from the queen. Because of such tact there was much less resentment when he did take control of the Order of Calatrava in 1487, that of Alcantara in 1494 and that of Santiago in 1499. A Council of the Military Orders was established in 1489 to take over the administration of the corporations.

E *Royal finance*

To maintain their hold on Castile the monarchs needed a sound financial base. Ferdinand and Isabella were not fiscal innovators. They relied on traditional taxes and did not significantly dent the noble and clerical exemption from taxation. Their main income derived from the **alcabala**, a sales tax first introduced in 1342, providing up to eighty per cent of the Crown's total revenue. The *servicio y montazgo*, a traditional tax on the sheep flocks of Castile, provided another profitable source of income, as did customs dues – another time-honoured royal right. The *cruzada*, a new tax on the Church granted by the papacy during the Granada war, continued to be collected after 1492 and contributions raised from the *Hermandad* (which raised an average of thirty million *maravedís* per annum between 1485 and 1498) and granted by the *Cortes* were valuable additions to the monarchs' revenue. (In 1500–04 alone, the Cortes provided subsidies of 300 million *maravedís*.) The ordinary revenue of Castile rose from seventy-three million *maravedís* in 1474 (of which only eleven million were collected, owing to the civil war) to 320 million *maravedís* by 1510 and, when the 'extraordinary' revenue of the *Hermandad* and the *Cortes* were added, the Crown's financial position should have been healthy.

   There were, however, huge expenses. The marriage of Catherine of Aragon to Prince Arthur of England, for example, cost sixty million *maravedís*, whilst the second expedition to Naples in 1500–04 cost 366 million *maravedís*. Grants and pensions were costing the Crown 112 million *maravedís* by 1504 (partly a result of the policy of buying noble support). The monarchs were obliged to resort to issuing *juros* or government bonds and the interest on these was taking up 131 million *maravedís* by 1516. Charles, the grandson of Ferdinand and Isabella, therefore succeeded to a throne that was just solvent but certainly not wealthy.

alcabala a 10 per cent sales tax

TABLE 4
Income of the Castilian Crown

1474	11m *maravedis*
1479	94m *maravedis*
1481	150m *maravedis*
1496	269m *maravedis*
1504	317m *maravedis*
1510	320m *maravedis*

F *Administration*

In administration, too, the monarchs preferred to adapt rather than to innovate. A series of councils staffed largely by **letrados** (civil servants trained in law) administered the main areas of government. The Council of Castile spawned committees for foreign policy, justice, finance, the *Hermandad* and Aragon and further councils were set up for the Inquisition (1483), the military orders (1489) and Aragon (1494). It used to be thought that the reliance on *letrados*, who tended to be of middle class or gentry origin, was a conscious attempt by the

letrados experienced lawyers, used as administrators by the crown

KEY ISSUE

How radical were Ferdinand and Isabella's reforms of the government of Castile?

See pages 55–6

monarchs to remove the nobility from government. Modern historians have pointed out that the role of *letrados* was already well established by the reign of Isabella (Henry IV had insisted that at least eight of the twelve members of the Council of Castile were *letrados*) and that the monarchs were simply interested in obtaining the best possible administrative ability.

Thus the monarchs tended to pursue conservative policies in dealing with the problems of Castile. What made them successful was the close attention paid to the operation of the policies, backed up by the personal appearances of the peripatetic monarchs. Yet all this could be so easily threatened by a major crisis – such as the succession crisis after 1504.

4 ∽ THE CONQUEST OF GRANADA

With the successful conclusion of the war against Portugal and the restoration of some degree of stability in Castile, Ferdinand and Isabella were able to turn their attention to the south. There, the Moorish kingdom of Granada bore constant witness to how incomplete had been the Reconquest. Several motives existed for the decision to destroy this last remnant of Muslim power in Spain.

A *Motives for the attack on Granada*

FEAR OF ISLAM
Fear of Islam was widespread in the late fifteenth century. The victories of the Ottoman Turks in the Balkans and the eastern Mediterranean seemed to signal an onslaught on Europe, an offensive in which the apparently wealthy and self-confident kingdom of Granada might play a leading role. The Ottomans had already made contact with the Moorish states of North Africa and with Granada, and a Muslim alliance would jeopardise Spanish trade in the Mediterranean, including the link with Ferdinand's own province of Sicily. By overcoming Granada the Spanish monarchs would not only improve the security of their own kingdoms but also win a significant local victory in the duel between Christendom and Islam. 'The dead weigh on me heavily', wrote Isabella of Spanish casualties during the war, 'but they could not have gone better employed.'

PATRONAGE
A second, and perhaps more pressing, reason for the conquest was to provide the monarchs with land which could be distributed as patronage amongst the Castilian nobility. Those nobles who had fought for Isabella in the civil war had to be rewarded and those who still harboured doubts about her succession had to be won over. The conquered land could be disposed of as Ferdinand and Isabella wished

and by 1492 over half the area of Granada had been granted to the Castilian aristocracy.

THE PARTICIPATION OF THE NOBILITY

Linked with this was a third factor. Nobles who could give vent to their warlike inclinations in a potentially lucrative invasion of Granada would be less likely to revolt or engage in conflicts among themselves. Hernando del Pulgar described this as 'exercising the chivalry of the realm'. The Muslims were an easily identifiable enemy and war against them would unite all Castilian nobles under the banners of Christianity and Isabella.

THE RESOURCES OF GRANADA

The monarchs may also have been influenced by a fourth considera- tion: the wealth of Granada. The mountainous Alpujarras region was famous for its mulberry bushes on which silk worms were reared. Granada silk was a valuable luxury commodity to Christians and Muslims alike and would make an important addition to the prosperity of Castile. Moreover, the merchants of Granada had a share in the distribution of the gold that reached the North African ports after being transported across the Sahara. European demand for gold was rising and access to this supply would be a useful windfall.

THE OUTBREAK OF WAR WITH GRANADA

The occasion for war occurred in 1481. During the 1470s, a series of truces had barely restrained the skirmishing between Christians and Moors along the borders of Castile and Granada. In April 1478 the Moors attacked the Christian town of Cieza, killed eighty of the inhabitants and captured the rest. Heavily involved in the war against Portugal, Ferdinand and Isabella were in no position to retaliate, to negotiate the release of the prisoners or even to afford to ransom their luckless subjects. They may even have been obliged to give up the annual tribute traditionally paid to the monarchs of Castile by Granada. Once the war with Portugal had ended, the monarchs were less willing to submit to such humiliations and began to make preparations for full-scale war. In 1479 they applied to Pope Sixtus IV for the coming conflict to be declared a crusade. The request was granted, conferring the status of martyr on those who died fighting and earning remission of sins (i.e. fewer years in purgatory) for all those who fought. Those who did not fight could obtain indulgence by contributing to war expenses. Tension heightened when the ruler of Granada, Mulay Hassan, refused to renew payment of the tribute. 'The coffers of Granada contain no more gold but steel', was his alleged reply to the demands of the Spanish. Alarmed by the Christian preparations, the Moors decided to strike first in order to improve their strategic position whilst there was still time. In December 1481, they seized a number of Christian strongholds on the border, including the town of Zahara. Ferdinand and Isabella welcomed this as a 'chance to put in

TIMELINE

1482 Opening of war against Granada

1492 City of Granada falls to Ferdinand and Isabella

1494 Ferdinand and Isabella given the title 'Catholic Monarchs' by Pope Alexander VI

1499 Moorish revolt in Granada

1502 Muslims in Castile told to convert to Christianity or be exiled

KEY ISSUE

Why did Ferdinand and Isabella decide to invade Granada?

hand forthwith what has long been in our minds', and prepared to invade Granada in 1482.

C *The Spanish victory*

The ensuing war lasted for ten years and was fought with a bitterness inspired by crusading zeal on the Spanish side and desperation on the part of the Moors. The Christians held the upper hand, deploying larger forces than the Muslims could muster (Spanish manpower exceeded 50 000 at times) and using cannon to reduce the castles and cities of Granada. Much of the credit for Spanish success can be attributed to Ferdinand who played an active part in the campaigns, directing strategy and leading armies in person. His Aragonese military experts possessed skills and technology (such as the new hand-held gunpowder weapons) which the Muslims could not match. Isabella was not the type of woman to sit meekly by whilst there was God's work to be done and she played a valuable part in the campaign by organising supplies and reinforcements. The practical partnership of the two monarchs was never seen to better effect than in the Granada war.

Militarily backward, Granada was fatally weakened by feuding within the ruling Nasrid dynasty. Mulay Hassan faced revolt by his son Boabdil and was then overthrown by his brother, al-Zagal, in 1485. During the following years Boabdil and al-Zagal fought each other, to the obvious satisfaction of the Christians. In 1489 al-Zagal surrendered to the Spanish, leaving Boabdil as ruler of a shrunken, devastated Granada. Appeals to the rest of the Islamic world brought no response and in 1491 Ferdinand's army closed in on the city of Granada. After an eight-month siege, Boabdil capitulated and in January 1492 the Spanish entered the Muslim capital. This was perhaps the greatest moment of the reign: the culmination of several centuries of Reconquest and a rousing triumph for the joint monarchs.

D *The results of the fall of Granada*

The collapse of Moorish resistance had a number of important results. The international prestige of Ferdinand and Isabella was hugely enhanced. At a time when Christianity appeared to be on the retreat in the face of militant Islam, in Spain at least the tide had turned. In 1494 Pope Alexander VI accorded Ferdinand and Isabella the title 'Catholic Monarchs', describing them as 'athletes of Christ'. Spanish adulation was unbounded: 'It is the extinction of Spain's calamities', crowed the scholar Peter Martyr and an observer of the fall of Granada wrote exultantly of the 'most distinguished and blessed day there has ever been in Spain'. The monarchs had temporarily united their kingdoms in a common cause, eradicated a persistent threat to the southern border of Castile, trained a formidable army in the techniques of modern warfare and assured their own supremacy in relation to the Castilian nobility. It may also have made the Castilians willing to

Historians and the quest for the origins of the Nation State

For many years it was a commonplace of historical writing that the late fifteenth century and early sixteenth century saw the birth of 'nation states' in western Europe. The key feature of this process was the emergence of 'new monarchy' in these states, which was characterised by the unification of hitherto separate dynastic lands, centralisation of political and military power in the hands of the monarch, innovative and more efficient methods of government, increased royal income, a reduction in the independence of the aristocracy and of the regions, more royal influence over the church and a foreign policy aimed at exerting control over peripheral areas of the state. The Spain of Ferdinand and Isabella, like the England of Henry VII, seemed to display all these elements. Historians applauded the unification of Castile and Aragon, the curbing of the volatile Castilan nobles, the creation of a system of government councils and the intrusion of royal power into the towns of Castile, financial solvency and the absorption of frontier areas such as Granada and Navarre. Modern historians have argued that the process of creating modern nation states was a far more protracted process than this traditional interpretation would suggest. Authors such as Kamen and Lynch see Ferdinand and Isabella operating within a medieval framework, developing and refining existing methods rather than creating new ones. They possessed neither the power, nor perhaps the will, to sweep away the conditions they had inherited. In particular, they ruled dynastic states – collections of territories brought together by the accidents of inheritance – with widely differing customs and structures, whose integration would take two or three centuries rather than two or three decades.

support Ferdinand's campaigns in Italy after 1494, an area which had hitherto been an exclusively Aragonese preserve.

E *The Muslims after 1492*

For the Muslims, the terms of the surrender were surprisingly generous. So generous, indeed, that it is possible Ferdinand was showing leniency to secure immediate compliance, with the intention of utterly crushing the Muslims at some convenient future time. (It must, however, be pointed out that the Muslims living in Aragon were well treated and gave Ferdinand no trouble during his reign.) Although the inhabitants of Granada became subjects of Ferdinand and Isabella, they were allowed to practise their own religions and customs, to trade freely, to own property and to emigrate in safety if they wished to do so. There was to be no forcible conversion to Christianity. Many of the élite of Granada preferred to cross to North Africa, carrying with them a desire for revenge and an ambition to liberate their co-religionists who remained under the heel of the Infidel.

The years after 1492 suggested that Muslims and Christians might live together amicably in Castile's new province. Areas depopulated by the wars were occupied by peasant settlers from Andalusia (35 000 to 40 000 immigrants moved south between 1485 and 1498) while Moorish farmers worked much as before, even if their masters were now Castilian rather than Moorish nobles. The Count of Tendilla was appointed Captain-General of Granada and pursued moderate policies, respecting the customs of the native population. Isabella's confessor, Hernando de Talavera, was created Archbishop of Granada. He, too, did not abuse the sensitivities of the Muslims and preferred to gain converts to Christianity by preaching and persuasion rather than by harassment.

F *Conversion to Christianity or expulsion*

In 1499 all this changed. In Early Modern Europe it was regarded as a sign of weakness for states to permit more than one religion inside their borders, and the monarchs and their advisers must have been concerned that the Muslims in the south were a potential threat. With the intention of investigating the matter, Archbishop Ximenes de Cisneros of Toledo, primate of Spain, accompanied Ferdinand and Isabella to Granada. Appalled by what he saw as Talavera's leniency, Cisneros embarked on a programme of mass 'conversion'. It has been shown that this was not part of the surrender agreement of 1492 and, in November 1499, the Muslims of the Alpujarras rose in revolt. Ferdinand crushed the outbreak in an energetic campaign in 1500 (although he seems to have had serious doubts about the wisdom of Cisneros' policy) and the Moors were offered the choice of conversion to Christianity or emigration. Most were too poor to leave. In 1502 Isabella ordered the expulsion of all remaining adherents of Islam, with all those remaining automatically becoming Christian. These ***Moriscos***,

Morisco a Spanish Muslim who had converted to Christianity

as they were known, were to be a source of anxiety for Spanish monarchs for decades to come. Unreconciled and unabsorbed, they remained a potential Muslim threat on Spain's strategic southern coast. Ferdinand and Isabella had created an intractable problem which was to last until the final expulsion of the *Moriscos* in 1609. Granada had been unified with Castile, but at the expense of a divided society.

5 ↪ THE ECONOMY OF SPAIN UNDER FERDINAND AND ISABELLA

With the decline of the Catalan commercial empire, Castile moved into a position of economic domination of Spain. The most profitable product of Castile was wool, grown on the merino breed of sheep which had been introduced to Spain from North Africa in about 1300. Sheep farming enjoyed a favoured status and was encouraged by the monarchs for both financial and economic reasons. Considerable revenue was derived from the *servicio y montazgo* tax on sheep and the export of wool provided customs duties. There was a ready market for merino wool in Europe and large quantities were shipped to northern ports such as Antwerp, where it was sold for textile manufacture. The aristocracy also preferred pastoral agriculture as few workers and little capital investment were necessary for sheep farming. The number of sheep rose from 2.7 million in 1477 to 3.5 million in 1526 and huge areas of the Spanish interior were turned over to grazing. This expansion was a mixed blessing for Spain. Most historians believe that the emphasis on sheep led to the neglect of arable farming, inducing grain shortages in 1502–08 which necessitated large-scale imports in 1506 and aided the outbreak of plague in 1507. Moreover, the **Mesta** (the corporation of sheep-owners) was granted privileges that were detrimental to arable agriculture. In 1489 the *canadas* or migratory routes used by the sheep flocks were enlarged. In 1500 a royal councillor was appointed to the new post of President of the *Mesta* and in 1501 a new law stated that flocks could use any land that had been used as pasture in preceding centuries for ever. Preoccupation with the export of raw wool meant that Spain failed to develop her own textile industry. Much land was deforested and subjected to erosion, a further example of the imbalance between pastoral and arable farming which was a long-term legacy of Ferdinand and Isabella.

The monarchs' policy towards trade and industry was also not entirely beneficial. The harsh treatment meted out to the Muslims of Granada, the *conversos* (Jews converted to Christianity) and the Jews resulted in the flight of many skilled workers and some capital from Spain. To compensate for this, efforts were made to recruit foreign experts, especially from Flanders and Italy. A further handicap to development was the system of **guilds**. In most areas of Europe these were in decline but in Spain they retained their privileged position, discouraging innovation and initiative and perpetuating old-fashioned practices. A third factor hindering progress was that Aragon and Castile remained separate economic units with customs barriers operating between them. Catalan merchants were treated as foreigners at the great Castilian commercial fair of Medina del Campo.

Some measures were taken to encourage Spanish trade. Agents were sent to London, Bruges and other cities to facilitate the sale of wool and convoys were organised to ship Spanish wool to northern Europe. Navigation laws were passed to stimulate the carrying of goods in Spanish ships. In 1483 the trade fair at Medina del Campo was reorganised and some improvements were made to the dilapidated road system, although too much of the responsibility for this fell on the small settlements along the highways rather than on the major towns that the repairs were intended to benefit.

guild an association of craftsmen to regulate standards and protect their interests against competition

By 1516, the Spanish economy was already in an unhealthy state due to lack of investment in home production, absence of commercial enterprise and an agricultural base too reliant on a single product – that of wool. The influx of gold and silver from the New World concealed these structural deficiencies for much of the sixteenth century, but when this dried up it became clear that Spain had not developed an economy to match those of the Netherlands, England or France.

6 ↪ CISNEROS AND RELIGIOUS POLICY

A *The problems of the Spanish Church*

The condition of the Church in Spain in the mid-fifteenth century was regarded with concern by the monarchs, especially Isabella who was renowned for her piety. Most of the seven archbishops and forty bishops lived lives of ostentatious luxury and ignored their spiritual and pastoral duties. Absenteeism was rife. Several archbishops and bishops had participated in the civil war, drawing on their huge estates and revenues to finance their political ambitions. For example, Don Alfonso Carrillo, Archbishop of Toledo, fought with the Portuguese army at Toro and could command an army of a thousand men and the loyalty of 19 000 vassals. The state of the religious orders was widely regarded as a scandal and the parish clergy were frequently poor and uneducated.

Royal policy towards the Church had three main priorities. First, the monarchs wished to obtain royal domination of the personnel of the Church. This meant wresting control of ecclesiastical appointments from the Papacy and ensuring that dependable and loyal men were appointed to senior posts. A second aim was to obtain a share of the vast wealth of the Church. The third priority was to reform the Church and raise its moral and educational standards.

B *Royal control of the Church*

In the aftermath of the civil war Ferdinand and Isabella carried out a number of measures to curb the political and military power of the Church, obliging it, for example, to hand over fortresses to the custody of royal appointees. This was followed by a determined royal offensive to gain control of the appointment of bishops, traditionally in the hands of the papacy. At a gathering of Spanish clergy at Seville in 1478, the monarchs obtained support for the reduction of papal influence and a programme of reform. When the bishopric of Cuenca fell vacant in 1479, Ferdinand and Isabella asserted their right to nominate the new bishop and Pope Sixtus IV gave in after a prolonged wrangle. Following up this success, in 1486 the monarchs secured from Innocent VIII the important right of *patronato* or patronage over Church appointments in the newly occupied lands of Granada. Using Spanish support for the papacy in the Italian Wars as a lever, Ferdinand extracted further concessions, this time over the Church in the New World. In a bull of 1508 Pope Julius II gave the monarchs the *patronato* over all Spanish territory in America, including rights to dismiss churchmen, tax the Church and ignore papal edicts. The papacy was thus excluded from influence in Spain's colonies, the Crown exercising a supreme headship. It was not until 1523 that Adrian VI admitted the power of Charles V to appoint to bishoprics in Spain itself, but the battle had effectively been won during the reign of Ferdinand and Isabella.

The monarchs were not slow to take advantage of their new rights by appointing reforming Spanish clergymen to the highest offices. The Queen's confessor, Hernando de Talavera, had constantly urged Isabella to improve the state of the Church and in 1492 he was appointed to the new archbishopric of Granada. There he practised what he advocated by preaching frequently, spending his revenues on the poor and providing work for the destitute. He abhorred idleness and even the poor blind were given employment blowing bellows for blacksmiths. Munzer, a German observer, recorded of Talavera that 'his continual studies, his constant labour and rigorous fasts had so debilitated his body that his bones were visible'. His place as the queen's spiritual adviser was taken in 1492 by Cisneros, who was made Archbishop of Toledo in 1495.

C *Reform of the Church*

With the active encouragement of Isabella, Cisneros set about improving the religious orders. This was a huge task as there were hundreds of monasteries and convents in Spain. At first, external visitors were sent round, but when this proved unsuccessful attempts were made to discipline the orders from within. In Cisneros' own order, the Franciscans, those who believed in strict adherence to the rule of St Francis (known as observants) gained ground at the expense of the Conventuals, who enjoyed a more relaxed existence. When Cisneros died in 1517 there were no Conventual religious houses left in Spain. The Dominicans, Augustinians and other orders followed this trend. Of course, there were failures. Many remote religious houses were scarcely touched by reform and four hundred Andalusian friars showed what they thought of the reforms by settling in North Africa and becoming Muslims, rather than give up their concubines.

Attempts to reform the secular clergy were also necessary. Talavera claimed that the Spanish bishops were guilty of absenteeism, simony and moral laxity. The lower clergy also left much to be desired. Isabella complained to the Bishop of Calahorra that, in his diocese, 'Most of the clergy are said to be in concubinage [living with mistresses] publicly and if our justice intervenes to punish them, they revolt.' In 1500 in Palencia the clergy had to be told not to 'gamble or fight bulls or sing or dance in public'. To combat such laxity, bishops were ordered to reside

PROFILE

CISNEROS (1436–1517)

Francisco Jimenez de Cisneros was born in 1436, the son of a minor royal official. He entered the church and in 1484 retreated into a remote monastery to devote himself to a life of prayer. There he acquired a reputation for high spirituality, wearing a hair shirt, fasting frequently and whipping himself. Isabella heard of his devotion and appointed him as her confessor in 1492. Cisneros was appointed Archbishop of Toledo in 1495, although he was so horrified at having to give up his contemplative life that he refused to accept the post for six months and even when he reluctantly agreed he refused to wear the conventional silks of the office and continued to dress in his rough friar's habit. He became Isabella's most trusted councillor and shared her concern to improve the condition of the Spanish Church. Faced with entrenched corruption and immorality, his crusade to raise standards met with only mixed success: he had to abandon attempts to cleanse his own cathedral when the clergy threatened armed resistance. Cisneros played an increasingly active part in the government of Spain, bringing a high level of commitment to whatever he undertook. His desire to eliminate the problem of the Moors in Granada encouraged Isabella's repressive policy towards them after 1500. Motivated by continuing hatred of Muslims he even led a Spanish expedition against Oran in 1509 when he was seventy-three and was reputed to have declared that 'the smell of gunpowder was sweeter than the perfumes of Arabia'. By the time of Isabella's death in 1504 Cisneros was the most respected statesman in Castile. He was appointed cardinal and inquisitor-general in 1507. When Ferdinand died in 1516, Cisneros was the natural choice to be made regent of Castile before the arrival of Charles Habsburg. He died in 1517, on his way to meet the new king.

in their sees and supervise their clergy. Parish priests were instructed to abandon their mistresses, preach sermons, wear appropriate clerical dress and provide their congregations with religious instruction. Here, too, the reformers ran into problems. The huge area of Spain made enforcement of reform difficult and even cathedral chapters sometimes resisted pressure to change their traditional modes of conduct. In 1496 the chapters (the governing bodies of the cathedral) of Castile appealed to the Pope and Ferdinand and Isabella had to resort to kidnapping their representatives to prevent them from leaving the country.

One of Cisneros' greatest achievements was the establishment of the University of Alcalà, completed in 1508, intended as a theological and cultural dynamo for the Church in Spain. The university offered a complete ecclesiastical education as well as specialising in medicine, languages and literature at a time when most Spanish universities concentrated on the study of law. Cisneros encouraged the production of printed books on spiritual matters and sponsored the compilation of the polyglot Bible. Published in 1522, this was a five-volume edition containing parallel texts of the Vulgate version and Greek and Hebrew versions. Alcalà became one of the great centres of European learning in the early sixteenth century, with scholars arriving from all over Europe to use its library (which included Arabic works captured in Granada) and to participate in the stimulating intellectual atmosphere of the university.

The overall impact of the reforms of the Church is disputed. Some historians, notably Henry Kamen, have argued that improvements only reached the religious orders and that the majority of the secular clergy (those not in monasteries) were totally unaffected. Certainly, there is little evidence that piety and morals were altered at a local level. Even Cisneros' own cathedral chapter of Toledo could not be fully reformed. In 1499, twenty-five of its members were reported to him for sodomy or concubinage and he seems to have taken no action. However, it can also be argued that the changes ordered by Isabella and Cisneros were sufficiently successful to protect the Spanish Church from the blast of anticlericalism and Protestant criticism later in the sixteenth century. It is not surprising that it was Spanish theologians who led the counterattack against Protestantism. Due to the reforms, the Spanish Church was better equipped than any other in Europe to face the challenge of the Reformation.

KEY ISSUE

What were the successes and failures of Cisneros's policies?

D *The Inquisition and the expulsion of the Jews*

During the early Middle Ages, Spanish Christians, Jews and Muslims had lived together in a state of mutual tolerance, or *conviviencia* as the Spanish called it. During the fourteenth century, however, religious tension had grown under the strain of economic depression and the Christian majority had turned on the Jewish minority. In 1391 thousands of Jews were massacred in Seville, Toledo, Barcelona and other cities. Many Jews converted to Christianity to avoid a similar fate. These **conversos** or 'new Christians' were still not safe from the virulent anti-Semitism that periodically gripped Spain in the fifteenth century.

conversos Jews who had converted to Christianity

REASONS FOR HATRED OF THE JEWS

There were a number of reasons for the widespread hostility towards the Jews and the *conversos*. First, Jews were identified in the popular imagination as Christ-killers and perpetrators of cannibalism and infanticide. Torquemada, the inquisitor-general, showed how they were classed with the worst enemies of the Church when he appealed to Ferdinand and Isabella for measures against 'Jews, blasphemers, deniers of God and the Saints, and equally sorcerors and necromancers'. Second, the Jews were hated for their role in Spanish society, being regarded as parasites and profiteers. Andres Bernaldez, a village priest, claimed, 'All their work was to multiply and increase … They never wanted to take manual work, ploughing or digging or walking the fields with the herds … but only jobs in the towns, so as to sit around making money without doing much work.' To many Spaniards the typical Jew was a money-lender or a rent- or debt-collector. A third reason for prejudice was that the *conversos* were believed to have adopted Christianity only as a cloak to conceal their continued practice of Judaism. Hernando del Pulgar, writing of the *conversos* of Toledo in 1485, said that they 'neither kept one law nor the other' and Bernaldez suggested that 'the greater part were secret Jews'. Despite this hostility, many *conversos* rose through their own abilities to high positions in Church and state. The fourth, and increasingly important, reason for suspicion was the growing Spanish obsession with *limpieza de sangre* or purity of blood. This was the belief that only those Spaniards whose blood was untainted by Jewish or Moorish influence were worthy to hold office. Anti-Jewish riots in Toledo in 1449 led to a decree that no one of Jewish ancestry was eligible for a place in the city government.

TIMELINE

1478	Inquisition established in Castile
1481	Inquisition re-started in Castile
1483	Torquemada named appointed Inquisitor-General of Spain
1486	Pope Innocent VIII gives Isabella right of *patronato* in Granada
1492	Jews expelled from Castile and Aragon Cisneros becomes confessor to Isabella
1495	Cisneros appointed Archbishop of Toledo

THE INQUISITION

To combat the alleged problem of the *conversos* in Castile, the monarchs turned to an institution which had first been introduced to Aragon in the thirteenth century – the Inquisition. This organisation, which possessed authority to investigate and punish cases of heresy, had been under papal control when first established. It had not been extended to Castile and by the mid-fifteenth century it was all but dead. When the monarchs decided to revive it and import it to Castile, they determined to bring it under royal supervision, making it independent of the papacy.

In November 1478 Pope Sixtus IV gave Ferdinand and Isabella the powers they sought by issuing a bull giving them authority to appoint inquisitors. After a delay of two years, inquisitors were commissioned to operate in Seville and in February 1481 they claimed their first victims when six *conversos* were burned as heretics. Some *conversos* fled, others tried to resist, but in the period 1481–88 Bernaldez recorded that 'the Inquisitors burnt over seven hundred persons and reconciled over five thousand and threw many into perpetual prison'. The harsh measures of the early inquisitors caused such an outcry that in April 1482 Sixtus IV denounced the Spanish Inquisition and ordered that appeals to the papacy be allowed. Ferdinand told the Pope that such interference was not acceptable and Sixtus had to admit defeat. This clearly marked another success for the monarchs in their struggle to control the Spanish Church.

It has been argued that the Inquisition was a device by which the monarchs could extend their general political control, as it had powers capable of overriding any other jurisdiction. However, there is little evidence of the political use of the Inquisition. It was employed to stop horse smuggling across the French border but, apart from isolated instances of that nature, it kept to its religious functions. Nonetheless, it was the only institution common to all of Ferdinand and Isabella's

Spanish realms. First established in Castile, it was extended to Aragon after the murder of an Inquisitor there in 1485. Here at least was some unification of Spain.

The organisation and procedure of the Spanish Inquisition made it unique both in Spain and Europe. At the head of the structure stood the inquisitor-general. The first of these was Tomás de Torquemada, appointed in 1483. Notorious for his implacable hatred of the *conversos*, Torquemada dominated the activities of the Inquisition until his death in 1498. Between 1507 and 1517 the post was held by Cisneros. Under the inquisitor-general was a six-member Council of the Supreme and General Inquisition or *Suprema*, chosen by the Crown and directly responsible to it. The Suprema supervised the activities of local tribunals, of which there were eventually thirteen in mainland Spain and others in Sicily, Sardinia and the Canaries. The main function of these tribunals was to seek out and punish *conversos* who still clung to Judaism. It must be stressed that the mission of the Inquisition was to combat heresy and therefore unbaptised Jews and Muslims were outside its sphere of influence. The procedure of the Inquisition involved the denunciation of heretics, the examination of the accused by the Inquisition (with the use of torture permitted) and, if found guilty, punishment by flogging, confiscation of property, service in the galleys or death by burning. It is not surprising that the Inquisition brought terror to many communities. In 1487 hundreds of *conversos* fled from Barcelona rather than face the rigours of the Inquisition's enquiries. However, as Kamen has made clear, the terror of the Inquisition was exaggerated by Protestant myth. Torture was used less than in ordinary courts and acquittals or mild penalties were far more common than floggings or burnings.

> **KEY ISSUE**
>
> *Why was the Inquisition introduced to Spain?*

THE EXPULSION OF THE JEWS, 1492

Even with the activities of the Inquisition, many Spaniards felt that a more drastic solution to the 'Jewish problem' was required. It was widely believed that the Jews encouraged the *conversos* to desert Christianity and return to their former religion. In addition, the war against Granada had engendered a spirit of militant crusade against non-Christian religions. In some areas there had already been attempts to banish Jews, as at Seville in 1483. The climax of the anti-Semitic hysteria came in March 1492 at Granada when an edict was issued by Ferdinand and Isabella giving all Jews in Castile and Aragon the choice of converting or being expelled from Spain. Accurate statistical information is in short supply, but it seems likely that about 150 000 of the Jewish population of 200 000 chose to leave. Many of those who stayed must have been converts in name only. Perhaps the most significant aspect of the expulsion was the economic loss to Spain. The Jewish emigrants took with them their commercial skill and experience and the absence of their enterprise contributed to the lack of economic vitality in Spain in the sixteenth century. As for the Jews, they continued to regard Ferdinand and Isabella with loathing for decades.

Around 1575, an eastern Jew wrote, 'Queen Isabel, the accursed, died weary of her life and half her body devoured by a cancer. God is just!'

7 ↭ THE FOREIGN POLICY OF FERDINAND AND ISABELLA

Until 1492 the commitments of the Castilian civil war and the Reconquest precluded the monarchs pursuing an active foreign policy. With the incorporation of Granada Ferdinand and Isabella could turn outwards and Spanish resources and troops were released for operations beyond Iberia. Foreign affairs were largely the responsibility of Ferdinand and he conducted relations with other states with a degree of unscrupulousness remarkable even in the atmosphere of duplicity and treachery which surrounded European diplomacy in the sixteenth century.

A *Aims*

It is perhaps dangerous to describe governments following a consistent foreign 'policy' in this period; rather, they tended to act as circumstances dictated and opportunities arose. However, Ferdinand did have certain constant aims. Of overriding importance was the need to check the growing power of France. A number of methods were used to achieve this: the construction of anti-French coalitions and marriage alliances (marrying his children to English, Portuguese and Habsburg royalty) the strengthening of Spain's northern border and military intervention to prevent French domination of Italy. In addition, Ferdinand followed a policy of cautious expansion onto the coast of North Africa and the reign of the monarchs also saw the beginning of the great Spanish Colonial Empire in America.

B *Acquisition of Cerdagne and Roussillon, 1493*

It was fortunate for Spain that the war with Granada was drawing to a close as Charles VIII of France reached adulthood and began to look for opportunities to fulfil his martial ambitions. Ferdinand was well aware that he could not hope to curb the French on his own and in 1489 he signed a treaty with Henry VII of England at Medina del Campo. A joint offensive was planned in which England would intervene to protect the independence of Brittany, which was being threatened by France, and Spain would recover Cerdagne and Roussillon. These two Catalan-speaking countries had belonged to Aragon until Ferdinand's father, John II, had been obliged to surrender them to the French in 1462 as a result of the civil war in Aragon. Both objectives failed: English forces (with some Spanish assistance) failed to save Brittany in 1492 and the Spanish were still too involved in finishing off Granada to make headway on the border with France. Charles VIII, however, did not seem to regard the retention of the two counties as a high priority and was prepared to barter them in exchange for Spanish neutrality during his projected invasion of Italy. At the Treaty of Barcelona in 1493, Cerdagne and Roussillon were handed back to Catalonia. This was a major success for the monarchs as it gave them control of the eastern ranges of the Pyrenees, denying France easy routes into the Iberian peninsula. The counties remained in Spanish hands until the Peace of the Pyrenees in 1659, when France occupied them once more.

C *Intervention in Italy*

The kingdom of Aragon had a long history of close involvement with Italy. A branch of the Aragonese royal house ruled Naples in the person of King Ferrante (1458–94), and Sicily was an important component of the Crown of Aragon. Thus, when Charles VIII invaded Italy and conquered Naples in 1494–95, Ferdinand could not stand idly by and see the French dominate the whole peninsula and then the western Mediterranean. A full account of the Spanish participation in the Italian Wars is given in Chapter 3, but there are several points which should be noted here. First, Ferdinand's skilful diplomacy did much to counter the triumph of French arms. In 1495 he allied with Pope Alexander VI, Venice, Milan and Emperor Maximilian I to force Charles to retreat. Later in the wars, Spain joined with Pope Julius II, a number of the Italian states and the Swiss in the Holy League of 1511–13, an alliance aimed at destroying French power in northern Italy, which gave Ferdinand the chance to seize Navarre. A second feature of Spanish intervention was the success of her armies. Castilian and Aragonese troops had gained considerable battle experience in the long war against Granada. In 1495 a veteran of that war, Gonzalo de Cordoba (known as 'El Gran Capitan'), was given command of the expeditionary force dispatched to fight the French. Cordoba was a brilliant general with an excellent grasp of strategy, a talent for organisation and an ability to develop new tactics. His string of victories made Spanish troops feared throughout Europe. Cordoba was a Castilian and it is significant that, as Aragon had assisted Isabella in her war against Granada, so Ferdinand was able to mobilise the manpower and resources of his wife's realm for 'his' war in Italy. Indeed Castilian troops and Castilian money were used to such an extent that Aragon was replaced as the dominant partner in Italian affairs.

The outcome of the Italian involvement was highly satisfactory for Spain. At the Treaty of Granada in 1500, Ferdinand and Louis XII agreed to partition Naples, but when war broke out soon after, Cordoba's victories forced the French to relinquish their claims to Naples at the Treaty of Blois (1505). Although France was still the strongest power in northern Italy at the time of Ferdinand's death in 1516, Spain was left in unchallenged possession of Sicily and Naples,

TIMELINE

1488 Spanish troops in Brittany to oppose France

1489 Treaty of Medina del Campo with England

1492 Columbus reaches America

1493 France gives up Cerdagne and Roussillon

1494 Treaty of Tordesillas

1503 Spanish victories over the French in Italy

1504 France acknowledges Aragonese possession of Naples

1509 Spain captures Oran

1510 Bougie, Tripoli and Algiers fall to Spain

1512 Ferdinand occupies Spanish Navarre for Castile

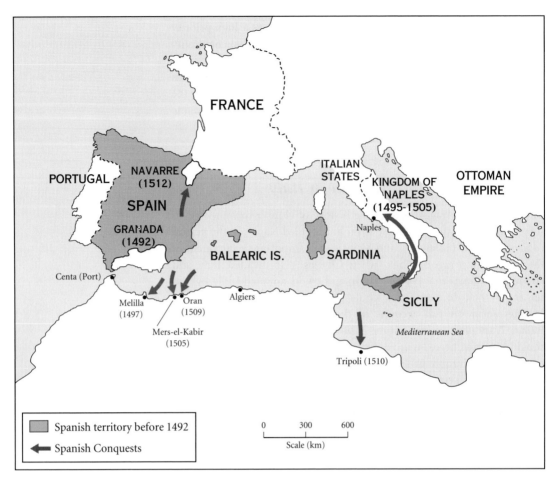

MAP 3
Spanish intervention in the Mediterranean after 1492

territories that were to provide her with grain, revenues and recruits during the sixteenth century.

D *The Acquisition of Navarre, 1512*

The wars in Italy also gave the Spanish a further opportunity to strengthen their border with France by gaining control of the small, nominally independent kingdom of Navarre. This state, like Cerdagne and Roussillon, had once been ruled by John II of Aragon. By 1494 Queen Catherine of Navarre and her French husband Jean d'Albret had been obliged to accept a Castilian protectorate over their territory, but they retained close links with France. In 1498 one observer noted that Ferdinand and Isabella 'do what they please' in Navarre and it was clear that Ferdinand was only waiting for a favourable opportunity to take over completely. In 1512 the chance came; France was heavily involved in war against the Holy League in Italy. Ferdinand demanded that

Spanish troops be allowed to pass through Navarre on their way to attack the French city of Bayonne. To permit this would mean Catherine and d'Albret losing their considerable estates in France and so they refused and signed a treaty with Louis XII. Claiming that this indicated aggressive intent (which was a complete fabrication) Ferdinand ordered an army of 17 000 men to occupy the part of Navarre which lay on the Spanish side of the Pyrenees in the summer of 1512. It is typical of Ferdinand's extraordinary diplomatic skill that he persuaded Henry VIII of England to provide a diversionary action by sending a force to south-west France to threaten the French while Navarre was occupied. The English army rotted with inactivity and achieved nothing for Henry. A dynastic pretext for this action was provided by Ferdinand's second wife, Germaine de Foix, who possessed a hereditary claim to Navarre. Pope Julius II agreed formally to depose Catherine and Jean, and in 1515 the kingdom was integrated into Castile, although Navarre retained its own institutions of government, its *Cortes* and coinage and the d'Albrets retained control over that portion of their kingdom on the French side of the Pyrenees. The acquisition of Navarre was a triumph for Ferdinand: Spain dominated the Pyrenees, and the whole Iberian peninsula with the exception of Portugal acknowledged his rule. By transferring Navarre from the kingdom of Aragon to Castile, he involved Castile in the defence of the northern frontier, although this did not perhaps indicate any growing unity between Aragon and Castile as much as Ferdinand turning his back on Aragon, given the greater resources and more pliable institutions of Castile.

E *North Africa*

To turn to the Mediterranean, the war against Islam was justified for Ferdinand as a religious crusade and as an extension of Spanish influence. In a letter of June 1509 he wrote that 'from my youth I was always very inclined to war against Infidels and it is the thing in which I receive most delight and pleasure'. There is even evidence that Ferdinand planned operations against Islam outside the obvious limits of Spanish national interest. In February 1510 he declared, somewhat ambitiously, that 'the conquest of Jerusalem belongs to us and we have the title of that kingdom'. However, it may well be that such statements are examples of Ferdinand's duplicity – he was endeavouring to prod the *Cortes* and the Pope into offering financial assistance for a crusade against the Turks when his true intention was to fight the French.

Following the conquest of Granada it seemed natural for the Spanish to carry the war across the Mediterranean into the Moorish states of Algiers, Morocco and Tunis in North Africa. The Portuguese had already seized important towns such as Ceuta and Ferdinand had no wish to be outflanked by his Iberian neighbours. By moving into North Africa Spain would protect her trade with Sicily and prevent the Moors from inciting or aiding disaffected elements in Granada. The emirates of North Africa seemed to provide an easy target, warring amongst themselves and lacking the modern powder weaponry which Ferdinand had employed so successfully against Granada. In 1494 Alexander VI granted crusading status to the projected offensive and in 1495 recognised Spanish rights in north-eastern Africa. The conquest was begun as a private enterprise by the Duke of Medina Sidonia, who occupied the city of Melilla in 1497, with the agreement of Ferdinand and Isabella. The danger created by the revolt in Granada in 1499–1501 gave a fresh impetus to action against Islam. Following the conquest of Naples in 1503–04, Spanish troops were made available from the Italian theatre and an expedition sailed to North Africa in 1505. The town of Mers-el-Kebir was taken and in 1509 an army led by Cardinal Cisneros captured Oran. Tripoli fell to the Spanish in 1510 and Algiers had to accept a Spanish protectorate. Cisneros wanted to launch total war against the Muslims but Ferdinand understood the financial and military difficulties of prolonged campaigning in the African interior. Instead, he was content to garrison a limited number of coastal strongholds, sufficient to discourage aggressive intentions by the Moorish states. Although strategically valuable, these Spanish outposts proved to be expensive to maintain and dangerously weak when compared to the alliance of the Ottoman Empire and Moorish emirates which Charles V faced in the late 1530s and 1540s.

See map on page 52

KEY ISSUE

How successful was the foreign policy of Ferdinand and Isabella?

F *The Atlantic*

The late fifteenth and early sixteenth centuries witnessed the beginnings of Spanish exploration of the Atlantic and the foundation of the Spanish Empire in the Americas. (Full treatment of this topic will be found in Chapter 4.) It must be stressed that Ferdinand and Isabella gave this aspect of policy a very low priority when compared with Italy or North Africa and the full significance of the discoveries was not appreciated until the years after the death of Ferdinand in 1516.

The Portuguese had been exploring the Atlantic for some decades and rivalry was an important motive in the development of Spanish interest in discovery. By the Treaty of Alcaçovas of 1479, the Portuguese acknowledged Spanish rights to the Canary Islands and a combination of royal and private initiative led to the conquest of Grand Canary in 1483, Palma in 1492 and Tenerife in 1493. The native populations of these islands were reduced by the fighting and slave-raiding and Iberian colonists arrived to exploit the potential for sugar-cane production. The islands were eventually to become an important staging post on the route to America.

Ferdinand and Isabella were interested in breaking into the lucrative Asian spice trade and it was to further this interest that they gave limited support to the plans of the Genoese navigator Christopher Columbus to sail westwards in search of an Atlantic route to the East. The successful voyage of reconnaissance in 1492 was followed by similar explorations and by 1516 a number of Caribbean islands (including Hispaniola, Cuba, Jamaica and Puerto Rico) had been settled by Spaniards and the Central American coastline had been explored. Later in the sixteenth century Spain set about exploiting the wealth of America in earnest, but the origins of Empire lie in the reigns of the Catholic monarchs.

It must be stressed that this was a Castilian Empire with the Aragonese excluded from trade and settlement in America. Although Ferdinand was King of Aragon he exercised his power through his wife's realm of Castile, given that it was far richer and more easily subject to royal authority. As a result even the possessions in Italy, which were officially attached to the realm of Aragon, were extended mostly by Castilian soldiers and exploited by Castilian office-holders. In the eyes of Europe, Spain was unified in its foreign policy – it is in diplomatic correspondence that the title 'King of Spain' first gained currency – but Ferdinand ensured that foreign policy was largely a Castilian matter.

8 ↜ THE SUCCESSION CRISIS

Ferdinand and Isabella had one son, John, and four daughters, Isabella, Joanna, Maria and Catherine. John married Margaret, the daughter of the Emperor Maximilian in 1497, and within six months he was dead, of sexual over-indulgence, it was rumoured. Margaret was pregnant at the time of her husband's death but she gave birth to a stillborn child. This left the monarchs' eldest daughter Isabella as heir. She was married to King Manuel of Portugal and they produced an heir, Miguel. However, Isabella died in 1498, leading the French observer Commynes to write of the 'miserable accidents which in a short space of time befell the king and queen of Castile, who had lived in so much glory and happiness to the fiftieth year of their age'. Worse was to follow. In 1500 the infant Miguel died, leaving the monarchs' second daughter, Joanna, as heir. Joanna was married to Philip 'the Fair', Duke of Burgundy and son of the Holy Roman Emperor Maximilian I.

This marriage had produced a son, Charles, in 1500. A Habsburg succession now seemed inevitable. Philip regarded Spain as something of a provincial backwater, disliked the Spanish and did not trust Ferdinand. Indeed, he joined Maximilian and Louis XII of France in an anti-Spanish alliance in 1504. In a will made shortly before her death in 1504, Isabella placed the government of Castile in the hands of Ferdinand until their grandson Charles should reach the age of twenty.

Isabella's death precipitated a prolonged succession crisis. Ferdinand announced the succession of Joanna, though with no mention of Philip. The latter set about constructing a party within Castile who would support him, led by the Marquis of Villena. The chronicler Bernaldez saw Villena and other such nobles as men who 'acted more out of greed for royal land than for the good of the kingdom'. However, English observers reported to Henry VII that Ferdinand was unpopular due to the high taxation for the war in Italy and that the people would welcome Philip.

In 1506, Philip landed in northern Castile and nobles rushed to join him. Ferdinand was obliged to withdraw from Castile and to hand the government over to Philip and Joanna, but the situation was transformed when Philip died at Burgos in September 1506 at the age of twenty-eight. Joanna's sanity, always fragile, now began to give way. She refused to leave Philip's lifeless body, having been informed by a monk that he would rise from the dead. In Castile a complete breakdown of government seemed likely. Nobles began to recruit and attack each other and without the strong hand of Ferdinand (who was engaged in reorganising the government of Naples) Bernaldez claimed that 'men knew they were as sheep without a shepherd'. Ferdinand returned to Castile with an army in 1507 and soon crushed the dissident nobles. He ruled as governor of Castile whilst the wretched Joanna, who could scarcely be persuaded to eat, wash or change her clothes, retired into mad obscurity. She survived until 1555, a pitiable inmate of the castle of Tordesillas.

Ferdinand had made a second marriage to a French princess, Germaine de Foix, in 1505 and still hoped for another heir. This did not materialise and when he died in 1516 all Ferdinand's possessions passed to his grandson, Charles. Charles was already Duke of Burgundy and when he was elected Holy Roman Emperor in 1519, Spain became inextricably involved in the politics of northern Europe. It was this international connection, rather than what had been a precarious dynastic union, which was to be of the greatest importance to Spain during the Early Modern period.

9 ↭ THE UNIFICATION OF SPAIN

By the time of Ferdinand's death in 1516, Castile and Aragon were scarcely more united than they had been in 1469. There was a measure of unification in terms of religion and foreign policy, and Granada had been absorbed, but Castile and Aragon were still undeniably distinct entities.

The institutions the monarchs had used to pacify Castile were confined to that realm. Ferdinand had tried three times to introduce the Hermandad into Aragon but three times he had failed. Rather than integrate Aragon with Castile, he had neglected his own kingdom. He had settled some serious disputes there – a land dispute between nobility and peasants known as the *remensas*, for instance – but he had been acting as an arbitrator rather than as a continuously involved politician. This can be seen by the amount of time he gave to his kingdom in a period when personal kingship was vital. He spent less than seven years visiting Aragon out of the thirty-seven years of his reign. Aragon effectively ran itself behind its protective hedge of liberties, the *fueros*.

The kingdoms of Spain retained separate institutions, laws, languages, coinage and economies. Aragon was in a political and commercial decline, whereas the vigour of Castile was finding outlets in imperialist undertakings in the New World and Europe. That Castile and Aragon had not been united would hardly have been a cause of disappointment to Ferdinand and Isabella, because their priorities were different. Stability in the kingdoms, eradication of religious minorities, the destruction of Granada, the frustration of the expansionist ambitions of the French kings and the furtherance of Spanish power in the Mediterranean were their major aims and in these they were successful. They laid the foundations of the Spanish Empire of the sixteenth century and won the admiration of contemporaries of all nationalities. In 1514 Ferdinand himself could remark, with some justification, that 'For over 700 years the Crown of Spain has not been as great or as resplendent as it is now, both in the west and the east, and all, after God, by my work and labour.'

> **KEY ISSUE**
>
> *What does the succession crisis reveal about the nature of Spanish unity?*

10 ⌐ BIBLIOGRAPHY

J.H. Elliott, *Imperial Spain 1469–1716* (Edward Arnold, 1963), **H. Kamen, *Spain 1469–1714* (Longman, 1991), *J. Lynch, *Spain under the Habsburgs, Vol. 1* (Blackwell, 1991) and A.W. Lovett, *Early Habsburg Spain 1517–1598*(Oxford, 1986) are all worth consulting for their extensive coverage of Spain in this period. *H. Kamen, *Inquisition and Society in Spain* (revised edition, Weidenfeld and Nicolson, 1985) and the same author's **The Spanish Inquisition: An Historical Revision* are the leading studies of the Inquisition. *J.N. Hillgarth, *The Spanish Kingdoms, Vol. 2* (Clarendon, 1976) contains some useful information. P.K. Liss, *Isabel the Queen* (Oxford, 1992) is a recent biography. In the *Access to History* series Jill Kilsby, *Spain: Rise and Decline, 1474–1643* (Hodder and Stoughton, 1989) is quite brief on the Catholic monarchs but **Geoffrey Woodward, *Spain in the Reigns of Ferdinand and Isabella, 1474–1516* (Hodder and Stoughton, 1997) is an excellent guide to the topic. J. Edwards, *The Monarchies of Ferdinand and Isabella* (Historical Association Pamphlet, 1996) is a very useful introduction. David Abulafia, **Spain and 1492* (Headstart, 1992) has some revealing insights into that momentous year in Spanish history. *David Nicolle, *Granada 1492* (Osprey, 1998) is a thorough and prolifically illustrated military history of the fall of the last Moorish kingdom.

11 ⌐ STRUCTURED AND ESSAY QUESTIONS

A *Structured questions.*

1. (a) By what methods did Ferdinand and Isabella attempt to secure control of Castile?
   (b) How successful were they in eliminating opposition?

2. (a) What were the aims of Ferdinand and Isabella's religious policy?
    (b) 'The Catholic kings sought the triumph of a renewed Catholicism at home and dynastic rights abroad rather than any unification of their kingdoms.' Do you agree?

B *Essay questions.*
1. What were the aims of Ferdinand and Isabella and how successful were they in achieving them?
2. How well-governed was Spain under Ferdinand and Isabella?
3. How secure was the unity of the Spanish kingdoms in 1516?
4. 'Ferdinand and Isabella joined Aragon and Castile in a dynastic but not a political union.' Discuss.
5. 'They pursued traditional aims by traditional policies.' Discuss this judgement on Ferdinand and Isabella.

Advice: *Answering structured questions*

In a structured question, the first part essentially requires just factual knowledge. You must, of course, choose the right material to answer the question and you must write it in a way that shows you understand the topic. This can be done by briefly setting events in their context and in the way that you link events together.

The second part of a structured question is more like the traditional form of an essay and there is advice throughout the book on how to tackle different approaches to essay writing – for example, a comparative question or a discussion one. It is in this part of a structured question that you will reveal your ability to analyse events and draw conclusions that you can support with appropriate evidence.

Example question:

1. (a) By what methods did Ferdinand and Isabella attempt to secure control of Castile?

It would be safest to include as wide a range of factors as possible, such as: the civil war, treatment of the nobility, the Hermandad, the Military Orders, the conquest of Granada, the towns, the Church and the Inquisition.

Remember that these questions usually account for two-fifths of the marks, so that if you have about thirty minutes to answer both parts of the question you would only have about ten minutes to answer the first part.

1. (b) How successful were they in eliminating opposition?

This is where your skills of analysis and judgement come into play. The subject matter is virtually the same as for the first part, but for this section you must draw conclusions about how much Ferdinand and Isabella actually achieved and how far problems remained for their successors. It should not be necessary for this part to repeat the factual detail you included for 1(a). For instance, in discussing the incorporation of Granada into Castile, you would not repeat a description of the conquest. You might instead comment on how Talavera's policy of religious compromise was replaced by the repression favoured by Cisneros, storing up trouble for the future.

12 ⤳ DOCUMENTARY EXERCISE ON THE CATHOLIC MONARCHS AND THE RELIGIOUS MINORITIES

Read the following sources about the relationship between Ferdinand and Isabella and the Jews and Muslims.

...and since the absence of these people depopulated a large part of the country, the queen was informed that commerce was declining; but setting little importance on the decline in her revenue, and prizing highly the purity of her lands, she said that the essential thing was to cleanse the country of that sin of heresy, for she understood it to be in God's service and her own. And the representations which were made to her about this matter did not alter her decision.

SOURCE A
From the Chronicle of Hernando del Pulgar, *recording the flight of* conversos *when they heard of the activities of the Inquisition in 1481.*

The Holy Office of the Inquisition, seeing how some Christians are endangered by contact and communication with the Jews, has provided that the Jews be expelled from all our realms and territories, and has persuaded us to give our support and agreement to this, which we now do, because of our debts and obligations to the said Holy Office: and we do so despite the great harm to ourselves, seeking and preferring the salvation of souls above our own profit and that of individuals.

SOURCE B
Letter from Ferdinand to the Count of Aranda about the expulsion of the Jews, 1492.

We neither are, nor have been, persuaded to undertake this war by desire to acquire greater rents nor the wish to lay up treasure; for had we wanted to increase our lordships and augment our income with far less peril, labour and expense, we should have been able to do so. But the desire which we have to serve God and our zeal for the holy Catholic faith has induced us to set aside our own interests and ignore the continual hardships and dangers to which this cause commits us; and thus can we hope both that the holy Catholic faith may be spread and Christendom freed of so relentless a menace as abides here at our gates, until these Infidels of the kingdom of Granada are uprooted and expelled from Spain.

SOURCE C
Letter to the Pope from Ferdinand and Isabella in 1485.

SOURCE D

Isabella giving her reasons for her policy towards the Muslims of conversion or expulsion.

...since the major cause of subversion of many Christians that has been seen in these our kingdoms was their participation and communication with the Jews, that since there is much danger in the communication of the said Moors of our kingdom with the newly converted and they will be a cause that the said newly converted may be drawn and induced to leave our faith and to return to their original errors...as already by experience has been in some in this kingdom and outside of it, if the principal cause is removed, that is, to expel the said Moors from these our kingdoms and lordship, and because it is better to prevent with the remedy than to wait to punish the errors after they are made and committed...it is right they be expelled.

1. *What is meant by (i) conversos (Source A), and (ii) 'the purity of her lands' (Source A)?*
2. *To what extent do Sources A, B and C agree that Ferdinand and Isabella were prepared to place their religious principles above financial and economic considerations?*
3. *Assess the reliability of these sources as an explanation of Ferdinand and Isabella's motives.*
4. *Using the sources and your own knowledge compare the reasons for the Catholic monarchs' attack on the Jews and on the Muslims.*

The Italian Wars

3

OVERVIEW

In 1494 Italy was a collection of rival states (of which Milan, Venice, Florence, the Papal states and Naples were the most powerful), each looking to extend its own influence at the expense of its neighbours. There had been no general war in the peninsula and no major invasion by a foreign power for forty years. In 1494 Charles VIII of France, with a dynastic claim on Naples and newly secure borders at home, took advantage of Italian disunity to invade. Initial success was astounding, but his attack soon triggered the hostility of Italian states, who feared French supremacy and also Spanish intervention as Ferdinand of Aragon pursued his own claim to Naples. Further French invasions followed under Louis XII and Francis I (the latter also having a dynastic claim on Milan, the 'shield of Italy'); consequently, Italy became the battleground of Europe as the armies of France, Spain, the Holy Roman Empire and the Italian states themselves fought for dominance. The French had managed to secure control of Milan by the Treaty of Noyon in 1516, but the Spanish were firmly entrenched in southern Italy. The instability of Italian politics made it the cockpit for European conflict in the years following 1494. From 1519 the wars in Italy merged into the wider struggle between the Valois and Hapsburg families, which is covered in Chapter 8.

1 ↵ THE CONDITION OF ITALY

In 1537 a Florentine named Francesco Guicciardini retired to a villa in the countryside near his home city to write an account of events in Italy during the previous half-century. The theme of Guicciardini's *History of Italy* was how the disunity and selfishness of the Italian states enabled foreign powers to invade the peninsula and turn it into an international battleground, inflicting 'innumerable horrid calamities' on its people. Yet before the wars began in 1494 the Italian states seemed to be at the height of their wealth and influence.

In 1454 the Peace of Lodi gave rise to the Italian League. The League was designed for two main purposes: to provide unity in the face of possible foreign attack (the Turks and the French were the main external threats), and to maintain a balance of power inside the peninsula so that no single state could achieve dominance. The League, carefully maintained by each state's resident ambassadors, helped to give Italy nearly forty years of comparative peace, leading Giovanni Bentivoglio, a citizen of Bologna, to praise it as 'this most holy League

See page 11

upon which depends the welfare of all Italy'. The League was maintained by each state posting resident ambassadors in the capitals of the others – with this major innovation in the mechanism of international relations, the Italians had developed Renaissance diplomacy.

The key to peace was the friendship between Milan, Florence and Naples, a coalition that restrained aggression amongst the smaller states and kept the peace among the larger. In 1482, for example, war broke out between Venice and the small neighbouring state of Ferrara. The intervention of Milan, Florence and Naples terminated the conflict and preserved the independence of Ferrara. The guiding hand of the League was Lorenzo de Medici 'the Magnificent', ruler of Florence. Guicciardini commented that his name 'was held in great esteem all over Italy, and his authority influential in discussions on joint affairs'.

The general peace enjoyed by the Italians brought the following description from the pen of Francesco Guicciardini:

> Italy had never enjoyed such prosperity, or known so favourable a situation as that in which it found itself so securely at rest in the year of our Christian salvation, 1490, and the years immediately before and after. The greatest peace and tranquillity reigned everywhere; the mountains and arid areas as well as the fertile plains were under cultivation; she was dominated by no other power than her own and not only did Italy abound in men, merchandise and riches but she was also famous for the magnificence of many princes, the splendour of many noble and beautiful cities and as being the centre of religion. She flourished with men adept at administering public affairs and had the highest standards of knowledge in all the arts. According to the standards of the day Italy was not lacking in military glory as well. Blessed with so many gifts she deservedly held a celebrated name and reputation among all nations.

Although peace and prosperity seemed to be the most significant features of Italy in the second half of the fifteenth century, there were several factors that belied this appearance and rendered the Italian states vulnerable to external aggression. First, they failed to unite in the face of foreign invasion. In 1480 a Turkish army occupied the Neapolitan port of Otranto and King Ferrante of Naples requested aid from the other powers. This appeal met with little response. Although the danger passed when the Turks evacuated Otranto in the following year, it had been clearly shown that the states could not rely on each other for assistance. Indeed, the disunity of Italy in 1494 was to be the most important asset to Charles VIII of France in his invasion.

Second, mutual suspicion of each other kept the Italian states in a state of constant preparation for war. The terms of the Italian League limited the size of the armies of the major states: the Papacy, for

Guicciardini's influence on views of the wars

Francesco Guicciardini was born in 1483, a member of an aristocratic Florentine family that played an important role in government. He trained as a lawyer and then served in various departments of the government and also acted as an ambassador. From 1516 he moved into the service of Pope Leo X and continued to serve the Papacy as a diplomat, provincial governor and general until 1534. During this time he wrote books on history and methods of government and also developed a friendship with his fellow-Florentine Niccolo Machiavelli. After 1534 Guicciardini returned to Florence and although holding positions in the various governments he devoted most of his energies until his death in 1540 to compiling his *History of Italy*. Guicciardini's book is still the single most important source for events in the Italian peninsula between 1494 and 1537. This is because he used techniques that have led some commentators to see the book as 'the first great work of modern historiography', as Felix Gilbert puts it. Guicciardini researched his subject in government and private archives, viewed these sources critically and compared them with each other where possible. He made his work as accurate as he could and gave it a clear chronological structure. He also included material on other nations where it was relevant to events inside Italy, giving the work great scope. Perhaps Guicciardini's greatest achievement was to include discussion of causation and motivation in an attempt to provide a reasoned explanation for the events that he described. The quality of the *History of Italy* has influenced judgements on the Italian Wars right up to the present day, although recent historians have begun to question some of Guicciardini's conclusions. For example Guicciardini emphasises the degree of stability and calm in the peninsula before 1494 to provide a contrast with the chaos after the French invasion, whereas current interpretations stress the precarious nature of the peace. Such re-assessments do not, however, diminish Guicciardini's standing as one of Europe's greatest historical writers.

KEY ISSUE

What were the 'modern' features of Guicciardini's historical writing?

example, was supposed to have 3000 troops, but Pope Paul II regularly deployed over 8000 as he strengthened the papal grip on central Italy.

A third feature of the Italian political scene was how unprepared the states were for war with foreign powers. At a time when other nations, France in particular, were constructing strong national armies, the rulers of Italian states tended to rely on mercenary bands led by professional commanders known as **condottieri**. The condottieri practised a formal and elaborate style of warfare in which the main objective was to suffer as few casualties as possible and merely

condottieri the leaders of mercenary bands who signed a *condotte* (contract) with a government, receiving pay in return for their military skills and troops

outmanoeuvre, rather than defeat, the opposing army, which was likely also to be composed of mercenaries. Guicciardini made a telling comparison between the army of Charles VIII of France and those of the Italian rulers. Charles's army was, he believed,

men-at-arms mounted troops wearing armour

...formidable not so much because of the number as for the bravery of his troops. For, his **men-at-arms** were almost all the subjects of the king and not low-born persons but gentlemen whom the captains could not enlist or dismiss at will; in addition they were paid by the royal government and not by their officers. Their companies were at full strength, the men in good health, their horses and arms in good condition... Each one competed with his companions to serve honourably, driven on by the thirst for glory which noble birth encourages and also because they hoped their bravery would be rewarded as merit was rewarded with promotion. The officers, almost all of whom were nobles and subjects of the kingdom of France, had the same incentives... they had no other goal than to win praise from their king.

All these things were different in the Italian army, where many of the men-at-arms were either peasants or commoners subject to some other prince and completely dependent on the captains with whom they contracted for their wages, and who had the power to pay and dismiss them. Thus they had no incentive to serve well. The captains were very rarely subjects of the states which hired them... they did not hire the number of soldiers for which they were being paid... they frequently transferred from one state to another, sometimes tempted by ambition or greed to be unstable or even disloyal.

Equally obvious was the difference between the Italian infantry and that of Charles, because the Italians did not fight in firm, well-organised units but scattered throughout the countryside, most of the time hiding in the cover of riverbanks and ditches. But the Swiss [who fought for Charles]... would face the enemy like a wall without even breaking ranks... The French infantry fought with similar discipline.

A fourth factor was the instability of the Italian state system. The 'concert of Italy' which existed after 1454 looked impressive but it concealed many unreconciled rivalries amongst the Italian states. Naples was concerned that Milan might help France to revive its claim to Naples, all the other powers (especially the Papacy) were alarmed by the growing economic and naval power of Naples, Venice feared that Milan might try to regain lands in Lombardy lost to Venice before 1454 and Florence was an economic rival of Venice and territorial rival of the Papacy. It was only the need to settle their own internal affairs that prevented other European powers from intervening before 1494.

The crisis of that year was triggered by a series of political developments. In April 1492, the death of Lorenzo de Medici removed a stabilising influence, even though he was not quite the diplomatic genius portrayed by Guicciardini. More important was the unstable state of affairs in Milan. The Duke of Milan, Gian Galeazzo Sforza, reigned in name only, with the real power in the state resting with his uncle the regent, Lodovico Sforza.

Gian Galeazzo Sforza was married to Isabella, the grand-daughter of King Ferrante of Naples and daughter of Ferrante's aggressive son, Alfonso. Ferrante of Naples was a cruel and untrustworthy individual who was reputed to keep the embalmed bodies of dead enemies to gloat over. Isabella sent a stream of complaints back to Naples that she and her husband were constantly insulted by Lodovico and his wife, Beatrice D'Este. Alfonso took this as an excuse to threaten Lodovico and by 1493 a Neapolitan attack on Milan seemed to be imminent. Fearful that Milan would lose such a war, Lodovico looked for a powerful ally. In April 1493 he declared himself to be an ally of France

LODOVICO SFORZA 'IL MORO' (1452–1508)

PROFILE

Born in 1452, the second son of Francesco Sforza Duke of Milan, Lodovico was given the nickname 'Il Moro' ('the Moor') during his childhood because of his dark skin and black hair. From the early 1480s Lodovico held effective power as regent and used his position to make the Milanese court one of the most magnificent in Europe. He was a patron of artists (including Leonardo da Vinci), scholars and musicians and sponsored the construction of waterways and fortifications. The people of Milan were taxed heavily to pay for these extravagant projects. Lodovico played a major role in the diplomacy between the Italian states, being on good terms with Lorenzo the Magnificent of Florence, Pope Alexander VI and, for a time, with Ferrante of Naples. Deteriorating relations with Naples encouraged Lodovico to look to France for aid, precipitating Charles VIII's invasion. Frightened by the scale of French success in 1494–95, Lodovico aligned himself with the Holy League and the exit of the French allowed him to strengthen his grip on Milan, especially as his nephew and nominal ruler Gian Galeazzo, had died in 1494. When Louis XII of France invaded Milan in 1499 Lodovico found himself undermined by the opposition of the Milanese people, who were tired of his demands for taxation and captivated by the rumour that French subjects did not have to pay tax! He enlisted the support of Holy Roman Emperor Maximilian (who had married Lodovico's niece) but his counter-invasion in 1500 was defeated by the French. Lodovico was captured and spent the rest of his life in French castles. He died in 1508 but both of his sons, Massimiliano and Francesco, later became Dukes of Milan.

KEY ISSUE

Which features of the Italian situation as described by Guicciardini might have encouraged European powers to invade?

and invited Charles VIII of France to enter Italy, defend Milan and conquer Naples, to which the French king had a hereditary claim.

It is likely that Lodovico presumed that the mere threat of French intervention would be sufficient to deter Naples, but Charles accepted the invitation. Thus it was Italians who opened the door to foreign action in Italy and in the following years mutual hostility among the Italian states was to give other rulers every opportunity and excuse to march their armies into the peninsula.

2 ↩ CHARLES VIII'S INVASION OF 1494–95

A *France – an expansionist state*

The invitation from Lodovico Sforza was an unmissable chance for Charles VIII of France, providing him with just the pretext he needed to interfere in the affairs of Italy. It also came at a time when his kingdom had the resources and opportunity for foreign adventures. For much of the fourteenth and fifteenth centuries, monarchs of France had been beset by two major problems: the occupation of large tracts of their country by English troops during the Hundred Years War and the threatening power of some of the great magnates who ruled their territories almost as independent states, and even made war on their sovereign. By 1494 both of these difficulties had receded. The English had been ejected from France (apart from Calais) by 1453 and had then lapsed into the confusions of the Wars of the Roses. The reign of Louis XI (1461–83) saw the danger from the feudal magnates diminish, especially after the death of Charles the Bold, Duke of Burgundy, who was killed by the Swiss at the Battle of Nancy in 1477. Louis was able to strengthen his eastern border by absorbing Burgundian territory. The power of the French monarchy was further increased when Charles VIII married Anne of Brittany and took control of her duchy in 1491, despite English intervention on behalf of the Bretons. Strong monarchy seemed to have returned to France and with it the possibility of an aggressive foreign policy.

B *The motives for Charles VIII's invasion*

The precise reasons why Charles VIII wished to invade Italy have been the subject of some debate. It is generally accepted that Charles's fanciful and erratic character played some part in the decision. The king fed his imagination with the epics of medieval chivalry. He dreamed of winning glory for himself by advancing into Italy and then using it as a base to drive the heathen Turks out of Europe and re-establish the Byzantine Empire with him at its head as 'Emperor of the East'.

On a more practical level, Charles had a claim to the Crown of Naples. The French-descended House of Anjou had ruled in Naples

CHARLES VIII OF FRANCE (1483–98)

Charles succeeded to the throne in 1483 on the death of his father, Louis XI. Aged thirteen at the time, his sister, Anne of Beaujeu, capably held the reins of government until Charles came of age in 1492. Charles seems to have possessed only limited intelligence –'very young, weakly, wilful, rarely in the company of wise men' was the scornful verdict of Philippe Commynes, one contemporary observer. His physical appearance also excited unkind comments: the Venetian ambassador described him as 'small and ill-formed in person, with an ugly face...short-sighted...and thick lips which are continually open. He stutters and has a nervous twitching of the hands.' Guicciardini cruelly pointed out that 'his limbs were so ill-proportioned that he seemed more like a monster than a man'. Once he had taken control of Brittany by marrying Duchess Anne, Charles turned his attention to the preparation and implementation of his invasion of Italy. The expedition gave him the opportunity to fulfil his dreams of conquest and glory. Charles was certainly no coward: at the Battle of Fornovo (1495) he was surprised by a force of Milanese cavalry whilst accompanied only by a single attendant. Drawing his sword he defended himself skilfully until his bodyguards arrived a few minutes later. In 1496–97 he considered launching new attacks on Italy, but these plans came to nothing. Tragedy struck Charles in late 1495 when his three-year-old son died of measles. Queen Anne's other pregnancies resulted in stillbirths or children who died in infancy. In early April 1498 Charles fell ill, but on 7 April felt well enough to watch some of his courtiers play tennis in a dry moat. On the way he accidentally smashed his head on a low doorway but proceeded to watch the sport for two hours before saying that he hoped never to sin again and then collapsing. He died nine hours later, lying in the moat on a dirty straw mattress. The contemporary Philippe de Commynes remarked, 'And so this great and powerful king died, and in such a miserable place, when he had so many magnificent houses.' His lack of children meant that the crown passed to Louis of Orleans.

until driven out in 1442 and Charles had inherited its claim. Given the ideas of the time, it was almost a duty as well as a matter of ambition to assert dynastic rights. Modern historians see the French invasion of 1494 not as a new departure in foreign policy but as another phase in a tradition of French intervention stretching back to the thirteenth century.

Italy was also the centre of European trade with the East and it has been suggested that Charles wished to advance the commercial interests of France in that area. This seems unlikely: fifteenth-century kings were generally moved by considerations of honour and territorial ambition, rather than economics.

Rome in particular had traditionally been a great lure to invaders from across the Alps. Not only was there the prestige of the Roman Empire to be emulated, which had attained greater prominence in the Renaissance, but Rome was also the centre of the Roman Catholic Church. Any prince who could dominate the Papacy would have a political advantage throughout western Europe, and with representatives of all rulers regularly at the papal court, Rome was the great diplomatic hub and listening post.

Additional spurs to invasion were provided by a leading Italian churchman, Cardinal Giuliano della Rovere, and a powerful Neapolitan nobleman, the Prince of Salerno. In the papal election of 1492, della Rovere had been defeated by Alexander VI, head of the Borgia family. Determined to harass his hated rival, della Rovere joined the clamour for French intervention. Similarly, the Prince of Salerno, who had led a baronial revolt against King Alfonso of Naples in 1485–86, encouraged the invasion plans. He arrived at the French court in 1489 and received estates and pensions from Charles VIII. By 1490 he was providing practical advice on Italian castles and rivers and within days Charles called for an investigation into the French claim to Naples. There was no Italian state, except perhaps for Venice, which was not engaged in internal feuds acting to smooth the path of the invading French.

C *French diplomatic preparations*

Aware that an invasion of Italy would be no small undertaking, Charles was careful to ensure that France was safe from attack during the operation.

(i) At the Treaty of Etaples in 1492, he promised an annual pension to Henry VII of England.
(ii) At Barcelona in 1493 he bought off Ferdinand and Isabella of Spain by returning the provinces of Cerdagne and Roussillon.
(iii) In 1493 concessions were made to Maximilian of the Netherlands (who became Emperor Maximilian I in that year): at the Treaty of Senlis two areas on France's eastern border, Artois and Franche-Comté, were surrendered by France.

Charles VIII was heavily criticised by some contemporaries for squandering the gains of Louis XI and, in the long term, weakening France's borders. Modern historians have tended to agree with this assessment, although David Potter argues that the Treaty of Etaples was a good bargain and the concession over borders in the Treaties of Barcelona and Senlis more generally 'liquidated problems and in some ways was unavoidable'.

D *The French invasion force*

It has already been shown that the Italian states were divided and militarily weak. Charles of France, in contrast, possessed the most formidable army in western Europe. The heavily armoured French cavalry was famous for its irresistible charges and Charles had hired a contingent of 8000 Swiss pikemen, the most feared and effective infantry in Europe. During the fifteenth and early sixteenth centuries, the Swiss cantons attempted to offset their lack of natural resources by hiring armies to any ruler who could afford them. The Swiss were to play a prominent part in the Italian Wars and the proximity of the battleground to such a recruiting source was one of the factors in the prolongation of the wars.

The decisive arm in Charles's 25 000 strong invasion force was, however, the artillery. Until the late fifteenth century, the typical artillery piece was a huge pipe of iron or bronze called a 'bombard'. This cumbersome instrument had to be transported on a large wagon drawn by oxen and then lowered onto a solid block of wood for firing. Ammunition consisted of stone balls which were difficult to move and expensive to manufacture, as they required the expertise of skilled

PICTURE 4
Engraving of a cannon *by Israel von Meckenen*

KEY ISSUE

What caused Charles VIII to invade Italy and how effective were his preparations?

masons. The French military expert Jacques de Genouillac had made advances in the design of artillery by 1494. Barrels were shortened and lightened and mounted on a two-wheeled gun carriage pulled by horses, greatly easing the problem of mobility. Wrought-iron balls were fired, which were to prove devastating against the high, thin medieval walls of many Italian towns. However, recent historical work has pointed out that where the French encountered lower and thicker fortifications surrounded by deep, wide ditches constructed with defence against artillery in mind, the outcome was not so clear-cut. Two modern Florentine fortresses, Sarzanello and Sarzano, for example, held out against the French guns until their ruler negotiated a treaty with the invaders.

E *The campaign of 1494*

Charles marched his army over the Alps in the summer of 1494 and met his siege train of forty guns, which had been transported by sea, in Genoa. The French passed through Milan and swept into Florence, the ally of Naples. The Florentines resisted and the military might of the invaders became apparent for the first time when they bombarded the walls of the frontier fortress of Fivizzano. Moreover, the French not only introduced a new technology but also a new savagery to war in Italy. The garrison and many of the inhabitants of Fivizzano were massacred when the town fell, Guicciardini commenting that this was 'a thing unheard of and very frightening in Italy, which for a long time had been used to seeing wars staged with beautiful pomp and display ... rather than waged with bloodshed and dangers'. Rather than experience similar treatment, a string of Florentine cities capitulated without a fight. The ruler of Florence, Piero de Medici, fled and the French king entered the city. The Medici had been growing less and less popular, so Charles was actually welcomed as the protector of Florentine liberties and received a contribution towards the cost of the war against Naples.

See documentary exercise on pages 80–1 for Guicciardini's description of the French artillery

The French then pushed on south, receiving the surrender of numerous cities as they went. Charles entered Rome on the last day of 1494 and Pope Alexander VI, 'oppressed by incredible anxiety and dread' according to Guicciardini, fled into the papal castle of Sant Angelo. The proximity and power of Charles forced Alexander temporarily to conceal his dislike for the French and he gave the French right of passage through his territory, as well as control of a number of fortresses. After spending a month in Rome, Charles continued his march towards Naples.

Once again, terror was used as an instrument of war. The walls of the Neapolitan border fortress of Monte San Giovanni, which had once endured a siege of seven years, were battered down in eight hours. The French, infuriated by the treatment of their heralds, who returned from negotiations without their noses and ears, subsequently slaughtered the garrison and fired the buildings of the town, 'induced by their innate fury, and also to warn others by this example not to dare to resist them', as Guicciardini remarked. King Alfonso, having only just succeeded his father Ferrante, abdicated in favour of his son Ferrantino. But the new king was forced to abandon the city of Naples, which Charles entered in triumph on 22 February 1495. The French overran almost the whole kingdom and Charles seemed to have achieved his objective.

The French assault had been extraordinarily successful. In a few months their army had marched the length of the peninsula, forced the strongest towns to yield and so intimidated the Italians that little effective resistance had been offered. The rottenness of Italian political and military conventions had been exposed for all to see, and after 1494 there could be no return to the insularity that had existed before the advent of Charles VIII. For Charles, however, success was to bring problems – problems that would expose his victory as being as fragile as the Italian peace he had so comprehensively shattered.

MAP 4
Italy in 1494

3 ⇆ THE INTERVENTION OF SPAIN

A *The Holy League against France*

Alarmed by Charles's domination of Italy, five powers formed a coalition in March 1495, with the aim of ejecting the French from Italy. Spain felt her grip on Sicily threatened and French occupation of Naples might well have serious strategic implications in the western Mediterranean. Hence, Ferdinand of Aragon was willing to commit troops to aid Ferrantino in the recovery of his kingdom. Also, he had long followed the policy of using his diplomatic mastery to restrict the French wherever he could. Pope Alexander VI and the Venetians both feared that permanent French control of Italy would inevitably weaken their own positions.

Even Lodovico Sforza was prepared to turn against his erstwhile ally. Gian Galeazzo had died in October 1494 – it is uncertain whether this was due to Lodovico's poison or, as was commonly claimed in this period, to sexual over-indulgence. Lodovico was recognised as Duke of Milan by the people and bought confirmation of his title from Emperor Maximilian. He felt secure and thus the powerful French presence in Italy was now potentially dangerous to him, rather than reassuring.

Across the Alps in his Austrian territories, Maximilian was alarmed by the scope of Charles's ambition and his interference in a traditionally imperial sphere of influence. Hence he too adhered to the Holy League or League of Venice, as this rather motley collection of allies is sometimes known. Fear of France was certainly all that held the coalition together, but it was still a diplomatic precedent of enormous importance for the future. As Mattingly says, 'It was in fact a Europe-wide coalition against France, the first decisive drawing together of the major states of Europe into a single power system.'

TIMELINE

1454	The Peace of Lodi appears to bring peace to Italy
1492	Death of Lorenzo de Medici, a key peacemaker in Italy
1494	Charles VIII of France invades Italy
1495	Charles VIII captures Naples but later retreats
1496	The French army left in Naples surrenders to the Spanish

B *The French retreat*

In the spring of 1495 Charles, concerned at the vulnerability of his lines of communication back to France and possibly bored with the whole enterprise, left a sizeable force to garrison Naples and returned north with the remainder of his army. The army of the League, made up largely of mercenaries provided by Milan and Venice and commanded by the *condottiere* Gonzaga of Mantua, moved to intercept the French. In July 1495 the two armies clashed at Fornovo. Although enjoying superiority of numbers, the Italians were badly mauled by the dash of the French cavalry and the firepower of their artillery. Both sides claimed victory, but Charles chose to retire across the Alps. In October, the Peace of Vercelli concluded the conflict between Charles and the League.

See map on page 77

C *The French loss of Naples, 1496*

In the south, however, fighting continued. The Duke of Montpensier, Charles's viceroy in Naples, faced massive problems. His unruly troops soon became unpopular among the people, supplies were a constant problem and his force was seriously weakened by an epidemic of syphilis, known to the French as *le mal de Naples*. Ferrantino and the Spanish commander Cordoba gradually reconquered Naples, aided by local revolts against the army of occupation. In July 1496 at the siege of Atella Cordoba captured Montpensier and French resistance came to an end.

Thus the conquests of 1494–95 had proved temporary. Charles planned to return to the peninsula to re-establish his position, but died in April 1498. However, this was not the end of French interest in Italy as his successor, Louis XII, also had ambitions in the peninsula.

See map on page 77

See map on page 77

KEY ISSUE

What problems had the French encountered in their expedition of 1494–95?

4 ∽ THE CAMPAIGNS OF LOUIS XII, 1500–05: THE CONQUEST OF MILAN AND THE LOSS OF NAPLES

Louis, Duke of Orleans, became king when his distant cousin Charles died in 1498 without an heir. Louis XII was a very different character from Charles VIII but he came to share his predecessor's obsession with Italy. Although more cautious than Charles, Louis had supported the 1494 venture because 'his greatest pleasure was following arms, which he loved the best of all things' according to St Gelais, a contemporary observer.

Louis inherited the French claim to Naples and added a claim of his own to Milan. He traced this through his grandmother, Valentina, who was the daughter of a Visconti Duke of Milan. Milan, just to the south of the Alps, was wealthy, owing to its position at the junction of trade routes, and was also of great strategic importance, guarding the Alpine passes as the 'shield' of Italy. Louis had laid claim to the duchy even before he was king, issuing coins as 'Duke of Orleans and Milan' and the Venetian ambassador reported that Louis thought of nothing but the destruction of the Sforzas and would give ten years of his life to achieve it.

Louis was encouraged in his ambitions by his most prominent adviser, Georges d'Amboise, Archbishop of Rouen, whose immediate aim was to be raised to the cardinalate and whose ultimate aim may have been the Papacy. Just as Charles had been invited into Italy by an Italian ruler, so Louis was given encouragement by Pope Alexander VI who, according to Guicciardini, was 'pricked on by his own interests which he knew could not be satisfied so long as Italy was at peace'. Alexander was desperate to extend the influence of the Borgia family, especially by helping his son Cesare to win territory in central Italy. French assistance would be invaluable in obtaining this. In return,

TIMELINE

1498 Louis XII becomes King of France
1500 The French take control of Milan Treaty of Granada: the French and Spanish divide Naples
1503 The Spanish defeat the French in Naples
1505 Treaty of Blois: Louis XII gives up his claims to Naples

PICTURE 5
Pope Julius II *by Raphael*

See map on page 77

arquebusiers soldiers who carried the early form of a gun known as an arquebus

Alexander could promise Louis aid in divorcing his barren and deformed wife, Jeanne, and marrying Charles VIII's widow, Anne, whose hand carried with it the Duchy of Brittany. In 1498, Cesare sailed to France, carrying the papal dispensation for Louis to marry Anne of Brittany and a cardinal's hat for d'Amboise. In France, Cesare married the sister of the King of Navarre and then accompanied the French army south into Italy.

Lodovico Sforza, who had betrayed his French allies by joining the Holy League and who now faced Louis' rival claim to his Duchy of Milan, was in an impossible position. His only firm ally in Italy was Federigo, the new King of Naples (the fourth in as many years), who was also fighting for survival. When the French attacked in 1499, Sforza fled to the Empire where he was received by Maximilian I and where he hired 10 000 Swiss mercenaries to help him regain his duchy. He re-entered Milan in 1500 to a rapturous reception from the people, who had rapidly grown tired of the financial demands of the pro-French faction who had taken power in his absence. The French responded to the challenge and at Novara in April 1500, Sforza's Swiss surrendered rather than fight their fellow countrymen in the French army. Sforza was captured and taken to France. The French now had a secure grip on Milan and were encouraged to attempt the conquest of Naples as well.

Rather than try an outright attack on Naples, which would certainly have brought a Spanish response, Louis decided to act through diplomacy. In November 1500, the Treaty of Granada partitioned Naples between France, which obtained the northern half (including the capital) and Spain, which annexed the south. It was typical of the cunning of Ferdinand of Spain that he negotiated this agreement behind the back of his cousin and ally Federigo, King of Naples since 1496. Disgusted by Spanish treachery, Federigo threw himself on the mercy of Louis XII, who allowed him to stay in France and even installed him as Duke of Anjou.

Territorial disputes between the two powers occupying Naples soon reached fever pitch and in 1502 the French attempted a military solution by invading southern Naples. Cordoba, the Spanish commander, was forced to retreat into the port-fortress of Barletta where he was besieged during the winter of 1502–03. Supplied and reinforced by sea, Cordoba broke out in April 1503 and encountered the French at Cerignola. This battle was remarkable for being probably the first to be decided by hand-held gunpowder weapons: the French cavalry and Swiss pikemen attacked with their customary vigour but were driven back by Spanish **arquebusiers** occupying a carefully chosen defensive position and protected by a ditch and palisade. Cordoba followed up his victory by capturing the city of Naples and in December 1503 he surprised the French army defending the northern bank of the River Garigliano. Using secretly assembled bridging equipment, the Spanish crossed the river and routed the French forces. The victories at Cerignola and Garigliano mark Cordoba as one of the greatest generals of the sixteenth century.

Those victories also forced Louis XII to agree to the Treaty of Blois (1505) by which he gave up his claims to Naples and acknowledged Spanish control of the kingdom. From this point on, it was clear that the French had no hope of sustaining their claim to Naples. The problems of distance and lines of communication running through hostile states were overwhelming. In contrast, Spain could supply her forces in southern Italy from well-established bases in Sicily. For France, the key issue in the wars was whether she could continue to dominate Milan and conquer fresh territory in the north.

KEY ISSUE

Why did Louis XII decide to renew the wars in Italy?

POPE ALEXANDER VI, CESARE BORGIA AND POPE JULIUS II (1494–1513)

PROFILE

One of the major reasons why Italy remained in a state of war for so long was the political ambition of the Papacy. The campaigns of Louis XII in Milan and Naples gave Alexander VI (1494–1503) an excellent opportunity, in the form of French diplomatic and military assistance, to further the interests of the Borgia family, by building up a block of hereditary territory in central Italy. The work of Michael Mallett has shown that Alexander was a skilful diplomat, not the debauched monster of tradition. It is true that Alexander wished to establish his son Cesare as Duke of Romagna but this did not necessarily conflict with the best interests of the Papacy. With French support, Cesare Borgia conquered the small states of the Romagna and established his own principality there. His government was harsh but efficient, and Cesare became the model for Niccolò Machiavelli's manual of ruthless statesmanship, *The Prince*. His father remarked that 'Cesare is a good-natured man; he cannot, however, forgive offences.' He also had designs on other states, notably Florence, but the death of Pope Alexander VI in 1503 undermined his position. He lost his possessions and died in an obscure skirmish in 1507.

Alexander VI's successor, Pius III, survived his election by only a few months. The papal tiara then passed to Giuliano della Rovere who took the title Julius II and held the Papacy between 1503 and 1513. Giuliano was the nephew of a previous Pope, Sixtus IV, who had showered the young Giuliano with favours, including six bishoprics in France and another three in Italy, and made him a cardinal when he was only twenty-eight – an interesting example of the **nepotism** practised by the Papacy at this period. Pope Alexander VI plotted to assassinate Giuliano, causing him to flee to France to seek the help of Charles VIII. By the time of his election it was already clear that Julius II was more of a soldier and a statesman than a cleric, revelling in the military and diplomatic battles of Renaissance Italy. Through administrative ability and personal energy, he succeeded in consolidating

nepotism giving posts to one's own family

the Papal states in central Italy (including fighting a successful war against Venice) and at the same time made the financial structure of the Papacy more efficient. He was prepared to ally with the French in the League of Cambrai but then turn against them in 1510–11 when he felt that they were becoming too dominant. Julius II was the subject of a scathing attack by the humanist writer Erasmus, whose *Julius Exclusus* has coloured opinions of this warrior Pope since the sixteenth century. In the context of his bitter campaign against Venice, M.S. Anderson comments that he was 'always a good hater'. Christine Shaw, who has written a recent biography of Julius, concludes that he was a forceful and successful ruler, although not a man of great spirituality.

5 ⟶ SHIFTING ALLIANCES AND FRENCH DEFEAT, 1508–14

The next stage of the wars in Italy saw the construction of the League of Cambrai, an ill-assorted alliance of states that had nothing in common beyond the wish to crush Venice. Emperor Maximilian had quarrelled with the Venetians and had been heavily defeated by them at Friuli in 1508. The subsequent truce left Venice in control of territories such as Fiume and Trieste, which the Habsburgs claimed. Eager for revenge, Maximilian allied with Louis XII, who saw the opportunity to enlarge his possessions in northern Italy. Julius II hoped to use foreign intervention for his own purposes: the Venetians had occupied a number of cities in the Romagna after the fall of Cesare Borgia and the Pope now demanded that they be handed over. The only military activity of any significance in the war was a battle between Louis XII's army and a Venetian force at Agnadello in May 1509. The French were victorious and in the south of Italy the Spanish gratefully accepted the chance to occupy a number of Venetian-held cities, thereby consolidating their position as the dominant power in the region.

Meanwhile, Julius II had used the opportunity presented by the French victory to regain the disputed cities in the Romagna. He then made a claim on the duchy of Ferrara, whose dukes were clients of the French. Thus a reversal of alliances took place, with the Pope constructing a new Holy League against France with the Papacy, Spain, Venice and Henry VIII of England as the main participants. Once again the chronic instability of Italian politics kept conflict in the peninsula simmering.

After a period of indecisive fencing between France and this next Holy League of Italian powers and Spain, founded in 1511, the military situation was transformed by the arrival of an energetic new French commander, the 21-year-old Gaston de Foix. Moving his army with speed and precision, Gaston secured control of most of northern Italy

MAP 5
The major battles of the Italian wars, 1494–1515

and then marched south to besiege Ravenna. A combined force of Spanish and papal troops moved to raise the siege and in April 1512 the two armies met outside the city. The French emerged victorious but at the cost of their brilliant young commander, killed at the moment of victory. Just as the dismissal of Cordoba (for exceeding his orders) had deprived the Spanish of a general capable of winning decisive victories, so the death of Gaston de Foix robbed France of a soldier of genius.

Despite their victory at Ravenna, problems mounted for the French. Emperor Maximilian sent an army into Italy in 1512 and the Swiss turned against the French and occupied the key French territory in Italy, Milan, in the same year. Unusually, they were acting on their own initiative rather than as mercenaries. Led by the formidable Cardinal Schinner, the Swiss were determined to take Milan to protect their southern boundaries and to secure their supplies of grain and wine. They defended their position in North Italy when they inflicted a heavy defeat on the French at Novara and installed Lodovico Sforza's son, Massimiliano, as Duke of Milan. However, that familiar instability of alliances in the Italian Wars now became apparent once again.

See map above

KEY ISSUE

Would you agree that of all the Italian powers it was the Papacy which did most to prolong the Italian Wars?

With France reeling from the defeat at Novara and Henry VIII's much vaunted triumph at the Battle of the Spurs during the English expedition to northern France in 1513, the time was ripe for a joint attack on the French by the League: the Swiss even went as far as to invade southern France. Failure to formulate a combined strategy meant that the opportunity was lost and the Swiss concluded a separate peace with France in September 1513. The Papacy and Spain followed suit in December 1513, the Emperor in March 1514 and England in July 1514. Nonetheless, France seemed to have failed in her bid for supremacy in northern Italy. But the death of Louis XII in early 1515 brought to the throne the young and aggressive Francis I who, just like Charles VIII and Louis XII, found that the disunity of the Italian states offered an excellent opportunity for military glory and territorial gains.

6 ✎ FRANCIS I'S DESCENT UPON ITALY

The character of the new French king is described in Chapter 9. His main aims in Italy were to increase his own reputation and that of France through success in battle and to avenge the defeats of 1513, re-asserting the French claim to Milan. According to his propaganda he also intended to deliver Constantinople from the clutches of the Turks.

Following the expulsion of the French in 1513, the Italian states had wasted the opportunity to prepare to resist future external interference. The Venetians had openly supported the French. In Milan the Swiss ruthlessly pressed their demands for payment for ejecting the French and this, combined with Duke Massimiliano's reckless expenditure on luxuries, alienated a population whose prosperity had already been ravaged by years of war. The Papacy was also playing its usual game of self-interest. Cardinal Giovanni Medici had been elected Pope as Leo X in 1513, and he set about promoting the interests of himself and his family. He was prepared to negotiate for French aid to further his ambitions in the peninsula but, in the event, opposed them when they invaded. Thus the French and the Venetians found themselves primarily opposed by Swiss and Italian troops.

Francis commanded an army of about 30 000 when he crossed the Alps into Italy in 1515. He scored an early success when he bribed nearly 10 000 of the Swiss defending Milan to return home. The French then approached Milan and in September they fought a two-day battle at Marignano against 15 000 Swiss who had remained loyal to their Milanese allies. The result remained in the balance until the Venetian army threatened the rear of the Swiss, forcing them to retreat.

The Battle of Marignano had important results. Massimiliano was retired to a comfortable exile in France and the people of Milan were obliged to pay a heavy indemnity to Francis for 'their great rebellions and acts of disobedience'. Francis became the new Duke of Milan. The Swiss came to terms with Francis at the Eternal Peace of Fribourg in 1516, by which they agreed never again to serve against the French and were paid a subsidy in return. Leo X was also anxious for an agreement with the new master of northern Italy and the two settled their differences at Bologna in 1516. Thus by 1516 the French seemed to have triumphed. They were firmly installed in Milan, the Swiss were happy to supply them with mercenaries, and the Pope was a pliable ally. Charles Habsburg, the new King of Spain following the death of Ferdinand, was willing to acknowledge Francis as ruler of Milan at the Treaty of Noyon in 1516. However, the election of Charles as Holy Roman Emperor in 1519 greatly increased the strategic importance of Italy and the peninsula became the principal theatre of war in the Habsburg–Valois conflict, which will be dealt with in Chapters 8 and 9.

See pages 273–4

KEY ISSUE

What were the motives and results of Francis I's invasion of Italy?

7 ∽ ITALY: THE PREY OF FOREIGN POWERS

The internal weakness that had made Italy a prey to foreign states since 1494 continued into the nineteenth century. During the intervening centuries, the epithet of the Austrian statesman Metternich applied very well to Italy – it was just a 'geographical expression'. At various times France, Spain and Austria controlled parts of the country and it was not until 1870 that the last foreign troops were removed from Italian soil. Indeed, the eventual unification of Italy owed considerably more to the intervention of foreign powers than it did to the efforts of her own people. Guicciardini's despair at the failings of his countrymen proved not only to be an astute depiction of the events of his own lifetime but also an accurate prophecy of the future.

8 ∽ BIBLIOGRAPHY

**M.S. Anderson, *The Origins of the Modern European State System 1494–1618* (Longman, 1998) – chapter 4 is a clear, concise account of the wars. Recent general surveys of Italian history in this period include *Denys Hay and John Law, *Italy in the Age of the Renaissance 1380–1530* (Longman, 1989) and Robert Hole, *Renaissance Italy* (Hodder and Stoughton, 1998). **Richard Bonney's *The European Dynastic States 1494–1610* (Oxford, 1991) places the Italian Wars in their international context. French involvement is well covered in *David Potter's *A History of France 1460–1560* (MacMillan, 1995). Military aspects are discussed in J.R. Hale, *War and Society in Renaissance Europe* (Fontana, 1985) and David Nicolle's *Fornovo 1495* (Osprey, 1996). There are numerous studies of Italian rulers, one of the most recent being *Christine Shaw's *Julius II: The Warrior Pope* (Blackwell, 1993). Others include M. Mallett, *The Borgias* (Bodley Head, 1969) and Sarah Bradford, *Cesare Borgia* (Weidenfeld and Nicolson, 1976). The classic study by *G. Mattingly, *Renaissance Diplomacy* (Jonathan Cape, 1955) has many insights. A recent, specialised collection of essays on Charles

VIII's invasion can be found in *The French Descent into Renaissance Italy, 1494–95: Antecedents and Effects*, ed. David Abulafia (Varorium, 1995).

9 ⌐ STRUCTURED AND ESSAY QUESTIONS

A *Structured questions.*
1. (a) Write an account of the events of the French invasion of Italy in 1494–95.
   (b) Why were the Italian states unable to prevent this invasion?
2. (a) Describe the French attempts to conquer Italy between 1494 and 1516.
   (b) Why did the French fail to make permanent conquests in this period?

B *Essay questions.*
1. Why did French armies invade Italy so frequently after 1494?
2. Why did foreign powers regard control of Italy as important between 1494 and 1529? (See also Chapter 8.)
3. 'It was the internal weakness of Italy which allowed foreign states to use the peninsula as their battleground.' Discuss.
4. Why did the Italian Wars last so long?

10 ⌐ DOCUMENTARY EXERCISE

This source question deals with the changes in military techniques that came about during the Italian Wars.

This new plague of artillery, developed many years before in Germany, had been brought to Italy for the first time by the Venetians during the war against the Genoese in 1380...The biggest of these artillery pieces were called bombards, which were subsequently employed throughout Italy since this new invention could be adapted for attacking towns. Some of them were made of iron, some of bronze, but they were so big that the large pieces could be dragged only very slowly and with the greatest difficulty; furthermore, men were unskilled in handling them...For the same reasons, it was difficult to plant them in position against cities; once placed, there was such an interval between one shot and another compared to later developments, that a great deal of time was consumed with very little reward. Consequently, the defenders of the place under attack had time to calmly make the necessary repairs and fortifications.

But the French developed many pieces that were even more manoeuvrable, constructed only of bronze. These were called cannons and they used iron cannonballs instead of stone as before, and this new shot was incomparably larger and heavier than that which had been previously employed. Furthermore, they were hauled on carriages drawn not by oxen as was the custom in Italy, but by horses, with such agility of manpower and tools assigned for this purpose that they almost always marched right along with the armies and were led right up to the walls and put into position there with incredible speed; and so little time elapsed between one shot and another and the shots were so frequent and so violent was their battering that in a few hours they could accomplish what previously in Italy had used to require many days. They used this devilish rather than human weapon not only in besieging cities but also in the field, together with similar cannon and other smaller pieces, but all of them constructed and manoeuvered with the same dexterity and speed.

SOURCE A
History of Italy 1494–1532
by Francesco Guicciardini.

1. *According to Guicciardini, what were the limitations of the guns used by the Italians before 1494?*
2. *Using the source and your own knowledge, explain the advantages possessed by the French artillery in 1494.*
3. *Having read the analysis of Guicciardini's influence on views of the wars (see page 63), assess the reliability of this source.*

Advice: *Narrative and analysis in essays*

The aim of an essay must be to provide an analysis rather than tell the story of what happened. However, it is particularly tempting to lapse into narrative when faced with a year-by-year series of events, as in the Italian Wars.

Below are three narrative paragraphs, extracts from an essay written in answer to question 1 above: 'Why did French armies invade Italy so frequently after 1494?' Criticise these paragraphs in detail and then rewrite them, converting them from narrative to an analysis relevant to the question. Use the same information, but use it selectively and as evidence rather than just a sequence of facts. Following each paragraph are relevant analytical points, which you should highlight.

(i) Charles VIII crossed the Alps into Italy in 1494. He was welcomed by the Duke of Milan, Lodovico Sforza. The French defeated the Florentine forces and the Medici ruler of Florence fled; Charles was then hailed by the Florentine people as the protector of their liberties. The French then arrived in Rome. The Pope, Alexander VI, persuaded them to pass through his lands quickly. In Naples the fortress of Monte San Giovanni was taken, King Alfonso abdicated and his son, who became King Ferrantino, fled. The powerful Neapolitan nobleman, the Prince of Salerno, was not sorry to see Alfonso and Ferrantino go.

Analytical points: *the ease of invading Italy owing to divisions amongst the Italians and the feebleness of their response.*

(ii) Louis XII's grandmother had been a member of the Visconti family, formerly rulers of Milan. Milan lay just to the south of the Alps and was the centre for the main roads leading to the Alpine passes. Milan was a wealthy trading city, handling brocades, wines and grain. Louis crossed the Alps in 1499. He won the Battle of Novara, where the Swiss troops working for Lodovico Sforza would not fight their fellow countrymen in the French army, and he took firm control over Milan. Louis felt secure now in northern Italy and struck a bargain with Ferdinand of Aragon to partition the kingdom of Naples.

Analytical points: *the importance of Milan and the inadequacy of its defences.*

(iii) Francis I became king in 1515 at the age of twenty-one. He crossed the Alps in the same year. The Swiss had taken Milan from the French in 1513 and used one of the Sforza family as a puppet duke, but Francis beat them in 1515 at the Battle of Marignano with the help of the Venetians. The French once again occupied Milan and the Pope, Leo X, made a settlement with Francis, the Concordat of Bologna, in 1516.

Analytical points: *the vulnerability of the French in Milan and their willingness/capacity to strike back if defeated.*

The Age of Discovery

4

Before the fifteenth century even educated Europeans had little understanding of the lands which lay beyond their continent. The existence of Africa and Asia was appreciated, but there was only the haziest knowledge of their shape and of the people who inhabited them. America was totally unknown. In the fifteenth and sixteenth centuries a combination of economic motives (the desire to reach the sources of spices, gold, and other high-value trading goods) and religious motives (an urge to find allies against the threat of Islam and to convert non-Christian peoples) impelled first the Portuguese and then the Spanish to venture beyond European waters. The Portuguese concentrated their efforts on opening up a route to Asia by sailing around the southern tip of Africa and then establishing control of the profitable trade in the Indian Ocean. The Spanish stumbled across the Americas when Columbus sailed across the Atlantic hoping to reach Asia by a western route, and they rapidly began to establish a huge land empire in central and southern America by attacking and destroying the indigenous populations there.

These voyages were made possible by a gradual improvement in shipbuilding and navigational techniques, which gave Europeans supremacy at sea. Weapon technology and ruthless determination also gave them an advantage over local populations and allowed them to dominate the globe as no other civilization had done before. By the end of the sixteenth century, most of the globe had been mapped and only Australia, New Zealand, Antarctica and the lands surrounding the North Pacific remained to be discovered. This chapter will examine the motives of the Europeans, the reasons why the Iberian states led the age of exploration and the effects that discovery had on Europe and on the conquered peoples themselves.

1 ↜ THE BEGINNINGS OF EUROPEAN EXPANSION

The speed and extent of this 'Age of Reconnaissance', as it has been called, was unparalleled. Other civilisations had carried out voyages of discovery: the Vikings had explored the North Atlantic in the ninth century, in the early fifteenth century the Chinese admiral Cheng Ho sailed to Sri Lanka, the Indian Ocean and probably the north coast of Australia, and Arab ships had cruised the east coast of Africa. The unique feature of the European age of discovery was that a single culture intruded into all the major continents simultaneously and linked the oceans of the world with a single system of navigation. Information about large numbers of other peoples was gathered in one area of the globe for the first time and the process was begun by which Europeans became the dominant military and economic force in the world.

The early explorers had little reliable factual knowledge to guide them. Some learning inherited from the classical world was becoming available. For example, the *Geography* of Ptolemy, an Egyptian who wrote about the Roman Empire in the second century AD, was translated from Greek into Latin in 1406. The great respect with which ancient scholarship was regarded during the Early Modern period meant that such writers were given a rather uncritical acceptance, even when their findings were highly dubious. Ptolemy, for example, believed that it would not be possible to reach India by sea because the Indian Ocean was encompassed by a large mass of land to the south.

More recent information came from the writings of the Venetian Marco Polo who travelled across Asia to China in the late thirteenth century. He resided in Peking for twenty years and composed a largely accurate account of the wealth and splendour of the Mongol Empire under Kublai Khan. Polo's *Travels* was printed in the late fifteenth century, giving it a wide circulation in Europe, and it is known that Christopher Columbus possessed a copy. Polo was, however, unique and even his knowledge was beginning to become outdated by the time European navigators came within striking distance of Asia.

Competing for the attention of would-be explorers and the educated public in Europe were fantastic travellers' tales, which were accepted just as readily as the account of Polo. The prime example of this type of book was the *Travels of Sir John Mandeville*. This extraordinary fourteenth-century work was packed with entertaining stories of men with eyes in their shoulders and mouths in their chests, others whose testicles hung below their knees and giant ants that hoarded gold. It included almost no geographical information of any value but retained a quite undeserved popularity throughout the fifteenth and sixteenth centuries, even when reputable descriptions of newly discovered lands were being published. Other writers gave lurid accounts of the fate that would befall ships venturing too far from Europe – falling off the edge of the world or boiling to death in the hot seas of the south. Mandeville and his imitators served only to obscure the truth about Asia and Africa.

Given this confusion between fact and fiction, it is not surprising that contemporary maps were of little help. The conventional depiction of the globe was the *mappa mundi*, which showed a disc-like world with Jerusalem at the centre and the known continents of Europe, Asia and Africa crudely arranged around it. The interiors of the latter two were filled with whatever the fertility of the map-maker's imagination provided as appropriate. As a practical aid to navigation the *mappae mundi* were useless.

Thus the explorers of the Early Modern period were taking a leap into the unknown in a very real sense. Whereas the space pioneers of the second half of the twentieth century have had a clear idea of their destination and been able to communicate with a base that can provide advice and assistance, men such as Columbus and Magellan left their home ports for months or years at a time with little navigational data and no prospect of aid if storms, reefs or hostile populations threatened the voyage. It is not surprising that losses of ships and men were heavy. The main questions to be considered with regard to the age of discovery are what motivated Europeans to face such hazards, what means they possessed to make their exploration successful, why it was that Spain and Portugal took the lead in the reconnaissance and what changes were brought about in Europe by the discoveries.

See pages 91–2

KEY ISSUE

Why was European geographical knowledge so limited at the start of the fifteenth century?

2 ⟿ THE MOTIVES

The explorers and conquerors sailing from Europe in the fifteenth and sixteenth centuries were driven by a mixture of impulses. The Spaniard Bernal Diaz wrote that it was his ambition to 'serve God and His Majesty, to give light to those who were in darkness and to grow rich, as all men desire to do'. In this remark Diaz highlighted the two most significant motives: the urge to spread and strengthen Christianity and the prospect of national and personal profit. Although contemporary piety demanded that the religious element should be stressed, economic factors were of greater importance in almost every voyage and it is these that will be considered first.

A *Economic motives: spices, gold, slaves and land*

It has been shown earlier that at the end of the Middle Ages Europe was in commercial contact with Asia. A highly profitable trade in luxury goods flowed from China, India and the East Indies (the latter being a convenient general term to cover Malaya, Sumatra, Java and Borneo) through the Indian Ocean, the Red Sea and the Persian Gulf and then overland to the ports of the eastern Mediterranean. There the goods were sold by Arab traders to the Venetian and Genoese merchants who conveyed them on to Italian ports for resale to the rest of Europe. By far the most important items in this trade were spices. Before the Agricultural Revolution of the eighteenth and nineteenth centuries, Europe was unable to grow sufficient feed to keep large numbers of livestock alive during the winter. Animals were therefore slaughtered in the autumn and the meat salted to preserve it for the coming months. Spices such as pepper (from India and the East Indies), cinnamon (from Sri Lanka), ginger (from China) and cloves (from the East Indies) helped to flavour the decaying flesh and also acted as a

TABLE 5
Price ratio of spices

Spice Islands	1
Malacca (collection point for spices from the Spice Islands)	2
Calicut (port in India)	4
Alexandria (port in Egypt)	80
Venice	250

preservative. Apart from this very practical application, European palates were also acquiring a taste for seasoned foods, a craving that could only be satisfied by the imports from the East. Other high-value, low-bulk items shipped from Asia included silks from China, emeralds from India, rubies from Tibet and sapphires from Ceylon. Even the humble rhubarb (from China) was valued in Europe for its alleged medicinal properties.

By the fifteenth century, however, a number of factors were conspiring to threaten this long-established trade. The huge costs of transport, which were increased by the number of hands through which the goods passed and the tolls exacted along the route, made spices highly expensive by the time they reached the Mediterranean.

Europeans longed for a method of supply that would reduce the price. Resentment had also built up at the virtual monopoly enjoyed by Italian merchants once the goods had reached the West, and other states began to search for ways of breaking this stranglehold. In addition, the route was vulnerable to interruption by hostile Muslim states in the Middle East, although G.V. Scammell has stressed that, if anything, the rise of the Ottoman Empire encouraged the trade by bringing stability to the region. Thus a cheaper and more reliable method of obtaining the products of Asia was needed. It was this motivation which encouraged the Portuguese to sail south along the coast of Africa and into the Indian Ocean, and prompted Columbus to sail west from Spain in his attempt to reach China by crossing the Atlantic.

The luxuries of Asia were not the only commodities over which Europeans wished to gain control: a shortage in the supply of gold meant that exploration of the gold-producing areas of West Africa might yield profitable pickings. The 'gold famine' in Europe was probably caused by two main factors. The expansion of trade inside Europe in the later Middle Ages created a need for more gold and silver coins and increasingly, European merchants were having to send gold and silver to the east in order to pay for imports from Asia. Silver could be supplied from the mines of Germany, Bohemia and Hungary but Europe lacked sources of gold sufficient to sustain her economic growth. Instead, gold was obtained from West Africa where it was extracted by surface mining and panning in the regions of the Upper Senegal River, the Upper Niger River and Ghana (the 'Gold Coast'), regions given the collective name of 'Guinea'. From these areas the gold was moved across the Sahara Desert by camel and sold to Italian and Catalan merchants in North Africa. The Portuguese had captured the city of Ceuta in Morocco in 1415 and hence probably had information on the source of the Guinea gold, which knowledge almost certainly stimulated their reconnaissance of the African coast. The search for precious metals was also a consistent theme in the Spanish exploration and occupation of America. Columbus was obsessed by the belief that his American discoveries were in fact outlying areas of China or Japan and that mountains of gold lay just over the horizon. As he wrote, 'Gold is the most precious of all commodities; gold constitutes treasure, and he who possesses it has all he needs in this world, as also the means

---

KEY ISSUE

Why were spices so expensive by the time they reached Venice?

of rescuing souls from **Purgatory**, and restoring them to the enjoyment of paradise.' It is hardly surprising that the Spanish gave a high priority to looting the civilisations of America and then exploiting the silver mines of the region. Personal profit coincided with Spanish national interest. 'I came here to get gold, not till the soil like a peasant', remarked Francisco Pizarro, the conqueror of Peru.

The search for the sources of spices and gold were the most important economic motives but there were a number of other potential benefits of exploration for the Europeans. Much of Europe was short of labour following the ravages of the Black Death in the fourteenth century. This was a particular problem for Portugal, which had a population of about one million at the end of the fifteenth century. One solution to this problem was to recruit additional labour in the slave markets of North Africa. Black slaves were transported across the Sahara with the gold caravans for sale to European and Arab buyers. Voyages down the African coast enabled the Portuguese to buy or capture slaves at source in West Africa and then ship them for use in the sugar plantations of Madeira and the Canaries or in Portugal itself. Recent work on the slave trade by Hugh Thomas has shown that many African rulers were happy to sell their criminals or prisoners of war in exchange for Portuguese goods. In the 1450s one captain of a Portuguese ship reported that he received ten or fifteen slaves in return for a single horse. By the end of the fifteenth century, blacks may have made up as much as ten per cent of the population of Lisbon; they were employed in a variety of occupations as builders, dockers and household servants. By 1540, about 10 000 slaves a year were being taken from West Africa, many of these being sent across the Atlantic to provide cheap labour in the Caribbean and Central America. The development of this profitable trade certainly encouraged Portuguese interest in Africa.

A less dramatic motive than the hunt for spices, gold or slaves was the urge to settle on land which was free from the obligations to a lord which were usual in Europe, and which could be farmed profitably. (There was already a precedent in the lucrative sugar plantations of the Atlantic islands.) The second American voyage of Columbus in 1493, for example, consisted of seventeen ships filled with 1200 settlers, attracted not only by the lure of gold but also the chance to acquire free land and a work force of local Indians who could be terrorised into submission. This process was repeated throughout the Spanish American possessions. On the Caribbean island of Hispaniola (modern Haiti and the Dominican Republic), for example, twenty-four mills were grinding cane sugar within a few years of discovery.

Purgatory In the Catholic faith the place in which the souls of the dead suffer for their sins before being admitted to heaven. At this time it was believed that the stay in purgatory could be reduced by the prayers of those on earth.

B *Religious motives: the search for Christians and for converts*

The second great motive for exploration was provided by religion. In the fifteenth century, Christendom felt under threat from Islam in

Eastern Europe and the Mediterranean. The fall of Constantinople to the Ottoman Turks in 1453 was the most obvious sign of this growing menace and throughout Europe demands were made for a counter-attack. The obvious location for this was Iberia. The Spanish and Portuguese had a long tradition of crusading against the Moors, both in the **Reconquest** of their peninsula and in fighting in North Africa. The important capture of the Moroccan city of Ceuta by the Portuguese in 1415, an event which greatly increased Portugal's awareness of Africa, was part of the centuries-old struggle in the western Mediterranean. It encouraged the Portuguese to sail south along the African coast in an attempt to outflank the Muslims and also to seek the aid of Prester John.

Reconquest the Christian re-capture of Spain and Portugal from the Muslims during the Middle Ages

This legendary Christian king was believed to live in Africa and the explorers of the fifteenth century hoped to enlist his support in the struggle against Islam. Stories of his wealth and power were numerous. It was said that 30 000 guests could be seated at his table made of emeralds and that twelve archbishops sat at his right hand. Fantastic as such accounts seem today, to the embattled Christians of late medieval Europe they offered the prospect of deliverance from the shadow of Muslim might – if only Prester John's kingdom could be discovered. The search for Christians was a constant stimulus to exploration. When Vasco da Gama dropped anchor at Calicut in India he declared that he had come 'in search of Christians and spices' and at once mistook a Hindu temple for a church and a Hindu goddess for the Virgin Mary.

In 1492 the capture of Granada, the last outpost of Islam in Iberia, by the forces of Ferdinand and Isabella of Spain released Christian troops for service elsewhere. Some carried the struggle into the Moorish states of North Africa but others chose to take Christianity to the newly discovered lands across the Atlantic. As J.H. Parry has commented, 'the feelings which rallied Spaniards against Granada developed into a bold and methodical imperialism'.

KEY ISSUE

Why did Europeans feel threatened by Islam in this period?

The urge to defend Christendom was one element of religious motivation. Another was the genuine desire to bring the teachings of Christ to those who had not heard them. The obvious agency to lead such a mission was the Papacy, but successive popes were preoccupied with European affairs and in any case lacked the resources or information to attempt mass conversion. Thus the responsibility tended to devolve onto national governments, a situation recognised by a papal **bull** of 1493 which instructed Ferdinand and Isabella of Spain to send 'virtuous and God-fearing men endowed with training, experience and skill, to instruct the natives ... and to imbue them with ... Christian faith and sound morals'. When the Spanish occupied huge areas of Central and South America, priests accompanied them, smashing the idols and abolishing the practices of the native religions. They then set about building churches and converting the local inhabitants. In New Spain (Mexico) alone there may have been five million converts by 1536, with friars baptising up to 1500 people in a single day. Of course, many of these could only have had the vaguest notion of the Christian message and the rituals and beliefs of the

bull an important decree from the Pope, sealed with his signet-ring (from the Latin *bulla* = seal)

Catholic Church were often combined with those of pre-Conquest religions. Thus the 'conversion' of the indigenous peoples was often merely an excuse for the Europeans to exert greater control over local populations. Nevertheless, the establishment of the Christian faith in the New World is one of the most remarkable aspects of the era of discovery. In contrast, the Portuguese made less impact in Asia. This was because they did not destroy the existing cultures as the Spanish did in America and also because they chose not to colonise large areas.

See pages 382–4

C *Renaissance motives?*

A third motive for participating in exploration is less easy to define. It has been argued that the spread of the values and ideas of the Renaissance contributed to the eagerness with which explorers and conquerors endured hardship and achieved almost superhuman feats. The emphasis of the Renaissance on the importance of the individual and the fame he could achieve provided a strong inducement to bold action. Hernando Cortes, who conquered the huge Aztec Empire in Mexico with a few hundred Spaniards, gained an education in Salamanca, one of the centres of the Spanish Renaissance. The theme of winning reputation runs through many of his recorded utterances: when he and his men landed on the coast of Mexico he urged them on with 'many comparisons with brave deeds done by heroes among the Romans'. This desire to emulate the achievements of the classical world was another feature of the Renaissance. Such is the theory. However, it seems far-fetched to believe that the Renaissance could work such a change in the basic patterns of human behaviour. Marco Polo had undertaken hazardous journeys without the benefits of a Renaissance education and there is no evidence that Francisco Pizarro read classical authors before taking Peru by storm. Another feature of Renaissance thought was the increasing desire for knowledge, even if this was somewhat uncritical and credulous at times. The invention of printing allowed the circulation of reports of voyages and discoveries and the diffusion of navigational information. For the first time, monarchs, sailors, soldiers, churchmen and scholars co-operated in enterprises that were studied and commented on throughout Europe.

See Chapter 5

KEY ISSUE

How important were each of the motives leading towards exploration?

3 ↪ THE MEANS

The great voyages of discovery of the fifteenth and sixteenth centuries were not the result of any single technological breakthrough, but rather the culmination of centuries of development in the skills of shipbuilding, navigation and seamanship. The details of these developments are sometimes complex but it is important to grasp them, as without maritime expertise the Europeans could never have penetrated to every ocean of the globe.

A *Ships*

The first requirement of any successful voyage of exploration is a ship capable of sailing long distances, investigating an objective and then returning safely to its point of origin. Until the late Middle Ages no vessel in Europe (with the arguable exception of the Viking longship) was capable of performing such a task. Mediterranean shipping was dominated by the galley – a sleek, fast vessel propelled by a combination of oars and sails and capable of manoeuvring in shallow or confined waters. Although favoured by the Italian states as both a merchant and naval vessel, the galley had definite limitations, which made it unsuitable as a vessel of exploration. The large number of oarsmen meant that considerable supplies of food had to be carried, severely limiting the range of the galley. The narrowness of the design restricted cargo space and the galley was vulnerable to the high waves of the open ocean.

The nations facing the Atlantic and the North Sea had evolved an entirely different type of vessel. These were broad, high-sided, stable ships, able to survive the pounding of heavy swells and to carry large amounts of cargo in their holds. They were propelled by large square sails which made handling difficult in contrary winds, or when delicate manoeuvring was required. Such unwieldy, clumsy vessels could be of little use in exploring unknown coasts. Instead, the Iberians developed a hybrid form of ship that borrowed features from Mediterranean and Atlantic designs and added rigging of Arab origin.

This vessel was the famous *caravel*, the most popular type of ship for voyages of discovery in the fifteenth and early sixteenth centuries. Originally used as a cheaply-constructed coastal trader and fishing vessel, the *caravel* had a shallow draught (that is, it did not need deep water), a light but seaworthy construction and the advantage of lateen sails, a triangular design which spread into the Mediterranean from the Red Sea during the Middle Ages. Lateen rigging gave an ease of handling in all winds that was crucial when sailing in uncharted waters. Sometimes square sails were also fitted to increase speed when sailing with the wind, this variation being known as a *caravela redonda*. Small in size (around 60–80 tons) and crewed by between twenty and thirty men, the caravel was sufficiently fast, nimble and sturdy to be favoured by explorers such as Columbus, who included two in his fleet of three ships for the first Atlantic crossing in 1492. (It is significant that his only non-caravel, the square-rigged *Santa Maria*, foundered on a reef and had to be abandoned.) The Venetian traveller C'a da Mosto, writing in the mid-fifteenth century, described caravels as the handiest vessels afloat.

The limited size of the *caravel* made it unsuitable as a cargo carrier and, once trading links with a newly discovered area had been established, merchant ships of a larger size were operated. These *carracks* were broad, heavy ships with considerable carrying capacity in their three or four decks. By the mid-sixteenth century, *carracks* of over a thousand tons were routinely plying between Europe and the Indian Ocean and America.

B *Navigation*

Medieval seamen had few navigational aids available to them. They relied on coastal landmarks and accumulated knowledge of natural phenomena such as cloud formations, flocks of birds, sandbanks and shoals of fish. Simple observation of the sun and stars was probably also used. Thus navigation tended to be by instinct and experience rather than through scientific means.

This rather primitive situation was improved by the advent of the magnetic needle in the Mediterranean in the twelfth century, allowing a reasonably accurate estimation of the direction of north. Attached to a card showing the main points of the compass and housed in a box for protection, the magnetic needle had become the principal method of navigation in the Mediterranean by the fifteenth century and was to be a vital tool for the early explorers. J.H. Parry has commented that 'the compass liberated the seaman from his dependence on clear skies'. For measuring the **latitude** of a vessel it was possible to use an instrument called an astrolabe which was sighted on the North (or Pole) Star, the elevation of the star above the horizon giving a measurement of the latitude of the observer. However, clear, calm conditions were required for effective use and thus it was of dubious value in the rough waters of the Atlantic. Most medieval seamen preferred to use the technique of 'dead reckoning' to plot their position. This involved estimating the speed (by throwing overboard a piece of wood with a rope attached and counting the knots tied along the rope at measured distances), direction (using a compass) and length of voyage elapsed (the evolution of more accurate sand-glasses was an important development for mariners in the fifteenth century), and then working out the location on a chart. However, in 1484 a body of astronomers advised John II that latitude might be calculated by measuring the height of the midday sun and then comparing it with a set of tables which had been worked out by a Portuguese man named Zacuto in 1478. It was typical of the highly organised nature of Portuguese exploration that a ship was despatched south to check the practicality of the calculation. Navigators could now arrive at the correct latitude and then sail east or west to their destination. (An accurate method of measuring **longitude** was not developed until the eighteenth century.)

This improvement in navigational techniques also enhanced the quality of maps and charts. In the Middle Ages, sailors in the Mediterranean were able to make use of *portolans* or maps showing the coastline with main ports, natural features and hazards such as reefs. Lines of direction radiated from important points on the map and thus with a compass, a portolan and an idea of his speed, the mariner could judge his location with reasonable accuracy. In northern European waters the *rutter* was more common: written sailing directions with

latitude the angular measurement north or south from the equator (at 0 degrees) to the poles (at 90 degrees)

longitude the angular measurement east or west, nowadays taken from a line running north–south through Greenwich (at 0 degrees) to 180 degrees west or east

gunpowder weapons weapons using gunpowder to fire a projectile, ranging from small hand-guns to large cannon

information on tides, shallows and currents. *Portolans* were, of course, no use when a ship was sailing outside European waters and so the new methods of navigating were important in increasing the confidence of explorers.

C *Weaponry*

Another important technical advance which improved chances of success was the development of **gunpowder weapons**. The *caravels* of the early explorers tended to be lightly armed, but once contact had been made with potentially hostile populations, ships sailed with greater firepower. In the fifteenth and early sixteenth centuries artillery on ships was of small calibre, useful mainly for killing enemy crew and bringing down rigging, but during the sixteenth century naval cannon became heavier and capable of sinking opposing vessels. These guns were mounted along the sides of a ship in 'broadsides', which could deliver a formidable weight of shot. European armaments technology made Portuguese and Spanish fleets almost invulnerable to attack by less developed ships. In particular, the populations of America had no ocean-going vessels and so the Spanish were able to land when and where they pleased. On land, too, gunpowder weapons often gave Europeans a significant advantage over more numerous but less well-armed peoples. An Aztec account of the Spanish conquest of Mexico reported that 'The Spanish fired one of their cannon and this caused great confusion in the city...the people scattered in every direction...It was as if they had eaten the mushrooms that confuse the mind or had seen some dreadful apparition.' However, this superiority should not be exaggerated, at least with regard to the early phases of discovery. Cortes marched into Mexico with only a few small cannon and thirteen hand-held firearms, so the effectiveness of gunpowder weapons was in their psychological impact rather than their capacity to inflict heavy casualties. Just as decisive in European victories were high-quality steel swords and armour (against which native populations deployed stone-edged wooden clubs and quilted protection) and sometimes, in America, the horses of the Spanish, which were unknown to the local populations. The conquistador Bernal Diaz attributed Spanish victories 'under God, to the horses'. The Americans were also over-awed by Spanish hunting dogs 'so fierce that in two bites they laid open their victims to the entrails'.

4 ↩ THE PORTUGUESE EXPERIENCE

It is one of the most remarkable features of the age of discovery that the lead in exploration was taken by the small and economically backward kingdom of Portugal. With a population of about one million in the fifteenth century, a dearth of fertile agricultural land, no tradition in long sea voyages and few good harbours, Portugal seemed to have little to recommend it when compared with, for example, the rich and commercially sophisticated Italian states. Virtually its only contributions to European trade were fish, salt, cork and olive oil. However, appearances were deceptive: Portugal possessed assets that made her unique.

First, the geographical position of Portugal was a great advantage. Situated at what J.H. Parry has graphically described as the 'street corner of Europe', Portugal absorbed influences from both the Mediterranean and northern Europe, leading, for instance, to the evolution of the *caravel*. The Portuguese also possessed a considerable inshore fleet to take advantage of the fishing grounds just off her coast. Only a small proportion of the population was involved in this activity but it did give Portugal a nucleus of tough, trained sailors manning handy, seaworthy craft. The caravels were small enough not to require much capital expenditure – an important point when the comparative poverty of Portugal is considered. Perhaps most important of all was the location of Portugal in relation to the wind systems of the North Atlantic. In summer the prevailing winds off the Portuguese coast blow from the north and north-east, driving ships down the coast of Morocco and out into the Atlantic. These 'north east trades' provided favourable sailing conditions for at least 1500 miles, as far south as the Cape Verde islands. By turning north, ships could then use the prevailing westerly winds to return to Europe on a more northern route. Iberia was thus an ideal starting-point for voyages south and west into the Atlantic.

A second advantage enjoyed by the Portuguese was political stability during much of the fifteenth and early sixteenth centuries. Moorish resistance had been overcome by Alphonso III (1248–79) and in 1385 Portugal, assisted by English forces, defeated her larger, expansionist neighbour Castile at the Battle of Aljubarrota. A permanent peace was established in 1411 and for much of the rest of the century, Castile's energies were taken up in civil war. Secure from external threat, prevented by geography from expanding in Europe and with the capable Avis dynasty providing firm government at home, Portugal could devote men, ships and money to exploration. Many of the early Portuguese expeditions were led by members of the nobility, who combined a thirst for personal glory through war and conquest, a chivalric desire to serve their lord, the king, and a hatred of non-Christians in roughly equal measures.

A third point to consider is that Portugal had several powerful motives for embarking on a period of exploration. It has already been shown that the Iberians were heirs of a crusading tradition. In addition, economic factors seem to have been especially strong. The gold famine hit Portugal particularly badly, with no gold coins being minted between 1383 and 1435, and thus the need to reach the sources of Guinea gold was pronounced. Success was apparent when the Lisbon mint began to issue a new gold coin, the *cruzado* (or 'crusade') in 1457.

A final reason for Portuguese leadership in the era of discovery was the Portuguese royal family. A succession of kings and princes, of

TIMELINE

1415 Portuguese capture Ceuta on African coast

1434 Portuguese reach Cape Bojador, landmark on west coast of Africa

1441 First slaves and gold brought back to Portugal from West Africa

1479 Treaty of Alcacovas: Portuguese right to explore Africa and Spain's control of the Canary Islands mutually agreed

1488 Bartholomew Dias reaches the Cape of Good Hope: way round Africa open

1494 The Treaty of Tordesillas: Pope Alexander VI divides lands yet to be discovered between Portugal in the east (Africa and Asia) and Spain in the west (most of America)

1498 Vasco Da Gama reaches India by sea, opening up the highly profitable Asian trade

1512 Portuguese reach and take control of Asian Spice Islands

1513 Portuguese occupy Macao, off the coast of south China

whom Prince Henry the Navigator (d.1460) is the most famous, acted as patrons of the Portuguese seamen, giving an organisation and discipline to the exploratory voyages. In 1469 Alfonso V made a five-year contract with Fernando Gomes, a Lisbon merchant, for the exploration of 400 miles of African coastline per year in return for trading rights there. Gomes successfully carried out his side of the bargain and became even richer in the process. Perhaps of greater importance was the work of King John II (nicknamed 'the Perfect'), who ruled Portugal between 1481 and 1495. In the mid-1480s, John despatched meticulously-planned expeditions to search for Prester

PROFILE

PRINCE HENRY 'THE NAVIGATOR' OF PORTUGAL (1394–1460)

Prince Henry was born the third son of John I of Portugal and an English princess, Philippa of Lancaster. In 1415 he fought at the Portuguese capture of the Moroccan port of Ceuta, thus perhaps arousing an interest in the possibility of exploring the African coast. Appointed governor of the Algarve in southern Portugal in 1419 he established his court at Sagres on the south-western tip of land. From there he financed and supervised the discovery and occupation of Madeira and the Azores, planned the reconnaissance of the African coast and supervised developments in shipbuilding and navigation, becoming what J.H. Parry calls 'the royal specialist in overseas activity'. He did not, however, participate in voyages himself, perhaps because that would not have been conventional behaviour for a member of the royal family. Prince Henry was a rather austere figure: the chronicler Azurara wrote that 'the expression of his face at first sight inspired fear in those unaccustomed to him', he never married and, unusually for a medieval ruler, he abstained from alcohol. His life was not a total success: in 1437 he led a disastrous expedition to capture Tangier and he attracted criticism for holding a number of monopolies including control of the soap industry! He died, deeply in debt, in 1460. Although the traditional picture of Henry as a Renaissance scholar who surrounded himself with the foremost geographical experts of the day has long been discarded, his contribution was certainly significant. For a decade after his death Portuguese exploration stagnated. His title 'the Navigator' was bestowed by later scholars. Urs Bitterli's comment is a fair one: 'although Henry the Navigator was not the trail-blazing pioneer of genius that is often depicted, he was undoubtedly a character who knew how to seize and exploit the opportunities offered by the age in which he lived'.

KEY ISSUE

Why is Prince Henry seen as such an important figure in the early Age of Discovery?

John and a route to the Asian spice sources. Not only did Bartholomew Diaz reach the southern tip of Africa whilst under his patronage, but John also sent Pedro de Covilha to India by an overland route to gather information which might be useful on future voyages. John even ordered his captains to erect limestone pillars at intervals along the African coast to claim the continent for Portugal. Such personal royal involvement was an important component in Portuguese achievement.

Having established why Portugal was in the forefront of European exploration, it is now necessary to consider the extent of the Empire acquired by Portugal, and some of the benefits and problems it created. It is convenient to divide the Empire into four areas: the Atlantic islands, Africa, Asia, and Brazil.

KEY ISSUE

What advantages did the Portuguese have over other European states?

A *The Atlantic Islands*

There are four main groups of islands off the African coast: Madeira, the Canaries, the Azores and the Cape Verde Islands. Active colonisation by Europeans began in the fifteenth century. Madeira (settled about 1420) was at first renowned for its quality timber but soon became more important for sugar production. Sugar-cane was imported from Sicily at the instigation of Prince Henry, who in 1452 supplied capital for the first sugar-crushing mill. The island also became the home of a profitable wine trade as a result of Prince Henry's introduction of the Malvoisie grape from Crete. The Canary Islands were disputed by Portugal and Castile and at the Treaty of Alcacovas in 1479. Portugal gave up her claim to them in return for Spanish recognition of her rights in the other three groups of islands. The Azores were explored in the 1430s, and were producing considerable quantities of grain by the end of the fifteenth century. The Portuguese began the settlement of the Cape Verdes in the 1460s, sugar becoming the main agricultural product of the islands. The Atlantic islands had another function, acting as staging posts in the long oceanic voyages to the Americas and Asia. Ships would put in for supplies of food and water and other necessary stores, increasing the economic and strategic value of the islands.

B *Africa*

The Portuguese made no comparable attempts to colonise the mainland of Africa due to the inhospitable climate, the vast scale of the continent and the tropical diseases which afflicted Europeans in the sweltering jungles of the west coast. Instead, forts and trading-posts were established as the explorers made their way south, the first probably being established on the orders of Henry the Navigator at Arguin Island in the 1440s. From these secure bases the Portuguese traded European textiles, weapons and trinkets for gold and slaves. By the late fifteenth century, an average of 400 kilograms of gold a year was being shipped to Portugal, whilst between 1450 and 1500 about 140 000 slaves were captured or purchased. As America was opened up in the sixteenth century, the demand for slaves increased and by 1600 about 60 000 Africans had been sent to the Portuguese colony of Brazil. Other destinations for this profitable trade were the Spanish possessions in the Caribbean and Central America. It was only in the 1560s that the Portuguese monopoly on this trade was challenged by the English trader John Hawkins. In addition to gold and slaves, other items of value obtained from Africa included ivory and pepper. After 1500 forts were also built on the east coast of Africa, these acting mainly as ports of call for shipping sailing to or from Asia.

C *Asia*

See map on page 98

Vasco da Gama's trail-blazing voyage to Calicut in India in 1498 was the signal for the start of a Portuguese maritime offensive to take control of the trade routes of the Indian Ocean. Da Gama was able to take advantage of the mutual hostility of the Indian states to gain political advantage and any opposition could be dealt with by a crude application of European firepower. The Portuguese strategy was based around the destruction of rival fleets at sea and the seizure of strategic points on land to provide naval bases and trading posts. The victory over an Egyptian fleet at Diu in 1509 secured mastery of the Indian Ocean and was followed by the capture of the port of Goa in India in 1510 and of Ormuz at the mouth of the Persian Gulf in 1515. A fort was established in Sri Lanka in 1518. Further east, Malacca, the collection point for spices from all over the East Indies, was occupied by the Portuguese in 1511, and in 1557 they began the creation of a city at Macao in southern China. By 1600, Portugal owned a network of fifty fortified points between southern Africa and Japan which, together with her naval power, allowed her to plunder, tax and monopolise certain trades almost at will.

Spain might have challenged this dominance, but in 1529 Charles V sold his claim to the spice islands to the Portuguese for 350 000 ducats. The Portuguese derived considerable profit from importing spices, especially pepper, to Lisbon and then selling them on to the rest of Europe. They also became the carriers of Asia, trading Chinese silk to Japan and Indian cotton to Africa, for example. However, the Portuguese position in the Indian Ocean was always rather precarious due to a shortage of manpower (the tiny Portuguese population could not meet the demands of her far-flung empire in Asia, Africa and Brazil), a lack of ships (Portugal produced little timber and ship losses on the long voyage between Lisbon and Asia were frequent) and a tendency to alienate local populations by unnecessarily harsh treatment. By the end of the sixteenth century, the Empire in the east was in decay, with the Dutch preparing to oust the Portuguese as the leading European power in the region.

D *Brazil*

The final component of the Portuguese overseas Empire was the South American possession of Brazil. Discovered by Pedro Cabral in 1500 (after his fleet had been blown off course in the Atlantic when bound for India), it lay in that portion of the Atlantic assigned to Portugal by Pope Alexander VI at the Treaty of Tordesillas in 1494. (In an act of arbitration between the rival Portuguese and Spanish explorers, the Pope had decreed a line 270 leagues west of the Azores – territory discovered to the west of the line was to be Spanish, leaving territory to the east to the Portuguese.) At first, Brazil seemed to possess little of economic attraction apart from red wood useful for dyeing. When the French began to show an interest in the area in the 1530s, John III of Portugal decided to encourage settlement of the coastal strip, and sugar-cane was introduced from Madeira. As the local Indian population proved inadequate to labour in the sugar plantations, African slaves were shipped to Brazil. By 1580 the Portuguese population of the colony numbered about 20 000 and sixty sugar mills were at work to supply Europe. As in Asia, the Portuguese in Brazil came under increasing pressure from the Dutch in the following century.

> **KEY ISSUE**
>
> *Why was the Portuguese empire a maritime empire?*

The rise of the insignificant nation of Portugal to the status of a global power is one of the most surprising developments in Early Modern Europe. Urs Bitterli describes it as 'an achievement unparalleled in history'. That the Portuguese could not sustain their expansion is hardly surprising, especially when comparison is made with her larger and more populous neighbour, Spain.

5 ⌐ THE SPANISH EXPERIENCE

A *Spanish motives*

Due to internal conflicts, the Spanish were slower than the Portuguese to take advantage of their favourable geographical position facing the Atlantic, but once they had started they displayed a ferocious commitment to discovery and exploitation of new lands. There are several reasons why it was the Spanish who followed the Portuguese lead so enthusiastically.

Spain was a recently united country in the late fifteenth century. The traditionally hostile kingdoms of Castile and Aragon had been brought together in an uneasy association by the marriage of Isabella of Castile and Ferdinand of Aragon. Energies previously dissipated in competition could now be harnessed and turned outwards. Ferdinand and Isabella were determined that their state should not miss opportunities such as those their Iberian neighbours were taking. As the Portuguese slowly navigated the African route to the East, the Catholic monarchs and their subjects began to consider the possibility of a western route to the Indies. The discoveries of Columbus stimulated this race.

See Chapter 2

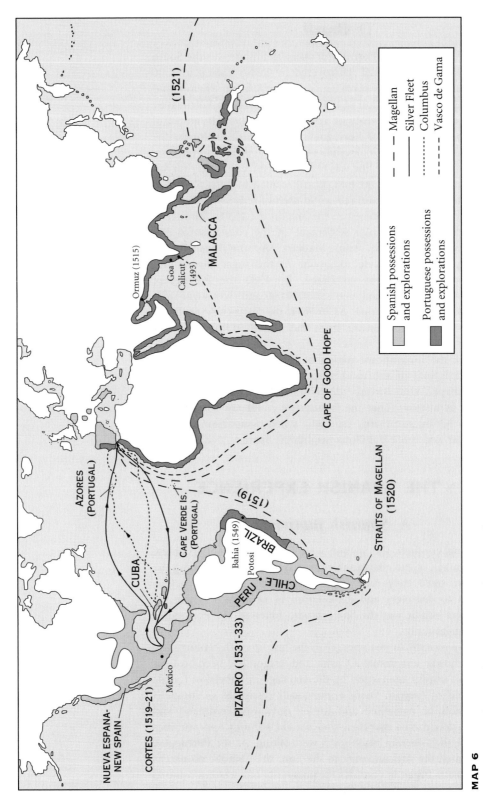

MAP 6

Portuguese and Spanish expansion in the sixteenth century

TIMELINE

1492	First trans-Atlantic voyage of Christopher Columbus reaches America
1494	Treaty of Tordesillas: Pope Alexander VI divides lands yet to be discovered between Portugal and Spain, allowing Spain to dominate America
1501	Amerigo Vespucci reaches the east coast of South America and shows that America is a separate continent
1513	The Spaniard Vasco de Balboa crosses the Isthmus of Panama and sights the Pacific Ocean
1519 –22	First circumnavigation of the globe by Spanish expedition led by Ferdinand Magellan
1519	The Spaniard Hernan Cortez sets out to conquer the Aztec Empire in Mexico
1532	Francisco Pizarro occupies the Inca Empire in Peru
1545	Discovery of a mountain of silver ore at Potosi (Peru) which helped to finance the Spanish drive for dominance in Europe

A second reason has to do with the nature of Spanish society. For centuries, the Spanish had battled against the Moorish occupiers of their country. In the atmosphere of the Reconquest, bravery, ruthlessness and Christian fervour were virtues to be admired and emulated. Although internal wars and then the assault on Granada occupied the Spanish for most of the fifteenth century, these conflicts continued to foster an aggressive militarism in the Spanish, and especially Castilian, nobility. After 1492 new outlets were needed for these urges and the prospect of fame, land and gold ensured that a steady stream of *hidalgos* (noblemen) were available to lead expeditions in newly discovered lands. Extended contact with a different culture, that of North African Islam, helped to equip the Spanish to deal with the civilisations they would encounter beyond Europe.

B *A colonial empire*

The nature of Spanish exploration differed markedly from that of the Portuguese. Even before their voyages commenced, the Portuguese knew that India, China and the Spice Islands existed. Their knowledge of the location of these areas was imperfect but they had clear objectives; the problem was how to reach them. Once they had reached the East they were content to capture strategic points and to use these to control trade. The early Spanish voyages, too, started with a clear aim: to reach the East by sailing across the Atlantic. It soon became apparent, however, that the discovery of America opened up territory completely unknown to Europeans. The Spanish then began to establish colonies in the new lands. As early as 1502 Ferdinand and Isabella commanded Columbus to return to the 'islands and mainland which are in the said Indies and supervise the preserving and peopling of them'.

The establishment of the Spanish Empire in America took a remarkably short period of time, little more than a generation. The

KEY ISSUE

Were Spain's reasons for embarking on exploration similar to those of Portugal?

See map on page 98

process began with perhaps the most famous voyage of exploration of all, the transatlantic passage of Christopher Columbus in 1492. Columbus, a Genoese by birth, was an experienced navigator who approached John II of Portugal in 1484 with a plan to reach China by sailing westwards. As the Portuguese were putting all their resources into the exploration of the African route to the East, Columbus was unable to secure the necessary financial backing. He then turned to the court of Ferdinand and Isabella and, after a long delay, obtained financial support. The voyage of 1492, made with three ships and less than a hundred men, convinced Columbus and the Spanish court that a short cut to the wealth of the East had been discovered. 'Oh, happy deed, that under the patronage of my King and Queen the disclosure has begun of what was hidden from the first creation of the world', wrote Peter Martyr. In fact, Columbus had touched on various Caribbean islands as far west as Cuba. Nevertheless, the gold and placid Carib Indians he brought back stimulated a rush of volunteers in search of riches and an easy life. Columbus made further voyages to America but he never found the route to China for which he searched so desperately and died, a disappointed man, in 1506.

Columbus had shown that there were lands worth exploring to the west, and in the early sixteenth century a number of expeditions vastly increased the geographical knowledge of Europe. Amerigo Vespucci, a Florentine who was sponsored at different times by both Spain and Portugal, sailed along the coast of South America in 1499 and 1501 and received such acclaim in Europe that the new continent was named after him. It was now clear that the lands in the west were a formidable barrier across the route to the East and to the outlying islands of Asia. This was confirmed in 1513 when a Spaniard named Balboa, searching for gold on the American mainland, crossed the isthmus of Darien and became probably the first European to see the Pacific. The huge size of this hitherto unknown ocean only became apparent when a Portuguese in the service of Spain, Ferdinand Magellan, sailed a small fleet around the southern tip of South America in 1519. Suffering appalling privations, Magellan struggled across the Pacific, only to be killed by hostile natives in the Philippines. However, one of his ships, commanded by Sebastian del Cano, limped back to Spain – the first expedition to circumnavigate the globe.

At the same time as these voyages were taking place, the Spanish were exploring and colonising the islands of the Caribbean and investigating the coastline of Mexico. Rumours of a vastly wealthy empire in the interior of Mexico soon reached the Spanish. In 1519 an expedition of about 600 Spaniards led by Hernando Cortes set out to find the source of these rumours. Cortes, an inspirational commander, marched into the heart of the huge Aztec Empire, killed its ruler, Montezuma, and captured and destroyed its capital, Tenochtitlan. The Spanish advantages over the Aztecs were the horse, well-made steel swords, cannon, help from local enemies of the Aztecs and considerable good fortune in that the Aztecs thought Cortes was the god Quetzalcoatl returning from exile in the east. Nonetheless, this was a staggering achievement for such a small force. The gold and silver of the Aztecs was looted and their lands occupied by the *conquistadores*. Mexico City arose on the site of Tenochtitlan. In 1522 Cortes was given the title of Governor of New Spain by Charles V and a fresh province had been added to the Spanish Empire in the New World.

Encouraged by this success, other Spanish adventurers set out to explore the interior of America. By the early 1530s, another empire ripe for conquest had been discovered, that of the Incas, located high in the Peruvian Andes and stretching 5000 km from north to south. In 1532 about 180 Spaniards led by Francisco Pizarro attacked and captured the Incas, who were fortuitously weakened by civil war, and in 1533 killed their Emperor, Atahualpa, and plundered the Empire. Although the Incas revolted in 1536 and the Spanish almost ruined their position through internal feuding, Peru eventually became another colony.

conquistador meaning 'conqueror', a term applied to the Spanish who invaded the Americas

KEY ISSUE

What advantages did Europeans possess over the native populations of America?

FRANCISCO PIZARRO (*c.* 1475–1541)

Pizarro was a typical, and highly successful, example of the tough *conquistadores* who brought huge areas of Central and South America under Spanish control. He was an illegitimate and illiterate member of a minor family of gentry from Castile who arrived in the Americas in 1502. He served in a number of expeditions and in the 1520s explored the coast of Peru in partnership with another *conquistador*, Diego de Almagro. Pizarro returned to Spain in 1528 and persuaded Charles V to appoint him as Governor of Peru. Back in the New World, Pizarro organised a small force to invade the Inca Empire. Using all his experience and considerable powers of leadership Pizarro drove his men over the Andes and into the heart of Inca possessions. When confronted by Atahualpa, the Inca Emperor, and a much stronger force, Pizarro was not afraid to take the initiative, attack the Incas during a parley and seize Atahualpa. Pizarro was thus able to control the Empire, remarking 'By having this man in our hands the entire realm is calm.' Pizarro promised freedom to his royal captive, but when Atahualpa had provided a huge ransom of 11 000 kg of gold and about twice that amount of silver Pizarro had him strangled as he was reckoned to be too dangerous to return to his own people. In 1533 Pizarro sacked and burned the Inca capital, Cuzco, and two years later founded Lima, the new capital of Peru. Pizarro's later years were split between attempting to suppress Inca rebellions and fighting his former partner Almagro for control of Peru. In 1538 Almagro was strangled on the orders of Pizarro's half-brother and his supporters responded by murdering Pizarro in 1541, a violent end to a remarkable career of conquest.

PROFILE

KEY ISSUE

Why is Pizarro seen as such a remarkable leader?

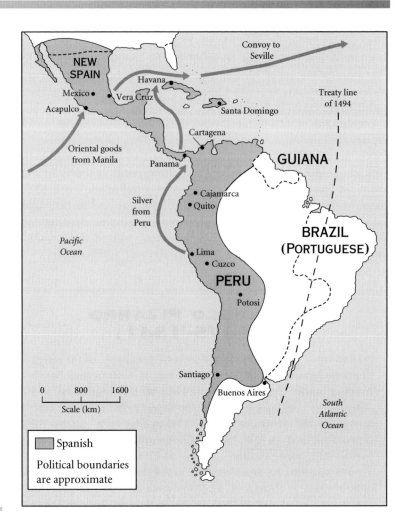

MAP 7

Spanish trade routes in the late sixteenth century

The conquests of Mexico and Peru opened huge areas for exploitation by the Spanish. As in the Caribbean islands, Spanish settlers allocated themselves vast estates or *encomiendas*, which were usually confirmed by royal grant. The holder of each *encomienda* owed military service to the Crown, and in return was-permitted to force the native population to work for him. The nature of this labour was mainly agricultural: natives were employed on plantations of sugar, cotton, vines and olives and in fields of barley, maize and wheat. Cochineal was regarded as being as valuable as gold, as it was used as a dye in the European textile industries. Cocoa was grown as chocolate and became an increasingly fashionable drink. European domestic animals flourished in the lush and ungrazed grasslands of the New World. Huge flocks of sheep and herds of cattle provided the settlers with all the meat they needed. Hides from the vast numbers of cattle in Mexico became the largest item by volume to be shipped back to Spain, providing a cheap and plentiful raw material for the leather industry there.

The impetus for the Spanish advance into the Americas was not, however, provided by profits from agriculture, but rather by the search for precious metals which could be sent to Spain at a great profit. Although the *conquistadores* had hoped for cascades of gold they were sadly disappointed. The native inhabitants of Hispaniola were soon stripped of their relatively small supplies of gold ornaments and then put to work panning for gold in the rivers of the island. The diminution of the work force and the decreasing returns of this source meant that Hispaniola was no longer a significant producer after 1530. The plunder of the Aztec and Inca Empires provided windfalls of gold but finds in Chile and Colombia proved difficult to operate due to shortage of labour and inaccessible seams. Nevertheless, the *conquistadores* continued to hack their way ever further into South America, lured by the legend of El Dorado, a ruler coated in gold, whose land could satisfy Spanish greed. Between 1500 and 1660 it is probable that about 300 tons of gold were transported from the New World to Spain.

Silver was a far more plentiful commodity. Once again, the native Empires were a fruitful source of loot and northern Mexico yielded considerable quantities of ore. The major finds were, however, in the central Andes, especially at Potosi where whole mountains of silver ore awaited excavation. This site was opened up in 1545 and although it was remote and difficult to reach (5000 m above sea level), soon there were some 13 000 workers (mostly Indians) on the site. The development of refining techniques using mercury, a method first used at Potosi in 1573, allowed more rapid exploitation of the silver. As much as 25 000 tons of silver were despatched to Spain in the period 1500 to 1660 (enough to triple European stocks), with large amounts also being retained for use in the New World. These shipments were of the highest importance to Spain, allowing her the financial strength to dominate Europe, but also providing her with the strategic problem of how to protect her silver convoys against envious enemies. The flow of silver gave the impression that Spain was wealthier than she was in reality and encouraged her to borrow beyond her ability to repay. Spain was not the only overseas market for New World silver. From the late sixteenth century, considerable quantities were sent from Acapulco in Mexico to Manila in the Philippines and from there distributed to China and other states in Asia. This trade made Manila an important commercial centre as silk, pearls and (ironically) gold were obtained from Asia and shipped back to America.

The profits from the export of silver and other goods and the affluence of many of the settlers engaged in farming allowed the construction of an impressive colonial structure. The Spanish founded new cities such as Lima in Peru and also adopted former Indian locations such as Mexico City. Buildings in the Spanish style were put up, and the settlers took a pride in the prosperity and size of their new cities. A number of vigorous industries began to grow. Shipbuilding became a prominent activity in the Caribbean and on the Pacific coast of America, meeting the need for coastal traders and even warships. Another area of economic growth was textiles. The merino sheep was introduced to Mexico, and by the end of the sixteenth century there were twenty-five cloth factories in the vicinity of Mexico City. Once again the unfortunate Indians provided slave labour in the textile factories.

The Spanish government was determined not to let the unruly *conquistadores* exist in a state of near-anarchy. The ruling oligarchies in the towns and cities of the New World proved to be a powerful obstacle to central authority, but the power of the Crown's representatives gradually grew. Each province was under the control of a governor who was advised by an *audiencia* or court of appeal, and also watched for signs of disloyalty or incompetence. The *audiencia* was staffed by lawyers who acted not only as judges but also as professional civil servants and provided the Spanish government with a competent and loyal bureaucracy. Huge distances and poor communications meant that government business was conducted at a grindingly slow pace, but considering such problems and the small number of personnel, the Empire was for the most part administered very effectively. Despite the problems of Spain in Europe, the Spanish colonies in the New World were to survive into the nineteenth century, until the urge for independence could be held back no longer.

KEY ISSUE

How did the Spanish Empire differ from that of Portugal?

ANALYSIS

European attitudes towards conquered peoples

Iberian reactions towards those races coming under their control ranged from admiration of the apparent unsophisticated innocence of native peoples to a harsh contempt for all non-Europeans and non-Christians. In both Africa and Asia the Portuguese and Spanish were not able to colonise large areas, so it is America that provides the best evidence. In his initial contacts with the inhabitants of the Caribbean, Columbus recorded an atmosphere of co-operation on both sides: 'I, in order that they might feel great amity towards us ... gave to some among them some red caps and some glass beads, which they hung around their necks, ... At this they were greatly pleased and became so entirely our friends that it was a wonder to see.' In some cases the newcomers were regarded as gods and welcomed as such. Despite such friendly early contacts, the Europeans soon made it clear that they expected to achieve political and religious domination and to exploit the native populations. This soon led to what Urs Bitterli has characterised as 'collision' between the two cultures. When Columbus left Hispaniola in January 1493 he erected a small fort containing about forty men. When he arrived back ten months later, he found that the fort had been destroyed and the settlers killed by the local population. During the next two years, the Spanish waged ferocious reprisal campaigns, resulting in the death of perhaps 100 000 Indians out of a population of about one million. In the following half-century the remainder of the native population was exterminated as a result of forced labour in gold mines and agricultural estates, imported diseases such as smallpox and disruption of traditional economic and family organisation. Hispaniola proved to be the pattern for 'collisions' throughout America.

The sufferings of the indigenous peoples in the Americas fired a debate in Europe on the extent to which the newly-discovered peoples should be considered humans and whether they possessed rights. Isabella of Castile had requested that the natives, as prospective converts to Christianity, should be well-treated and after her death King Ferdinand passed The Laws of Burgos which stated that Indians should be well-treated, paid for their labours and converted to Christianity. The Papacy took a similar line. In 1537 Pope Paul III declared that 'the Indians are true men'. However, such pronouncements could usually be safely ignored by ruthless *conquistadores* and settlers who were thousands of miles from Spain.

All too often, then, the uncaring attitude of the triumphant Europeans meant catastrophe for indigenous populations. The Indian population in Mexico declined from perhaps twenty-five million in 1519 to about 2.6 million in 1568 and in Peru the population, which was probably about eight million in 1530, had fallen to about 1.3 million in 1590. In both cases, this was a result of epidemic disease, war and oppression. The conscious and also the unthinking brutality of the Europeans caused genocide on a massive scale.

6 ∽ EUROPE AND THE WORLD

It can be argued that the opening up of the rest of the world by European explorers in the fifteenth and sixteenth centuries was the single most important development in early modern European history.

It is true that the discoveries of the Portuguese and Spanish had little immediate impact on the vast mass of the European population; new goods from America such as peanuts, tomatoes, turkeys and tobacco were regarded as mere curiosities for decades and the trade in luxuries from the East remained the preserve of the rich. The Holy Roman Emperor Charles V never mentioned the New World in his memoirs, written in 1552. Throughout the sixteenth century, Europe, Africa and Asia were regarded as more important politically and culturally than America.

Portugal, 'an immense and fragile empire' as the French historian Braudel described it, enjoyed a period of commercial supremacy and domination of the Asiatic trade. In 1504 Venetian merchants found no spices at Alexandria or Beirut, whilst in the same year five Portuguese ships entered Falmouth harbour in south-west England carrying 380 tonnes of pepper and spices from Calicut. In the early sixteenth century, Portugal shipped seventy-five per cent of Europe's spice imports. In the long-run traditional patterns of trade re-asserted themselves to some degree, but the wealth of Portugal (based on Lisbon whose population soared from 40 000 in 1490 to 165 000 by the end of the sixteenth century) proved to be an irresistible temptation to Philip II of Spain, who advanced his claim to the Portuguese throne in 1580 and annexed the country.

Spain rose to a position of European pre-eminence owing to the flow of American silver and the credit this enabled her to enjoy. For over a century she was the most feared power in Europe, thanks to her ability to finance armies and fleets from her imperial resources. As G.V. Scammell has commented, 'to her enemies she was an object of terror, hatred and revulsion'.

The Empires and the wealth of Spain and Portugal encouraged other European states to grasp at land outside Europe. By the second half of the sixteenth century, England and France were laying the foundations of empires in North America and the Dutch were energetically looking for trading opportunities both there and in South America and Asia.

In terms of European civilisation, accepted views on history, geography and theology were challenged and revised. The Europeans gained a new self-confidence and a belief in their own superiority, summarised neatly by the remark of Hernan Perez de Oliva when he wrote in 1528 that 'Columbus set sail to unite the world and give to these strange lands the form of our own'. This arrogance was to grow in subsequent centuries and would eventually allow the numerically small peoples of Europe to assert their dominance in every continent on earth. In the short term, apart from some examples of enlightened administration, this dominance was to bring the peoples subject to Europeans little more than interminable labour, a new religion variously imposed on them and new diseases to which they had no resistance. In the long term, there was to be the cultural and economic legacy of imperialism which played so great a part in shaping the modern world.

See pages 382–4

KEY ISSUE

How was Europe changed by the Age of Discovery?

7 ↜ BIBLIOGRAPHY

**J.H. Parry, *The Age of Reconnaissance* (Cardinal, 1973), J.H. Parry, *The Spanish Seaborne Empire* (Hutchinson, 1976), C.R. Boxer, *The Portuguese Seaborne Empire 1415–1825* (Hutchinson, 1969), *G.V. Scammell, *The World Encompassed* (Methuen, 1981) and **G.V. Scammell, *The First Imperial Age* (Unwin Hyman, 1989) are all wide-ranging surveys of the age of discovery. **D. Arnold, *The Age of Discovery 1400–1600* (Lancaster Pamphlets, 1983) and *D. O'Sullivan, *The Age of Discovery 1400–1550* (Seminar Studies, Longman, 1984) are briefer, but still very useful. J.H. Elliott, *The Old World and the New* (OUP, 1970) considers the Spanish Empire in America. U. Bitterli,

Cultures in Conflict (Polity Press, 1989) has some interesting material on the clashes between European and indigenous cultures around the globe. *F. Fernandez-Armesto *Columbus* (OUP, 1991) is the best biography of Columbus. *Hugh Thomas, *The Slave Trade* (Picador, 1997) is a magisterial work of history stretching from the fourteenth to the nineteenth century. T.Wise and A. McBride, *The Conquistadores* (Osprey, 1980) and J. Pohl and A. McBride, *Aztec, Mixtec and Zapotec Armies* (Osprey, 1991) contain interesting material on the military aspects of the Spanish conquest of America. The 500th anniversary of Columbus's trans-Atlantic voyage resulted in a crop of films on the controversial Genoese. The best is *1492: The Conquest of Paradise*, which has some interesting sequences on maritime techniques and the impact of the Spanish in the New World.

8 ↩ STRUCTURED AND ESSAY QUESTIONS

A *Structured questions.*
1. (a) What evidence is there that the expansion of Europe accelerated in the late fifteenth and early sixteenth centuries?
    (b) How do you account for this acceleration?
2. (a) What evidence is there that the search for new trade routes was an important motive for the Portuguese and Spanish voyages of exploration in the fifteenth and sixteenth centuries?
    (b) How important was this aim compared to religious motives?

B *Essay questions.*
1. What technical developments aided the Europeans in their voyages of discovery?
2. Why did so many of the voyages of discovery start from Portugal and Spain?
3. Why did Europeans make voyages of exploration in the fifteenth and sixteenth centuries?
4. How did the discovery of the New World affect Europe in the sixteenth century?
5. Does profit or piety better explain European overseas exploration in the fifteenth century?

9 ↩ DOCUMENTARY EXERCISE

Different individuals had varying motives for seeking new lands across the sea. Read the following sources and then answer the questions below.

Henry the Navigator (1394–1460), organised many of the early voyages of exploration along the west coast of Africa.

See profile on page 94

You should note well that the noble spirit of this prince, by sort of natural constraint, was ever urging him both to begin and to carry out very great deeds. For which reason, after the taking of Ceuta he always kept ships well armed against the Infidel, both for war and because he had also a wish to know the land that lay beyond the isles of Canary and that cape called Bojador ... he sent out ships to those parts, to have sure knowledge of them all ...

The second reason was that if there chanced to be in those lands some population of Christians, or some havens, into which it would be possible to sail without peril, many kinds of merchandise might be brought to this realm, which would find a ready market ... and also the products of this realm might be taken there. Such trade would bring great profit to our countrymen.

The third reason was that, as it was said that the power of the Moors in that land of Africa was very much greater than was commonly supposed, and that there were no Christians among them, nor any other race of men; and because every wise man is obliged by natural prudence to wish for a knowledge of the power of his enemy, therefore the said Prince Henry exerted himself to cause this to be fully discovered, and to make it known definitely how far the power of those infidels extended.

The fourth reason was because during the thirty-one years that he had warred against the Moors, he had never found a Christian king ... who for the love of our Lord Jesus Christ would aid him in the said war. Therefore he sought to know if there were in those parts any Christian princes, in whom the charity and love of Christ was so ingrained that they would aid him against those enemies of the faith.

The fifth reason was his great desire to make increase on the faith of our Lord Jesus Christ and to bring to him all the souls that should be saved ...

But over and above these five reasons I have a sixth that would seem to be the root from which all others proceeded: and this is the inclination of the heavenly wheels.

SOURCE A

Azuzara, a 15th-century Portuguese chronicler writes an account of the motives of Henry the Navigator.

1. *Who were the Moors?*
2. *In your own words outline the six reasons Azurara mentions.*
3. *Which reasons seem to be the most plausible?*

They had no proper weapons, and did not know what these were. When I showed them swords their ignorance was such that they seized them by the blades and cut their fingers ... some wore a few grains of fine gold in their ears and noses which they gave us without difficulty ... I must add that this island belongs to Your Highnesses as securely as the kingdom of Castile. It only needs people to come and settle here and to give orders to the inhabitants who will do what ever is asked of them. I myself, with the few men at my disposal, can travel all through these islands without risk. I have already seen three of my men land alone, and by their mere presence cause the flight of a whole crowd of Indians, although they had no intention of harming them...They know nothing about the art of war and are so cowardly that a thousand of them would not stay to face three of our men. One can see that they are well able to do whatever is asked, and they need only to be given orders to be made to work, to sow or to do anything useful. They could build towns and get used to wearing clothes and to behaving like ourselves.

SOURCE B
Extract describing an encounter with Indians in the Caribbean, written by Columbus.

Q

1. *In what ways would Columbus's description make the New World seem attractive to Europeans?*
2. *Using your own knowledge and the source, explain whether this is likely to be a reliable picture of the newly-discovered lands in the Caribbean.*
3. *What does the passage reveal about European attitudes to newly discovered peoples?*

5 The Renaissance

OVERVIEW

'The Renaissance' refers to the great renewal of artistic creativity in Italy, and especially the city of Florence, from 1400 onwards. By 1500 the Renaissance was also established in Rome, underway in Venice, and had started to make its influence felt across all of Europe. By then the artists included such outstanding figures as Leonardo da Vinci, Michelangelo and Raphael; this latter period has become known as 'the High Renaissance'. But the Renaissance was also a rebirth of interest in the classical civilisations. A group of scholars known as **humanists** revived the study of ancient Rome and the great Latin authors such as Cicero. They found writings that had previously been lost, and edited and corrected ones that were still in general use. They were not just scholars, studying the Romans (and later the Greeks) for their own sake: they looked to these classical civilisations for guidance on how to communicate most effectively, and on how best to conduct their political and moral lives. They then built their findings into the education system; our study of history, literature and languages is a long-term effect of what they did. In the unstable, exciting world of the Italian city-states, the humanists pointed to ancient Rome as the model of how to live a civilised life. But they did not just copy the Romans. The humanists' own writings changed the way people viewed politics, religion and society, first of all in Italy and then throughout Europe. Leading historians in the nineteenth century identified this as the birth of modern civilisation. Although this sweeping judgement is disputed by many more recent historians, the Renaissance is still viewed as an intellectual and artistic movement of key significance.

humanist a student of the humanities or arts subjects, particularly the classics of the ancient world

1 ⌐ THE ITALIAN HUMANISTS AND THE ORIGINS OF THE RENAISSANCE

The term 'Renaissance' is derived from the Italian word *rinascità* meaning 'rebirth'. The sixteenth-century art historian, Vasari, coined it to describe what he saw as the replacement of the stereotypes of medieval art in about 1400 by a new, more vigorous and freer creativity based on a 'rebirth' of Roman and Greek classical principles. It is Vasari's depiction of artistic genius which has been passed down to us in familiar images of the Renaissance, such as Leonardo da Vinci and his *Mona Lisa*. The true origin of the Renaissance as a movement, however, was to be found in classical scholarship.

Around 1400 there began a craze for book collecting, following on from a renewal of interest in classical literature led by the great poet Petrarch in the fourteenth century. Scholars mainly based in the central Italian city of Florence, such as Poggio Bracciolini, scoured monastic libraries to find older, more authentic versions of the writings of Latin authors or, where they were really lucky, to rediscover classical texts which had been lost altogether. This was not just a fad. These enthusiastic scholars saw themselves as overthrowing the errors of centuries. Generations of their predecessors had relied on texts full of errors, having been copied out wrongly by scribes; or their way of thought had been cramped by medieval scholasticism, a Christianised version of the thought of Aristotle, the Greek philosopher. Turning away from such scholastic philosophy, the critical scholars of early fifteenth-century Italy were known as humanists because they taught that the humanities in the form of classical literature – including history, **ethics**, poetry, rhetoric and grammar – are the basis of civilised life. The humanists also saw that the classics came from another distinct age, the glories of which they were confident they could revive; medieval scholars had not been able to place classical texts in any clear context or chronology.

ethics the study of moral conduct, especially in public life

It was the humanists' belief that, before any understanding could develop, there had to be a good grasp of pure and elegant Latin. Matteo Palmieri, writing in 1432, rejoiced in 'seeing our youth entering on the study of Latin by such order and method that in a year or two they come to speak and write that language with a fluency and correctness which it was impossible that our fathers could ever attain to at all'. This celebration of a classical language may seem odd for us with the current emphasis ever more on modern languages, but in the period around 1400 Latin was of enormous importance as the international language and the medium of all scholarship. If you wanted to communicate you had to be effective in Latin. So the humanists studying Latin were concerned with rhetoric (the ability to express oneself) and with the moral problems involved. The academic subject which serves a similar purpose today would be English.

KEY ISSUE

Why was it thought to be so important to collect and edit Latin texts?

The career of Coluccio Salutati (1331–1406) may provide the answer as to why a renewed emphasis on elegant and accurate Latin took on such significance. He was a lawyer and a public servant, as well as being a leading humanist. He worked as chancellor (in effect, head of the civil service) in three Italian cities, the final one being Florence where he held office from 1375 to 1406. Salutati did not pursue his humanist study of Latin purely as a private hobby; he also introduced it into his public service. He particularly admired Cicero, the great writer from the age of Caesar, and modelled his diplomatic correspondence and speeches on Cicero's fine rhetorical Latin. In doing so, Salutati set a trend. His rivals in other cities and his successors in Florence competed to write the best, most classical Latin. The rulers of Italy, appreciating the prestige and the subtleties of humanist diplomacy, encouraged this competition. Humanist scholarship and power politics could now come together in a fertile relationship.

Salutati did not just provide the practical model of the humanist in political work; he also found in Cicero a justification for what he was doing. Cicero promoted the principle of *negotium*, the idea that scholars should not hide in their ivory towers but should be active in the world, letting their learning influence their public life (especially their work in government) and be influenced by it themselves. In contrast, Petrarch, who had dominated attitudes towards classical Latin in the mid-fourteenth century, had not known all of Cicero's writings and anyway was committed to the principle of *otium*, retreat from the world into neutral and undisturbed pursuit of the truth. With the discarding of this semi-monastic ideal, the fifteenth-century humanist was dedicated to public life, or *negotium*.

A cynic might point out that *negotium*, in the form of government service, paid better than *otium*, but there are historians who cannot believe that the burst of Renaissance creative energy that ensued was mercenary. Hans Baron in particular has argued that the Renaissance grew from *civic* humanism, that is, not just professional government service but the humanist's patriotic dedication to his community. For Baron, the model humanist was Leonardo Bruni (1370–1444) who led the civil service of Florence as chancellor for seventeen years from 1427. He not only believed in *negotium*, but saw his adopted city, Florence, as the most advanced form of community, a republic to be contrasted with most Italian city-states ruled by princes or tyrants. His views were clear in all his writings, particularly in his *History of the Florentine People*, which glorified the republic and confirmed the Florentines in their growing conviction that, owing to their ideals and their skills, they were entitled to be regarded as the New Romans. So political idealism as well as political activity may have been crucial to the achievements of the Renaissance humanists.

The Baron thesis certainly clarifies the origins of the Renaissance. It tells us that it had to begin in Florence, set apart by its vigorous republican institutions. It even tells us more precisely when it began – civic humanism was galvanised in the 1390s when Florence was threatened by Gian Galeazzo Visconti, Duke of Milan. There was a display of patriotic rhetoric that continued even after the threat to Florence was removed by the death of Gian Galeazzo in 1402. According to Baron, Bruni and other civic humanists found their inspiration, and therefore the inspiration of the Renaissance, in the liberty of Florence.

There are problems with the Baron thesis. Bruni was not exclusively dedicated to the republic of Florence – he spent part of his career working in the Curia, the papal civil service in Rome, which provided jobs for many humanists. Bruni's writings do not all coincide neatly with the political events that are supposed to have stimulated them. The liberty of Florence itself may have just been a rhetorical invention, used to disguise the narrowing **oligarchy**, the small group of influential men who really controlled Florentine affairs.

Perhaps Florence needed the humanists, with their classical dignity and reassuring rhetoric, not to express an authentic republicanism but

oligarchy government dominated by a few people or families

to hide just how precarious the city's republican institutions had become. From failed popular revolt (the Revolt of the Ciompi in 1378) to unofficial monarchy (discreet dominance by the Medici family from 1434), Florence passed through a period of profound transformation. The humanists, with their optimism and eloquence could make the transition smoother. Likewise, a little later in Rome the popes were seeking to re-establish themselves after the Great Schism; it was logical that the reassurance and persuasion of the humanists' commanding Latin could be employed there as well. Bruni was not the only humanist to move between Florence and Rome in search of employment. Therefore, with the trend established, the other princes of Italy started to compete for the services of the best humanists and the Renaissance gradually spread. The humanists were clearly not identified as being necessarily republican. That was in part because Cicero, whose writings were central to the humanists' political thinking, had been much more concerned with the public good (which could be served by a prince) rather than the specifics of republican government. It is the case, nevertheless, that the best humanists in the early fifteenth century remained mostly in Florence. That may well be because it was there, in that precariously republican city, that their skills were most needed.

See page 2

At the opposite end of the scale from Baron, P.O. Kristeller has argued that the humanists were first and last rhetoricians, defined purely by their style of communication – speech-writing – rather than by any specific moral or political convictions they had in common. However, this does under-estimate the humanists' genuine response to the classical world they studied and the intellectual innovations stimulated by it.

See pages 122–4

The work of the humanists had a social purpose; rhetoric is not necessarily the same as propaganda, it can express something more enduring than what is called for by passing political interests. The humanist Barbaro was one amongst many arguing that wealth was necessary for the exercise of virtue in supporting your family and your community. There had been much wealth amassed in medieval Italy, but the Church disapproved and there had been guilt to go with it. Now the Renaissance offered the idealisation of wealth and, for better or for worse, liberated the conscience of the Italian ruling class.

The humanists did not just debate issues relevant to the moral and social dilemmas of their employers. They helped to develop a new moral vocabulary. For instance, in the Middle Ages the word *virtù* carried more or less the sense of what we mean by virtue, or sometimes manliness. In the hands of the humanists, *virtù* became the moral duty to develop all one's individual potential to the full, including political acumen. The humanists were idealising the pursuit of power.

The Renaissance was neither just an event amongst scholars nor a style of propaganda. We have seen how much the humanists had to offer to Florence in particular and to the Italian élite in general. Gradually, over the course of the fifteenth century an Italian, and finally European, network of humanists grew, visiting one another and corresponding. There were places where this network was concentrated

KEY ISSUE

Was civic humanism anything more than propaganda?

– Florence in the early 1400s, Rome in the early 1500s – but no single centre. We must turn now to the unique environment in Italy in which this network flourished and made sure that the Renaissance was not just a local or a passing fashion, but an environment which made the relationship between patrons and humanists, power and imagination, extremely fertile.

ANALYSIS

secularism politics and morality independent of religion

Jacob Burckhardt and the Renaissance

Jacob Burckhardt is the nineteenth-century Swiss historian who did more than any one to establish the view of the Renaissance that is still argued over today; his great work was *The Civilization of the Renaissance in Italy*, published in 1860. For Burckhardt, the political and social turmoil of city-states in late medieval Italy, along with the revival of classical learning, led to 'the discovery of the world and of man'. He meant a new concern with the here and now and a lessening of respect for the religious thought and authorities which had dominated the Middle Ages. He saw Renaissance humanism as the origin of modern **secularism**, as a decisive break with the Middle Ages, and he saw the Renaissance as the origin of modern individualism, where people's roles as independent and free individuals, their own decisions, their own achievements mattered, rather than just their identity as members of a group such as a monastery, a noble family, or a guild. He also referred to the Renaissance 'state as a work of art', being 'the fruit of careful reflection and adaptation', meaning that Renaissance rulers and humanists thought critically about the way in which a state was constituted, rather than just accepting it as given, an inheritance from forebears or something ordained by God. But in many ways, Burckhardt was writing as a nineteenth-century figure looking for the origin of his own world, increasingly characterised by secularism and individualism. The word humanism itself had only been coined in 1806. There was no unified, single movement (except perhaps the 'civic humanism' later claimed to be identified by Baron, but which in any case was limited to early fifteenth-century Florence.) Burckhardt under-estimated the influence of religion; even the most dedicated students of classical philosophy such as the neo-Platonists were trying to find a way of synthesising it with Christianity. Much of the 'discovery of the world' had to wait for the scientific revolution of the seventeenth century. Burckhardt himself acknowledged later in his career that he had exaggerated the extent of individualism in Renaissance society, where people were often driven by the uncertainties of political life to seek greater security in family networks, guilds or other associations. We get a greater sense of prominent individuals in the Renaissance than in previous eras because portraits and memoirs appeared then for the first time in large numbers; but the portrait was as often as not a family group and the memoirs a local chronicle rather than an autobiography. Burckhardt thought that the thirst for individual fame was specific to the Renaissance, but the medieval chivalric knight knew that thirst just as well. Given such criticisms, it may seem a mystery why Burckhardt is still read today. It is probably because he was the historian who first effectively characterised the Renaissance as an essential phase in the development of Western civilisation as a whole, rather than as something confined to scholarship or the arts. His conclusions may be argued over, but he set the agenda for debate that is still very much alive.

2 ↶ THE ITALIAN ENVIRONMENT

Italy was at the forefront of Europe in urban development. There were independent cities elsewhere in Europe, especially in the Rhineland and the Netherlands, but few which were as wealthy as their Italian counterparts, or as politically sophisticated. The city was the centre of everything. As one Remigio put it around 1300, 'Destroy his city and a citizen is like a painted or a stone image, because he is thereby shorn from the vigour and work that he once had.' The obvious exemplar for such dedication to the city was that greatest of all city-states, ancient Rome. When the humanists proclaimed the values of ancient Rome to willing listeners, and when Renaissance artists, sculptors and architects offered their services, the cities, and not just Florence, supported their 'vigour and work'. There had to be some measure of stability, though, before the men of the Renaissance could get their message across.

The trouble with the medieval Italian cities being a law unto themselves was that their citizens could not always agree on what that law should be. There were struggles between the various families, neighbourhoods or guilds within the cities. It was quite normal for a home to incorporate a watchtower, patriotism not always extending to a complete street let alone the city. (In a number of towns youths would gather to let off steam by throwing rocks at one another, a practice not unknown today but rarely accepted as an official sport.) With the faction fighting being so violent, it was always likely that any politically active intellectual would end up in exile for his pains, as happened to the great poet and philosopher, Dante, driven out of Florence in 1301. However, this served to make civic unity an even more desirable, if elusive, ideal. As Waley has put it, 'As hungry men dream of food and frozen men of warmth, so the men of the Italian republics dreamed of concord.' Humanist writings made it seem as though that concord and greatness were attainable by city-states – the political reality underneath was still uncertain, but by 1400 not so uncertain as to give the lie to the rhetoric or spoil the dream.

Republican governments were being replaced by **despots**. There were exceptions, primarily Venice and Florence, but the former was still more a maritime empire than an Italian city-state and, as we have already seen, the Florentine republic was sliding towards rule by one family – the Medici. Despotism had become the norm by 1400. For Burckhardt these despotisms were the seedbeds of the Renaissance and, through that, the modern world, owing to the despots' willingness to abandon tradition, to be individualists and to adapt the state to more modern needs. These generalisations have been much qualified by more recent historians, but it is true that despots provided a working environment for humanists, once the fashion to employ them had caught on. The despots needed humanists to adorn their courts in order to give them an air of legitimacy.

> **despot** individual wielding all the power in a state

Elsewhere in Europe, princes found security in their ancient title, with inherited land as the measure of status and authority. In Italy it was more political skill that counted, with money as the measure of power; but neither gave sufficient security. (An exception was feudal Naples but that was the part of Italy least affected by the Renaissance.) A humanist chancellor and a programme of general spending on the arts could give a despot some dignity to bolster his position. Sigismondo Malatesta, the vile dictator of Rimini, was the patron for one of the most perfect of Renaissance buildings, Alberti's Tempio Malatestiano. More significant was to be the attitude of Lorenzo de Medici, the ruler of Florence from 1469 until 1492. He knew how he had earned his nickname, 'Il Magnifico'. He commented on the 663 755 gold florins he had spent on the arts, charity and in taxes (it is not odd that he made no distinction as they were all seen as being of public benefit): 'I think it casts a brilliant light on our estate and it seems to me that the monies were well spent and I am very well pleased with this.' So there was certainly the need and the will to spend on Renaissance culture, and there was also the money.

Italy was already immensely wealthy by the early fourteenth century, owing to its trade with the East. If anything, it started to decline from that time, a situation worsened by the onslaught of bubonic plague after 1347, with no preventive measures possible. The population of Florence, around 95 000 in 1338, had dropped to 40 000 by 1427. Economic and **demographic** downturns do not seem promising for a great cultural movement, but actually they may have helped. The fewer people to inherit accumulated wealth, the greater amount there was to inherit per capita and to spend on culture. And while there were fewer trading opportunities, this allowed for more idle money to be spent on culture. In general, Italy's wealth had accumulated sufficiently during the earlier Middle Ages to afford cultural extravagance during the period of its relative decline.

> **demography** population statistics, or the study of them

The men who had made this wealth, competing with nobility who had inherited their status, needed legitimacy as much as rulers. Humanists reassured them that wealth could be a mark of distinction if spent wisely and that true nobility sprang from merit rather than just birth. Also, classical learning could be seen as evidence of merit and status. In Florence, the communal schools were so bad that the wealthy employed private tutors and therefore a good education was socially exclusive. Alberti remarked that a grasp of Latin 'is so important that someone unlettered, however much a gentleman, will be considered nothing but a country bumpkin'.

See page 131

Even the less well educated merchants were generally literate, and that in itself also challenged the clergy's monopoly over learning and education. In Italy with its great merchant cities, laymen were becoming more independent of the Church and its domination over cultural and moral life. The humanists provided laymen with a specifically lay culture. John Stephens has commented that in their provision of cultural and moral guidance the humanists can be seen as the heirs of the priests. This does not mean, however, that the élite of Italy started to abandon Christianity, even though their respect for priests diminished.

Burckhardt thought that the worldliness of wealthy Italian patrons and the revival of interest in the pagan gods of ancient Greece and Rome in art and writing showed that the Renaissance was undermining Christianity in Italy. But he ignored the fact that the vast majority of Italians were entirely traditional in their Christian devotions and he underestimated the capacity of the Renaissance élite to reconcile their secular interests with religious beliefs. One Florentine businessman gave a regular percentage of his takings to charity, marking 'to God' in his accounts. Another would commission a religious painting by a Renaissance artist and donate it to the parish church, thereby earning prestige, of course, as well as religious merit. A modestly clad Virgin Mary was still a far more common figure in Renaissance art than a naked Venus and it has been estimated that ninety per cent of Renaissance paintings were of religious subjects. The social and intellectual context of Renaissance art was still Christian. In literature, too, the values of the Renaissance did not seem necessarily to contradict Christianity; even the pagan philosophy of Plato was to be reconciled with Christianity by Marsilio Ficino, as we will see. The Renaissance was to flourish in an environment which was not demonstrably less Christian than other parts of Europe.

The maintenance of Christian belief in the environment of the Renaissance did not stop Italian churchmen being worldly in many of their interests. The Marquis of Mantua showed the tone of Italian ecclesiastical life in the 1460s in a comment to his son: '*Although* you are a cardinal, be religious and observe your obligations.' With the Pope in Rome and as many dioceses in Italy as the rest of Europe put together, the Church provided rich pickings for the Italian élite. For example, the Medici began as rulers of Florence but in the early sixteenth century they were to provide two popes. Bishops were as interested as secular rulers in the worldly glory that could come through learning and the arts. The Italian Church, as much as the governments of Italy's cities, was to give employment to humanists such as Bruni and to artists, and thereby provide an institutional basis for the Renaissance.

It was not just the social and institutional environment in Italy that fostered the Renaissance. There were also the physical remains of classical civilisation abounding in what had been the heart of the Roman empire. Much of what the tourist sees today has been dug out of the ground since the Renaissance, but the great landmarks, such as the Colosseum, were magnificently visible even then and challenged the men of the Renaissance to look closely at the culture which had produced them. There were numerous reminders of that culture in objects such as the *sarcophagi*, Roman marble tombs decorated with **relief** sculpture, which had often been taken over for Christian burials and so were conveniently situated for study in cloisters and quiet

relief sculpture or a design projecting slightly from a flat surface

MAP 8
Italy at the close of the fifteenth century

churchyards. Given these plentiful remains, it is surprising that Italians had not tried to copy their Roman ancestors earlier. But having something in view is one thing, taking the trouble to look is another. It was the literary inspiration of the humanists that caused Italians to appreciate the classical remains around them. Clearly the development of Italy, in its urban society and politics, its economy, its religion and its culture, created an environment favourable to the Renaissance. This does not mean that it was an inevitable cultural event. It depended much for the form it took on the work of those key humanists in Florence around 1400. However, once established, the Renaissance could spread relatively easily through the rest of Italy, and its message of classical revival could spread through every aspect of the culture of the Italian élite, particularly the visual arts.

> **KEY ISSUE**
>
> *What made the Italian environment uniquely favourable to the Renaissance?*

3 ∽ THE VISUAL ARTS IN THE EARLY RENAISSANCE

A textbook can only inadequately describe the changes in the arts that came about during the Renaissance. It is necessary to go to an art gallery to look at a Renaissance collection or, best of all, to go to Italy and experience the variety and exuberance of the works that Italians painted, sculpted and built in the period after 1400. All a textbook can do is to suggest some of the social conditions in which creativity flourished and some of the breakthroughs made by key artists.

Artists in the Middle Ages did not have a distinct social status. They were classed as craftsmen. The value of their paintings was usually determined by the costs of the materials rather than the artistic quality; the most valuable painting was the one most laden with gold leaf. Even when they created what today would be thought of as a masterpiece, they won no more fame for it than their fellow craftsmen did for making cloth or nails. In contrast, there was to be nothing anonymous about Renaissance artists. The greatest of them developed distinct styles and were recognised for it, sometimes to the extent of being cultural heroes. Gradually artists ceased to be ordinary craftsmen and rose in social status, as members of the Italian social élite competed for their services. This was made easier by the greater social mobility in Italy, specifically in Florence, a city of shopkeepers as Peter Burke calls it, in contrast with much of the rest of Europe where birth was all-important.

This fame of individual artists, however, should not be confused with the romantic image of the artist working in heroic isolation. All Renaissance artists were trained in a *bottega*, or workshop. As apprentices they would learn basic techniques from their master who would then employ them in the painting of background detail. The workshop of the medieval guilds had not been entirely abandoned. However, the aspiring Renaissance artist would leave his workshop and look at the work of other masters. He would learn from the style of other artists in order to create his own. It is this combination of individualism and co-operation that made Renaissance art so fertile in new ideas. We shall consider some of these new ideas in relation to painting first, then in sculpture and finally in architecture.

It was the work of Masaccio (1401–28) that provided the model for Renaissance painters. Even the confidently individual Leonardo da Vinci (1452–1519) acknowledged that he took much inspiration from the Brancacci Chapel in Florence, which contains Masaccio's most famous work. He was not the first to break away from medieval conventions; a hundred years earlier Giotto had won fame for introducing into painting the movement and emotion of a dramatic situation with some space for the action. But Masaccio was the first to paint everything systematically as seen from a one-point perspective, with the size of the objects portrayed according to whether they were close to the viewer or far away. This technique enabled the artist to model images in three dimensions and to get away from the flat stereotypes of medieval art; it gave the space in which the image of living people could be created. Such a technique might, however, allow only for clever illusion. Masaccio offered something more. He peopled the space his technique created with beautifully composed figures expressing human dignity. This was the same dignity found in classical sources and celebrated by the humanists. Indeed, Masaccio took inspiration directly from classical sources; he looked at Roman statues as well as at living people when he was designing the figures in his painting. For all the fame of his successors, he was the original Renaissance artist.

There are more contenders for the title of original Renaissance sculptor. In 1401 in Florence, there was a competition to decide who should create the sculpture which was to adorn some new doors for the baptistery, that prominent building next to the cathedral which was thought by many to be Roman. The winner, against stiff competition, was Lorenzo Ghiberti (1378–1455). One of the doors he created was to be called by Michelangelo the 'Gate of Paradise'. He worked to themes suggested by the humanist Bruni and used perspective to give an appearance of depth to the sculpture in relief, that is, projecting slightly from the flat surface of the doors. He was even the first artist to announce his individuality by writing about himself. So Ghiberti has some claim to being the originator of Renaissance sculpture.

He was, however, rapidly surpassed by his pupil, Donatello (1386–1466) who went on to look more closely at classical examples and at the human body and then, with unique skill in handling stone or bronze, to create masterpiece after masterpiece. He was to break much more completely from the stiffness of medieval sculpture, incorporating into his work dramatic expression and a sense of fluid human movements. Donatello's study of David after the slaying of Goliath was the first nude statue since classical times. His portrayal of the mercenary Gattemalata astride his horse was the first equestrian statue since that of Marcus Aurelius 1100 years before. As well as completing much fine work himself, he established many of the possibilities that later Renaissance sculptors were to explore.

More extraordinary perhaps than any other in his contribution to the Renaissance was Filippo Brunelleschi (1377–1446). It was he who first developed the systematic perspective that was to be employed in such a significant way by Masaccio. It was he who was Ghiberti's closest challenger in the competition over the design of the baptistery doors. He even sculpted a crucifix in a way that Donatello had said could not be done. But he is remembered most often as the first Renaissance architect. He accompanied Donatello in his study of classical remains and learnt not just the classical details, but the rules of proportion that had given Roman architecture a sense of harmony as well as grandeur.

A century earlier the Florentines had begun to build a magnificent cathedral but they had not completed it. Brunelleschi provided the solution to the problem of covering the central space by designing a dome which surpassed the engineering even of the Roman Pantheon. When they were homesick, Florentines came to say that they longed for the cathedral and its dome. Bunelleschi had originated Renaissance architecture by learning from Roman techniques and architectural values. He also brought to his fellow Florentine citizens something of Roman greatness.

Masaccio, Ghiberti and Donatello, Brunelleschi – in their careers can be found much of what characterised the artistic Renaissance. It is hard to explain how such a cluster of genius arose in one generation after 1400 and in one city, with a population rather smaller than modern Surbiton. Some would put it down to extraordinary fortune. Some art historians see it as the logic of art's internal development, one idea stimulating the next. But the intellectual atmosphere created by the Florentine humanists with their call to revive Roman culture both helped the artists to develop their own ideas and conditioned an audience to welcome their innovations. In the end that audience counts almost as much as the creators. It was the ruling class of Florence, or at least the guild of cloth merchants looking to surpass other guilds in its patronage, that was to make the decision over the baptistery doors. It was the ruling élite, first of Florence and then of Italy as a whole, that was to pay for Renaissance art and was therefore in a position to make the final choice as to its direction.

The importance of the patron has been much debated. Baxandall argued that patrons pretty well determined everything in an artistic commission, and contracts do show that artists were heavily restricted in their choice of materials, dimensions, subject matter and even composition. They had to paint in a visual language that their patrons could understand, and what seems individual to us in a painting today may in fact portray common gestures, rituals and even dances of the period. However, this does not adequately explain change in artistic styles or why some artists were so much more original, and so much more sought after than others; the recognition of an individual artist's creativity rather than dull conformity to a patron's wishes did count.

While some Renaissance patrons might have been very prescriptive in their commissions, many displayed an unusual tolerance for innovation (in contrast with the way popular taste lags behind *avant-*

garde art today). It may be that, in the fifteenth century at least, it was the development of perspective that made the exploration of new possibilities so exciting to patrons and artists alike. A modern analogy of technical breakthrough leading to greater acceptance of stylistic innovation would be film – there is much produced that is conformist, but there is also room for great originality and creative flair, despite the need to give paying customers what they want.

See exercise on patronage on pages 139–44

Lisa Jardine has recently argued that Renaissance art was the product of a society overwhelmingly concerned with commodities, 'worldly goods' rather than more abstract values. She points to the rich fabrics and furnishings featuring in so many paintings: 'the Virgin and Saints enjoy the same luxury level of lifestyle as those who give the artist his instructions'. It is clearly the case that patrons were concerned with the projection of their status, but this is not the whole story. Lisa Jardine states that she is looking for the origins of 'our own exuberant multiculturalism and bravura consumerism' in the Renaissance. In doing so, she may be writing more about the preoccupations of our own age, as Burckhardt wrote about his, than about the Renaissance itself. Piety mattered as well as wealth and status (and aesthetic pleasure). Patronage of paintings by laymen became important from the thirteenth century onwards, because friars enlisted the support of laymen in decorating their new churches and bringing bible stories to life. As John Stephens has put it, art, like the classics, 'supplied food to satisfy a hunger for moral improvement awoken by the friars'. It was a way of justifying, even consecrating the possession of wealth, as well as displaying it. Even if the subject of a painting was secular the display of wealth could simply appear vulgar if 'worldly goods' were too ostentatious: Alberti, in his treatise on art in 1435, which did more than any other to lay down the rules, made moderation, balance and harmony the aim, and his criticism of unnecessary detail and excessive use of gold or other costly materials was well heeded. Through Renaissance art patrons sought an addition to their dignity and moral standing, not just a reflection of their everyday reality.

KEY ISSUE

What was so radically new in the visual arts of the early Renaissance?

4 ↩ THE DEVELOPMENT OF RENAISSANCE THOUGHT

A discussion of the humanists and the artists of the early Renaissance should give a sense of the values of the movement that was going to affect the whole of élite culture in Early Modern Europe. Those values, however, were not fixed. Apart from innovative thinkers and artists stimulating each other, the gradual retrieval of the classical past proved a continuing source of inspiration.

More and more classical texts were collected, edited and made available to those educated enough to read them. They could be consulted in new libraries, such as the St Mark's Library founded by Cosimo de Medici in 1437 and the first one to be endowed by a layman since Roman times. Scholars' use of different versions of classical texts enabled them to arrive at more accurate editions. The works of the Roman poet Virgil, for instance, had been known throughout the Middle Ages but it was not until 1470 that an edition appeared that was reliably close to the original. Artists as well as scholars could be inspired by what they found in libraries. Painters could read the Roman author Pliny on the theory of art, which partly made up for the fact that no original Roman painting had yet been unearthed. Architects could read Vitruvius whose writings, largely forgotten for 1500 years and then brought to light in an Alpine monastery around 1410, became the standard textbook of classical architecture. But the most significant fertilisation of Renaissance thought came from the rediscovery of Greek.

In some ways classical Greek thought, at least that of the great philosopher Aristotle and the mathematician Euclid, had never been lost. It had been absorbed into medieval thinking, but only through Arabic translations and had been overlaid by the logical intricacies of scholasticism, the philosophy of the Middle Ages. The original Greek texts were available in the Byzantine Empire but the Christians of the Church of Rome in western Europe put up a sort of cultural wall against the Greek Orthodox Church of the Byzantine Empire in eastern Europe. Then around 1400, the Italian humanists reacted against what they felt was the obscure thinking of the medieval scholastic philosophers based on garbled versions of the great ancient Greek philosopher, Aristotle. So the humanists saw the need to renew and clarify classical Greek thought as well as Roman. The trouble was that no one understood Greek. Petrarch had a copy of Homer's poetry and he would kiss it to acknowledge its greatness, but he could not read it. He hired a monk called Pilatus to translate it, but the monk, ill-advisedly standing too near to a ship's mast in a storm, was killed by lightning and no successor could be found. It was not until 1396 that a scholar from Constantinople, Emanuel Chrysoloras, became the first Professor of Greek at Florence and began the gradual process whereby the Greek language and Greek thought were re-introduced into western Europe during the fifteenth and sixteenth centuries. Texts were brought from Constantinople, and a great burst of interest followed the visit of scholars from there, travelling to Italy for the Council of Florence in 1438, which attempted to reunite the Roman Catholic and Greek Orthodox churches. And after the fall of that city to the Ottoman Turks in 1453, refugee scholars came permanently. The cultural effects were enormous. The Greeks had been the originators of science, of medicine, of drama (tragedy and comedy), of history and of geography in western thought. The insights of that classical world opened up a new world of ideas as the Renaissance developed. It seemed to many that the greatest insights came from Plato.

We think reality is the world we see around us. Plato, writing about 400 BC, thought that the world we see is just the shadow of what is real and that the job of a philosopher is to see through this messy world to the real perfection that lies beyond, a perfection which we would call

> **KEY ISSUE**
>
> *Why did the study of Greek lag far behind the study of Latin and why was it so important to the development of the Renaissance?*

spiritual. Modern science makes it hard for us to appreciate this but Marsilio Ficino (1433–99) managed to do so; he established a group of neo-Platonists in Florence who were to turn the Renaissance into a philosophical as well as a literary and artistic movement.

Ficino and his fellow neo-Platonists influenced all the men of Renaissance culture around them. Both Cosimo de Medici and his grandson Lorenzo Il Magnifico, the unofficial rulers of Florence, were friends as well as patrons to Ficino. Botticelli developed the symbolism of his painting from Ficino's ideas, especially in his masterpiece known as *Primavera*. Poets such as Poliziano absorbed the ideal of Platonic love – not just non-sexual affection as it is thought of today but the neo-Platonists' vision of spiritual love transcending the merely physical. Theological debate was sharpened by the neo-Platonic ideas about the soul as the immortal essence of man.

One of Ficino's main aims was to explore such ideas in order to reconcile Platonic philosophy with Christianity. One of the most remarkable of Ficino's disciples, who went too far with the theology, at least for the Pope's liking, was Pico della Mirandola (1463–94). He also gave a definition of man that seemed to go further than the earlier views of the Renaissance humanists on the dignity of man. In 1486 he wrote as if God were speaking to newly created man:

> The nature of other creatures, which has been determined, is I
> confined within the bounds prescribed by Us. You, who are
> confined by no limits, shall determine for yourselves your own
> nature, in accordance with your own free will, in whose hand I have
> placed you...We have made you neither heavenly nor earthly, 5
> neither mortal nor immortal, so that, more freely and more
> honourably the moulder and maker of yourself, you may fashion
> yourself in whatever form you shall prefer. You shall be able to
> descend among the lower forms of being, which are brute beasts;
> you shall be able to be reborn out of the judgment of your own
> soul into the higher beings which are divine. II
> ...Whatever seed each man cultivates will grow and bear fruit in
> him. If the seeds are vegetative, he will be like a plant; if they are
> sensitive, he will become like the beasts; if they are rational, he will
> become like a heavenly creature; if intellectual, he will be an angel
> and a son of God...

Q

1. *What distinguishes man from the beasts (lines 1–5)?*
2. *All humanists regarded man as being able to improve himself in some way. In what way is Pico going further in this optimism than the civic humanists of the early Renaissance (lines 5–11 and refer back to pages 110–15)?*
3. *There is a view that the Renaissance became increasingly élitist. Is there any evidence from Pico's writings above to support or to contradict that view?*

During the fifteenth century, the subject of the Renaissance seemed to have become Man rather than people, the ideal or perfect form of humanity rather than the citizens of ancient Rome or contemporary Florence. At the start of the century the status of artists had risen; by the end of the century some were thought of as geniuses. They were men like Leonardo da Vinci, Raphael and Michelangelo – the heroes of what is known as the High Renaissance at the end of the fifteenth century and the beginning of the sixteenth century.

5 ᴄ THE HIGH RENAISSANCE

Leonardo da Vinci (1452–1519) is still the model of 'a genius'. Although he often failed to finish what he started, he always did enough to show his unique insight, whether it was in military engineering or the anatomy of the human body, in his theoretical grasp of the principle of the helicopter or in his painting. The people he portrayed in art were created with techniques such as the clever use of light and shade and newly introduced oil painting, but Leonardo's people are more than that – even when armed only with a piece of charcoal Leonardo could make his subjects seem full of complex meaning and beauty. He was so highly regarded in the end that Francis I saw it as a great boost to his own prestige when he tempted Leonardo to come and live near him at Amboise.

One of the few artists to rival Leonardo was Raphael (1483–1520). He spent most of his career in Rome where he decorated the papal apartment with frescoes (painting onto fresh plaster). His subjects included 'The School of Athens' showing Plato and other Greek philosophers, illustrating the Greek emphasis that the Renaissance had acquired. Raphael painted many versions of the Madonna and Child – his Mary and Jesus was so ideal as to be almost too sweet but for the firmness of his composition. With Raphael, there was no sense of ordinary citizens featuring in his art, even though his portraits were unsentimental and full of vitality.

Michelangelo (1475–1564) was concerned even less with the ordinary citizen in his art. He was consumed by the ideal, expressing contempt for Flemish art, which, for all its brilliant technique, was far too concerned with realism. When Michelangelo sculpted he did not just copy from nature; he felt that there was a figure already in the block of marble struggling to free itself. Like the neo-Platonists, he saw his role as seeking a reality beyond what was ordinarily visible. On the ceiling of the Sistine Chapel in the Vatican, he depicted the Creation of Man itself, the most familiar image since then of divine and artistic inspiration. Around the Bible stories shown on the chapel's ceiling, Michelangelo painted characters from mythology and a series of heroic male nudes which were thought to be unsurpassable as portrayals of the human body. Being unsurpassable was the problem – for all the glory that Michelangelo had brought to art he made it difficult for lesser artists to find new things to express within the Renaissance tradition. He and the other great artists of the High Renaissance had, as it were, said it all. Apart from the Venetians, who were developing their own tradition, the artists of the Italian Renaissance gradually turned to mannerism – imitation or exaggeration of the *maniera* or style developed in the High Renaissance, particularly by Michelangelo.

6 ↫ HISTORY AND POLITICAL THOUGHT

The neo-Platonists dominated later Renaissance thought, but not exclusively so. The development of humanist ideas in a rather different direction can be seen in the writing of history. The later Renaissance historians, such as Francesco Guicciardini (1483–1540), continued, like Bruni before them, to imitate classical historians such as Livy and to study harsh political realities. Although they often had a political or moral motive for writing history, historians like Guicciardini used their sources with some discrimination and excluded what was most obviously myth from their analysis. Rather than speculating a great deal about the intervention of God or the Fates, they wrote about down-to-earth causes and human motivations. Although not as scientific in their methods of research, they resembled modern historians more than they did their medieval predecessors, the usually superstitious and uncritical monastic chroniclers. They were aware that institutions and customs varied and changed, whereas the chroniclers tended to view everything as resembling their own time and place. Rather than fleeing everyday reality like their contemporaries the neo-Platonists, Renaissance historians tried to meet it head on – ever more unpleasant though this became with the onset of the Italian Wars after 1494.

When he came to write his *History of Italy* in the 1530s Guicciardini, for all that his account was minutely detailed, was not engaged in scholarship for its own sake. He was trying to explain why Italy, once great, had collapsed in the face of foreign invasion and internal disorder after 1494. A friend of his was to employ history in a more radical way as part of an early type of political science, designed to show how the disorder might be reversed. He was a Florentine named Machiavelli.

PROFILE

NICCOLÒ MACHIAVELLI (1469–1527)

Born in 1469 into a family of declining wealth and status, Machiavelli knew that he would be successful only through his own talent, rather than privilege. From 1498 he joined the republican government of Florence, renewed after the Medici had fled in 1494. He was for a time in charge of Florence's citizen militia, and he was a close observer of politics in various courts, being sent on numerous diplomatic missions to Louis XII of France, Emperor Maximilian, Cesare Borgia (the ambitious son of Pope Alexander VI) and Pope Julius II. However, in 1512 the Medici returned, with Spanish help, as Dukes of Florence. The Republic was no more and Machiavelli was forced into retirement at his country farm. He was bored by the rural routine and was only happy when he could shut himself away in his study, put on robes of state and, through his books, converse with the classical authors about history and politics. For him, it was through his humanist imagination that the doors of power could once again be opened. This is in contrast to the humanists of a century before, such as Bruni. Their classical learning had opened the doors of power to them in reality, not just in imagination. Machiavelli did not, however, intend to remain only in the realm of imagination. He was quite prepared to work for the Medici, and so in 1513, almost as a job application, he wrote a manual on how to be a successful ruler, calling it simply *The Prince*. The Medici ignored it and it was not published until 1532, although it then came to be regarded as the most scandalous product of the Renaissance. Machiavelli's other works included *Discourses on Livy* (1515–17), *The Art of War* (1519–20), *The History of Florence* (1520–25), and two mildly obscene comedies *Mandragola* (1518) and *Clizio* (1524–25). He died of a stomach complaint in 1527.

Before Machiavelli most writing on politics had told a prince how to be good. In *The Prince* Machiavelli told him how to be effective, how to demonstrate his **virtù** rather than what we would call virtue.

> **virtù** fulfilling your individual potential, sometimes translated as prowess

1	... since my intention is to say something that will prove of practical use to the inquirer, I have thought it proper to represent things as they are in real truth, rather than as they are imagined. Many have dreamed up republics and principalities which have never in truth been known to exist; the gulf between how one should live and how one does live is so wide that a man who neglects what is actually done for what should be done learns the way to self-destruction rather than self-preservation. The fact is that a man who wants to act virtuously in every way necessarily comes to grief
10	among so many who are not virtuous ... ... there are two ways of fighting: by law or by force. The first is natural to men, and the second to beasts. But as the first way often proves inadequate one must needs have recourse to the second ... ... as a prince is forced to know how to act like a beast, he should learn from the fox and the lion; because the lion is defenceless against traps and a fox is defenceless against wolves. Therefore one
17	must be a fox to recognise traps, and a lion to frighten off wolves ...

The most prominent example in *The Prince* is Cesare Borgia, the son of Pope Alexander VI. He conquered an anarchic and violent region known as the Romagna and appointed one Remirro de Orco to restore peace and stability. Machiavelli describes how Cesare reviewed the situation once that was done:

1. *How does Machiavelli justify his approach (lines 1–10)?*
2. *For Machiavelli, virtù involved acting like a lion or a fox as necessary (lines 11–17). What political characteristics did these animals symbolise?*
3. *How does Cesare's disposal of Remirro (lines 18–24) illustrate those political characteristics? What might have happened if such brutal action had not been taken?*
4. *Compare Machiavelli's view of mankind as expressed above with that of Pico della Mirandola, as quoted on page 124.*

> Knowing also that the severities of the past had earned him a 18
> certain amount of hatred, to purge the minds of the people and to
> win them over completely he determined to show that if cruelties
> had been inflicted they were not his doing but prompted by the
> harsh nature of his minister. This gave Cesare a pretext; then, one
> morning, Remirro's body was found cut in two pieces on the piazza
> at Cesena, with a block of wood and a bloody knife beside it. The
> brutality of this spectacle kept the people of the Romagna for a
> time appeased and stupefied.   24

Machiavelli cannot be judged by *The Prince* alone. He developed a much more complete philosophy in a substantial work known as *The Discourses* inspired by the writing of the Roman historian, Livy. He made clear his cyclical theory of history – all states move from rule by a prince through rule by an aristocracy to rule by the people. The last stage necessarily degenerates into anarchy until a leader emerges, ruthless and effective enough to make himself prince, and the cycle begins again. Given this theory, a prince acting like Cesare Borgia was an antidote to anarchy, perhaps an evil but a necessary evil.

From one point of view, Machiavelli was the first political scientist. He developed his theory quite systematically, backing it up with evidence drawn from history and from contemporary affairs, and trying hard to exclude any prejudices. This does not mean that his conclusions would all be accepted today, but a refined version of his method has a following.

From another point of view Machiavelli signalled the end of the Renaissance in Italy. The tremendous Renaissance optimism, culminating in neo-Platonism, was turning to the pessimism about mankind contained in *The Prince*. Machiavelli's little manual was to win him nothing but condemnation. However realistic he might have tried to be, in the end he was powerless. That was to be the fate of other Renaissance men as their social and political context changed out of all recognition.

KEY ISSUE

Why was Machiavelli so controversial?

7 ⇦ THE CHANGING SOCIAL AND POLITICAL CONTEXT OF THE RENAISSANCE

From its beginning, the Renaissance had been associated with the ruling élite in Italy rather than with the people as a whole. However, that élite had been broadly based. In Florence, the Medici became the major patrons but there were other bankers besides them, and merchants made rich by the *arte della lana* – the Florentine cloth industry – and powerful guilds, all of whom could support scholars and artists. However, as society became ever more stable and economic opportunities diminished there was less social mobility and the Renaissance élite grew more exclusive. Even more exclusive were the smaller courts to which the Renaissance spread and where so much depended on the whims of individual rulers. Nevertheless, while the ruling élites retained their tradition of patronage and while the individual princes were discriminating and in control of their own destinies, the Renaissance continued to develop. But the Italian social and political environment was not secure against foreign invasion.

In 1494, the French invaded Italy and from then until 1559 the peninsula was the battleground of the great powers of Europe. In Florence the effects were devastating. The then head of the Medici family, Piero, was forced to flee in 1494, having bungled the diplomacy with regard to the invasion. In his place a Dominican monk named Savonarola came to dominate the Florentines through his powerful preaching. He told them that the invaders were the scourge of God punishing them for their sins. Amongst their sins could be numbered those editions of pagan authors and those paintings that were not austerely religious enough. Savonarola organised bonfires of such vanities and converts to his exclusively religious cause included Pico della Mirandola and even the painter of that pagan nude in *The Birth of Venus*, Sandro Botticelli. It seemed as though the era of the Renaissance had ended and the era of repentance had begun. However, this was not yet so. Savonarola eventually lost his influence and was burnt at the stake in 1498. The republican government which succeeded him not only employed Machiavelli but also commissioned that great symbol of republican defiance, Michelangelo's statue of *David*, the giant slayer. The trouble was that the republic could not slay giants and, as we have seen, it succumbed to Spanish dominance and the restoration of the Medici, their power now openly ducal rather than disguised by republican forms. After one brief outburst of renewed republicanism in 1527–30, Florence settled down into a dull stability. The city became essentially provincial, and the Florentine Renaissance was over.

The Italian Wars brought internal disruption and domination by either the French or the Spanish to many other city-states besides Florence. For a while, the Italian princes had formed leagues and tried to play one power off against another, but their famed diplomacy proved to be no protection. Those princes had used culture to express their power; during the Italian Wars it gradually became a substitute. A Spanish-style rigidity set into court life which inhibited innovation. Princes, compensating for their diminishing power, wanted to control artists rather than to befriend them or sympathise with their aims. This can be seen in the way that the free atmosphere of the open *bottega* or artistic workshop of the fifteenth century turned into the rule-bound formality of the private academies, many of which were organised for the princes of the sixteenth century. There was less wealth to pay for culture as the wars took their toll on the Italian economy. The rhetoric which had joined the early humanists with the ruling élite degenerated

See Chapters 3, 8 and 9

See pages 61–6

into servile praise or vicious satire, both of which were well exemplified by one Aretino (1492–1556) who was avidly read or lividly banned all over Italy. As the princes' foreign policies became futile, the civil services, which had fostered the talents of the early humanists, became far more concerned with just keeping the people under control, and in the end that needed guns not rhetoric.

At first Rome, with the wealth and prestige brought to it by the Papacy, seemed immune from this. It had maintained that immense confidence in which the Renaissance flourished. While wars raged across Italy, the artists of the High Renaissance, such as Raphael, worked in Rome and humanists could still find employment for their talents. However, this atmosphere was not to last. Confidence became diplomatic over-confidence and Rome was sacked in 1527 by a mutinous imperial army. In an action symbolic of the way in which the world was changing, a soldier scrawled LUTHER across a Raphael fresco in the Vatican. The atmosphere after the sack was one of pessimism. There had been an astonishing array of talented artists and scholars in Rome between 1500 and 1527, who were now largely dispersed. Michelangelo did not abandon Rome, but around 1536 he painted his sobering vision of the *Last Judgement* in the Sistine Chapel, contrasting sharply with the hope in his image of the *Creation* painted before the Sack of Rome. Political circumstances cannot entirely determine what may have been a fundamental change in artistic values, but they can confirm a trend.

Only in Venice did the Renaissance outlast the middle of the sixteenth century. That republic was ruled by a closed group of aristocratic families, but scholars and artists tended to work in harmony with them, rather than being controlled by them as was the trend elsewhere in Italy by that time. There was also that necessary degree of openness to outside influences and freedom to allow for innovation. The maritime republic escaped foreign domination. Also the Counter-Reformation was limited in its impact there – this is best illustrated by the case of Veronese who was prosecuted for painting the *Last Supper* as an entertaining, lavish dinner party: he merely changed the title to *the Feast in the House of Levi* and all was well.

It was not just the more creative environment in Venice that helped to prolong the Renaissance there. The city's artists also had a distinct contribution to make owing to their tradition of *colore*, expressing much more through colour than through the drawing or *disegno* which characterised earlier Renaissance art. The leading artist in Venice, and indeed the European art world of his day, was Titian (1489–1576). He painted masterpieces right up to his death at the age of eighty-seven. But by then even the Venetian Renaissance was on the wane.

The Serene Republic, as it was known, had entered into its period of relative decline by the end of the sixteenth century. The economy was being hit by foreign competition and the Venetian aristocrats were turning their attention away from the city and towards the villas they were building as rural retreats, 332 of them being constructed in the seventeenth century. Machiavelli had hated his rural retreat, craving the excitement of power. In contrast, the Venetian élite seemed to be happiest away from the strains of the city. The Renaissance, which had thrived amidst urban life and its politics, was no longer an Italian phenomenon.

The Renaissance did not just expire, though, as it came to an end in Venice. Ways of transmitting it had been developed as it spread through Italy and it was carried across the Alps, albeit in a modified form, beyond the social and political environment in which it had originated.

KEY ISSUE

Why and when did the Italian environment cease to be favourable to the Renaissance?

8 ➣ THE TRANSMISSION OF THE RENAISSANCE

The Renaissance was transmitted through education. This made it durable despite the changes in its social and political context. The earliest humanist educators included Vittorino da Feltre who founded a school in Mantua in 1423 and Guarino da Verona who founded his school at Ferrara in 1436. These schoolmasters provided the model of Renaissance education. The curriculum was based on the study of classical texts, mainly in Latin, although Greek was introduced as well. To some this might not sound exciting, but the subject matter – the speeches, history and poetry – was well adapted to the needs of a wide range of pupils, medieval education having been directed mostly towards would-be churchmen. The Roman ideal of 'a healthy mind in a healthy body' was adopted, games being an important part of the curriculum. In Vittorino's school, girls as well as boys were admitted, and poor students who showed promise studied in the school on an equal basis with the children of the rich, even with the Gonzaga family which ruled the city. However, it was more normal as the Renaissance developed for the majority of pupils to be boys and to be drawn from the wealthier section of society. Privilege did not mean that the boys were always pampered. Some teachers taught through encouragement but many were to regard regular corporal punishment as a more effective teaching aid than gentle words. Still, most of the pupils who left such schools carried with them a respect for humanist learning, however painfully acquired, which kept the Renaissance alive.

Humanist schools originated in Italy but they were not confined to the peninsula. The Renaissance educational ideal spread all over Europe. In England, for instance, it was embodied in the grammar schools, which were set up in the sixteenth century. In their efforts to attract the élites of Europe to send their children to Catholic schools, and so hold the pass against Protestantism, the Jesuits employed the classical curriculum of the Renaissance. (And, even though the study of classics has declined, the humanist ideal of a balanced curriculum survives in modern schools.) All over Europe in the Early Modern period the ruling classes, from those who ran the shires in England to the nobility of Poland or the burghers of Swiss cities, came to experience the Renaissance through their education; it was their common culture.

Critical to the success of these Renaissance schools was the fact that they had an increasing number of books available. This was due to printing. It can be argued that printing, developing from the second half of the fifteenth century, was vital for the Renaissance both to last and to spread. The movement had begun in part as a reaction against the errors of medieval scribes. Before printing, there had been the danger that once the generation of energetic early humanists had passed there would have been a lapse back into the old ways of copying errors, and without printing, the libraries, those storehouses of Renaissance knowledge, would not have become so widespread or have been built up so quickly. In the *scriptorium* where scribes toiled, the Renaissance could have been worn away. It could flourish in the printer's workshop in any part of Europe. Scholars often gathered in such workshops 'in an almost incredible mixture of the sweatshop, the boarding house and the research institute' with a view to the market for books (writing was a much more commercial enterprise than painting) and the circulation of their ideas. Peter Burke, however, warns against assuming that printing simply transmitted a neatly packaged Renaissance to the rest of Europe – it was not just what a book said but how it was interpreted, as with Erasmus's Greek New Testament.

The spread of the Renaissance was not just a technical matter of educational systems and movable type: it represented an ideal. In its early form of civic humanism, it had been confined to the urban élites of Italy. The feudal aristocracy north of the Alps had very different interests and clung to their own Gothic culture rather than importing the ideas of the Renaissance from Italy. However, the Renaissance ideal in Italy was not static. In succession to the civic humanist came 'the Renaissance man', a character much more likely to be international in his appeal.

The Renaissance man is the archetypal all-rounder. He is learned and courteous, poetic and well-dressed, but he can also run, jump, swim, ride and fight, all to perfection. The model of this universal man, if he can ever have existed, was Leon Battista Alberti. Modesty was not one of his qualities, as he showed in the 1460s when he wrote about the extraordinary variety of qualities he possessed as a great architect and a leading theorist of painting, among his other attributes. The ideal of versatility appealed to competitive men of many European élites. The ideal was embodied in what amounted to a textbook for the aspiring Renaissance man, *The Book of the Courtier* by Baldassare Castiglione.

Castiglione was a diplomat and government adviser who worked for various princes and finally for the Pope. He was admired by many of those with whom he came into contact, including the Emperor Charles V. He was an international figure and so when *The Courtier* was published in 1528 it was greeted with much interest. It was based on Castiglione's experiences at the court of Urbino, a tiny principality in central Italy, sustained mainly by what its Duke could earn as a leading mercenary. Those earnings were good and paid for the construction of

See pages 18–19

See page 137

one of the finest palaces in Europe in which a refined court of noblemen and intellectuals was assembled. Castiglione claimed to be describing how those courtiers related to one another, what they did and what they talked about in their debates:

1	Noble birth is like a bright lamp that makes clear and visible both good deeds and bad, and inspires and incites to high performance as much as fear of dishonour or hope of praise; and since their deeds do not possess such noble brilliance, ordinary people lack
5	both this stimulus and the fear of dishonour...
6	I have very seldom known men who are good at anything who do not praise themselves. It seems to me that it is only right to allow them to do so, since when a man who knows he is of some worth sees himself being ignored, he grows angry at the way his qualities
10	are hidden from sight...
11	There are also many other sports, although they do not directly require the use of weapons, are closely related to arms and demand a great deal of manly exertion. Among these it seems to me that hunting is the most important, since in many ways it resembles warfare; moreover, it is the true pastime of great lords,
16	it is a suitable pursuit for a courtier...

Q

1. *These extracts of dialogue identify three of the distinguishing features of a courtier. What reasons are given for including noble birth (lines 1–5), self-praise (lines 6–10) and an appreciation of hunting (lines 1–16)?*
2. *How might such dialogue make the courtier acceptable in aristocratic circles anywhere in Europe?*

The Courtier did not say anything startlingly new; it summarised the attitudes of the early sixteenth-century Renaissance with regard to the arts, learning and neo-Platonic philosophy. Although it was set in the real court of Urbino, the atmosphere was more of a fantasy world of wit and wisdom, which was not rooted in any one place. *The Courtier* was a package of ideas easily exported to the rest of Europe, especially given its endorsement of aristocratic principles. It was part of the change of focus of the Renaissance from the city and urban politics to the country villa and the social life of the nobility. By the end of the century it had been translated into all the major European languages and had inspired a number of imitators such as one in English called *The Governor* by Sir Thomas Elyot. The Renaissance man was very much the fashion.

In many respects, however, northern Europe retained its own traditions. The Flemish school of painting, for instance, had developed independently of the Italian Renaissance and was to continue as an influence throughout the Early Modern period. Indeed cultural influences in the Renaissance did not just move one way: the Italian painters of the High Renaissance had been taught how to use oils by Flemish artists and Italian musicians emulated Flemish composers and performers. In architecture, decoration was often classical in the Italian fashion in the sixteenth century and some Italianate features such as a study became common, but on the whole the plans of buildings, their basic structure, remained true to native styles. Again, as with printing, Burke stresses these adaptations involved in the reception of Renaissance culture; it was not simply a copy of the Italian Renaissance transmitted across the Alps.

Northern humanists had their own purposes, for instance in celebrating national identity in contrast with most Italian humanists' concern with civic identity. The German Conrad Celtis planned a *Germania illustrata* and claimed in 1487 that 'not only the Roman empire and arms, but also the splendour of letters has migrated to the Germans'. However, the most distinctive feature of the northern Renaissance in the realm of learning was Christian humanism, the use of humanist techniques to edit and interpret the Bible and other religious texts. One man more than any other merged northern piety with Italian learning to create Christian humanism – Erasmus of Rotterdam. He deserves special attention as he came to represent the northern Renaissance as a whole, his achievements showing how the Renaissance could be transmitted and how it was transformed as it passed north of the Alps.

9 ↜ ERASMUS AND CHRISTIAN HUMANISM

PROFILE

ERASMUS (c.1466–1536)

Erasmus was the greatest of the Christian humanists. He was born in Rotterdam, the illegitimate son of a priest, and was educated at a school in the Dutch town of Deventer where most of the teachers belonged to the Brethren of the Common Life, a group of laymen who did not take monastic vows but who cultivated monastic ideals of prayer and poverty. Although Erasmus later criticised his teachers he had permanently absorbed their devotion to a simple piety. At first, Erasmus seemed destined to be a monk and, under pressure from his guardian, entered the monastery of Steyn. However, he found life there intolerable, hating the rigid formality and the excess of ceremonies, which he felt obstructed religious devotion rather than inspired it. Above all, he needed freedom and he leapt at the opportunity to leave the monastery in 1494 to act as a bishop's secretary. From then on, as he grew more famous, if not wealthier, through his writings, Erasmus was to wander Europe, never settling down for long, refusing offers of professorships or rich bishoprics rather than risk being tied down. He journeyed between the Netherlands, France, Italy, Germany, Switzerland and England, and his capacity for friendship with princes and scholars and endless, elegant letter writing maintained a cultural network which covered half of Europe. He was the most truly international scholar of his day. In writings renowned for their style and wit, he worked to advance classical learning and to reform the Church. However, his hopes of gradual and peaceful reform were shattered by the violent divisions in the Church brought on by the Reformation. At first he tried to keep his distance, but only won the distrust of both Catholics and Protestants. He came out against Luther in 1524 but remained isolated from hardline Catholics. His last years were spent in Basle and Freiburg, as he sought to preserve his freedom, which seemed increasingly threatened, and fed ever more works to the printing presses which had spread his fame wherever Latin was read. Huizinga described him as 'the international pivot on which the civilisation of his age hinged'. However, in many ways his age had already passed before he died in Basle in 1536.

Just as he travelled from country to country, so Erasmus rejected any fixed system of ideas and continually sought to extend the frontiers of his knowledge. From his youth he could not accept what he saw as the sterility of scholastic theology and once commented that the theology lectures he attended at Paris in the late 1490s were the time to catch up on his sleep. He saw the light of clear reason instead in the classical texts, which had been collected and edited by the humanists of Italy. He imitated the classical authors in his own writing although making Latin alive and energetic again rather than purely mimicking. As Mann Phillips put it, 'He felt more at home with antiquity than the world into which he was born.' However, the classics he valued were always those which illuminated Christian thinking. When he jokingly referred to 'St Socrates' he was not sanctifying the pagan ways of the Greek philosopher but commenting on how much Socrates' thought prefigured Christianity.

The fruit of Erasmus's extensive survey of classical literature was the *Adages*, published in 1500. The *Adages* were quotations culled from classical Roman authors to illustrate all that was best in Latin style and thought. If Erasmus had never published anything else, he would still have been famous for the *Adages* as, more than any other single work, it introduced educated northern Europeans to the classical learning of the Renaissance.

For Erasmus himself this was of secondary importance. However highly he valued reason and classical learning, they were just the means to an understanding of virtue, which in turn would reinforce faith. This was Christian Humanism. Erasmus never gave up reading and editing classical texts but his primary concern was clear from 1504 when he published the *Enchiridion Militis Christiani*, the *Handbook of a Christian Soldier*. He was arguing for a simplified Christian life, getting to know Christ as a person through reading the Gospel, interpreting charity as love for one's neighbour rather than merely participation in the externals of religious ritual. This personal, ethical approach to religion was termed the 'Philosophy of Christ' but, while 'philosophy' sounds intellectual and exclusive, Erasmus expressed the hope that education would lead to the participation of everyone through knowing the Gospels, such that 'Out of these the farmer should sing while ploughing and the weaver at his loom'. Erasmus had absorbed some of Pico della Mirandola's ideas about man's divinely granted capacity for self-improvement, but he saw himself as working for the potential of all mankind, rather than just for a humanist élite.

For all his emphasis on personal religion in the *Enchiridion*, Erasmus did not attack Catholic doctrine or the main religious services such as the Mass – he respected tradition and saw the need to treat it with a sense of proportion and to purge it of abuse rather than to abandon it. But the alternative to 'handbook' as a translation of *Enchiridion* is 'dagger' and this was an intentional ambiguity. Erasmus was not just setting out the personal approach to religion but also fighting against the ignorance and profiteering that he saw as being so prevalent in the Church and so burdensome to the faithful. A demand for reform was a consistent theme in his career, although rather than using protest as a weapon he generally chose wit and satire. His most popular satire was his *Encomium Moriae*, the *Praise of Folly*, which he wrote in 1509 as a joke for his friend, Sir Thomas More, with whom he was staying at the time.

The middle section of the book consists of Folly personified as a preacher describing the foibles and feebleness of different types of people. Folly encourages sympathy for some such as teachers; 'surely a tribe whose lot would seem most disastrous, the most wretched, the most godforsaken, if I did not soften the horrors of that miserable profession with a sweet touch of madness'. With regard to others the satire was more biting:

> ...In the first place, [monks] believe it's the highest form of piety to be so uneducated that they can't even read. Then when they bray like donkeys in church, repeating by rote the psalms they haven't understood, they imagine they are charming the ears of their heavenly audience with infinite delight...But nothing could be more amusing than their practice of doing everything to rule, as if they were following mathematical calculations which it would be a sin to ignore. They work out the number of knots for a shoe-string, the colour and number of variations of a single habit, the material and width to a hair's breadth of a girdle...Yet another monk will produce such a pile of church ceremonies that seven ships could scarcely carry them...

The *Praise of Folly* was not remarkable only because of the impact of its satire. Folly was personified to show not only how people might degenerate for want of reason, but also how they need more than reason to be fully human. Humour, joy, love, all irrational emotions which make life worth living are aspects of Folly. The final section of the book deals with that most sublime foolishness, the necessary transcendence of reason that is faith. Erasmus's humour and satirical outrage, like his classical learning, were brought into the service of the Philosophy of Christ.

KEY ISSUE

In what ways did Erasmus's Christian humanism differ from the Italian humanism of the preceding hundred years?

Q

1. *What does Erasmus's satire imply is wrong with this type of religious life?*
2. *Why might such satire have been so popular amongst Erasmus's readers?*

When Erasmus wrote his *Praise of Folly* in a few days, he was just taking time off from his major labour, which was his work on the Bible and other religious texts. In 1499 on one of his visits to England, he had noted the work of the humanist John Colet on the writings of St Paul. Colet had himself suggested similar work to Erasmus but the great Latin scholar declined on account of his ignorance – he knew no Greek, which was necessary to read scripture in the original. The seed was sown in Erasmus's mind, however, and he set himself the task of learning Greek even though, as he complained in one of his letters, it nearly killed him. By 1504 he had read the *Annotations* on the New Testament by the great Italian scholar of half a century earlier, Lorenzo Valla, and he decided that he would complete the great task which Valla had begun. He published a series of commentaries on books of the New Testament, which emphasised the simple lessons to be learned as against the complex interpretations argued over by the scholastic commentators of the Middle Ages. But his most important task was to purify the text of the New Testament itself.

In 1516 Erasmus published his version of the New Testament in its original Greek. This Greek New Testament was no perfect work of scholarship, having been rushed in the end, but it had a revolutionary impact equalled by little else published in the Early Modern period. For centuries the Church had based its doctrines on the authority of the official version of the Bible, the Latin Vulgate. Over those centuries of scribal copying, many errors had crept into the Vulgate until, in 1516, Erasmus proposed to correct them through employing humanist techniques on the Greek original. He saw it in terms of the sweet light of reason. His preface to the Greek New Testament anticipated 'the easy triumph of pure knowledge and Christian meekness' (Huizinga). Instead, the Protestant reformers were to use the Greek New Testament in their attack on the doctrinal authority of the Church of Rome and so usher in centuries of religious strife.

Through works such as the *Praise of Folly*, Erasmus had become the leading critic of the abuses of the Church, of idle monks and false relics, of all the paraphernalia involved in the exploitation of the faithful. He had no automatic respect even for the Pope – in 1513 he had written *Julius Exclusus* in which he pictured the warlike Julius II being turned away from the gates of Paradise by St Peter. He had done his best to use humanist scholarship to strip away the errors of centuries in the name of Christian truth, but although he had inadvertently prepared the way for the Protestants, he had assumed that reasoned argument and lively wit would lead to gradual, peaceful reform and the last thing he wanted was to threaten the unity of the Church.

Erasmus's position was one of moderation but once the storm of the Reformation had broken after Luther's protest in 1517, there was little understanding of that. He believed in civility, containing argument within courtesy, and he was reluctant to consider divisive religious questions beyond the capacity of man to answer. Such beliefs gained him no respect amongst the religious combatants. In the 1520s and 1530s, the Protestants vented their fury on him for his refusal to side

See page 161

with them, whilst many Catholics blamed his satires and scholarship for helping to set off the Reformation in the first place. Even when Erasmus did openly oppose Luther in 1524 over the issue of free will, he was still attacked by Catholics for being too timid. In the early years of the century, the best days of Christian humanism, Erasmus had regularly prophesied the dawning of a 'golden age'. There were no more such prophecies once the Reformation crisis had taken hold.

Although some historians, especially Huizinga, have criticised Erasmus for his indecisiveness when faced with Protestant rebellion and Catholic reaction, he was determined to stick to his own moderate course, however the religious zealots reacted. Starting in 1519, he published regular editions of his *Colloquies*, dialogues in which he continued to contrast the ridiculous with the worthy sides to human behaviour in all their social as well as religious forms. The *Colloquies* expressed Erasmus's belief in the value of liberty and its responsible use. His message and his style may have affected little the controversies of his own age, but they have had an enduring effect on authors throughout succeeding generations.

By the time of his death in 1536 Erasmus's message had less and less contemporary impact in an increasingly dangerous world. In England his old friends the Christian humanists, Thomas More and John Fisher, had been executed for their loyalty to the Church of Rome, whilst his fellow Christian humanist and sparring partner in France, Lefèvre d'Etaples, had been forced to flee on suspicions of heresy. By the time of Erasmus's death the Christian humanists were no longer the dominant intellectual force they had once been. In aspects of education and style the humanist influence survived; but the age of the Renaissance had given way to the age of the Reformation.

KEY ISSUE

What made Erasmus so successful in the first two decades of the sixteenth century, and why did his reputation suffer from the 1520s onwards?

10 ↰ BIBLIOGRAPHY

**R. Hole, *Access to History Themes: Renaissance Italy* (Hodder and Stoughton, 1998) or *Alison Brown, *The Renaissance* (Longman, 1988) are good introductions. **L. Martinez, *Power and Imagination* (Knopf, 1979) discusses politics and culture. Lisa Jardine, *Worldly Goods – A New History of the Renaissance* (Macmillan, 1996) characterises the Renaissance as the product of a consumer society; in contrast John Stephens's *The Italian Renaissance* (Longman, 1990) stresses the moral values it embodied. *The Renaissance in National Context*, ed. Roy Porter and Mikulá Teich (CUP, 1991) shows the spread and diversity of the Renaissance in Europe. **James McConica, *Erasmus* (Past Masters, 1991) is a short and stimulating essay. *J. Huizinga, *Erasmus* (New York, 1924; Princeton paperback, 1984) and of course **J. Burckhardt, *The Civilization of the Renaissance in Italy* (Basle, 1869; English translation, Phaidon, 1944) are two great historical classics.

11 ↶ STRUCTURED AND ESSAY QUESTIONS

A *Structured questions.*
1. (a) What was new about art and scholarship in Florence in the early 1400s?
   (b) Why did the Renaissance develop first in Italy?
2. (a) How did the Renaissance spread north of the Alps?
   (b) Why was Erasmus such an important figure in the Northern Renaissance?

B *Essay questions.*
1. What was Renaissance humanism?
2. What impact did politics have on the development of the Renaissance?
3. Assess the significance of two of the following: Marsilio Ficino, Castiglione, Machiavelli.
4. What did the Northern Renaissance owe to the Italian Renaissance?
5. 'Erasmus' greatness was as a scholar and a wit rather than as a reformer.' Discuss.

12 ↶ DOCUMENTARY EXERCISE ON ARTISTS, PATRONS AND PRESTIGE

Rather than simply being objects of great beauty, Renaissance paintings were intended to be 'read' and interpreted, and they can therefore be used as historical sources as much as can be written documents. A Renaissance artist was not some lonely genius pursuing his own isolated vision of perfection. He generally worked for a patron and, although there was room for artistic originality, he had to bear his patron's intentions clearly in mind as he created the work of art. The portraits illustrated represent social and political purposes which were motive forces in the Renaissance. To work out what some of those purposes were, study the portraits and their background and then answer the questions which follow.

See pages 121–2

Source A This belongs to the early Flemish Renaissance. It was painted by van Eyck in Bruges in 1434 – the inscription on the back wall translates as 'Jan van Eyck was here, 1434'. He was one of the pioneers of oil painting which allows an artist to portray objects and people with greater detail and heightened realism, a technique which the Flemish were to teach to the Italians later in the fifteenth century. The couple shown here are Giovanni Arnolfini and his wife Giovanna Cenami, and clues in the picture indicate that the occasion was their marriage or at least their betrothal. The single candle in the chandelier symbolises marriage and the dog represents faithfulness. The arrangements of the hands suggest that an oath was being taken. It may be the earliest known equivalent of the wedding photograph. Modern viewers

often conclude that Giovanna was already pregnant, although other paintings of the time, with women holding bunches of material in a similar manner, suggest that it may have been more the fashion of the time and place to appear that way.

Source B Painted between 1459 and 1463, this fresco shows the journey to worship the newborn Jesus by the Magi, the Wise Men, sometimes known as the Three Kings. The most important Florentine confraternity – a club with religious and social functions – was dedicated to the Magi. The significant figures in the fresco, however, are portraits of those who had been involved with the last attempt to unite the Roman Catholic and Greek Orthodox Churches at the Council of Florence in 1439. It had been a failure, but had placed Florence under the European spotlight, along with the Medici, the banking family who ruled Florence at the time. They were technically of no higher rank than any other citizens but used their money and connections to pull strings and govern the city. The older man at the front of the detail shown is Cosimo de Medici, the head of the family, and to his left is his son Piero, known as 'the Gouty', who

commissioned the fresco. The child next to Cosimo, his horse facing the viewer, is Lorenzo, who was to take over the family business and the city following his grandfather's death in 1464 and his father's in 1469. (He was included in this commemoration of the Council of Florence, even though he had not been born at the time.) His political and cultural prestige was to win him the title of Lorenzo the Magnificent. Two rows behind Lorenzo there is a figure with an inscription on his hat; it reads 'Opus Benotti', the work of Benozzo, who was the artist, so this is his self-portrait. The fresco adorns the walls of the chapel in one of the Medici palaces in Florence.

Source C Pope Sixtus IV (1471–84) had been a friar from a poor background who rose rapidly through the ranks of the Church to become Pope in 1471. He had hoped to organise a crusade against the Turks, but as the chances of that faded he sought to dominate Italy instead, engaging in conflicts with Florence (1478–80), Ferrara (1481) and Venice (1483). The Turks took advantage of the turmoil and established a base at Otranto in southern Italy for a year (1480–81). Meanwhile, Sixtus consolidated his political grip on the Church by what had become a traditional method, appointing his nephews as cardinals. The nephews are pictured here in 1480 standing alongside

(Picture 9) Pope Sixtus IV,
his nephews and Platina *by
Melozzo da Forli*

the Pope, while the kneeling figure is Bartolomeo Platina, the leading
humanist who helped Sixtus to re-establish the Vatican library, still one
of the great libraries of the world. The library was also the first to be
open to the public. Platina points to the inscription which praises the
Pope for this and for rebuilding so much of Rome. At nearly 4 m in
height, the fresco dominated the Vatican library. The artist Melozzo da
Forli was particularly well known for his command of perspective, the
technique perfected by Brunelleschi at the beginning of the century,
which gives the illusion of three dimensions on a two-dimensional
surface.

Source D Federico da Montefeltro was illegitimate but became
Count of Urbino, a small territory in eastern Italy, on the death of his
half brother in 1444; by 1474 he had elevated himself to the title of duke
by marrying his daughter off to a nephew of Pope Sixtus IV. He had not
gleaned his great wealth from his subjects – he was a mercenary, hiring
out his services for cash on a short-term contract, never as an ally, and
had fought both for and against most of the major powers of Italy. He
was also a great patron of the arts. His library of manuscripts was more
extensive than most universities and his palace at Urbino was one of the
greatest works of Renaissance architecture. He is shown here, painted
by the Flemish artist Juste de Gand, wearing orders of chivalry such as
the garter just below his knee and the ermine around his neck. Above
his lectern is a hat encrusted with pearls (possibly a gift from the Shah
of Persia who was urging him to undertake a crusade against the
Turks), his helmet is laid by his feet, and his son Guidobaldo, richly
bejewelled and holding a sceptre, stands at his knee. The sceptre has

SOURCE D
(Picture 10) Federigo da
Montefeltro with his son
Guidobaldo
by Juste de Gand

'Pontifex' written on it, referring to the grant of the ducal title by the Pope.

Source E The Emperor Charles V rated the Venetian artist Titian so highly that he knighted him in 1533 and on one occasion astonished his courtiers by bending down to pick up a brush which the artist had dropped. This showed how far artists had climbed the ladder of status; it would have been unthinkable before the Renaissance that a nobleman, let alone the Emperor himself, would have stooped for a painter, who would have been routinely classed along with other manual workers. But an artist of Titian's skill and renown could enhance the status of his sitters, or even the Emperor himself. At the battle of Mühlberg in 1547 Charles had, it seemed, destroyed the forces of Protestantism in Germany. In the 1548 Augsburg Interim he was trying to capitalise on this triumph and to impose a settlement which would restore both his imperial authority and Catholicism. He summoned Titian to Augsburg to help him project his newly restored image, and this painting was one of the results. It shows Charles in the armour he wore at the battle, astride a horse in the manner of equestrian statues of triumphant Roman emperors. It was the first equestrian painting of a monarch, and was felt to confer such authority

See page 239

SOURCE E

(Picture 11) Charles V at the
Battle of Mühlberg *by Titian*

that it became the fashion for portraits of princes during the following
century.

Q

1. *The scene of the Arnolfini Marriage (A) is quite a modest
bedchamber, but look at the clothes the pair are wearing, the fixtures
and fittings of the room such as the chandelier and the mirror, and
casual details such as oranges at the window, which must have been
imported from the Mediterranean, or the pattens (which look like
sandals and were worn to keep shoes free from the mud of the streets)
which have been left presumably where they were kicked off. What do
such details convey about the social position and attitudes of the
couple?*
2. *In the Journey of the Magi (B) the Medici family are prominent,
but shown dressed and equipped similarly to the other Florentine
riders in the procession. What political considerations may have
influenced the way in which the Medici were portrayed?*
3. *What does the protrait of Federigo da Montefeltro (C) tell us
about his values and the position he was trying to make for himself
amongst the rulers of Italy? Why might his young son have been
included in the portrait, and holding a sceptre?*
4. *Why was Platina included in a group portrait of Sixtus IV and his
nephews (D), and how do his place in the painting, his pose, and his
expression reflect on the Pope?*

Q

5. *Given that* Charles V at Mühlberg *(E) is a battle scene, what features that you might expect to see in such a painting are missing? What image might Charles have hoped this portrait of him would project a year after the battle, when a peace settlement was being decided?*

6. *'Paintings can reveal aspects of a period or a personality which no written documents can.' Discuss this comment with reference to the paintings A–E and any other Renaissance paintings you know.*

6

The German Reformation

In 1517 Martin Luther, an obscure monk and lecturer at the University of Wittenberg in northern Germany, published his ninety-five theses (debating points) attacking the sale of indulgences by the Church, which he thought was a public scandal. The printing press spread his ideas all over Germany and beyond. Germans, without an effective central government to protect their interests, felt particularly vulnerable to Church money-raising schemes and so rallied to Luther's cause with enthusiasm. This seemed like the latest instalment in an age-old quarrel between laymen and the Church, but in 1520 Luther made clear in a series of crucial pamphlets that he was not just objecting to corruption in the Church but was attacking many of its most fundamental teachings. He also denied the authority of the Pope in Rome and in effect called for the German princes to take over and reform the Church. This was the point at which reform became Reformation, a revolution against the Church of Rome. Loyal Catholics, led by Emperor Charles V, tried to suppress Luther and his protest, but Luther stuck to his beliefs and was protected by his prince, the Elector of Saxony.

Meanwhile Luther's supporters multiplied, some understanding his message, some reading into his protest what they wanted to see. Many German humanists became Lutheran preachers, celebrating a simpler, more scripturally-based religion, stripped of what they saw as useless rituals. Peasants broadened the Lutheran protest against the Church into social rebellion against lords (although these peasants were to be condemned for their uprising by Luther himself and crushed in the savage Peasants' War of 1524–25). The councils of the free, imperial cities were under pressure from vocal Lutheran citizens to bring in the Reformation, but were in any case happy enough to take control over the Church and its clergy where it was safe to do so. Finally, an increasing number of German princes were prepared to defy the authority of the Emperor as well as the Pope. However, none of these groups were completely united – many remained loyal to the Pope and Catholicism. The loyal Catholics were slow to organise effective opposition to Luther, but the Catholic princes did manage to hold the line against Lutheranism in much of southern Germany and the Rhineland. Before this happened Luther and his supporters, or Protestants as they were known from 1529, intended to transform the whole Church, but as their advance lost momentum they started to establish their own independent Protestant churches.

Throughout the rest of Europe other leaders of the Reformation emerged and Protestantism spread, challenging the old ways. Rulers everywhere, whether Protestant or Catholic, became concerned with ensuring the religious unity of their states – a process known as 'confessionalisation' from the confessions of faith (declarations of religious belief) which subjects had to accept. Where communities remained religiously divided, religious wars were often the result. The legacy of these has been seen nearly five centuries later in Northern Ireland. With Protestantism unable to triumph completely and Catholicism failing to recover all its lost territories, the Reformation brought an end to the unity of western Christendom.

1 ⌁ THE INDULGENCES CONTROVERSY

In resolving his personal crisis Luther had developed the central doctrine of what was to be called Protestantism. Its consequences for the Roman Catholic Church, of which Luther was still very much a member, were enormous. Justification is when you are free of sin and righteous enough in the eyes of God to enter heaven, and Luther's reading of St Paul was that justification depended on faith alone, or *sola fide* to give the formal Latin term. That faith was entirely in the gift of God; no human effort, no good works, would make any difference. Christ's once-and-for-all sacrifice on the Cross had been sufficient to redeem mankind. Sharing in that ultimate sacrifice through faith, irrespective of your actions in life, would win you salvation and a place in heaven: this is known as the theology of the Cross, and it made much of the apparatus of the Church redundant. The relics and pilgrimages and saints' festivals and multifarious services, all of which the Church promoted and on which it depended for much of its income, were threatened. The Church offered these as opportunities for the Christian to work his way to heaven, to secure salvation by works, not, it must be said, as an alternative to faith but as an addition to it. However, Luther's life as a monk had convinced him that working your way to heaven was impossible and, according to his doctrine, the attempt was irrelevant anyway. Justification 'by works' became meaningless when seen in contrast to justification 'by faith *alone*'.

A problem with which Luther had struggled was the Law – the Ten Commandments and so forth. As a monk he had never felt able to obey it completely, so assumed that he must be damned. Now he realised that the Law was merely there to show humans that it was useless to try and rely on themselves; like a torch in the dark it served to show up human inadequacies. Obedience being an impossible task, total reliance on faith channelled to the individual through the grace of God was the only alternative. This did not mean that humans were not bound by rules such as the Ten Commandments. Luther thought that a consequence of justification would be sanctification: people with faith

sola fide justification or salvation 'by faith alone'

THE YOUNG MARTIN LUTHER (1483–1546)

Luther was born in Saxony in north-eastern Germany. His father was a miner, eager to make himself a successful businessman and to make a professional man – a lawyer – out of his son. Martin certainly had every educational opportunity, despite the financial struggle involved, finally taking his Master's degree in law at the University of Erfurt in 1505. But he was not to be a lawyer; another event in 1505 was far more significant than Martin's law degree, at least according to his own later reminiscences. When on a journey, he was caught in a thunderstorm so dramatic that he feared for his life. He fell to his knees and vowed that if he survived he would dedicate his life to God by becoming a monk. Shortly afterwards he entered a branch of the Augustinian order.

Martin's life as a monk was one of constant struggle. He felt he could only satisfy the implacable God, whose terrifying power had taken physical form in that thunderstorm, by purging himself of sin. He tried everything the Church offered to achieve that – constant prayer, devotion to Church services and especially the Mass, penance in the form of self-denial practised to the extent that he damaged his health by not eating or sleeping enough. But it did no good; his sense of sin was overwhelming. The constant emotional strain made him a most unusual monk: he came to a point where he even felt hatred for God. In 1508, he joined the Faculty of Theology at the recently founded University of Wittenberg. In the ten years after he became a university teacher at Wittenberg, Luther found his ideas growing clearer as he expounded them to his pupils. When studying St Paul's Epistle to the Romans he lighted on the sentence 'He who through faith is righteous shall live'. Suddenly he realised that all his attempts to purge his sins and be righteous were useless because righteousness can come only through faith and faith comes freely given by God.

Luther no longer hated God. He wrote later of his experience, 'I felt that I was altogether born again and had entered paradise itself through open gates.' Luther's flash of insight while shut away in his study came to be known as the 'tower experience'. Historians now debate when it occurred, being able to agree only that it was between 1513 and 1519. Some also doubt that it was as dramatically sudden as Luther later made out, but the implications of Luther's insight turned out to be dramatic enough to shatter the religious unity of western Europe.

would naturally grow holier, although owing any goodness they achieved solely to God and taking no credit for themselves. Those without faith needed to have the Law applied to them to keep them under control.

The implications of all this were not immediately apparent. Luther himself saw it as a matter for further study and scholarly debate. For the Protestant Reformation to begin, there had to be an incident to bring Luther and his ideas to the attention of the Church authorities and the people at large beyond the cloisters of Wittenberg University. That incident was to be the Indulgences Controversy.

In 1517 there appeared on the borders of Saxony a Dominican preacher named Johann Tetzel who displayed more of the character of a salesman than a friar. He was selling indulgences, which were, in effect, much sought-after passports to heaven. According to the doctrine of the Church, these indulgences worked as a result of the Pope drawing on the 'treasury of merits', the accumulated good works of saints through the ages, which could make up for the ordinary person's lack of righteousness. Such an indulgence was attractive because it could save you many agonising years in purgatory where your impurity would normally have to be burnt out of you before you were fit to enter heaven. Developments of the doctrine of indulgences as recently as 1476 had meant that they could be bought on behalf of someone already dead, who would then gain instant access to heaven as well. In between his vivid impressions of the groaning of his listeners' parents in purgatory, Tetzel would chant, 'As soon as the gold in the basin rings, right then the soul to Heaven springs.' Although it was not publicly known at the time, the money raised was to be spent on the rebuilding of St Peter's in Rome and to pay off the debts the Archbishop of Mainz had taken on when buying his archbishopric.

The ruler in Wittenberg, the Elector of Saxony, had banned Tetzel from his lands, not because of any religious qualms, but because he wanted no competition for the funds he could raise through his own relics collection. But the people were prepared to travel to buy indulgences and Luther, for one, watched them go with dismay. He was by no means the first to suggest that this sale of indulgences was an abuse, but his assault on them was to develop into an attack on the fundamental doctrines of the Church at that time.

On 31 October 1517 in Wittenberg, Luther published his *Ninety-Five Theses* (debating points) on the subject of indulgences, perhaps doing so in the traditional manner by nailing them to the church door. Some of the theses engaged people's support in a fairly simple emotional way. For instance, Luther wondered why the Pope, if he had the power to release souls from purgatory, did not do so out of charity rather than charging for it. This made Tetzel's offer seem less of a bargain and more like just another stratagem by which the Church squeezed money out of its overburdened members. But the more important underlying point, later made clearer by Luther, was that the Church was not just abusing its right to issue indulgences – it probably did not have that right in the first place, even if its purposes were moral and the indulgences were

KEY ISSUE

What was at the heart of Luther's rejection of medieval Catholicism?

free. For Luther, no action or works by a mortal, whether the Pope or the recipient of an indulgence, could affect God's decision on whom to admit to Heaven, as only faith freely given by God actually counted.

The impact of the *Ninety-Five Theses* was immediate. Through the recently established printing presses they became known throughout Germany and beyond. They caught the popular imagination, being discussed in taverns and market places as well as universities and cloisters. To many Germans it was as though Luther, that hitherto obscure professor, was a David challenging the Goliath of the corrupt Roman Catholic Church, intent on exploiting Germany. Clearly the Church had to stop Luther before that valuable source of income – indulgences – was lost forever amidst the popular furore. As Luther clarified his ideas during 1518 and 1519, it became clear that what he was saying posed a threat to the structure of the Church as a whole.

The problem for the Church was that Luther acquired influential protectors from the start. In the spring of 1518 he won over the support of some of his own superiors in the Augustinian order. More importantly, the Elector Frederick of Saxony was proud of the university he had established at Wittenberg and he was not going to allow any foreign Church authorities to suppress one of his professors. Also, he was under the influence of a close adviser, Georg Spalatin, who had much sympathy for Luther.

The Church authorities, being unable to move against Luther directly, decided to try a mixture of persuasion and threats. Luther was summoned to Augsburg in October 1518 to meet with the papal legate (ambassador) in Germany, Cardinal Cajetan. The cardinal appealed to Luther not to disturb the peace of the Church with his dangerous ideas, and reminded him of the danger of opposing the Pope and being judged a heretic. But such a threat was an error. Luther's first instinct when the controversy began had been to apologise to his bishop for any disruption he had caused. He had even written to the Pope in May 1518, '...I fling myself at the feet of your Holiness...I shall acknowledge your voice as the voice of Christ...' Now he saw that he was being forced to make a choice between his vision of the truth and his personal safety. From his early days as a monk Luther had not been one for the easy way out. He was no revolutionary by temperament but he was obstinate. He refused to deny what he saw as the truth and so he defied Cajetan. He even attacked the Pope's right to decide issues of doctrine without clear biblical proof.

1519 was no easier year for the Church authorities. In January the Emperor Maximilian died. The Pope, Leo X, wished to prevent Maximilian's grandson Charles, who already ruled the Netherlands and Spain, from becoming Emperor and thus the dominating power in Europe. A critical voter in the forthcoming imperial election, and even a possible candidate, was the Elector Frederick of Saxony. The Pope sent the Elector a golden rose, the highest sign of papal favour, and certainly did not choose to cause irritation by pressing too strongly for the arrest of Frederick's protégé, Martin Luther. Political force clearly could not succeed. It was hoped that intellectual force would prevail instead – thus a champion of orthodox Catholicism, Johannes Eck, challenged Luther and his supporters to a public debate.

The two sides met in the summer of 1519 in Leipzig. At first Luther, trying to keep a low profile, was represented by his university superior and now follower, Andreas von Karlstadt. But Karlstadt could not stand up to Eck's rigorous cross-examination. Luther had to speak for himself as only he had the certainty of basic principles necessary to refute aged dogmas being presented by Eck as obvious truths. With the atmosphere now heightened by Luther's intervention, Eck played his trump card. He exposed the likeness between some of Luther's ideas and those of Jan Hus, the Bohemian burnt as a heretic a century before. In disputing the authority of the Pope, Luther had earlier appealed to a General Council of the Church, viewed by many as the highest ecclesiastical authority. This did not help him now – Hus had been condemned in 1415 by a General Council at Constance and, by implication, Luther's ideas stood condemned as well.

It looked as though Luther would have to give in or deny even the authority of a General Council. He chose the latter course, as certain as ever that it was his duty to uphold the truth as it was revealed to him by God through the holy scriptures. Luther had been forced into a position where he would recognise only one authority with regard to religious belief – not the Pope, not a General Council but scripture alone. *Sola scriptura* (by scripture alone) was to take its place alongside *sola fide* (by faith alone) as a foundation of Protestant belief.

Luther had not planned to subvert the established order of the Church. It was the authorities' reactions to his views that had forced him to develop his arguments in debate with Cajetan and Eck to the point where he denied the tradition and the hierarchy of the Church. They had foolishly pushed Luther into a corner without having the power in Germany to crush him. An important condition of the success of the Reformation was the vulnerability of the Church and the mistakes its leaders made.

Luther was now reliant solely on scripture – not the faulty, official version, the Latin Vulgate, but the Greek New Testament published by Erasmus in 1516 which, in his view, showed up the errors of Catholic theology. He had not been a willing revolutionary but he now took the initiative, publishing pamphlet after pamphlet on what was wrong with the practice and the teaching of the Church and how these could be put right. In particular, there were three pamphlets from 1520 in which he worked out the implications of *sola fide* and *sola scriptura* and thus launched the Reformation.

> *sola scriptura* 'scripture alone' rather than the tradition of the Church authorising what to believe

KEY ISSUE

Was it Luther or his opponents who created the Reformation crisis?

2 ✒ THE 1520 PAMPHLETS

A *Address to the Christian nobility of the German nation*

Luther asserted that 'the Pope almost seems to be the adversary of Christ called in Scripture the Antichrist'. Not only had the popes failed the Church, they had also brought the world near to chaos by claiming the authority of secular princes as their own. Luther regarded the worldly corruption of the Church as a secular matter, so he appealed to those princes to lead the Reformation. His protest was necessarily bound up with politics.

The politics, however, were not Luther's first concern. The greater part of the pamphlet was devoted to moral outrage at the abuses of the Church, the sexual permissiveness, the luxury and exploitation. Attacks on abuses were nothing new but Luther went on to attack the Church at its doctrinal roots.

Luther denied that priests were any more sacred than ordinary men, or that they could act as intermediaries between their congregations and God. Instead, he wrote of 'the priesthood of all believers' – any man who had faith could be saved and consequently he was his own priest. This did not make ministers redundant in Luther's eyes, but it did mean that they acted as representatives of their congregations rather than superiors. With the priests' role so diminished it was as though a religious revolution was being launched on behalf of laymen. More of the doctrinal details of this revolution were to be made clear in Luther's next major pamphlet.

B *The Babylonish captivity of the Church*

See pages 516–17

The title refers to the enslavement of the Jews by the Babylonians described in the Old Testament, the implication being that the true Christians of the Church had been enslaved by the Roman tyranny of the Pope. Luther's purpose was to show how it had all been achieved through what he saw as fraud. In doing so he attacked Catholicism at its heart, the seven sacraments. It was this pamphlet that was most controversial and that shocked moderate Catholic reformers like Erasmus into realising that Luther was not just a reformer of abuses but a religious revolutionary.

The most important function of the Church had been to administer the seven sacraments, which took the believer through a series of rituals from birth to death. Luther believed that these had been used to make believers reliant on priests; for four of the sacraments he could find no basis in scripture at all. He claimed that there were only three genuine sacraments – baptism, the **Eucharist** and penance – although he later reduced the figure to two when he dispensed with penance.

Most controversial was Luther's doctrine of the Eucharist. He retained the Eucharist as a sacrament but condemned the theory of

Eucharist the ceremony derived from the Last Supper, with the consecration of bread and wine

transubstantiation in terms of it being a complete transformation of the bread and wine, and the idea that the priest was miraculously re-sacrificing Christ during the ceremony. For Luther, Christ's sacrifice had taken place once and for all upon the Cross, the priest was no miracle worker and the bread and the wine remained bread and wine. Another feature of the Catholic Eucharist was that the laity took communion in only one kind, i.e. the bread, with the wine reserved for the priest. Luther insisted that all were spiritually equal and so should receive communion in both kinds, i.e. both bread and wine.

Luther, however, did not break so free from Catholic tradition as to think that the Eucharist was purely a symbolic act. He believed that Christ was physically present in the Eucharist, not replacing the bread and wine but entering into them. He explained the physical presence of Christ in the bread and wine as being like the presence of heat in hot iron. This view was justified later by followers with the theory of the 'ubiquity' of Christ, that is the capacity of Christ's crucified body to cut miraculously and invisibly across space and time and so be present in the Eucharist as a renewed experience of the original physical sacrifice.

Many people today find this hard to grasp and so did a lot of Luther's contemporaries. Not only Roman Catholics condemned his view; some Protestants also saw the notion of the physical presence of Christ in the Eucharist as the superstitious nonsense of someone who had not broken cleanly away from the corrupt beliefs of the medieval Church. But, for Luther, the words of Christ at the Last Supper clearly supported him and, to understand his emotional conviction, think back to his story of God's power in that thunderstorm which made him vow to enter a monastery. He always did have a strong sense of God's physical intervention in the world.

What Luther had lost was his terror of that awe-inspiring power of God. The last of his major 1520 pamphlets expanded on how such terror could be transformed into joy.

> **transubstantiation** the Catholic belief that in the Eucharist the bread and the wine are physically transformed into the Body and Blood of Christ

C *The freedom of the Christian man*

Without compromising any of his beliefs, Luther was to make this work one of his most uncontroversial in tone. Rather than attacking any of his opponents, he was trying to share his sense of liberation. The freedom he celebrated was freedom from those laws of God that no mortal could satisfactorily obey. This did not mean that Luther expected the faithful to stop trying to obey the laws of God – they would naturally go on doing so owing to their love for God and their awareness of the imperfection of the world and themselves – but they could rest assured that, insofar as they failed, Christ would make up for it. This was a freedom from the consequences of human inadequacy.

Luther was even conciliatory towards the Pope, perhaps as an idealistic gesture or because Elector Frederick was worried by the violence of the controversy. Still, Luther's conciliation was strictly limited. He sympathised with Pope Leo X as being amongst evil counsellors, like

Daniel amongst the lions, but he also made clear that he expected Leo to abandon his former position completely and join in the Reformation. Such a notion was, of course, laughable in Rome. Indeed Pope Leo, preoccupied by politics closer to home, gave little attention to the Lutheran affair and is unlikely to have had any perception of the new theology being expounded in the 1520 pamphlets.

By the end of 1520 that new theology was near completion. It was unsystematic; Luther responded spontaneously to ideas and events, and there were many details to be argued over, but the essentials were there. In 1521 Luther's teaching was brought together in *Loci Communes*, a textbook written by Philip Melanchthon, Luther's close supporter in Wittenberg.

From the basis of *sola fide* and *sola scriptura* Luther had worked out the priesthood of all believers, the need for only three (later two) sacraments, the rejection of transubstantiation and the meaning of Christian freedom. He was not revolutionary through and through, as his cautious treatment of baptism and the Eucharist show, but he had been sufficiently radical to destroy much that had underpinned the structure of the medieval Catholic Church. The question became whether Luther would have the chance to preach his theology further or whether he would be crushed by the authorities of Church and Empire.

> **KEY ISSUE**
>
> *In what ways were the 1520 pamphlets most radical?*

3 ∽ UNDER THE BAN OF CHURCH AND EMPIRE

'Arise, O Lord, and judge your cause. A wild boar has invaded your vineyard . . . Arise all ye saints, and the whole universal Church, whose interpretation of Scripture has been assailed . . .' These were the opening words of a papal **bull** named *Exsurge Domine* which threatened Luther with **excommunication** if he did not repudiate his heresy within sixty days. But Luther was to demonstrate how little he respected or feared papal authority when his time was up on 10 December 1520. He staged a bonfire on which he burnt the bull and then fuelled the flames further with the books of canon law, which defined the legal powers of the Church. Luther's words soon became more fiery as well: 'The Emperor and princes must take up arms against the Roman Antichrist and the Roman Sodom. We must wash our hands in their blood.' But the greater likelihood at this stage was the reverse, that Luther's enemies would wash their hands in his blood.

Here again the steadfast protection of Luther by Elector Frederick was critical for the beginnings of the Reformation. Hoping to ensure a favourable hearing for Luther and to forestall a final excommunication, he arranged for his controversial professor to put his case before the Emperor at the meeting of the **Imperial Diet** at Worms in April 1521. Luther went willingly – he said that he would not refuse to go if there were as many devils at Worms as there were tiles on the roofs. He no doubt had it in mind that this was the big opportunity for his plain

bull an important decree from the Pope, sealed with his signet-ring (from the Latin *bulla* = seal)

excommunication exclusion from the Eucharist, in effect expulsion from the Church

Imperial Diet the parliament of the Holy Roman Empire

speaking of God's word to win over the young Emperor Charles V and assembled princes. He may well also have put some trust in the safe-conduct granted by the Emperor.

At Worms, however, even Luther's confidence faltered. Faced by the ritual and the challenge of the occasion Luther wondered whether he alone could be right. He asked for a day to think things over. When he came back to face all the powers of Germany his resolve was as strong as ever: '... my conscience is captive to the Word of God, I cannot and I will not recant anything, for to go against conscience is neither right nor safe. So help me God. Amen.' The safety he was thinking about was not of this world. That made him all the more difficult for ordinary politicians to deal with.

The Emperor listened patiently to Luther but was not moved by what he had said. Charles V had a high sense of duty both with regard to the faith of his ancestors and to his imperial role as defender of the Church. Ironically, he could also score a propaganda point against the Pope by being first to act decisively against the rebellious monk. Luther was put under the ban of the Empire; in other words, outlawed. But before this was formally decided the princes had already turned to business more pressing than complex theological disputes – making complaints against papal taxation. Elector Frederick had tactfully withdrawn from the Diet and Luther himself had started to travel home, free to do so owing to his imperial safe-conduct. It was all very well for the Emperor to formally condemn Luther but he had no practical means of stopping him writing and preaching. It looked as though Luther was going to slip through the political holes in the German constitution.

On the way home from Worms, however, it looked more as though Luther had slipped into the hands of his enemies. A group of mysterious horsemen kidnapped him and the rumour spread rapidly that he had been assassinated. As it happened, it was the Elector Frederick being cautious again. He had had Luther abducted for his own safety and he was subsequently installed in a castle of the elector's called the Wartburg. There Luther grew a beard and was known as Junker George. It soon became clear that he had not been assassinated – he started to translate the Greek New Testament into German and to turn out anti-Catholic pamphlets at the rate of about one a fortnight. The impact of these is shown in a comment of Chieragato, the Pope's ambassador to the Diet of Nuremberg in 1522: 'Luther's doctrine has already so many roots in the earth that a thousand persons could not pull it up; certainly I alone cannot.' We must now turn to the reasons why Germany was such fertile ground for Luther's protest.

TIMELINE

1517 *Ninety-Five Theses and beginning of Indulgences Controversy*
1518 Luther meets Cardinal Cajetan
1519 Disputation with Eck
1520 Publication of the three key pamphlets
1521 Diet of Worms

KEY ISSUE

Why did Charles V choose not to lead the German Reformation?

4 ↜ GERMANY'S GRIEVANCES AND PROPHECIES

The abuses of the Church did not cause the Reformation but they made it less able to defend itself. The Church had become preoccupied with preserving and funding its huge bureaucracy and this led to constant haggling with those who would have to pay. Even those who were otherwise loyal Catholics continued to haggle while the Lutheran storm broke. When the princes at Worms turned away from the Lutheran affair, they compiled a list of no less than 102 complaints, known as *gravamina* or grievances, against papal extortions and abuses. One grievance complained of the Pope appointing to Church offices the unqualified and the unlearned, such as bakers and donkey drivers, even when they could speak no German. Another grievance stated: 'We also regard it in the highest degree objectionable that His Holiness the Pope should permit so many indulgences to be sold in Germany, a practice through which simple-minded folk are misled and cheated of their savings.' The princes at the Diet of Worms might have accepted the imperial ban on Luther for heresy, but they had other things on their minds, which to them were more important.

Grievance lists had been compiled as early as the Diet of Frankfurt in 1456. Other countries – France, England, Spain – had long since limited papal control over their national churches, but Germany did not have a central authority with sufficient strength to do so. There had been an attempt in the Concordat of Vienna of 1448 to restrict papal authority, but it only applied to Habsburg lands. The same slackness in the imperial constitution which made it so difficult to suppress Luther had, ironically, allowed the Papacy to extend its powers in the first place. The people as a whole bitterly resented papal taxation and, well before Luther, they welcomed parodies of the Papacy in carnival displays and woodcuts, their equivalent of cartoons. This anti-papalism did not automatically mean the rejection of Catholic doctrine. But it did mean that the enemy of the Pope might well be seen as the friend of the German people.

It was not only the Papacy that was looked upon as an object of resentment. The whole German clergy came under fire for living a luxurious life at the expense of ordinary lay people. In towns, the clergy could be disliked for living a privileged life distinct from the rest of the community. The grievances of the craft guilds of Cologne in 1513 included statements such as 'Clerical persons should from now on bear the same civic burdens as burghers...Let the clergy pay taxes on the wine they tap for themselves...The council should instruct the preachers of the four **regular orders** to preach nothing but the true word of God and to utter no lies or fables...'. Preachers who criticised the clergy received a favourable hearing in towns and cities all over Germany.

regular orders monks

For peasants, the money they had to pay to the Church, the tithe, was a burden they found it difficult to shoulder, given ever greater efficiency in the collection of other dues they owed to lords and princes. Peasant protest had already begun before 1521. For instance, in 1476 Hans Böhm, the so-called Drummer of Niklashausen, had attacked the established clergy and at the same time demanded that 'it must come about that the common people have enough to give all an equal sufficiency'. Böhm and his movement were exterminated by the Bishop of Würzburg but the sign of peasant protest, the *Bundschuh* or clog, was still to be seen at Worms when Luther was defending himself there, and there was popular clamour in support of him. Those who were anti-clerical, or whose general social protest included anti-clericalism, did not necessarily understand Luther's doctrine but they would voice support for a man who appeared to be cutting the clergy down to size.

Social and economic problems were of great importance but they did not automatically lead to the German people becoming rebels, religious or otherwise. Their reactions were fashioned by popular beliefs. The Drummer of Niklashausen, for instance, did not begin his campaign with a programme of social reform but with his claim that he had had a vision of the Virgin Mary. As his peasant followers approached Würzburg they responded to the threat of the bishop's cannon by saying, 'Our Lady will protect us from harm. You cannot hurt us.' (They were proved wrong.) Luther had no visions of the Virgin Mary but he was seen by many as a man inspired by God, whose religious mission could overturn the normal order of things.

That overturning of the normal order of things was not thought just to be possible owing to divine intervention: it was expected. Prophecy was a central element in popular belief. The prophecies of Joachim of Fiore (1132–1202) were still popular in the sixteenth century. He believed that the world was in the 'Age of the Son' but would pass into the 'Age of the Spirit' which would be an era of full and genuine freedom when the old order would pass away. More specifically, for several generations before the 1520s, a 'holy man' had been expected who would begin the reform of the Church. This inspired reform literature, amongst which was the *Reformatio Sigismundi*, written in *c.*1438 but published in eight editions between 1476 and 1522. It combined warnings with recommendations of what needed to be done:

1	The hour will come for all faithful Christians to witness the establishment of the rightful order. Let everyone join the ranks of the pious who will pledge themselves to observe it. It is plain that the Holy Father, the Pope, and all our princes have abandoned the task set them by God. It may be that God has appointed a man to set things right. Let no one, neither princes nor cities, make
7	excuses for not heeding God's warnings ...
8	Take a good look at how bishops act nowadays. They make war and cause unrest in the world; they behave like secular lords, which is, of course, what they are. And the money for this comes from pious donations that ought to go to honest parish work, and not to be spent on war. I agree with a remark made by Duke Frederick of Austria to the Emperor Sigismund in Basel: 'Bishops are blind; it is
14	up to us to open their eyes ...'
15	It seems to me that great evils have arisen in the western part of Christendom since Pope Calixtus imposed the rule of celibacy. It may be a good thing for a man to keep himself pure, but observe

the wickedness now going on in the Church! Many priests have lost their livings because of women. Or they are secret sodomites. All the hatred existing between priests and laymen is due to this. In sum: **secular priests** ought to be allowed to marry. In marriage they will live more piously and honourably, and the friction between them and the laity will disappear... 23

secular priests parish priests

1. *How might the* Reformatio Sigismundi *have affected attitudes towards Luther and his enemies (lines 1–7)?*
2. *What does the second paragraph above (lines 8–14) have in common with Luther's Address to the Christian Nobility of the German Nation (see page 152)?*
3. *Why should hatred between priests and laymen be due to celibacy (lines 14–23)? How might this attack on clerical celibacy have helped to prepare the way for Luther?*

KEY ISSUE

How significant were anti-papalism and anti-clericalism in preparing the way for the Reformation?

The *Reformatio Sigismundi* fitted in to the popular tradition that reform must come but its appeal was largely confined to the literate (between five and ten per cent of the population), although it could reach others through being read aloud. More important were the oral tradition and the pictorial representations in woodcuts which adapted and popularised bible stories and sustained beliefs in prophecy. In this tradition, the 'holy man' would be the new Elijah who would identify the Antichrist, launch the last battle against Satan and announce the second coming of Christ and the last judgement. There was a feeling that the end of the world was at hand. When the image of Luther appeared in woodcuts as a 'holy man', in the robes of a doctor of theology or a monk, sometimes with the halo of a saint or the dove of the Holy Spirit above his head, the response to him could be rapid and dramatic.

Despite this mood of expectation, however, Germany's grievances and prophecies did not amount to a reform movement for Luther simply to take over. For all the criticism and the hopes for future reform, the beliefs and rituals of the Catholic Church were still seen as the only route to salvation. Luther did not build on a tradition of dissent: there had been virtually no heresy trials in Germany since the 1470s. Instead there were many examples of a growth in conventional religious enthusiasm. Since the fourteenth century, laymen in the Netherlands and north-west Germany had been joining the Brethren of the Common Life (a religious association fully Catholic in its doctrine) and reading devotional literature such as Thomas à Kempis' *The Imitation of Christ*. In Upper Austria, the number of Masses endowed to be said for the dead increased greatly, reaching a peak in 1517. There were mass pilgrimages, such as one to Mont St Michel in 1457, made up mostly of children from southern Germany. For all that the Imperial Diet complained about the selling of indulgences, they only sold because there was a ready market for them amongst the people of Germany. Bernd Moeller has suggested that 'the late fifteenth century in Germany was marked by greater fidelity to the church than in any other medieval epoch'.

This does not seem to fit into the picture of a Germany ready for the Reformation owing to grievances and prophecies. However, Steven Ozment argues that both the devotion to the beliefs and rituals of the Church and much of the criticism of its personnel sprang from a terrible underlying spiritual anxiety. Laymen were trying ever harder in their Catholic devotions and the confession of sins, until Luther arrived on the scene, writing pamphlets, standing defiant at Worms and appearing in woodcuts. He was the 'holy man', armed with his Bible, who could relieve spiritual anxiety and offer an alternative route to salvation. Euan Cameron rejects Ozment's emphasis on spiritual anxiety, arguing that there is far more evidence of the Church being easy-going, reassuring people that correct ritual observance and perhaps an occasional indulgence would earn them their places in heaven. He even thinks that in his later years Luther exaggerated his own early torments. Instead, Cameron suggests that Luther's appeal to the people flattered them and it is this that explains the enthusiasm of their response: 'Lay people saw some of the best talents in the Church turn towards them for approval and support. Nothing could have been more surprising or more intoxicating.' Certainly the weakness of the response to Luther's protest by Catholic theologians was in part due to their reluctance to appeal to the people for judgement of issues which they thought should be discussed only in a closed group of theologians and clerics.

If support for Luther had depended simply on lay people feeling flattered, his protest might have petered out. But there was one early source of support that proved crucial in turning Luther's popular protest into the Reformation movement – the humanists. They were the first to close ranks in support of Luther and most of the early Lutheran preachers were of a humanist background. As the officers of city councils or as counsellors to princes, they were to give the Reformation much of its political force. However, while it was of critical importance, the relationship between Luther and the humanists was not clearcut.

> **KEY ISSUE**
>
> *How did popular beliefs encourage the spread of Lutheranism?*

5 ↳ LUTHER AND THE HUMANISTS

The Christian humanists had many reasons for rallying to Luther's cause. They saw Luther's ideas pitted against **scholasticism**, which they already despised as being barbaric and futile. One humanist, Mosellanus, wrote in 1519 that Luther had 'hissed the Aristotelian theology off the theological stage'. The Christian humanists had had immediate sympathy with Luther's doctrine of *sola scriptura* which seemed close to their own intellectual ideal of going *ad fontes*, back to the original sources to seek understanding, which in this case was the scriptures. As we have seen, Luther relied on Erasmus's Greek New Testament of 1516 and much of what he had to say about inner faith seemed to correspond well with Erasmus's philosophy of Christ.

> **scholasticism** the dominant philosophy of the Middle Ages

> See pages 135–7

There were reasons other than religious ones for humanists to support Luther. When he wrote of Germany 'which nation with its noble nature is praised for its constancy and faithfulness in all history', some humanist nationalists welcomed his protest as another blow struck on behalf of German pride. In 1500, one of their number, Conrad Celtis, had republished an ancient Roman text, Tacitus's *Germania*, which had rapidly become a cult work, detailing the resilience of the Germans 1500 years before. Elsewhere Celtis wrote,

'Resume, O men of Germany, that spirit of older times wherewith you so often confounded and terrified the Romans.' Clearly such nationalism could reinforce Luther's cause. However, its influence should not be over-estimated. This nationalism was not of the modern sort, which is concerned with political unity and national self-determination. German nationalism in the time of Luther would perhaps be better termed national sentiment – it was made up of a literary mythology about inherent German greatness and was not a practical programme of national political unity. Still, those who read the works of the German nationalists had been made more receptive to a stand against a foreign power such as the Papacy. All they needed was a controversy to make their suspicion of the power of the Church yet more intense.

For the humanists that controversy was not in the first instance about indulgences. The Church was already being rocked by the Reuchlin affair. Johann Reuchlin was a scholar specialising in the study of Hebrew as a way of furthering understanding of the Old Testament. But in 1510 he had been attacked, on the grounds that he was slipping into Judaism, by Pfefferkorn, a new Christian eager to prove that he really had put behind him the beliefs of his own Jewish ancestors. The controversy grew in proportion as the theologians of Cologne weighed in on the side of Pfefferkorn while some humanists, although not the cautious Erasmus, backed Reuchlin, seeing the attack on him as an attack on the whole *ad fontes* way of intellectual enquiry. The humanists had the better of the argument in terms of propaganda. Their *Letters of Obscure Men*, written by Crotus Rubeanus and Ulrich von Hutten in 1515 and 1517, made a mockery of their opponents. They even gave us a new word – obscurantism – to describe the sterile thinking of closed minds. When Luther made his stand there were plenty of humanists, especially the younger, more radical ones, who were prepared to see him as another Reuchlin in need of defence against a Church which might suppress any new, critical thinking.

It was the younger and more radical humanists who were to provide not just a sympathetic reception to Luther but practical action on his behalf. They were the group from which were largely drawn the pamphleteers, the preachers and finally the pastors who were to campaign for him and establish Lutheran congregations far and wide across Germany. This pool of intellectual talent had grown in the previous generation as new schools and universities in Germany multiplied. In fact, the pool was probably too large for the number of jobs available so career frustrations could have fuelled support for Luther. Moeller has laid great stress on the importance of the humanists: 'Without them [Luther] would have failed as did many before him who had tried to stand up against the old Church. One can state this pointedly: no humanism, no Reformation.'

However, as the Reformation developed, differences emerged. Some of the radical humanists felt that Luther had not abandoned medieval superstition in his belief concerning the physical presence of Christ in the Eucharist: they were to gravitate towards the Swiss Reformation.

See pages 170–1

Others, especially the older, more conservative humanists, came to feel that Luther was not going to purify the Church but rather to wreck it.

Before 1517 the humanists had been critical of the clergy and scholastic theology, but they had been fundamentally Catholic in their beliefs and many remained so. Even Reuchlin, the victim of the Cologne theologians, was shocked by Luther's attack on the seven sacraments. Many humanists, used to the civility of intellectual debates, were appalled by the violence unleashed by the Reformation. Mutianus wrote, 'I for one do not love the fanatic stone throwers.' A central element in the thinking of many humanists was the possibility of man's self-improvement; that contrasted with Luther's belief in man as being totally worthless in himself and entirely dependent on God's grace. Erasmus, among others, could not resolve that conflict.

Erasmus tried to remain detached from the Reformation debate, although at first he suspected that the attack on Luther was an attack on Christian humanism. He grew increasingly distressed, however, as he saw Luther 'rending the seamless robe of Christ' in threatening the unity of the Church, especially with his revolutionary attack on the seven sacraments in *The Babylonish Captivity of the Church.* In 1524 Erasmus at last committed himself in a diatribe against Luther on the issue of free will. Erasmus argued that it was vital to believe in free will if man was to have any purpose on earth, or he would just be a puppet. In his reply Luther praised Erasmus's eloquence but condemned his argument: 'it is as if rubbish, or dung, should be carried in vessels of gold or silver'. Luther argued that all things are decided according to God's 'immutable, eternal and infallible will. By this thunderbolt free will is thrown prostrate and utterly dashed to pieces.' This debate on free will clearly showed the gulf between the optimism of the humanist Erasmus and the pessimism of the Lutheran vision of man.

> See pages 137–8

The humanists were split, some, like Erasmus, rejecting Luther's vision and others being converted to it. Luther had gained much from the humanists but he had not compromised with them. He retained his distinctive view of what the Reformation meant. The question after 1521 was whether all those flocking to the cause of the Reformation would continue to share his view.

> **KEY ISSUE**
>
> *Why did the humanists support Luther, but only in part?*

6 ᔕ THE CRISIS IN WITTENBERG

Luther was uncompromising over what he saw as essential doctrine but he was quite prepared for the details of Catholic religious practice to change only slowly, if at all. However, there were those in Wittenberg who wished to hurry the Reformation on and make a cleaner break with the Church of Rome. While Luther was in the Wartburg castle there was little he could do about it. In the autumn of 1521 the changes in Wittenberg began. For instance, monks began leaving their monasteries, their vows having been made redundant by the doctrine of *sola fide*. Events took a more radical turn with the arrival in December of the Zwickau prophets.

In 1520 the town of Zwickau had witnessed an extraordinary experiment led by Thomas Müntzer, who had declared that there was a kingdom of Christ to replace all authorities, secular as well as religious. The magistrates had acted against Müntzer, who fled. Three of his followers became the Zwickau prophets who appeared in Wittenberg. They accused Luther of being cowardly and demanded a complete cleansing of the churches. This involved the removal of all statues and paintings of saints, and even whole altars, which might be worshipped idolatrously instead of all worship being focussed on Christ. This stripping of the churches of images and any other distractions, known as iconoclasm, threatened to take a hysterical turn and to degenerate into iconoclastic riots. Even peaceful iconoclasm was serious, being an attack upon property and not just upon doctrine.

Andreas von Karlstadt, Luther's university superior and failed debater against Eck, was carried along in the mood of exultation created by the Zwickau prophets. Philip Melanchthon, closer to Luther and of a more moderate disposition, really did not know what to do. There was the danger that Elector Frederick would use force to stop the attacks on church property. Luther had to intervene personally. He wrote from the Wartburg in January 1522, 'Without spilling blood or drawing the sword, let it not be doubted that we shall gently extinguish these firebrands.' Luther returned to Wittenberg in March 1522 to extinguish the firebrands with his preaching.

On eight successive days he preached what were known as his Invocavit sermons. Here are some extracts from one of them:

Q

1. *How might this sermon have curbed the Zwickau prophets, or at least those who had responded to their message?*
2. *Why did Luther want to avoid making ordinances or general laws (lines 4–5)?*
3. *What problem did the very existence of the Zwickau prophets indicate with regard to relying solely on the Word of God for authority?*

We must first win the hearts of the people. But that is done when I   1
teach only the Word of God, preach the gospel, and say: Dear
lords or pastors, abandon the Mass, it is not right, you are sinning
when you do it; I cannot refrain from telling you this. But I would   4
not make it an ordinance for them or urge a general law. He who   5
would follow me could do so, and he who refused would remain
outside. In the latter case the Word would sink into the heart and
do its work. Thus he would become convinced and acknowledge
his error, and fall away from the Mass; tomorrow another would
do the same, and thus God would accomplish more with His Word
than if you and I were to merge all our power into one heap...
Take myself as an example. I opposed indulgences and all the
papists, but never with force. I simply taught, preached and wrote
God's Word; otherwise I did nothing. And while I slept or drank
beer with my friends, the Word so greatly weakened the Papacy
that no prince or emperor ever inflicted such losses upon it. I did
nothing: the Word did everything.   16

The *Invocavit* sermons worked. For a time, at least in Wittenberg, Luther had taken back control of the Reformation. The influence of the

Zwickau prophets was brought to an end. Karlstadt left Wittenberg and was to wander Germany in peasant clothing, rather ineffectively preaching a simple, spiritual religion.

Luther always emphasised the importance of sermons and he himself produced at least 3000 of them. In 1518 he had described the 'ears alone' as the organs of the Christian. Lutheran preachers all over Germany reached the illiterate as well as the educated and, even for those who could read, they added that extra emotional charge which established the Reformation. However, the direction of the Reformation, and Luther's own role in it, owed much to what he called 'God's highest and ultimate gift of grace by which He would have His Gospel carried forward' – the printing press.

KEY ISSUE

How effectively did Luther deal with the crisis in Wittenberg in 1522?

7 ⤴ THE REFORMATION AND THE PRINTING PRESS

It has been argued by Elizabeth Eisenstein that printing did not just spread Protestant ideas but helped to shape the Reformation in the first place. Printing ended the scribal corruption, the copying errors, of the Middle Ages. The new accuracy made it easier to define theological positions exactly and easier for Luther to attack the corruption of doctrine. With regard to *sola scriptura*, an appeal to the Bible as the sole authority had been made before Luther by other reformers such as Wycliffe; but an evangelical, or Bible-based, religion only became possible once the Bible could be mass produced. In September 1522 Luther published the *September Testament*, his translation into ordinary German of Eramus's Greek New Testament. (Other translations of the Bible had been on the market for some time but they were based on the corrupt official version, the Vulgate.) Within twelve years 200 000 copies of the *September Testament* had been sold and by then, in 1534, Luther had completed his translation of the Old Testament as well.

See pages 18–19

The Church had faced heresy before and had generally contained it slowly but surely, but now it seemed defenceless. The printing presses gave it no time. Luther said that it had taken a fortnight for his *Ninety-Five Theses* to spread across Germany. In the sixty years since printing had been invented, literacy had grown to a rate of perhaps twenty per cent in towns. The literate layman's appetite for books was inflamed by the Reformation controversy and the output of books was to increase by six or seven times between 1518 and 1524. Also, there were innumerable fly-sheets or woodcuts to recall or amplify what the people heard from reformed preachers. There were Catholics writing against Luther, but they were outnumbered twenty to one by those writing in favour of him. Luther himself used the press as a weapon in personal contests with his opponents and it was not all a matter of theology – he caricatured Dr Eck as Dreck (dirt) while Johannes Cochlaeus became Rotzleffel (snot spoon). The demand for what Luther wrote was immense. The thirty tracts published by Luther between 1517 and 1520 amounted to some 300 000 copies. In the early years of the Reformation, the Lutherans won the battle of the books hands down.

Through the press Luther could also give shape to the services and methods of the new, emerging Church. In 1523 he published a reformed Mass, the *Formula Missae et Communionis*, and in 1526 his German Mass, the *Deutsche Messe*, appeared. Other reformers, starting with Karlstadt in 1521, had adapted church services in their own way but, through the printing press, Luther was able to issue the authentically Lutheran version. He also published many hymns, which were to characterise Lutheran worship. Vital for less able preachers, who might get things muddled, he wrote the *Kirchenpostille*, a series of textbook sermons. By 1529 he had completed his *Small Catechism*, a question and answer instruction manual for use in the home, and his *Great Catechism* for more thorough education. Luther did not just drink beer with his friends while the Word did it all, as he claimed in the *Invocavit* sermons. He wrote down what he was convinced the Word was and got it printed.

Printing did not ensure Luther's total control over the Reformation. The press could spread the ideas of one man more quickly and certainly than ever before, but it also magnified the explosion of differing ideas which resulted from the break-up of the medieval Church. Luther had calmed the radicalism in Wittenberg but there were restless radicals elsewhere who would not conform and other reformers, particularly in southern Germany and Switzerland, who had independent minds. Also, it was not so much what Luther published which counted but the varying reactions to it. We must now look at the impact of the Reformation upon the different types of people who made up the German nation.

> **KEY ISSUE**
>
> *How crucial was the printing press to the development of the Reformation?*

8 ⌐ THE REFORMATION AND THE PEASANTS

See page 158

Luther recognised the need to communicate through woodcuts 'for the sake of simple folk' and we have seen how there was already a tradition of anti-papalism in these cartoons. Scribner has likened these woodcuts to 'homemade gin: cheap, crude and effective'. However, he has also shown that much of the message that got through to the peasants was a negative view of the Papacy rather than a positive representation of Luther's teaching. For example, the depiction of Christ on the Cross might indicate *sola fide*, but this could not be an unambiguous image as the Crucifixion was also important in Catholic devotion. Luther was the 'holy man' and his fellow ministers might be seen as worthy preachers, but in many woodcuts an even more dynamic image would be that which showed the Pope and his supporters in all their viciousness. The Pope was pictured as the Antichrist heralding the end of time and the last judgement; he was to be seen as the seven-headed beast of the apocalypse or the 'whore of Babylon'. Another favourite image was the wheel of fortune, or 'the world turned upside down', showing the mighty being overthrown and the meek being raised up. There was an air of expectancy that, with papal power being overthrown, society would be transformed. Lutheranism was thought of by many peasants not in terms of theology but of godly rebellion.

See exercise on pages 182–7

The brief, futile Knights' War of 1522, when two Protestant imperial knights, Ulrich von Hutten and Franz von Sickingen, had led an attack on the Archbishop-Elector of Trier, had shown how religious and social discontents could merge. By 1524 not only was the Reformation shaking Germany but also the grievances of peasants against their lords had reached a new intensity such that rebellion, when it came, was devastating. Particularly in the south and south-west of Germany, peasant communities in the course of the previous century had been losing their freedom. It was made difficult to move from one estate to another. Especially controversial was the use of the forest which the peasants regarded as free territory and which the lords were trying to regulate, inventing the crime of poaching. The labour services demanded of the peasant by his lord in return for land were not legally specified and so could be gradually stepped up. The peasant of southern Germany, who had been free in most respects, was gradually being turned into a serf.

This departure from customary freedom was a long-term trend. What made it unbearable by 1524 was that the population was rising by as much as 0.7 per cent a year so that there was an increasing demand for fertile land which could not be met, whilst recent harvests had been failing at the rate of about one in four. Added to this was an increased burden of taxation to pay for the wars against the Turks.

The growing resentment of the peasants found a particular object in the ecclesiastical landlords, mainly abbots, who took tithes as well as rents. In 1525 one grievance against the Abbess of Buchau asserted that every peasant should be 'as free as a bird on a branch and may move to and live in towns, markets and villages unhindered by any lord. She (the Abbess) has forcibly squeezed our freedom from us and has monstrously burdened us with ruin, death taxes, marriage restrictions and serfdom, defying God's decree and all reason and even her own edict of freedom.' Luther's protest seemed like a manifesto of liberation against such ecclesiastical oppression. Peasants were much more concerned with their daily, material existence than with theological complexities. Luther's call for spiritual equality, given 'the priesthood of all believers', was readily extended by the peasants to a demand for social equality.

The Peasants' War began with an uprising near Schaffhausen on the Swiss border. It spread rapidly, reaching its peak in the spring of 1525 with all of southern Germany in turmoil, except for Bavaria where the dukes had kept lords more under control and the status of the peasants more stable. The uprising, although it seemed so general, was not one organised revolt but a series of provincial rebellions sparking others off – five main ones, each with its own character and its own independent peasant army.

MAP 9
The Peasants' War

KEY ISSUE

How far was Luther's protest responsible for the Peasants' War?

---

customary law law established by precedent and custom over many years

---

godly law law supposedly derived from God and so superior to any human law

---

Despite regional variations one set of peasant grievances gained particularly wide circulation – the *Twelve Articles of Memmingen*, adopted by a peasant parliament in Memmingen in March 1525. The bulk of the articles were demands for the peasants' rights to be restored and the drift into serfdom halted. This was in line with earlier peasant demands based on an appeal to custom. However, the mark of the Reformation was clearly visible. One article called for congregations to elect their own ministers, which indeed had been an early reform favoured by Luther. But, more than that, instead of an appeal solely to **customary law** there was also an appeal to **godly law**. The preamble to the *Twelve Articles* began: 'There are many antichrists who, now that the peasants are assembled together, seize the chance to mock the gospel.' It continued with the point that the peasants seeking Christian justice could not be labelled rebels; those who opposed them were the rebels against God. The peasants had seen the woodcuts where the Pope as Antichrist had been cast down and now they were going to cast down antichrists as well.

Peter Blickle has recently emphasised the significance of this appeal to godly law. Peasant demands were no longer limited by custom; the social and political order became an open question. Godly law could form an ideology which united townsmen and miners, all the unprivileged, with the peasants. As the uprisings spread northwards more and more cities became involved, while to the east the miners of the Tyrol joined with the peasants. Blickle has argued that the uprisings ought to be termed the Revolt of the Common Man rather than the Peasants' War. When Michael Gaismair, a rebel leader, wrote his *Tyrolean Constitution* he envisaged a Christian democratic republic. All social privileges were to disappear, as would all barriers between people, literally meaning the destruction of castle and city walls. The economy was to be self-sufficient and controlled by locally elected officials. All that was to be left of the social order was the Common Man.

The *Tyrolean Constitution* and all similar rebel programmes were utopian. In some regions, however, the peasant mood was simply that of destruction, especially where there was inadequate leadership or where the rebels were in the grip of religious hysteria. In Thuringia on the borders of Saxony, the latter was the case as Thomas Müntzer, who had earlier inspired the Zwickau prophets, was in control there. He advocated a form of communism ('Everyone should properly receive according to his need') and swift justice for any lord who did not co-operate ('He should be hanged or have his head chopped off'). But this was not demanded in the name of a fair society; it was in preparation for the second coming of Christ on earth. Lords had to be disposed of because they had forced the peasants to concentrate on material existence and had prevented them from learning how to read the Bible. Müntzer was so confident of victory that he just made more certain the defeat of his peasant army and his own destruction at the hands of Landgrave Philip of Hesse and Duke George of Saxony at the Battle of Frankenhausen in May 1525. Some peasant armies of up to 15 000 strong held out until the following year but they were picked off one by one and the revolts came to an end.

By this stage Luther had lost all sympathy with the peasant rebels. He claimed that his message had been wickedly misinterpreted. He had preached only spiritual equality and he had consistently opposed rebellion against princes who, even if they were tyrants, had been appointed by God to keep sinful men in order. He had some justification for his claim that his words were twisted, but he had helped misinterpretation to occur. His fighting talk encouraged rebellion. He had criticised lords and princes, calling them the 'biggest fools or the worst scoundrels on earth'. He used the rhetoric of freedom and communal solidarity, which had far more explosive effects in southern Germany than Luther had anticipated from his vantage point in the north. He tried to halt the revolt, publishing his *Friendly Criticism* of the *Twelve Articles of Memmingen* in April 1525, but he could not control disturbances which had been set in motion by peasant grievances galvanised by the Reformation and the idea of 'godly law'. Frustrated, he published a furious tract in May 1525 entitled *Against the Thieving, Murdering Hordes of Peasants*, in which he invited the princes to destroy the peasants and show no mercy until they submitted. It seemed as though the popular Reformation had ended in disaster. However, the Reformation remained very much a popular force, even after 1525, in the great cities of Germany.

9 ↩ THE REFORMATION AND THE CITIES

In 1521 there were sixty-five imperial or 'free' cities, not under the control of any prince and owing allegiance direct to the Emperor. Of those fifty-one became Protestant at some stage. The Reformation was not imposed on these cities by merchants or magistrates; in nearly every documented case popular support was registered. For instance, in Ulm in 1530 when the citizens were asked to vote on whether to maintain the Reformation or return to Catholicism, eighty-seven per cent of the votes were in favour of the Reformation.

It was in cities that the growth in late medieval piety had been concentrated. The cities themselves and institutions within them were regarded as sacred societies. In Ulm in 1508, for instance, a blasphemer had been banished for fear that God would punish the whole community if he stayed. The guilds and confraternities within cities had their chapels and their patron saints. So the Church did not monopolise religion; the views of lay people counted and they could be highly critical. Anti-clericalism was common, the clergy often regarded as parasites and, being unmarried, disturbingly alien from the ordinary community.

People in the cities were able and willing to respond to Luther's message. There was a relatively high degree of literacy and the printing presses producing Lutheran literature were to be found in the cities, so books and pamphlets were readily available.

Print in many ways, though, was a supplement to preaching. A characteristic of city life has been termed 'sermon addiction', given that some would sit through sermons of four hours in length. Many cities and towns endowed preacherships – thirty-one per cent of the towns in Württemberg, for instance – in order to satisfy the public demand. This fitted in well with the Lutherans' greater emphasis on preaching and, as some citizens' petitions show, led to quite a sophisticated under-standing of Luther's message.

Some specific preachers prepared the way for Lutheranism. In Nuremberg in 1516 Johannes von Staupitz, Luther's monastic superior, preached on the powerlessness of man to find the route to salvation for himself. This was not fully Lutheran but it was an important element in the reformer's thinking which was thus current in Nuremberg even before the Indulgences Controversy. While Staupitz preached largely to an élite, in Strasbourg from 1478 to 1510 there had been an enormously popular preacher called Geiler von Kaisersberg who had attacked abuses in Church and state and who had based all his arguments on the Bible. The Lutheran reformers, therefore, had not invented the evangelical approach.

Not only were the cities of Germany sensitive to religious ideas, they were also growing in political awareness. Most cities had had to struggle with the authority of a local bishop. By the 1480s not only had those struggles been won but the cities, in order to protect themselves against the power of territorial princes, had won the right to attend the Imperial Diet and even to meet separately from the princes. Many city councils had acquired sophisticated civil servants working in chancelleries, in many ways the model for modern bureaucracy. And those civil servants were often humanists. The cities were independent enough to decide religious issues for themselves and, where there were humanists, they had the men capable of presenting the arguments. This was in sharp contrast to the Reformation in the countryside. As Euan Cameron puts it, 'It was much easier for city tradesman to learn about the Reformation, become enthusiasts for it, and then press reform measures upon the city fathers living a few streets away, than for farmers or villagers even to hear a reforming preacher, let alone to lobby a distant prince or king on that preacher's behalf.'

As well as political awareness, the cities' attitude towards the Reformation was also affected by social change. The development of trade had damaged the medieval ideal of unity and had led to increasing divisions between rich and poor. The result was social tension, but also a greater chance of movement between classes. This led to the emergence of groups which Steven Ozment has described as 'the ideologically mobile', that is people made more receptive to new ideas by social change. This could be because of social grievance (workers or the poorer clergy), ambition (certain guilds, newly rich merchants) or ideals (university students, humanists). These groups were the most enthusiastic when Lutheran preachers arrived in town.

City councillors were less enthusiastic about reform, fearful of innovation and also of the wrath of the Emperor or Catholic princes. However, in few cities was there a concerted attempt to crush the Reformation. Overriding any question of religious zeal was the determination amongst most city councils to maintain the peace and their own positions. Lutherans were generally permitted to preach, as an attempt to prevent them could risk a riot.

When an attempt was made to replace Lutheran preachers, there could be difficulties other than popular opposition. In Strasbourg in 1523 the preacher Matthew Zell was dismissed, but only other Protestants could be found to replace him. Similarly, in Lubeck the council gave in to popular demands for preachers but could find no Catholic priests to fill the posts. There was little the city councils could do to help the Catholic Church when it was unable to help itself.

Gradually one city council after another gave in to popular demands for reform. First of all, the council would demand the preaching of the 'pure Word of God'. This was ambiguous as moderate Catholics could claim they wanted the same, but it does show the influence of *sola scriptura*, an emphasis on scriptural authority, and it was a signal that Protestant preachers would be given free rein. Ultimately, under mounting popular pressure, the council would not only tolerate Protestant worship but also declare the whole city reformed and Catholicism banned. This occurred even in Nuremberg, the most stable and authoritarian of cities, because, although there was little social tension, it was feared that the precious unity of the city might be threatened by religious strife. The formal occasion for the adoption of the Reformation was usually a disputation, when leading reformers and Catholic theologians would debate in front of the city magistrates – who would then declare that they had been convinced by the weight of the Protestants' arguments.

The timescale for this did differ considerably and depended much on the city's strategic position in relation to any neighbouring Catholic princes or the Emperor. Nuremberg's calm Reformation (master-minded by the humanist reformers, such as Lazarus Spengler, who ran the government) was one of the earliest, established in 1525. At the same time Strasbourg was less calm, experiencing pressure from much more radical guild members, but able to give in without fear of Catholic reprisals and even to provide refuge for some of the more extreme radicals, because it was on the borders between France and Germany and thus remote from imperial power. In Regensburg, even though Protestant ideas were widespread there as early as 1522, there was no formal Reformation until as late as 1542, for fear of neighbouring Catholics, the dukes of Bavaria.

The city councils were pushed towards Reformation by popular pressure but there were also advantages for them in giving in to it. It saw the completion of civic control of ecclesiastical affairs, which had been developing during the Middle Ages. For example in 1523, the city of Leisnig established a 'common chest', a treasury which handled the income from Church property and devoted it to charity. As well as these practical powers, Protestant preachers also reinforced the status of the magistrates, quoting scripture on the sanctity of the magistrates' office. The public image of city councils was much enhanced when they had accepted the Reformation, as they were then revered as the guardians of it.

Although the Reformation was established in this way in the majority of German cities, there were differences in the forms it developed, roughly along a north–south divide. In the north of Germany, in such cities as Stralsund, religious change was part of a democratic movement with citizen committees trimming the powers of the councils as well as forcing the introduction of the Reformation. The nature of the Reformation there was strictly Lutheran, with few independent-minded reformers.

In the south there tended to be much greater emphasis on the solidarity of the community as a whole, with the councils helping to impose strict religious discipline and organised charity. This is possibly because, as Thomas Brady has suggested in *Turning Swiss*, the cities of southern Germany were following the model of the Swiss cities. There were also reformers in the south who were not always prepared to toe the Lutheran line. For instance, Martin Bucer, active in Strasbourg from 1523, established not just a corps of Protestant preachers and teachers but also officials known as lay elders to discipline the faithful and deacons to look after social welfare. He was taking more social and political initiative than Luther allowed; Church and state were much more clearly separated by Luther. These reformers in the south were also influenced by the Swiss Zwingli who rejected various Lutheran doctrines, especially the idea of the physical presence of Christ in the Eucharist.

See pages 316–21

This variety and vitality in the urban Reformation was not to last. The cities found themselves caught between the Lutheran princes of the Schmalkaldic League and the Catholic princes led by the Emperor. With the victory of the Emperor at the Battle of Mühlberg in 1547, many cities lost their freedoms – Charles V abolished twenty-eight city constitutions and introduced 'trusty' small councils. When the Emperor was in turn defeated, the cities that did not remain Catholic found that they had to toe an orthodox Lutheran line instead. The popular element in the Reformation had finally given way to mass conformity as the age of the free city came to an end.

See pages 237–9

While it had lasted, the urban Reformation had followed a fairly consistent pattern – the arrival of a Protestant preacher and the circulation of Protestant literature, an enthusiastic popular response, the acceptance of the Reformation sooner or later by the city council, which then made it official after a disputation. There were broad variations in the pattern, as we have seen in the north–south divide. However, each city followed its particular path to the Reformation, and indeed a few cities, such as Cologne, remained Catholic. (The city council of Cologne identified with the fiercely Catholic university and the cathedral clergy were also a powerful force there; ironically the impulse for reform came most strongly from two archbishops of Cologne in the sixteenth century who turned Protestant and tried to take the city with them but failed.) There were also 2000 territorial cities, many of which must have seen lively variations in the people's experience of the Reformation, albeit under princely control.

KEY ISSUE

Was it only in the cities that the Reformation was truly popular?

Changing histories of the Reformation

ANALYSIS

The first historians of the Reformation, starting in the sixteenth century itself, were Protestants or Catholics writing the history of their own churches. Their concern was religious history. Then during the eighteenth century there was a reaction against conventional church histories. Enlightenment historians often characterised the Protestant reformers as liberals just like themselves, attacking the medieval superstition and power of the clergy. Church histories continued to be written (and still are) but this shift from the religious history to the political history of the Reformation was consolidated in the mid-nineteenth century in the work of Leopold von Ranke, seen by some as the first truly

See quote by Robert Watson pages 417–18

professional historian. He thought he could avoid the theories and prejudices of his age by scrupulous work in the archives rather than believing what he was told and by painstaking accumulation and open-minded assessment of the evidence. The questions he asked, however, still fashioned his view of the Reformation. He was most interested in high politics, in the decisions of princes and the debates in the Imperial Diet. His works were first read in Germany from the mid-nineteenth century onwards, at a time when nationalist fervour was mounting and Luther was seen as a hero of the German nation inspiring the princes to liberate their fatherland from foreign control.

The princes continued to take centre stage in explanation of the Reformation for a century after Ranke, right up to the 1960s. Then the German historian Bernd Moeller, followed by others such as the British A.G. Dickens, changed the focus from high politics to urban history, looking more to the great German cities for 'the creative and irrevocable events' in the development of Protestantism, especially in its early stages. In the cities were to be found the German humanists, as reformist preachers and city government officials. It was to cities that ordinary people came to hear about and argue through the new religious ideas. It was their clamour that then forced the Reformation upon their city councils and it was the cities' printing presses that spread Reformation ideas throughout Germany and beyond.

By the 1980s, however, the pioneering work of Robert Scribner and others opened up further areas of the social history of the Reformation. The presses were not just printing pamphlets for the literate. They also turned out woodcuts by the thousand which, as Scribner showed, were essential in adding to the words of popular preachers, modifying and transmitting the ideas of the Reformation to a largely illiterate population in the countryside as well as in the cities. The history of the Reformation is not just concerned with the literate élite but also with the peasants who adapted it to meet their own ideas and needs. But in the 1990s attention shifted once again to the princes, with historians such as R. Po-Chia Hsia examining the way in which they sought to impose social control on the peasants and townsfolk as part of the process of confessionalisation during the later sixteenth century and beyond. The historians of each succeeding generation bring new concerns and questions to bear on the significance of the Reformation.

10 ↫ THE REFORMATION AND THE PRINCES

Before the recent growth in studies of the cities, the princes of Germany were given the credit for introducing the Reformation. While they were of increasing importance in later years, they were slow to dedicate themselves to the cause in the 1520s. Even Frederick the Wise of Saxony, Luther's protector, did not clearly adopt Lutheranism himself until he was on his deathbed in 1525, and the non-committal Frederick had been Luther's only princely supporter in the first seven years of the Reformation.

This does not mean that princes were necessarily hostile to Luther and all he stood for. We saw earlier how the princes at the Diet of Worms turned as rapidly as possible from the Lutheran affair to their grievances against the Papacy. At the Diet of Nuremberg in 1523, they demanded more national control and 'the preaching of the pure Gospel according to true Christian understanding'. But they nearly all remained Catholic, unwilling to break completely from tradition or to risk conflict.

See pages 154–5

There were just three notable exceptions to this. In 1524 Luther's close associate, Philip Melanchthon, had managed to convert the 20-year-old Landgrave (i.e. Count) Philip of Hesse who was to be the most dynamic of Lutheran politicans. In 1525 the Elector Frederick's successor, John of Saxony, declared himself a firm Lutheran and the Electors of Saxony were to remain so for over two centuries. Also in 1525 the Grand Master of the Teutonic Order, a crusading order of knights in north-east Germany, converted to Lutheranism, secularised the order's estates and declared himself Duke Albrecht of Prussia. Eventually, over half of Germany was to be ruled by Lutheran princes – but it was nearly thirty years before that came about.

It is impossible to be completely certain how far individual faith caused any one prince to convert to Lutheranism. However, some historians have stressed the material gains involved. When a prince became Lutheran he would take over Church lands and use them for his own purposes. This does not necessarily indicate simple greed. Philip of Hesse used former monastic revenues to finance a new university at Marburg and to set up a hospital for the poor and sick at Haina. In all, sixty per cent of the revenues he acquired were spent on such charitable endeavours and much of the rest of it went on the upkeep of the Lutheran Church. In any case, an acquisitive prince could take over ecclesiastical revenues and yet remain a Catholic, as Ferdinand and Isabella demonstrated when they took control of the crusading orders of Spain.

Alongside the 'church lands' motive there was the expansion of the prince's sovereign powers. When a prince adopted Lutheranism he no longer had to share his authority with Pope or bishops, and his defiance of the Catholic Emperor further demonstrated his independence. This was part of the development of the Early Modern state, not yet the secular state of modern times but no longer the medieval state with its recognition of universal authorities such as Pope and Emperor. The princes of Germany were not to make themselves completely free of imperial authority but Luther had assured them of their sovereign importance when it came to religion in his *Address to the Christian Nobility of the German Nation* in 1520. Luther had declared that Church and state were separate, but in fact that served the prince's authority. The Church had no right of interference in secular affairs while the prince had a duty to maintain good order in the Church and to supervise its activities as a matter of paternal concern for his subjects.

The duty of supervising the Church, and the power it gave to the prince, was a positive inducement to convert to Lutheranism. More negative was fear of religious strife. In the sixteenth century, toleration was regarded as a sign of weakness rather than as a virtue – heresy was tantamount to treason and could easily lead to civil war. To maintain civil peace it was felt that the people had to be of one religion, the prince's religion. This led to conservatism, a reluctance to adopt what might be heresy. However, as Protestantism spread amongst the people of Germany, and Catholicism seemed incapable of standing up to it, the balance shifted and it became the safe policy for many princes to become Lutheran. Before making any move, however, most princes would be very sensitive to the opinions of their parliament or Estates, upon whom they depended for support and taxes. There was an alternative, the systematic suppression of Protestantism and the Estates as undertaken by the dukes of Bavaria, but it often seemed more risky than defying the Emperor, given the threat of popular disturbances.

It was not difficult to defy the Emperor as he was regularly distracted by his commitments in other parts of Europe and the Mediterranean. For instance, he could not be present at the Diet of Speyer in 1526 as he was in Spain, concerned with the new hostile League of Cognac led by France. Even his brother, Ferdinand, who had special responsibilities in Germany, was keeping an anxious eye on the Ottoman invasion of neighbouring Hungary. This meant that Philip of Hesse and John of Saxony could attend the Diet of Speyer in 1526, sporting Lutheran lapel badges with impunity. The princes as a whole could not agree to enforce the Edict of Worms against Luther, so the only conclusion was that each prince should conduct himself 'as answerable to God and to His Imperial Majesty'. This gave no right to reform but was a great encouragement to it none the less.

Despite this lack of decisive action by the Emperor, however, the reformed princes were worried about possible aggressive action by Catholic princes. In 1525, the League of Dessau had been set up, bringing Catholic princes together, including Duke George of Saxony, the cousin and rival of the Elector. In response, in 1526 Philip of Hesse and John of Saxony joined the Lutheran League of Torgau along with princes from Brunswick-Lüneburg, Brunswick-Grubenhagen, Mecklenburg, Anhalt-Zerbst and others. Unfortunately, these minor princes rejoiced in long names rather than powerful armies, so the Lutherans felt no security. In 1528 war almost broke out owing to the Pack affair:

Pack, Duke George's vice-chancellor, leaked false details of a Catholic attack, which prompted a pre-emptive strike by Philip of Hesse and John of Saxony. When the error was realised, Philip got the blame, as it was thought that he had been trying to force John into an attack in spite of the latter's wish to restrict the League of Torgau to a defensive purpose. The Catholics were outraged. Their fears that Lutheranism could only lead to conflict seemed to have been confirmed and they demanded that it be eradicated.

In 1529 at the Diet of Speyer the Catholic princes called for a halt to reform and for Catholicism not to be hindered anywhere, although they saved their most aggressive words for the Zwinglians and other 'debasers of the sacraments'. The response to this was the Protestation, from which Protestantism took its name: 'In matters relating to God's honour and the soul's felicity each must stand before God and answer for himself.' The Protestants on this occasion were Philip of Hesse, John of Saxony, four other princes and the delegates of fourteen cities.

The Emperor's response to the Protestation was initially muted. He was on his way back to Germany and a far more immediate problem in 1529 was the fact that the Ottomans, who had destroyed the kingdom of Hungary in 1526, were now at the gates of Vienna. However, his position was stronger in 1530. The Ottoman siege of Vienna had been unsuccessful, peace with France had been renewed in 1529 and in 1530 the Pope had submitted so far as finally to crown Charles as Emperor. On the Protestant side, Philip of Hesse's grand vision of an alliance stretching from France to Transylvania had come to nothing, while John of Saxony continued to insist only on a defensive stance. Some Protestant powers, especially Nuremberg, declared that they had no right to resist the Emperor at all. Charles had decided that the time had come to settle the Lutheran question once and for all.

Charles invited the Lutherans to present their beliefs to a Diet at Augsburg in 1530. It was the diplomatic Melanchthon who prepared the Lutheran statement of belief, called the Confession of Augsburg. Melanchthon steered clear of contentious issues, such as the status of the Pope, and concentrated on points such as clergy being allowed to marry, on which he hoped there could be agreement. But however impressive the common ground, the two sides were not to be reconciled. Luther, observing the Diet from a place of safety a few miles away, did not approve of compromise, as for him it was a matter of pure and simple truth. Likewise, the Catholic theologians were not going to paper over the cracks – their rejection of the Confession, known as the Confutation of Augsburg, was accepted by the Emperor. It looked as though the question could only be resolved by war.

In 1531 the Protestants prepared themselves by forming the Schmalkaldic League. Luther, always reluctant to oppose a secular ruler, at last gave his personal approval to resistance to the Emperor. However, there was to be no war as yet – the Emperor once again found himself preoccupied by the Ottoman threat and a truce (the Nuremberg Standstill) was agreed in 1532. For the next twenty years there was to be much jockeying for position between princes and

See Chapter 11

TIMELINE

1522 Knights' War
1524 Peasants' War
–25
1525 Elector Frederick dies
     Catholic League of Dessau formed
1526 Lutheran League of Torgau
     First Diet of Speyer
1528 Pack affair
1529 Second Diet of Speyer – the Protestation

     Siege of Vienna by Turks
1530 Diet of Augsburg
1531 Foundation of Schmalkaldic League
1532 Nuremberg Standstill
1555 Peace of Augsburg

See Chapter 8

PROFILE

See page 321

LANDGRAVE PHILIP OF HESSE (1504–67)

Philip ruled over Hesse, an important territory in western Germany, and from 1525 dedicated his career to furthering the cause of the Reformation. He was a tireless organiser, bringing together leagues of Protestants in Germany, urging on his more cautious partners such as the Electors of Saxony, and sending envoys as far afield as England, France, Venice and even Turkey in search of allies. He tried to unify the reforming party, bringing together the rival theologians, Luther and Zwingli, at the Colloquy of Marburg in 1529, to persuade them to reach a compromise, although without success. In 1534 he struck a significant blow against the Habsburgs when he led the campaign to restore the Protestant Duke Ulrich of Württemberg to his territories in south-west Germany. His dynamism was crucial to the political and military success of the Reformation.

But it is not just modern politicians whose private lives can compromise their public achievements. Philip was unhappily married to Christina of Saxony and had fallen in love with Margaret von der Saal. Unwilling to commit adultery, he consulted Luther, who surprisingly advised him to take Margaret as his second wife, arguing that bigamy was not forbidden by scripture. The marriage took place in secret in 1540, but the news soon leaked out and the result was moral outrage. Support for Philip melted away, and he was forced to come to terms with the Emperor. However, relations deteriorated again from 1542 onwards when Philip returned to the attack, seizing the territories of the Catholic Duke Henry of Brunswick-Wolfenbüttel. When the Emperor saw his chance in 1547 he attacked the Protestant princes, taking first Elector John Frederick of Saxony and then Philip into custody. Philip was released in 1552 and returned to Hesse to continue the reform of the Church, but he was no longer the leading figure in Reformation politics he had once been. He gave assistance to Protestants in the Netherlands and France as the religious wars began in those countries, still trying and still failing to unite the forces of the Reformation. He died in 1567.

KEY ISSUE

How far did the Reformation become purely a political issue once the princes had taken over?

Emperor until the final reckoning of the Peace of Augsburg in 1555. There the princes won the right to decide whether their territories were to be Lutheran or Catholic, a principle known by a Latin phrase *cuius regio...eius religio* (his territory, his religion). The Reformation was by now definitely princely, rather than popular. How far this could foster genuine Lutheranism will be examined in the next section. However, it is clear that Lutheranism could not have survived without princely protection against hostile forces. There again, as Fischer-Galati has

MAP 10

Germany divided, 1555

shown, the Ottoman threat conditioned the success of the Lutherans, taking the pressure off them at almost every critical moment. This did not escape Luther's notice – the cause of God could be served by the unwitting Infidel as well as by Christian princes.

11 ∽ THE LUTHERAN CHURCH AND CONFESSIONALISATION

In the end, Luther had to rely on the princes to organise and protect a new, reformed Church. This involved a double disappointment for him. He had assumed that the changes he had demanded would entail the reform of the old Church rather than the creation of a new one. By the end of the 1520s it was clear that the Church was in schism (split) for the foreseeable future – a new Lutheran Church now existed in rivalry with the old Church of Rome and later in rivalry with other Protestant Churches. The separate Lutheran Church had come into existence almost by default. Each of the rival churches, with their own confessions of faith, were staking out their territory, a process known as confessionalisation.

The other side to Luther's disappointment related to the organisation of the Church. At first he had laid down that 'a congregation which has the Gospel must and should choose and call from amongst itself someone to teach the Word on its behalf'. However, in too many cases the people clung to their old ways and their old, unconverted Catholic priests. Or, more immediately dangerous to the Lutheran Reformation, the people went too far, turning to the *schwärmerei*, the 'dreamers' or extremist sectarians who seemed to Luther to be about to destroy the Reformation before it had become established. Even where a minister was doctrinally reliable, he sometimes demanded too much independence from the secular authorities, as was shown by complaints from city councils such as Speyer where Lutheran ministers were seen to be as arrogant in asserting their authority as Catholic priests. (Indeed, amongst a sample of 176 Lutheran ministers investigated by Scribner, three-quarters had formerly been Catholic priests.) Where Luther had hoped there could be freedom and spontaneous Christian brotherhood, there had to be discipline.

The first step was to organise visitations, inspections of parishes to check up on preaching and the conduct of services. Also, the people were questioned on articles of faith to see how much they understood. The first visitation to be carried out in Saxony was underway by 1527. The results horrified Luther. In 1529 he wrote, 'Men have been hearing the pure Word for ten years now but they act as though nothing had changed.' Steps were taken to remedy this. Officials known as superintendents were appointed to act as permanent inspectors. In 1532 church authorities were formally established in Saxony, with most responsibility vested in visitation committees made up of theologians and lawyers appointed by the prince and given the job of examining ministers and their progress in the parishes. This system was adopted in most Lutheran principalities. It could be taken to extremes, as in a 1544 visitation in Württemberg where pastors and local officials were invited to inform on one another.

The quality of pastors was gradually improved, and they became a university-trained, professional class. However, they were socially exclusive, if not in the same way as the Catholic clergy – a sample of clergy in Württemberg shows that sixty-three per cent were the sons of pastors, and they were very much under the thumb of the state. The universities they had trained in had largely lost their autonomy to princely control, and they themselves were in effect becoming officials of the state bureaucracy.

Through such state control, discipline was established and the flexible boundaries between Churches – in parts of Westphalia Catholics and Protestants had even shared the same church buildings – were turned into rigid lines of division with no compromise allowed. But, although social élites mostly worked together with princes, this tightened control neither inspired greater zeal nor remedied the problems that had horrified Luther in 1529. In comparison, the Calvinist system was to be much more dynamic, bringing ministers closely into cooperation with each other and with the lay elders, the

See pages 335–7

leaders of their congregations. Another contrast was to be seen in Denmark where the Lutheran Reformation was established by the 1530s, and in Sweden from the 1540s. There it was found necessary to retain bishops for church government to be properly managed – and, of course, to serve the interests of the state.

Neither Calvinist organisation nor Lutheran bishops could maintain perfect unity in their churches but the loosely organised Lutherans of north Germany were to split into factions in the generation after Luther's death in 1546. The Philippists, the followers of the more liberal Philip Melanchthon, were bitterly opposed by the Gnesio-Lutherans, the followers of the much more uncompromising Flacius Illyricus. As one faction gained the upper hand over the other, Lutheran ministers were required to show their understanding and acceptance of the 'correct' position or face disciplinary action. This factional competition greatly disrupted the work of the Lutheran clergy, and even when a compromise was reached in the Formula of Concord, finally adopted in 1580, it was more a formal unity, indicating confessionalisation, than the spontaneous sense of common purpose which had been so strong in the early years of the Reformation.

The various visitations and inspections of the Lutheran Church were not just concerned with the conduct of the clergy and their ability to state the accepted dogma, but also with the knowledge of the people. Lutheran schools had been set up to spread literacy so that the scriptures could be read and the main articles of the faith understood. Gerald Strauss has shown how limited in effect Lutheran teaching methods were. The visitation records for later in the sixteenth century show little optimism about the impact of Lutheran ideas upon ordinary people. In Geislingen the people showed 'contempt for the sermon, catechism and the Lord's Supper, also sacrilegious behaviour on the Sabbath . . . they open their shops on Sunday and do their buying and selling as though we had no divine and secular laws against these sins'. In the countryside around Hamburg the inspectors found 'unbelievable self-indulgent wickedness and contempt for preaching, for the holy sacraments'. At the time of the Peasants' War many of the people had adapted Lutheranism to their own needs, or a muddle of Catholic beliefs survived – church bells were rung to ward off storms, however much the pastor might complain of such Catholic superstition, and there is one extraordinary example of a much revered relic of Luther, a miraculously incombustible image of him. Whether they were clinging in this way to the remnants of Catholic belief or were simply indifferent, Strauss concludes that Lutheran indoctrination of the people was a failure.

Like so many other movements Lutheranism suffered from 'routinisation', the exhaustion of early enthusiasm and its replacement by dull routine procedures. However, despite all the weaknesses of the Lutheran Church as an institution, Lutheranism had made an indelible impact on the history of Early Modern Europe. The medieval Church had been undermined. By the later sixteenth century, seven out of every ten inhabitants of the Holy Roman Empire were at least officially

Lutheran. Even though Lutheranism itself was largely confined to Germany and Scandinavia the initial split in the Church led to the development of other Protestant churches and reactions within Catholicism. The Lutheran protest had contributed to popular turmoil in Germany in the 1520s and substantial changes in the cities. The constitution of the Holy Roman Empire, the looseness and tensions within which had allowed for the spread of Lutheranism in the first place, was permanently affected by the religious divisions amongst princes and cities. In Europe as a whole, little in the way of intellectual attitudes, diplomacy, ecclesiastical or social policy was left unaffected by Luther's challenge.

> **KEY ISSUE**
>
> *In what ways did the Lutheran Church change in the later Reformation?*

12 ↬ BIBLIOGRAPHY

**K. Randell, *Luther and the German Reformation, 1517–55* (Hodder and Stoughton, 1988) and *M. Mullett, *Luther* (Lancaster Pamphlet, 1987) are the best introductions to the topic. *A. Johnston, *History at Source: The Reformation in Europe* (Hodder and Stoughton, 1997) contains an excellent range of documents. **Euan Cameron, *The European Reformation* (Clarendon, 1991) is the best, most complete recent overview. S. Ozment, *The Age of Reform* (Yale, 1980) is best on the background to the Reformation. **R.W. Scribner, *The German Reformation* (Macmillan, 1986) summarises more recent approaches to the Reformation and his *Varieties of Reformation* (Historical Association Pamphlet, 1994) corrects the excessive emphasis on Luther and shows the many-sided nature of the movement. *Alister McGrath, *The Intellectual Origins of the European Reformation* (Blackwell, 1987) is the most accessible account of the theology. *The Early Reformation in Europe*, ed. Andrew Pettigree (CUP, 1992) shows how the Reformation varied in its form and impact from country to country.

13 ↬ STRUCTURED AND ESSAY QUESTIONS

A *Structured questions.*
1. (a) Who supported Luther during the early Reformation and who opposed him?
   (b) Why were the Catholic Church and the Emperor unable to crush the Reformation in Germany?
2. (a) What was the role of the German princes in the Reformation?
   (b) 'The Reformation could only really take root in the cities.' Discuss.

B *Essay questions.*
1. How revolutionary was Luther?
2. 'Luther lost control of the Reformation almost as soon as it had begun.' Discuss.

3. How far was the Reformation more a princely than a popular movement?
4. 'Without the work done by Erasmus and other humanists, Lutheranism could never have developed.' Do you agree?
5. Why did the Reformation begin in Germany?

Advice: *Constructing an argument*

It is important to construct an argument before you start writing an essay. This will help you to avoid lapsing into narrative, and will give your essay a clear sense of direction. Your argument should build from relevant point to relevant point without contradiction or repetition.

Consider the question 'How revolutionary was Luther?' At first sight that is not an easy question because 'revolutionary' is not a word with one precise meaning. You might be tempted to write an answer simply summarising what Luther did and leave the reader to make up his or her own mind. However, an essay is a test of your judgement. If you are methodical it is not difficult to develop your own case. Try the following procedure:

(i) Break down the question into component parts, which could form the basis of your plan. In this case they might include:

How revolutionary was Luther with regard to:

- doctrine?
- government of the church?
- politics?
- society?

(ii) In just a couple of sentences, jot down a summary answer to each of the component questions. One sentence could state whether Luther *intended* to be revolutionary in the sense of breaking away from medieval tradition.

Another sentence could suggest whether or not he had a revolutionary *effect*, whatever his intention.

Take into account how far Luther's position changed as the Reformation developed.

(iii) You can sharpen your argument through comparison. Think through what your answers to the component questions would have been if the subject had been Erasmus or Müntzer. By reference to other reformers you can put Luther into perspective.

(iv) Now review your short answers in order to come up with your overall argument.

A good argument has to be clear and consistent but it does not need to be dogmatic. You might take the view that Luther was revolutionary in some ways and not in others. You could argue that his protest had far more revolutionary effects than he had ever intended. Remember that element of change – it could be that Luther became more or less revolutionary as the years went by.

(v)   As you write your essay bear in mind the following:

- The first sentence of each paragraph should be a point relating directly to the question and advancing the argument which you have thought out. In the rest of the paragraph you can then present the evidence which supports or extends your point.
- As you write you should be refining your argument, dealing with any exceptions or differing points of view.

14 ⌐ SOURCE EXERCISE ON WOODCUTS IN THE REFORMATION

See pages 164–5

In *For the Sake of Simple Folk* Robert Scribner examined woodcuts, the political cartoons of the sixteenth century, to explore the images of the Reformation that would have been accessible to those who were illiterate or had little experience of theological arguments. Although some woodcuts were designed by leading artists such as Cranach and Holbein, Scribner likened their impact to 'homemade gin: cheap, crude and effective'; they clearly played an important role in creating popular support for Luther. Scribner and other historians have emphasised the distinction between the complexities of what Luther stood for and how some of his supporters (let alone his enemies) interpreted what he was saying. Woodcuts provide vital clues as to how Luther was perceived by the mass of ordinary people, popular Lutheranism, as opposed to the official Lutheranism which historians used to think was the only story.

Source A This contrasts Christ ascending to heaven with the Pope tormented by monsters, plunging into hell.

CHRISTVS.   ANTICHRISTVS.

SOURCE A
(Picture 12) Two woodcuts from Passional Christi und Antichristi *by Lucas Cranach the Elder, 1521*

Source B Luther is pictured as the classical hero Hercules, with the Pope slung alongside the skin of a lion as a trophy around his neck. He is bludgeoning the theological and philosophical authorities of the Middle Ages.

Source C Monsters and visions from the Bible's prophetic *Book of Revelation* had passed into popular mythology (and have remained there, as is evident in numerous horror movies). One such monster was the seven-headed beast of the apocalypse. The Pope and other Catholic clergy are shown as the beast, seated on the kingdom of the devil seen here as a locked chest as used by indulgence sellers, with the devil crawling from underneath. A papal bull authorising indulgences hangs on the cross, along with the instruments used to torment Christ.

SOURCE B
(Picture 13) Luther as Hercules Germanicus *by Hans Holbein the Younger, 1528*

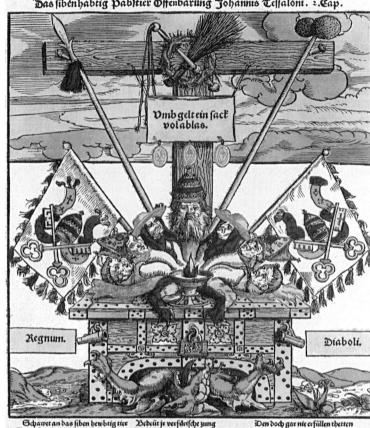

Das siben habtig Pabstier Offenbarung Johannis Tessaloni. 2.Cap.

Vmb gelt ein sack vol ablas.

Regnum.   Diaboli.

Schawet an das siben hewbtig tier   Bedeüt je verfürische zung   Den doch gar nie erfüllen thetten
Gantz eben der gstalt vnd manier   Das thier was aim pardel gleich   2 pies/pallium noch annatten
Wie Johannes gesehen hat   Bedeüt des Bapst mördische reich   Bann/opfer/peicht/stifft zů Gotsdiensi
Ein tier an des meres gstat   Das auch hinricht durch tiranney   Land vnd leüt Künigreich rent vñ zinst
Das hat siben vngleicher haubt   Alles was jm entgegen sey   Das es alles hat in sich verschlunden
Eben wie diß pabstier gelaubt   Auch so hat das thier peren füß   Das thier entpfieng ain tödlich wunden
Die waren all gekrönt bedewt   Deüt das das Euangelé fülß   Deüt das Doctor Martin hat gschriben
Die blatten der gaistlichen lewt   Ist von dem bastum vndertretten   Das bapstum tödlich wund gebliben
Das thier das het auch zehen horen   Verschart/verdeckt vñ zerknetten   Mit dem otten des Herren mund
Deüt der gastlig gwalt vñ ennoten   Das thier het auch aine löwen mund   Gott geb das es gar gee zů grund.
Das thier trüg Gottes lesterung   Bedeüt deß bapstum weiten schlund   Amen.

SOURCE C
(Picture 14) The seven-headed papal revelation, *artist unknown, c. 1530*

Source D Johann Tetzel is seen carrying the Bull of Indulgence in his right hand as he encourages ordinary Germans to hand over their money to him. The last two lines in the verse shown translate as 'As soon as gold in the basin rings, Right then the soul to heaven springs.' Instead of a horse, Tetzel is riding a monstrous hybrid and a vulture circles above his head in place of the dove representing the Holy Spirit.

Source E This shows a monk perhaps about to give alms to a widow and her child. Then a first flap lifted reveals the monk to be no shepherd tending his flock but a wolf eating a sheep. The lifting of a second flap shows the monk eating money, rather than giving it in alms.

Source F Luther is shown in the pulpit pointing to Christ on the Cross and the simple Protestant rite of the Eucharist, with only Christ and the symbol of the sacrificial lamb on the Communion table. The

O jhr deutschen mercket mich recht/
Des heiligen Vaters Papstes Knecht/
Bin ich/vnd bring euch jtzt allein/
Zehn tausent vnd neun hundert carein/
Gnad vnd Ablaß von einer Sünd/
Vor euch/ewer Eltern/Weib vnd Kind/
Sol ein jeder gewehret sein
So viel jhr legt ins Kästelein/
So bald der Gülden im Becken klingt/
Im huy die Seel im Himel springt/

SOURCE D
(Picture 15) Johann Tetzel,
*anonymous contemporary
caricature*

SOURCE E
(Picture 16) Monkish
covertousness, *artist
unknown, 16th century*

SOURCE F

(Picture 17) The supper of the Evangelicals and the damnation of the Papists *by Lucas Cranach the Younger, 1540*

SOURCE G

(Picture 18) The Pope as a wild man
by Melchior Lorch, 1545

faithful receive Communion in both kinds, i.e. bread and wine, from ministers dressed simply, without elaborate vestments. The group in the centre is receiving the wine, which had been reserved for the clergy alone in the Catholic rite. Meanwhile Luther looks down on the Pope and the Catholic clergy cast down into the gaping, flaming jaws of hell, depicted as a monster.

Source G Here the wild man, a terrifying creature of popular mythology, wearing the papal tiara and holding the key of St Peter, spews out poisonous creatures to plague the earth.

Q

1. *Which of these woodcuts are likely to have been intended for a more educated audience? Which would have been most readily understood by a mass audience?*
2. *Why do monsters figure so prominently in these woodcuts?*
3. *'Popular woodcuts show that it was anti-clericalism, and particularly resentment of the Church seizing Germany's wealth, which galvanised support for Luther far more than a positive understanding of the new doctrines he preached.' Discuss this comment with reference to these sources and your wider knowledge.*

7 Popular culture, gender and the witch hunts

OVERVIEW

Popular culture is one of the newer areas of research by historians. There has been academic interest in folklore since the eighteenth century but customs, rituals or tales of the past were then studied for their romantic cultural value or even merely for their quaintness, rather than to find out their original meaning. Since the beginning of the twentieth century, historians have been examining popular culture as the key to past ways of thought. Some social historians are still sceptical; for them it is the material conditions of life that really matter. However, borrowing from the ideas of anthropologists, who are used to studying societies with ways of thought alien to our own, more and more has been done to piece together the beliefs, values and basic concepts of ordinary people in the past.

These all-embracing ways of thought of past peoples are generally known as *mentalités*, the name given to them by the French historians who pioneered their study. The study of *mentalités* tells us about people's values in the past, how they related to religion, nature and each other. It is connected with the rituals that gave communities a sense of identity, some solemn, some riotously celebratory. It shows how those communities, through the force of custom, policed the activity of individuals. It includes gender, the different roles assigned to women and to men, and sexuality – so much that is thought simply to be 'natural' actually has a cultural aspect and changes through time or from place to place.

Popular culture and beliefs were at the heart of the way people conducted their lives, how they felt about them and sometimes how they died. Le Roy Ladurie has shown us how a carnival could be used for upper-class plotting and massacre at Romans in 1580, and the witch hunts which had swept across much of Europe by the end of the sixteenth century are a dramatic example of how the culture of the learned could interact with that of the people to disastrous effect. Much of popular culture, however, concerns communities coming together and expressing their solidarity. The locations for shared ideas and entertainments might be the church, the tavern or the home, or the streets.

1 ∽ POPULAR CULTURE IN THE CHURCH BEFORE THE REFORMATION

The Church might seem to be the classic example of the learned élite imposing its culture on the people. However, in many ways the people used the church physically and symbolically for their own purposes.

Church ceremonies eased people through the transitions of life from birth (baptism) to death (the last rites and the funeral). A woman who had just given birth was thought to be ritually 'polluted' until she was re-introduced into the community through a special blessing known as 'churching'. There was an 'art of dying' to cope with the final, traumatic hours of life, contemplating the Virgin and the saints. For those left behind, collective mourning, with the tearing of clothes and wailing, may have been a more effective ritual way of dealing with loss than the repressed, private grief which is thought more tasteful in much of the modern world.

Church services also followed the seasonal calendar, which governed agricultural communities to help to ensure fertility. During the rogation days in the Spring, when buds could still easily be devastated by frost or storms, the priest would lead his congregation in procession around the parish 'beating the bounds', calling on God's protection for those within the bounds.

The church was frequently adorned with gargoyles. They could be a functional part of the guttering but they also served to ward off the malevolent natural spirits that inhabited the mental universe of the people. The graveyard around the church was not just consecrated land where the dead could lie in peace. It was an open space to be used for dancing and for sports, a practice condemned by sixteenth-century reformers. Within the church there was not necessarily the reverential hush that we might expect today. There were no pews and angry reformers have again left us a picture of a congregation wandering around, gossiping and even playing with their dogs during a service. A congregation was not simply disciplined and passive.

This does not mean that the people discounted religion. Indeed, Lucien Febvre in *The Problem of Unbelief* doubted whether atheism was conceptually possible before modern philosophy and science, the word atheist in the sixteenth century being an insult rather than a genuine description of anyone. However, this view is now thought too sweeping – there were at least a few humanists, under the influence of some classical authors, who doubted the immortality of the soul or were generally sceptical about religion. There were also occasional protests by individual peasants or artisans that the whole of religion was just a money-making racket. Nonetheless the expression of such views was rare, either because Febvre was broadly right, because of fear of the consequent outrage, or because church services gave an identity and security to the community. In any case official church teaching could be given a twist by popular interpretation.

In the fifteenth century, the holy family had been much promoted as an object of veneration. However, Joseph was popularly viewed as a figure of fun. He was seen as a cuckold – Jesus was not his child – and many a joke was cracked about his lack of virility. What was being reinforced in this popular humour was the biological and social role of the father. In the decoration of a crib at Christmas, a practice that had grown in popularity since the thirteenth century, the vulnerability of the baby Jesus at his birth was emphasised and along with it the need to care for the young. The cultural trappings of the holy family served to reinforce the norms of family life.

The saints in general gave expression to popular culture as well as to official theology. The Feast of St John falls in midsummer and was celebrated with great bonfires, the Fires of St John, especially in northern Europe where the lengthened days of the season were of such importance. The night before a saint's festival was an opportunity for eating and drinking which could last the whole night through. These were called wakes, when time was turned around and night became day. Such celebrations were part of the making of holy days into holidays which acted as markers amidst the ordinary time of the year. Taking into account Sundays as well as the number of such holidays, the ordinary time for working was actually limited to just 200 days during the year.

Churchmen were not separated off from popular culture. They exploited it, as in the church at Augsburg where popular drama was used, which even included stage machinery with an angelic figure being lowered through the roof. A variant of their own was the Feast of Fools when the clergy would perform mock church services, leading an ass dressed up on holy vestments around the church. Such a performance was not intended as a mockery of church services but as comic relief, to allow due seriousness to be sustained for the rest of the year. When the Feast of Fools came under attack during the fifteenth century, one French cleric defended it using the metaphor of a wine barrel needing air holes to stop it exploding.

Popular culture in the church was made out of the materials of official religion, but something new was also created. The norms of traditional society were reinforced, and celebrations, acting as a safety valve, could make ordinary life more acceptable and stable. This was so at least until the reformers, both Catholic and Protestant, took control in the sixteenth century.

> **KEY ISSUE**
>
> *How far was the Church responsible for forming popular culture?*

2 ⇝ TALES IN THE TAVERN OR THE HOME

> ***veillée*** a gathering to gossip or tell stories while engaged in sedentary work

Inside the tavern or the home, or at the ***veillée*** in France when women sewed and men sharpened their scythes, there took place the joking and the gossip now lost to the historian. However, there were also the bards or ballad singers, some of whose traditional stories – variations on stock characters and situations made recognisable by standard phrases about dying heroes or forlorn lovers – finally found their way into print. Such stories can tell us much about the *mentalités*, the values and fears of the society that responded to them.

One such tale, transmitted in taverns or simply retold at home or at the *veillée* and known in over a hundred versions in Germany, France and elsewhere, is that of Aschenputtel, or Cinderella as she has become known. The story is made up of five standard elements: abuse by relatives (the wicked stepmother and stepsisters); supernatural assistance (the fairy godmother); meeting with the hero (the prince); the recognition test (the fitting of the slipper) and marriage to the hero. These elements could be varied according to the creative skill of the performer and the liking of the audience. The recognition test, for instance, could be the fitting of a slipper, the wearing of a ring or the plucking of an apple. The idea of a recognition test itself floats from story to story, turning up in King Arthur and the sword in the stone, for example. In Cinderella however, the recognition test reflects the anxiety about a woman being matched up with a suitable husband, which is why matchmakers were to be found in some societies. In the variation where only Cinderella could pluck the apples, having been starved by her stepmother, there surfaced the peasant fear of malnutrition. Remarriage was frowned upon in Early Modern society – hence the 'wicked stepmother and stepsisters' element. Involved in this is a universal emotional problem of the stepmother being seen as an intruder into the family circle. But it was also a matter of property settlements and dowries and deciding who should have precedence. Behind every fanciful tale there were the emotional and material realities of life.

Robin Hood, one of a number of outlaw heroes in the different regions of Europe, was already popular enough by 1405 for a Franciscan friar to complain about people listening to rhymes about him in preference to going to Mass. Historians have debated whether he actually existed. He may have just been an offshoot of courtly romance or he may have been a historic outlaw, a primitive **social rebel** acting as a nucleus for a series of legends which grew in the re-telling, rather like the later American hero, Jesse James. If he did exist, it is likely that he operated in Barnesdale in Yorkshire in the early fourteenth century rather than Sherwood Forest in the late twelfth century, which is where later tradition and modern films have placed him. However, the reality of Robin Hood is of less importance than his impact on the popular imagination.

social rebel identified by the élite as a criminal, by the people as a hero fighting oppression

Robin's adventures took place in the greenwood. The contrast of his life there with that of a settled village or town was the eternal contrast of nature against culture. In this he merges with 'the green man', the personification of nature, who, however, suffers the fate of nature being subdued by culture when his image is caged and then burnt. Robin's representation of nature also helped him to acquire Maid Marion as the legend developed, her role being identified with that of the queen of the May. More specifically, Robin Hood was free of legal restraints, flouting

KEY ISSUE

What insights can peasants' tales give us into their concerns and priorities and in what ways must the historian be cautious in his analysis?

yeomen a small landowner

the strict forest laws that prevented peasants from hunting and taking advantage of the abundance of nature.

In *Robin Hood and the Monk* a religious element is added. Christ is referred to as 'hym that dyed on a tre', identifying him with the forest, and Robin, relying on the 'myght of milde Marye', risks all in showing his outlaw's face in church in order to attend Mass. Religion seemed to be the property of the Church rather than the people and that could always breed resentment, if only occasionally actual heresy. In his guise as a social rebel Robin also stood up to financial exploitation by the Church. The earliest villain was not Prince John or the Sheriff of Nottingham but the Abbot of St Mary's.

Tales of Robin Hood would seem to offer clear insights into popular culture. Historians, however, are uncertain as to the original audience and authorship for these ballads. There are aristocratic elements in the tales but it seems likely that **yeomen** and their minstrels were responsible for them, that is, small landowners rather than the peasants who made up the mass of people. This is another case where the boundary between popular and élite culture is blurred.

ANALYSIS

Class and the origins of popular culture

Debates about many specific aspects of popular culture thrive but the central issue for many historians is that of class. Robert Mandrou has studied the stories and songs in the cheap booklets read by the minority of literate peasants but presumably also read aloud in taverns. He reckons that it was an escapist culture full of futile beliefs and miraculous occurrences imposed by the dominant classes in order to keep the people quiet. For Geneviève Bollème this same literature shows the basic concepts of the people with regard to life and death, freedom and oppression; in her view the people developed their own culture. Peter Burke in his *Popular Culture in Early Modern Europe* stresses that élite culture and popular culture did not occupy watertight compartments. A courtly display, such as the masque, could have its origins in popular entertainment. Classically inspired poets such as Ariosto were published in shortened versions for popular consumption. Anyway, the ruling classes joined in popular culture, singing the songs, telling the tales and processing in the carnival until the eighteenth century, when the idea of what was 'vulgar' and to be avoided really took hold. Roger Chartier in turn has emphasised that it is the reception of a custom or story that matters more than its origin – it can be transformed when integrated into a new social setting. He calls this forging of something new from a jumble of different sources *bricolage*. One example would be the way in which official Church rituals were re-worked into popular culture.

Whether peasants or small landowners, those who shaped popular culture were responsive to the events of the larger world. When Gaston de Foix was killed at the Battle of Ravenna in 1512 ballads sprang up about him, transmitting the news of his life and death. However, when news was assimilated into popular culture a pattern was often imposed on it. The ballads about Gaston de Foix were reworkings of those about King Rodrigo, the heroic fighter against the Moors of centuries before. Likewise, Louis XII of France was celebrated for his relatively peaceful, prosperous and just reign in the early sixteenth century; but Louis XII was also benefiting from the favoured place in ballads of St Louis, a predecessor as King of France. In popular culture, names carried a magnetic quality. The Emperor Frederick had inspired many tales of his return from sleep in a mountain in order to save Germany (another theme which crops up in the King Arthur legends); this could be seen as prophetic of the Elector Frederick of Saxony saving Germany by protecting Luther. The mass of people were aware of current events and politics mostly through the matrix of popular culture.

If anything was to alter that matrix of popular culture, it was printing. Printing fixed tales in a permanent form when previously they had gone through as many variations as there were story-tellers. Alien ideas, whether from another class or another region brought in by the *colporteurs*, the travelling salesmen of cheap booklets, could weaken the local tradition, but popular culture survived. Even into the twentieth century, folklorists have collected tales quite distinct from any printed versions.

Mentalités

ANALYSIS

A problem with the study of popular belief systems or *mentalités* is the difficulty of being precise. They are not like events with a set of causes and consequences. It is hard to categorise *mentalités*, saying where one ends and another begins through the years or from one region to another, because there are problems with the evidence – a folk tale known in 1700 may well have already been current in 1500 or earlier, but it will remain uncertain. Also there are 'middle-men' to beware of, the literate observers who reported the visual events of a sixteenth-century carnival or wrote down a tale which may have circulated orally for centuries. They may not have understood what was going on and so garbled the evidence. The historian has to try and reconstruct the way of thought of a largely illiterate society through literary means. That is why many judgements are less certain and generalisations more tentative than in other areas of historical study.

3 ↬ RITUALS ON THE STREETS

Rituals are not confined to religion. In different forms they structure much of everyday life. For instance, a kiss is not just a kiss – it can be a sign of profound commitment. In the Middle Ages a vassal did homage to his lord by kissing him full on the lips, although this had largely disappeared by 1500, possibly because it was increasingly seen as something sexual. The parties to a peace settlement, however, still kissed each other on the cheek, an action derived from the kiss of peace in church. We still say 'kiss and make up' even when no kissing is involved. A handshake too may seem to be just a 'natural' gesture, but its significance varies from place to place and time to time. In Britain today it generally indicates a formal introduction; in France it is a regular way of greeting colleagues at work. It also has a history. It may have existed in the sixteenth century, but it had largely been replaced by bowing as an indicator of social standing. In turn the Quakers in the seventeenth century and beyond insisted on it as a sign of democratic equality, and however unconscious of it we are, that is how it remains. The absence of words does not signify an absence of meaning. Gesture and deportment communicate much about class. Renaissance writers such as Erasmus and Castiglione stressed the need for noble bearing, which meant calm steady gestures in contrast to the arm flailing of a peasant. Jesuits reinforced their reputation for providing exclusive education by training their pupils in the self-control of their body language.

Collective rituals also embodied the social structure, bringing the whole community together. For instance, after the cult of the Eucharist had intensified in the 1200s there followed the great processions of the Feast of Corpus Christi (the body of Christ), when all the dignitaries and representatives of the guilds marched in order of precedence through the streets (see the painting of the Venetian Corpus Christi procession on page 21). There were often floats in the procession with costumed characters representing bible stories, which evolved into the mystery plays. There is debate about whether such a procession was in effect a mirror (reflecting the way the town was ordered) or a model (the élite showing the community what they thought it ought to be like, with everyone put in their place in the procession). It probably varied – an identical ritual performance need not signify the same thing from place to place or from time to time.

When the Reformation came, it was not only beliefs that changed but also the religious practices that had helped to give a community its identity. For instance, Protestants abolished the Corpus Christi processions wherever possible. There then began what Natalie Zemon Davis has identified as 'the Rites of Violence', with Protestants and Catholics being outraged by displays of the opposing group's culture and rituals. Protestants might trample on the Catholics' consecrated bread, the host, while Catholics might burn Protestant bibles. Both sides would kill in order to purify the community. Religion and

See pages 474–6

popular culture were closely integrated. This could strengthen the solidarity of the community but, when there was religious conflict, the associated cultural symbols signalled a split in the community rather than its unity.

Collective rituals were not solely derived from religion, with disorder as the only alternative. When a gang of youths appeared on the streets of a town or village around 1500, yelling and beating drums or anything else they could find in order to make 'rough music', they were not necessarily just drunk. It was quite likely that a *charivari* was under way.

A *charivari* was the ceremonial mocking of those who had offended the norms of a community. It was often provoked by great disparity in age between marriage partners, the elder usually being a widow or widower. This was disliked because a young person was being removed from the pool of eligible partners. In the case of re-marriage, there was the 'Cinderella syndrome' again – the rights of the children of a previous marriage were not guaranteed. So while the *charivari* might appear riotous, letting off steam and simply acting as a social safety valve, it was in fact seeking to re-assert the traditional order of things.

The youths who took part in a *charivari* were organised in abbeys of misrule. These were quite elaborate youth groups, even possessing their own judges and mock coinage. Their functions not only included the *charivari* but also the bearing of burning brands in procession and dancing for the fertility of the land and the people. If they wished to mock someone who did not comply with their social norms, they might make an effigy and burn it – Guy Fawkes is a relic of this. The abbey of misrule in Romans was responsible for the maypole and it taxed and policed all weddings. An essential part of a marriage was the 'bedding' of the couple. In Artigat the village youths burst into the bedroom of the newlyweds Bertrande de Rols and Martin Guerre at midnight in order to serve the couple with *resveil*, a drink full of herbs and spices to ensure ardent and successful love-making. Whatever their different functions, the abbeys of misrule and other organised gangs of youths channelled the energies of the young, who generally did not settle into family life until quite late in their mid-twenties in the sixteenth century. Youths between puberty and marriage, a potential source of disorder, were thus tamed and made useful.

A *charivari* might take place at any season but the most important performance on the street, in southern Europe at least, took place in the run up to Lent, the period of compulsory fasting before Easter. This was the carnival – or *carnevale* (farewell to flesh). It was a time of riotous good living before the repressive season of abstinence from meat and sex. It was an occasion on which ordinary hierarchy ceased to exist, when the world was turned upside down.

The carnival might begin with a masquerade, dancing with faces painted or masked so that ordinary time and society would be suspended. In the carnivals of southern France the *reynages* would then take over, mock kingdoms such as the abbeys of misrule, complete with mock kings, queens, ministers and laws. These reynages would take on

KEY ISSUE

What were the purposes of a charivari?

animal emblems, possibly totems of ancestors but also with a social point to make; an earthbound animal such as a sheep being suitable for a largely lower class *reynage*, a bird such as an eagle fitting the social pretensions of a more upper class *reynage*. There would be feasts and sports, running and horse races or tilting at rings with their suggestive sexual imagery. But it was not purely a period of licence to have a wild time.

This was a time when norms would be reinforced with much hilarity. A cuckold or a husband beaten by his wife would be led through the streets seated backwards on an ass. If sex roles were to be re-affirmed, though, they first had to be reversed. In the processions through the streets there would be transvestism, men in particular aping the 'unruly woman' who might threaten to disrupt the male ordered society. As well as sex roles, food had to be put in its place by first inverting it. An 'official' price list might be issued with strawberries costing nothing and hay or rotten herring as the most expensive. Young people often dominated these festivities, the emphasis being on renewal, on the old making way for the new. There were grotesque masks and gestures. The lower body (sex and gluttony) was celebrated at the expense of the upper body (reason and piety). Violence was also brought into the

PICTURE 19
The struggle between Carnival and Lent *by Pieter Breughel the Elder*

open – only in play unless something went wrong or there was malicious disruption – which would culminate in a duel between Carnival, in the shape of a self-indulgent, fat old man, and Lent, in the form of a crabbed old woman.

See Picture 19

All this was not anarchy, despite all the tension and joy and fear. It was the logical, quite strict inversion of what was normal, which could imprint the structure of normality onto people's imagination. The world would be turned the right way up again come Ash Wednesday. Lent, the crabbed old woman, always won her duel, or Carnival might be tried and symbolically executed. Built into every carnival was its own ending. It could only exist in extraordinary time, which served to highlight the nature of ordinary time and society.

Carnival was the occasion when sin was brought out into the open in order to be banished before Lent. There was a focus on excess in food and sex (the deadly sins of gluttony and lust) but sin also included anything disrupting the customary order of things. That is why the carnival at Romans in southern France in 1580, studied by Le Roy Ladurie, could become an occasion for real violence. First there was a protest by a carnival *reynage* representing lower status townsmen against those newly claiming nobility and so seeking tax exemption. Then there was a response from the authorities who used the tension of mock violence to breed a fear of real anarchy – which finally justified crushing, and even massacring, the protesters. When mixed with politics in this way, the functions of carnival could be manipulated, but Keith Thomas has stressed carnival's importance in more primitive rural communities with no experience of politics as such. Carnival was a safety valve, releasing the tension that could build up in a hierarchical society where the people had no outlet through politics. (This was not a new idea – see page 190 for the fifteenth-century French cleric who used the image of allowing holes in a wine barrel to stop it exploding, with reference to the Feast of Fools.) And, for all its inverted references to everyday life, the Russian theorist Mikhail Bakhtin stresses that carnival had a value as an experience of sheer exhilaration, a second life in itself distinct from hierarchy and the dull grind of ordinary, ordered existence.

KEY ISSUE

What was the significance of carnival?

4 ↜ GENDER AND SEXUALITY

Carnival, as we have seen, regulated gender relations. A common feature was men dressing in what we would think of as pantomime women's clothing, satirising women who would not submit to male authority. They were also mocking what was seen as the sexual rapaciousness of women. The image of middle-class Victorian women, for whom sex was thought to be simply an embarrassment and to whom an orgasm was unknown, was a complete reversal of the sixteenth-century stereotype of women desperate for sex and ensnaring men to get it.

The science of the time mostly reinforced this stereotype. Women's wombs were depicted as 'hungry', clamouring to be filled. The word hysteria was derived from uterus and signifies the breakdown of self-control. Women were thought to be men gone wrong. The leading sixteenth-century anatomist, Vesalius, identified female genitalia as men's turned outside in and thus imperfect imitations. Galen (a second-century Greek physician) had argued that men and women were sexually equal: his ideas were revived in the Renaissance but did little to dent the prevailing stereotype. Aristotelians were of the opinion that a man's semen was entirely responsible for the foetus with the woman being merely the carrier, and that optimum conditions during intercourse would ensure the conception of a son. However, women could still be blamed for spoiling the process – Henry VIII clearly did not hold himself responsible for failing to produce a son for so long.

A woman's sexual honour was bound up with what happened to her, rather than her intentions. In various parts of Europe one way in which a band of youths displayed solidarity and daring, and allowed initiates to prove their virility, was through the gang rape of a woman. If she was an abandoned wife or otherwise not respectable, this was deemed her fault, compounded if she was made pregnant, as this was thought impossible without an orgasm, and an orgasm showed pleasure in the sexual act. After such a dishonour the only recourse for the victim was to become a prostitute, although after 'retirement' in her thirties, she might find a husband.

Not all prostitutes were victims all the time. In Renaissance Italy were to be found the great courtesans. They did not charge by the hour or the night, but were kept in state by wealthy lovers, showered with gifts, and honoured by the nobility, cardinals and even popes. Their beauty was idealised in the neo-Platonic tradition of the time, being seen not just as attractiveness but as an embodiment of spiritual qualities. (Physical beauty has its history too – the medieval ideal of a small and slender woman was giving way to a fuller, plumper shape, and the skin had to be pure white rather than the tan which indicated hard peasant labour under the sun.) Renaissance men who were rich enough vied with each other for the favours of courtesans, whose wit, learning and beauty were legendary. One of the most famous examples, Tullia d'Aragona, was much embarrassed when one suitor she thought too young for her tried to kill himself, ineffectively as it turned out, in her presence. All the courtesans themselves were vulnerable as their physical charms faded. Most tried to save for their retirement and many had daughters to carry on the family business.

The history of women first revealed the many social consequences of gender stereotyping, and historians are now increasingly looking at how such stereotyping applied to men. A man was expected to have close virile friendships, with displays of mutual affection, while too devoted an expression of passionate romantic love for a woman could put his masculinity into question. An ordinary young man on the streets was expected to fight, whether he wanted to or not, rock-throwing battles known as *sassaiole*, for instance, being staged energetically throughout

See pages 123–4

northern Italy. Such violence was dangerous enough, but was more systematically so in the form of feuds between clans, such as the clash of Montagues and Capulets, which was based on a medieval feud in north-east Italy. Gradually violence as the proof of masculinity was brought more under control, at least for the élite, through the code of duelling, which was elaborated in the sixteenth century – relatively cleaner and quicker but still satisfactory to male honour. A courtier, as envisaged by Castiglione, in addition wrote Renaissance love lyrics and treated all about him with courtesy and careful self-control. This had the ambiguous effect of confirming his élite social status as a civilised man, but could also be seen as the feminisation of social life, which he then had to balance with an enthusiasm for hunting and martial prowess.

The regulation of young men's sexuality was regarded as a serious problem, particularly where late marriage (i.e. in the late twenties or thirties) was the custom. One solution was to establish municipal brothels, which could distract young men from assaulting the honour of 'respectable' women. The authorities in fifteenth-century Florence placed the brothel right in the middle of town, perhaps also to distract young men from each other. A special magistracy in the city, the Office of the Night, arrested 17 000 men for sodomy between 1432 and 1502, 3000 being convicted. The evidence given at the trials implicated nearly two out of every three Florentine men under forty. Many were not investigated further, and the penalties were light for those convicted. It seems to have been the norm that a single man in his twenties or thirties would have sexual partners from among men under twenty, and that this would cease once he got married. If the strict honour code was adhered to, the older man being active and the younger one passive, this was not regarded as a serious offence or a slur on the older man's masculinity. The younger man was supposed to give up his 'effeminate' ways and prove himself once he was past twenty. (Machiavelli joked about a handsome man: 'When young he lured husbands away from their wives, and now he lures wives away from their husbands.') In contrast, in 1496 when a 63-year-old confessed to playing the passive role, the authorities were so shocked that they sentenced him to be burnt, and then commuted the sentence to imprisonment to avoid the embarrassing publicity which a burning would bring. The Florentines had a rich sexual vocabulary but no word for homosexual; the notion of a separate homosexual identity or subculture only emerged in western thought in the nineteenth century. Similarly, sex between women is documented in the Early Modern period, but was not taken much notice of by male authorities or commentators. As Michael Rocke has argued, 'little trace, if any, can be found then of the categories that today largely define sexual experience and personae'. What is often thought to be simply natural varies across time and place in the way that it is culturally defined.

Tolerance for extra-marital sex of all kinds was to be increasingly restricted as social discipline tightened in the Reformation and Counter-Reformation, and as the new scourge of syphilis spread.

Official brothels were closed and, although prostitution remained widespread, it was generally criminalised. The same fears of illicit sex, along with a growing belief that water was dangerous to health, led to the closing of public baths. That also pre-empted 'bath pregnancies', whereby, as Sara Matthews Grieco put it, 'women were supposedly inseminated by adventurous sperm wandering about in warm waters'. (This also had a predictable effect on hygiene, despite the élite's alternative of wiping, powdering and perfuming and attempts to keep themselves clean at meals. The image of the Middle Ages as one of unrelieved dirt is better deserved by the Early Modern period.)

There were also attempts made to restrict courting practices such as 'bundling', whereby a couple could become intimate through foreplay, stopping short of either full sex or a commitment to marry. Both Protestant and Catholic authorities condemned such customs and urged total parental control over sexuality and choice of partner. Patriarchy – the stern if supposedly benevolent rule of a father over his family – was to be reinforced in the sixteenth century. Children were thereby reined in, and so, of course, were women.

> **KEY ISSUE**
>
> *What were thought to be the main differences between feminine and masculine identities in this period?*

5 ↝ THE ROLE OF WOMEN IN THE SIXTEENTH CENTURY

The image of women based on popular beliefs about their biology was added to by bible stories, especially those of Eve and of the Virgin Mary. It was thought to be all too easy for a woman to fall back into the sin of Eve, while Mary presented an ideal almost impossible to emulate. The solution was the guidance of a strong husband. The alternative for a respectable Catholic woman was to enter a convent, and convents had long been centres of independent female living, even female power. Some abbesses controlled wealthy estates and in Germany they could be territorial rulers. Groups of women called *beguines* preferred to live in religious groups but otherwise carried on ordinary lives. Medieval women saints, such as St Catherine of Siena, had thought nothing of upbraiding popes and princes for failing in their religious duties. All this changed with the Reformation. In Protestant territories convents and *beguinages* were closed, and nuns married or pensioned off. Women lost their chance of authority in the Church. That said, an understanding of scripture was expected, so there was a drive in most Protestant lands to educate girls, if only to read. Even under Counter-Reformation Catholicism the independence of female religious declined. The proportion of women saints fell by a third, and a late sixteenth-century example such as St Teresa in Spain had to tread carefully not to fall foul of the Inquisition. Nuns were more strictly enclosed and convents placed under closer supervision by the male authority of the bishop. The model Catholic women taught her children true religion and obeyed her husband and the priest.

There were examples of powerful women in the sixteenth century, such as Elizabeth I. However, she was the 'Virgin Queen' and portrayed almost as a goddess, i.e. in a position to rival the Virgin Mary as an ideal, and thus not taken as a role model for ordinary women.

Ordinary women were expected to marry and submit to their husbands. They were then treated as legal nonentities, to be represented by their husbands in civic affairs or the courts. Any dowry or other property they brought to the marriage was managed by the husband, although legally it did revert to the wife if she was widowed. Olwen Hufton has identified some of the features of the 'ideal' marriage: 'He creates wealth, she saves; he seeks a living, she keeps house; he deals openly with the world, she keeps herself apart from all but a few; his virtue is enhanced by skill in discourse, hers by silence.' Rebels against this ideal were treated harshly. 'Scolds' might be gagged or ducked. Adultery in a man was a trivial offence (although less so as the Reformation took hold) while in a woman it could be savagely punished. The murder of a husband was far more serious than the murder of a wife: in England murdering a husband was classed as petty treason because he was the ruler of the household.

Before 1500 there had been a larger number of economically independent women, particularly in retail trades. There were loopholes in the law that had allowed them to be 'officially' unmarried when trading. They had even occupied official positions as grain inspectors or toll collectors, and a widow might take her husband's place as a guild member. Both men and women are recorded as being physicians. Gradually however, many of these opportunities were closed off. Loopholes disappeared as the medieval law codes of many cities were replaced by Roman law, with its emphasis on patriarchal authority. City officials and physicians were required to have university degrees or other formal education denied to women. A woman's work was increasingly confined to tasks such as spinning and 'low' trades such as fish-mongering – the words 'spinster' and 'fishwife' came to denote respectively women so unfortunate as not to have a husband or so unrespectable as not to be controlled by one. Such restrictions came early in parts of Germany or later elsewhere, and were not enforced in England until the eighteenth century. In 1501, Strasbourg city council declared that all widows or unmarried women had to have a male guardian for their financial affairs. But there were exceptions – on special pleas women might be permitted to do 'men's work' if a husband were disabled or children were starving. More exceptionally still we have the memoirs of Glückel of Hameln in the seventeenth century, who inherited nothing but debts from her husband but then managed to build up a Europe-wide trading operation. However, even she lost all she had when she married again a husband who then went bankrupt.

In towns from 1500 onwards, only the men were perceived as workers; however hard the labour, household and family duties were not seen as work, even when they involved spinning and taking in boarders to earn extra cash. This may be connected with the expansion of the market economy taking men away from the household and also with the Protestant idea of a vocation, whereby ordinary work, assumed to be male, was dedicated to the glory of God. Women were to serve God through reproduction, not production. Luther made this point with polemical force: 'Women are created for no other purpose than to serve men and be their helpers...Let them bear children to death; they are created for that.' Nonetheless among poorer families, and particularly in northern Europe where the extended family was not so much the norm, women still had to go outside the household to work. In towns they were mostly in domestic service. In the country agricultural wage regulations show that they were paid half the rate of men; if they were paid in kind they received no meat or beer, unlike the men. They rarely found themselves doing lighter work: women could often be engaged in heavy labour such as skinning and stretching in the wool industry. But viewing the decline in the status of women from about 1500, Merry Wiesner warns against seeing the Middle Ages as a golden age: 'Women's economic activities were increasingly restricted during the Early Modern period, but their legal dependence on father or husband, unequal access to family resources, and inability to receive formally acknowledged training, had adversely affected their economic position in the Middle Ages and would continue to do so into the twentieth century.'

The image of the stern husband as patriarch is a forbidding one, and Lawrence Stone's work on the family has suggested that there was little affection expressed by husbands for wives or by parents for children. However, there are studies showing bereaved spouses or parents showing sustained personal grief and even turning to physicians for help with ensuing depression. Any formal power relationship can be modified by mutual consent or emotional bonds. Or there is always transgression. There were hen-pecked husbands whatever the homilies said about stern husbands and submissive wives. However, transgression could be dangerous. Sometimes, women who did not fit the pattern of respectability were identified as witches, and the penalties for that in the Early Modern period grew more terrible than they had ever been before.

KEY ISSUE

What was the economic and legal status of women in the sixteenth century, and how far was it getting worse?

6 ᔈ WITCHES

We know about witches in this period largely from legal records. Margaret Murray, working on this evidence over half a century ago, argued that the authorities were trying to crush a surviving pagan religion, its main ceremony held at the witches' sabbath, an orgiastic gathering presided over by a horned god identified by Christians as the devil. That theory has largely been discredited given the lack of evidence of a sabbath ever having taken place outside the imaginations of the witch hunters and their victims, who, broken down by torture, would admit to anything. There were magical practices amongst the people of

Europe but nothing as systematic as a pagan religion, and the idea of the Sabbath rarely featured in the original accusations by a witch's neighbours.

The witch hunters were the believers in devil-worshipping witches, as we shall see, but that does not mean that they invented witches. Popular witch beliefs were prevalent in Early Modern Europe, although it is not entirely clear whether they had been learned from priests or semi-educated story-tellers in the late Middle Ages, or whether such beliefs are simply natural to a peasant society. For instance, the image of the Ancient Roman witch, the *striga*, seems to have survived in the form of the follower of the goddess Diana (or Holda in Germany) who would leave her home and fly out by night across towns or villages. It is hard to tell whether this is just a myth preserved in popular tales or whether some women convinced themselves that they were able to fly. (It could be that the sensation of flight was brought on by applying special unguents, which contained alkaloids capable of inducing hallucinations. As G.R. Quaife puts it, 'the so-called witches' ointment may have had little to do with a diabolic cult but it was an effective element in the lifestyle of the early modern drug addict'.) Whatever the psychological realities behind beliefs such as night flight, witches were not thought of in the popular mind as being worshippers of the devil. Magic, good or bad, seemed generally independent of official Christian theology.

Only one group of witches, which does seem to have constituted a cult in Friuli in Northern Italy, has been properly documented, and they saw themselves as the opposite of evil-doing witches. They were the *benandanti*, 'good-walkers', who claimed that they left their bodies by night in order to battle against evil. They became *benandanti* if they were born with the caul (the membrane around the embryo) intact. They told the Inquisition how, when they were in their early twenties, they were summoned to battle by a mysterious captain and had no choice but to go. They saw their magic as specifically serving Christ. However, this did not fit in with the official theology of the Inquisition which judged all magic to be evil.

In 1580 one of the *benandanti*, Moduco, told the Inquisition this, shortly after investigations had begun:

> I am a *benandante* because I go with the others to fight four times a year, that is during the Ember Days, at night; I go invisibly in spirit and the body remains behind; we go forth in the service of Christ, and the witches of the Devil; we fight each other, we with bundles of fennel and they with sorghum stalks ... In the fighting that we do, one time we fight over the wheat and all the other grains, another time over the livestock, and at other times over the vineyards. And so, on four occasions we fight over all the fruits of the earth and for those things won by the *benandanti* that year there is abundance.

By 1649 another of the *benandanti*, Michele Soppe, was telling a different story to the Inquisition:

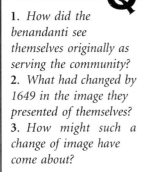

1. *How did the benandanti see themselves originally as serving the community?*
2. *What had changed by 1649 in the image they presented of themselves?*
3. *How might such a change of image have come about?*

The place was in the country near Malisana during the dance and conventicle of the witches, in that field where they gather, about two years after I began to go to the ball, in the presence of all the witches and warlocks who were assembled there. It happened like this: the devil asked me if I wanted to give my soul up to him; in exchange he would grant me all the favours that I desired. At the devil's request I replied that I surrendered my soul to him…Also, at the request of the devil I twice denied Jesus Christ and his holy faith; every time I went to the witches' ball I kissed the devil's arse, just like all the witches and warlocks, and I did all the things the others did.

The *benandanti* were specific to one small region, but all over Europe there were 'cunning' folk, healers and diviners, people who had supernatural powers which could serve the community. The historian of the *benandanti*, Carlo Ginzburg, believes them to represent the survival of a pre-Christian tradition of shamanism, communing with good or evil spirits, which also accounts for night flight as noted above. There is no evidence, however, of 'cunning' folk, being aware of any systematic alternative to Christianity.

The services of 'cunning' folk were much sought after, but whoever could cure could also kill. When someone used magical powers to harm people, livestock or the soil, he, or more usually it was thought to be she, was guilty of what was called **maleficium**, the casting of harmful spells. It was *maleficium*, not devil worship, which was an idea originating in popular culture.

maleficium causing harm through malevolent magic

The *benandanti* were men, but overall around seventy-five to eighty per cent of those accused of witchcraft in Europe at this time were women. This reflects the enduring fear of women, particularly old women, marginal to society.

Women were suspect in the first place because, just as they had power over life, so it was feared they had power to bring death. On the whole, they were the healers who gathered herbs, made up the medicines and perhaps muttered the incantations taught to them by their mothers. Such a woman could kill as well as cure by using her skills. In Augsburg a high proportion of witchcraft accusations were made by mothers against lying-in maids who cared for a baby after birth, while the mother was weakened and regarded as being in a ritually 'polluted' state. Witchcraft could be blamed if the baby sickened and died, and Lyndal Roper has argued that post-natal depression in the mother or envy of maternity expressed by the maid may have played a significant psychological role.

As we have seen, women were sexually stereotyped as having only a fragile control over insatiable lust. This threatened order in the community and the family in particular. It may have been less of a concern in popular culture than among celibate, clerical witch hunters, projecting onto women their own repressed sexual desires.

While women were perceived as a threat, their real position might be one of defencelessness. Not possessing the social or legal standing of a man, a woman might turn to spells in her own defence, attempting *maleficium*. If she were brought to court, even when she had not attempted *maleficium*, her word would be treated as of much less value than that of a man.

Old women in particular (at that time those over forty or fifty) were subject to witchcraft accusations. They were thought to be useless to the community in general, marginal and therefore dangerous. A fear might have been that they would prey sexually on young men – if a *charivari* did not scare them off doing so. If they were widows there might be property disputes regarding their inheritance. In a dispute with neighbours, particularly if charity was refused, an old woman, made strange by senility, might mutter curses and pay for it dearly when she was brought to trial as a witch. Age, however, may just indicate how long it took for individual suspicions to build up and coalesce into community support for a witchcraft accusation – trial evidence shows that suspicions were regularly voiced twenty years or more before a formal accusation was made.

Witchcraft accusations were the most savage assaults on the position of women as it deteriorated during the sixteenth century and beyond. But women too would spread rumours about a suspect neighbour or make formal accusations. There may have been specific reasons, such as the tensions arising from maternity discussed in the Augsburg example above, but more generally women might have felt the need to prove their own normality, their own willingness to accept the assumptions of a patriarchal society. This is due in part to the fact that women, as well as men, were subject to all the demographic, economic and religious changes that disrupted communities in the Early Modern period.

After 1500 there were an increasing number of accusations of *maleficium*. Each accusation had its specific cause, a personal quarrel, a mysterious death, a wild old woman prone to dangerous cursing. An accused witch was usually a bad neighbour. But there were also more general causes. The plague continued to strike sporadically, so the threat of devastating misfortune was always present and could make people more ready to accuse others of the evil arts. More specifically, sixteenth-century communities were disrupted by the growth of population and by changes to family and commercial life. This gave rise to elusive anxieties, which could be relieved by finding a scapegoat in the form of a witch.

Religious insecurities at the time of the Reformation had their effect. Alan McFarlane and Keith Thomas see the decline of Catholic almsgiving as a source of guilt: that guilt could be relieved by labelling the beggar turned away from the door as an evil-doer, even a performer of *maleficium*. Keith Thomas has also shown how the Catholic Church, with its many sacramental practices, was a source of counter-magic, whereas the law was the only recourse for Protestants. This does not explain why accusations of *maleficium* also increased in Catholic countries, but in those cases there was the Counter-Reformation. This

See pages 377–9

KEY ISSUE

In what ways were witches real?

demonology the study of demons and the Devil

was not just the counter-attack on Protestantism but also a drive to impose official religion more firmly on the masses, leaving less scope for either magic or counter-magic. Both Protestant and Catholic reformers also sought to impose tighter social discipline and curb immorality; the guilt this inspired may have boosted witchcraft accusations as a form of scapegoating. Peasant notables, in particular, who were better educated in official religion and who had benefited from the economic developments of the period, may have been more willing to identify with the élite and turn to the courts, rather than trust the traditional counter-magic employed by their less educated, poorer neighbours. Also, while accusations of *maleficium* were intensified by religious and economic changes, they were also encouraged by the way they fitted in to the panic amongst churchmen and judges about the devil being loose in the world. Popular culture and learned **demonology** thus merged in the ideology of the witch hunters.

7 ⌐ THE WITCH HUNTS

Up to the eleventh century, Christian writers had dismissed witchcraft as an illusion but throughout the succeeding centuries, details were added to what Levack has called a 'cumulative concept of witchcraft'. Witches were clearly capable of *maleficium* but many other features were added to their original image amongst the people.

According to these developing academic beliefs, witches were supposed to commit the most heinous crime of killing and eating babies. It was asserted that they could change themselves into the shapes of different animals. From the followers of Diana, they acquired the power of flight on a broomstick or perhaps a goat. They were thought to fly to a sabbath and worship the devil in an inverted form of Christian worship, as the *benandanti* were supposed to do once the Inquisition had finished with them. A feature peculiar to England and Scotland was the 'familiar', an animal who would do the witch's bidding and leave a tell-tale sign, the mark, a spot of insensitive skin where the familiars could suckle the witch's blood. By the mid-fifteenth century inquisitors were finding most of these characteristics, or persuading themselves that they were, in their witch hunts in mountainous regions. One inquisitor at Como at the foot of the Alps in northern Italy claimed forty-one victims in one year. For him and his like, *maleficium* was not just one brand of popular magic; it was an indication that a sabbath-attending servant of the devil was at work.

There was nothing amongst the dominant ideas of the time that could erode the concept of the witch. Such supernatural malice and service to the devil contradicted nothing in the general philosophical assumptions of the period. Some neo-Platonic philosophers of the Renaissance, who believed in harmonious natural forces dominating the world – good demons in a sense – criticised the beliefs about witches, but their voices were in a minority. Another intellectual trend at the time was a re-examination of the thought of St Augustine, which was to inspire Luther but also contained within it a demonology, which served to reinforce the concept of the witch. Stuart Clark has shown how there was an increasing obsession during this period with inversion – if Christ inspired reverence then His inverse, the devil, along with his servants the witches, consequently inspired all the greater fear.

Given such ideology, it is not so surprising that two particularly enthusiastic witch hunters, Heinrich Krämer and Jakob Sprenger, managed to panic Pope Innocent VIII into issuing a papal bull in 1484 empowering them to pursue witches with all vigour in Germany and, by implication, making general what had hitherto been local hunts. They followed this up in 1486 with the publication of *Malleus Maleficarum*, an encyclopaedia of what inquisitors could expect witches to be getting up to. These celibate clerics seem to have been particularly obsessed by fears of castration by magical means. Some details, about the sabbath for instance, were actually left out, but with the addition of the work of Paulus Grillandus, published in 1524, the picture of the devil-worshipping witch was more or less complete. Again printing had played a vital role. The inquisitor and the judge could now run a trial according to the textbooks, and the realities of the crimes being investigated mattered less and less.

The Church had provided the image of the witch but the judges had added to it. They had teased out new details during trials that could be fed back into the textbook image, and there was no shortage of details, given that witchcraft was the *crimen exceptum*, the exceptional crime warranting the suspension of normal procedures. Rules on evidence, disinterested juries and the reliability of witnesses were ignored. The unsupported testimony of hysterical children could identify someone as a witch and bring him or her to the stake. But in many cases there were no witnesses of events, merely circumstantial evidence, and there was always the need to find out the names of other witches. Torture, which had been part of ordinary legal procedure since the thirteenth century, would be applied and confessions extracted from those accused of witchcraft.

The full range of torture instruments was used – thumbscrews, racks, the strappado where the body was suspended from a pulley and jerked violently in mid-air – but the *tormentum insomniae*, sleep deprivation, was the one guaranteed to make the suspected witch break down, supply any details of her attendance at the sabbath which might satisfy the relentless interrogator, and provide a list of names of others who could be tried for witchcraft and tortured in turn. With torture forcing confessions, it is not surprising that judges found their worst fears to be realised. The answers to their leading questions confirmed for them the truth of the textbooks such as the *Malleus Maleficarum*. Where the victim had a lurid imagination, and many were accused in the first place because they were old and confused or were displaying symptoms of psychosis, new details could emerge on, say, the consumption at sabbaths of fried bats, a witches' delicacy in Alsace. Such detail could be used to amplify the theologians' theory of witchcraft. There were also those names of other witches that showed conclusively that Satan had a legion of followers who could overwhelm Europe unless they were mercilessly crushed. There was no room for doubt. In cases where torture was used, the conviction rate was around ninety-five per cent.

The conviction rate in England's secular courts was much lower than was general on the Continent, being around fifty per cent or below. This seems to have been due less to English scepticism than to differences in legal procedure. In secular courts on the Continent there had been a judicial revolution. Restorative justice, whereby the injured party had to sue for justice and suffer penalties if he or she could not prove their case, gave way to retributive justice, with the state prosecuting the criminal. This meant that victimless crimes, such as simply being a witch, even without any evidence of harm to others, could be prosecuted on the Continent, whereas in England one individual had to accuse another and provide evidence of actual injury. Also, torture was not a part of ordinary legal procedure in England. This did not exclude witch scares altogether in England, but they were fewer and quicker to end than on the Continent. In Scotland, which shared some of the Continental procedures such as torture, three times as many were executed for witchcraft as in England.

Spain was another country where the witch hunts were few and relatively controlled. Given its reputation for religious bigotry in the Early Modern period, this has puzzled some historians. Brian Levack has emphasised that witch-hunting hysteria grew in the most uncontrolled fashion where the courts concerned were both secular and local. In Spain the highly centralised, ecclesiastical courts making up the Spanish Inquisition handled witchcraft cases and kept hysteria

PICTURE 20
*'Witch kisses the Devil's arse'
from* Compendium
Maleficarum *by Francesco
Maria Guazzo, 1608*

under control. Indeed, there were Spanish inquisitors among the sceptics concerning witchcraft. In 1610, the witch craze broke out in the Basque country. Inquisitor Salazar, sent to investigate it, reported that 'there were neither witches nor bewitched until they were talked and written about'. This scepticism was fostered by the Spanish Inquisition's long experience of false denunciations for heresy; with its own, more sophisticated measures for dealing with religious deviance, it was less prone to panic.

A witch-believing peasantry more ready to make accusations because of religious and economic changes, a learned demonology which absorbed the popular idea of *maleficium* into devil worship, the dissemination of that demonology through printing, a judicial revolution and the use of torture, with local, secular courts ready to be caught up in hysteria – these were the preconditions for the witch hunts. Countries, such as England and Spain, which did not share them all, escaped more lightly. But these preconditions were established by the early years of the sixteenth century and yet there was a lull of nearly half a century before witch hunts started to spread like epidemics across Europe from the 1560s onwards. There is no perfect correlation, but the insecurity brought on by intensified religious conflict may have been a trigger in many areas. By the 1560s some Protestants, in particular the Calvinists, were becoming more evangelical and more expansionist. By then the Catholic Church had also started to re-organise itself and the Counter-Reformation was under way. Particularly hard hit by witch hunts were the border lands of France, Germany and Switzerland and these were the areas most disputed by Catholics and Protestants. Johann von Schöneburg, the Archbishop-Elector of Trier, for instance, was a militant supporter of the Counter-Reformation, first hammering the Protestants after he began his reign in 1581. Then between 1587 and 1593, he had 368 witches burnt, leaving two villages with only one female inhabitant apiece. When one of his judges proved too lenient he had him tried for witchcraft, tortured, strangled and burnt. Such intensive witch hunts reached a peak in both Protestant and Catholic lands in the 1620s when the Thirty Years' War had brought with it renewed religious conflict. The worst was over in western Europe by 1650, when religious conflict in Europe was starting to die down.

Politics were often an aspect of witch trials. In the fifteenth century, the Duchesses of Bedford and Gloucester had been accused of witchcraft in the midst of political intrigues. In France, Joan of Arc's claim of supernatural inspiration had laid her open to charges of witchcraft by her political enemies. But by the late sixteenth century, the politics had changed. No longer were leading politicians just seeking to overcome opponents. With the decline of the Church as an independent institution in the Early Modern period, politicians sought to exercise an increasing moral authority. Christina Larner showed how witchcraft legislation was often accompanied by measures to regulate morality. Witch hunts may have been part of a general moral panic which included fears about infanticide, incest, adultery and sodomy, as efforts were made to regulate the lives of the peasantry and the

> **KEY ISSUE**
>
> *How did the cumulative concept of the witch as devil worshipper arise?*

unrespectable hordes of the towns. They were in part also a feature of the emerging godly state, taking on the moral authority formerly exercised by the Church.

Witch hunting did not end completely once the godly state had established itself or when religious conflict died down in the mid-seventeenth century. In Poland, where the Counter-Reformation did not become militant until the late 1600s, the witch hunts were delayed and lasted from 1680 to 1750. But this was exceptional, because by then educated Europe had dropped the late medieval demonology that justified it all. This was not because of the reasoning of critics. In the sixteenth century Johann Weyer had put forward strong arguments for apparent cases of witchcraft being the product of torture and psychological delusion. James VI's retort was all too typical in suggesting that Weyer himself must be a witch. The spread of practical scepticism through centralising judicial institutions, such as that of the Spanish Inquisition, was the first reason for the decline in witch hunting. In France, for instance, the authority of the Paris parlement (supreme court) was extended over outlying areas during the seventeenth century and it brought witchcraft trials under stricter control; the Paris judges may still have retained an abstract belief in witchcraft, but they regarded most accusations as the result of feuds or the hysteria of provincial officials or peasants. Ultimately, however, the disappearance of the demonology resulted from the triumph amongst the educated classes of a scientific, mechanistic world view which took hold in the **Enlightenment** of the eighteenth century. There was no room for devil-worshipping witches in a universe that God had made to run like clockwork, according to scientific laws.

This change of ideas did not happen as smoothly as some historians such as Keith Thomas seem to have assumed. Repeal of witchcraft legislation was often a highly contested political issue rather than a matter of common consent among the élite, as Ian Bostridge has shown was the case in the England of the 1730s. But the balance gradually shifted from disbelievers in witchcraft being themselves accused of the black arts, to those who retained a belief being stigmatised as reactionary, ignorant and prey to provincial superstition.

But this brings us back to where we started – the relationship between popular culture and the learning of the élite. We have seen how the prevalent popular belief in *maleficium* was merged with the devil worship that was worked out schematically by theologians and amplified by judges, and this was the precondition for the horrors of witch hunting. But recently Robin Briggs has argued powerfully that the importance of witch hunts, let alone any 'witch craze' has been much exaggerated. The estimated number of victims has been revised down from the once commonly accepted hundreds of thousands to about 40 000. The demonology found in the *Malleus* and other texts played a far smaller role in most trials than used to be thought; more common were accusations of *maleficium* by neighbours rather than by witch hunters from outside the community, so Continental cases were not always so different from English ones. The distinct importance of

Enlightenment the movement towards the end of the Early Modern period which proclaimed the triumph of reason and condemned superstition, which included many religious beliefs

popular beliefs is shown by their survival long beyond the collapse of élite demonology, when there were still witch prickers ('brodders' in Scotland) who specialised in finding the devil's mark. Suspected witches were still subject to the 'swimming' test – when they sank they were innocent, if also possibly drowned. One Ruth Osborne did die as a result of such a test at Tring in Hertfordshire as late as 1751. The witch beliefs completed in sixteenth-century Europe had staying power as part of popular culture until improved communications and widespread urbanisation eroded their rural environment.

> **KEY ISSUE**
>
> *Why did witch hunting become so intensive in the later sixteenth century?*

8 ↪ BIBLIOGRAPHY

**P. Burke, *Popular Culture in Early Modern Europe* (Temple Smith, 2nd ed., 1997) has been the key text for twenty years. *Edward Muir, *Ritual in Early Modern Europe* (CUP, 1997) analyses non-verbal culture. *Merry Weisner, *Women and Gender in Early Modern Europe* (CUP, 1994) is an excellent synthesis of huge amounts of new research. N.Z. Davis, *The Return of Martin Guerre* (Harvard, 1983) is a good example of 'micro-history', revealing how a society functions through one incident/locale. (Daniel Vigne's film about Martin Guerre is also well worth seeing.) E. Le Roy Ladurie, *Carnival in Romans* (transl. Penguin, 1981) is another good example of micro-history. *C. Larner, *Witchcraft and Religion* (Blackwell, 1984) contains a series of brilliant essays; one entitled *'Crimen Exceptum?' The Crime of Witchcraft in Europe* is the best short analysis available. **B. Levack, *The Witch hunt in Early Modern Europe* (Longman, 2nd ed., 1995) is the most reliable synthesis of recent scholarly views. *Robin Briggs, *Witches and Neighbours* (Harper Collins, 1997) is a powerful critique of many of the generalisations made about witchcraft accusations. C. Ginzburg, *The Night Battles* (transl. Routledge and Kegan Paul, 1983) is a case study of the *benandanti*.

9 ↪ STRUCTURED AND ESSAY QUESTIONS

A *Structured questions.*
1. (a) What were the main elements in a sixteenth-century carnival?
   (b) How far did popular culture ever escape official control?
2. (a) Why were the majority of those accused of witchcraft women?
   (b) What are the most likely reasons for the increased frequency of witchcraft accusations in the Early Modern period?

B *Essay questions.*
1. 'Popular culture at the time of the Reformation did not exist in its own right. It was dependent on the culture of clerical and noble élites.' Discuss.

2. How important was the religious element to popular culture in the Early Modern period?

3. In Early Modern Europe what were the main characteristics of the role of women, and how and why did it change?

4. How had the stereotype of the witch developed and become so firmly established in Europe by the beginning of the sixteenth century?

5. Whose interests, if any, did the witch craze serve?

10 ↬ EXERCISE ON POPULAR CULTURE

The study of popular culture is different from political topics – the events are not in chronological order, the lines of cause and effect are not as clear and there have to be broader, more risky generalisations. To help to organise your ideas on the topic, find two or more pieces of evidence in connection with the following statements. At least one example should support and one should qualify the generalisation made. The material can be drawn from this chapter, other chapters or general reading. The evidence can then be collated and considered during group discussion to decide what can be stated with some certainty and what needs to remain tentative.

(i) 'Popular culture could not escape control by official religion.'
(ii) 'The main purpose of popular culture was to express the identity of the community – and to control individuals who might be different and threaten that identity.'
(iii) 'Printing ended the autonomy of popular culture.'
(iv) 'Popular culture consisted of ways of letting off steam. It kept society stable by acting as a safety valve.'
(v) 'Popular culture is, in many respects, just another term for popular superstition.'

The material discussed in this exercise could then be used in answering essay question 1 above.

11 ↬ PICTURE EXERCISE ON GENDER AND THE FAMILY

See pages 139–45

Paintings, engravings and woodcuts were often made with the purpose of advancing status or an ideological position. They can also reveal social assumptions, which may have been conscious or partly subliminal. The painting illustrated here is an example that can be 'read' as evidence of contemporary attitudes about gender roles and the family. Study it and then answer the following questions.

PICTURE 21
Family group *by anon.*
North Netherlands painter,
1559

Q

1. *What does the body language of the man, the position of his arms, and the expression on his face reveal about his (idealised) role as a husband?*

2. *In contrast, how does the way the woman is holding herself indicate her gender role and status?*

3. *Framed by the heads of the couple and the gesture of the man towards the woman can be seen Adam and Eve through the window. Eve is standing, looking down on the seated Adam and is reaching down the apple from the tree with which to tempt him. Her gesture towards Adam is a variation on that of the husband towards his wife. What do you think this biblical reference is meant to say about the relationship of the couple in the foreground?*

4. *The children playing with toys are a smaller detail in the painting. How do they still command attention from the viewer? What might their position in the painting indicate about their relationship with their parents?*

8

Charles V

OVERVIEW

'Roman King, future Emperor, *semper augustus*, King of Spain, Sicily, Jerusalem, the Balearic Islands, the Canary Islands, the Indies and the mainland on the far shore of the Atlantic, Archduke of Austria, Duke of Burgundy, Brabant...Count of Habsburg, Flanders and Tyrol, Count Palatine of Burgundy... Landgrave of Alsace, Count of Swabia, Lord of Asia and Africa.' Thus ran just some of the titles of Charles I of Spain, more commonly known as Charles V, the Holy Roman Emperor. The list conveys the extent of Charles's territories, stretching from Spain to Italy, Austria, the Netherlands and Franche-Comté and, across the ocean, the vast, only partly discovered bulk of the New World. Some of the titles are purely honorific, such as Lord of Africa and Asia, while the title 'Roman King, future Emperor' conveyed great prestige but no territory. The latter is very important. By virtue of his titles Charles could legitimately see himself as the leader of Christendom with all that would entail in the fight against the **Infidel** and heresy. But the support for such a claim to leadership came from a strictly limited territorial base, albeit one that dwarfed the possessions of other European rulers and provoked them out of fear or rivalry to oppose him at any opportunity. The only link between Charles's territories, acquired by dynastic accident, was his person; hence the more accurate and contemporary term to describe his Empire – '**monarchia**'.

Charles respected the individual traditions and privileges of his territories. The only central institutions were the councils, which travelled with Charles, making the role of secretary of vital importance. As he travelled between his dominions he was endlessly distracted from one problem to the next – he visited Germany nine times, Spain six times, the Netherlands on ten occasions and Italy on seven. Members of the royal family acted as viceroys, but there was widespread dissatisfaction in most areas at Charles's continual absences and some problems that only he could solve. Thus Spain rose in revolt while he was in Germany from 1519 to 1522 to establish himself as Holy Roman Emperor. Returning to Spain from 1522 to 1529 he took a firm grip on government there, but had to resist two invasions of Italy by Francis I and abandon any chance of settling the Lutheran question in Germany. In 1535 his great triumph over the Ottomans at Tunis was immediately undermined by a further war with Francis I. He constantly had to press his dominions for ever greater funds – the Netherlands yielded much but he had to go carefully after a tax revolt in Ghent in 1540, and finally had to rely on piling up debt and taxing Castile on a scale which inflicted serious damage to its economy.

However, in the late 1540s, with Francis I excluded from Italy and a stand-off with the Turks in place, Charles was able to turn his full

Infidel a disbeliever in the true faith, usually applied by Christians to Muslims

Monarchia the disparate territories ruled by Charles V

KEY ISSUE

What problems were caused by the extent of Charles's territories?

| Habsburg lands | Boundary of the Holy Roman Empire |
| Habsburg acquisitions with date | Military routes connecting Habsburg dominions (north western route later known as the Spanish Road) |

1   Hungary – 1526
2   Tunis – 1535
3   Milan – 1535
4   Guelders – 1543

MAP 11
The Empire of Charles V

attention to Germany. Military victory over the Protestants in 1547 was not followed up by a sustainable religious settlement and Charles was defeated in 1552–53 by Protestant rebellion and by renewed French intervention in Germany. Unable to face settling with the heretics, he left Germany to his brother Ferdinand, who had been his deputy there throughout the reign, and passed on his other dominions in the Netherlands, Italy, Spain and the New World, to his son Philip. By 1556 he had abdicated from all his titles and retired to a monastery in Castile. His territories had been more extensive than any European ruler since Charlemagne 700 years before, but the responsibilities they brought with them had proved too great for Charles V.

1 ↩ CHARLES IN SPAIN

In January 1516, Ferdinand of Aragon died and Charles became King with his mother Joanna the Mad, who lived on as a shadowy figure at Tordesillas until 1555, technically sharing the Crown. It was not until September 1517 that Charles arrived in his new kingdom, because first the Netherlands had to be safeguarded from attack by offering concessions to the French in the Peace of Noyon. Cardinal Cisneros, the regent of Spain after Ferdinand's death, had been urging Charles to arrive as soon as possible because of widespread discontent in the country.

The nobility sought to take advantage of the power vacuum before Charles's arrival to re-establish the control they had lost under Ferdinand and Isabella, and the towns were ready to fight to defend their privileges. Cisneros's attempt to raise a permanent army was defeated by both towns and *grandees*, who saw that it would have made the Crown militarily independent and Cisneros had to give way to prevent serious trouble.

grandees the most important nobles

The young, ugly and awkward king did not make a favourable first impression and his actions soon confirmed the worst fears of Spaniards. Cisneros died before he was dismissed but Burgundians were installed in key positions. To avoid breaking his promise not to give offices to foreigners, Charles issued them with letters of naturalisation, a device that naturally caused widespread resentment. The most glaring affront was the appointment of a seventeen-year-old Burgundian as the Archbishop of Toledo.

Cortes the equivalent of parliament, there was a separate one for each of the Spanish kingdoms

In spite of the tension, the Castilian *Cortes* (parliament) was persuaded to vote an exceptionally large *servicio* (tax) of 600 000 ducats payable over three years. Charles immediately left for Aragon where the more entrenched nature of the *Cortes'* privileges, the *fueros*, delayed his recognition as king and a grant of 200 000 ducats for eight months. In Catalonia, the process took a year and produced 100 000 ducats. Before he could visit Valencia in 1519, Charles received news that required him to leave for Germany to ensure his succession as Holy Roman Emperor. Such a journey required ready cash.

servicio non-noble Spanish tax

To provide this money, the Castilian *Cortes* was summoned, in defiance of tradition, to the northern town of Santiago to vote a second *servicio* before the expiry of the first. The town of Toledo refused to send anyone and the instructions given to the deputies of Salamanca summed up the feelings of the *Cortes*: 'adjourn the *Cortes*... stop offices going to foreigners... do not agree to any servicio... the king's duty is to govern... by his presence, not by his absence'. It was only by the most intense pressure, and by adjourning the *Cortes* to La Coruna where Charles was preparing to set sail, that the court managed to secure a subsidy. The money was never collected and the alienation of Charles's Castilian subjects was now complete.

A *Revolt: Comuneros and Germania*

Charles abandoned his Spanish kingdoms as they flared into revolt. The causes of the rebellion did not lie merely in his tactless handling of the *Cortes* or appointment of foreigners. Resentment had been growing in the towns for years as a result of the Crown's failure to protect them against the attacks of the great aristocratic families. A myth developed of an earlier golden age and Charles was urged to 'act in everything like the Catholic lords, King Ferdinand and Queen Isabella'.

The accession of a foreign king and emperor was unwelcome in three respects: he would be absent for much of the time, his empire was centred on distant north Europe, and his advisers treated the Castilians 'as Indians'. Thus the *Comunero* movement which developed in the

CHARLES V (1516–56)

Charles was the eldest son of Philip of Burgundy and Joanna of Spain, sometimes called Joanna the Mad. He spent his entire childhood in the Netherlands and became Duke of Burgundy at the age of six. The Burgundian court had an elaborate code of chivalry expressed in the **order of the golden fleece** and this heavily influenced Charles. He believed strongly in the idea of knightly honour and fighting for the Christian faith and this sometimes led him into naive behaviour, as in 1528 when he challenged Francis I to single combat for breaking his word over the Treaty of Madrid. Charles was very devout and spent much time in prayer before taking important decisions. He believed firmly that all human affairs are determined by God and this gave him a fatalistic outlook.

Unfortunately, although Charles had strong opinions about the correct behaviour of a king, his appearance did not match up to the image. He had a misshapen jaw (the Habsburg jaw) which meant that his teeth didn't meet and he could not chew properly. He was also notoriously greedy and as a result suffered from terrible indigestion and very painful gout, which at times meant that he had to be carried around on a litter. Charles never liked making decisions, but this became more pronounced as his reign progressed, and he also began to suffer from bouts of depression. In 1553–54 he suffered a breakdown, becoming obsessed with his collection of clocks and leaving the direction of policy to his sister, Mary of Hungary. The verdict of modern historians on Charles has been harsh, many seeing him as a mediocre failure, but up to the end of the nineteenth century he was admired for his military campaigns, for the size of his empire and for his moral superiority, which was proved by his voluntary abdication of all his titles and possessions in 1555–56.

PROFILE

Order of the Golden Fleece the highest chivalric order in the Netherlands

PICTURE 22
King Charles V with his hunting dog *by Jakob Seisenegger, 1532*

towns was essentially reactionary, united in a hatred of present conditions and groping after a previous, more satisfactory, state. The *Comunero* demands asked that Charles return to Spain and marry soon; he should remove foreigners from his entourage; the *Cortes* was to be given a major role in government and to meet every three years; taxes and the expenses of the court should be reduced. None of these demands were revolutionary but even so Charles's position in Castile was soon in grave danger.

Following the lead of Toledo, riots broke out in most of the major towns of Castile. In Segovia the deputies who had voted for the new taxes were murdered. Royal authority broke down and the *grandees*, further angered by the appointment of Adrian of Utrecht as regent despite Charles's promise to appoint no other foreigners, did nothing to help the royal cause. The rebels found leadership in men such as Juan de Padilla, members of the lesser nobility of the towns, from whom the deputies to the *Cortes* were drawn.

A crisis was reached after the accidental burning of the great centre of Medina del Campo, which was blamed on government forces. In outrage, fourteen of the eighteen cities represented in the *Cortes* set up a Holy Junta and in September 1520 their forces seized Tordesillas and Joanna, the legal queen. If she had been persuaded to support the *Comuneros* in writing, it would have legitimised the uprising and made the loss of Spain a real possibility. This was the climax of the rebellion, but Joanna would sign nothing and the *Comuneros* could not agree on a common course of action. At this opportune moment, Adrian of Utrecht made some skilful concessions to win over the *grandees*. The Constable and Admiral of Castile were appointed co-regents; it was agreed that the collection of the *servicio* would be suspended and that no more foreigners would be appointed.

These concessions, combined with the increasingly radical nature of the revolt as it spread to the estates of the *grandees* and threatened their privileges, brought them over to the government's side. Old antagonisms between the towns and the nobility surfaced and at Villalar in April 1521, the Castilian nobles and their retainers destroyed the *Comunero* army and executed Juan de Padilla and other leaders. The revolt was stopped just in time to prevent its exploitation by Francis I who had invaded Navarre. Castilians joined the Aragonese in repelling the invader who was crushed at the battle of Pamplona in June 1521.

The fragmented nature of the Spanish peninsula was clearly illustrated in the revolt of the *Comuneros*, not only by the failure of the Castilian towns to overcome their rivalry but also by the failure to link up with a major rebellion which broke out simultaneously in Valencia. This revolt of the *Germania* (brotherhood) never posed as great a threat to Charles because it was a class conflict, which was dealt with by the nobility.

The *Germania* had been set up to repel attacks by **Barbary pirates** but its leaders took the opportunity of a plague outbreak in Valencia in 1520 to seize control of the city and the surrounding countryside. The violence of the rebels ensured their eventual defeat at the hands of the

---

KEY ISSUE

What mistakes by the young king prompted the revolt of the Comuneros?

Barbary pirates Muslim pirates oprating out of ports on the north African coast

nobility, even though the rebellion spread across the whole kingdom and over into Majorca. The main forces of the *Germanía* were defeated in October 1521, but resistance continued into 1523 and it was not until December 1524, after the execution of hundreds of rebels, that a general pardon was finally issued.

The reason why the revolt was allowed to continue for so long was because the government attached less importance to Valencia. A challenge to royal authority there lacked the force of a similar challenge in Castile and the nobles could therefore be left to control the revolt themselves.

Charles could not take the credit for the crushing of either revolt. He was reliant on the co-operation of the nobility, without which his reign would not survive. Winning over the social elite was Charles's priority when he returned to Spain in July 1522.

B *The government of Spain*

Charles remained in Spain for seven years. This was to be the most settled period of the reign, during which he married, remodelled the administration and underwent a decisive shift in outlook. When he left Spain once again he was no longer a foreign monarch; he had adopted it as his spiritual home even if he was present there for only eight of his remaining twenty-nine years. Spain had become the centre of his empire and the home of his family. In choosing Spain, Charles tied the interests of his dynasty to the Mediterranean and Atlantic, leaving the Austrian homeland of the Habsburgs, and therefore the imperial crown, to his younger brother Ferdinand.

The other major feature of these years is the decisive relegation of Aragon to a secondary role. Charles continued the policy of Ferdinand in regarding Castile as 'the head of all the rest' because it was wealthier and more populous and also because it was easier to extract revenue from it. The revolt of the *Germanía* did not affect the privileges of the Aragonese. The nobility continued to exercise great power over their tenants and, in contrast to Castile, the *Cortes* retained the right to discuss grievances before taxation, a privilege it was not worth the Crown contesting, given the poverty of the eastern kingdoms. Aragon kept its liberty at a price, however. As J.H. Elliott saw, the history of Spain in fact became the history of Castile. Castilians became reconciled to the new, alien regime by the opportunities it opened up and by Charles's increasing attachment to his eventual homeland, while the Aragonese found themselves ever more isolated from affairs of state, especially after Charles's death.

Castile was still seething with discontent. It was vital to rebuild support for the monarchy rapidly because the treasury was in ruins: the *Comuneros* had taken the Crown's ordinary revenue for 1521–22 and the *servicios* had not been collected. Charles had to reduce hostility to his government and thus gain acceptance for his new taxes. A number of reforms were therefore adopted, including the replacement of

corregidores officials appointed by the Crown to supervise the affairs of Castilian towns

KEY ISSUE

How did the revolt of the Comuneros *affect the* Cortes *and the nobility?*

letrados university-trained lawyers who worked for the government

unpopular or corrupt officials. The towns retained their privileges but the **corregidores** were re-established. The *Cortes* was allowed into partnership with the Crown. In return for taxes, it was responsible for handling revenue, which provided opportunities for members of the *Cortes* to enrich themselves, although it became little more than a tax-voting assembly. The deputies' salaries were paid from the taxes they voted, and Charles refused to consider 'grievances before supply', i.e. he would not listen to their complaints until they had agreed to supply him with the taxes he needed.

A partnership was also effected with the nobility. They were rewarded by being confirmed in their social position and privileges, above all in their exemption from taxes, but were increasingly excluded from the government of Spain. The price of this exclusion was that the nobility was allowed to govern the countryside with very little interference. Peace was brought to Castile but at considerable cost, with severe limitations on central policy and on the Crown's ability to make changes. However, with a compliant *Cortes*, Charles could now afford a standing army and was therefore less dependent on the power of the nobles.

The Spanish Empire had no institutions in common and no imperial bureaucracy. Any attempt at reform of the administration had to take account of the privileges of each territory and also the prolonged absence of the Emperor. But throughout Charles's huge empire there was a need for central direction and co-ordination of policies. Gattinara, the imperial chancellor, therefore developed the conciliar system of Ferdinand and Isabella by reforming the Council of Castile, creating the Councils of Finance and the Indies and remodelling the Council of War. Later, in 1555, a Council of Italy was created which completed the system. The councils were bureaucratic committees composed mainly of **letrados** (university-trained lawyers) for the administration of royal policy. They communicated with the Emperor through a secretary who thereby acquired considerable power. The most important of these was Francisco de los Cobos, secretary of the Council of Finance, who was largely responsible for the administration of Spain in Charles's absence. An Andalucian of humble origins, he amassed a vast fortune, but he was a reliable and efficient servant and as such enjoyed Charles's fullest confidence. Cobos was a rival of Gattinara's and this led to a decline in the latter's influence from about 1527. After Gattinara's death, Charles became his own chancellor, with Cobos responsible for Spanish and Mediterranean affairs and Nicholas Perrenot, Lord of Granvelle, his leading adviser on the Netherlands and the Empire.

The secretaries acted as filters for incoming correspondence and decided whether a dispatch should go direct to the Emperor or to the appropriate council for discussion first. The system also gave council members, especially the secretaries, enormous patronage, as they controlled access to the Emperor. Corruption was rife and the bureaucracy grew to parasitic proportions. Although it worked adequately in ordinary circumstances, the conciliar system found it hard to respond to crises. This is clearly seen in the Council of Finance.

C *Finance*

The Council of Finance was created in 1523 to supervise and control all income and expenditure, and to establish regular and efficient means of raising money. In fact the enormous scale of Charles's commitments meant that all the council could do was to stave off bankruptcy by a series of desperate measures, such as the sale of offices or the seizure of private shipments of bullion. The government of each of Charles's territories was in theory self-supporting but in practice by the end of the reign several, such as the German territories, were reliant upon the subsidies of other areas. In addition, there were the constant wars against France and the Turks, which were an impossible financial burden.

Castile came to play an increasingly vital role in the financing of the Empire, not because it was particularly rich, rather the reverse, but because of the ease with which money could be extracted from it once the *Cortes* of Castile had been humbled. The influx of bullion from the New World, although not significant until the end of the reign, was channelled through Castile and this was a readily obtainable source of wealth. For this reason above all, Castile became the centre of Charles's empire and the most frequently tapped supply of funds. The results for Castile itself were less than favourable.

See pages 400–3

Initially, Charles relied most heavily upon the Netherlands and Italy for money as these were the wealthiest parts of his empire. However, the scale of the tax demands placed upon them led to revolt in Ghent in 1539 and to the viceroy of Naples complaining that further claims would be 'to squeeze juice from a stone'. In 1540 Charles wrote to his brother Ferdinand, 'I cannot be sustained except by my realms of Spain', and in effect this meant Castile, which henceforth bore the brunt of imperial expenditure. This was done with the agreement of the nobility as they were exempt from taxation. The *Cortes* invariably voted the huge sums demanded of them because they were unaffected. The unevenness of the tax burden was recognised by the rulers. In 1545 Philip wrote to his father, 'The common people who have to pay the *servicios* are reduced to such distress and misery that many of them walk naked.' Charles made an attempt to spread the distribution of taxes more widely in 1538 when he summoned the nobility and clergy to attend the *Cortes* and proposed the introduction of a new tax on foodstuffs, the *sisa*, which would be payable by all. The nobility refused to abandon their tax-free status and as a result were never again summoned to the *Cortes*, which found itself powerless to refuse the increasingly arbitrary demands of the Crown. The nobles' financial privilege had been bought at the expense of their political influence over government policy.

juros government bonds which could be bought and which gave a fixed rate of interest

Instead Charles relied more heavily on *servicios*, non-noble taxes, and on a number of more dubious expedients such as the sale of **juros**,

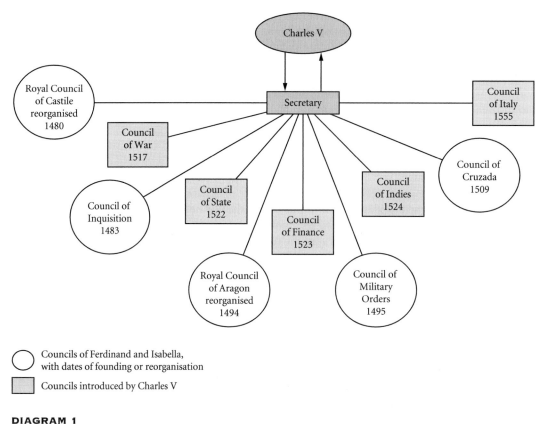

DIAGRAM 1
The government of Spain under Charles V

government bonds which carried a fixed annual interest and which meant mortgaging future revenues for present gain. He also used the services of foreign bankers whose interest rates climbed steeply as the reign progressed. To pay this interest, specific items of revenue were assigned to each debt and thus it was that by 1554 all revenue had been anticipated (earmarked for debt repayment) up to 1560. Castile's resources were swallowed up to meet expenses, most of which had little to do with Spanish interests.

D *The economy*

Charles presided over the start of Spain's 'golden age' when it became the most powerful state in Europe with an admired and feared army, a vigorous cultural life and an expanding overseas empire that produced unimagined wealth. But he has also been criticised by historians such as Koenigsberger for distorting the Spanish economy and failing to provide the right circumstances for growth, with the result that Spain eventually became an economic backwater from which it has only recently emerged.

His overriding need for money made it impossible for Charles to develop a coherent economic strategy. The opportunities afforded by the opening up of the New World ought to have given Spanish, particularly Castilian, trade and industry a great stimulus. In fact it proved totally unable to cope with the demands of the colonists and it was foreign merchants who benefited the most.

There was little understanding of economic forces and at one stage Charles agreed to a ban on all exports of cloth except that to the Indies in an effort to keep domestic prices down. This caused such a depression in the textile industry that the ban had to be lifted after five years.

The reasons for the high prices prompting the export ban are uncertain, but it has been claimed that the influx of bullion was partly responsible. Bullion helped to finance Charles's wars and to provide an extravagant lifestyle for the nobles but it was not used for investment in industry and provided no lasting benefit to the economy. Heavy taxation discouraged industrial investment, which was despised, and the greatest financial return was to be obtained by buying *juros*. It was the pressing demands of warfare that led to the failure to develop an economy in the New World to the benefit of Castile, or to build up the Castilian economy for future benefit. Money was always required immediately and this effectively prevented any long-term strategy.

See pages 25–6

Some parts of the Spanish economy did flourish in Charles's reign. Seville and its hinterland enjoyed the fruits that a monopoly of the Atlantic trade gave them; the ironworks of the Basque region flourished; ceramics, leather and silk were all in demand. However, Spanish agriculture was neglected and backward. Too much emphasis was placed on the rearing of sheep, encouraged by the government because of the taxes it produced, but with the consequence that, with an expanding home market as well as the Indies, Castile was regularly importing wheat by 1560. Increased demand led to higher prices and the consequence of the Empire for the ordinary Spaniard was a decline in living standards.

In general it can be said that opportunities were missed to put the Spanish economy on a sound footing that would have enabled it to meet the demands of imperialism. That Spain managed to maintain an illusion of strength as Europe's greatest power until 1660 says more for the long-suffering of the ordinary people than it does for the inherent strength of the economy. Decline, when it became evident, was swift and almost irreversible.

With hindsight, it is easy to see Charles's handling of the Spanish economy as his greatest failure. Henry Kamen points out how other countries profited from Spain's failures. Armaments were imported from Italy and textiles from England to provide for Spanish colonists' needs. The *Cortes* of Valladolid complained in 1548 that 'Spain has become an Indies for the foreigner'. By the seventeenth century five-sixths of the trade from Cadiz was no longer in the hands of Spaniards. In criticising Charles's lack of imagination, however, we must bear in mind his very imperfect understanding of economic forces and his desperate need for ready cash. Investment in industrial enterprises was a risky business with a slow and uncertain return. On the other hand, bullion was very acceptable to foreign financiers, who would lend large sums on the security of future shipments. As is often the case with governments, short-term advantage triumphed over long-term planning.

The 1520s and 1530s saw both the circumnavigation of the world by Magellan's expedition and the conquest of Mexico and Peru by Cortes and Pizarro. For the Indians the effect of conquest was devastating: the cruelty of the Spaniards, their diseases and their labour demands combined to reduce the native population of Mexico from about 25.2 million in 1518 to 2.65 million in 1568. The belated recognition by the government that the labour force was being destroyed led to the decision to import black slaves from Africa, with incalculable results. It also led to the passing of the New Laws in 1542 which freed, at least in law, all Indian slaves in the New World and set up an organised system of *audiencias* (courts) and officials under a viceroy. Despite its imperfections, this system worked reasonably well and can justifiably be seen as one of Charles's successes.

| See Chapter 4 |

Spain achieved its greatest glory under Charles and his descendants. For 150 years the rest of Europe feared and respected its power. The foundations of this power were, however, less solid than they appeared. The enormous scale of Charles V's commitments, above all the struggle in Germany and eastern Europe, led to a distortion of the Spanish economy for reasons which had no connection with Spain. The country was saddled with an intolerable burden of debt, which led to successive bankruptcies in future decades. Specifically Spanish interests, above all in the Mediterranean, were neglected for problems in the rest of the *monarchia*, so that Spain's glory was also her weakness. The privileges of Empire could not be divorced from its burdens.

KEY ISSUE

Did Spain gain or lose more from the reign of Charles V?

2 ↬ THE NETHERLANDS

Charles's ancestral home, the Netherlands, where his reign began and ended, provided crucial resources for the Emperor's wars in the first part of his reign. He made relatively frequent, but brief visits to the Netherlands (ten visits totalling twelve years) and relied heavily on the capable services of his aunt, Margaret of Austria, and sister, Mary of Hungary.

The Netherlands was the most urbanised part of Europe. It was the richest of Charles's territories, with a flourishing cloth industry and enterprising merchants. For many years Charles was dependent on the subsidies they granted him. In 1559 Soriano, the Venetian ambassador, wrote 'These lands are the treasuries of the King of Spain, his mines and his Indies, they have financed the enterprises of the Emperor for so many years in the wars of France, Italy and Germany.' Already, however, this was no longer true. As in Spain, Charles taxed his subjects until they would pay no more. In so doing he provoked serious

The Monarchia

Charles believed he had received his inheritance from God as a sacred trust and that it was his responsibility to maintain the unity of Christendom and to fight the Infidel. This view was shared by Mercurino Gattinara, his imperial chancellor from 1518 to 1530, who wrote to Charles immediately after his election as Emperor in 1519:

> Sire, God has been very merciful to you: he has raised you above all the Kings and princes of Christendom to a power such as no sovereign has enjoyed since your ancestor Charles the Great (i.e. Charlemagne). He has set you on the way towards a world monarchy, towards the uniting of all Christendom under a single shepherd.

Gattinara had a vision of a true union of all Charles's territories, hoping that he would eventually be the legislator of the whole world, building on the ideas of Dante. Gattinara himself was the only link between the territories (apart from Charles) because he exercised jurisdiction over all of them and presided over all councils. He saw Italy as the centre of Charles's empire and the struggle for Milan as therefore of the first importance. If Charles could win Italy and the friendship of the Pope, he would be able to dominate Europe. Gattinara died in 1530 at an auspicious moment, when it seemed as if his dream was realised. Charles did not appoint another chancellor, taking on the duties himself, but he had absorbed much of Gattinara's outlook.

However, the concept of a universal empire had to come to terms with political realities. Although contemporaries were unaware of it, the era of universalism was past. The Reformation was about to destroy the unity of Christendom so dear to Charles's heart and political power was increasingly being vested in nation states such as France and England. The Holy Roman Empire from which Charles derived his prestigious title was in fact where he enjoyed least power, as the princes sought to win autonomy. The size of the *monarchia* and the threat it posed to other states meant that Charles was engaged in a constant struggle with hostile forces and his twin aims of defeating the Infidel and eradicating heresy were to remain unrealised. Crusades and chivalry were things of the past; Charles had to face a world where the most Christian King of France would ally not only with Protestants but also with the Turks.

opposition, especially in Ghent, and, more seriously, stirred up hostility to the notion of foreign rule. This was kept in check during his reign because of his personal popularity as a Burgundian but it surfaced with great vigour when his son, a Spaniard, took over. The Low Countries resented the fact that the money they voted was not always spent in their interests. They particularly disliked the war with France.

Charles was eager to bring the provinces of the Netherlands into a closer union and to provide them with a more efficient and centralised government. Each province had its own estates (parliament) and this made effective control more difficult. In 1531 the Council of State set up a Council of Finance to co-ordinate the collection of taxes, and a High Court of Appeal. Both were strongly opposed, as was a plan in 1534 to create a standing army paid for by each province, for 'if we accept the proposal we shall undoubtedly be more united, but we shall be dealt with in the manner of France', i.e. with a loss of local liberties.

Charles realised that to insist on reforms might endanger his sources of revenue and therefore refrained from pushing his claims too far. He was forced to concede the **redress of grievances** before supply and to watch every demand for money being haggled over and whittled down. The provincial estates were even allowed to build up their own administrative machinery to control the collection and expenditure of the taxes they voted. The government derived one major advantage from its failure to centralise and that was the continuing local nature of the estates. Whilst there was no political unity, there would be no concerted opposition to challenge the position of royal authority.

redress of grievances complaints brought to the monarch in parliament or its equivalent for him to remedy

This became increasingly important as the government increased its demands for money against a steadily rising tide of discontent. War disrupted trade and was therefore damaging to the economy and the Netherlands was very vulnerable to attacks from France, so there were constant demands for peace. These were ignored by Charles and as a result there were riots in Bois-le-Duc in 1525, Brussels in 1532 and in 1537 Charles's birthplace Ghent began a tax strike that had flared into open rebellion by 1539.

Ghent was a city in decline and the demands for subsidies in the French war of 1537 had been too much. The whole of Flanders was equally dissatisfied but the revolt failed to become general because the guilds set up a democratic dictatorship and terrorised the government's supporters in the upper classes, thus frightening potential leaders in other areas. Charles took the revolt seriously enough to come in person in 1540 to crush it. Ghent lost its charter, was forced to pay a heavy fine, a quarter of the town was pulled down to make a fortress and representatives of all classes had to beg pardon barefoot and on their knees. Such harsh punishment was intended to deter potential imitators, and the excessive tax demands continued. The Netherlands claimed that in five years it had given Charles extraordinary grants of eight million ducats, yet he still left his son Philip with a sizeable debt.

In religion, Charles acted with severity. The laws against heresy (*placaten*) became increasingly harsh throughout the reign, although Lutherans were already being burnt in 1523. Despite this, Lutheran and radical preachers found a ready audience among the artisans of the towns and heresy continued to spread and flourish.

Superficially, Charles's reign was successful in the Netherlands. Certainly he extended its territory by annexing Tournai (1521) and Cambrai (1543) from the French and creating six northern provinces by the defeat in 1543 of William, Duke of Cleves, the successor to Charles of Egmont, Duke of Guelders. The Netherlands thus became a coherent unit, at least in geographical terms. However, there was no political union and little sense of a common identity, as the course of the Revolt of the Netherlands in the latter half of the century was to show. Charles detached the Netherlands from the Empire, with which it had little in common, and created the prospect of a powerful North Sea Empire by the marriage of Philip to Mary Tudor in 1554. The frustration of this hope by Mary's childless death in 1558 left the Netherlands as an isolated outpost of a Spanish Empire that was firmly centred on the Mediterranean. In such a context, with a foreign king as ruler, the latent discontent, which had scarcely been suppressed under Charles, was to surface with explosive force that would require great tact to manage. Charles's legacy to Philip in the Netherlands was a potential powder keg.

KEY ISSUE

What problems did Charles leave in the Netherlands for his successor?

3 ↪ HABSBURG–VALOIS RIVALRY, 1521–29

See pages 273–7

France was constantly threatened by the vast span of Charles V's empire. Consequently it engaged in a series of wars against Charles, mainly in Italy, to prevent his domination of the peninsula, which Charles's capture of Milan in particular would represent. Charles had begun his reign at a disadvantage compared to the already victorious Francis I. Three years later, however, the tables were turned when Charles became Holy Roman Emperor and immediately took precedence over his rival.

This rivalry with Francis I was at the heart of Charles's problem as Emperor. Francis would never accept his claim to leadership of Christendom, and French interference in Italy and support for the Pope could prevent Charles from dominating the Papacy and securing the alliance he hoped for, which would be essential if he was to make his dream of leadership a reality. French propaganda portrayed Charles as bent on the domination of all other princes, and this image endured far more than Gattinara's more constructive idea of *monarchia*. The threat to Francis was more of a psychological one than a reality. Charles had no desire to conquer France, and no hope of doing so. However, Francis had to maintain his prestige by constantly diverting Charles from problems in the Empire and against the Turks, by forcing him to engage in costly wars over Italy.

Northern Italy, and specifically Milan, was crucial to Charles because it provided a route from Spain to Austria along which troops could pass when necessary. It was also important to have a safe overland route to the Netherlands. Milan was the key to this too. (The 'Spanish Road' was to increase in importance under Philip II.) If Charles lost control of Milan to France, the different elements of his empire would be isolated and effective action would become extremely difficult. The only alternative route to the Netherlands was by sea, which was also vulnerable to the French, and it therefore became important to secure the co-operation of England, which was forthcoming in the early 1520s at least.

Not only was Charles a threat to Francis but the reverse was also true. Charles had the difficulty of co-ordinating men and money from scattered territories, with France eager to exploit any weakness in the chain. Meanwhile, France as a unitary state did not experience the same logistical problems and could strike at whichever part of the Empire seemed vulnerable. Charles was a man of integrity and he found the unscrupulous Francis very hard to deal with, especially when the latter allied with the great enemy of Christendom, the Ottoman Empire.

There were also other irritants to drive the two sides apart. Italy had been a battleground since the fifteenth century and only domination by one side would end the conflict there. Charles wished to regain Burgundy, the ancestral home of his dynasty, annexed by France in 1477. Similarly, the incorporation of Navarre into Castile was not recognised by France. These old disputes could be revived whenever circumstances seemed appropriate (as when France tried to take advantage of the revolt of the *Comuneros* by reasserting claims to Navarre). However, the main bone of contention was Italy.

The French were active once more in Italy from 1521, but the Imperial forces routed them at Pavia in 1525 and captured Francis himself. In the ensuing Treaty of Madrid he agreed to surrender all claims on Italy and the Netherlands, and to return French Burgundy.

TIMELINE

The struggle for Italy, 1516–29

1516	Treaty of Noyon: an annual tribute of 100 000 ducats to France to prevent invasion when Charles goes to Spain
1521	French troops invade the Netherlands and war resumed in Italy Charles takes Tournai
1522	Battle of Bicocca: Charles takes Milan
1523	Anglo-imperial attack on France failed
1524	Francis I invades Italy and takes Milan. Allied to Pope
1525	Battle of Pavia: French defeat, Francis I captured Charles's alliance with Henry VIII breaks down
1526	Francis I released after signing the Treaty of Madrid On return to France, he repudiates the treaty League of Cognac: France, Pope and Venice
1527	Imperial troops sack Rome
1528	Naples besieged by French, blockaded by Genoese Andrea Doria, Genoese naval commander, switches to Spanish side, ensuring Spanish naval supremacy in western Mediterranean
1529	Battle of Landriano: Charles defeats French Treaty of Cambrai Francis I renounces claims to Italy, agrees to marry Charles's sister, Eleanor

TIMELINE

The defeat of Francis I

1530	Pope crowned Charles Holy Roman Emperor
1530–35	Francis makes alliances with Charles's enemies, including the Turks
1535	The Duke of Milan dies, childless
1536	Francis invades to try and prevent direct Habsburg rule in Milan
1537	Charles attacks France.; neither side makes any gains
1538	Ten-year Truce of Nice arranged by the Pope
1542	Francis I declares war again
	Fighting on three fronts: Milan, the Pyrenees and the Netherlands
	Large parts of the Netherlands devastated
	Charles takes Cambrai from the French and the six northern provinces of the Netherlands from their ally, the Duke of Cleves
	Henry VIII captures Boulogne
1544	Peace of Crèpy
1547	Francis I dies

Once given his freedom, and taking the risk that Charles would not harm his sons left as hostages, he went back on all that he had promised. After another French invasion of Italy and another defeat (at Landriano in 1529), the ensuing Peace of Cambrai once more recognised Habsburg domination of Italy, although Charles gave up his claim on French Burgundy. (During this period of fighting in 1527 the Sack of Rome by mutinous imperial troops had taken place, described in a documentary exercise at the end of the chapter.) When the last Sforza Duke of Milan died in 1535, Francis made his final bid to stop the duchy becoming a hereditary possession of the Habsburgs. He failed, and the 1538 Truce of Nice, brokered by the Pope, in effect confirmed Charles's victory in the Italian Wars. That was not the end of all fighting in Italy, but the main focus shifted to the north and the border lands between France, the Netherlands and Germany. There, the final round of fighting between Francis and Charles began in 1542 and ended in stalemate in 1544.

Ultimately, Francis I had not been able to tolerate Charles's claim to dominance. The latter might protest, as he did in 1536 that 'There are those who say that I wish to rule the world, but both my thoughts and my deeds demonstrate the contrary', but this was hardly enough to dissuade Francis from trying again and again to engineer the downfall of his great rival.

The French threat was the most troublesome distraction from Charles's other problems. Decisive action against the emergent German Protestantism had to be postponed and the internal needs of Charles's empire were sacrificed to the struggle against 'the most Christian' King of France. In 1529, the Turks had directly threatened the hereditary Habsburg lands in Austria but, for Charles, war against France took priority and he continued to demand troops for Italy from his brother Ferdinand, a request which was met but which strained the younger man's loyalty. In Germany, the Lutherans were offered an amnesty in

TIMELINE

The defeat of Charles V

1552 Treaty of Chambord: Henry II allied with the German Protestants who allow him to take Metz, Toul and Verdun

1553 Charles fails to recapture Metz

1556 Charles abdicates

TIMELINE

Stalemate

1557 Battle of San Quentin: Spanish victory France and Spain bankrupt

1558 Spanish ally, England, loses Calais to France Both sides desperate for a break from fighting

1559 Treaty of Câteau-Cambrésis Spanish control of Italy accepted but France keeps Metz, Toul, Verdun and Calais

KEY ISSUE

Did either Spain or France gain an advantage from their prolonged warfare?

return for their support of the Empire and to relieve the pressure on Ferdinand. The struggle against France in Italy took precedence over other concerns.

In 1547 Francis I died, shortly before Charles's great triumph at Mühlberg. It looked as if the Habsburg–Valois struggle had been decided in favour of the former. Charles had no equal in Europe and the stranglehold on France was tighter than ever; yet within six years Charles was a broken man, seeking only to escape from the trials of the world.

Francis I was succeeded by Henry II whose anti-Habsburg feelings had been encouraged by his years as a captive in Spain. He abandoned the struggle in Italy in order to concentrate on Charles's weakest spot by allying with the German Protestants, who agreed that Henry should have the key Rhine bishoprics of Metz, Toul and Verdun in return for his support in the war against Charles. After coming to terms with the Protestants, which he found deeply humiliating, in the winter of 1552–53 Charles made a valiant but unsuccessful attempt to recapture Metz, which, as he wrote to his sister Mary, gave the French 'a clear road to the Rhine and so they will be able to cut off my communications from South Germany to the Netherlands and Franche-Comté'.

His failure, coupled with the victory of the Protestants, convinced Charles that God had deserted him and he began to seek the best way to abdicate. The siege of Metz had been ruinously expensive (having cost two million ducats) and money could no longer be raised, even at interest rates of nearly fifty per cent. Charles decided that a younger man must tackle the problems and his reign ended with the final phase of the conflict with France unresolved.

Charles's son, Philip II, began his reign with a five-year truce with France which lasted barely a year before Pope Paul IV, who nursed a fanatical hatred of the Habsburgs, re-opened the conflict by trying to oust Philip from Naples, and summoning the French to his aid. Philip II issued the order for bankruptcy in 1557 (although it was never carried out) and Henry II was close to it. Exhaustion prompted both sides to peace. Two factors combined to improve the prospects of a lasting peace. The break-up of Charles V's inheritance removed the irritant of encirclement from France, and the death of Philip's wife, Mary Tudor, in November 1558 broke the Spanish–English alliance which was so dangerous to France.

The Peace of Câteau-Cambrèsis (1559) was a triumph for Charles V's southern struggles against the French. Italy, with the exception of Venice, became almost a Spanish province. Spanish dominance in the peninsula was secured and with it the 'Spanish Road' to the Netherlands. All France retained were five fortresses in Savoy. In the north, the advantage was with the French. Henry II retained Metz, Toul and Verdun and did not restore Calais to the English, while Philip withdrew from occupied towns in northern France. Many of the provisions of the treaty lasted for a century, as France was riven by forty years of internal strife, allowing Spain unchallenged dominance of western Europe.

4 ↜ THE STRUGGLE WITH THE OTTOMANS

For centuries Christendom and Islam had co-existed with uneasy relations on the frontiers. Islam had come closest in Spain, where the Moors were only finally defeated in Granada in 1492. Then the main threat came from the Barbary pirates and their raids on shipping and the coast. But this was no more than an irritant for a long time. This secure state was shattered by the emergence of the aggressive Ottoman Empire, which was committed to conquest and expansion. The fall of Constantinople in 1453 opened the way to the Mediterranean and in 1522 Rhodes fell – the last bastion of Christian power, except for Cyprus, in the eastern half of the sea. The previous year had seen the conquest of Belgrade, exposing the Danube, a route that would take the Turks deep into Europe and enable them to threaten Vienna, at the heart of the hereditary Habsburg lands.

See Chapter 10

Thus, within a few years of assuming power, Charles V was faced with the task of preventing further incursions by the Turks. He was in the front line of any attack and inevitably the activities of the Sultan were a cause of constant concern. Ferdinand bore the major responsibility for defending central Europe, although Charles assisted him when he could; it was in the Mediterranean that Charles was more closely involved. One of his most cherished wishes was to lead a crusade against the Turks, but the politics of Christendom never allowed this. Instead, Charles was denied the opportunity to take decisive action against the Turks in his home territory of the western Mediterranean by the scale of his commitments elsewhere. The reverse was also true. The pressure of the Turks on the eastern flank of the Empire prevented harsh measures against the German Protestants until it was too late.

A *The Mediterranean*

For Charles's Spanish subjects in the south, firm action against the Turks was essential if they were not to be in continual fear of attack from Barbary pirates, who became immeasurably more threatening in alliance with the Turks and with the possibility of internal revolt by the *Moriscos.* In 1516, the pirate Barbarossa had established himself in Algiers and become a vassal of the Sultan. In 1532 he became grand admiral of the entire Turkish fleet. This exposed the coasts of Italy and Spain, which suffered constant raids, and threatened Charles's communications. This was especially serious in Sicily as it acted as a granary for other parts of the Empire. Charles was unable to take action against Barbarossa until the 1530s when he had the help of the Genoese. There was no Spanish fleet that could compare with that of the Turks and no effort was made to build one. However, when Charles arrived back in Spain in 1533 after an absence of four years, he was anxious to fulfil his religious mission and to please his Spanish subjects by striking a blow at the Turks.

Moriscos the converted but not fully assimilated descendants of the Moors of Granada

See pages 308–9

This became more urgent after 1534 when Barbarossa made a daring attack on Italy that brought him close to Rome, and on his return captured Tunis. This was too serious to be ignored and Charles decided to lead an expedition in person to conquer Tunis, the gateway to the western Mediterranean, thus winning glory for himself as well as protecting the western Mediterranean. La Goletta and Tunis were taken in 1535 and eighty-five of Barbarossa's galleys – the bulk of his fleet – were captured. Although spectacular, the victory did not alter the balance of power. Barbarossa escaped to Algiers and within a few weeks had organised an attack on Minorca. Charles lacked the naval strength to follow up his acclaimed triumph and in 1536 the French entered into open alliance with the Sultan, which opened French ports to his ships.

War with France in 1536 prevented a continuation of the Mediterranean campaign until after the Truce of Nice in 1538. Charles then arranged an alliance with the Venetians and the Pope but distrust between these allies led to their defeat by the Turks at the Battle of Prevesa off the Greek coast in 1538. The Venetians made a separate peace with the Turks and without their galleys it was impossible for the western alliance to offer effective resistance to the Turkish fleet. Charles decided to strike at Algiers – the heart of Barbarossa's power. He regarded his mission as a holy war and again led his troops in person. Unfortunately the campaign in 1541, which started out too late in the year, was a disaster. One hundred and fifty ships were lost in a storm and Charles was forced to retreat with his army almost intact, partly because his own captivity or death could not be risked. This was a great blow to his reputation and put an end to serious moves against the Turks in the Mediterranean.

In 1543–44 the Turkish fleet wintered in Toulon and Christian slaves were sold in the market. In 1551 Tripoli was taken with ease by the new leader of the Turkish fleet, Dragut, providing another useful link in the chain with Algiers. Alarmed by the threat to Sicily, Charles removed Spanish and Italian troops from Württemberg, thus directly encouraging the German rebellion of 1552. What saved the western Mediterranean from complete Turkish domination was its distance from Turkey, the internal dynastic problems of Suleiman, and war against Persia. Charles V and Suleiman I faced similar problems. Their empires were too big to make concerted action in one area a possibility for long. Both linked up with the other's enemies but in the end the empires were too far apart for a decisive confrontation between them. Charles had dreamed of a crusade against Constantinople. Instead he had been unable to safeguard even his own territories.

B *Eastern Europe*

The naval power of the Turks was worrying but posed a less serious threat than the huge armies which Suleiman could muster for attack on central Europe. While German attention was focused on the Diet of Worms in 1521, Suleiman was busy capturing Belgrade and thus exposing Hungary to his attacks. The challenge was delayed for four years, but in 1526 he returned in force and wiped out the Hungarian army, together with its king, Louis II, at the battle of Mohacs. As brother-in-law to the childless Louis, Ferdinand claimed the crowns of Bohemia and Hungary despite the opposition of the powerful noble John Zapolyai who wanted the throne himself. Zapolyai won the support of Suleiman by swearing allegiance to him, presenting Ferdinand with a double threat. In 1529, the most serious attack on Habsburg power was launched. Vienna was besieged for three weeks until the onset of autumn forced the Turks to withdraw. It was the immense distances involved which saved the Habsburg lands, because the campaigning season was between eight and ten weeks long. The further the Ottomans penetrated into enemy territory, the longer were their lines of communication: the campaigning season became progressively shorter and the likelihood of further conquest more remote. Charles also made diplomatic contact with the Shah of Persia as a way of pressurising their common enemy.

In 1529, Ferdinand's pleas for aid had been largely ignored as Charles concentrated on securing his coronation before tackling the German problem. By 1532, when there was news of the approach of another large Turkish army, he was ready to show more positive support. A large army was assembled which confronted the Turks at Guns and forced them to retreat. The advantage was not followed up because the German troops refused to cross the frontier into Hungary. This failure was deeply disappointing to Ferdinand: inevitably his interests lay in central Europe and his devotion to Charles's wishes was often strained as the latter's attention was heavily concentrated on the western Mediterranean. For his part, Charles had not welcomed Ferdinand's election as King of Bohemia and Hungary because of increased conflict with the Turks and he was most concerned to ensure peace on his eastern flank so that he would be able to deal with other matters. Ferdinand's negotiations with Suleiman were therefore not unwelcome and the latter part of the reign saw a diminution of the Turkish threat, with the exception of the early 1540s when a fully Turkish administration was established in eastern Hungary. Uneasy co-existence could bring trouble. As late as 1683 the Turks were besieging Vienna. The problem was contained in the sixteenth century, but not solved.

The most serious effect of Turkish activity in central Europe was seen in Germany. Distraction by the Infidel was to cost Charles dear in his dealings with the heretic Lutherans.

> **KEY ISSUE**
>
> *How successfully did Charles deal with the Turkish threat?*

5 ⌐ THE HOLY ROMAN EMPIRE

Charles was unanimously elected Holy Roman Emperor in 1519 in succession to his grandfather Maximilian. The title remained in the Habsburg family until it died out and it is therefore easy to regard

Charles could rarely concentrate on one problem at a time.
The following shows some key years of the reign when he particularly
suffered distractions from one problem to another.

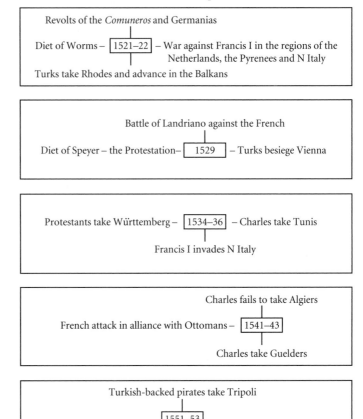

DIAGRAM 2
Charles's distractions

Charles's election as a foregone conclusion. This was not the case. The seven electors (Cologne, Mainz, Trier, Bohemia, the Palatinate, Brandenburg and Saxony) guarded their independence and the issue was in doubt to the end. The electors were persuaded to choose Charles by a combination of factors: he was prepared to spend most money in bribes – the election cost him nearly one million gold gulden; the Pope supported his main rival, Francis I, and Charles was unlikely to be able to interfere too much with the privileges of the princes given the scattered nature of his territories.

Thus Charles became the pre-eminent ruler in Christendom. It was a dubious honour. The empire entailed far more responsibilities than privileges since the title brought with it no actual power, only prestige, and it was in the Empire that Charles was finally to be defeated.

Germany was the largest nation in Europe, with great resources. However it was impossible to use these for common political objectives because of its internal disunity. There were more than 2500 different authorities, mainly knights but also great princes, church leaders and cities, acknowledging no overlord but the Emperor. The Emperor was limited by the Diet, which represented the electors, the princes and the free imperial cities. Without the cooperation of the Diet, the Emperor was powerless unless he could muster troops of his own to enforce his will – this was very seldom possible and even then he relied on the support of at least some of the Diet's members. In the early sixteenth century, both Maximilian and Charles made attempts to reform the Empire to make it a more coherent unit but these plans came to little, mainly because the princes were unwilling to surrender any of their power. There was a general desire for a united Germany in theory, but not at the expense of anyone's privileges. The development of a religious split in the Empire made an already difficult situation impossible for its ruler.

A *The Protestant threat*

Charles was deeply hurt by the appearance of heresy within his territories and pledged himself in 1521 to its eradication: 'To settle this matter, I am determined to use my kingdoms and dominions, my friends, my body, my blood, my life and my soul.' Unfortunately for him, it was politically expedient for many of the princes to adopt Lutheranism and without their active support, Charles could do little. The crucial middle years of the 1520s were devoted to settling Spain and by the time Charles turned his full attention back to the Empire, the Lutherans had established themselves too firmly to be dealt with easily. Charles's desire to give them a fair hearing and win them back by compromise through the action of a General Council also played into the Protestants' hands because it gave them over twenty years to build up their strength before an open confrontation took place.

Charles returned to Germany in 1530 for the Diet of Augsburg, fresh from his coronation as Emperor by the Pope and at the peak of his power. Peace had been secured with France and he was now anxious to settle the religious problem so that a united empire could face the Turkish threat. It was not to be so simple. The Catholic majority in the Diet was not prepared to use force against the Protestants until a General Council of the Church had met, something to which Pope Clement VII was resolutely opposed. Despite a desire for compromise on both sides, the Augsburg Confession, a Protestant statement of faith written by the conciliatory Melanchthon, was too much for Charles to accept. When the Protestants withdrew from the Diet, it was decided to return to the Edict of Worms after a delay of six months. In response, the Protestants formed an alliance known as the Schmalkaldic League in 1531.

Further action against the Protestants was postponed by the approach of a huge army under Suleiman. A religious truce meant that all the estates sent help to Charles, enabling him to halt the Turks at Guns. This was the first of a series of temporary truces granted to the Protestants as Charles required all his strength for the international situation. In 1534 Charles acquiesced in the loss of Württemberg to the Protestants because he was preparing to attack the Turks in the Mediterranean.

The Schmalkaldic League grew in power throughout the 1530s. It established contacts with France, England and Denmark, while carefully preserving an appearance of loyalty to the Emperor. Charles was more concerned about relations with France and the Turks and, as a result, his policy in Germany throughout the 1530s consisted of periodic denunciations of heresy combined with toleration in practice, while a solution was left to the General Council he repeatedly pressed upon the Pope. This absence of direction meant that the Protestants were able to make steady gains. By 1545 all of north-east and north-west Germany was Protestant, as well as large parts of the south. In 1544 Frederick II of the Palatinate became a Protestant. With all the secular electors except Bohemia favourable to Protestantism and the Elector Archbishop of Cologne leaning in the same direction, the possibility of a Protestant empire could no longer be ignored. It was time for Charles to take positive action. Fortunately for him, events had been moving in his direction for some time.

The Schmalkaldic League began to break up after 1540. From 1541 Landgrave Philip of Hesse, its most dynamic leader, was at the mercy of Charles V after he made a bigamous marriage (with the support of Luther) to avoid the sin of adultery! Bigamy carried the death penalty and so Philip was forced to support the Emperor. This gave rise to hopes for peace at the Colloquy of Regensburg in 1541. Two months of amicable talks between theologians of both sides failed to secure a compromise that either would accept. This was a turning point for Charles; he had based his whole policy on the idea of peaceful compromise and its failure left him bitterly disillusioned. Charles did not understand how strong religious passions were, especially on the question of the Eucharist. Issues which might have been peacefully settled by compromise twenty years before were now too deeply entrenched; only military victory or toleration would solve the problem now. As the latter was unacceptable to Charles in the long term, it left force as the only option.

Accordingly, Charles began to look for allies among the princes, but in the meantime he remained outwardly conciliatory in order to secure the help of the Protestants for the last war against Francis I. In the Peace of Crèpy (1544), Francis not only agreed to co-operate over the calling of a General Council but also agreed not to form alliances with the German Protestants. Suddenly they were isolated and Charles increased his advantages by making important alliances. The support of Bavaria was secured by promising Ferdinand's eldest daughter for Duke Albert's eldest son. Most important of all, the Protestant Duke Maurice of Saxony was promised his cousin's title as Elector of Saxony if he went over to Charles. For once the Pope (Paul III) was in full support of the Emperor and was generous with troops and money. All was now

See page 361

prepared for full-scale war against the heretics. Already, in 1543, a campaign against the Duke of Cleves had forced him to abandon the reformation of his territories.

A Venetian ambassador at the court of Charles V reviewed the situation in July 1546:

> Concerning the Emperor's disposition towards the States of Germany, every one is at present certain that war is in contemplation... The causes which are said to have moved the Emperor to this, are: first, the little regard which the German States have for some years past shown to his orders, by not attending the Diet; and secondly, the fear that the heresy which infects some of them, should spread over them all, and finally pervert his dominions in the Low Countries, which are the chief sources of his greatness... The Princes of Germany have never liked Charles V; probably because he continually avails himself of their counsels, without treating them in the deferential and considerate manner, which Maximilian and all the former Emperors accustomed them to expect.
>
> They complain that he has wasted power in disputes with his fellow Christians, instead of turning it to account against the Turk, as was his duty; that he is now about to make war upon themselves, and that under the pretence of religious zeal, he intends to conduct a foreign army into Germany, to trample on their ancient liberties.

1. What distinction can be drawn between the motives for war attributed to Charles V and what the princes believed to be the case?
2. From your reading on Charles V so far, do you think the princes' fears were justified?

B *Resort to force*

The Schmalkaldic League was slow to realise that Charles had changed his policy. This was partly because they had no wish to fight the Emperor. Luther's insistence on obedience to secular rulers was part of his appeal to the princes but also made it harder for them to challenge their own overlord. By September 1546 the Emperor's army from the Netherlands, Hungary, different parts of the Empire and Italy was united. The failure of the League to win a quick victory before the armies united demonstrates its lack of effective leadership. There was no common ultimate objective and considerable distrust existed between the cities (who refused to pay for the troops) and the princes.

Charles won control of south Germany with little difficulty. Then in April 1547 he took the Lutherans by surprise and at the Battle of Mühlberg he crushed the army of the league, captured Elector John Frederick and gave his electoral title and the land which went with it to Maurice of Saxony. Mühlberg gave Charles control of the whole of Germany and his triumph was completed when Philip of Hesse surrendered in June. Germany was at his mercy; Francis I, Henry VIII and Luther were all dead. It seemed as if Charles could do as he pleased.

KEY ISSUE

Why did Charles wait so long before taking decisive action against the Protestants?

MAP 12

War in the Empire

Paradoxically, the very completeness of his triumph ensured that it would be temporary. The Pope had already withdrawn his support and the Catholic princes were not prepared to see Charles consolidate his position at the expense of the Protestants if it would also adversely affect their own power. Charles had shown his strength in combination with a number of the princes but if they all combined against him, he was powerless to enforce his will. Charles's position had been untenable from the start. An alliance with the Protestant Duke Maurice in a religious war was always bound to break down.

A Diet was summoned to Augsburg in the autumn of 1547 and the Emperor proposed the formation of a league of princes with himself at the head, in which each member would contribute to the cost of a standing army to enforce the laws of the Empire. This was not a new idea – it was based on the earlier Swabian League – but it was defeated by the opposition of the princes who recognised how much Charles would be strengthened. The Elector of Brandenburg summed up their feelings: the Empire 'would be reduced to servitude'.

The religious question was also unresolved. The General Council at Trent, which first met in 1545, was a disappointment for Charles because it was not seeking a compromise solution to the Protestant problem, but a restatement of the Catholic faith in opposition to Protestantism. Charles attempted to solve the German problem himself by drawing up the Augsburg Interim in 1548, a compromise that allowed clerical marriage and communion in both kinds, i.e. both bread and wine; but there were no substantial concessions and the interim was disliked by everyone. The Pope saw it as an attack on his own position and rights, while for the Protestants it was a wholly inadequate addressing of the depth of their religious convictions.

This double failure by Charles to resolve the political and religious problems of the Empire made him consider the future in a new light. The victory at Mühlberg had only been possible with the help of money and troops from the Netherlands and Spain. Any future emperor deprived of these resources would find governing the Empire even more impossible than Charles himself. Such reasoning led Charles to question the position of his brother Ferdinand and, in so doing, to split the Habsburg family down the middle.

C *Dynastic quarrels*

Charles had promised to work for Ferdinand's election as King of the Romans which would give him the right to succeed Charles as emperor; a promise that was fulfilled in 1531 after Charles's coronation as Emperor. Since then, Ferdinand had been Charles's devoted regent, putting his brother's concerns above his own even when there was serious danger,

---

FERDINAND, KING OF THE ROMANS FROM 1531, EMPEROR 1558–64

PROFILE

Three years younger than Charles, Ferdinand was born and brought up in Spain and did not meet his older brother until 1517. He was much more popular in Spain than Charles, having been brought up as a Spaniard and to remove him as a possible threat to Charles, the treaty of Brussels was signed in 1522, by which Ferdinand gained control of the Habsburg lands in Austria and acted as Charles's regent in the Holy Roman Empire. In 1521 he married Anna, daughter of the King of Bohemia and Hungary.

Ferdinand was of a gentle, quiet disposition and tended to be overshadowed by the more aggressive Charles. Like his nephew, the future Philip II, he was very reserved and did not believe in displaying emotion. He was a moderate who was ready to compromise and also a skilled negotiator, which was of great importance in the management of the Empire. He was very loyal to Charles, at some cost to his own interests, but was not prepared to sacrifice the prospects of his children.

especially from the Turks. This was not easy for a proud and ambitious man but Ferdinand recognised that his power had come from Charles and that he gained from the Emperor's prestige. Relations between the brothers had been especially good during the 1540s and in the Schmalkaldic War. It therefore came as a great blow to Ferdinand when Charles proposed that his own son, Philip, should succeed Ferdinand as Emperor instead of the latter's son, Maximilian. In this way Charles felt that the two sides of the dynasty could be kept closely linked and Spanish resources could be made available for imperial purposes.

This provoked a bitter family quarrel. Eight months of negotiations at Augsburg during 1550–51 eventually produced the Augsburg Agreement in which Ferdinand accepted the idea of alternating the succession in the Empire between the two branches. The agreement did not please Maximilian or the princes, who felt that their rights as electors were being ignored and who were not prepared in any case to accept the succession of Philip, a foreigner with no knowledge of Germany. The level of opposition was such that eventually Philip renounced his right to succeed Ferdinand. In return, Milan was detached from the Empire and added to the Spanish kingdoms. Charles had alienated his brother to no purpose and at a time when he was to face the most serious challenge to his power.

D *The revolt of the princes*

Charles's cavalier attitude to the rights of the electors and his humiliating imprisonment of John Frederick of Saxony and Philip of Hesse produced fears about the future liberties of the princes which sparked off revolt. The northern princes formed themselves into a league in 1550, for the defence of Lutheranism and the liberation of Philip of Hesse. This became much more dangerous for Charles when Maurice of Saxony joined, having not received the bishoprics of Halberstadt and Magdeburg which he had been promised. Also the Protestant princes secured the alliance of Henry II of France in return

See page 281

for the bishoprics of Metz, Toul and Verdun. Such a combination had always been Charles's greatest fear but for a long time he refused to take seriously the reports of a movement against him. His contempt for the princes after Mühlberg convinced him that they would never dare to attack him.

Accordingly he left any preparations for war much too late. Troops were even withdrawn from the Empire because Charles wanted to take the Duchy of Parma. Maurice took the city of Magdeburg and Henry II walked into the Rhine bishoprics with no effective opposition. Charles was nearly captured in Innsbruck in May 1552 and the humiliation of flight gave him a shock from which he was unable to recover, although in the short term he showed great resolution in mustering resources from Spain, the one territory that could supply them. Charles now distrusted Ferdinand but had no one else to rely on to negotiate with the princes. Peace within Germany became vital as the external threats mounted. The pirate Dragut was terrorising Naples, Ferdinand became involved in another Turkish war in Hungary, with French help the imperial garrison was driven out of Siena and there were hostilities on the Flemish border.

Maurice of Saxony was also ready to negotiate because he lacked the resources to follow up his victory over the Emperor. In August 1552 temporary agreement was reached in the Treaty of Passau. Charles was not prepared to accept the existence of Lutheranism as inevitable and permanent; the furthest he would go was to offer a truce in religious matters until the next Diet. Maurice and his allies were compelled to make do with this so that attention could then be turned to the French.

The failure of the siege of Metz (November 1552–January 1553) was a bitter blow to Charles. He had hoped to drive the French out of the Empire and then resolve the problems in Germany by force. This was now impossible and the scale of his problems outstripped his resources. Even the long-suffering Castile could do no more – its revenues were already anticipated for the next three years. In the Empire the rule of law had broken down and Albert Alcibiades of Prussia, described as 'an enormous, insane, wild beast', was able to terrorise the country. Deeply disillusioned and with a feeling that God had deserted him, Charles decided that he was unable to solve the problems of the Empire and that he must withdraw from it. In January 1553 he went to the Netherlands and never returned to Germany. The final acts of the reign were to be those of Ferdinand, although Charles's abdication was not accepted by the electors until 1558.

> **KEY ISSUE**
>
> *How did Charles's triumph at Mühlberg lead so quickly to defeat?*

E *The Peace of Augsburg*

The first priority was to restore order. Leagues were formed which included both Catholic and Protestant princes. In July 1553 Albert Alcibiades was defeated at the battle of Sievershausen by Maurice of Saxony who was fatally wounded. Order was restored but only because the princes had wanted it. The reliance of the Emperor on the power of the princes was made plain, but so was their commitment to the continuing existence of the Empire and their willingness to preserve it. Ferdinand recognised that he could not coerce the princes within their own territories and this acceptance of political reality made the solution of the religious problem a possibility.

The Diet met at Augsburg in February 1555. Charles refused to attend: 'My reason is only this question of religion, in regard to which I have an unconquerable scruple.' In April 1555 he repeated his opposition to compromise, protesting against anything which 'could infringe, hurt, weaken or burden our ancient true Christian and Catholic faith'. In theory, this absolute stand was the position of both sides at the Diet. The ultimate aim was Christian unity, but in the meantime peace was a temporary necessity. The Catholics recognised that they could not subdue the Lutherans by force, while the latter felt that their faith would become universal once it was freed from persecution.

The final solution was not tolerant in any real sense. It made provision only for Lutherans and Catholics, ignoring the growing strength of the Calvinists. Each prince was allowed to choose his own religion and thus determine the faith of his subjects – summed up in the formula *cuius regio, eius religio* (his territory, his religion). There was to be no missionary activity or protection of co-religionists in other territories. No territory ruled by a bishop which was Catholic in 1552 was allowed to become Protestant.

This pragmatic solution subordinated religion to politics. It was only possible in a nation such as Germany, which had little real unity. Religious unity was preserved – but only within the bounds of each principality. More than anything else, this destroyed the medieval concept of the unity of the Empire and opened the way for the destructive conflicts of the next century.

Charles regarded his defeat in the Empire as his greatest failure and, on his own terms, this was so.

6 ⌐ THE ABDICATION OF CHARLES V

After his defeat at Metz, Charles sank into apathy and despair. He was aroused by the death of Edward VI in July 1553 and the succession of the still unmarried Mary. This gave rise to the possibility of leaving Philip with an empire that would revolve around Spain, England and the Netherlands, effectively strangling the hated France. This was a worthy inheritance for his beloved son and Charles felt he could then abdicate with a clear conscience. His plans had to be postponed for a time, however, because Henry II launched a savage attack upon Hainault in 1554. But then events in 1555 convinced Charles he must go. His mother died in April, Mary turned out to be barren, the religious peace of Augsburg was agreed in Germany and the new Pope, Paul IV, was fanatically anti-Spanish. To Charles, it seemed as if the same problems were reappearing and that he had failed in all his objectives.

On 25 October 1555, in the great hall of the castle at Brussels where he had begun his reign, Charles V abdicated with great solemnity: the crowd 'could not restrain their tears and sobs'. In a private ceremony in January 1556 he renounced his rights to Spain. He continued as Holy Roman Emperor in name only until February 1558 when the electors agreed to choose Ferdinand instead.

Charles retired to Spain with his sisters Mary and Eleanor. He built himself a modest house near the remote monastery at Yuste and there he died in September 1558.

7 ⌐ CHARLES V – A FAILURE?

Charles V was one of the great figures of his time. 'His personal moral character towered far above that of the princes of his age' (H. Holborn). He took the highly unusual step of abdicating voluntarily, feeling that his reign had been a failure, which in itself shows his integrity. Charles undoubtedly did fail in his two main objectives of suppressing heresy and leading a crusade against the Turks, but this should not blind us to his achievements. The Turkish menace was withstood; Lutheranism had to be accepted as permanent but German Catholicism was saved at a crucial moment and revived in the latter part of the century; the opening of the Council of Trent in 1545 suggested that at last Pope and Emperor would join forces to renew the Church. Also, the great biography by Karl Brandi, the foundation of modern studies of Charles V, focuses attention on Charles in northern Europe, where his setbacks were greatest. He might be thought more of a success if he is viewed as a Mediterranean monarch rather than as a world emperor.

Charles's real failure as a ruler lay not in the inability to achieve his ideals, which were unrealisable, but in the legacy he left to his successors. Warfare was an almost constant backdrop to the reign, distorted the economies of Spain and the Netherlands and in the latter caused serious unrest. In Germany the imperial title was preserved but only with the failure to gain real power and the effective fragmentation of the Empire.

Charles was a man of ideals with a deep sense of religious calling and purpose. He told Philip to 'exterminate heresy, lest it take root and overturn the state and social order' and he sought for peace so that he could purge the stain of heresy from his lands. Throughout his reign, the prize of victory seemed to come within his grasp (e.g. in 1525, 1530 and 1547) only to be snatched away by a new combination of forces working against him. The tragedy of Charles V was that he had a vision of Christendom united under one Pope and one Emperor working in harmony, which the extent of his dominions appeared to make a real possibility. In reality, the very power that he wielded was so threatening to others that it led to constant division and warfare, precisely what Charles sought to avoid. As N.M. Sutherland comments, even 'successive popes were not sorry to see Charles V ruined by the problem of heresy whose resolution might have greatly increased his power'. Vision and failure were inextricably interwoven from the start and it was no disgrace when Charles realised this and abandoned the struggle to men whose responsibilities were less and whose vision was narrower.

> **KEY ISSUE**
>
> *Was the imperial title more a burden than a privilege?*

8 ⌐ BIBLIOGRAPHY

**H.G. Koenisberger, revised M. Rodríguez-Salgado, *New Cambridge Modern History, Vol. 2* (Chapter X) (CUP, 1990), *M. Rady, *Emperor

Charles V (Longman Seminar Studies, 1989) or *S. MacDonald, *Charles V, Ruler, Dynast and Defender of the Faith, 1500–58* (Hodder and Stoughton, 1992) are the most concise general surveys. Karl Brandi, *The Emperor Charles V* (Harvester, 1980) is the classic biography, while *A.F. Alvarez, *Charles V: Elected Emperor and Hereditary Ruler* (Thames and Hudson, 1975) is more readable. J. Lynch, *Spain Under the Habsburgs, Vol. 1* (Blackwell, 3rd ed., 1991) and *H. Kamen, *Spain 1469–1714: A Society of Conflict* (Longman, 1983) show the effect of his rule on Spain. H. Holborn, *A History of Modern Germany: The Reformation* (Knopf, 1959) covers the conflict with the German princes well. *R. Bonney, *The European Dynastic States 1494–1660* (pp. 109–24) (OUP, 1991) offers incisive comment on the whole topic.

9 ↪ STRUCTURED AND ESSAY QUESTIONS

A *Structured questions.*
1. (a) What was Charles's policy towards the Protestants?
   (b) 'Charles V was a failure as Holy Roman Emperor.' Do you agree?
2. (a) What were the causes of the revolt of the *Comuneros*?
   (b) How successfully did Charles V govern Spain?

B *Essay questions.*
1. To what extent were Charles V's problems of his own making?
2. 'A resounding success.' Is this a fair judgement of Charles V's rule as King of Spain?
3. Why did Charles V never create a unified administration for his empire?
4. Was Charles's conception of his role as Emperor unrealistic in the sixteenth century?
5. What were Charles V's aims against the Turks and how far did he realise them? (*See Chapter 10 to help with this answer.*)

Advice: *Structured questions and the broader picture*

In a structured question, the level of analysis expected to reach the highest grade will be less sophisticated than that required for a full essay. However the same skills are still required and the more evidence you can give of understanding the broader picture and making connections, the more highly you will be rewarded. The points you make must be relevant – no credit will be given if they are not – but you should demonstrate that you understand the context in which decisions were made and events occurred.
   Example question:

1.(a) What was Charles's policy towards the Protestants?

You would need to give a coherent account of what Charles did about the Protestants during his reign. Include factors such as his hatred of heresy, his desire to win the Protestants back and the scale of Charles's commitments. You do not have the time to narrate all the events but you should show how his policy changed from condemnation of Luther at the Diet of Worms in 1521, through the years of compromise and uncertainty while he was distracted by war against France and the Ottomans, until he turned to military confrontation with the Protestants from the mid-1540s onwards. You should not use this section to make judgements; that comes in the next part.

1. (b) 'Charles V was a failure as Holy Roman Emperor.' Do you agree?

You should assess the success of Charles's policy towards the Protestants and then consider other factors which made him a success or a failure before drawing a conclusion. For instance, you need to discuss the weak constitutional basis of imperial authority which Charles inherited. And while it was Protestantism that became the major challenge, do not ignore the French and Ottoman threats to the Empire. (In the end it was the seizure of Metz by Henry II of France that finally broke Charles.) Make sure you write relevantly – Spain, in particular, was not part of the Holy Roman Empire, however important it was as one of Charles's dominions, so you can only bring it in to make comparative points. One might be the greater authority he enjoyed there in contrast with his weak constitutional position in the Empire.

Advice: *Discussion essays*

Many A-level essays have the word 'discuss' before or after a statement or quotation. Variants include 'comment' or 'do you agree?' but they are all the same type of question and are inviting a 'yes/no' answer. If a one-word answer makes sense, it is a discussion essay, e.g.: ' "A resounding success". Is this a fair judgement of Charles V's rule as King of Spain?' Note that in this example 'discuss' or 'comment' is not included in the title.

You may have strong views on the question asked but the examiners would not have asked the question unless there was an opposing case, so even though you should express at least qualified support for one side or the other, it is essential to look at both sides. To put it another way, you must do both the 'yes' and the 'no' side.

For this type of question, examiners often choose areas of current controversy among historians. If you have familiarised yourself with recent interpretations on a topic and can demonstrate your knowledge of leading ideas, this will be a great advantage.

Planning a 'yes/no' essay is relatively easy as a structure is already provided, since you must consider each side in turn. If the question is in two parts, each of these must also have a 'yes' and 'no' side. In your conclusion you should then explain which side of the argument you favour and why.

Consider this question:

'"More a Mediterranean Monarch than a European Emperor." Discuss this view of Charles V.'

(i)   To plan the essay, first assemble arguments with supporting evidence in favour of the statement.

(ii)   Next, assemble arguments with supporting evidence against the statement.

(iii)   Having assembled your arguments, you must arrange them in order. There are two ways of approaching this. *Either* put the 'yes' case first with arguments ranked in order of importance and then do the same for the 'no' case, *or* weave the two together – this can be more difficult as there are seldom times when there is a straight alternative but if you can link the contrasting views throughout the essay, it will make more effective reading.

(iv)   Finally, you come to the writing of the essay. Use your introduction to explore the difference between a Mediterranean monarch and a European emperor, i.e. what the examiner wants you to contrast. Then follows the bulk of the essay with the argument for each paragraph clearly stated in the first sentence and followed by some selected supporting evidence (remember that you are not giving Charles's life history). From your weighting of the essay, one should be able to tell which side you are favouring. In your conclusion you must then state what your answer to the question is, with any reservations.

PICTURE 23
'The death of Bourbon at the Sack of Rome' *by Meemkerck, engraved in 1527*

10 ∽ DOCUMENTARY EXERCISE ON THE SACK OF ROME, 1527

In 1527 starving soldiers in Charles's army, under the command of the Duke of Bourbon, moved south and sacked Rome in an orgy of looting and destruction that appalled the rest of Europe. They had not been paid for months and Rome was the richest prize they could take. There were three groups of soldiers in the attacking army: German Lutherans, Spanish Tercios and Italians. The Constable of Bourbon was killed in the first assault on the city and was therefore unable to restrain the wilder excesses of his troops that followed.

The responsibility of Charles V for the sack has been much debated. He was in Spain at the time, and there is no evidence that he approved the march on Rome. However, he took no steps to prevent the catastrophe, and the outcome was of benefit to him in subduing the opposition of the Pope.

Everywhere cries, the clash of arms and the shrieks of women and children, the crackling of fire and the crash of falling roofs. We were numb with fear...

SOURCE A
A Frenchman, Grotier.

Burned is the great chapel of St Peter and Sixtus...the heads of the Apostles are stolen...the sacrament thrown into the mud...reliquaries trampled under foot...I shudder to contemplate this, for Christians are doing what even the Turks never did.

SOURCE B
Cardinal Salvati.

There was a statue of the Madonna dressed in a robe of huge pearls...the sacristy was full of treasures...there was a cross of the finest gold covered with pearls and precious stones which was of great value...nothing was saved.

SOURCE C
Sister Orsolo of the Monastry of Santa Cosimata.

In the destruction of Rome, the Germans showed themselves to be bad enough, the Italians were worse, but worst of all were the Spaniards.

SOURCE D
A Citizen of Narvis.

It was the Spaniards who broke open the tomb of Pope Julius II, who had been dead for fourteen years, and dragged out the corpse to plunder it.

SOURCE E
An eye witness.

It was showed in some cases that the Lutheran Germans showed more pity, being prepared to defend the virtue of women. It was enough for them to lay their hands on booty.

SOURCE F
A commander of the imperial army.

On the sixth of May we took Rome by storm, killed 6000 men, plundered the houses, carried off what we found in churches and elsewhere, and finally set fire to a good portion of the town. A strange life indeed! We tore up, destroyed the deeds of copyists, the records, letters, and documents of the Curia. The Pope fled to Castel Sant'Angelo...For three weeks we lay siege until, forced by hunger, he had to surrender the castle...The Pope had to sign the surrender treaty that the secretary read to him. They all bemoaned themselves piteously and wept a lot. Here we are, all of us rich. Less than two months after we occupied Rome, 5000 of our men died of the plague for the corpses remained unburied. In July, half dead, we left the city for the Marches to find cleaner air...
In September, back in Rome, we pillaged the city more thoroughly and found great hidden treasures. We remained billeted there for another six months.

But the sack of Rome was not just a terrible outrage. It was to have a profound effect on the whole of the Catholic church.

SOURCE G
Jacob Burckhardt in 1860.

A singular feature was to emerge from the devastation of Rome namely, a spiritual and secular renewal.

SOURCE H
Charles V's secretary.

Every single horror of the sack is a precise, necessary and providential punishment for each of the iniquities that soiled Rome.

SOURCE I
German poster, May 1527.

She has fallen, fallen that great city in which the **Red Whore** long resided with her cup of abomination.

Red whore compares the Pope to the whore of Babylon, the symbol of corruption in the Book of Revelation

The disaster was not completely unexpected. There had been a series of predictions throughout the 1520s that the destruction of Rome was imminent.

At the close of 1526, Aretino published in Mantua a book of predictions for the year 1527 which, in addition to vitriolic attacks on Rome and the Papal court, contained, it would seem, an actual premonition to the sack of Rome...

Much has been made of the public displays and crank behaviour of an itinerant street cleaner, nicknamed Brando, who harassed Clement. On Holy Thursday, April 18, 1527, during the Papal blessing from the gallery of St Peter's, he appeared naked by the Statue of St Peter and cried out: 'Bastard, sodomite, because of your sins Rome will be destroyed. Confess and mend your ways. If you do not believe this, wait and see in two weeks' time...'

'It had reached such a point,' wrote the Tuscan historian Varchi, 'that not only monks from the pulpits, but ordinary Romans went around the public squares proclaiming in loud threatening tones not only the ruination of Italy but the end of the world. And there were some people who, convinced that the situation could not get any worse, said that Pope Clement was the Antichrist'...Cardinal Francesco Gonzaga announced the news in his letters: 'One can safely say that our father in heaven wants to scourge Christianity...' (Rome, May 7); 'There is every reason to suspect that from day to day new suffering and devastation will occur, and that the whole world will go to ruin and be annihilated...' (Ostia, May 16). The fall of Rome inescapably signified the start of the complete upheaval of the world.

SOURCE J
André Chastel, The Sack of Rome, 1527 (1983).

1. *Read Sources A, B, C and F and write a short account of the sack of Rome.*
2. *In what way did the attackers treat churches and sacred objects? Suggest reasons for their actions.*
3. *Read Sources D and E. How would the sack affect Italians' views on the domination of the peninsula by the Spanish?*
4. *Read Sources G, H and J. How was the sack regarded by contemporaries? What effect did it have on the Church?*
5. *What similarities can be seen between Lutheran (Source I) and Catholic (Sources H and J) opinions of the sack? Are there any differences?*
6. *'The Sack of Rome changed nothing politically but had a profound effect on the future of the Roman Catholic Church.' Discuss. (See also Chapter 12: 'The Counter-Reformation'.)*

9

Francis I and Henry II

See pages 283–6

OVERVIEW

New Year's Day, 1515, heralded the accession of a new King of France, who was wistfully remembered later in the sixteenth century as *le grand roy Francoys*. In an age of personal monarchy, the fate of the country rested to a tremendous extent on the character of the king. Francis I was twenty years old, fiercely ambitious and determined to be the pre-eminent prince of Christendom, outshining his rivals Henry VIII of England and Charles of Ghent, later King of Spain and Emperor. He had inherited a country where the great and often threatening fiefdoms on its borders had been taken under royal control – Burgundy to the east (1477) and Britanny to the west (1491) – and which was the largest and most fertile country in Europe. With this power base secure, immediately on his accession Francis prepared an invasion of Italy, to regain the great prize of Milan and cover himself with glory in war. Neither his early success nor his later setbacks were conclusive: he was still struggling with his rivals as his reign drew to a close thirty-two years later.

But while foreign affairs preoccupied him – along with court life, his many building projects and his mistresses – he was forced to pay attention to domestic affairs as France moved into an era of rapid change. Although Francis and his immediate predecessors owed much to the reforms of Louis XI (1461–1483), traditional royal government and administration was still a ramshackle affair and Francis found that he needed to overhaul it to raise the money for his fabulously expensive wars. Francis knew well his obligations to protect justice and the Church in France, but he treated the state mainly as a war machine. There has been debate then and now as to how far he compromised with the existing system in his reforms or whether he asserted a new overriding royal authority.

For contemporaries, though, the most obvious change was in religion as the Reformation began to take root in France. In the first part of his reign, before the religious battle-lines of the Reformation were clearly drawn up, Francis could not accept that French reformers posed the same threat as foreign heretics such as Luther, and he restrained the royal courts and the Sorbonne (the University of Paris) as they sought to stamp out all those with unorthodox ideas. But as the Reformation spread amongst the lower classes and became more radical in the 1530s, Francis stepped up the persecution of Protestants to preserve the Catholic faith of his ancestors and the unity of the realm. However, foreign policy – specifically the need to ally with German

Protestant princes – continued to distract him until his death in 1547. His son Henry II continued his policies, although by the time of his early death, killed in a joust in 1559, he bequeathed a France newly at peace and free from external threats – at the price of all French claims on Italy. However, France was instead now threatened within by noble factions which could not be subdued by Henry's teenage heirs or his widow, Catherine de Medici, and by religious divisions which tore apart communities all over France. The reigns of Francis I and Henry II were seen as an era of greatness, but the seeds had been sown for an era of destruction during the ensuing French Wars of Religion.

1 ∽ DOMESTIC POLICY

In 1515 the population of France probably stood at about fifteen million but, as the country recovered from the ravages of the Hundred Years' War, it began to increase steadily. This in turn stimulated French agriculture, urban development and trade, although the landless poor did not share this new wealth as prices rose and an era of cheap bread ended. These trends were only hazily understood at the time, and indeed few Frenchmen would have been able to visualise their country as a whole. Many of the great frontier provinces had only recently become a part of the French kingdom – for example, Brittany in 1491 (and that was formally annexed only in 1532). Aristocratic families still held sway over their lands and threatened the security of the king, regional differences abounded and Frenchmen did not even share a common language. The idea of a French nation had only just emerged in the later Middle Ages, and it centred very much on the monarchy.

The monarch was the fount of honour. He raised nobility to the peerage, or knighted them, and awarded honorific posts in the central and provincial administrations. The king led his nobility in war and this began to forge a French identity; during the Italian Wars soldiers were said to be fighting for *la patrie* as well as their king and myths of the heroic origin of the French abounded, particularly descent from the Trojans. The king was the protector of the **Gallican** Church, which was loyal to the Church of Rome but fiercely defensive of its French character and privileges. Printing had enhanced the monarch's authority over his subjects – a printed royal **edict** at least gave local élites a stronger sense of being direct subjects of the king rather than just vassals of the local lord – and this added to France's growing identity as one nation. However, the government institutions Francis inherited from his predecessors were as yet far from constituting a streamlined national bureaucracy, despite some measure of centralisation having been achieved by Louis XI (1461–1483). In order to govern this sprawling, developing country, Francis needed to make central government and local administration work as best he could.

Gallican the name given to the Church and its privileges in France

edict a law issued by the king

PICTURE 24
Portrait of Francis I on
horseback *by François
Clouet*, c. 1540

A *Central government: institutions*

By the early sixteenth century, there were three particularly important
organs of central government: the King's Council (*Conseil Etroit*), the
Grand Conseil and the *Parlement* of Paris. These institutions had once
formed part of the medieval Great Council, the *Curia Regis*, but they
now enjoyed very different functions and were to develop even more
under the administration of Francis I.

The King's Council was the most important, consisting of the
monarch and his advisers. In the past, these had been royal princes, the
higher nobility and the most important officers of state, but now
membership was usually by royal invitation. By the fifteenth century,
the king was anxious to prevent complete aristocratic domination of
the council, and Francis continued in this. The value placed on the
maîtres des requêtes, who were trained lawyers, shows this concern.
Under Francis an inner circle of advisers also developed, known as the
Conseil des Affaires, which was consulted over crucial issues.

Since 1497 the *Grand Conseil* had taken over part of the judicial
business transacted by the King's Council. It acted as a court of appeal,
intervened in (jurisdictional) conflicts between courts and checked on
complaints against royal officials. Although relatively inexpensive,
people found it frustrating to use because, like the King's Council, it
followed the monarch on his travels round the kingdom. However, this

maîtres des requêtes
lawyers used as royal
officials in central
government or as
emissaries to the
provinces

proximity was to the king's advantage and made it more attentive to his wishes than the **Parlement**. The *Parlement* of Paris was a supreme court, rather than a parliament. It had remained in Paris since the thirteenth century but was still considered a part of the King's Council.

The *Parlement's* jurisdiction had once covered the whole kingdom, but as France had extended her boundaries, a number of provincial *Parlements* were added. As a court of law, the *Parlement* judged all offences concerning the king's person, his rights and his lands, from treason to rape and highway robbery. It also acted as a court of appeal from less important royal tribunals. But in addition, its powers embraced social, economic and ecclesiastical matters, from ensuring that Paris received enough corn and fuel, public hygiene and upkeep of roads to controlling the price of bread, fixing wages and academic matters. No papal bull could take effect in France until it had been registered by the *Parlement*. Its most influential role, in a political sense, was probably in ratifying royal legislation.

It is important to remember that this institution was very different from the English parliament. The *Parlement* was made up of royally-appointed judges, not elected MPs. Historical precedent, however, allowed the *Parlement* to resist the monarch on occasion, particularly when it was able to claim that a royal decree contradicted one of the fundamental laws of the kingdom. When this occurred it would submit remonstrances (objections) to the king who would either modify his suggestions or issue a *lettre de jussion*, which was an order to register his edict without any more delay. This could lead to further remonstrance and *lettres de jussion*, only terminating with the king appearing in person to register his enactment. Such an event was known as a **lit-de-justice**, meaning that the king was temporarily assuming the power he had delegated to *Parlement*. (As you read this chapter note examples of the clashes between *Parlement* and the king.) During the captivity of the king in Madrid following the battle of Pavia in 1525 the *Parlement* had grown assertive in opposing the wishes of the regent, the king's mother, Louise of Savoy. It was even preparing to prosecute the chancellor, Duprat, the king's leading official. But on his return in 1527 Francis insisted that the *Parlement* register a decree without protest which stated its clear subservience to the Crown. In the end the

Parlement the equivalent of a supreme court; the jurisdiction of the Paris *parlement* covered central France, but there were six provincial *parlements* in outlying regions

lit-de-justice the personal appearance of the king in *parlement*, seated on the bed or throne of justice, when the judges were forced to obey him without delay

King		
Conseil Etroit	*Parlement*	*Grand Conseil*
Main decision-making body. The chancellor, assisted by *maîtres des requêtes*, turned its decisions into edicts and practical policies.	Equivalent of a supreme court. Registered royal edicts in the statute book.	A court of appeal, dealing with complaints against royal officials and supervising the courts.

TABLE 6
Central government in France

Parlement could not resist an adult king determined to impose his authority.

The Estates General was the closest equivalent to the English parliament. Composed of delegates representing the three orders of society (clergy, nobility, and commoners, known as the third estate), it claimed the right to ratify treaties and approve taxation. The fact that the Estates General had not been summoned since 1484 seems to be another example of the growth of royal power at this time. The king made treaties and raised taxes on his own authority. However, there was little demand for it to be otherwise. While there was no national parliament, there were local parliaments, the Provincial Estates. In addition the French nobility, unlike the English, were exempt from many taxes and benefited from royal gifts and pensions, ever more important at a time of inflation. Given access to the 'royal trough', as J. Russell Major puts it, they had little motive to demand an Estates General to resist the king's tax demands.

During the reign of Francis, the bureaucracy became more extensive and it was more sophisticated and complex than the machinery of government in England. The Chancery, headed by the chancellor, turned the council's decisions into laws. Chancery secretaries were assisted by the *maîtres des requêtes* (trained lawyers under the chancellor's control). There were fifty *maîtres* under Francis and they proved to be a vital link between senior departments of state. They benefited socially, many being ennobled. Francis increased the number of people holding office under the crown; it has been estimated that there was an average of one office-holder to every 3000 inhabitants in his reign. (But the reach of government was to grow much further – at the height of royal power under Francis's successor Louis XIV (1643–1715) there was to be one office-holder to every 400 inhabitants, and by 1980 modern government was represented by one official to every twenty inhabitants.)

Francis also increased central administration by creating offices and then selling them, thereby increasing his revenues, a practice known as venality. An office in this sense had a definite meaning: it was a permanent government post. Whereas Francis was quite restrained in selling titles of nobility, it was he who turned the sale of offices into a system. He sold offices to those anxious to acquire social status or gave them away as rewards so that the recipients were then free to sell them if they wished. This created serious problems for his immediate successors, as offices tended to become the property of a limited number of families. However, in the short term it was financially advantageous and resulted in loyalty to the king.

B *Provincial government*

In contrast to this increasingly bureaucratic central authority, local government in early sixteenth-century France was irregular and regionalised. This did not, however, prevent it from playing a vital role in the development of royal authority.

As well as the one in Paris, there were six provincial *Parlements* in 1515, which had developed since 1443: Toulouse, Rennes, Bordeaux, Dijon, Rouen and Aix-en-Provence. They had similar powers to the *Parlement* of Paris and each one had to register royal decrees. A law registered in Paris could not become law in Provence, for example, without first being registered by the *Parlement* of Aix-en-Provence. They were viewed with suspicion by their parent body in Paris because, rather than acting as one sovereign judicial body, they tended to defend provincial interests against royal governors or the central power. They were often more troublesome to the king, being remote from the centre of authority in Paris and capable of using extended delaying tactics if they disliked a royal edict. But as with the Paris *Parlement,* in the end the king could impose his own authority. Members of the *Parlement* of Rouen had a reputation for being drunk or at least hungover and selling justice for cash or sexual favours. When it opposed important royal legislation in 1540, Francis suspended it and passed on some of its powers to magistrates in Bayeux. The *Parlement* was reinstated in 1541, with its members promising better behaviour in the future. This was the tactic of a short sharp shock, followed by compromise with the local élite, which was generally the way local disturbances were dealt with. It showed how royal authority could intervene when necessary, but permanent direct rule by central government was not an option. Parts of Normandy had come close to anarchy and the *Parlement* was needed to restore order.

Much responsibility for provincial administration lay outside the direct control of the Crown. For example, most of the great provinces, which had formerly been independent political units on the edges of France, retained their Estates or provincial parliaments. Unlike the Estates General, the Provincial Estates still played an important role in the life of the country. Although they only met once a year for a week or less, many Estates had succeeded in gaining control over the levying of money within their areas and were able to play a leading part in the life of the province by constructing roads and public buildings, fixing and levying customs duties and sometimes organising a rudimentary police force for the countryside. J. Russell Major highlights the vital (and in practice independent) role of the Estates in the government of the provinces. He also argues that what was only a slow rise in royal taxation in line with inflation shows how effective the Estates must have been in haggling with royal commissioners and cutting back royal financial demands. In contrast, Knecht points to the numerous occasions where the Estates tried to resist tax demands but won only temporary delays. The king would generally bargain only about the means of raising money, not about the amounts. Knecht states that 'the effectiveness of the Estates under Francis was limited to matters of secondary importance to the Crown; where its financial interest was at stake, they were virtually powerless'. In the absence of the Estates General there could not be united opposition to the king, who could

See pages 283–6

pick the Estates off one by one if necessary. But was there such a conflict of interest between the king and Estates as this debate assumes? Both Russell Major and Knecht think in terms of winners and losers. However, whatever the rhetoric and the argument over precise amounts, it was in the interests of the king to make reasonable financial demands whenever possible, and so strike a workable deal with the Estates in order to minimise tax evasion and passive resistance.

Of all the Crown appointments in the structure of local government, the provincial governors were the most important. Their jurisdiction did not cover the whole country but they were active in the border provinces and vital to the exercise of royal authority there. They were usually of the higher nobility; under Francis they included his sons, uncle and favourites (including the husbands of his mistresses!). They could be dismissed at the whim of the king. In 1542 Francis annulled the powers of all governors, saying that they had become too excessive. In this way he removed one of the governors, Montmorency, with the minimum offence to him personally and shortly afterwards restored the powers of the other governors. However, the king had shown who was ultimately in control. None the less, on a day-to-day basis the patronage that governors could wield, both at court and in the provinces, made them potentially independent and therefore dangerous

MAP 13
Sixteenth-century France

to the Crown if a king failed to lead and curb them. In general Francis I faced little open resistance to his authority by the nobility, except in the case of the Constable of Bourbon whom he provoked into open rebellion.

THE CONSTABLE OF BOURBON

Charles, Constable of Bourbon, was the greatest nobleman of France at the start of Francis's reign. He had been in dispute with his cousin Suzanne over part of the Bourbon inheritance, but had happily resolved that by marrying her. His lands then formed an almost independent territory in central France, where he had the right to raise troops and taxes and dispense justice. He also held lands in Germany and so owed allegiance to the Emperor as well as to the King of France. As constable he was in charge of the army in peacetime and by right would take the place of honour by leading the vanguard of the army in battle. To begin with, Francis treated the constable with all the courtesy due to his rank, but it must have been difficult for him to tolerate such an independent power within the kingdom.

In the campaign of late 1521 the first expression of the king's resentment came when Bourbon was denied command of the vanguard. Then the following April Duchess Suzanne died leaving no surviving children – the constable expected to retain her lands in accordance with her will, but Francis announced that as her line was at an end some must revert to the Crown. More dangerously, the king's mother, Louise of Savoy, was Suzanne's closest blood relative and she laid a claim to all her estates. Louise proposed the same solution as in the dispute between the constable and Suzanne – that of marriage. However, the constable rejected her, as at forty-four Louise was unlikely to bear children and his line would also come to an end, his estates passing to the Crown on his death. Romantic historians present Louise's pursuit of her claims against the constable as the consequence of spurned love, but it is more likely that she had her heart set on the Bourbon lands rather than on his person. Also, Francis suspected (rightly) that the Emperor Charles V had offered his own sister in marriage to the constable and that would allow his great enemy access to the heart of France. The constable had shown no sign of pursuing the Emperor's proposal, but, under pressure from the king, the *parlement* ordered the seizure of the Bourbon estates in August 1523 without waiting to clarify the legal justification. The constable then severed his allegiance to the king. He had already been plotting with the Emperor and Henry VIII to secure support for a rebellion, but the plot misfired and the constable fled the country.

Having lost his French lands and offices, he entered the service of the Emperor. Commanding imperial troops, he invaded Provence in 1524, but was forced to withdraw. Finally in 1527 as he struggled to keep control of mutinous troops, he was killed in the first assault of the Sack of Rome. Without a clear set of goals his rebellion had served only to strengthen Francis's position. His fellow nobles had felt no solidarity with him, seeing it as his personal quarrel with the king, and they were content for their own part to follow Francis on the campaign trail and compete for royal favours and honours at home. The constable's failure illustrates one of the mainstays of Francis's authority – the lack of any coherent, significant challenge to it.

bailliages local units of administration and justice

Local administrators below the rank of provincial governors were the *baillis*. They staffed the **bailliages**, of which there were about eighty-six. The officials working within these *bailliages* were not well paid and had to rely on fees and gifts. The king thus ensured an active, if corrupt, system of local government.

The *maîtres des requêtes*, who helped the Chancellor of France run his departments, were a link between the *bailliages* and central government. They were sent on tours of inspection around the provinces, dealt with complaints against royal officials and if they found anything amiss they were supposed to report back to the King's Council. Their role was important in the development of centralised government in France, although they were not permanent inspectors like the later *intendants* of the seventeenth century.

KEY ISSUE

In what ways, if any, were central and provincial administration improved by Francis?

Francis made no startling innovations in central and provincial government, probably because foreign and religious problems seemed more pressing. However, we can identify a move towards centralisation and specialisation, the use of trained expert officials, and increased efficiency, especially where royal finances were concerned.

Provincial administration

King ———————————————→ Provincial *Parlements*
                                        (in some provinces)

Provincial governors

                                        Mâitres des requêtes

Provincial Estates
(in some provinces)

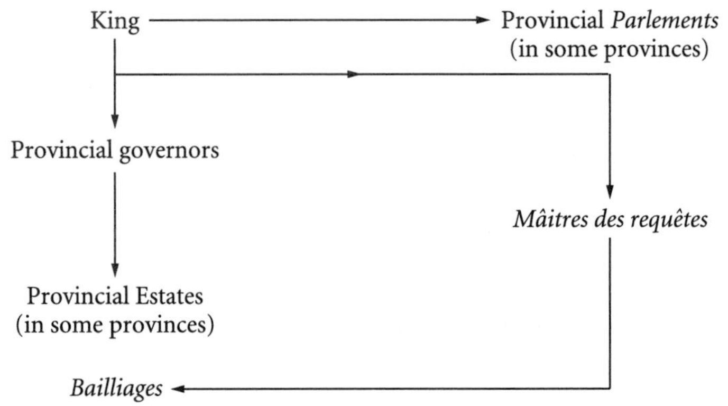

DIAGRAM 3

Provincial administration in 16th-century France

Bailliages ◄————————————

C *Financial administration*

Francis had a significant advantage over his contemporary rulers – the power to tax at will. Ever since Charles VII had managed to turn a limited concession by the Estates into an established right, kings of France had collected the **taille**, the main direct tax, on this basis, and it was later extended to include the **gabelle**, a tax on the salt which was vital for the preservation of food. This increased the king's revenue enormously. With all its inconsistencies, the *taille* represented half of the Crown's revenue and grew steadily in importance. The sales tax known as the *aides* brought in about a third as much as the *taille* and the *gabelle* about a sixth.

Indirect taxes were collected by the practice of tax-farming. By this system the king authorised an individual, often the highest bidder, to collect and keep a particular royal tax after prior payment to the king of a fixed sum. This pleased both financier, because he could make a profit, and king, because he received the money without any administrative problems and expense. A different method was used for the *taille*. An assessor and collector were elected from a parish. When the parishioners had been assessed, the amounts owed were read out in church and the following Sunday taxes were paid. Few escaped, as the assessor would suffer if the expected amount did not reach Paris. So, although the system seemed corrupt and in need of reform, it did work.

Francis was extravagant in every sphere of life but it was his foreign policy and wars that were the single heaviest item of expenditure. His first campaign into Italy leading up to the battle of Marignano cost 1.8 million livres. By 1517 Francis's debt equalled his regular annual income but he continued naively to pay out huge sums such as the 200 000 livres he spent in 1520 on entertaining Henry VIII at the Field of the Cloth of Gold.

In order to build up a treasure chest to fund his wars, and blaming corrupt officials for his shortage of cash, Francis embarked on a programme of fiscal reform. In 1523 he established a new central treasury, the *Trésor de l'Epargne* (headed by the *trésorier*) into which all his revenues from taxation and royal lands were deposited. The *trésorier de l'Epargne* was accountable direct to the king, whereas before a dozen officials with overlapping jurisdictions were much more prone to inefficiency and corruption. This innovation gave Francis supreme control of financial matters but money still did not reach the t*résorier* as plentifully or swiftly as the king would have wished. In order to tighten control further, Francis decreed in the Ordinance of Rouen in 1532 that the coffers holding the money collected by the *trésorier* should remain at the Louvre rather than follow the king and that there should be three locks on each one, requiring three key-holders to be present whenever they were opened so that they could keep an eye on each other.

Francis extended these reforms again in 1542 when he was once more at war with the Emperor. This time he established sixteen *recettes générales* which were financial and administrative regional offices,

taille the main tax on individual wealth, from which the nobility were exempt

gabelle a tax on salt

TABLE 7
Taille in livres

1524	2.4 million
1544	4.6 million

collecting all forms of royal income previously collected separately and which, with a warrant from the *Trésorier de l'Epargne*, were authorised to make payments locally to speed up administration.

Centralisation by the subordination of all the royal 'receivers' to the *trésorier* who in turn had to refer to the king, uniformity by bringing together revenue from taxation, royal lands and other sources, and simplification by more efficient methods of collection: achieving this had taken Francis twenty years, in a rather staccato way. This has been seen as the gradual working through of a master-plan for reform, but Philippe Hamon has shown that it was more a response to changing conditions and personnel. Still, although the system was by no means perfect, a framework for the future had been established.

Nevertheless, because of his constant need for ready cash Francis resorted to several expedients to see him through a crisis. He practised venality, the sale of offices. He borrowed heavily from the Italian bankers of Lyon, requested forced loans from towns exempt from the *taille*, borrowed from his own tax officials and, much to the horror of the *Parlement*, sold Crown land.

The financial crisis of 1521–23 showed Francis's powers of ingenuity. War with the Emperor proved expensive and France's revenues were stretched beyond their limits. The king's chief financial minister was Jacques de Beaune, Baron de Semblançay, who sensibly warned his master in September that the money left in the treasury would only last for another month. The war continued over the winter into 1522, with Francis moving from one expedient to another. Finally, the following September, the scheme known as the **rentes** *sur l'Hôtel de Ville de Paris* was established. This was an early type of public credit. Francis borrowed 200 000 livres from Paris against the security of the municipality's revenue – which was trusted much more than the king's treasury – and each contributor was assured of a life annuity or *rente* at 8.5 per cent. It was an ingenious idea for the time – in total it brought in 725 000 livres, other *rentes* being sold in 1537 and 1543. Based on a system of mutual trust, this system has been acclaimed by some, even if Francis, reacting only to the immediate needs of war, allowed the practice to drop.

> **rentes** bonds based on the revenues of Paris used to finance government borrowing

> **KEY ISSUE**
>
> *Did Francis's financial reforms merely complicate the system?*

Such ingenuity did not solve Francis's problem and in 1523 he was once again without resources to pay for his campaigns. He now began to suspect his officials of embezzlement and so in January 1523 he set up the *Commission de la Tour Carrée*, another expedient to look into fiscal administration and claw back money siphoned off by officials.

Semblançay, the king's loyal finance minister, was the principal target. However, the final verdict of the commissioners was that the king owed his minister 1 190 374 livres! This was just a temporary reprieve. In 1527, Semblançay was arrested and thrown into the Bastille. His trial was a farce, for his judges were handpicked by the king, rather than by the *Parlement*. He was hanged at Montfaucon in August and aroused the sympathy of the Parisians due to his dignified manner and age (he was eighty!). Historians can only speculate as to Francis's motives. He may have come to resent this older and wiser minister, or perhaps he wanted to break up the network of banking families from Tours that dominated finances, of which Semblançay was a part. Since his capture by the Spaniards in 1525 Francis had attempted to recover from his debts; it was a time of national crisis when he was in search of scapegoats, and it served 'to encourage the others' to stay in line. But this hardly justifies judicial murder. The affair shows Francis at his most ruthless.

For a short time after the Peace of Cambrai in 1529, France was at peace with her neighbour and Francis seized the opportunity to refill his coffers. By 1536 the 1.5 million livres saved by Francis had been absorbed in the war against the Emperor which cost over three million livres, and the same was true in 1542. Again, Francis used every expedient to raise cash, including extending the *gabelle*, or salt tax.

Francis was fortunate that he endured relatively few instances of resistance to royal taxation compared with his contemporaries or his successors in seventeenth-century France. He only levied one new tax and even this was not entirely new. This was the *solde des 50 000 hommes* levied on all towns. What was new in 1543 was that from then on it was to be levied annually, even in peacetime. Although the paying of the tax created problems, as for example in Lyon where they had to borrow from Italian bankers to do so, there was no unified resistance to it.

There were only a few instances of popular rebellion against taxation, despite the financial strain on the French people. In 1542, in western France people took up arms against Francis's attempts to reform the salt tax in the Edict of Châtellerault of 1541. This introduced a single salt tax to be levied at the salt marsh. Severe penalties also aimed to eradicate fraud and smuggling and, by a further edict in April 1542, the king tried to increase the yield of the *gabelle* by simplifying the levy. To the government this might have been reasonable and fair but to those affected it seemed to threaten their whole way of life. Ten thousand men, aware that the king was occupied with war against the Emperor, took up arms and forced the royal commissioners to retire.

The measure of Francis's concern is shown by the fact that, despite being at war, he himself came to La Rochelle to pass the final judgement when the rebellion was over. The rebels expressed their remorse and Francis reminded them of the seriousness of their crime, particularly at a time when he was defending the kingdom. But he concluded that he could not refuse them a pardon if they truly repented and he did not wish to be seen to treat his subjects in a similar vein to Charles V and the people of Ghent.

See page 226

Francis's treatment appears very magnanimous compared with the policies of Charles and Henry towards their rebels, but it has to be remembered that he could be little else when this part of the country was particularly vulnerable to English attack, and although the ordinance of 1542 was revoked, a similar policy was put into practice in 1544. Magnanimity was not characteristic of his policy towards rebels. In November 1544, following a rebellion at Lagny-sur-Marne over the *gabelle*, he ordered the Seigneur de Lorges to sack the town and

TABLE 8

Annual increase in royal taxation

Louis XII:	2.38%
Francis I:	1.44%
Henry II:	5.7%

KEY ISSUE

How damaging were Francis's financial expedients?

See pages 257–8

KEY ISSUE

What effect did faction have on government?

forbade the inhabitants from taking de Lorges or his troops to court whatever atrocities they committed.

Francis has enjoyed the reputation of being a shrewd businessman because he left several million livres in his treasury despite his many years at war. However, this is misleading because when he died Francis owed the Lyon bankers 6 860 844 livres. His income in 1547 was 7 183 271 livres. Royal income from taxes had risen only slowly in comparison with his predecessor Louis XII and his successor Henry II. Francis had in reality left a huge debt for his successor to pay off. Despite his various fiscal experiments he had failed to improve the financial situation of the Crown, not through lack of ability but because both his time and money had been absorbed by foreign affairs.

D *Faction*

Even though the unification of the kingdom was well advanced by the reign of Francis, there was still opportunity for the powerful families who continued to control various parts of France to challenge the authority of the Crown. This could and did occur in different ways but it needed a strong and effective king to suppress it. A case study of this is the rebellion of the Constable of Bourbon.

An example of faction, with leading noblemen gathering supporters to compete for power and patronage, came from within the king's family and intensified in the last years of Francis's life, particularly as his health deteriorated. There was rivalry between his two surviving sons, the Dauphin Henry and Charles, Duke of Orléans. After the death of their eldest brother in 1536, Charles became Francis's favourite son and the rift between the two brothers widened in 1541 when Montmorency, the chief royal minister, fell from favour. Henry remained loyal to him throughout but Charles fell under the influence of the king's chief mistress Madame d'Etampes, Montmorency's greatest enemy. The war of 1542 made the situation even worse; whereas Charles conquered Luxembourg, Henry had to retreat from Perpignan. Had the Treaty of Crèpy in 1544 been implemented, Charles might have become Duke of Milan, married the Emperor's daughter and gained four French duchies from his father. This was very insulting to the prestige of the dauphin but, fortunately for him at least, Charles died in 1545.

Following this, Francis and Henry did grow closer, but on his accession to the throne one of Henry's first moves was to restore Montmorency. Francis had found that power struggles could occur even within his own family and again the importance of the personality of the king is emphasised. Francis had contained the problem; a weaker monarch might not have done. This was an omen for the future.

Faction abounded in the last five years of Francis's life, probably because, although still in control, he was a sick man as an ultimately fatal illness took its toll. It showed that the fragile position even of an authoritative king such as Francis could be challenged, and that he always had to be vigilant even amongst his most trusted advisers and friends.

Francis I – A Renaissance prince?

The young king, Francis I, appeared to be the model Renaissance prince, aided by his handsome, powerful physique (apart from his bandy legs below the knees) and his personal charm and tastes. Castiglione, in the *Book of the Courtier*, that handbook of courtly Renaissance living, had predicted that when Francis came to the throne 'just as the glory of arms flourishes and shines in France, so also with the greatest brilliance must that of letters'. Although he lacked a classical education Francis did indeed love books, and so built up one of the finest manuscript libraries in Europe, which was to form the nucleus for the modern *Bibliothèque Nationale*. He protected the Christian humanists from the *parlement* and the Sorbonne who thought their work heretical; in a sense he temporarily saved the Renaissance from being overwhelmed by the struggles surrounding the Reformation. In 1530 he established the *Lecteurs royaux*, four royal lectureships in Greek and Hebrew which were the basis for today's *Collège de France*. The great writer Rabelais proclaimed 'thanks be to God, learning has been restored in my age to its former dignity and enlightenment', although it should be remembered that Rabelais's views may have been coloured by wanting to win the king's favour and that the lecturers were paid only irregularly and denied permanent accommodation.

See pages 268–70

Francis certainly wanted to project the image of a great Renaissance patron; during his invasion of Italy in 1515 he saw the style and prestige enjoyed by Renaissance princes there and understood the need to compete with other princes to secure the services of the most acclaimed artists. His first coup was to tempt the aged Leonardo da Vinci to France in 1516 to live near the royal Château of Amboise for what turned out to be the last three years of his life. Other Italian artists followed, such as G.B. Rosso and Francesco Primaticcio who decorated the Palace of Fontainebleau, which Francis was reconstructing in Renaissance style, with a series of paintings exalting the king as soldier and patron in the manner of the triumphant art of ancient Rome. Sometimes they catered to his taste in erotic art, Venus or naked nymphs being frequent subjects. In the latter part of his reign, Francis secured the services of the sculptor Benvenuto Cellini who made for him the fabulous salt cellar portraying the earth and the ocean, one of the most exquisite small works of the Renaissance. His collection of paintings culminated in what we see today at the Louvre. Francis's image became better known than any of his predecessors through portraits, especially those by Clouet (see Picture 24), and the numerous copies of them.

Francis also built on a grand scale. Before his day decorative motifs had been imported from Renaissance Italy, but now the principles and structure of Renaissance architecture were more fully understood, and Francis himself was reputed to collaborate with his architects in the design of his buildings. Construction work was undertaken at a number of royal châteaux. The greatest work towards the end of his reign was at Fontainebleau and Francis also partly remodelled the Louvre and several other royal châteaux. The new Château of Chambord was inspired by a Medici villa near Florence. The style of court life within these palaces changed. The court, a community of some 10 000 people which was larger than all but twenty-five or so towns in France, remained the centre for elaborate feasting, hunting, jousting and other sports in which Francis loved to show off. But during his reign courtly manners and the art of conversation, as recommended by Castiglione, also became highly prized, making a clearer social distinction between court nobles and their rougher country cousins. When the court arrived at a town during its frequent tours of the French provinces – it was important for the king to have as much contact as possible with all parts of his realm – there would be a triumphal entry with processions and pageants. The king was still portrayed in these as the embodiment of all the virtues as in the Middle Ages, but he was now also presented as Caesar.

Renaissance princes have been depicted as creative in political as well as cultural and social life. Francis certainly made innovations, but these reforms now seem to have been reactions to circumstance rather than part of a master plan. While, for his benefit, French writers debated how absolute were the powers of the king, there is little evidence of any influence derived from the political thought of the Italian Renaissance. Francis could sound like Machiavelli – 'If I had only to deal with the virtuous...', he

See pages 283–4

PICTURE 25
Château de Chambord

said in explaining why he intended to bribe the imperial Electors, 'but in times like the present, [a man] has no means of attaining his object except by force or corruption.' However, this is crude self-justification rather than a sign that he had read Machiavelli's works. Francis was a Renaissance prince in the image he projected, the style in which he lived, and the patronage he exercised, rather than in the substance of his political thought or action.

KEY ISSUE

How far was Francis I a model 'Renaissance prince'?

2 ⤆ RELIGIOUS POLICY

A *The Concordat of Bologna*

As Francis was King of France during one of the most turbulent periods in the history of the Roman Catholic Church, religion was bound to be an important issue. When he came to the throne the French Church enjoyed the unusual privilege of relative independence from Rome. The question was whether he would be able to maintain this and cope with the challenge of Protestantism.

The Concordat of Bologna was an agreement made by Francis with Pope Leo X in 1516, by which the king permitted papal taxation in France in return for the right to nominate bishops. It has been said that it gave the king control over the French Church, so much so that there was never any inducement for him to ally with the Protestant reformers against the authority of the Pope. However, Knecht has shown that the relationship of Church and state in France was already one of close mutual dependence, whatever the relationship between king and Pope. After the passing of the Pragmatic Sanction in 1438 which increased the development of Gallicanism (the independence of the French Church from Rome), by 1471 Louis XI was controlling clerical appointments and by 1515 this royal control was an accepted fact – technically the French Church was free to nominate bishops and abbots for itself, but the king would make known his preferred candidates and few were brave enough to disagree. The Concordat of Bologna merely formalised royal control. It was in fact a major concession to the Pope for reasons of foreign policy, to further Francis's ambition to take the kingdom of Naples. However, it was a concession that aroused some of the most concerted opposition Francis had to face.

The Paris *Parlement* was a staunch defender of Gallican privileges and delayed registration of the concordat. In January 1518 the king received a memorandum from two representatives of the *Parlement* which repeated the objections to the concordat: fear that all benefices would become liable to papal taxation, and of large-scale papal interference in the French Church. Francis was thrown into a fit of rage. He roared that there would only be one king in France and no senate as in Venice, and threatened to turn the *Parlement* into a nomadic institution, making it 'trot after him like those of the Grand Conseil'. The two *Parlementaires* were ordered to leave but when they pleaded for respite, they were told that if they were not gone by 6.00 am the following morning they would be thrown into a pit by twelve archers and left there to rot for six months! Rumours then spread that Francis planned to establish a new *Parlement* at Orléans. Royal intimidation finally triumphed: on 22 March 1518 the concordat was registered, though under protest.

The *Parlement* had capitulated, but Francis still had to face the opposition of the Sorbonne, then the Faculty of Theology of the University of Paris, that bastion of Gallicanism, which had a vested interest in a system that reserved a third of vacant benefices for graduates. The Sorbonne was important as the leading theological school in Europe and its support was vital in influencing public opinion. But under threat of banishment it too capitulated.

Did the concordat do nothing, then, to increase the Crown's control of the Church? Although recognising the king's right to appoint to major benefices, it did not give him unlimited power:

> Henceforward, in the case of vacancies now and in the future in cathedral and metropolitan churches of the said kingdom [of France] whoever is king of France shall within six months counting from the day on which the vacancy occurred present and nominate to us and to our successors, as bishops of Rome or to the Apostolic See to be invested by us, a sober or knowledgeable master or graduate in theology, or a doctor or graduate in all or in one of the laws taught and rigorously examined at a famous university, who must be at least twenty-seven years old and otherwise suitable...
>
> ...and should the king not nominate a person with such qualifications, neither we, nor our successors nor the Holy See shall have to invest such a person...If, within the stipulated six months, the king should present to us, our successors or the Holy See a secular priest or a regular priest of another order or a minor under twenty-three years or someone unsuitable in another way, such a person will be rejected by us and will not be invested with the office.

1. *Why did age limits have to be stipulated?*
2. *How far could these clauses of the concordat really limit the royal power?*

If the limitation embodied on the concordat had been adhered to, the Crown would not have gained as much control over the Church as it did. But the Pope did not quibble over details of the application because the authority of the Holy See, undermined by the Pragmatic Sanction, was now much restored – 'the thorn removed from the eye of the Church', as it was put at the time. Even though Francis did not gain long-term advantage in Italy through this concession to the Pope, he refused to abandon the concordat. To do so would have meant the appearance of giving in to the Gallican opposition, and under the concordat he was at least appointing to Church offices as of right rather than relying on political pressure as under the Pragmatic Sanction. It had become a matter of principle.

B *Reform and reformation within France*

KEY ISSUE

What advantage did the king gain through the Concordat of Bologna?

In the early sixteenth century, as in other parts of western Christendom, there existed the paradox of a lowering of standards within the French Church, combined with the flourishing of humanist ideas at the highest academic levels. Jacques Lefèvre d'Etaples was one of the leading French humanists. Deeply concerned about the state of religion, he deliberately chose to become a teacher and to keep in touch with events rather than to retreat to a monastery. In 1512 he published an edition of St Paul's epistles. Lefèvre was important because he was the first French Christian humanist (classical scholar who aimed at instilling new life into the Christian religion by going back to the original scriptural text). He was following the example of Erasmus, who had visited France in the 1490s. Lefèvre's influence was tremendous, particularly after he joined the household of the Bishop of Meaux.

If French humanism was to revive the French Church properly, it needed support from the top. The higher clergy were not particularly inspiring but there were a number of exceptions. The best known is Guillaume Briçonnet, Bishop of Meaux. Appalled at the state of his diocese when he visited in 1518, he immediately set about remedying the situation and was soon joined by Lefèvre and a group of *evangelical* preachers who became known as the Circle of Meaux. Briçonnet, inspired by Bishop Giberti of Verona, imported a printing press and divided up his diocese into twenty-six zones, allocating preachers to each of them for Lent and Advent, while he himself preached every Sunday in his cathedral. Unfortunately this annoyed the local Franciscans, who were dependent for their survival on payment for their services as preachers. In the long term it had far greater significance: they accused the bishop and his evangelical circle of heresy and put their claim before the Sorbonne and the *Parlement* of Paris. Their fate rested on the definition of heresy.

France could not escape the infiltration of Luther's works for long. Although the Sorbonne sympathised with his attack on indulgences, they could not tolerate his later ideas. Finally, on 15 April 1521 the university issued its *Determinatio*, condemning Luther's ideas as heresy, but it was too late to retrieve the seeds that had already been sown.

But what precisely did the critics mean by heresy? Was it just Lutheranism or did it include evangelical humanism practised in France before 1519? The dividing line between evangelical humanism and Lutheranism is difficult to pinpoint in the 1520s. Both emphasised the importance of the writings of St Paul and an improved understanding of scripture. There were points where they differed; for example, Lefèvre could not accept Luther's reduction in the number of sacraments, but other members of the Circle of Meaux, notably Guillaume Farel, soon became totally convinced Protestants. The scholar and preacher Louis de Berquin was a disciple of both Erasmus and Luther. To the Sorbonne, there was no question about it; both were detestable. So the infiltration of Luther's ideas into France in the early 1520s put a slur on the more orthodox reformers at Meaux.

C *Francis I and the question of heresy*

As the 'Most Christian King' Francis could not tolerate heresy; it would have completely contradicted his aim for national unity. However, Francis's interpretation of heresy did not coincide with that of the Sorbonne and this was to be the cause of future problems. Francis liked to portray himself as the ideal Renaissance monarch and from the beginning of his reign he had been an enthusiastic patron of humanism. He enjoyed the company of well-educated men and his household included several humanists: his secretary Guillaume Budé, his doctor Guillaume Cop and his old tutor François de Rochefort.

Francis invited Erasmus to France in 1517 to take charge of a college devoted to the study of classical languages, although he declined. Francis's invitation was stressing the importance of the study of the classics in reaching a correct understanding of scripture, but to the Sorbonne only the Latin Vulgate was respectable. There were also close links between the court and the Circle of Meaux due to the influence of the king's beloved sister, Marguerite, who became Queen of Navarre in 1527. She sought Briçonnet's spiritual guidance and corresponded with him from about 1521, becoming acquainted with the ideas of Lefèvre. Her influence on the king must not be underestimated.

Francis was none the less hostile to the German heresies spread by Luther. In June 1521, he instructed the *Parlement* to examine all printers and booksellers and check that nothing was published without the university's approval. When this proved difficult to impose, Francis followed it up by a proclamation issued on 3 August 1521. This stated that anyone owning Luther's works had one week in which to hand them over to the *Parlement* or face a fine and imprisonment. This proved to be little more effective than the first measure.

One reason was the difference of opinion between the king and the Sorbonne and *Parlement* in their interpretation of heresy. The best example of this is the treatment of a young scholar, Louis de Berquin, who was found in possession of Luther's books in 1523. Berquin's own works were examined by the Sorbonne and proclaimed heretical: he was reported to the *Parlement* and arrested on a charge of heresy. In the meantime, the university had seized the opportunity to examine works by Lefèvre and Erasmus. Whereas Francis did not wish to be seen protecting heretics, this he refused to tolerate. So he referred the case to his *Grand Conseil* and Berquin was released. Francis had over-ridden the Sorbonne's traditional right to judge doctrine.

It has been said that Francis failed to crush heresy at this stage because of the inconsistency of his policy. But, as we have seen, heresy in France in the early 1520s was not clearly defined. Francis's policy was consistent in that he was constantly ordering the authorities to stamp out heresy: the problem was that their interpretation differed from his, and Francis's patronage of evangelical humanism provided a breeding ground for the infiltration of more Protestant ideas.

The *Parlement* had an equally rigid view of heresy. In 1525, it seized its opportunity to become involved in the persecution of heretics during Francis' captivity in Spain after the Battle of Pavia. Although *Parlement* met at the invitation of the regent, Francis's mother Louise of Savoy, it took advantage of her vulnerable position and criticised a number of royal policies that had been pursued since the beginning of the reign. Although no direct accusation was made, it implied that Francis was guilty of protecting heretics and demanded that Louise pursue a tougher policy of persecution. Only in religion did she go some way to satisfying their demands: having applied to the Pope, Clement VII, she set up the *juges délégués* which formed a commission made up of two *Sorbonnistes* and two *Parlementaires* with powers to deal with all heresy cases without consulting the ecclesiastical courts. So heresy jurisdiction was now directly under the control of the orthodox extremists.

The new machinery was immediately put into action against the Circle of Meaux, which resulted in the king making one of his few interventions in the domestic affairs of the realm from captivity. No doubt Francis had been warned of what was happening by his sister who had recently visited him in Spain. He ordered proceedings against Lefèvre and other defendants to be suspended until his return, but the *Parlement* ignored this and the *juges délégués* were ordered to continue with their work. Berquin was also harassed in the king's absence: he was arrested for a second time in January 1526 and accused of heresy, but sentence was not passed as it became known that the king had been released.

On his return, Francis expressed his disapproval of the persecution by appointing Lefèvre as librarian at his new Château of Blois, allowing Caroli to resume preaching in Paris and demanding Berquin's release. The following year, 1527, he abolished the *juges délégués*, which led hopeful reformers to believe that he was moving closer to Luther, particularly as the Emperor now had control of the Pope. This was not the case; all Francis was doing was once again showing the Sorbonne and *Parlement* who was ultimately in control of the kingdom.

Early in 1528 Duprat, Archbishop of Sens, put forward a list of harsh penalties for heresy and in July a horrific device known as *l'estrapade* was first used for putting heretics to death at Meaux. Instead of being burned at the stake, the victim was suspended by means of iron chains over the flames, into which he was alternately lowered and raised so as to prolong the agony. This was obviously meant as a deterrent to heretics and was by all accounts quite successful.

1528 also heralded the first of a series of **iconoclastic** attacks in Paris, when a statue of the Virgin and Child was deliberately damaged. Francis offered a large reward for information about the culprits, showing the extent of his concern. This event is significant because it

iconoclasm the destruction or removal by Protestants of sacred images, such as paintings or statues

KEY ISSUE

Why did Francis need to struggle with the Parlement *and the Sorbonne over religion?*

was the first of many such acts and reveals that the more fundamental ideas of the radicals were already being absorbed by the lower classes, and that seemed much more threatening to the royal authorities.

D *Heresy and politics, 1530–47*

Parlement and the Sorbonne believed that heresy would never be eradicated from the whole of France, whatever legislative action the king might take, as long as it was allowed to flourish at court. There followed a series of contests between king on the one hand and *Parlement* and the Sorbonne on the other. This led to the final downfall of Berquin in April 1528: *Parlement* took advantage of the king's absence from Paris and Berquin was burned on the Place de Grève.

These frequent contests between the king and the Catholic extremists did not mean that Francis tolerated heresy. The spread of heretical ideas would not only threaten the unity of the kingdom but also jeopardise his delicate diplomatic negotiations. It was at the king's own request that, on 30 August when Francis and Pope Clement VII met at Marseilles, a bull was drawn up to quicken the procedure in heresy trials, and a later one made special provision for the punishment of ecclesiastics. These were meant to be used only in emergencies, but this very soon occurred.

After Nicolas Cop, the rector of the University of Paris, had delivered his traditional sermon on All Saints' Day, 1533, in the Church of the Mathurins, the Sorbonne complained to *Parlement* because he had referred to the ideas of Lefèvre. Fearing the worst, Cop vanished, taking with him the university's seal; he was followed by his young friend John Calvin. Three months later he turned up in Basle. In the aftermath of this incident there broke out a wave of persecution. Having made around fifty arrests, *Parlement* informed the king of the terrifying growth of heresy in the capital. Once the king had returned he was able to assess the situation for himself – persecution soon ended.

Tranquillity remained till the Affair of the Placards broke out in the autumn of 1534. On the Sunday morning of 18 October, Parisians on their way to Mass were aghast to find that Protestant **placards** attacking the doctrine of the Mass had been put up during the night in various public places. The Parisians' hysteria grew when it was reported that identical broadsheets had been found in the Château of Amboise where the king was in residence and in five provincial towns, Orléans, Blois, Amboise, Tours and Rouen. To make matters worse, the placards did not flaunt Luther's more moderate view but Zwingli's extreme position on the Mass, which denied the physical presence of Christ in the sacrament altogether. (The followers of Zwingli in France were known as sacramentarians.)

The Affair of the Placards was a significant event in itself for two reasons: first in showing that the Eucharist had ceased to be merely an academic debate, and second in the reaction of the people to the placards; it can be seen that the Reformation in France was becoming

placards in this context bills posted on walls and doors attacking the Catholic Mass

more popular and more easily defined. In short, it polarised people's opinions.

Almost immediately there followed a swift campaign of persecution on a scale as yet unknown to French reformers. A special commission of twelve *Parlementaires* was set up to judge heresy cases (along with a subcommission to deal with suspects within the *Parlement's* own ranks). By the end of November six dissenters (labelled Lutherans whether they were or not) had been burned in Paris. Francis was actually complimented by the Sorbonne for his zeal in dealing with this bout of heresy! Then on 13 January, shortly after Francis had returned to the capital, some copies of the *Petite Traité*, a sacramentarian tract, were discovered in the streets. Although seemingly of less significance than the first episode, this incident was more provocative considering the measures being taken to stifle heresy. It was probably this flouting of his authority that made Francis ban all printing on the same day till further notice and to order a procession for 21 January.

This must have been one of the most dramatic demonstrations of orthodoxy that the capital had ever witnessed as shrines and relics were carried through the streets. The relics included the crown of thorns and, in pride of place, the blessed sacrament, which the placards had insulted, reverently borne under a canopy by the king's three sons. Immediately behind walked Francis, his dismay at recent events openly expressed by his black attire, bare head and the lighted torch in his hand symbolising his own orthodox Catholic view of the Eucharist. After a service at Notre-Dame, he urged his subjects to denounce all heretics, and ended the day by burning six heretics. Further legislation was passed against those who harboured and concealed heretics.

The traditional explanation of Francis's harsh reaction was the appearance of a placard on his own bedchamber door. Although contemporary accounts differ over detail, it is almost certain that at least one such placard was found in the king's apartments at Amboise. Was this a crime grave enough to provoke such a violent campaign of repression in a town as far away as Paris? Also, unauthorised persons drifted in and out of his apartments with ease. Nothing in his behaviour suggests an outburst. He did not rush back to the capital but travelled at his usual leisurely pace.

Was Francis then responding to the international situation? This is unlikely as he was sounding out the German Lutheran princes at the time and the persecution could hardly have been more embarrassing; this incident also ruined his anti-Habsburg coalition.

It was the *Parlement* of Paris who acted first over the Affair of the Placards and who quite legally ordered the search for the culprits in the king's name. Previously, as for instance over Cop's sermon, the king had called a halt to persecution ordered in his name. This time he did not, and the reason must be that he felt *Parlement* to have correctly assessed this Protestant challenge. The placards were a violent attack on a fundamental belief of the Catholic faith and were on display to all the king's subjects. Their language was abusive even for the sixteenth century and it quite clearly showed the radical path that the French

Reformation had been taking since the mid-1520s. Paris was in an uproar in response, with rumours flying that the reformers were going to seize the Louvre, set fire to churches and slay the faithful at Mass. So for once the *Parlement* and the Sorbonne got their way. As the 'Most Christian King', Francis could hardly ignore the seriousness of the offence or the popular hysteria it had provoked. He acted astutely in giving his blessing to the persecution.

It has been traditional to see the Affair of the Placards as marking a radical change in the king's attitude to heresy, from one of toleration to one of persecution. But Francis had never tolerated what he considered to be heresy; he had merely disputed the definition of heresy with the Catholic extremists. Francis did not immediately break off negotiations with the German princes or stop patronising humanists. The king's attitude towards heresy did harden, but there were still disputes as to who should be labelled a heretic, persecution was not stepped up again significantly until the 1540s, as we shall see, and it was only as a result of Calvin's influence in the 1550s that French Protestantism really took shape and became a clear target. But Francis had identified a new enemy as a result of the Affair of the Placards – the sacramentarians, who were regarded as so radical as to be traitors as well as heretics.

E *The growth of persecution*

To foreign ambassadors, Francis claimed that persecution in France was political and not religious: he had gone no further than any other ruler in stamping out sedition, which, given his views of sacramentarians, was at least part of the truth. None the less, in much of the 1530s he did suspend persecution while he needed the alliance of the German Protestant princes. Then, after the Truce of Nice in 1538, he was freed from the constraints of foreign policy and turned his full attention to the problem of heresy.

The **Parlements** needed more power if heresy was to be eradicated. So on 1 June 1540 the Edict of Fontainebleau gave the *Parlements* what they had long wanted, control of heresy cases. This proved insufficient and finally in July 1543 Francis decided that the power of search and arrest would now be shared by the secular and ecclesiastical authorities, and further decrees continued to be issued until the end of the reign, with one aim – to hunt down heretics. The numerous draconian measures taken suggest that it was becoming increasingly difficult to stifle the growing Protestant challenge.

As in the rest of Europe, French Catholics were bewildered and confused by the contradictory doctrines put forward by the different reformers. The Sorbonne, increasingly frightened by the threat of Protestantism despite the king's policy of persecution, attempted to define the doctrine of the Catholic Church in a series of twenty-five articles, published in July 1543. These were an orthodox statement of traditional Catholic practice with regard to dogma, worship and organisation. This Confession of Faith gave the campaign against heresy a clearer sense of direction. The dangers of the printing press as a means of spreading subversive ideas had long been recognised. In 1543 the Sorbonne drew up the first *Index of Forbidden Books*, consisting of sixty-five titles amongst which were the works of Luther, Melanchthon and Calvin.

Persecution intensified during the last years of the reign and the number of prosecutions for heresy by the *Parlement* of Paris increased. Heretical ideas spread deeper into the kingdom and penetrated a wider spectrum of the population in the late 1530s and throughout the 1540s. In particular, the lower classes and the burghers and artisans of the towns were 'contaminated'. In 1545, five commissioners were assigned to particular areas with full powers of search and punishment. Heretics were hunted down all over France but none more viciously than the inhabitants of the Provençal villages of Merindol and Cabrières who were massacred in 1544. They were actually *vaudois*, heretics whose beliefs had persisted through the Middle Ages into the sixteenth century and who had decided to ally with the Protestants.

As we have seen, it is nevertheless too much of a simplification to say that until 1534 Francis was well-disposed towards reformers, protecting them from persecution by the Sorbonne and the *Parlement* and that after the Affair of the Placards, he suddenly rounded on them to unleash a savage campaign of repression which continued until the end of the reign. Before 1534 he had been highly selective in whom he chose to protect. After 1535 the constant U-turns in foreign policy had their effect on religious policy, as did the enduring influence of his sister, Marguerite, who sympathised with the reform movement, and the continuing contest over the definition of heresy. Although there were significant changes towards the end of the reign, Francis remained more a Renaissance prince than a Counter-Reformation king.

TIMELINE

1516	Concordat of Bologna
1521	Sorbonne condemns Lutheranism
1523	Berquin first arrested
1525	*Parlement* seizes initiative in persecution of heresy
1528	Berquin executed
1533	Cop's sermon
1534	Affair of the Placards
1540	Edict of Fontainebleau

KEY ISSUE

Was Francis consistent in his religious policy?

3 ↪ FOREIGN POLICY

Much of the detail of Francis's foreign policy has been dealt with in relation to the Italian Wars and Charles V. Here we shall review some of the main features, assessing Francis's goals and achievements.

See pages 227–30

A *The issue of Milan*

For most of his reign, the key issue for Francis was Milan, which was of great strategic importance, dominating the Alpine passes into Italy. He felt that he had a hereditary right to the duchy and that he had to retake it and avenge the defeat of his predecessor, Louis XII, by the Swiss.

Francis's invasion of Italy on becoming king in 1515 was an unqualified triumph. As the Swiss blocked the obvious routes across the Alps, Francis chose a pass used only by local peasants and their herds, so that he was able to take the Milanese by surprise at Villafranca. A Venetian eyewitness commented that the Alps had seen nothing comparable since Hannibal's famous crossing! His defeat of the seemingly invincible Swiss at Marignano covered him with glory and he retook Milan.

However, Francis's pre-eminence was short-lived. Charles of Burgundy became King of Spain in 1516 and put himself forward to succeed his grandfather as Holy Roman Emperor in 1519. Francis put himself forward as a rival candidate. He spent 400 000 crowns to try and bribe the electors, but to no avail. It seemed as though he suffered from too great a sense of his own grandeur, but he actually had more practical motives. He wrote that he wished to gain the Empire 'to prevent the said Catholic king from doing so. If he were to succeed, seeing the extent of his kingdoms and lordships, this would do me immeasurable harm; he would...doubtless throw me out of Italy.' Even in the case of the imperial election, the issue was Milan. A standard view has often been that Francis's prime objective was to break out of the new Habsburg encirclement of France. This would make sense but there is no direct evidence for it and Francis's policies may just have been a continuation of his predecessors' overriding concern with Italy.

KEY ISSUE

What errors did Francis make in his foreign policy before his capture at Pavia, and were they avoidable?

By 1522 Milan was in Habsburg hands, after Francis had tried to take advantage of Charles by attacking Spain during the Revolt of the *Comuneros*. Still, the French successfully resisted an Imperial invasion in the region of Marseilles and Francis managed to re-take Milan in 1524. However, there was not to be another Marignano – in 1525 Francis was defeated and captured at the Battle of Pavia. He had shown great personal bravery during the battle but the consequence for him was imprisonment in Madrid.

B *The consequences of defeat*

By the Treaty of Madrid in 1526, Francis was forced to concede Milan to Charles and he promised to return the Burgundian territories taken by Louis XI. He was then freed, leaving behind him his two young sons as hostages. Francis's comment that they would be treated well and have the opportunity to learn Spanish may have been bravado rather than lack of paternal feeling. Charles thought he had won hands down, but Francis was not to give in so easily.

In May 1526 the Viceroy of Naples visited Francis, having heard that he intended to disregard the Treaty of Madrid and hoping to persuade him otherwise. This was his official answer:

> It has been resolved that the Viceroy will be called to the Council 1
> tomorrow, and after his demands have been heard, they will be
> answered. First, should he speak of the king's promises, oath and
> obligation, he will be told that the King is under no obligation
> whatever and that he is not bound to keep his promises, since they 5
> [the Imperialists] did not trust his word, but kept him under guard,
> setting him free only after they had received hostages. Nor is he

obliged to keep promises which may be attributed to him, since they were extorted from him under the fear of life imprisonment
10 and of death consequent on the grave illness caused by melancholy into which he had fallen.

He feared also that his mother would not be able to carry the regency for long, given the onerous nature of the task and her sorrow over the King's capture. He was afraid too, that the kingdom would fall into ruin and civil strife and that his children,
16 who are young, would be cheated of their inheritance.

> **Q**
> 1. *What does this extract tell us about Francis's attitude towards his children (line 15)?*
> 2. *How real was the threat of 'ruin and strife' (line 15)?*
> 3. *What does this show us about sixteenth-century diplomacy?*

Taking as an excuse Charles's capture of the Pope after the Sack of Rome, Francis declared war again in 1528. However, the defection of the Genoese admiral to Charles and defeat at Landriano in 1529 brought about the Peace of Cambrai in the same year. This left Milan firmly in Charles's hands and Francis with a huge ransom of two million gold écus to pay to secure the release of his sons. But it was not a complete defeat for Francis – his right to the Burgundian territories in France was at last recognised. With the ransom paid at last, on 1 July 1530 the two French princes were taken by boat to freedom across the Bidassoa river. They had differing responses to the way in which they had been treated and the opportunity to learn Spanish. The elder, Francis, bade a polite farewell to his captors. When it came to his turn the younger, Henry, later to be Henry II and victor over Charles V, made his feelings clear by farting.

C *The last conflict in Italy*

After six years of careful diplomacy, negotiating with such diverse potential allies as the Pope and the Ottoman Emperor, Francis again attempted to take Milan in 1536. This was extremely rash as there were already promising negotiations with Charles in progress, with the possibility of one of Francis's sons becoming Duke of Milan after the death of the last of the Sforzas in 1535.

Francis did capture some Italian territory and won glory in repelling an Imperial attack on Provence. However, in financial terms it was disastrous; within a year Francis had spent all he had saved since 1532. Charles had certainly been defeated and Francis now had a foothold in Italy, but most of Provence was laid waste and the succession of Milan, over which the war had been fought, remained as doubtful as ever.

The influence of the king's favourite, Anne de Montmorency, on foreign policy cannot be overestimated at this time. He changed Francis's strategy in the Habsburg–Valois conflict from aggression to defence and now went even further by attempting a reconciliation between his master and the Emperor. The main objective of French foreign policy, the recovery of Milan, remained the same, only the method was now different.

The consequence was the Truce of Nice in 1538 arranged by Montmorency and the Pope. Francis and Charles refused to meet each

TIMELINE

1515	Battle of Marignano
1522	Milan in Spanish hands
1525	Battle of Pavia
1526	Treaty of Madrid
1529	Peace of Cambrai
1536	Francis invades Italy
1538	Truce of Nice
1542	Charles V and Henry VIII invade northern France
1544	Peace of Crèpy
1552	Henry II takes Metz, Toul and Verdun
1557	Battle of St Quentin
1558	French take Calais
1559	Peace of Câteau-Cambrésis

other initially at Nice, even in front of their spiritual father. Perhaps it was fortuitous, for when Francis's wife, Queen Eleanor, went alone to meet her brother Charles, a wooden pier, specially constructed between the boats, collapsed and the queen, the Emperor and many of their retinues were flung into the sea.

Francis retained Savoy and Piedmont but the peace achieved little else. While Montmorency remained in power, the spirit of friendship was maintained and in 1539, when Charles was faced with a revolt in Ghent, Francis invited him to take a short cut through France and entertained him royally on the way.

D *Conflict in northern Europe*

In October 1540 when Charles formally invested his son, Philip, with the Duchy of Milan, Montmorency's policy appeared to have failed and he was sent from court in disgrace. Without him at the helm, Francis reverted to his old ways and war broke out once again.

This time Francis faced a two-pronged attack by Charles V and Henry VIII on northern France. The imperial army came within leagues of Paris before retiring owing to exhaustion. Francis was criticised at the time for not doing anything to halt the imperial advance but it could also be argued that he showed sound judgement in reserving his army for the defence of Paris, given that the war was on two fronts.

Just how far foreign policy could override other considerations was shown by Francis's alliances with the Turks to attack Charles V, any thought of crusade displaced by the principle that your enemy's enemy is your friend. Thomas Cromwell commented that Francis would ally with the Turk and the devil if that was the way to regain Milan. In 1543 the Ottoman emperor put a Turkish fleet under the command of the feared Admiral Barbarossa at Francis's disposal. This was a great help militarily but a diplomatic embarrassment, especially as Francis was forced to allow Barbarossa to take over the port of Toulon on the French Mediterranean coast as his winter quarters. Tax concessions did little to placate the inhabitants, who had to abandon their houses to the Turks while Barbarossa established a mosque and a slave market.

The Peace of Crèpy in 1544 restored the status quo but a significant change had come about in the shape of the Habsburg–Valois conflict. By the time Francis died in 1547 the main arena was now to be northern Europe.

E *Success or failure?*

In the end Francis had gained little. Had he been foolish to challenge Habsburg power on the Italian peninsula? Certainly this Italian dream seems to have been almost an obsession which had driven him on, as at Pavia when it would have been more sensible to retreat. It was, of course, a matter of prestige and, although Francis possibly put his priorities in the wrong order, he was right to recognise the importance of military glory in the eyes of his subjects and the rest of Europe. But Francis could still have offered a challenge to Charles's authority, considering the Emperor's other distractions, by pursuing a more defensive policy. This was apparent during the ascendancy of Montmorency but the balance swayed once more in Charles's favour when Francis took over again and reverted to the offensive. He could not afford to wage war abroad, in terms of manpower or money, for such a continuous length of time and the kingdom paid the penalty in terms of financial weakness in the future. It is debatable whether Francis's foreign policy brought any advantages to France. In the short term there was the prestige and satisfaction of thwarting the Emperor on occasion, but in the long run Francis gained little in terms of territory and prosperity to balance the losses sustained. He was also continually distracted from the domestic affairs touching royal authority and the religion of France which were to dominate the latter half of the sixteenth century.

> **KEY ISSUE**
>
> *Did France gain at all from Francis's foreign policy?*

4 ↪ THE REIGN OF HENRY II, 1547–59

A *Government reforms and finance*

For two months after Francis's death on 31 March 1547 elaborate religious and court rituals were performed before he was finally buried alongside his ancestors at St Denis. The effigy of the dead king was even served meals for eleven days, symbolic of his continuing authority while his 28-year-old son Henry prepared himself for the kingship he would assume following the funeral. He needed little preparation however. He immediately dismissed from court his father's mistress, the Duchesse d'Etampes, and to the chagrin of his queen, Catherine de Medici, installed his own mistress Diane de Poitiers. Twenty years his senior, she had enchanted him when he was an adolescent and he remained loyal to her for the rest of his life. She ensured that her friends and relatives benefited greatly in government posts and pensions. Henry recalled his old friend Anne de Montmorency – who had been out of favour ever since the failure of his peace policy following the 1538 Truce of Nice – and Montmorency was made a duke and peer. The sons of the Duke of Guise also came to prominence. They were a family well connected internationally, being related to the dukes of Lorraine (an independent principality at that time) and James V of Scotland through his marriage to their sister Mary. Francis, Duke of Guise from 1550, Charles, Cardinal of Lorraine and their four younger brothers were unusually effective as a close-knit team in their quest for power and patronage. They never wielded the influence held by Montmorency, but one of the brothers, Claude, married the daughter of Diane de Poitiers and they worked through her. Lesser nobles in turn sought advantage by attaching themselves to Montmorency, Diane or the Guises. Such factions were a normal part of court life while Henry was there to keep ultimate control. But when his early death in 1559 removed the

PICTURE 26
Henry II *by François Clouet*

restraint imposed by his personal authority, factional conflict was to slide easily into civil war.

As well as changing personnel, Henry instituted a series of major administrative reforms within a month of coming to the throne. He appointed four secretaries of state, each responsible for communications with the local authorities in a quarter of France and each also handling foreign policy concerning the states adjoining their respective quarter of the country. This ensured that the king was more fully informed of what was going on both within France and beyond its borders. Henry next created the post of controller-general, an inspector of the government's financial accounts, intended to combat corruption and promote efficiency. He also sent officials known as *intendants* to assist provincial governors with financial and judicial affairs. While often welcomed by the governors who needed expert help, they also extended royal influence into the more remote parts of the country and the following century were to be built up into the chief agents of royal authority.

Henry's first reform of taxation was not such a success. In 1548 he reorganised the rates and collection of the *gabelle*, the hated salt tax. Angry crowds lynched tax collectors (including some unfortunates who just looked like one) and looted the houses of the rich, and soon a rebellion was spreading over western France. It was crushed with great severity by Montmorency, the citizens of Bordeaux in particular being subject to harsh penalties. Henry, though, thought better of the reforms to the *gabelle*, reverted to the old system and restored the privileges of Bordeaux. This backtracking illustrates the conclusion of Henry's recent biographer Frederic Baumgartner: 'Henry, like most kings of the early modern period, thought of himself as absolute but was unable to rule absolutely, nor did he make any strong effort to do so.'

Henry racked up all other taxes gradually and without provoking resistance through risky innovation. In 1523 royal taxation had totalled between seventy-one and seventy-two million livres; under Henry it reached between 131 and 132 million per year. However, once Henry was engaged in wars in Germany and Italy and given the effects of inflation, this was nowhere near enough. He consolidated his loans on the Lyon financial market in 1555 in an agreement known as the *Grand Parti de Lyon*, fixing the annual interest he was to pay at 16%. But he could not keep up the payments and, although not formally bankrupt, in 1557 found it increasingly difficult to obtain any further credit. Given this situation and defeat that year at the battle of St Quentin, he knew he had to make peace. However, 1559 saw both the peace settlement of Câteau-Cambrèsis and the king's death: Henry's debts survived him and enfeebled the monarchy just when it was at its most vulnerable.

See page 281

KEY ISSUE

In what ways did Henry II build on his father's government reforms?

B *Religious policy*

Henry has the reputation of having escalated religious persecution. In 1547 he established a new tribunal in the *Parlement* to deal with heresy cases. It became known as the *chambre ardente*, the burning chamber. It heard 215 cases between 1548 and 1550 when it was closed, with thirty-seven condemned to death, and there were additional trials in the provincial *Parlements*. He followed this up in 1551 with the Edict of Châteaubriant which instituted the *mercuriale*, a session in the *Parlement* every three months to root out any heresy amongst its own members. It tightened up censorship of books, authorised the seizure of heretics' property, one-third to go to any informers, and ordered all teachers and officials to obtain a certificate to prove that they were Catholic church goers. Finally, in 1557 he issued the Edict of Compiègne, which established the death penalty for obstinate sacramentarians (meaning Calvinists), for going to Geneva or publishing books there, and for illegal preaching or participation in forbidden religious services. These measures restricted but did not halt Calvinist conversions. For a time some Calvinists did flee, but they tended to end up in Geneva where their faith and organisation was reinforced, before returning to France. Later the judges responsible for enforcing the Edicts of Châteaubriant and Compiègne expended more effort in quarrelling over who had the right to try cases rather than actually trying them. Furthermore, hard on the heels of each edict was war abroad, which distracted the attention of the king from heresy at home.

Henry was most concerned with heresy spreading amongst the population at large or those who judged them. He took few steps to eradicate it amongst the old nobility. In 1557 he asked the Pope to establish the Inquisition in France and three inquisitors were appointed – including the Cardinal of Châtillon whose Protestant sympathies were more than rumours. The Cardinal's brothers, Admiral Coligny and d'Andelot, all nephews of Henry's old friend Montmorency, were Protestant sympathisers as well. D'Andelot was openly converting his followers and tenants to Calvinism, but apart from keeping him under house arrest for a time and making threats, Henry did nothing. It was the conversion of a large proportion of the French nobility which was to enable the Calvinists to put up the fight that they did in the opening years of the Wars of Religion.

See page 364

Although allied with Pope Paul IV (1555–59) towards the end of his reign, there had been no earlier co-operation between Henry and Pope Julius III (1550–55). There were quarrels over Church appointments, and Julius wanted to reconvene the Council of Trent (the General Council of the Church intended to advance a Counter-Reformation by equipping Catholics with good discipline and clear doctrine). Unable to feel solidarity with other Catholic rulers, Henry opposed the Council, being far more interested in maintaining German Protestants as allies against Charles V. The row between king and Pope grew so bitter that at one stage Henry was threatening an independent Church of France in imitation of Henry VIII's Church of England, while Julius thundered that he would declare Henry deposed. Relations were patched up, but Henry had made no effort to advance the Counter-Reformation. He did nothing to improve the standards of the clergy to win back some of the hearts and minds lost to Calvinism. Choosing bishops for political reasons, not for their capacity to inspire the faithful, Henry appointed a lower number of theologians and a higher number without a university degree than any king of the century. He had failed to understand that repression alone, even if it had been pursued as a consistent policy, could not stop religious differences from deepening.

KEY ISSUE

How effective were Henry II's religious policies?

C *Foreign policy*

Henry continued his father's foreign policy – he would do anything to undermine Emperor Charles V. But his first objective was to neutralise the English, who were troublesome allies of the Emperor and had taken Boulogne in 1544. He breathed new life into the Auld Alliance with Scotland, sending an army there to put down a rebellion and menace

England from the north, and in 1548 the niece of the Guise brothers, Mary Queen of Scots, landed in France to marry the Dauphin Francis. Henry then struck directly at the English in Boulogne and had regained it by 1550.

By this time Henry's attention had turned once again to Italy where Charles V was attempting to dislodge Henry's ally, Ottavio Farnese, from Parma. But he did not repeat the mistakes of his predecessors by attempting a full-scale invasion of Italy directly into the shifting sands of the peninsula's changing alliances and uncertain logistics. Instead his forces picked off some small northern Italian towns and maintained Siena in rebellion against its Spanish garrison from 1552 to 1555, so tying down imperial forces. Taking a leaf out of his father's book, Henry also persuaded the Turks to send a fleet to harass the Emperor and his allies in Italy in 1552. But his most important move was in the north. He negotiated an alliance with the German Protestant princes who bitterly resented the religious settlement imposed on them by the Emperor in 1548 in defiance of German liberties, and who were not as cowed by that defeat as the Emperor had hoped. In 1552 Henry invaded the Empire as arranged and seized Metz, Toul and Verdun, the three cities which could guarantee the security of north-eastern France. He 'watered his horses in the Rhine' but tactfully went no further as that would have antagonized his German allies. The Emperor, horrified, hurried from Italy and in November, far too late in the season, began a siege of Metz. Francis of Guise inside the city resisted successfully and the gouty, tired Emperor was forced to lift the siege in January 1553. Henry was triumphant, and Charles V moved towards his abdication in 1555–56.

Before this, however, the Emperor managed one last political coup. In 1554 his son Philip II who was to inherit Spain and the Netherlands, married the new Queen of England, Mary Tudor. The tables had been turned. Scotland was tied to France by marriage, but now England was similarly tied to the Netherlands, perhaps permanently, Henry feared, if Philip and Mary had children. But there was no immediate conflict. When Philip took over from his father in 1556 he needed a breathing space to establish himself. Henry, in dire financial straits, accepted the five-year truce of Vaucelles.

The truce lasted barely five months. In Italy the new, and slightly unhinged, Pope Paul IV had declared war on Philip II. Henry saw this as his opportunity to take Naples, but his forces rapidly got bogged down in the Papal states and nothing was achieved before the great disaster at St Quentin on 10 August 1557. Philip II had invaded northern France, routed and captured Montmorency outside St Quentin, and went on to take the city. It was only Philip's caution and shortage of money that stopped him marching on Paris. Henry recalled his troops from Italy and desperate to redeem the situation in some way, struck against Calais. In January 1558 the English lost their last foothold in France.

All parties to the conflict were now financially exhausted and the Peace of Câteau-Cambrésis was agreed in April 1559. It was the pivotal peace settlement of the sixteenth century. Henry gave up the French claims on Milan and Naples. Lands which were the gateways to Italy were restored to Philip's ally the Duke of Savoy, who in turn agreed to marry Henry's sister Marguerite. The Italian Wars were at last over. It looked like a triumph for Philip, and the settlement was deeply unpopular in France. However, Baumgartner judges that 'from a strategic point of view the French had gained vastly more from Câteau-Cambrésis than they had lost'. Metz, Toul and Verdun remained in French hands – solid additions to French security rather than the fantasies of conquest in Italy. Following the death of Mary Tudor and the rejection of his proposal of marriage to her successor Elizabeth I, Philip felt able to abandon his English allies. So Calais remained in French hands, and Philip married Henry's eldest daughter.

A great tournament was held in Paris in June to celebrate the royal marriages and the peace. Despite soothsayers' warnings of impending doom, Henry insisted on entering the lists himself. He was struck by a lance, which penetrated his vizor; splinters were driven into his forehead just above the eye, and he died ten days later. The international peace settlement he had been celebrating was to last for thirty years, but that was because France plunged into the factional and religious strife which Henry had been unable to foresee – the French Wars of Religion.

> **KEY ISSUE**
>
> *Was Henry II's great achievement in foreign policy not to get bogged down in Italy?*

5 ⤖ BIBLIOGRAPHY

**R.J. Knecht, *Renaissance Warrior and Patron: The Reign of Francis I* (CUP, 1994) is the standard text and **R.J. Knecht, *French Renaissance Monarchy* (Longman Seminar Studies, 2nd ed., 1996) provides a concise version with useful documents. **M. Rady, *Access to History: France 1494–1610 Renaissance, Religion and Recovery* (Hodder and Stoughton, 1988) is an excellent guide to the main issues. *David Potter, *A History of France, 1460–1560: The Emergence of a Nation State* (Macmillan, 1995) is a fine synthesis of recent scholarship. *J. Russell Major, *From Renaissance Monarchy to Absolute Monarchy: French Kings, Nobles and Estates* (The Johns Hopkins University Press, 1994) is the most recent statement of his important views. *Richard Bonney, *The European Dynastic States 1494–1660*, pp. 99–109, (Oxford University Press, 1991), gives a good summary of Francis's foreign policy. *Mark Greengrass, *The French Reformation* (Blackwell, 1987) makes clear the various strands of reform. *Frederic Baumgartner, *Henry II, King of France 1547–1559* (Duke University Press, 1988) is the best recent biography.

6 ᔦ STRUCTURED AND ESSAY QUESTIONS

A *Structured questions.*
1. (a) What were the priorities of Francis I?
   (b) Did Francis I leave the French monarchy stronger or weaker at the end of his reign in 1547 than at the beginning in 1515?
2. (a) How did the policy of Francis I and Henry II towards heresy change during the course of their reigns?
   (b) 'In their pursuit of glory in war Francis I and Henry II neglected both French government and the French Church.' Discuss.

B *Essay questions.*
1. How far was Francis I a traditional rather than an innovative ruler?
2. How far were Francis I and Henry II able to utilise the power of the monarchy?
3. 'He subordinated religion and national interests to the pursuit of personal glory.' Is this a valid comment on the foreign policy of Francis I?
4. 'A failure, but a glorious failure.' Do you agree with this assessment of the reign of Francis I?
5. 'Because of his early death Henry II has been overshadowed by his father Francis I, but Henry was the more effective monarch.' Discuss.

7 ᔦ DOCUMENTARY EXERCISE ON FRANCIS I: AN ABSOLUTE MONARCH?

Was Francis I an absolute monarch, i.e. a monarch recognising no legitimate restraint on his authority?

This question has long fascinated historians. Absolutism is usually applied to seventeenth-century France, particularly to the reign of Louis XIV. Can it also apply, however, to Renaissance France? Certainly the doctrine of royal absolutism was to be found in the early sixteenth century in the work of contemporary writers.

Two of these, Claude de Seyssel, an important churchman, and Guillaume Budé, a leading humanist scholar, illustrate the two schools of thought at the time. Seyssel, in his *La Monarchie de France*, admired the moderation of the French monarchy because it was checked from exceeding its powers by the aristocracy, which he identified with the sovereign courts. Budé's *L'Institution du Prince* saw the role of the aristocracy differently. To him they were privileged but should not share power with the king. Budé realised the importance to the king of wise advice but stated that he was free to reject this as long as he was not overriding the precedents set by his predecessors.

The authority of the king in France is regulated and restrained by three checks... The first is Religion, the second, Justice and the third, Police...

With regard to the first, it is an indisputable fact that the French have always been, and still are... pious and God-fearing... For that reason it is both proper and necessary that whoever is king should make it known to the people by example and by visible and outward signs that he is a zealot, an observer of the Faith and of the Christian religion, and that he is resolved to use his power to strengthen and sustain it... So long as the king respects... the Christian religion he cannot act as a tyrant. If he is guilty of such an act, it is permissible for a prelate or any other devout man who respects the people, to remonstrate with and to upbraid him.

Justice, which is the second check... indubitably carries more weight in France than in any other country in the world, especially because of the institution of the Parlements, whose principal role is to bridle the absolute power which the kings might seek to use.

The third check is that of the Police, by which is intended those many laws that have been passed, and subsequently confirmed and approved from time to time, which help to preserve the kingdom as a whole and the rights of the individuals who compose it.

SOURCE A

From La Monarchie de France, *Claude de Seyssel.*

1. *How far could the French Church, according to Seyssel, act as a check on the authority of the king?*
2. *In what way is this merely a rhetorical check?*
3. *Using examples from the chapter, how would you describe Francis's relationship with the Parlement?*
4. *Did the Parlement act as a check on the king, as Seyssel argues?*
5. *What does Seyssel mean by the 'Police'?*
6. *Were there any other checks on the authority of the king in practice?*

Contemporary historians also debate as to how absolute, if at all, was the French monarchy under Francis I. J. Russell Major has described early sixteenth-century France as 'popular and consultative' and is sceptical of the existence of absolutism except in theory. R.J. Knecht argues that, although Francis's absolutism was limited in comparison with that of Louis XIV in the late seventeenth century, the king 'frequently acted in an authoritarian manner allowing no room for opposition or even criticism'. David Potter goes further in asserting the practicality of absolutism, pointing out that absolute monarchy had a much broader base than the king alone, as it benefited those in royal service as well.

Russell Major's argument rests on the following:

(i) 'The French Renaissance monarchs ruled according to the law, not in defiance of it.' He argues that their claim to the Crown 'was based on law, not force' and that they in turn respected the rights of their subjects.

(ii) '...they [French kings] accepted the decentralisation of the state, and made little effort to centralise it'. For example, newly acquired lands kept their own institutions and laws, provincial governors attempted to usurp royal power, and there was the establishment of local *Parlements* and the continuation of provincial estates.

(iii) '...they were inherently weak, not strong'. France had neither an adequate army nor an adequate bureaucracy.

(iv) '...that the dynamic elements in society were the nobility and the bureaucracy, not the bourgeoisie'. The Renaissance monarchs did suppress rebellious nobles but not indiscriminately. In fact the nobility were the natural advisers and companions of the king and therefore their economic status improved accordingly.

(v) '...the basis of a king's power lay in the support he could win from the people, not in a standing army or a bureaucracy'. Kings restored order after a period of civil unrest through the use of assemblies and there was no other 'safe, logical alternative to their rule'.

In the new edition of his biography of Francis (1994) Knecht puts more emphasis on the limitations to Francis's absolutism than he did previously:

'Francis was undoubtedly a strong monarch, but he could not ignore the foundations of medieval privilege on which his monarchy rested...The enforcement of the law depended on a willingness to obey...' But he still stresses Francis's 'strongly authoritarian disposition'. 'He seems not to have considered himself bound by tradition and to believe that he had the right to depart from existing ordinances, institutions and methods of government.'

Russell Major argues that Francis's overhaul of the financial administration was a failure, shown by the need to keep on making changes every ten years or so. Knecht believes that Francis's reforms tightened up royal control considerably and that 'the degree of royal absolutism that existed in early sixteenth-century France may be measured by the amount of fiscal control exercised by the king. How far was he free to tax his subjects at will? Francis...had more control over the purses of his subjects than any of his fellow monarchs.'

Potter places more emphasis than Knecht on the institution of the monarchy rather than on the personality of an individual king. He argues that despite the insecurity of a king when facing a strongly armed opponent, and the difficulties of governing a large country without the benefit of modern communications, 'nevertheless, the legal basis of Absolute Monarchy, the capacity of the crown to recover from repeated shocks, and the benefits available to men of energy and ability in its service, proved decisive. Thus a powerful identity of interest existed well before the fifteenth century between the king and the array of officials which staffed the high organs of administration. The

Absolute Monarchy was in this sense the vehicle in which a substantial political elite rode in order to control the machinery of order, power, patronage and private interest.'

Q

1. *List J. Russell Major's five arguments disputing the existence of absolutism and apply them to the reign of Francis I, finding examples for and against each one.*
2. *Can you think of occasions when Francis displayed the 'strongly authoritarian disposition' suggested by Knecht?*
3. *Using examples from the chapter, how far would you judge that Francis exercised absolute power in connection with taxation and finance?*
4. *What evidence is there in the case of Francis I that 'a substantial political elite', as described by Potter, backed the concentration of power in royal hands?*
5. *How far did absolutism exist in the reign of Francis I?*

The Ottoman Empire

OVERVIEW

At about half past one in the morning of Tuesday 29 May, 1453, **Sultan** Mohammed II gave the order for the final assault on Constantinople. The first attack by his irregular troops, the *Bashi-Bazouks*, was beaten off after two hours. A second assault by trained regiments of Turkish troops also failed. Finally, a way in was discovered through a small gate and Mohammed's elite troops, the *janissaries*, fought their way into the city. The last Emperor of Constantinople, Constantine XI, threw himself into the battle and was never seen again.

Constantinople had been one of the great cities of Europe for over a thousand years, since the Roman Emperor Constantine had made it his capital. Although its importance had declined, it remained a great centre of Christian culture and of trade and its capture by an Islamic ruler horrified and terrified Europe.

For the next 150 years, the **Ottoman** Empire can fairly be described as more successful and powerful than any other state in Europe. Under Suleiman the Magnificent (1520–66), the state dominated the Balkans, the Middle East and much of North Africa. The Ottoman navy controlled the eastern Mediterranean and the Black Sea and its armies were considered invincible.

It seems surprising, therefore, that so few historians have written at length on the Ottoman Empire. In part, this reflects a traditional European stereotype of the 'cruel Turk' and a lack of understanding of Islamic culture and society. Modern historians, such as the French historian of the Mediterranean, Fernand Braudel, and the Turkish historian, Halil Inalcik, have justly drawn attention to the remarkable impact of the Ottoman Empire. The American historian, Stanford Shaw, is equally convinced of the strength and importance of the Empire, but points out its rapid decline after the death of Suleiman the Magnificant. In particular, he stresses the limits to further expansion imposed upon it (the army had to return to the heart of the Empire each winter), the cultural and intellectual divisions which made the Empire suspicious of innovation, and the rise of factional divisions in its government. But even today, serious historical research is discouraged by the inaccessibility of the major archives and the skill in languages that is required before they can be used.

Despite these problems, it is now accepted that the major events of the sixteenth century, such as the Hapsburg–Valois rivalry and the Reformation were, directly or indirectly, deeply affected by the Ottoman threat. Not only this, the Ottoman system of government

Sultan the sovereign ruler of an Islamic state, most usually referring to the Ottoman (Turkish) emperor

janissaries professional soldiers recruited as children from the Christian peoples of the empire

Ottomans the dynasty which ruled the Turkish Empire

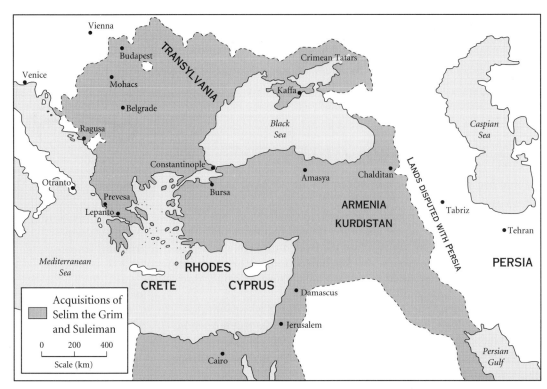

MAP 14
The Ottoman Empire in 1571

was so different and arguably so much more effective than that of, for example, Charles V, that a study of the Ottoman Empire provides an invaluable point of comparison and contrast to the rest of Europe.

1 ↩ THE RISE OF THE OTTOMAN EMPIRE TO 1453

Throughout European history, nomadic tribes have drifted from Central Asia towards Europe and Asia Minor. These tribes have often posed a serious military threat, particularly because of their skills as horsemen. Tribes of Turkic race began to colonise Anatolia (modern Turkey) from the end of the eleventh century onwards. Anatolia was the frontier zone between the Christian and Islamic worlds and great opportunities were available to successful fighting tribes as there was a chance of plunder and relative freedom from government. The frontier therefore attracted the most aggressive and militaristic elements amongst the Turkic tribes and successful leaders gained great prestige. The violent nature of this frontier society was reinforced by militant religion – the Turkish Muslims sought justification in Islamic law (the

Shari'a) for fighting people who did not share their faith, just as crusaders claimed it was a Christian duty to fight the Infidel.

One of the most successful *ghazis* amongst the Turks was Osman, who lived in western Anatolia, destroyed a Byzantine army in 1301 and established the Ottoman dynasty. His grandson, Suleiman, crossed into Europe and the victory of Suleiman's brother, Murad, over the combined armies of Serbia and Bosnia at Kosovo in 1389 confirmed the Ottoman Turks as the greatest power in the Balkans. Only the cunning diplomatic intrigues of the Byzantine emperors of Constantinople, and the sudden danger posed by the armies of Timur (Tamberlaine), who invaded Anatolia in 1402 and destroyed a Turkish army at Ankara, delayed the now inevitable fall of Constantinople for the next fifty years.

> **the *Shari'a*** the Islamic law code

> ***Ghazis*** holy warriors whose duty was to fight against non-Muslims until they submitted

2 ∽ THE CAPTURE OF CONSTANTINOPLE

The capture of Constantinople in 1453 brought enormous prestige to Mohammed II. To the world of Islam, he was now Mohammed the 'Conqueror', one of the greatest *ghazis* (holy warriors) in history. The Turkish historian, H. Inalcik, has written, 'The Islamic world came to regard Holy War as the great source of power and influence'. Mohammed also saw himself as the heir to the Roman tradition of a universal empire. In 1466, George Trapezuntius, a Greek scholar, wrote, 'No one doubts that you are Emperor of the Romans. Whoever is legally master of the capital of the Empire is the Emperor and Constantinople is the capital of the Roman Empire'. Mohammed undoubtedly believed that control of Constantinople would provide a springboard for the conquest of the whole Christian world.

Not only did the city have great prestige, but its location – where Europe meets Asia and the Black Sea joins the Mediterranean – had made Constantinople traditionally a great trading centre. Although Islam preached the duty of Holy War, its laws forbade the forced conversion of Christians and Jews, once conquered. As long as these subject communities paid tribute and did not offend Islamic law, they were left in peace. This relative tolerance within the Empire meant that a great opportunity now existed to rebuild Constantinople as the most thriving, open trading centre of the eastern Mediterranean, once united in the Byzantine Empire and now being gradually reunited under Ottoman rule. In his *History of Mohammed the Conqueror* Kritoboulos, a contemporary Greek historian, described the Ottoman Sultan's policy as follows:

See page 299

KEY ISSUE

What was the importance of the possession of Constantinople?

Q

1. *What does this tell us about Mohammed's aims for Constantinople?*
2. *How did his attitude towards other religious faiths differ from those found elsewhere in Europe?*

> When the Sultan had captured the city of Constantinople, almost his first care was to have the City repopulated. He also undertook the further care and repairs of it. He sent an order in the form of an imperial command to every part of his realm, that as many inhabitants as possible be transferred to the City, not only Christians but also his own people and many of the Hebrews.

3 ↶ THE EXPANSION OF THE OTTOMAN EMPIRE, 1453–1520

A *Mohammed II*

Mohammed II and his successors Bayezid II (1481–1512) and Selim I 'the Grim' (1512–20) continued the expansion of the Ottoman state. By 1464, Mohammed had eliminated the small states of Trebizond on the Black Sea and the Morea (the Peloponnese in Greece), both of which were ruled by families with a claim to the Byzantine inheritance. His main threat to the west, however, was Venice. The Venetians possessed a far stronger navy than the Ottoman Empire, which had traditionally been a land power. They were also, however, reliant on the goodwill of the Turks to maintain their trade and had been granted important trading concessions in 1454. The Venetians were reluctant to commit themselves to a lengthy war against the Ottoman Empire. Over the next century and a half, there were many wars, but economic necessity invariably forced Venice to make peace and the Venetian Republic could never be relied on in any European coalition against the Turks.

Despite this, with the support of the pope and in alliance with the Hungarians and the Albanian chieftain, Scanderbeg, the Venetians went to war in 1463. This war clearly demonstrated the superiority of the Ottoman military system. In 1468, Scanderbeg died and Albania passed under Ottoman control, and in 1470 Euboea, off eastern Greece, was seized. The Venetians hoped to take advantage of the hostility of other Islamic states towards the Ottoman Empire, which Mohammed wished to bring under direct control, specifically of Uzun Hasan, the ruler of the so-called 'white sheep' of eastern Asia Minor. These nomadic tribesmen lived in remote and mountainous districts and were particularly formidable opponents. In 1472, the Venetians allied with Uzun Hasan and one of the remaining bands of crusaders, the Knights of St John, whose naval base at Rhodes constantly menaced Ottoman trade in the Aegean. The response to this challenge emphasised the formidable nature of the Ottoman army. Over 70 000 men were sent against Uzun Hasan, who was defeated in 1473. Ottoman power, as a result, now extended to the Euphrates (in modern Iraq).

After this overwhelming victory, the Ottoman army advanced to within sight of Venice and the peace treaty of 1479 confirmed Ottoman control of the Balkans and forced the Venetians to pay an annual tribute. Mohammed had also been able to turn eastwards to subdue the remaining Genoese colonies on the shores of the Black Sea and the Crimean Tatars to the north of it, which by 1475 confirmed complete Ottoman control of the region.

The last years of Mohammed's life were dominated by the twin aims of subjugating Rhodes and invading Italy. On 4 December 1479, the siege of Rhodes began and on 11 August 1480, Otranto in southern Italy was seized and the pope prepared to flee to France. Only the death of Mohammed in 1481 caused these campaigns to be abandoned. This may well have been fortunate for the Turks, since an advance into Italy would almost certainly have unified Christendom in the defence of Rome and the shrine of St Peter.

Even so, Mohammed's achievement was remarkable. Ottoman rule in the Balkans and Asia Minor was to last for four centuries.

B *Bayezid II*

The reign of Bayezid II, 1481–1512, is generally seen as one of consolidation. He succeeded to the throne only with some difficulty and relied on the support of the élite troops of the army, the *janissaries*, to whom he was forced to offer bribes when he came to the throne, establishing a most unfortunate precedent. He did succeed in extending Ottoman power beyond the Black Sea and by 1503, Moldavia and Wallachia (modern Romania) had become vassal states. Moreover, economic pressures forced the Venetians to make peace after the war of 1499–1503 and Bayezid must take credit for the effective foundation of the Ottoman navy.

Along with these advances, the growing importance of the Ottoman control of the great trade routes was becoming ever more clear. This had the result of almost doubling public revenues in Bayezid's reign.

Despite this, he must be considered a failure in two areas. First of all, the war with the *Mamluks* (1485–91) was unsuccessful. The **Mamluks** were the rulers of Egypt and Syria and at no time during this conflict was any major Syrian town captured. Bayezid failed, therefore, to win the military prestige of his predecessor, which was so vital for any successful Sultan. Much more critical, however, was the growing threat of heresy and war in the eastern part of the Empire. There are many variations of religious belief within Islam, but the most fundamental division is between the *Sunni*, the orthodox majority which included the Ottoman sultans, and the *Shi'ites*. In the thirteenth century a militant sect arose amongst the *Shi'ites*, known as the *Safavids*. Under the leadership of Ismail (1487–1524) Persia emerged as a strong **Safavid** state on the eastern border of the Ottoman Empire. There were many sympathisers with these *Shi'ites* within the Ottoman Empire, causing constant threats of rebellion, which did in fact break out in 1511. At critical points fear of such rebellion and the Persian threat to the east was to divert the Ottomans from their struggle with the Christian states of the western Mediterranean and central Europe.

mamluks originally slaves deputising for the rulers of Egypt and Syria, they had eventually taken over as the ruling dynasty

safavids a Shi'ite sect opposed to the rule of the Ottomans who belonged to the Sunni branch of Islam

C *Selim I*

The *janissaries* felt that Bayezid was too ineffectual to cope with the Persian threat and he was forced to abdicate in favour of Selim I (1512–20). Selim shared Mohammed's vision of a world empire and had the forceful and martial spirit required to put these aims into practice. After seizing the throne, he ruthlessly executed all other possible claimants to it and paid substantial 'tips' to the *janissaries* to secure their loyalty. The *janissaries* were based in Constantinople and Selim did not rely on a landed aristocracy in the manner of western Europe. He saw his main danger as coming from Ismail and the *Safavids*. On 13 August 1514, Selim won a bloody but decisive victory at Chaldiran near Lake Van in Anatolia (modern Turkey) and temporarily occupied Tabriz, Ismail's capital. He did not maintain the occupation but kept control of the high plateau of eastern Anatolia, which provided an excellent natural barrier against invasion. Although the *Safavid* state continued to exist, it was significantly weakened and pressure on this frontier was, for a time, reduced.

This was only the start of Selim's outstanding career as an energetic conqueror. He once wrote to Tuman Bey, the *Mamluk* ruler of Egypt, that he intended to become the ruler of east and west like Alexander the Great and between 1515 and 1517 he launched a series of dramatically successful campaigns in Syria, Egypt and Arabia. The *Mamluks* had originated as a military class of slaves and had managed to impose themselves as the rulers of Egypt and Syria. By 1515, however, their fortunes were in decline. In the Red Sea, the Portuguese fleet posed a major threat and had established bases at Socotra on the Gulf of Aden and Ormuz in the Persian Gulf. The great fear of all Muslims was that they would seize the holy cities of Mecca and Medina. The Arab population of these cities became increasingly convinced that the *Mamluks* could not defend them effectively, particularly after the Portuguese defeated the *Mamluk* navy in 1509. Any Muslim leader who could effectively defend the holy cities would dramatically enhance his reputation as the champion of Islam.

In 1516, Selim marched into Syria. In the only significant battle near Aleppo on 24 August, the *Mamluks* were routed, thanks mainly to the superiority of Turkish artillery and musket fire. On 27 September, the important city of Damascus was occupied and Selim's army marched into Palestine. After a slight hesitation, the Sinai peninsula was crossed in only 5 days at the beginning of 1517. On 22 January, the *Mamluk* army was defeated. 25 000 were killed and by the end of 1517 Egypt was under effective Ottoman control.

The capture of Syria and Egypt brought enormous wealth to the Empire. These were areas of great economic value themselves and they also controlled vital trade routes. Even more important was that the Ottoman sultans were now the protectors of the most holy cities of Islam, Mecca and Medina and the guardians of the pilgrimage routes, a position which brought enormous honour and prestige in the Islamic world. The Sultan now bore the title 'Servant and Protector of the Holy Places'.

KEY ISSUE

How important to his authority was the Sultan's role as the protector of orthodox Islam?

4 ↶ THE CIVIL AND MILITARY ORGANISATION OF THE OTTOMAN EMPIRE IN THE FIFTEENTH AND SIXTEENTH CENTURIES

A *The power of the Sultan*

A description of the growth of the Ottoman Empire does not in itself explain the rapid expansion of Ottoman power. In its organisation, the Ottoman state possessed qualities that were not to be found in its European rivals. An examination of the civil and military organisation of the state is essential if its growth is to be understood.

There is no doubt that the actual power of the sultans was far greater than that of the major European monarchs. Islamic law and tradition regarded strong royal authority as the basis of the whole social system. The main task of the monarch was to protect his subjects from exploitation by the more powerful members of the community. One of the most striking features of the Ottoman Empire was the absence of a powerful, hereditary aristocracy. The problems of particularism (local loyalties and privileges) and a potentially rebellious aristocracy were far less than in France and the Low Countries, for example. An Ottoman bureaucrat and historian, Tursun Bey wrote in the fifteenth century, 'Without a sovereign men cannot live in harmony and may perish altogether. God has granted this authority to one person only and that person, for the perpetuation of good order, requires absolute obedience'.

B *The administration of the Empire*

In order to rule effectively, however, any ruler needs a reliable and efficient administration. The method adopted by the Ottoman rulers was to use slaves as the vast majority of the ruling class of the Empire. Most slaves were obtained by the **devshirme**, which was a levy of Christian children, the word having its origin in the Turkish word meaning 'to collect'. The main sources for this levy were the Christian villages of the Balkans. Urban areas were excluded and so were only sons. A levy was taken every three or four years and between 1000 and 3000 children were taken. These were converted to Islam and underwent a rigorous process of selection.

Some of the children from this Christian levy were used for military service, as will be described later in this section. However, the best were selected for the direct service of the sultan at the *Topkapi Sarayi*, the sultan's palace in Istanbul. They received a rigorous education in the Koran, Arabic, Persian, Turkish, music, and mathematics, and also learned horsemanship and archery, along with artistic skills, such as miniature painting or bookbinding. One of them once wrote that the aim of this education was to produce 'the warrior statesman and loyal Muslim, who at the same time should be a man of letters and polished

devshirme the levy of Christian children who were converted to Islam and were technically slaves, although forming the élite of the army and government service

speech, profound courtesy and honest morals'. Many of these slaves stayed within the palace and served the sultan directly. Others became provincial governors, or entered the religious establishment.

The most important office of state was that of Grand Vizier. The Grand Vizier was the sultan's deputy in all matters of state. He conducted the Imperial *Divan* (Council) every day except Friday (the Muslim holy day) and its decisions were sent to the sultan for approval. The Grand Vizier was given the Sultan's seal of office and the council dealt with finance, foreign policy and government appointments. From the late fifteenth century, the Grand Viziers were drawn from the palace slaves, and, however powerful over others, they were always completely dependent on their masters, the sultans. Machiavelli was, therefore, entirely correct when he described the Ottoman Empire as an 'absolute monarchy dependent on slavery'.

No state in the fifteenth and sixteenth centuries had the effective power of the modern state, but the use of slaves did bring great advantages to the sultans. The slaves did identify their interests in general with those of the central government and lacked the power bases in the provinces that made many territorial aristocrats, who served other European monarchs, actively suspicious of any expansion of central authority. Quite simply, the power and influence of the slaves depended on a strong and stable government.

C *The army*

Slavery was not only the basis of the civil administration of the Ottoman state; the core of the army – the *janissaries* – were also recruited by the *devshirme*. The use of slaves in the standing army dates back to the capture of Adrianople in 1361, when prisoners of war became the first *janissary* corps. Mohammed II increased the size of the corps to 10 000 and it was to be the nucleus of his army. The sultan chose the commanders personally and the corps took its orders directly from him, wherever it was serving in his empire. The *janissaries* were supposed to be on a war footing at all times. They lived in barracks, trained regularly and were not allowed to marry. Estimates of their numbers vary, but in Suleiman the Magnificent's reign there were probably around 12 000. In battle, they held the centre of the sultan's army. Most *janissaries* were infantry, but there was an élite of about 6000 cavalry who acted as the sultan's personal bodyguard. *Janissaries* tended to be devout Muslims and Muslim preachers were attached to them to maintain their zeal as g*hazis*, or holy warriors. The advantages of a trained, disciplined and fanatical standing army cannot be overestimated in early modern Europe. Although the loyalty of the *janissaries* was already being undermined by the end of the sixteenth century and the practice of bribing the corps, dating back to the accession of Bayezid II in 1481, still existed, at their best they were loyal servants of the sultans and lacked the attachment to a particular locality and region that so often existed elsewhere in Europe.

Although the *janissaries* provided the élite of the Ottoman army, they were in fact only a minority of its total strength. Indeed, the entire provincial administration of the Empire was designed to provide for its military needs. The typical Ottoman province was organised under the *timar* system. A **timar** was a piece of land held for life by an individual from the sultan in return for military service. The system originated in the first place in response to a shortage of currency. The soldiers would collect their income in kind from a village, which released the government from any obligation to pay them a salary. The main aim of this system was to provide a large number of *sipahi*, or light cavalry, for the army. In the sixteenth century, it is estimated that there were about 40 000 *timar*-holding *sipahi*.

The successful functioning of the *timar* system stemmed from the view of property ownership in the Ottoman world. Virtually all the land in the Empire was regarded as the property of the Sultan; in 1528 about 80 per cent of land was owned by the Crown. The **sipahi** were not given the land itself, but only the right to collect a fixed amount of revenue from it. They lived in their villages, but did not farm and could not take any land from the peasants. They could arrest a wrongdoer, but had no power to administer punishment, which was the responsibility of the local judge.

The power of the *sipahi* over the peasantry was therefore very limited. The peasant was protected by the state and an independent legal system. The *sipahi* provided their own horses and carried a bow, sword, shield, lance and mace. Large *timars* would be expected to provide an extra horseman and the wealthier *timar* holders wore armour. In campaigns, they formed the light cavalry on either wing of the army, whose aim was to outflank and encircle the enemy. While the *janissaries* held together the centre of the Sultan's armies, the *sipahi* would attack on the flanks. The Ottoman armies were particularly well placed in battle to use the speed of the *sipahi,* who were far more mobile than heavy European cavalry, to surround their enemies in a classic pincer movement. The campaigning season lasted from March to October and generally the *sipahi* were very anxious to return home at the end of the season. Their horses would be exhausted and they had received no money wages. It was at this time that the Ottoman army was traditionally at its weakest.

The *timar* system offers a further example of the powers of the central government. The government controlled the granting and revocation of *timars*. Although the son of a *timar* holder inherited his father's military status and received a *timar* similar in size to his father, *timars* could not be passed on to sons, as the land was the property of the state. Also, any *timar* holder who did not perform military service for seven years would lose his military status. In other words, a strong hereditary aristocracy, which could pass on its land and wealth, did not exist in the Ottoman Empire.

The advantages of this system were the subject of letters written by Ogier Ghiselin de Busbecq, a horticulturalist (he introduced the lilac

timar land granted by the Sultan to a cavalryman to support him while serving in the army

sipahi cavalrymen (free rather than slaves), who formed the other major element of the Ottoman army, alongside the *janissaries*

and tulip to Europe) and imperial ambassador in Constantinople from 1554 to 1562. He wrote to a fellow ambassador in Portugal:

Q

1. *How did the Ottoman system enable the Sultan only to take note of 'merit', 'character', 'natural ability' and 'disposition'?*
2. *What might have been the purpose of these letters home by Busbecq's comparing the Ottoman system with that in Christian states?*
3. *What problems might the Ottoman system eventually produce?*

The Sultan's headquarters were crowded by numerous attendants, including many high officials. All the cavalry of the guard were there and a large number of *janissaries*. In all that great assembly no single man owed his dignity to anything but his personal merits and bravery, no one is distinguished from the rest by his birth, and honour is paid to each man according to the nature of the duty and offices which he discharges. Thus there is no struggle for precedence, every man having his place assigned to him in virtue of the functions which he performs. The Sultan himself assigns to all their duties and offices, and in doing so pays no attention to wealth or the empty claims of rank, and takes no account of any influence or popularity which a candidate may possess, he only considers merit and scrutinises the character, natural ability and disposition of each. Thus each man is rewarded according to his deserts, and offices are filled by men capable of performing them. Those who hold the highest posts under the Sultan are very often the sons of shepherds and herdsmen, and, so far from being ashamed of their birth, they make it a subject of boasting, and the less they owe to their forefathers and to the accident of birth, the greater is the pride which they feel. They do not consider that good qualities can be conferred by birth or handed down by inheritance, but regard them partly as the gift of heaven and partly as the product of good training and constant toil and zeal...

Thus, among the Turks, dignities, offices and administrative posts are the rewards of ability and merit; those who are dishonest, lazy and slothful never attain to distinction, but remain in obscurity and contempt. This is why the Turks succeed in all they attempt and are a dominating race and daily extend the bounds of their rule. Our method is very different; there is no room for merit, but everything depends on birth, considerations of which alone open the way of high official position.

KEY ISSUE

Why was the authority of the Ottoman emperors greater than that of many Christian rulers?

5 ⌐ THE PEOPLE OF THE EMPIRE, 1450–1580

A *Status and stability*

It was clearly understood that the stability and prosperity of the people was essential if the military and economic strength of the Empire was to be maintained. The military and administrative classes were exempt from taxation and were legally totally separate from the wealth-producing classes, who were known as the *reaya*, literally meaning 'flock'. The sultan was seen as the guardian, guide and protector of the *reaya* and in return they were the financial backbone of the Empire. To move from the **reaya** to the military classes required the permission of the sultan, which was very rarely granted. The laws of the Empire stated that, 'The *Reaya* and the land belong to the Sultan'. There was, therefore, no powerful aristocracy holding great legal powers over the peasantry, such as existed in most European countries.

There is no doubt that one of the reasons for the outstanding speed of Ottoman expansion was that the peasantry in the Balkans was treated with far more justice after the Ottoman conquest than had been the case under previous Christian rulers. Before the Ottoman conquest, the peasantry had been subject to many harsh and varied burdens, imposed by local aristocrats or monasteries. The sultans abolished all of these. For example, it was no longer legal to demand forced labour from the peasantry and obligations, such as the transportation of firewood and hay, could no longer be imposed. Instead, all the peasantry paid one poll (head) tax, which replaced all their former duties to their lords. For many of the peasantry, therefore, Ottoman rule provided a stability and security that they had never known under Christian rule, when the Balkans in particular had been notoriously unstable. Only those who resisted Ottoman rule were subjected to intimidation and violence.

reaya town-dwellers and peasants, the mass of people not in the army or government service

B *Religion*

Moreover, although it was seen as the duty of all *ghazis* to extend *Darulislam* (the abode of Islam) by campaigning in the non-Islamic world, which was known as *Darulharb* (the abode of war), Islamic tradition totally rejected the idea of forced religious conversion of Christians and Jews. There were occasions when Christians converted *en masse* to Islam, for example in Bosnia. However, Bosnia was an area with a tradition of heresy and religious dissidence and there is no evidence of forced conversion.

The Orthodox Churches in eastern Europe rejected the authority of the pope in Rome. Attempts to reunite the Orthodox and Roman Catholic Churches were bitterly resented by most of the Orthodox Churches, who generally preferred Islamic rule to rule from Rome. The most gifted and respected opponent of union with the Roman Church was the scholar George Scholarius Gennadius. After the fall of Constantinople, it was discovered that he had been bought as a slave by a wealthy Turk in Adrianople, but Mohammed the Conqueror insisted on his return to Constantinople and in January 1454, as Emperor, he installed Gennadius as **Patriarch** of the Orthodox Church. Mohammed was clearly aware that he could capitalise on the hostility of his Greek Orthodox subjects toward the Catholic Church.

Mohammed's aim was to use the patriarch as the head of the Greek Christian community within his empire. The patriarch's role was not simply that of a religious leader; he was to be the political leader of the

patriarch in the eastern Orthodox Churches supreme authority lay with the patriarchs, the Greek Orthodox following the Patriarch of Constantinople

Orthodox community and would be responsible for maintaining their political loyalty.

The system, known as the *millet*, was later extended to the Armenian Christians and to the Jews. They were to be self-governing communities within the Empire under the authority of their religious leader. The sultan would hold him responsible for their good behaviour. The leading figures within the Orthodox Church, who formed the Holy Synod, were granted freedom from taxation and deposition and freedom of movement. Ecclesiastical courts would deal with all disputes of a religious nature between Orthodox Christians, such as marriage and divorce. Only criminal cases and those involving a Muslim went to the state's courts. In return for these privileges, it was to be the duty of the Church to discipline Christians who did not pay their taxes or disobeyed the state. Christians were supposed to wear a distinctive dress and could not carry weapons.

Although the status of the non-Islamic peoples within the Empire was clearly inferior, they did enjoy the right to practise their religions and maintain their culture. In this, Islamic society was notably more tolerant than that of most of Europe.

The Ottoman Empire also provided a refuge for religious groups who were persecuted in the rest of Europe. Many of the Jews expelled from Spain came to the Ottoman Empire and settled in large numbers in cities such as Salonika. They were often welcomed because of their intellectual and scientific expertise and their trading links with the west. Members of the Mendes family, who were originally from Spain, came to Istanbul in 1553 in flight from religious persecution and effectively controlled the European spice trade. One of their relatives, Don Joseph Nasi, became one of the wealthiest men in the Ottoman Empire. He gained a monopoly of the wine trade and was made Duke of Naxos, which was a very important wine-producing area. Not only could the Jewish community provide much intelligence and advice about conditions in the west, but they were often naturally very sympathetic towards anti-Spanish and anti-Habsburg policies.

KEY ISSUE

How did the empire benefit from these religious policies?

See pages 307–8

The American historian Stanford Shaw has written of Mohammed II, 'To the mass of people he offered an end to the feudal oppression of their former Christian masters, security of life and property, and an opportunity to preserve their old traditions and ways as well as their religion through the *millet* system.' It can be said that, until the 1580s at least, Mohammed's successors maintained the spirit of these policies with some success. In many ways Muslims who were not members of the administrative classes were no better off than Christians. *Shi'ite* Muslims were more of a threat to the state than Christians.

C *Economic life*

One of the greatest advantages that the Ottoman Empire possessed over its main rivals from 1450 to 1580 was its superior wealth. Despite the discovery of America and the opening of the route to India via the

African coast by the Portuguese, major trade routes were still concentrated on the eastern Mediterranean, through which Europe had to import valuable commodities that it could not produce for itself. Constantinople itself stands at the crossroads of land routes from Asia and the sea route from the Black Sea. The acquisition of Syria and Egypt increased the wealth of the Empire partly through control of their resources and brought a virtual monopoly of all the traditional trade routes. This gave enormous advantages. The Venetian Republic, which would have been such a formidable opponent, was heavily dependent on the Ottoman Empire for the maintenance of its trade and became increasingly cautious about commitment to a long war. Moreover, the wealth of the Empire made it more capable than its European rivals of sustaining the enormous cost of sixteenth-century warfare.

When Constantinople fell in 1453, it had lost most of its former population and glory. Its population had fallen to below 30–40 000, which was far smaller than could be contained within its massive fortifications. Moreover, since the city had not surrendered voluntarily, it was pillaged according to Ottoman tradition, and much property was destroyed. Mohammed was determined to restore the city as a great imperial capital. First of all, immigration was encouraged. Christian traders and artisans were brought in from captured commercial centres, such as Trebizond. The leaders of the Greek Orthodox, Jewish and Armenian communities were ordered to live in the city. By the 1470s, about 60 per cent of the population was Muslim, about 25 per cent Greek Orthodox and about 15 per cent Jewish. Each group had its own quarter within the city. Turks wore white turbans, Greeks blue turbans and Jews yellow turbans. During the next century, the population of Istanbul rose spectacularly. It became by far the biggest city in Europe, with a population twice the size of Paris and four times that of Venice. One simple reason for the growth of Constantinople was that it was now the political and administrative centre of a great empire. The growth in population created great demand, especially for the grain of the territories which surrounded the Black Sea, which increased their dependence on the goodwill of the Ottoman Empire.

The unique situation of Constantinople, whose harbour – the Golden Horn – was the only safe anchorage between the Black Sea and its outlet into the Mediterranean, enabled the Ottoman state to establish virtually complete control of the Black Sea trade. Italian ships were subjected to close inspection each time they passed into or out of the Black Sea, and the influence of Genoa as a result declined dramatically in the sixteenth century. Certain vital and valuable commodities were traded through the markets of Constantinople. For example, the Khan of Crimea, a tributary state of the Empire, shipped 1000–1200 tons of salt every year. Even more important was the slave trade, which was the chief source of income for the Khan and his Tatar horsemen. The Tatars raided for slaves far into Russia and Poland and these were shipped to the slave markets of Constantinople. A tax of four gold ducats on each slave raised 100 000 gold ducats each year.

TABLE 9

Constantinople's estimated population

1478	80 000
1530	400 000
1600	700 000

As well as being a focal point of the Black Sea trade, Constantinople became the centre of an extensive road system. The Turkish historian, H. Inalcik, has written, 'Not since the fall of the Roman Empire has any state in Europe devoted such care to its system of roads.' Undoubtedly, the Ottoman road system was vastly superior to that of western Europe. Between six and ten caravans arrived each year from Iran and there were also caravans from Basra, Aleppo, Ragusa and Poland. Military roads, which basically followed Roman routes, were driven through the Balkans to the important centre of Adrianople and then to Sofia and Belgrade. By wagon, the journey from Belgrade to Constantinople took one month. Charitable foundations known as *waqfs* were endowed with property to provide the income to pay for road maintenance. These built hostels and maintained roads and bridges. Money was also allocated to pay forces of soldiers whose job was to guard the roads against bandits. Perhaps the most ambitious feature of this trade network was the construction of *caravanserais* where caravans – convoys of traders – could be lodged. These could have as many as 200 rooms and space for 5000–6000 horses.

Trade with Europe had traditionally been handled mainly by the Venetian Republic and this remained largely the case, at least until 1564. But the sultans gave great privileges to the city state of Ragusa (modern Dubrovnik) which was a tributary state of the Empire and a useful counterweight to the Venetians. In October 1564 the French were granted trading rights – a typical example of the alliance of convenience between the Ottoman Empire and the French, with their shared dislike of the Habsburgs – and by 1600 there were 1000 French ships in the Mediterranean.

Of course, the expansion of the Ottoman Empire greatly boosted its economic resources. Of particular significance was the capture of Syria and Egypt. In 1528 they alone provided one-third of the imperial revenue. They also enabled the Empire to acquire control of more vital trade routes. By 1517, with the capture of Aleppo, all outlets for Persian silk were in Ottoman hands.

An even more important acquisition in many ways was the port of Alexandria in Egypt. In the sixteenth century, spices still dominated world trade. The main source of these was the Far East and one of the major markets was Europe, which did not produce pepper, ginger, cinnamon, nutmeg, cloves and frankincense, but did have an inexhaustible demand for them. It has often been suggested that the opening of trade routes around the Cape of Good Hope by the Portuguese such as Vasco da Gama in the late fifteenth century destroyed the economic importance of the Mediterranean. The reality is far more complicated. Indeed, the French historian, Fernand Braudel has written, 'The circumnavigation of the Cape of Good Hope did not strike an immediate death blow to the Mediterranean spice trade.'

The Portuguese did attempt to block the trade routes through the Persian Gulf and the Red Sea, but Portugal was a small state and could keep a fleet of only twenty ships in the Red Sea, which had been sufficient to undermine the *Mamluk* rulers of Egypt and Syria but not enough to stop the Ottomans re-opening the trade routes from the Far East to Alexandria, Damascus and Beirut. The importance of the spice trade was a vital factor in the Venetian reluctance to sustain a long war against the Turks and it was only in the early seventeenth century that the Dutch succeeded in taking over the bulk of this trade, ending the economic stranglehold by the Ottoman Empire. Until then the economic resources of the Ottoman Empire in the sixteenth century were undoubtedly far greater than any of its European rivals.

The government was concerned to protect the peasantry and, in the Balkans at least, the peasantry was far more prosperous than in previous centuries. The aristocracy was too weak to exploit them, so a higher proportion of peasants' income went to the state, rather than being creamed off locally. Above all, the Turks appreciated the vital importance of Constantinople, whose wealth, splendour and rapidly growing population provided a massive market for trade and for the agricultural region around the Black Sea. Success in war created a stable trading area on which Christian Europe was still dependent for all kinds of goods. The wealth of the Empire was combined with an administrative and military system generally superior to that of other European states.

With such administrative and commercial superiority firmly established by 1520, it is hardly surprising that the reign of Suleiman – the highly able sultan who succeeded to the throne in that year – saw the Ottoman Empire at a pinnacle of power and success. The sultan was known as Suleiman the Magnificent.

> **KEY ISSUE**
>
> *Why was the Ottoman Empire in the sixteenth century so much wealthier than all other European states?*

6 ⌐ THE REIGN OF SULEIMAN THE MAGNIFICENT, 1520–66

A *The accession of Suleiman the Magnificent*

Suleiman the Magnificent was born in 1494 or 1495. We know little of his childhood, but we do know that his father, Selim the Grim, was a ruthless man, who forced Bayezid, his own father, to abdicate and then strangled his two older brothers and five nephews to ensure that he had no rivals for the throne. Suleiman played a minor role in the government of the state during his father's reign; we know that he was for some time governor of the important city of Adrianople.

Selim became increasingly cruel and tyrranical; seven Grand Viziers (chief ministers) were beheaded in nine years. News of his death in September 1520 was kept secret until Suleiman could get to Constantinople where, understandably, his accession to the throne was viewed with some relief.

B *Suleiman's advantages as a ruler*

Suleiman inherited a very advantageous position. There were no rival claimants to the throne and so he avoided a bloody struggle for power

PICTURE 27
Sultan Mehmet Celebi

See Chapters 8 and 9

and gained the immediate loyalty of the *janissaries*, who were probably at their most powerful and effective as a fighting force at this time. Selim the Grim, Suleiman's predecessor, had doubled the size of the Empire. Egypt and Syria were not simply the source of vast revenues which made Suleiman the wealthiest ruler in Europe, they also provided the money and expertise to enable Selim to develop a great shipyard in Constantinople which was to be the basis of Ottoman naval power. Moreover, none of the principal rivals of the Ottoman Empire in the eastern Mediterranean or the Middle East was in a position to challenge Suleiman effectively; both the Venetians and *Safavids* had been humiliatingly defeated quite recently and had no desire to fight.

Therefore, if there were to be effective opposition to Suleiman, it would have to come from western Europe. There is no doubt that Suleiman gained enormous benefits from the suspicions and rivalries amongst the major European powers, which prevented a unified front being formed against him, despite the consistent and sometimes frantic efforts of the papacy. In particular, Suleiman was aided by the rivalry between France and the Habsburgs, which dominated Europe at this time. To ally with the infidel Turks was an act which would draw the condemnation of all Christian Europe, but Francis I repeatedly, if sometimes secretly, sought Suleiman's assistance. After the Battle of Pavia in 1525, the French ambassador in Constantinople asked Suleiman to attack the Habsburgs by land and sea or face the prospect of complete Habsburg supremacy in Europe. The Venetians echoed this view. In 1532 Francis I admitted to the Venetian ambassador that the Ottoman Empire was the only power that could prevent the complete domination of Europe by Charles V.

At this time, the Ottoman and French fleets began to cooperate in the Mediterranean. On 18 February, 1536, a trade agreement, subsequently named the 'capitulations', was negotiated between the two powers, which was followed soon after by a secret military alliance, and when the Ottoman fleet besieged Corfu in 1537 it was reinforced by the French navy. After papal pressure, Charles and Francis did make peace in July 1538 and promised to organise a crusade, but the alliance between the French and the Ottoman Empire was a natural one against a common foe, and in 1543 formal military cooperation took place. It was relatively ineffective, but served to illustrate the continuity of the links between the two states, although French policy was regarded as shocking by the rest of Europe, particularly when the Ottoman fleet wintered at Toulon.

Suleiman was also aided by the emergence of Protestantism in Europe. Indeed, it has been argued that the Protestant Reformation would have been crushed by Charles V if he had not been continually distracted by the Turkish threat. This is not to suggest that Protestant reformers had any sympathy for Islam. In typical fashion, Luther described the Turks as the 'scourge of God', Mohammed the Prophet of Islam as the 'servitor of the devil' and once claimed 'that the spirit of Antichrist is the Pope, his flesh the Turk'. Nevertheless, Luther opposed the idea of a crusade against the Turks. He regarded crusades simply as

SULEIMAN THE MAGNIFICENT (1520–66)

Suleiman the Magnificent came to the throne on 30 September, 1520. Known as Suleiman Kanun, 'the lawmaker', to his own people, he is remembered both for the constant expansion of Ottoman power during his reign and for the firmness and justice of his administration at home. The pattern of his life reflected these two concerns. Each summer he would lead his armies on campaigns to the distant frontiers of his empire. The winter, in contrast, would be devoted to administrative activities and he would stay in Constantinople, rarely visiting any of his provincial capitals. During this time, he was renowned as an outstanding interpreter of Islamic law who regulated the laws of property, the duties of his servants and the terms and conditions of military service. He was also a great patron of the arts, and builder of fine mosques, roads and bridges. At twenty-six, on his accession, Suleiman was still a young man, as was the Emperor Charles V, who was to be his great rival. Despite his many personal qualities, he was as determined as his father to prove his military superiority over the neighbouring states.

In the first ten years of his reign, Suleiman won a series of spectacular military victories, which took his armies to the gates of Vienna. The remainder of his time was spent in Constantinople. With regard to his family life, Suleiman's mother, Hafiza, ruled over the harem, in which there were over 200 women, which was in fact a modest number when compared with other sultans. Suleiman also seems to have generally confined his attentions to a small number of particular favourites. The most important by far was known as Roxelana. She came to have a dominant influence over Suleiman. The other great influence on Suleiman was Ibrahim, his Grand Vizier from 1523. Ibrahim was the son of Christians from western Greece. As a child, he was captured by Turkish pirates and enslaved. He was both a close companion and the second most important figure in the state. He once said, 'Although I am the sultan's slave, whatsoever I want is done.' While he retained the sultan's favour, this was certainly true. However, in the 1530s, after the death of Suleiman's mother, Roxelana's influence increased rapidly and it is likely that she was responsible for the execution of Ibrahim in 1536. Unprecedentedly, she also persuaded Suleiman to make her his legal wife. She dedicated herself to advancing the fortunes of her favourite son, the inadequate Selim, against Suleiman's other children. As a result, when Suleiman died in 1566, his legacy was to be squandered by Selim as his successor.

PICTURE 28
Turkish floral design

a means of furthering papal financial and military influence. Moreover, the German Lutheran princes utilised Charles's need for military support against the Turk to gain concessions from him. Inevitably, therefore, the divisions within Christendom brought about by the Reformation were exploited by the Turks, who were well aware of the close identification of the Habsburgs with the Catholic faith. Therefore, Suleiman's only consistent opponents were the Habsburgs. Charles V, and later Philip II, contested control of the Mediterranean where their fleet was under the command of the Genoese admiral, Andrea Doria, while Ferdinand faced the army of the Ottoman Empire in Hungary. The clash between the two empires was not simply a clash between two rival dynastic states; it was also a clash between two civilisations in expansionist phases. Suleiman was an Ottoman *ghazi* and the leader of a state which was geared to religious wars. The Habsburgs were the chief defenders of Catholic Europe, despite the frequent suspicion of the papacy, and as Iberian rulers, leaders of its expansion into the Americas and Asia. Suleiman was also the inheritor of the traditions of the Roman Empire as the conqueror of Constantinople, which had been its capital, and certainly hoped to capture Rome itself. Charles V as Holy Roman Emperor, on the other hand, inherited another tradition of universal monarchy from Charlemagne.

There is no doubt that Suleiman possessed significant military and economic advantages over the Habsburgs, but there were certain weaknesses in his system that might be exploited. First of all, there was the constant threat from the *Safavid* Empire to the east, which had a reservoir of potential support in the large number of *Shi'ite* sympathisers in eastern Anatolia within the Ottoman Empire. Second, despite the development of an Ottoman navy, the Christian powers were regarded as having superior naval resources. In particular, the island of Rhodes, which was held by the Catholic Knights of St John, was a nest of Christian pirates, who constantly disrupted Ottoman trade in the Aegean Sea. Finally, Suleiman set out on campaigns from Constantinople each campaigning season and the *sipahi* cavalry needed to return for the winter. This meant that much of his fighting was conducted at a great distance from his home base and campaigns often had to be broken off after only a few weeks so that the troops could be home for the winter.

Despite this, Suleiman's armies enjoyed a record of almost uninterrupted success. So great was the prestige of his armies that his enemies were always very reluctant to initiate war against him. Ottoman diplomatic techniques were also perhaps more sophisticated than those of their Christian rivals. In the Crimea, Transylvania, Hungary, North Africa and Ragusa, the Ottoman Empire controlled client states on its distant frontiers. These might be ruled by Christians or by Muslims, but all were clearly dependent on Ottoman friendship. In Hungary and Transylvania the alternative to Ottoman rule was the Habsburgs, while the Crimean *Tatars* and *Ragusa* were dependent on trade with Constantinople.

Militarily and economically, the Ottoman state commanded far greater resources than its rivals. The sultan did not need to fear over-mighty subjects. Although there were religious tensions within the Empire, they were tackled in a far more flexible fashion than was usual in western Europe. Quite simply, in the time of Suleiman there was no aspect of government in which the Empire was clearly weaker than its European rivals and in most it was far stronger.

> **KEY ISSUE**
>
> *What was the significance of the divisions and rivalries amongst Suleiman's potential opponents?*

C *The campaigns of Suleiman the Magnificent, 1520–66*

THE FIRST SUCCESSES: BELGRADE AND RHODES

In order to establish himself as a worthy *ghazi* in the Ottoman tradition, Suleiman needed swift and spectacular military success. In the Balkans, his primary military target was Hungary. The city of Belgrade provided the major barrier to rapid advance along the Danube and Mohammed the Conqueror had been checked there by the Hungarian king, John Hunyadi, in 1456. Belgrade was at last captured by the Turks on 8 August, 1520, which opened the way for a future assault on the plains of Hungary itself.

The Greek island of Rhodes was controlled by the crusading order of the Knights of St John. They threatened the stability and prestige of the Ottoman Empire in many ways. They were notorious pirates, who fulfilled their religious vows and filled their pockets by attacks on Ottoman shipping in the Aegean Sea. In particular, they disrupted trade with Egypt, which was of such economic importance to the Empire. Moreover, they weakened the prestige of the sultan amongst devout Muslims by their success in transporting Christian pilgrims to the Holy Land. Rhodes was attacked in the summer of 1520. It possessed strong fortifications and over 60 000 defenders, many of whom were experienced soldiers. Eventually, the island fell in December 1522. It seems that the slaves and servants of the Knights of St John, most of whom were of the Orthodox faith, aided the Sultan's forces and preferred Ottoman to Catholic control. The threat of the Knights of St John was not removed altogether. They were allowed to evacuate to Malta and their control of this island, in alliance with Charles V, proved a constant menace to the forces of the Ottoman Empire. But the eastern Mediterranean, apart from some Venetian outposts, was now under undisputed Ottoman control and Christian piracy diminished in importance.

THE WESTERN FRONTIER: THE CONQUEST OF HUNGARY

After the defeat of Francis I by Charles V at Pavia in 1525, Suleiman considered a land and sea assault against Italy but eventually decided to attack Hungary. This was a well-considered choice. In the fifteenth century, under John Hunyadi and Matthias Corvinus, Hungary had been considered a formidable military state and an effective opponent of the Turks. Under their successors, Ladislas (1490–1516) and Louis

TIMELINE

1453	Fall of Constantinople
1520	Fall of Belgrade
1526	Battle of Mohacs
1529	Siege of Vienna
1532	Hungarian campaign
1533	Peace in Hungary
1551	Campaign in Transylvania
1562	Peace with Emperor Ferdinand
1566	Sulaiman's final Hungarian campaign

(1516–26), Hungarian power declined. The aristocracy strongly opposed any extension of royal power and its leader John Zapolyai was himself ambitious for the throne. In 1514, there had been a peasant rebellion that was brutally suppressed by the gentry, who followed their victory by imposing on the peasantry a particularly harsh form of serfdom. Hungary was therefore ruled by a weak king, who was dominated by an irresponsible aristocracy, who in turn harshly exploited the peasantry.

In 1526 the Ottoman armies invaded Hungary. On 29 August the Hungarian army was destroyed at the Battle of Mohacs. The discipline of the *janissaries* and the superiority of the Turkish cannon proved too much for the Hungarian cavalry, and King Louis was killed as he fled the battlefield. John Zapolyai offered to acknowledge Ottoman overlordship and pay a tribute if he was left in control of the country and this was agreed by Suleiman. Hungary was a great distance from Constantinople and a puppet ruler suited his interests. The Turkish army withdrew and the French granted recognition to Zapolyai. The Crown was then disputed between Zapolyai and Archduke Ferdinand, Charles V's brother, who had married Louis's sister. He invaded Hungary and drove Zapolyai from Buda in 1527.

The sultan agreed to restore Zapolyai to the throne and the second Turkish campaign into Hungary was launched in 1528. Buda was recaptured on September 3 and John Zapolyai was restored to his throne, while Suleiman's interests were protected by the establishment of a garrison of *janissaries* at Buda and the payment of an annual tribute.

Suleiman's armies then advanced to Vienna, which was besieged from 27 September until 15 October, 1529, when the end of the campaigning season forced the Ottoman army to retire. Vienna itself was safe but its suburbs had been destroyed and isolated Ottoman raids penetrated as far as Regensburg in Bavaria and Brno in Bohemia, causing great panic throughout Europe. Ferdinand was also fortunate that the Peace of Cambrai with France enabled Charles V to send him reinforcements. Nonetheless, it is probably true that Vienna was beyond the effective campaigning range of the Ottoman Empire. The organisation and government of the Empire required Suleiman to winter in Constantinople, from which each new campaign was begun. It was always late summer before his army arrived in Hungary and it had to return home in October, not simply because of climatic problems, but also because the cavalrymen, the *sipahi,* had to return to their lands, the *timars.*

In 1533, peace was made after mediation by Poland. Archduke Ferdinand recognised Suleiman as 'father and suzerain', while the Grand Vizier was his 'brother' and equal in rank. He also abandoned his claims to all of Hungary, although he was to retain control of part of northern and western Hungary along the border with the Habsburgs' Austrian lands. Suleiman had made only minor concessions and had established a stable border and recognition of his superior status. In 1540 John Zapolyai died. The succession issue was very complicated

and Hungarian opinion was divided between the supporters of
Ferdinand and Zapolyai's young son, John Sigismund. Suleiman
decided to settle this issue and invaded in 1541. In August he made his
camp at Buda, having destroyed all opposition, and established a new
Ottoman province, with Buda as its capital.

After further Ottoman attacks in the 1540s, a five-year truce was
declared in 1547 and Ferdinand agreed to pay an annual tribute of
30 000 gold pieces for those parts of northern and western Hungary
which he still controlled. Meanwhile John Sigismund was to rule
Transylvania, which was effectively an Ottoman puppet state.
Hostilities reopened in 1551 and continued in an indecisive fashion.
Suleiman was preoccupied in the east and Ferdinand lacked the
military strength to take advantage of this. The peace of 1562 more or
less repeated the terms of 1547.

After this, the frontier stabilised. Ferdinand concentrated on the
construction of a strongly fortified frontier and strengthening the
defences of small towns. He avoided pitched battles and forced the
Ottoman Empire into a war of long sieges. For example, when
Suleiman was persuaded into one last campaign against the Habsburgs
in 1566, he left Constantinople on 1 May and travelled for ninety-seven
days before meeting serious resistance. It then took 34 days to capture
the small town of Sigetvar, which fell on 29 August. Even if the sultan
had not then died it would have been impossible to continue the
campaign. It seemed as if the Ottoman Empire was incapable of further
expansion in this area.

What accounts for the success – and limits – of Suleiman's advance into central Europe?

THE EASTERN FRONTIER

The second major area of conflict for Suleiman the Magnificent was his
eastern frontier. There was always the threat of social and religious
unrest in Anatolia. In this part of the Empire there were many Turkish
aristocrats who resented the domination of the slaves of the *devshirme*
and also many peasants who were economically insecure and
sympathetic to the *Shi'ite* doctrines of the *Safavid* Shah Tahmasp.
Charles V had tried to exploit these problems by sending envoys to the
Safavids in 1529. By 1533 Suleiman had decided that an eastern
campaign was essential for his security. He also feared that Tahmasp
would block the vital trade routes, and needed to defeat the man who
was executing *Sunni* Moslems, of whom Suleiman was the great
protector.

In 1534 Tabriz was captured, although this remote and isolated city
in the mountainous region of Azerbaijan was later abandoned. Later in
the year Baghdad, a city of great wealth and prestige in the Muslim
world, was also captured. Suleiman stayed there until the spring of 1535
and it became the centre of a new province (in what is modern Iraq)
with a garrison of 2000 *janissaries*. By 1538, Basra in the Persian Gulf
also accepted Ottoman authority. The important Basra–Baghdad–
Aleppo trade route was now firmly under control and Syria fully
protected. Suleiman had, however, failed to commit the Safavids to a

KEY ISSUE

What was the importance of the eastern front for Suleiman?

decisive battle. The threat was greatly diminished but had not entirely disappeared.

There was no further serious conflict until 1548, although there was much skirmishing on the frontiers. In the summer of 1548, Suleiman marched once again on Tabriz, but found that the Shah had abandoned it rather than commit his army to battle. The fortress of Van was taken but over the next years the Shah recovered some ground. In April 1554 Suleiman again attacked and devastated much of the frontier, as an alternative to the destruction of the Shah's army.

After this, peace negotiations were opened and conducted at Amasya in May 1555. Suleiman abandoned his claim to Tabriz but retained Iraq, most of Kurdistan and western Armenia. These campaigns against the *Safavids* were largely undertaken in remote and mountainous regions, where water and food were scarce and the winters exceptionally harsh. Although Suleiman was never able to inflict another decisive defeat, such as Selim's victory at Chaldiran, he greatly extended and strengthened the frontiers of his empire. Considering that he was fighting, as in Hungary, at an enormous distance from his capital, his success was remarkable.

THE MEDITERRANEAN: THE CREATION OF OTTOMAN NAVAL POWER

The third major frontier and war zone for the Ottoman Empire was the Mediterranean. Even at the time of Suleiman's accession, the key islands of Rhodes, Crete and Cyprus were not in Ottoman hands and the eastern Mediterranean could not be navigated safely. Of course, the capture of Rhodes did improve the position. Equally important was the emergence of Muslim pirates, usually known as *corsairs*. These saw themselves as maritime *ghazis* and the North African coast provided many potentially useful bases for them. Most important was the city of Algiers. In 1516, two Turkish *corsairs* established themselves in Algiers. One was killed in 1518; the other, Hayreddin Barbarossa, became the most famous and effective Muslim sea captain of the sixteenth century.

Although the Barbary pirates placed themselves under Suleiman's protection, initially Barbarossa and his followers acted more or less independently. Algiers became the greatest threat to Habsburg dominance in the western Mediterranean and a haven for pirates and renegades of all races. In particular, many *moriscos* fled from repression in Spain to Algiers and took with them their hostility to the Spanish. In 1529, Barbarossa seized the Peñón d'Argel, the fortified island at the entrance to the harbour of Algiers, which had been a Spanish base. Despite this, the Spanish–Genoese alliance which brought Andrea Doria's fleet over to Charles V seemed to tip the naval balance against the Ottoman Empire, especially when Doria captured outposts in Greece in 1532.

But Suleiman's response was to appoint Barbarossa Governor General of Algiers and Grand Admiral of the Ottoman fleet in December 1533 and to begin to construct a new fleet. At a stroke, he had gained an experienced and gifted naval commander and a valuable

BARBAROSSA (C. 1482–1546)

Khair ud-Din, known as Barbarossa, was one of four brothers. He became a potter, another a trader like their father, and two others sea rovers and mercenaries. One of the latter was killed, but the remaining one, Arouj, began to make his fortune serving in the wars between the local rulers of North African cities. Barbarossa joined him and they took advantage of the local knowledge and thirst for revenge of Moors expelled by the Spanish from Granada to organise raids on the Spanish coast. However, as in 1515, when they were called in by the Muslim rulers of Cherchel and Algiers to aid them against the Spanish, they were equally capable of turning on their employers and murdering them in order to seize their cities. During a similar maneouvre in 1518, Arouj found that the local Muslim ruler had enlisted Spanish support and he lost his life in the fight. To secure and extend his own power, Barbarossa now turned to the Ottoman Sultan, Selim I, who named him his deputy in the region. On the accession of Suleiman the Magnificent, Barbarossa continued to serve in that capacity, projecting the power of the Ottomans across the Mediterranean far further than their land army could ever have done. Apart from the temporary loss of Tunis to Charles V in 1535, he held the Spanish at bay and consolidated Ottoman control over the local rulers of North Africa. When he died in 1546, his son, Hassan, succeeded him as the sultan's deputy and admiral.

base in the western Mediterranean. In 1534, Barbarossa recaptured the outposts in Greece seized by Doria and expelled the King of Tunis who was an ally of Spain. An invasion of Italy seemed imminent and a struggle for control of the central Mediterranean ensued.

See page 232

The recapture of Tunis by Charles in 1535 was certainly a major blow, but Barbarossa's navy was not significantly weakened. In September 1538, at Prevesa, near the entrance to the Adriatic Sea, Barbarossa was able to exploit the distrust within the combined imperial and Venetian fleets and the hesitations of Doria to inflict a significant, if not overwhelming, defeat. This confirmed Turkish dominance of the eastern Mediterranean and in October 1540 Venice was forced to surrender her remaining possession in the Morea. On the other hand, Barbarossa's expedition to the western Mediterranean in 1543 was equally unsuccessful. Initially the French cooperated in the unsuccessful siege of Nice, but Francis I was not a reliable ally. After Barbarossa occupied Toulon for a while, he retired without significant success.

The death of Barbarossa in 1546 caused a temporary halt to naval activity but excellent sea captains such as Turgut Reis, known more

KEY ISSUE

*How crucial was
Barbarossa to Ottoman
power?*

See page 409

familiarly as Dragut, remained. He took Tripoli in North Africa from the Knights of St John in 1551 and established himself as its ruler. Moreover, an attempt by Philip II to remove him ended in a disastrous rout at the island of Djerba in May 1560. One of the last great campaigns of Suleiman's career was the attempt to capture Malta from the Knights of St John in 1565. The capture of Malta would have given the Turks control of the central Mediterranean and it was only with great difficulty that the Christian forces raised the siege in September.

SULEIMAN'S MILITARY ACHIEVEMENTS

Suleiman's reign saw the continued expansion of his empire by land and sea. In the end it was not the military skill of his opponents that contained him, but the problems of time and distance. By land and sea the Ottoman Empire continually proved superior to its opponents, despite campaigning on very distant frontiers.

Many of the advantages that Suleiman enjoyed on land also applied at sea. Charles V was dependent on the unreliable Doria, who was always concerned to protect the interests of his city, Genoa, even when they clashed with those of his Habsburg allies. The Venetians too wavered in their commitment and rarely opposed the Turks for long periods. When Suleiman was unable to exercise power directly, he was able to delegate it to others, such as Barbarossa, who were well-chosen, dependable and effective.

7 ↝ THE DECLINE OF THE EMPIRE

It is easy to say that after 1566, the great days of the Empire were ended. It is certainly true that Suleiman's successors were not as competent as his predecessors. Selim II (1566–74) was nicknamed the 'Sot' (the 'drunkard') and neither he nor Murad III (1574–95) provided strong leadership. Moreover, the Ottoman navy at Lepanto (7 October, 1571) suffered a devastating defeat by a Holy League made up of Spain, Venice and the papacy, formed to rescue Cyprus, which the Ottomans had attacked in 1570. Such a spectacular setback seems an obvious illustration of the Ottomans' declining power. Some historians have argued that only the defection of Venice from the Holy League in 1573 prevented their decisive defeat in the Mediterranean.

The historian Andrew Hess strongly and effectively disputes the view of Ottoman decline. First of all, he points out that the Venetians were never able to recapture Cyprus, which fell to the Empire in 1571. Moreover, the Ottoman fleet was rebuilt to its former strength with remarkable swiftness. A colourful over-statement of the situation by the Grand Vizier, Mohammed Sokullu, in 1572 was bravado, but the underlying confidence was justified: 'The Ottoman State is so powerful, if an order was issued to cast anchors from silver, to make rigging from silk and to cut the sails from satin, it could be carried out for the entire fleet.' Indeed, the collapse of the Holy League after Lepanto, when

Conflict between Islam and Christianity

As we have seen, the Ottoman sultans earned much prestige by being the model *ghazis*, or holy warriors, and the territory beyond the frontiers of Islam where they won glory was know as *Darulharb*, the abode of war. In turn, Christians saw their wars against the Ottomans not merely as defensive but as crusades to drive them back and retake the holy places of Palestine. Some see such historical enmity as an enduring feature of the two religions, and Samuel Huntington has argued that this 'clash of civilisations' (including others, not just Islam and western Christianity) has such deep roots that it has succeeded the Cold War as the main pattern of conflict in today's world and can be expected to continue throughout the twenty-first century. It is clear that religion (along with ethnicity) is vital to social identity, with the result that in parts of the world now – just as in the sixteenth century – when there is a dispute over territory or power, religion can be used to rally support and identify 'the other', the enemy.

However, as the religious wars of western Europe in the sixteenth century demonstrate, and similarly the struggle between the *Sunni* Muslims and the *Safavids*, clashes can be more terrible within a civilisation than between them. When battle-lines have been drawn up between Islamic and Christian states, propaganda by each has tended to be reductionist, demonising the other religion, but they are complex traditions, which at other times can generate support for peace and co-existence, not just a potential for conflict – the *convivencia* of medieval Spain, for instance, or the permission granted by the Ottomans to Christians and Jews to practise their religion within the Empire. Many Orthodox Christians after all welcomed the security brought to them by Ottoman rule. As Francis I's alliance with Suleiman showed, where political and material motives do not coincide with religious ones, the political and material may well take priority over any 'clash of civilisations'.

Venice deserted it, and the rapid reconstruction of the Ottoman fleet illustrate that the traditional Ottoman advantages of economic superiority and a divided opposition still applied. No long-term strategic gains were attained by the Holy League. In fact, Ottoman naval expansion continued along the North African coast. Tunis was recaptured in 1574 and, along with Tripoli and Algiers, guaranteed the Islamic dominance of this coast. Expansion continued towards Morocco, which greatly worried the Portuguese. At the Battle of Alcazar on 4 August 1578, the Portuguese king, Don Sebastian, was killed and Morocco became a tributary state of the Ottoman Empire. It was not, therefore, until the truce of 1580 with Spain that the expansion of the Ottoman Empire in the Mediterranean ceased and this truce left North Africa under almost unchallenged Ottoman control, again through client rulers.

Nonetheless, weaknesses in the Ottoman system which were to become clear in the seventeenth century can in fact be seen as early as the reign of Suleiman himself. One of the great criticisms of the Ottoman system in the next century was the growing importance of court intrigue and favouritism. In particular, the Sultanate of Women, in which factions within the Emperor's harem secured advancement of their own favourites, is seen as a significant factor in the declining quality of the government of the Empire.

Even more important were the growing economic problems that the Empire was beginning to face. Inflation disrupted the Empire in the second half of the sixteenth century and weakened the *timar* system, in particular. The *sipahi* no longer received sufficient income to sustain themselves in the army and the lands they had depended on, the *timars* were often granted to favourites and government officials in place of salaries or pensions. Despite the tradition of treating the peasantry well, they suffered a growing burden of taxation and this showed itself in the Balkans, with the spread of banditry and in the repeated uprisings in Anatolia. In 1590, the Spanish ambassador in Venice wrote, 'The Empire is so poor and so exhausted that the only coins now circulating are aspers made entirely from iron.'

> **KEY ISSUE**
>
> *Why did Suleiman's legacy not promote further success for the Ottomans?*

8 ↩ BIBLIOGRAPHY

There is by no means the range and variety of books on the Ottoman Empire that there is on the other great monarchies of the sixteenth century and the work of many of the most distinguished historians is not easy to find. The two most recent surveys are **A. Stiles, *The Ottoman Empire, 1450–1700* (Hodder and Stoughton, 1989) and *M. Kunt and C. Woodhead (eds.), *Süleyman the Magnificent and His Age* (Longman, 1995). *F. Braudel, *The Mediterranean and the Mediterranean World in the Age of Philip II* (Fontana, 1975) is a classic and Braudel has many interesting comments about the Ottoman Empire, although somewhat buried in detail. *P. Holt (ed.), *Cambridge History of Islam* (CUP, 1977) is a mine of information and can be used as a reference book. **H. Inalcik, *The Ottoman Empire: the Classical Age 1300–1600* (Weidenfeld and Nicolson, 1973) is the most accessible book by a native Turkish historian. S. Runciman, *The Fall of Constantinople* (CUP, 1955) is deservedly regarded as a classic and gives a dramatic and highly readable account of the events of 1453. **S. Shaw, *The History of the Ottoman Empire and Modern Turkey, Vol. 1* (CUP, 1976) is another good introduction, while *Anthony Bridge, *Suleiman the Magnificent* (Granada, 1983) is highly readable.

9 ↤ STRUCTURED AND ESSAY QUESTIONS

A *Structured questions.*

1. (a) What were the main features of the system of government of the Ottoman Empire?
   (b) What advantages did this system of government bring to the Ottoman Empire in comparison with rival European states?

2. (a) What were the key breakthroughs made by the Ottomans in their expansion into Europe and across the Mediterranean in the century after 1450?
   (b) Why was the resistance to the advance of the Ottoman Empire so ineffective?

B *Essay questions.*

1. In what ways did Ottoman power menace Europe in the sixteenth century?
2. What were the distinctive features of the Ottoman system of government in the sixteenth century?
3. Why was the expansion of Ottoman power so rapid in the sixteenth century?
4. Were the successes of Suleiman the Magnificent the result of the strengths of his empire or the weaknesses of his opponents?

Advice: *Dealing with concepts such as strength and weakness in essay writing*

Almost all questions on the Ottoman Empire tend to deal with the issues of strengths and weaknesses. Often there will be questions on the expansion of the Empire and what made this possible. The danger here is to answer such a question by chronological reference to the key events. As a result, the essay will show *how* rather than *why* Ottoman supremacy was achieved. A good way to plan such an essay is to ask two questions: first, what makes a great power and second, what was distinctive about the Ottoman Empire when seen in comparison with other European powers? Using such criteria one should look at:

(i) the way in which the Empire was governed and the quality of its rulers and their policies in domestic and foreign matters;
(ii) the military organisation of the Empire's armies and navies;
(iii) its economic strengths and weaknesses;
(iv) the religious policies of the Empire, which provide an interesting contrast with other European states.

This approach naturally leads on to a comparative perspective. Strength and weakness are relative concepts and are often best assessed by use of comparison.

10 ↫ DOCUMENTARY EXERCISE ON THE DECLINE OF THE OTTOMAN EMPIRE

The power of the Empire did not suddenly evaporate, but after 1580 it was not seen as the great threat that it had been in the reign of Suleiman. Even the *janissaries* were now allowed to marry and learn a trade and changed from a loyal standing army to a privileged and rebellious caste. The other European states were fascinated by the Empire and quick to note its changing features. The Empire's power declined very slowly. As late as the 1680s, Vienna was besieged again, but as early as the 1590s the growing problems of the Turks were reported to the rest of Europe. The Venetian Republic maintained ambassadors at Constantinople, who provided some of the most interesting first-hand accounts of the Empire's problems. In 1592, Lorenzo Bernardo was sent as the Venetian Ambassador to Constantinople. Extracts of his report appear below, providing a representative contemporary analysis of Turkish decline:

> Three basic qualities have enabled the Turks to make such remarkable conquests and rise to such importance in a brief period: religion, frugality and obedience. In former times, all Turks held to a single religion whose major belief is that it is 'written' when and how a man will die, and that if he dies for his God and his faith he will go directly to Paradise. But now the Turks have not a single religion, but three of them. The Persians are among the Turks like the heretics among the Christians. Then there are the Arabs and Moors, who claim they alone preserve the true, uncorrupted religion, and that the 'Greek Turks' (as they call these in Constantinople) are bastard Moslems with a corrupted religion, which they blame on their being mostly descended from Christian renegades who did not understand the Moslem religion...
>
> As far as frugality, which I said was the second of the three sources of the Turks' great power, at one time the Turks had no interest in fine foods, in splendid decoration in their houses. But now that the Turks have conquered vast rich lands they too have fallen victim to the corruption of wealth. They are happy to follow the example provided by the Sultan, who cares nothing about winning glory on the battlefield and prefers to stay at home and enjoy the countless pleasures of the harem. Modelling themselves on him, all the splendid pashas, governors and generals, and the ordinary soldiers too, want to stay in their harems and enjoy their pleasures and keep as far as possible from the dangers and discomforts of war...
>
> Obedience was the third source of the great power of the Turkish Empire. They are all slaves by nature, and the slaves of one single master; only from him, can they hope to win power, honours

and wealth and only from him do they have to fear punishment and death...

Four years ago I found the Turks less obedient than they had earlier been. This time I learned that the situation had deteriorated still further...

The *janissaries* set fire to the houses of Jews in Constantinople and burned down a quarter of the city. For all this they were never even threatened with punishment.

1. *Explain the reference to the 'Persian heretics' and the 'Greek Turks'.*
2. *How valid is the ambassador's analysis of the traditional strengths of the Ottoman Empire?*
3. *What aspects of the Turkish system of government were clearly not working effectively by the 1590s?*
4. *What other factors in Turkish decline does the ambassador ignore? Why might this be so?*

11 ⤸ MAP EXERCISE

Geography is clearly a vital factor in helping to explain both the successes and the failures of the Ottoman Turks. Find a map of the Mediterranean in which the physical geography of the whole region is shown clearly. Then answer the following questions:

1. *How does the map help to explain the importance of Constantinople, Belgrade, Rhodes and Malta?*
2. *Why did Barbarossa's control of Algiers pose such a problem to the Spanish monarchs?*
3. *What would you see as the key frontier zones between Christians and Muslims?*
4. *Is the geography of the region the most important explanation for the establishment of these frontiers?*
5. *How far from Constantinople were the land borders of the Ottoman Empire?*
6. *How large was the Ottoman Empire in comparison with that of Charles V?*
7. *How did the size of the Empire affect its power?*

11 The Swiss Reformation

In 1518, a year after Luther made his protest against indulgences, Huldrych Zwingli (1484–1531) became a preacher at the Great Minster in the Swiss city of Zurich. There he gradually moved away from the Church of Rome, finally making the breach clear in 1523. He claimed to have developed his views independently of Luther and certainly his doctrine was sufficiently original to make the Swiss Reformation distinct from the Lutheran Reformation in Germany and Scandinavia. The importance of the Swiss Reformation does not derive only from the fact that it was different. It was its international impact that was to set it apart. Zwingli's Reformation gradually spread throughout northern Switzerland and into southern Germany, although he was to be killed in battle in 1531, having failed to secure any further gains. Ironically, the first religious initiative to originate in Zurich that was to spread across much of Europe in one form or another was not Zwingli's, but that of the so-called Anabaptists.

The Anabaptists' name derives from their denial of the sacrament of infant baptism in favour of the baptism of adults who could make a confession of faith. This was not just a minor doctrinal variation; it symbolised the Anabaptists setting themselves apart from normal society and the state, given that baptism introduced the individual into the community as well as into the Church. They formed sects, cut off from the 'impure' society at large, rather than churches, which tried to include whole communities. The Anabaptists were the mainstay of the Radical Reformation and were to be attacked by the leaders of the Magisterial Reformation, that is those who were loyal to princes or town councils, such as Luther and Zwingli.

Eclipsing both Zwinglianism and Anabaptism in long-term significance was the movement established in Geneva by John Calvin (1509–64). He was the leader of the second generation of reformers, bringing the Reformation to its high point through his intellectual and organisational energies. The success of Calvinism was international. Geneva having been secured, Calvinism was to spread first into France, Calvin's homeland, and then to the Rhineland, the Netherlands, England, Scotland and into eastern Europe as far as Transylvania. While Calvin's clarity of doctrine and the strength of his missionary organisation obviously played a role in this expansion of the Reformation, historians have now begun to question whether this is a sufficient explanation. A vital feature of Calvinism was the way in which it adapted itself to various national settings, developing in ways which Calvin himself never envisaged. More than that, it has been claimed to be the foundation of the modern world in unintentionally fostering democracy, revolutionary theory and capitalism. We must bear these ideas in mind but we must also remember that they were far from the minds of the Swiss reformers themselves. They had their attention focussed sharply on religious issues and when drawn, mostly unwillingly, into affairs of politics or economics they often reflected the age they lived in rather than being set to transform it.

1 ✍ THE REFORMATION IN ZURICH

A *The establishment of reform*

In Zurich the environment was as favourable to the Reformation as it could be in any city. The magistrates were used to regulating Church activities and were open to discussion about reform. The city was controlled by its guilds and so had a broad electorate of about 2000 out of 6000 citizens – there was no small ruling group of conservative Catholic families, as in some other cities, to stand in the way of religious innovation. But the reformer of Zurich, Zwingli, was still very cautious when in 1522 he criticised the Catholic practice of fasting during Lent, and followed this by an attack on celibacy, the first public signs that he was moving away from Catholic tradition.

ZWINGLI (1484–1531)

Huldrych Zwingli was born in 1484 at Wildhaus in Toggenburg, a region loosely attached to the Swiss Confederation. He was bright and his family scraped together the money to see him educated: so he was set to climb the ecclesiastical career ladder. Unlike Luther, he does not seem to have been obsessed by the problem of sin. Although he was quite a conscientious priest, he was not above the ordinary abuses of the Church. When he left Glarus, his first parish, in 1516, he paid a substitute and took the profit on the salary. Finding the priest's vow of celibacy a burden, he had an affair with a barber's daughter – quite acceptable behaviour at the time, although Zwingli later had to defend himself against enemies who claimed that he had seduced a virgin. He was not outraged by the corruption of the Church, abandoning his former ways only when he became intellectually convinced that Catholic doctrine had to be purified.

It was Christian humanism that first changed the way Zwingli thought. From the earliest days of his education he had assimilated a humanist style and love of the classics. In 1516 Zwingli began to read the New Testament in Erasmus's Greek version which brought into question standard interpretations. He also met Erasmus and corresponded with him, while growing in his appreciation of Erasmus's *Philosophy of Christ*, with its emphasis on the knowledge and imitation of Christ Himself, as opposed to mechanical, outward piety. Like Erasmus, Zwingli saw the need for reform in the Church, although unlike Erasmus he was later prepared to break with Catholicism to put it into effect. In 1519 Zwingli took up a prestigious appointment as preacher in the Great Minster of Zurich and was almost immediately faced by the trauma of ministering to the dying during a plague epidemic. He wrote a poem about it, declaring his absolute dependence on God – 'I am your vessel to be restored or destroyed' – quite independently of the ceremonies of the Church. From 1522 he was to lead Zurich's break with Rome. More interested in the sanctification of the whole community than the salvation of the individual that had preoccupied Luther, he co-operated with the city council to impose a strict control over the Church and people of Zurich. His drive to expand the Reformation in Switzerland led him into conflict with Catholic **cantons** and ultimately to his early death at the Battle of Kappel in 1531.

Canton self-governing region of Switzerland

Having tested the water over fasting and celibacy in 1522, Zwingli started to make his general position clear in an open letter, known as the *Apologeticus Archeteles*, which he wrote to the Bishop of Constance that summer. He set out to prove that he was not a heretic but he also attacked the authority of the Pope, the errors of General Councils and the unnecessary rituals of the Church. Zwingli was now as clearly an adherent of the Reformation as Luther. Having stated his position, he had to defend it, so the Council of Zurich agreed to a public debate on 29 January 1523.

In preparation for this debate, Zwingli wrote his *Sixty-Seven Articles*. They detailed his beliefs and what he saw as the regrettable innovations of the medieval Church. Amongst other things he attacked the powers of the Papacy and the use of excommunication, the sale of indulgences and the idea of purgatory, the worship of saints and pilgrimages to curry favour with God. He claimed the backing of an indisputable authority: 'We have the infallible and impartial judge, Holy Scripture, in Hebrew, Greek and Latin.' Zwingli's opponent, Fabri, urged the reformer not to set himself against the rest of the world, but Zwingli was as unimpressed by that argument as Luther had been – he would not surrender the truth for anything. The people of Zurich were also unimpressed by Fabri's arguments. The doctrine of the Reformation was established in Zurich in 1523.

The council took action but in a limited way. The monasteries were gradually taken over, the monks often accepting a pension and leaving quite willingly, the buildings being put to other uses, such as hospitals for the poor and schools. All preaching was to conform to the evangelical model established by Zwingli. But churches remained Catholic in appearance and the Mass was still celebrated in the traditional way even though Zwingli had condemned the doctrine behind it in his *Sixty-Seven Articles*. In part, the council did not want to be too hasty in alienating Catholic neighbours and there were hopes that the Pope himself could be persuaded to repay certain debts he owed to Zurich. Also Zwingli urged that reform should be carried out slowly so as not to leave the weaker brethren behind. But some of the more eager brethren forced the pace.

In September 1523 a cobbler named Hans Hottinger overturned a crucifix which stood on a road outside Zurich, on the grounds that you should worship only Christ and not a material image of Him. This started a series of writings and disputations, with Zwingli continuing to have the commanding voice. He was tactful though, suggesting that images be covered over until the council ordered their removal. That duly occurred in June 1524. The careful, organised removal of altarpieces, statues and crucifixes was iconoclasm of a sort but it was most unlike the frenzied iconoclastic riots which were to break out in other parts of Europe. The ultimate effect was the same – the churches were no longer Catholic to look at but were bare and simple, which the reformers hoped would concentrate hearts and minds on Christ and His Word alone.

Only one feature of Roman Catholic worship was left but it was the most significant – the Mass. Condemned by Zwingli two years previously, it was at last abolished by the council in April 1525. This did not mean that Zwingli had dispensed with the sacraments. Like Luther he cut them down from seven to two – baptism and the Eucharist. But the Eucharist, now no longer the Catholic Mass, was a simple service commemorating the Last Supper, with only ordinary bread and wine distributed from a Communion table rather than from an altar. This showed the reformers' rejection of the Catholic doctrine of **transubstantiation**. For Zwingli, the Eucharist was a necessary outward sign of faith but there was to be no magic about it. All the outward signs of Reformation worship had now been established in Zurich in a way that was rather more austere but still much the same as in the Lutheran cities of Germany.

> ## KEY ISSUE
> *Why did it take several years to establish the Reformation in Zurich?*

> **transubstantiation** the Catholic belief that in the Eucharist the bread and the wine are physically transformed into the Body and Blood of Christ

B *Zwingli and Luther – the split in the Reformation*

Despite their common Protestantism Zwingli always distanced himself from Luther. In 1523 he wrote, 'The Papists say, "You must be Lutheran, you preach just as Luther writes." I answer, "I preach just as St Paul writes, why not call me a Pauline?"' At this stage, Zwingli's aloofness was probably a matter of policy as well as doctrine. He did not want his enemies to brand him as a heretic too easily by associating him with Luther and so endanger Zurich's international position. Also Zurich could be an independent centre of reform in the Swiss Confederation, being remote from the political orbit of Lutheran Saxony. However, while the humanist Zwingli wholeheartedly agreed with the position of *sola scriptura*, authority from scripture alone, he showed no sign of being sympathetic to Luther's central doctrine of *sola fide*, justification by faith alone. McGrath suggests that Zwingli was suspicious of it given his own emphasis on sanctification, meaning the gradual making holy of the whole community, a renewal of the early Church's scripturally-based morality. (This of course had its appeal for civic leaders, those 'godly magistrates', who were to put this reform into effect.) But the two reformers never made explicit any differences over *sola fide*. Just as the abolition of the Mass was the final symbolic break with Catholicism, so it was the problem of the Eucharist which was to divide Zwingli and Luther and split the Reformation permanently.

In the bible story of the Last Supper, Christ indicates the bread and says, 'This is my body'. As we saw in Chapter 7, Luther took this in its physical sense – he thought that, in the Eucharist, Christ's body is physically present in the bread although without it changing in substance, as heat can be said to be physically present in red-hot iron. Zwingli saw this as an unwarranted compromise with the Catholic doctrine of transubstantiation. More of a humanist than Luther, he was less prepared to interpret the Bible in such a literal way. He took the words 'This is my body' to mean 'This represents my body'. This re-interpretation of Christ's words meant that, in the Eucharist, the bread was purely symbolic of Christ and did not contain Him in any way. Zwingli thought that a sacrament was like an oath, the means 'by which a man proves to the church that he either aims to be, or already is, a soldier of Christ...'. The division of opinion between Luther and Zwingli was profound. For Luther, even a non-believer would consume Christ physically in the Eucharist, albeit blasphemously, whereas for Zwingli, the significance was in the believer's response to the Eucharist because the spirit of Christ was already alive within him. Parties unable to agree on this essential point of doctrine began to form around the two reformers.

Most of the reformed areas of northern Germany took their lead from the Wittenberg reformer but in south-west Germany and Switzerland Zwingli had the greatest following, his party becoming known as the **sacramentarians**. This geographical division was not just a matter of which reform centre was closest. Thomas Brady has argued in his book *Turning Swiss* that the south-west German cities gravitated towards the Swiss Reformation as they tended to identify themselves constitutionally and socially with the Swiss cities. However, uppermost in the minds of the people at the time was the war of words between the two reformers. In a series of publications Zwingli stated his position in a cool and reasonable tone. He even praised Luther as the David who had slain the papist Goliath. But he also schooled his followers well in the *Prophezei*, a theological college opened in 1525 and designed to turn

sacramentarians
followers of Zwingli and later Calvin who denied any physical presence of Christ in the Eucharist

out a superior brand of sacramentarian preacher. Finding that Zwingli was consolidating his position, Luther put heat into the debate. He wrote in 1527 that Zwingli 'neither holds nor teaches any part of the Christian faith rightly and he is seven times more dangerous than when he was a Papist'. Such hostility within the ranks of the reformers was dangerous at a time when the Catholics were organising their forces for a counter-attack.

As early as 1526, the tireless champion of Catholicism, Johannes Eck, had won a victory at a disputation in the Swiss city of Baden. He had even had the support of some Lutherans against the Zwinglians present. (Zwingli had decided it was too dangerous to attend in person.) Nine of the Swiss cantons, mainly rural ones for which civic reformation had little appeal, declared their support for Catholicism. After the 1529 Diet of Speyer it looked as though the whole of Protestantism, as it had then become known, was in danger from the Emperor and the Catholic princes. The most dynamic Protestant leader, Philip of Hesse, saw that safety lay in unity so he summoned a conference of all the leading reformers to try and hammer out a compromise between the Lutherans and the Zwinglians. The Colloquy of Marburg, as it was called, opened in October 1529.

Here is some of the dialogue spoken at Marburg:

> Luther (in response to the argument that Christ's physical body cannot be in more than one place at a time): 'I repeat again that I do not accept mathematical dimensions as applicable to Holy Scripture, because God is greater than all the mathematicians.'
> Oecolampadius (the reformer of Basle and a supporter of Zwingli): 'Where, doctor, does it say in the Bible that we should close our eyes to its meaning?' Luther: 'If we debated for a century it would make no difference. Show me the text and I will be satisfied. We must not interpret in our own way the words of our Lord.'
> Zwingli (on a verse from the Bible that supported his case): 'This passage breaks your neck.'
> Luther: 'Don't be too sure. Necks are not so easily broken. You are in Hesse here not in Switzerland.'

Q

1. *What obstacles to compromise do the above illustrate?*
2. *What was the significance of Luther's last comment?*

The Colloquy of Marburg was not a complete disaster. The reformers came away with greater respect for one another, and of fifteen articles under discussion they had been able to agree on fourteen of them but not, of course, on the article concerning the Eucharist. This being the critical issue, the Swiss Reformation was to remain permanently distinct from Lutheranism and the two parties of reformers had to fight their battles against Catholic reaction separately.

KEY ISSUE

What made Zwingli's view of the Eucharist so controversial?

C *The Reformation in Berne*

Far more critical than the attitude of Lutherans for the survival of the Swiss Reformation was the attitude of the rulers of Berne. It was the most important **canton** both in terms of size and military resources and it carried much weight within the Swiss Confederation. Zurich was one of Switzerland's leading cities but, with five mountain cantons to the south remaining fiercely Catholic (in receipt of papal pensions and without major cities to spearhead the Reformation) and with the power of the Habsburgs not far away, Berne's support was vital.

The Council of Berne – equally annoyed by Zwingli's campaign against supplying mercenaries to the French and by Cardinal Schinner's support of the Pope – at first stalled, trying to avoid disturbance by maintaining Catholic worship while permitting evangelical preaching. This simply allowed the Zwinglians to gather enough support to dominate the council after the 1527 elections. In January 1528 a formal disputation between Catholics and reformers was held in Berne. Zwingli was present with distinguished supporters from northern Switzerland and southern Germany. It was more a triumphal declaration of opinions by the reformers than a disputation. The council declared that Berne was now reformed. Soon the Mass was

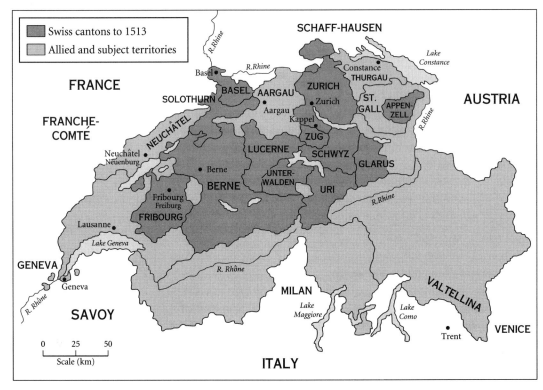

MAP 15
The Swiss Confederation

abolished and images of saints were removed from the churches. Like much of the Reformation it was strictly urban led and rebels against it in the surrounding countryside had to be put down. But given Berne's dominant position in Switzerland, there was no power that could reverse the reform. That was the best guarantee for the Swiss Reformation, not just for Zwinglianism but for the Calvinism of Geneva in the next generation.

D *Zwingli and politics*

Zwingli saw the need to be active in politics in order to further the Reformation. He sometimes attended council meetings and influenced voters to ensure that the necessary legislation was passed to abolish the Mass and remove the trappings of Roman Catholicism from the churches. He also made his views known on non-religious issues, such as his campaigns against supplying mercenaries to the French. This involvement in politics has sometimes been seen as a move to create a theocracy, a state controlled by priests or, more specifically, by Zwingli himself. Zwingli would have denied this indignantly.

In 1523 in his commentary on the *Sixty-Seven Articles*, Zwingli made it clear that Church and state were to be separate. The popes had failed to maintain that distinction, he thought, and so had become politicians rather than spiritual leaders. Zwingli stated a view similar to Luther's that the secular authorities should be obeyed by everyone; he did not claim any special authority for priests.

There were instances, however, where spiritual and secular affairs overlapped, one such being marriage. When a couple wanted to separate they were both abandoning a union made before God and breaking a civil contract. So to decide divorce cases it was necessary for clergy and magistrates to join together. But this is far from an indication of theocracy – in the marital court there were four magistrates and only two ministers.

Public morality was also of concern to both the clergy and the magistrates. In March 1530 a code of conduct was issued which affirmed that church-going was compulsory, restricted the sale of alcohol and forbade certain games which might lead to disorder. (Surprisingly, chess was thought to be one such game.) This could be interpreted as Zwingli taking control of the lives of Zurich's citizens, even as something approaching totalitarianism. However, such legislation was not new; many medieval cities had passed laws governing public morality. Besides, the councillors of Zurich had issued the code of conduct quite willingly – it had not been imposed by Zwingli.

E *Zwingli and war*

One final area where Zwingli was politically active was with regard to neighbouring cantons. He supported the foundation of a defensive league of seven reformed Swiss cities in 1527 called the Christian Civic Union. He was keen to spread the Reformation and pressed Zurich's council to be expansionist in its policies in territories jointly administered by several cantons. The five Catholic cantons of central Switzerland asserted that only a majority vote amongst the thirteen cantons could make such innovations in religion and in 1529 they formed the Christian Alliance with Ferdinand of Austria to protect their position. The scene was set for conflict.

The specific cause of war was the right of Unterwalden, one of the Catholic cantons, to appoint the new governor of the Freie Aemter in 1529, one of the jointly administered territories, of strategic importance to both Protestants and Catholics. Zwingli was determined to stop the Catholics gaining this advantage so he threatened to leave Zurich unless the council agreed to a declaration of war. The councillors, keen enough on expansion and confident of Zurich's superior military strength, did not need too much persuading and in June war was declared on the Catholic cantons. The problem was that Zwingli's influence did not extend to Berne which doubted that faith could be brought 'by means of spears and halberds' and which did not want to disrupt the Swiss confederation with civil war. Berne forced a compromise on the combatants. The Catholic cantons did agree to give up their Christian Alliance and also that local majorities in jointly administered territories could decide on reform. But this first Peace of Kappel of 1529 had frustrated Zwingli's hopes that war would lead to a united Protestant Switzerland.

Zwingli did not give up. He continued to work towards the political downfall of the Catholic cantons. He was encouraged by Philip of Hesse's aggressive stance towards the Catholics in Germany after the Diet of Augsburg in 1530 had failed to solve the religious problem there. He had hopes that Francis I would see the light and join the evangelical cause. He was well pleased by the economic blockade imposed by the Protestant cantons on the Catholics in 1530. The trouble this time was that it provoked the five Catholic cantons of central Switzerland to declare war before Zurich was ready to resist them. Zwingli might have been politically active but that does not mean that he was altogether politically realistic.

Earlier in his career Zwingli had been an army chaplain and had come to despise war fought for human profit. But this war was fought for God and Zwingli went with the army, such as it was, to join in the fighting. The Battle of Kappel in October 1531 was a disaster for the forces of Zurich and Zwingli himself was killed. His enemies quartered his body, burnt it and mixed the ashes with dung. Zwingli became one of the early victims of those religious wars that were to plague Europe for generations. As an active citizen as well as a reformer he had tried to transform Zurich, with a view to transforming all Switzerland, and had entered politics as necessary. The result was that the Swiss Reformation had both furthered the civic aspect of the Reformation and also helped to embroil it in political conflict.

TIMELINE

1518 Zwingli arrives in Zurich
1523 Sixty-seven Articles Disputation – Reformation established in Zurich
1524 First iconoclasm in Zurich
1525 Mass abolished in Zurich
1528 Berne adopts the Reformation
1529 Colloquy of Marburg War between Protestant and Catholic Swiss cantons First Peace of Kappel
1531 Second war Zwingli killed Second Peace of Kappel

After the second Peace of Kappel in November 1531 Zurich gave up its expansionist policies in north-eastern Switzerland and allowed its contacts with German Protestant forces to lapse, leaving Bucer of Strasbourg as the leading reformer of southern Germany. Zwingli was succeeded in Zurich by Henry Bullinger, a dedicated, effective reformer like his predecessor, but more prepared to keep out of politics. With Berne maintaining a low profile, the Reformation in Switzerland was only to develop political and international aspects again when John Calvin began work in Geneva. In the meantime, the Radical Reformation, which had begun in Zurich in the mid-1520s, was to have both political and international impact.

KEY ISSUE

Why and with what success did Zwingli involve himself in politics both within Zurich and in Switzerland as a whole?

2 ⤳ THE RADICAL REFORMATION

A *The origins of Anabaptism*

Zwingli insisted that reform must be introduced gradually so as not to leave behind those of a naturally conservative temperament. He recognised the need for order and so worked in co-operation with the magistrates. Not all of Zwingli's followers in the years after 1523 saw it his way. Instead, some followed his emphasis on the Bible as the sole authority and took it to what they saw as its logical conclusion. Not finding any clear instance of infant baptism in the scriptures they insisted that it should be abandoned and replaced by the baptism of adults. On this issue they refused to tarry for those more conservative or for the decision of the magistrates. This group became known as Anabaptists.

The simple ceremony in Zurich in 1525 when Conrad Grebel re-baptised George Blaurock, who then re-baptised others present, would seem to many people today to be entirely inoffensive. To Zwingli and most of his contemporaries, it threatened anarchy. Infant baptism meant that everyone in a community became a member of the Church; adult baptism meant that every individual could choose for himself whether to join – or not to join – the Church and that might lead to competing religious sects with a divided community as a result. Zwingli, like Luther, felt the need to argue from circumstantial evidence in the Bible that infant baptism must be the rule and he condemned his former followers who had become Anabaptists.

Baptism was not the only issue. The Anabaptists wanted to separate themselves off from the official Church in other ways. Instead of Zwingli's gradual process of sanctification of the whole community, they insisted that believers should mix amongst only the select sanctified few. They tried to stop paying tithes, the dues paid to support the officially appointed ministers. They wanted to elect their own ministers rather than have them vetted by the authorities. In being a threat to the existence of an official Church, the Anabaptists were necessarily a political threat as well. Anabaptist involvement in the Peasants' War of 1525 served to confirm this.

confession statement of faith

The political threat was made even clearer by the Schleitheim **Confession** of 1527. Once persecution had begun, the Anabaptists could not form a single coherent movement but this was the nearest they came to a manifesto of their views. In some ways it was a moderate document. Rebellion was rejected as a means to religious reform. The basic Protestant belief in the authority of the Bible was upheld against the spiritualists, those who relied on individual inspiration alone. But there was also the extreme view that once an adult was baptised and began to live the life of a perfect Christian, disciplined only by his religious brethren, the state would become irrelevant. The Anabaptist was not to serve the state in any office, he was not to bear arms in support of the state and he was not to swear oaths of loyalty. For sixteenth-century rulers this was unacceptable as it threatened their power at its roots.

Zwingli continued his attack on the Anabaptists in words, justifying the existence of the state as the only way of keeping order in a corrupt world. He condemned the notion that a perfect Christian life was possible given that all men are necessarily sinners. He denied the existence of free will, which the Anabaptists claimed they were exercising when they chose the path of righteousness. The authorities were to go further than words in Zurich and elsewhere as Anabaptism spread, in seeking to persecute the recalcitrant Anabaptists out of existence.

B *The persecution of Anabaptists*

In 1526 the council in Zurich passed a law prescribing the death penalty for unrepentant Anabaptists. The following year a leading Anabaptist, Felix Mantz, was drowned in Lake Zurich, a punishment thought appropriate for one who insisted on adult baptism. As a result the Anabaptists left Zurich, dispersing to remote Alpine communities or other parts of central Europe and along the Rhine. Remembering the religious radicals who had helped stir up the Peasants' War, other authorities followed Zurich's lead and few parts of Europe were safe for Anabaptists. In 1528 an imperial edict imposed the death penalty on them and one of the few things agreed by Lutherans and Catholics at the Diet of Speyer the following year was that this should be followed up as a matter of urgency.

In only a few areas were the Anabaptists tolerated. Bucer persuaded the authorities in Strasbourg that they should remain unmolested; he regarded the Swiss Brethren, as they were known, as sheep who had gone astray and should be coaxed back into the fold. Up to 2000 of them found refuge in Strasbourg, although only until 1534 when the Lutheran line, which excluded such radicals absolutely, was accepted by the city. Another area where Anabaptists found toleration was in the lands of Philip of Hesse. As he showed at the Colloquy of Marburg in 1529, he was interested only in uniting Protestants in order to stand up to the threat posed by the Catholics. His lack of dogmatism regarding the variations of Protestantism seems to have been shared by some of the noblemen of Moravia where, there being no strong central authority to interfere, sympathetic lords could provide a haven even for those radicals who practised a primitive communism.

Even though these areas of toleration existed, the Anabaptists were dispersed. They lost what coherence they had had in Zurich as a small movement. They were no longer the champions of rural communities with regard to free elections, tithes and village autonomy and thus they lost their mass support. Persecuted and generally scattered in small groups, they became more socially as well as religiously **sectarian**. The more persecuted and scattered they were, the more their faith was confirmed. Their sufferings were the sufferings of Christ and were to be welcomed rather than feared. In Augsburg in 1527 the so-called Martyr's Synod was held, in which missionary work was called for as a matter of urgency; they believed that the world was about to end and the faithful must be gathered in before the Day of Doom arrived. They also anticipated martyrdom as the Bible prophesied that the Antichrist would strike before Jesus came again to judge the world. They were right about the martyrdom; the more martyrs there were the more convinced were the survivors of the righteousness of their cause.

> **sectarian** cut off from the larger community

As Anabaptism became more fragmented, greater scope developed for a black legend to develop about them. Horror stories relating to one group or a few individuals could be taken as isolated examples; where stories were simply fabricated there was no way of giving them the lie. One story had Anabaptists making love on an altar to prove their purity. The truth of such a story was taken for granted; it fitted in well enough with their generally assumed deviancy. In contrast Balthasar Hübmaier worked with landed nobility in Moravia and upheld the authority of the state. But he was not remembered for his relative moderation; he was burnt at the stake in 1528 and his wife drowned. Much more notable news from Moravia was the establishment of the *Bruderhof* by Jacob Hutter. He judged that property was selfish and all should be abandoned to God. A system of communal farming was established without any private property. Hutter even managed to win the support of some lords who exempted the Anabaptists from taxes and services. But, however peaceful, voluntary and unusual this communal experiment was, it caused an early version of a 'red scare'. Philip Melanchthon, Luther's close supporter, was loud in his condemnation of all aspects of Anabaptism and, in particular, their supposedly widespread communism.

The Anabaptists were few in number, under one per cent of the population and often in groups of five or six. They were drawn from different classes but there were few powerful men amongst them. Artisans and yeoman farmers predominated in most areas with a few aristocrats in Moravia and more peasants in Württemberg and other areas nearer to Switzerland. In general, their aim was to separate themselves off from the larger, sinful society rather than to subvert it. Still, they were regarded as a profound threat to true religion and the

KEY ISSUE

Why were Anabaptists almost universally condemned?

social order. The fear they inspired seems out of all proportion to their capacity to do harm. But a liberal society was inconceivable to most in Early Modern Europe and any threats to authority had to be dealt with severely before the radicalism spread like an epidemic. Also, if one was disputing the issue of the danger of Anabaptism with the like of Philip Melanchthon, he might well have strengthened his argument by referring to the Peasants' War (in which the radicals won a reputation for violence however uncharacteristic that was for most) and later to the blood-letting at Münster in 1535.

C *Apocalypse at Münster*

There was a strong pacifist strain in Anabaptism. Ironically, that was regarded as a threat by rulers who needed to command troops made up of their subjects. However, as Anabaptism fragmented, its characteristics could vary enormously. Melchior Hoffmann represented a more militant strain, looking to the violent transformation of the world rather than withdrawal from it. He wandered in the Rhineland and as far as Sweden prophesying a violent **apocalypse**, the triumph of the 144 000 virgins at the end of time, and all this to take place in 1533. He identified himself with the Anabaptists although, like those known as Spiritualists, he relied much on an 'inner light' for religious guidance rather than the Bible. In 1533, by which time the destruction of the world was already overdue, he found himself in prison where he was to die in 1543. But his followers, the Melchiorites, most of them in the Netherlands, continued to await the day of wrath he had prophesied.

apocalypse the revelation of the end of the world

Their opportunity to prepare the way for it came in 1534 in the German city of Münster just over the border from the Netherlands. The year before, after a struggle to free itself from the power of its bishop, the Reformation had triumphed in Münster. The city's mayor, Bernt Knipperdolling, had met Melchior Hoffmann in Sweden and approved of the radicals. From the beginning of 1534 Melchiorites poured into the city. Jan Matthys, a baker from Haarlem, and Jan Beukels, formerly a Leiden tailor, took charge, forcibly re-baptising the population; Matthys declared the abolition of private property. Resistance to these measures was overcome by a mob which supported the Melchiorites, having been stirred up into apocalyptic belief by the earlier struggles to introduce the Reformation and by the threat of the Bishop of Münster who was gathering his forces to besiege the city.

Under siege conditions, an ever greater hysteria seized Münster. Matthys believed God had commanded him to face the Bishop in battle and had granted him invulnerability for the purpose. He went forth and was killed. Jan Beukels then became the dictator of the city. He made sins punishable by death, including that of scandal-mongering or complaining. Polygamy was introduced and Jan himself married sixteen wives, although that number was reduced when he had one beheaded for impertinence. He declared himself to be King Jan and reigned over his holy city-kingdom in the grip of terror and famine as the siege continued into 1535.

Finally the besieging forces, the Catholic Bishop now aided even by the Lutheran Philip of Hesse, found weak spots in the walls and took the city by storm in June 1535. After a slow, painful death, the corpses of King Jan and Knipperdolling were suspended in a cage from a church steeple as a sign that there had been a day of wrath but not the one the Melchiorites had anticipated. It was a symbolic day of wrath for all Anabaptists. Whatever their various, often pacifist, views they were identified with the dangerous and lunatic regime at Münster.

KEY ISSUE

How did persecution affect the radicals?

D *The survival and diversity of the Radical Reformation*

After Münster, the persecution of Anabaptists intensified. Some 2000–3000 lost their lives in the Netherlands within forty years. This did not exterminate them, however. They lived quietly, seeking to avoid the gaze of the authorities rather than preaching their beliefs too enthusiastically. There was very little unity amongst them, but numbers were kept up through missionary work such as that of Menno Simons in the Netherlands and northern Germany between 1536 and his death in 1561, showing how the faith could be preserved under severe persecution. In 1572, just over a decade after his death, his followers, the Mennonites, were granted toleration in Holland and later in parts of Germany.

The various Anabaptist sects – the Mennonites, the Swiss Brethren, the Moravian Brethren and other subdivisions – were not the only radicals to emerge in the aftermath of the Reformation. There were other yet more exclusive groups, sometimes more extreme, sometimes more intellectual. There were the Spiritualists who rejected even the Bible, 'that paper pope' as they called it, in favour of inner spiritual revelation. There were the Evangelical Rationalists, an offshoot of Italian humanism, who rejected the trinity and were the first **Unitarians**.

Some historians now dispute the significance of the Radical Reformation. Even the term itself, given currency by G.H. Williams' exhaustive study *The Radical Reformation*, published in 1962, has come into question. Interest in the radicals grew in the 1960s amidst an atmosphere of anti-authoritarianism, when the dissenters of four centuries earlier acquired a new academic importance. This merged with a particular interest in America, given that some of the sects, such as the Mennonites, had migrated there to escape persecution in Europe and still exist. The atmosphere has changed since the 1960s, and more emphasis has now been placed on how marginal the radicals were to the larger society of Early Modern Europe, and how little institutional and political impact they really made.

The radicals, however, cannot be written off by historians any more than Luther or Zwingli could ignore them. They had deep roots in the

Unitarians those who deny the Trinity, believing that God is alone divine and not three-in-one, sharing His divinity with Christ and the Holy Spirit

heretical sects of the Middle Ages, as C.-P. Clasen has shown, and they have persisted through to the modern day, when they are allowed to practise their brand of religion unmolested. In the sixteenth century, they demonstrated what Christian freedom could mean in a way that the 'magisterial' reformers had not anticipated. They also did much, however unintentionally, to fashion the Reformation when they forced the realisation that organisation and discipline were vital if the reformed Church were not to splinter into innumerable wayward sects. More than any other reformer, it was John Calvin who provided that organisation and discipline.

KEY ISSUE

Was the Radical Reformation in the end of any importance?

3 ⟳ GENEVA AND CALVINISM

PROFILE

JOHN CALVIN (1509–64)

Born in 1509 to an upwardly mobile family in the northern French town of Noyon, John Calvin was all set for a lucrative career in the Church or the law. However, in the course of his studies, he came under the influence of Christian humanists; like Zwingli he was much influenced by Erasmus's *Philosophia Christi*, an emphasis on the inspiration of scripture for living a fully Christian life. It is not certain when exactly he broke with Catholicism, but he was implicated with Protestants in 1533 and had to flee France. He wandered for two years, visiting Swiss reformers and the Duchess Renée of Ferrara, a French princess who created a small refuge for Protestant thinkers in her husband's Italian duchy. By 1536 he was also ready to publish the *Institutes of the Christian Religion* which was to be the religious handbook of all Calvinists. The reformer of Geneva, Farel, was delighted when Calvin, diverted by troop movements from his original route to Strasbourg where he intended to study, passed through Geneva. At first, Calvin would not agree to stay in that troubled city, but Farel accused him of refusing the task God had decreed for him. Reluctantly Calvin conceded, although two years later, having trodden on too many political toes, he withdrew from the city and finally arrived in Strasbourg in 1538. Then, in 1541 he was summoned back to Geneva, as the political scene had changed and reform had begun to falter without him. He was none too keen in his response – 'it would be far preferable to perish for eternity than be tormented in that place of torture' – but he knew his duty and went.

He established a Church organisation which became the most successful model for newly reformed churches throughout Europe. His clear exposition of theology in ever-expanding editions of the *Institutes* gave a strong identity to Calvinist churches and a sense of mission to those persecuted for their faith. Refugees flooded into Geneva and then out again to spread the Word; he had made the city the most dynamic centre of Protestantism by the middle of the century. Calvin never ran Geneva – he did not even become a citizen – but his views could never be ignored, and from 1555 his supporters were dominant on the council. E.W. Monter observed, 'Calvin was not so much a personality as a mind...In most cases (his) influence was based upon the fact that he knew more about something than anybody else, expressed himself about it more readily, and seldom changed his mind.'

Calvin had few intimate friends and was not renowned for his sense of humour, but he did have a human side. He had married while in Strasbourg, with his colleagues telling him that his irritability would otherwise make him insufferable. When in 1549 his wife died, she who had become the 'most excellent companion of his life', he was desolate. On his own deathbed in 1564, he made clear that his opinion of Geneva had not much improved in the intervening years: 'I have lived here amid continual bickerings...For you are a perverse and unhappy nation, and though there are good men in it the nation is perverse and wicked...'

PICTURE 29
John Calvin, *Flemish school*

A *The* Institutes of the Christian Religion

John Calvin wrote the *Institutes of the Christian Religion* in part to prove that evangelical religion need not give rise to Anabaptism or the disaster that had befallen Münster. It was the single most important book to be written by any of the Protestant reformers. Luther's thought had emerged through innumerable pamphlets and, although his helper Philip Melanchthon had tried to impose some order on Lutheran ideas in his *Loci Communes*, it was Calvin's *Institutes* that provided a truly systematic statement of Protestant thinking. He announced it as 'the Basic Teaching of the Christian Religion comprising almost the whole sum of godliness and whatever it is necessary to know on the doctrine of salvation'.

Calvin had the advantage of being a second-generation reformer, summarising a Protestant position after nearly twenty years of debate with Catholics. He also had the intellectual power to know the Bible and the writings of early Church fathers so well and to clarify his ideas so effectively that he could never be forced to back down on a theological point or express uncertainty. The *Institutes* was to expand through several editions from the six chapters of 1536 to a completely reorganised eighty chapters in 1559, but in order to explain in greater detail or deal with objections rather than make any change to the underlying principles.

Much of the material in the *Institutes* was in line with Lutheran teaching, for instance on the priesthood of all believers and *sola scriptura*. *Sole fide* was declared to be 'the principle article of the Christian religion', although Calvin never gave it as much emphasis as Luther, being preoccupied like Zwingli with the reform of urban communities rather than individual salvation.

On the subject of the sacraments Calvin agreed with the other reformers (once Luther had dropped penance) that there were only two – baptism and the Eucharist. However, Calvin was distinctive in his doctrine of the Eucharist. He rejected the early Zwinglian teaching, which seemed to reduce the Eucharist to nothing more than a commemoration of the Last Supper. He denied that it was 'a vain and empty symbol' and asserted that the believer is 'fed with the substance of Christ'. On the other hand, he could not accept that the believer was fed with the *physical* substance of Christ, as Luther maintained. For Calvin, Christ could not be contained within corruptible material things so it was as a real but spiritual substance that He fed the believer at the Eucharist. Calvin also felt that the whole debate got off the point of the Eucharist's importance as a seal of God's promised grace. As he said of the working of the Eucharist, 'I rather experience than understand it.' Luther was more dogmatic about his understanding and fell out with Calvin on this issue. There were other points of difference, but it was the debate over the Eucharist that once again stopped reformers from joining forces and led to the setting up of separate Protestant Churches. For a time the Eucharist was one of the critical issues keeping Zwinglians and Calvinists apart as well, although a compromise was to be reached by 1549.

In the *Institutes* Calvin developed the traditional doctrine of predestination. St Augustine had written that God has predestined those who are to go to heaven (the elect) while leaving the rest to a fate determined by their sin, and Luther had followed him in this view. Calvin's doctrine, though, earned the name of *double* predestination, given that God made a definite decision as to who to consign to hell (the reprobate), as well as who to select for heaven. For Calvin, this was arguing a basic principle, the overwhelming majesty of God, through to its logical conclusion. For his opponents it turned God into a harsh and even capricious figure who was prepared to create men just to cast them into everlasting flames.

The controversy it provoked made double predestination a far more significant issue than Calvin had ever intended. He did not claim that it had any practical effects in that no man could tell who was elect and who not. He said that, as long as someone claimed to be a Christian, acted like a Christian and participated in the sacraments, he or she must be assumed to be elect. In the case of those who failed such tests, it might just mean that they had not yet been brought to Christ. He was insistent that his doctrine would be the basis of a Church that included the whole community, not a sect. (He nonetheless loathed the 'pigs and dogs among the children of God'.) As for the individual's own salvation, the simple existence of faith was assurance of being elect. But moderate statements like this did not lessen the argument over the doctrine. Calvin found himself giving it more and more space in later editions of the *Institutes* as he justified himself against his critics. It was to become one of the distinctive features of Calvinism, even though much of that was due to the emphasis given to it by Beza, Calvin's successor. He insisted on arguing it through as a first principle according to the rules of Aristotelian logic, as opposed to the balanced view of the message found in the scriptures on which Calvin had focussed. Balance, as T.H.L. Parker has stressed, was difficult to maintain amidst the religious turmoil of the sixteenth century.

> **KEY ISSUE**
>
> *What made the* Institutes of the Christian Religion *distinctive?*

B *Geneva in the sixteenth century*

Geneva was a frontier city of some 10 000 people between France and Switzerland. It was part of the Duchy of Savoy and technically under the direct control of its bishop, but by the 1520s was seeking to free itself and enter into a pact with one or other of the Swiss cities.

In the 1530s, once the Genevans had allied themselves to Berne and driven off their ineffective bishop, Pierre de la Baume, it was independent but it was not yet stable. Its three councils and its four chief magistrates, the Syndics, governed the city but they were still split into factions, and the future of the Church in Geneva was not clear. The Genevans themselves did little in the way of reform beyond overthrowing the power of the clergy. Berne, however, intervened and sent the reformer Guillaume Farel under a safe conduct to Geneva. Exploiting fears of the bishop's return and the popular unrest which had led to iconoclasm in the churches, Farel persuaded the authorities to suspend the Mass in 1535 and the Reformation in Geneva had begun. Savoy soon threatened further attacks in 1535 and 1536 but Berne's commitment proved firm enough to fend that off. As in the case of Zurich five years earlier, the power of Berne proved crucial in defending the independence of reformed cities in the region of Switzerland.

Farel, however, had not triumphed completely. There was a faction opposed to him known as the Articulants who rejected any religious regulation by Protestant clergy just as much as they had rejected that by Catholics. John Calvin having joined him in 1536, the following year the two reformers put forward their blueprint for the reform of the Church, the twenty-one *Articles on the Organisation of the Church and its Worship at Geneva*. The councils accepted the *Articles*, although with some modifications, to reduce clerical control. Participation in communion (the Eucharist) was to be compulsory, not once a week as the reformers wanted, but once every three months. The reformers had provided for the excommunication of any whose views were heretical or behaviour outrageous – that was accepted by the all-important Small Council but the councillors insisted that they should have a role in deciding when such a penalty should be imposed.

The reformers had largely got their way but they failed to recognise the strength of feeling with regard to the renewal of clerical control in a city that had so recently staged a revolution against the clergy governing it. A Confession of Faith was put to the people with demands that every individual was to sign it. There was much reluctance to accept such orders from foreign reformers. There were refusals to sign and rumours spread through the city that Farel and Calvin were agents of the French seeking some political advantage.

The reformers became impatient and in 1538 tried to deny communion to those who refused to sign the Confession of Faith. The council, increasingly dominated by the hostile Articulants, then stepped in to restrain the reformers from exercising an independent power. They were not permitted to deny communion on their own decision to anyone and, as an indication of who was in charge, the council decreed that the Church of Geneva should adopt certain of the services of the Church of Berne. Farel and Calvin responded by refusing to celebrate the Eucharist on Easter Day. The situation was not eased by a friend of Farel's referring to the magistrates as a bunch of drunks. Relations between the reformers and the secular authorities had broken down and the only solution was for Farel and Calvin to leave Geneva.

Calvin had displayed a clear vision of doctrine and the requirements of a strong, disciplined Church but he had shown little political sensitivity. Geneva needed direction after its revolutionary years in the early sixteenth century but would not submit quickly to a new clerical yoke. Therefore in 1538 Calvin continued his journey to Strasbourg which he had broken off two years earlier, but he went there as an exile from Geneva.

> **KEY ISSUE**
>
> *Why did the authorities in Geneva find it so difficult either to accept Calvin or to dismiss him altogether?*

C *Calvin in Strasbourg*

In Strasbourg the Reformation was well established and the city's leading reformer, Martin Bucer, welcomed Calvin, who became pastor there to the Protestant exiles from France. In 1539 he published a new edition of the *Institutes* three times the length of the original. As a result of this work Calvin's reputation as a leading Protestant thinker was spreading and becoming international.

As his failure in Geneva had shown, however, Calvin had much to learn about the setting up of a reformed Church. It was from Bucer that he learned how to reconcile the authority of the Church with that of the magistrates and councillors through the close involvement of the latter in Church government. Calvin saw how important education could be in informing both mind and character when he taught in Jakob Sturm's academy in Strasbourg. Sturm's academy was to be a model for Geneva's own twenty years later. Calvin, already the master of doctrine, was now learning more about institutions.

While Calvin was in Strasbourg Geneva was once again suffering from lack of direction. The two leading ministers who had replaced Farel and Calvin proved to be inferior as preachers and organisers. An attempt was made by Cardinal Sadoleto to bring the Genevans back within the Catholic fold. In 1539 he wrote a letter to the city regretting past abuses and suggesting that all could be rectified once the Genevans had returned to the faith of their forefathers. It seemed that only Calvin could offer a satisfactory reply to this. From his exile he strengthened the Protestant case in Geneva by writing to Sadoleto, pointing out the doctrine rather than just the abuses which, he said, lay at the root of the Catholic Church's corruption.

It was not just the religious situation that opened a way back to Geneva for Calvin; political circumstances were also very different. Two of the four syndics (chief magistrates), who belonged to the Articulants faction and had opposed Calvin, were disgraced after they bungled some negotiations with Berne. In 1540 the remaining two syndics of the Articulants faction got themselves involved in a brawl in which a man was murdered. One syndic was executed and the other, trying to escape through a window, slipped and was killed. The supporters of Calvin now had the upper hand politically and, given that the two ministers who had taken over in Geneva had given up and left, arrangements were made to invite Calvin to return, which he reluctantly did in 1541.

D *The Calvinist Church*

As soon as he returned to Geneva in 1541, Calvin picked up where he had left off to the extent of preaching on the verse of the Bible where he had ended his last sermon in the city three years previously. Immediately, Calvin presented to the council his plan for a reorganised Church in his *Ecclesiastical Ordinances* of 1541.

Learning from Bucer, Calvin proposed four types of officers in the Church. These were:

(i)　*Pastors.* Their duties were to preach, to teach, to administer the sacraments and to guide the people in a Christian way of life. They were to be chosen by those who were already pastors and their appointment was to be confirmed by the council. The council added the words 'as it thinks fit' to the sentence about its confirmation of appointments. It was clearly not going to be regarded as a rubber stamp, and Calvin, with his newly learned tact and diplomacy, accepted that.

(ii)　*Doctors.* Their task was to instruct the people in true doctrine, so taking some of the load off the shoulders of the pastors.

(iii)　*Deacons.* Looking after the sick and the needy was their role. In line with humanist reforms in other cities, both Catholic and Protestant, an aim was to keep beggars off the streets through poor relief, an early version of the welfare state. This was especially necessary given the ending of support for the poor in Geneva through Catholic alms-giving.

(iv)　*Lay elders.* These were to be twelve worthy citizens whose duty was to supervise every person's conduct, issue warnings and, where necessary, report those who were not up to the mark to the Company of Pastors. They were to come from every part of the city so that they could keep an eye on all of it. They were chosen by the Small Council from amongst their fellow councillors in Geneva. Calvin was not setting up a Church in rivalry to the authorities of the state; rather he was incorporating those authorities into the Church.

These lay elders were not Calvin's invention; the reformer of Basle, Oecolampadius, and Bucer in Strasbourg had both used them. However, they gave Calvinism its characteristic of strong social control, given that the lay elders joined with the pastors in the consistory, a court to supervise beliefs and morals, which the *Ecclesiastical Ordinances* established as follows:

1. *What were the organisational strengths of the consistory?*
2. *How was pressure gradually built up on the wayward or rebellious in order to make them conform?*
3. *Of these three paragraphs which one was added to Calvin's original proposals by the Council and why?*

> A day should be fixed for the consistory. The elders should meet once a week with the ministers on a Thursday to ensure that there is no disorder in the Church and to discuss together any necessary action to put things right...
>
> If any one fails to come to Church to such a degree that there is real dislike for the community of believers manifested, or if any one shows that he cares nothing for the ecclesiastical order, let him be reprimanded, and if he is reasonable let him be sent back in a friendly way. If however he goes from bad to worse, after having been warned three times, let him be cut off from the Church and be denounced to the magistrate...
>
> All this must be done in such a way that the ministers have no civil jurisdiction nor use anything but the spiritual sword of the Word of God as St Paul commands them; nor is the authority of the consistory to diminish in any way that of the magistrate or ordinary justice... In cases where, in future, there may be a need to impose punishments... the council... will judge and sentence according to the needs of the case.

Menna Prestwich has argued that 'Calvin's revolutionary innovation was to require his churches to be established on the basis of a consistory'. In Zurich there was already a court similar to Calvin's consistory, but it had not been able to impose the same social and moral control as Calvin's consistory did in Geneva. In 1546 for instance, Amblard Corne, a leading citizen of Geneva, a syndic and president of the consistory itself, was reprimanded for dancing at a wedding. (Dancing was thought to be dangerous to sexual morality.) Corne submitted. In any one year up to one-fifteenth of the citizens were summoned to the consistory. Many reformers urged their flocks to learn the Lord's Prayer and other essential features of their religion, and to live morally, but none had previously established such a system to ensure that it happened. The consistory records show that for the most part, however, it was occupied with resolving family quarrels or disputes between citizens. It was an arbitrator bringing peace to the city and a counselling service, not just a disciplinary body, although it was at its most radical in the Reformation of Manners, the attempt to curb the carnivalesque aspects of popular culture. It was the consistory that was to be the key element in Calvinist churches all over Europe. As far as possible involving the leaders of a community ('the aristocratic principle of the consistory', as Beza called it), it was able to impose religious order on the rest of that community.

See pages 195–7

If one of the pastors was wayward he could be summoned before the consistory, but more than this threat was needed to maintain the standard of spiritual leadership. Calvin had a low opinion of his fellow pastors. He wrote in a letter in 1542: 'Our other colleagues are rather a hindrance than a help to us: they are rude and self-conceited, have no zeal and less learning.' Calvin could dominate the Company of Pastors in Geneva through force of intellect and character but he saw the need to create a strong corporate identity. The Company of Pastors therefore met once a week to study scripture and once every three months for what was known as the *grabeau*. The *grabeau* was a session of mutual criticism. In the words of T.H.L. Parker it 'was a little day of judgement when, flattery and convention laid aside, each man saw himself through the eyes of his fellows, and, if he were wise, harboured no resentment but knew the uniquely joyful release of voluntary humiliation'. This is an idealistic view of a most effective psychological technique. With the prospect of the *grabeau* each pastor would be more thoughtful in his approach to his work and his life in general. Each time a pastor admitted a weakness the Calvinist values of the company as a whole could be reinforced. The *grabeau* caused the individual to merge much more into the group.

The consistory and the *grabeau* gave Calvinism the institutional strength that Lutheranism lacked. Lutheran pastors had no similarly effective way of disciplining their congregations and they were themselves only irregularly supervised by superintendents and visitation committees. But important as the consistory and the *grabeau* were as institutions, it was Calvin who animated them and the Calvinist Church in general.

KEY ISSUE

What were the features of the Calvinist Church that enabled it to penetrate society so thoroughly?

E *Calvin and his opponents*

After the turmoil of the years before he arrived back in Geneva, most citizens were prepared to conform and listen to their irritable but nevertheless inspiring preacher. But Calvin still faced opposition within Geneva. There were theological opponents who protested that his pronouncements on some issues were too extreme. As before his exile in Strasbourg, more difficult to deal with were the political opponents who would not submit to Calvin's moral authority and who wanted to limit his power as much as possible.

A serious theological challenge came from a former monk called Jerome Bolsec, who met Calvin in a face-to-face debate in 1551. Bolsec argued that 'Scripture does not say we are saved because God has elected us, but because we have believed in Jesus Christ.' This was a direct attack on the doctrine of predestination. Calvin's response was to overwhelm Bolsec with his superior knowledge of the Bible and St Augustine. The minutes of their debate record that 'M. Jerome did not know what to say'. In 1551 Bolsec was exiled from Geneva so that 'the sacrament might not be polluted by him'.

It was the council that exiled Bolsec. They still wanted to limit Calvin's authority but not at the expense of allowing views that might be heretical to spread. This was as much for the sake of social unity as religious unity – the experience of many other cities and countries demonstrated how religious differences could lead to violence.

The most outrageous opponent of such unity was Michael Servetus. He was a disbeliever in the trinity, like some of the other radicals discussed earlier. He wandered from country to country taking on an assumed name once his writings had made him notorious. He learned medicine and even became physician to the Archbishop of Vienne, but his urge to enter theological debate was irrepressible. He recognised Calvin as one of his most serious opponents and exchanged letters with him until Calvin decided he was irreformable. When Servetus had been recognised in France in 1553 he was forced to go on his travels again and decided to go to Geneva to hear Calvin preach. He was recognised there and brought to trial for heresy. Calvin's condemnation of him was backed up formally by the various reformed churches that were consulted, and Catholics and Lutherans alike were united in approval of the execution of this arch-heretic. (He was burnt even though Calvin argued for more merciful beheading.) Calvin's international reputation was much enhanced by the Servetus case.

Calvin could rely on the council to crush heretical opposition but the council was the source of much political opposition for a decade and more after his return to Geneva. From 1545 a faction known as the Libertines emerged, so named because they would not submit to Calvin's moral authority. One of the most awkward of the Libertines was Philibert Berthelier. He and his friends would interrupt Calvin's sermons with coughing. When Calvin complained, Berthelier threatened to burp and fart instead. This was an irritant but the powerful Favre family was even more difficult to control. Members of the family were accused of a variety of sins from sexual immorality to playing darts instead of attending Easter communion. The Favres were continually called before the consistory where their 'astounding insolence' was recorded in the minutes along with their extensive use of obscene gestures. A particularly dedicated opponent to Calvin was M. Favre's son-in-law, Ami Perrin.

Perrin had been a supporter of Calvin when he had returned to Geneva in 1541 but he became one of the leading Libertines. This was not just due to a moral unruliness or his family connection with the Favre clan. Perrin was ambitious and came to see Calvin as a rival for political influence. Perrin's political career had its ups and downs – he was in prison for a time and was charged with treason in 1547 after some negotiations with the French – but by 1553 his fortunes reached a high point when he became first **syndic** as well as captain-general and the Libertine faction took control of the council. The issue on which

syndic Genevan magistrate – there were four

they chose to challenge Calvin was that of excommunication. Calvin viewed the exclusion of someone from the most important service of communion as a spiritual matter but, given that membership of the Church and citizenship were then so closely interlinked, it was a sensitive political issue as well.

Berthelier, along with two others, had insulted one of the pastors and had been excommunicated in 1552 without any objection from the council. This willingness to accept the consistory's decision over excommunications was in line with council policy since 1541. However, Perrin and his supporters asserted themselves in 1553, insisting that, after due apologies, Berthelier be allowed to take communion. The controversy over this dragged on for eighteen months. Calvin offered his resignation but Perrin and the others would not accept it. They had no fundamental religious opposition to the reformer but they did want to see him thoroughly tamed. The weakness of Perrin and his supporters, however, was that they could find no legal basis for denying the consistory the right to decide on excommunication. Then in February 1555 Perrin and his supporters lost the elections.

The Perrin faction had been too disruptive and too greedy, monopolising government posts for its own supporters. Finally, there was a brawl in May 1555 during which Perrin seized the black baton, the symbol of authority of his successor as first syndic – an act of treason. He fled the city and was condemned to death in his absence. The religious issue had clearly not been the only one, but the overthrow of the Perrin faction meant an end to Libertine opposition. From 1555 until his death in 1564, Calvin dominated the Church in Geneva and his supporters controlled the councils. This was due to Perrin's errors but also to the fact that Calvin had by now become indispensable; many religious refugees (who tended to support Calvin) had been awarded citizenship to broaden the tax base, and a new generation of Genevans had grown up who were much more willing to conform than the revolutionary generation of the 1520s and 1530s.

Calvin was triumphant and it seemed to some that Geneva was a new theocracy, a state ruled by its priests. This is an exaggeration. It was not Calvin himself or the Company of Pastors that passed judgement but the consistory, which included the lay elders nominated by the council. Anyway, most cases ended not in punishment imposed by the consistory but in reconciliation. Calvin had fought over the issue of excommunication because he thought it vital to the spiritual purity of the Church. He recognised that purely secular issues were no concern of the clergy and, unlike Zwingli, he did not attend all council meetings. When he did attend he did not necessarily get his own way, as on the occasion when he demanded the arrest of the ambassador from Savoy on a charge of seduction. This would have been diplomatically unwise and the council politely rejected his advice. Insofar as Calvin did play a dominant role in Geneva after 1555, it was because the rulers of the city respected his religious leadership rather than because they were blindly obedient or forced to obey.

TIMELINE

1536 First edition of the *Institutes*
Calvin arrives in Geneva

1538 In Strasbourg for three years

1541 Return to Geneva
Ecclesiastical ordinances
Consistory and *grabeau* established

1551 Calvin defeats Bolsec in debate

1553 Servetus arrested in Geneva and burnt

1553 Perrin and supporters assert their authority

1555 Perrin and supporters lose election and Perrin flees

1559 Genevan academy founded

1564 Death of Calvin

It is true that the religious sphere was broad in the sixteenth century and that can make Calvin seem more interfering. There was a brief attempt to replace taverns with religious eating houses where grace would be said and there would be no idle gossip or swearing; this move, however, proved to be too unpopular, showing the resilience of popular culture. There were many cases of the control of an individual's morals such as when Bonivard, the official historiographer, was forced to marry his housekeeper who had seemed too much like a concubine. Bonivard was in fact impotent and his wife and her lover, a servant, were executed for adultery in 1565. Such cases seem to us to bear the mark of a repressive regime. However, it was not all Calvin's doing: for instance, the magistrates had taken most of the initiative in the Bonivard case. Calvin did not impose himself on Geneva: for all the opponents he had to face and the riots which Genevans were prone to stage, in general the city was prepared to accept his guidance.

> ## KEY ISSUE
>
> *Why did Calvin face opposition in Geneva and how did he overcome it?*

F *The expansion of Calvinism*

By the 1550s Calvin had fallen out with Luther over the Eucharist but had come to an agreement with Bullinger, leader of the Zwinglians, in the *Consensus Tigurinus* of 1549. This had been spurred on by political necessity – in 1547 Emperor Charles V had defeated the Protestants in Germany and was a greater threat than ever before. Calvin kept up a constant correspondence with his fellow reformers, encouraging them and firmly letting them know his views. Although the Catholic cantons steadfastly refused to accept it, the Swiss agreement was to be extended in 1566 with the Second Helvetic Confession. Calvinism had become dominant in the Swiss Reformation but its mission extended to the whole of Europe, in particular to France.

Geneva became home to large numbers of exiles, Calvin amongst them. In the 1550s alone there were 5000 immigrants to the city which itself only had a population of 10 000. Some of those immigrants had come to Geneva to be trained as missionaries for service in their own countries. There were to be 120 missions, peaking in 1559, with thirty-two to France alone.

Calvinism spread through these missions but Calvin was aware that the training was inadequate, given that the Company of Pastors, only numbering eighteen in Geneva and its rural parishes, was hard pressed to attend to its normal duties let alone prepare missionaries. One of his long-term aims was finally realised when the money was raised for an academy, which opened in 1559. It incorporated the old school of Geneva and also offered courses at a higher level, principally in theology, which the missionaries needed to offer the certainty to their congregations which Calvin offered to his. Based on Sturm's academy in Strasbourg, and making use of experienced teachers from the academy at Lausanne which had just been closed, it was to become a most effective 'School of Christ', rivalling the Jesuit colleges which did so much to spearhead the Counter-Reformation.

As well as the academy, Geneva's printing presses were crucial to the spread of Calvinism. Not only Calvin's works were published, but also those of the exiles writing for their home markets. The psalms for French Protestants printed in 1561 and 1562 made up one of the biggest printing ventures in the sixteenth century. There was economic incentive here as well, with printing becoming the growth industry in Geneva.

The missionaries and Calvinist books were by no means guaranteed a friendly reception in the countries where they went. In France, for instance, persecution had steadily become more consistent and more severe since the 1520s. Calvin let his followers know what he expected of them in his *Letter to the Nicodemites* in 1544. Nicodemus had come to Jesus in secret, and Calvin urged those who had embraced the reformed faith not to hide the fact behind a pretence of Catholicism. The only choice was to face up to persecution or to flee. Either way, it was a hard path to take, but it may have been made easier by the Calvinist theories of **providence** and predestination. There was the conviction that Calvinism would necessarily triumph over what were seen as the Catholic forces of darkness. Divine providence was recognised when the French Protestant military leader, Coligny, found a vital ford across the Loire: it was hailed, without irony, as being like Moses' crossing of the Red Sea. And if the individual had to face martyrdom for his faith, he went to his death in the belief that he was predestined to be one of 'the elect', chosen by God. In his letters Calvin kept stressing how martyrdom was a sign of God's favour, and should be greeted warmly.

providence the belief that everything that happens conforms to God's plan for the world

Calvin's teaching was to suffer persecution rather than offer resistance to it, but he has a reputation for having established a revolutionary ideology. It is true that Calvinists were involved in armed resistance to sovereigns in France and the Netherlands but, as can be seen in Chapters 14 and 15, this was due to local political circumstances rather than to Calvin's political thought. Out of these conflicts there did arise some revolutionary theory, but its authors (such as Calvin's successor Beza who sanctioned resistance to a tyrannical king by 'lesser magistrates' at least) were writing after Calvin's death. Calvin himself was as conservative as circumstances would allow, believing like Luther that authority was ordained of God, and no doubt conscious of the memory of Münster and the danger of Calvinists being portrayed as subversives and radicals. He occasionally cited Old Testament examples of resistance, but at most reluctantly agreed that members of a royal family could restrain a king. In any case, more important for the survival of Calvinism in a hostile environment was its organisation.

See pages 349–51

When a few Calvinists, perhaps ten or twelve, had been converted in any one place, they gathered together in a conventicle for Bible reading and worship. Once there were enough to form a congregation a pastor was requested, often sent from Geneva, and a full parish organisation was set up, including a consistory. Calvinist leaders in a locality would gather together in a colloquy to discuss common problems and policy.

DIAGRAM 4

Calvinist Church structure

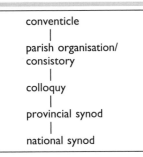

conventicle
|
parish organisation/
consistory
|
colloquy
|
provincial synod
|
national synod

KEY ISSUE

What made Calvinism capable of such extensive expansion?

Beyond that, when there were enough churches in a province to warrant it, an assembly called a provincial synod could be held and ultimately a national synod established.

Such a structure brought with it both flexibility and strength. The conventicles could spread in an almost cellular way, members of one moving off and setting up another. If one conventicle was destroyed through persecution, there were many others that could continue to grow and develop. Calvinism combined flexible organisation locally with coherent organisation at a regional and national level, giving it great political strength.

Lutheranism, its organisation totally dependent on secular authorities and without the same emphasis on providence, predestination and a willingness to face martyrdom, could never be as resilient as Calvinism. In the 1520s Lutheranism had benefited from a euphoric belief in the apocalypse, the reformers seen as fore-runners of the imminent, glorious second coming of Christ; a degree of apathy had set in when the apocalypse had not materialized. The Calvinists, belonging to the second generation of reform, also believed in an apocalypse but were prepared to work more slowly, surely and optimistically towards it.

TABLE 10

Luther, Zwingli and Calvin: a comparison

	Luther	Zwingli	Calvin
Sola fide	Key doctrine	No contradiction but no enthusiasm	Endorsement but not much emphasised
Sola scriptura	Key doctrine	Key doctrine	Key doctrine
Priesthood of all believers	Key doctrine	Key doctrine	Key doctrine
Eucharist	Physical presence of Christ	Symbolic	Spiritual presence of Christ
Predestination	Accepted	Accepted	Double predestination, in time a key doctrine
Exposition of doctrine	Stream of pamphlets; poorly structured *Loci Communes* by Melanchthon	*Sixty-Seven Articles*; much followed later in sermons/pamphlets	*Institutes of the Christian Religion*; 1559 edition in particular a masterpiece of compression and clarity
Organisation	Reliance on secular authorities	Collaboration with city council	Consistory and *grabeau*, colloquys and synods as well during expansion
Political thought	Obedience to authorities, although from 1530 accepted princes had right to resist emperor	Obedience to authorities, but urged war on cantons which resisted the Reformation	Obedience to authorities, only exception being resistance by members of royal family. Calvin's successor, Beza, sanctioned resistance by 'lesser magistrates'.

The classic example of the development of a Calvinist structure was France, where Calvinists were known as Huguenots, a name deriving from the pro-Swiss faction in Geneva. Conventicles were set up with support from both inside and outside France. The government tried to close the frontier but booksellers and missionaries got through, often displaying ingenuity and heroism. Farel escaped from Metz on one occasion disguised in a cart full of lepers. Calvin had delayed the setting up of consistories. He was cautious and had hopes of converting the rulers of France first in order to prevent any backlash. However, the growth of the Calvinist Church was running beyond Calvin's control, particularly in Paris.

The Church in Paris was founded in 1555 and three years later there were demonstrations of 3000–4000 Huguenots singing psalms on the left bank of the Seine. This was provocative enough but some Calvinists were even more militant, anticipating civil war. It was also in Paris that the structure of the Calvinist Church was completed, with the meeting of a national synod in 1559. Calvin, still cautious, had opposed this meeting and, although he sent it advice, the synod reached its own decisions with regard to discipline and a Confession of Faith.

Up to ten per cent of the French population converted to Calvinism, mainly drawn from amongst artisans and urban professional élites. Similarly, up to half of the French nobility, bringing their supporters and dependent peasantry with them, had converted, but they very much followed their own policies. They provided the Calvinist churches with a military organisation parallel to the Church structure – a captain to protect the consistory, a colonel for the colloquy, a general for the synod. Caught up in faction fighting with Catholic militants and with a crisis of Crown authority as well as religious conflict, they led the Huguenots of France into thirty years of civil war. Whatever Calvin's hopes for orderly conversion, Calvinism had become a revolutionary force.

See Chapter 15

The same was to occur in the Netherlands, ruled by Philip II of Spain. The contacts with Geneva were limited. In the 1560s there were no missionaries sent to the Netherlands although some preachers from there had visited Geneva. Most of those urging reform in the Netherlands were the so-called 'hedge-preachers', who would attract large numbers of people to leave the more closely regulated towns in order to attend a *prêche* in the countryside where they could hear 'the Word of God'. Calvin would probably have approved of the evangelical *prêche* but, as Phyllis Mack Crew has made clear, 'these early hedge-preachers were certainly Reformers in spirit, but they were not formal Calvinists'.

prêche unofficial meeting to listen to sermons

In 1567 the Duke of Alva had arrived in the Netherlands to punish the iconoclastic rioters and others who had rebelled in 1566. His persecution of those of the reformed faith (irrespective of whether they had been responsible for the riots or not) encouraged the imitation of Calvinist organisation in France which had successfully stood up to Catholic attempts at repression, although a fully Calvinist organisation did not emerge in the Netherlands until the Synod of Emden in 1571.

See Chapter 14

The roots of the Reformation in the Netherlands had not been specifically Calvinist but it was Calvinism that provided a structure strong enough to withstand persecution. Also, stories of Calvinist martyrs made the Dutch and the Flemish more willing to die for their faith as one of 'the elect'. This did not mean that the Calvinists took over the Netherlands. They remained a minority of well under ten per cent and were often engaged in disputes with the secular authorities similar to those Calvin had been involved in during his first years in Geneva. The Dutch Calvinist Church was also divided by religious controversies, which culminated in the ferocious disputes at the Synod of Dort in 1618. However, Calvinist zeal and organisation were key elements in the resistance to Philip II during the Dutch Revolt to come. Even magistrates in the north of the Netherlands who remained Catholic but were anti-Spanish accepted that Calvinism should be the official religion of their newly independent United Provinces.

Scotland's Reformation was more Calvinist in origin owing to the mediation of its leading reformer, John Knox. In the mid-1550s, after a spell as a French galley slave, Knox was in Geneva where he learned about the Calvinist faith and organisation. He was to call it 'the most perfect school of Christ'. He held the author of the *Institutes* in high regard and when he returned to Scotland he argued for a Reformation on Calvinist lines, a goal which was achieved in 1560 when the Protestant Lords of the Congregation had driven out the French forces of the regent, Mary of Guise, and passed the Reformation through the Scottish parliament. Knox was largely responsible for the *Scots Confession*, which made clear the reformed faith, and the *First Book of Discipline* which established the organisation of the Kirk, the Scots Church. However, in establishing the Reformation in Scotland Knox did not consult Calvin in Geneva, and the Scottish reformer was much less cautious than Calvin would have liked. In 1557 Knox had published his *First Blast of the Trumpet against the Monstrous Regiment of Women* in Geneva, an uninhibited attack on female Catholic rulers. Calvin was much embarrassed by this undiplomatic piece of propaganda. Also, Knox went much further in urging resistance to Catholic rulers than Calvin would allow. Knox and the Scottish Reformation were Calvinist but Calvin had no control over either.

Scotland provides an interesting variation in the pattern of Calvinist expansion. In most areas it spread in towns, primarily amongst those who were literate. In the case of the Palatinate, for instance, R. Po-Chia Hsia has described it as 'an abstract, intellectual religion of the élite'. Peasants tended to convert only at the behest of local nobility or where rural industry opened up a village to outside influence. However, in the Gaelic-speaking highlands and islands of Scotland Calvinism was adopted by rural congregations remote from towns or lords. The reason was a highly sophisticated oral tradition. Culture was transmitted by story-tellers throughout the generations, and Calvinist preachers inserted themselves into this tradition. They were winning hearts and souls for forty years before there was even a first translation of the New Testament in Gaelic (in 1603).

In England Queen Elizabeth had no liking for Calvinism, and she particularly disliked Knox for his authorship of the *Monstrous Regiment*. Also many exiles who had left during Queen Mary's reign had returned to England from Zurich or German cities, bringing reformed but not directly Calvinist ideas with them. Still, several of the bishops of the Church of England were influenced by Calvin's views, adapting his ideas on Church order and discipline, and that influence was to grow, if anything, during the religious disputes of the next century.

Germany was more resistant to Calvinist inroads than other areas of northern Europe, as Lutheranism was well established in north Germany and the Counter-Reformation was at last becoming organised in parts of south Germany such as Bavaria. However, by the 1550s the Lutherans had started to lose ground as a consequence of bitter in-fighting over doctrine following Luther's death in 1547. Calvin's own reputation in Germany grew when he was dragged in to another dispute about the Eucharist in 1552. A vital conversion to Calvinism was made in the person of Frederick III (1559–76), the Elector Palatine, a leading prince of the empire controlling extensive territories along the Rhine. The effective discipline of Calvinism appealed to him as visitations (official inspections) had shown how insecure the Reformation was in the Palatinate, and how much social as well as religious division there was between Lutherans and those still Catholic on the one hand and Anabaptists on the other. He made his capital city, Heidelberg, almost as important a refuge for exiles as Geneva and the Heidelberg Catechism of 1563 became the most important statement of the reformed faith for the Empire and later the Netherlands and also eastern Europe.

Again, however, Calvinism was adapted rather than simply adopted. This flexibility when circumstances required it was one of its great strengths. The Heidelberg Catechism was largely Calvinist but it also displayed the influence of Zwinglians and some followers of Melanch-thon. Although consistories were introduced, they never had the importance in the Palatinate that they had in Geneva or elsewhere. Power was concentrated in a state-controlled Ecclesiastical Council which had influence at every level of church organisation and so penetrated society more thoroughly than any other political institution. Also, the Elector's physician, Thomas Erastus, provided a political theory that asserted the supremacy of the state. The Calvinist Church in Geneva had never become a theocracy or defied the state, but Calvin had won for it some independent control over excommunication. Erastianism in the Palatinate ensured that the Church bowed to the state in everything, including excommunication.

By the first decades of the seventeenth century, Calvinism had become the religion of twenty-eight German states, albeit generally small ones, which looked to the greater strength of Calvinist institutions and the services of Calvinist administrators as protection against Spanish militarism and an aggressive Counter-Reformation. Princes of smaller states could also look to Calvinism to bolster their authority over their people. For Johann VI of Nassau-Katzenelnbogen, Calvinist schools were 'seminaries of the Republic: their mission was to instil discipline in children, to lay the foundations of social discipline, to honour God, and to produce the best soldiers' (R. Po Chia-Hsia). 'Court Calvinism' though, did not always lead to the conversion of the country, given the hardening of religious divisions by 1600. For instance, the Elector of Brandenburg converted in 1613, but he could not carry his Lutheran nobility with him and the Estates resisted his attempts to institute Calvinist reforms.

Calvinism spread eastwards into Poland, where ten per cent of the nobility converted to it, although that did not last owing to unusually weak organisation and a Catholic resurgence. In Bohemia Calvinism influenced the home-grown **Bohemian Brethren**. In Hungary the anti-Habsburg Magyars embraced Calvinism, largely in its Heidelberg form although with much local variation; the upper nobility and German speakers stuck to Lutheranism. In Transylvania Prince Bethlen Gabor (1613–29) established Calvinism as the state religion and played his part in the attempt to fend off the power of the Catholic Habsburgs in the Thirty Years' War. Calvinism even had an effect as far east as Istanbul where one of the **patriarchs** of the orthodox Church, Cyril Lucaris, sympathised with its teaching.

Only in the most firmly Catholic and the most firmly Lutheran countries in Europe was Calvinism limited. Wherever there was religious confusion, the certainty of the Calvinist faith and the strength of its organisation enabled it to take root.

Bohemian Brethren Hussites, religious dissidents who prefigured the Protestant reformers

Patriarch Leading bishop in the Orthodox Church

KEY ISSUE

How far did Calvinism come to differ from the views of Calvin during that expansion?

H *The historical impact of Calvinism*

Calvinism dominated the second, expansionist stage of the Reformation. Lutheranism was largely confined to Germany and Scandinavia whereas Calvinism spread, as we have seen, across much of Europe. Certainty of faith, a belief in divine providence and strength of organisation were crucial to this, but there were other ways in which Calvinism was distinctive.

Especially in his clinging to the doctrine of a physical presence in the Eucharist, Luther seemed to be still in the grip of scholastic thinking and therefore intellectually more conservative than Calvin, perhaps even making a false start to the Reformation. However, Steven Ozment has posed the question of whether Calvinists were really Protestants at all. Calvin asserted the centrality of 'justification by faith', but Calvinist discipline laid so much emphasis on a Christian morality, just as Zwingli had done, that it seemed as though 'works' were once again a way to heaven. The logical problem in this was dealt with by Calvin, who said that we 'should rely wholly on the free promise of righteousness (i.e. justification by faith alone). We do not, however, forbid the Christian from under-girding and strengthening his faith by signs of the divine benevolence towards him.' He meant that you could not earn your way to heaven piecemeal through good works, but you could reassure yourself that you were heading that way, i.e. 'elect' rather than 'reprobate', by living a godly life and working towards the sanctification of the community you lived in. Luther, in his overwhelming emphasis on faith, had cut away the Catholic sanctification of the works of everyday life; Calvin's revolution away from Catholicism seemed to have come full circle in restoring sacred significance to actions in everyday life. Ozment calls this 'the "re-Catholicizing" of Protestant theology at its most sensitive point'. It would be fairer to say it was re-Catholicising in effect rather than in underlying doctrine.

It may be that Calvin filled a gap in Christian life left by the destruction of medieval Catholicism. On the other hand, there are those who feel that his emphasis on the dignity of labour and a sense of purpose in everyday activity – in contrast with the prevailing aristocratic ethos of despising work – was vital to the creation of the modern world. Calvin described this divine calling to work in the *Institutes:*

> The Lord bids each one of us in all life's actions to look to his calling. For He knows by what restlessness human nature is inflamed, what waywardness carries it here and there, how its ambition longs to embrace various things at once. Therefore, lest through our own stupidity and rashness, everything is turned topsy-turvy, He has appointed duties for every man in his particular way of life ... It is enough if we know that the Lord's calling is in everything the beginning and foundation of well-doing.

Q

1. Why did Calvin judge a 'calling' to be necessary?
2. How might this sense of a 'calling' have affected a Calvinist's attitude towards his everyday work?

work ethic viewing hard work as a moral duty

For Max Weber, a sociologist writing at the beginning of this century, the 'calling' became the Calvinist **work ethic** and worldly success was thought by some to be evidence of being one of 'the elect'. That in turn operated as the 'spirit of capitalism' and so Calvinism was crucial to the development of the modern capitalist world. Weber recognised that there were capitalists before Calvinism, but he argued that they were prone to squander what they had gained and money-making was generally regarded as unethical. In contrast, more austere Calvinist entrepreneurs would reinvest profits and develop their businesses in a sustained way, and success could be interpreted as God favouring those who were 'elect'.

The problem with the Weber thesis is the narrow range of supporting evidence. He studied Calvinist capitalists in late seventeenth-century England who may have devoted themselves to economic activity owing to political exclusion following the Civil War as much as to any religiously-based vocation. Studies of capitalists in the Early Modern period show characteristics other than a strict Calvinist morality – some examples, Catholic as well as Protestant, have flight from religious persecution as the common denominator. Amongst the commercially enterprising Dutch, Calvinism was the official religion, but only a small minority were committed Calvinists and they were not identified with the mercantile interests. Calvin himself urged the faithful to share what they had rather than to pursue profit for themselves, and later Calvinist literature was also critical of unrestrained capitalism. He did take a liberal view on interest paid on borrowed capital, condemned as usury in the Middle Ages, but there again the Catholic controversialist Eck had found justifications for the Catholic bankers, the Fuggers, to charge interest. It seems that economic circumstances, just as much as political, could lead to the development of doctrine on both sides.

While the economic impact of Calvinism on the modern world is doubtful, its political impact on Early Modern Europe is more certain. Calvin, for all his caution, had set in motion an international conflict. It was not just that his creed became revolutionary within a number of countries in the hands of his successor Beza and others. Calvinists across Europe looked to each other for support in their various battles, given that they feared an international Catholic conspiracy against them. Catholic princes in turn, such as Philip II of Spain, saw an international Calvinist conspiracy threatening them. Even when it was political ambition rather than religious zeal that motivated the conflicts and even when the battle-lines between Catholics and Protestants became confused, the religious wars of the century after Calvin lasted longer and bred more bitterness because of the determination and the ability of Calvinists to stand up to the Counter-Reformation.

Calvin died in 1564, urging his fellow pastors that they should change nothing. That was not possible given changing historical circumstances as well as the liking of his successor, Beza, for crude propaganda which over-emphasised predestination and encouraged armed resistance to a Catholic government, if only by lesser magistrates. By 1600 Geneva itself had declined as a 'holy citadel'. Morale was low in the Company of Pastors and Perrot commented that: 'The School has gone cold.' However, by then Geneva had done its work. Europe, from Scotland to Transylvania, was the home of an aggressive Calvinism.

KEY ISSUE

What were the main features of the moral, economic and political significance of Calvinism?

---

4 ↵ BIBLIOGRAPHY

*G. Potter, *Zwingli* (Historical Association Pamphlet, 1989 ed.), **K. Randell, *Calvin and the Later Reformation* (Hodder and Stoughton, 1988), and *Euan Cameron, *The European Reformation* (Clarendon, 1991) are excellent introductions. Bruce Gordon, 'Switzerland' in *The Early Reformation in Europe*, ed. Andrew Pettegree (CUP, 1992) gives the national context. *G.R. Potter and M. Greengrass, *John Calvin* (Edward Arnold, 1980) contains useful documents and comment. Alister McGrath, *A Life of John Calvin: A Study in the Shaping of Western Culture* (Blackwell, 1990) is a full and robust account, although quite specialist. **International Calvinism 1541–1715*, ed. M. Prestwich (OUP, 1985) is an outstanding collection of essays, but *Calvinism in Europe 1540–1620*, ed. A. Pettegree, A. Duke and G. Lewis (CUP, 1994) and M. Greengrass, *Continental Calvinism* (Macmillan, 1995) are useful additions.

5 ⤸ STRUCTURED AND ESSAY QUESTIONS

A *Structured questions.*
1. (a) What did Zwingli contribute to the Swiss Reformation?
   (b) Why did Zwingli and other 'magisterial' reformers wish to destroy the Radical Reformation?
2. (a) What were the main differences between Lutheranism and Calvinism?
   (b) Why did Calvinism play the most prominent role in the international expansion of Protestantism?

B *Essay questions.*
1. Assess the significance of Zwingli's contribution to the Reformation.
2. Compare Luther and Zwingli *or* Luther and Calvin as Protestant reformers.
3. Why were the Anabaptists subject to such a rigorous persecution and what were its effects?
4. What made Calvin so distinctive as a reformer?
5. 'A Protestant Rome'. How accurate is this as a description of Calvin's Geneva?

6 ⤸ DOCUMENTARY EXERCISE ON CALVIN'S POLITICAL THOUGHT

Read these extracts and then answer the following questions. Bear in mind the changing political context in which Calvin was writing.

The Lord has not only testified that the office of magistrate is approved by and acceptable to him, but he also sets out its dignity with the most honourable titles and marvellously commends it to us... [Magistrates] have a mandate from God,... Accordingly there should be no doubt that civil authority is a calling, not only holy and lawful before God, but also the most sacred and by far the most honourable of all callings in the whole life of mortal men..

SOURCE A
From the Institutes *on the office of magistrate (1543 edition) – a term applying to rulers in general.*

We are not only subject to the authority of princes who perform their tasks towards us uprightly and faithfully as they ought, but also to the authority of all those who, by whatever means have control

SOURCE B
From the Institutes *on obedience to magistrates (1543 edition).*

of affairs, even though they perform only a minimum of the prince's office... [God] says that those who rule for the public benefit are true patterns and evidence of His benevolence; and those who rule unjustly and incompetently have been raised up by Him to punish the wickedness of the people; that all equally have been endowed with that holy majesty with which He has invested lawful authority.

SOURCE C
From the Institutes *on the best form of government (1543 edition).*

If the three forms of government which the philosophers discuss (monarchy, aristocracy and democracy) are considered in isolation, I will not deny that aristocracy, or a system compounded of aristocracy and democracy, far excels all the others: not indeed in itself, but because it is very rare for kings to control their will that it never is at variance with what is just and right; or for them to have been endowed with sufficient prudence and shrewdness to know how much is enough. Therefore man's weakness causes it to be safer for a number of men to exercise government so that each one can help, teach and admonish the other. If one of them asserts himself unfairly, there are a number of censors and masters to restrain him.

SOURCE D
From the Institutes *on resistance to kings (1543 edition).*

For if the correction of unbridled despotism is the Lord's to avenge, let us not at once think that He has entrusted it to us, to whom no command has been given except to obey and to suffer. I am speaking here of private individuals. If there are any magistrates appointed by the people to moderate the power of kings – as in ancient times the ephors were set against the Spartan kings, or the tribunes of the people against the Roman consuls, or the demarchs against the senate of the Athenians; and perhaps, as things now are, such power as the three estates exercise in every realm where they hold their chief assemblies – I am so far from forbidding them to withstand, in accordance with their duty, the violence and cruelty of kings, that, if they connive with kings in their oppression of their people, then I declare that they are guilty of the most wicked betrayal of trust...

In the following letter, Calvin was writing with reference to the Tumult of Amboise, a plot in 1560 involving some Huguenots who aimed to seize the young king, Francis II. There was a question as to whether Calvin had supported the plot:

Seven or eight months before the event, a certain person [La Renaudie, the organiser of the plot]... consulted me, whether it was not lawful to resist the tyranny by which the children of God were then oppressed... I strove to demonstrate to him that he had no warrant for such conduct according to God, and that even in worldly terms such measures were ill-organised, presumptuous and could have no successful outcome...

...if a single drop of blood were spilled, floods of it would deluge Europe; it were better we should perish a hundred times, than expose Christianity and the gospel to such shame. I admitted, it is true, that if the **Princes of the blood** demanded to be maintained in their rights for the common good and if the **Parlement** joined them in their quarrel, that it would then be lawful for all good subjects to lend them armed assistance. The man afterwards asked me, if one of the Princes of the blood, though not the first in rank [referring to the prince of Condé], had decided upon taking such a step, we were not then warranted to support him. I answered in the negative. In a word I adopted so decided a tone in condemning all his proposals that I was convinced that he had completely abandoned them...

If I should be asked why I did not more formally oppose the proceedings, I answer, that first of all I thought there was no great necessity for doing so, because I despised the enterprise as a childish affair...yet it is an undoubted fact that at that time people heard me preach several sermons in which I combated their cause with as much vehemence as I was master of. This can easily be verified, inasmuch as these sermons were copied word for word as I delivered them with the date of the month and the day, whence, it is evident, that I did not play a double part, nor avail myself of silence to spring a mine under ground.

princes of the blood
members of the royal family

Parlement the equivalent of a supreme court

SOURCE E
From a letter dated 16 April 1561, from Calvin to Admiral Coligny, one of the leading Huguenot nobles in France.

Q

1. *What was Calvin's attitude in general towards rulers or 'magistrates' and what reasoning lay behind that attitude (Sources A and B)?*

2. *What were Calvin's reasons for preferring a government made up of aristocracy, or aristocracy and democracy? Might his political experience in France and Geneva have influenced his opinion (Source C)?*

3. *On what grounds and by whom could a king be resisted, according to Calvin (Sources D and E)?*

4. *How definite is Calvin on whether that resistance should be passive or active (Extracts D and E)?*

5. *What do you think was Calvin's purpose in writing to Coligny (Source E)?*

6. *How far would you judge from the above evidence that Calvin himself was the author of a Calvinist revolutionary theory?*

12

The Counter-Reformation

In the immediate aftermath of Luther's protest it looked as though the Church of Rome might be ruined. Protestantism seemed to be unstoppable in Germany and it was threatening to spread throughout Europe. However, after decades of ruinous delay, the Catholic Church began to take corporate action. A General Council of the Church – a parliament of bishops and leading theologians – met at Trent in northern Italy in three sessions between 1545 and 1563. Its decrees gave Catholic militants a cause to be sure of, a new morale and a new discipline. Given its renewed vigour, the Roman Catholic Church could not only survive but fight back. With the help of crusading Catholic princes and new religious orders, especially the Jesuits, it found itself able to reclaim souls and territories previously lost to the Protestants. The term which best suited this renewal and attack seemed to be 'the Counter-Reformation'.

The term 'Counter-Reformation', however, is regarded by many as being inadequate, even misleading. It was coined by those accustomed to thinking about strategies and counter-offensives, about military matters. This cannot do justice to a spiritual movement that was positive, not merely reactionary and which had its origins long before Luther made his protest and which, diverse enough in Europe, spread with Catholics around the world to America, Asia and Africa, far from the battle against Protestants.

The Council of Trent itself seems to shrink in its relative importance amidst the many and various reform initiatives in what is now sometimes renamed the Catholic Reformation. This movement went further institutionally and spiritually than the reform of the Catholic Church itself – Catholic missions in the countryside found that many of the people of Europe held to magical, even semi-pagan beliefs, which made their work seem even more necessary. It is debatable whether the traditional heroes of the Counter-Reformation – the councillors of Trent, the popes, Philip II of Spain – solely determined the future of the Roman Catholic Church, or whether it was the case that Catholicism was developing slowly and diversely, not simply being driven by events in the religious conflict of the period. It is certainly necessary to look for the origins of Catholic renewal before the Council of Trent and before Luther even thought of making his protest.

1 ↶ THE REFORMERS

Long before 1517 there had been those seeking to revitalise the Church. There were groups of pious laymen, referred to in general as 'the devout', such as the Brethren of the Common Life, and also individual Catholic reformers such as Erasmus. Because Luther's protest was louder and more radical, it tended to obscure the quiet work of reform going on within the Church.

See pages 134–5

When Luther visited Rome in 1510, he discovered that the heart of the corruption of the Church was to be found in Italy, where the popes played out their power politics and where, for many, the Church was nothing more than a financial racket. While partly true, this is not the whole story. Already reformers were at work. New brotherhoods had been founded at Vicenza in 1492 and 1493 and at Genoa in 1497. These were men gathering together to pray and to fast, and by their example to make an impact on the society around them. In a hierarchical society, the scale of that impact depended in part on the rank of the reformers. That is why the foundation around 1514 of the Oratory of Divine Love, a sort of reform club, was so important. The list of those associated with this Oratory reads like a roll-call of the leaders of the Catholic Reformation. Giberti, Sadoleto, Thiene – these would all reform dioceses, advise the popes on reform or create new monastic orders. One, Reginald Pole, was even a connection of the English royal family.

See pages 362–3

Another member of the Oratory was Gasparo Contarini. He had no intention of becoming a priest at all. He was a Venetian aristocrat and statesman, and stayed so until the mid-1530s. But, inspired by a friend who became a hermit, he tried to measure and direct his active public life by his interior faith. He became a cardinal in the end (1535) and led a Catholic delegation in one of the last attempts at compromise with the Lutherans (the Colloquy of Regensburg, 1541), where he hoped in vain that a negotiated settlement might be reached. Contarini and Pole as well, while working within the Catholic fold to restore the Church, had some sympathy with the basic Protestant belief in justification by faith alone. In this they drew, as Luther had, on the ideas of St Augustine. They, and other Catholic reformers who thought like them, became known as the *spirituali*.

spirituali Catholic reformers who sympathised with some Lutheran doctrines but remained loyal to the Church

The most austere member of the Oratory, with no sympathy whatever for Protestant views, was Gian Pietro Carafa. He had shown his dedication to the Church at the age of fourteen, when he attempted to run away from home in Naples to become a monk. This adolescent commitment was to remain with him as he aided in the foundation of the Theatine order, and later on as he worked out new ways of isolating the contagion of heresy: a reorganised Papal Inquisition (1542) and an *Index of Prohibited Books* (1559). He was the leader of the *zelanti*, those bitterly opposed to any compromise, dedicated to the crushing of Lutheranism. In 1555 Carafa became Pope Paul IV.

zelanti Catholic reformers whose overriding concern was to combat heresy

See page 359

KEY ISSUE

Was Catholic reform having any impact before the need to react to Luther?

order monastic organization

Clearly, the men of the Oratory were to be of great significance in the attempt to strengthen the Church in the face of Protestant attack. But their reform club was founded before they had ever heard of Martin Luther. Furthermore, within the Oratory there were very different attitudes towards Luther's ideas when they had heard of him. The split between the *spirituali* and the *zelanti* was to become apparent during the crisis of the early 1540s. Before then 'the devout' continued their attempt to regenerate the Church, not just by example, but also by aiding the setting up of new orders of reforming monks and priests and making their protest to the Pope about the state of the Church.

2 ⌐ THE NEW ORDERS

The development of new **orders** at the beginning of the sixteenth century took place largely in Italy, remote from the centre of Lutheran controversy in Germany. Many of 'the devout' favoured this development as they were particularly dissatisfied with the old orders where monks and nuns had grown complacent, performing rituals mechanically, enjoying good collective incomes and failing to set an inspiring example to the people. One group of 'the devout' was the *Camaldolesi*, an eleventh-century order revitalised by Venetian noblemen who became hermits in 1510 to escape the corruption they saw all around them. More positive were the Theatines (founded 1524), a group of ordinary priests receiving training as reformers, and the *Somaschi* (1528) who dedicated themselves to caring for the sick, for orphans and for those prostitutes who would turn to God. Such social concern was one way of bringing religion to the people. Dramatic preaching was another way, a speciality of the Barnabites (1530). A new order of nuns called the Ursulines (1535) stayed firmly in the community, continuing to live with their families and devoting themselves to the education of girls. The simple fact of these new foundations and their activities shows that there was a reforming spirit alive in the Catholic Church. But few could be compared for their impact with the Capuchins and the Jesuits.

The Capuchins (1529) were not strictly a new order at all, but an offshoot of the Franciscans. St Francis (1181–1226) had set a standard of humility and skill in preaching which was thought to be unsurpassable. He and his followers had been instrumental in saving the newly growing towns of Europe from drifting away from the Church. Matteo da Bascio wanted to follow his example in bringing the Christian message to the people, and symbolised this by wearing a pointed hood or *capuccio* supposedly like that of St Francis. His followers, the Capuchins as they became known, did the same. Their zeal disturbed many of their self-satisfied fellow Observants, a branch of the Franciscans, who tried to crush the new offshoot, but unsuccessfully. The Capuchins were lucky to have powerful patrons, such as the Duchess of Camerino, whose uncle, conveniently enough, was Pope Clement VII. Surviving the factional politics of the Church, the friars with their pointed hoods became familiar and welcome figures throughout Catholic Europe. They were skilled in preaching and in the use of down-to-earth language. But they were most renowned for their fearlessness in combating deprivation and disease. Right from the start in Camerino, the Capuchins had nursed those afflicted by the plague despite the risk of infection to themselves. This selflessness was to be the mark of these friars; they brought their living faith and their Church to the people in the most practical way possible.

The Jesuits (1540) were the most out-going of all the new orders, following the example of their first 'general', reared in the tradition of the Spanish Reconquista, Ignatius Loyola. A unique blend of commitment to obedience to the Pope with the freedom to go anywhere and to adapt to local circumstances (unlike ordinary monks confined to one place and with a set routine), they have been seen as the most dynamic element of the Counter-Reformation. They consolidated the Church in the Catholic south and reclaimed lost souls in parts of the Protestant north; their first aim, however, had been to combat the Infidel Turk and they became the leading missionaries to the newly explored lands of South America and the Far East. They shared with the other new orders the spirituality of the early Catholic Reformation and are too often seen exclusively as part of militant reform from the 1540s onwards. Their methods and successes will be dealt with in looking at how the Catholic Reformation reached the people and, in detail, as part of a documentary exercise at the end of this chapter.

Whether in caring for the sick or the destitute, in preaching or in teaching, the new orders had started to reinforce not just the spirituality of clerics, but also the involvement of laymen. Left as mere spectators of church rituals the ordinary churchgoer in Italy, north and south, might have found the Protestant declaration of the 'priesthood of all believers' very enticing. This is not to suggest that the new orders or any of 'the devout' intended specifically to pre-empt Protestantism in the early days. In fact they were reacting to the same problem as Luther – how to channel the growing piety of the age. But it cannot be denied that, in keeping that channel Catholic, 'the devout' helped to save the Church of Rome from collapsing in the face of the challenge from Germany.

Before such collapse could definitely be averted, though, 'the devout' had to find ways of increasing their power. Otherwise their work might have been local to Italy, sporadic and ultimately of limited effect. Only power could spread and consolidate reform. For power it was necessary to look to the princes of Europe and to the popes.

> **KEY ISSUE**
>
> *In what ways did the new orders help to restore the Church?*

3 ⌐ POWER AND REFORM BEFORE TRENT – THE PRINCES

Princes frequently professed themselves to be good servants of the Church, but they usually preferred to be its masters. There has been much mythology in talk of 'new monarchies' in the early sixteenth century, but it is true that princes were slowly if unsteadily increasing their powers at the expense of privileged groups such as the Church. Hand in hand with this mastery went the possibility of bringing power into the service of reform.

See page 46

A traditional example of power supporting reform is the work of Cardinal Cisneros de Ximénez, the Archbishop of Toledo. He was a committed crusader confessing that for him, 'the smell of gunpowder was sweeter than the perfumes of Arabia'. However, he was also dedicated to reforming the Church as well as adding new territories to it. He drew on the support of the Catholic kings, Ferdinand of Aragon and his wife the devout Isabella of Castile, in order to reform monastic orders in Spain, establish a new university at Alcala and encourage the biblical scholarship of Christian Humanists. His attempts at reform were, however, of limited importance in the end. They were local to Spain, the land of the reconquista, where racial and religious purity were seen as one in the fight against the Moors, and where the Spanish Inquisition had been safeguarding that purity since 1478. Nonetheless, Cisneros' work does reveal some willingness by princes to back reform.

Such commitment to reform was present but even rarer in other parts of Europe. In England some Franciscan friars were reformed, but for Henry VII churchmen were largely seen as useful Crown servants. For Henry VIII, this was even more marked in his patronage of Cardinal Wolsey, the personification of such abuses as absenteeism and pluralism, although Henry did at least cultivate the friendship of reformist figures such as Erasmus and Sir Thomas More and could be a pious man on occasion. Just how secular Henry was in his public interests, however, is shown in his execution of More when his old friend refused to acknowledge the king's supremacy over the Church.

Across the Channel Louis XII of France and his successor Francis I found war and its attendant chivalry to be far more suited to their ideals than reform of the Church. But Francis did take an interest in the Church in 1516. His agreement with Pope Leo X in the Concordat of Bologna guaranteed him much control over the personnel and revenues of the Church in France. It was secular interest rather than spiritual renewal which lay behind this. In contrast, Francis's sister Marguerite was a patron of the reformist circle of the Diocese of Meaux but this was local and élitist. The key figure in the Church in France in the early years of the sixteenth century was Cardinal Georges d'Amboise. He had been made a papal legate in 1501 with the supposed purpose of reforming the Conventuals, a branch of the Franciscans. However, as the Italian Wars continued to absorb attention and cash, it became clear that the suppression of a monastery was as useful for the confiscation of its wealth as for any improvement of religion.

See pages 265–7

It was difficult to reform a monastery in Germany. At Deddingen the monks broke a reformer's carriage to pieces. At St Ulric's, Augsburg, a would-be reformer found himself jailed for a fortnight. In the Tyrol the great fifteenth-century churchman, Nicholas of Cusa, the Bishop of

Brixen, was continually obstructed by the local duke who rather liked the unreformed habits of a convent and its nuns. The developing piety of many Germans was flouted and frustrated. This paved the way for Luther's protest and in turn for the conviction of the Emperor, Charles V, that reform was vital for the maintenance of the Church and the Holy Roman Empire. The problem for Charles was that he was too late. For the first twenty years of his reign he had been preoccupied with the wars against the French and against the Turks. In these same years up until 1542, the reforming instinct in Germany had quickly found its main expression in Luther's new doctrine and the adherence to it of many free cities and some powerful princes. Charles V's belated attempts to reform were futile. He sent Matthew Held to the German princes and cities in 1536 to offer reform; Held was soon reduced to plotting war against the Protestants. Charles backed compromise with the Protestants at the Colloquy of Regensburg in 1541. The attempt failed and with drastic consequences, as we shall see. Charles then had to press even harder for what he had long expected was the only solution: the Pope had to reform his own administration and summon a General Council to spread that reform throughout the whole Church.

Charles was right. Princely authority was insufficient to organise reform. Some princes were just not interested. Others, as Charles had been, were preoccupied with what seemed to be more urgent secular matters. To reform the 'members', the body of the Church, so much depended upon the 'head', the Pope. The problem that remained was that popes often acted more as Italian princes than as vicars of Christ.

KEY ISSUE

Why did Catholic princes before Trent fail to make Church reform a priority?

4 ⌐ POWER AND REFORM BEFORE TRENT – THE POPES

Renaissance popes have often been portrayed as sensual, power-thirsty betrayers of the Church. This portrayal made a good argument for the Protestants and it still makes a good story, but it is not the whole truth. Princes and bishops had taken advantage of the Great Schism to whittle down the powers of the Papacy through the movement known as conciliarism which held that General Councils, not popes, governed the Church. The Councils of Constance (1414–17) and Basle (1431–49) nearly succeeded in making the popes puppet rulers of the Church. But at Basle the conciliarists quarrelled amongst themselves and conciliarism faded. Authority once again passed to one pope, resident in Rome.

In the aftermath of conciliarism the popes had one principal aim – security against attack. In pursuit of that, they self-consciously acquired not spiritual virtues but the refinement of the worldly arts of the Renaissance, which raised the status of churchmen, as they had done that of merchants and princes. It was also the case, as with Cisneros, that gunpowder smelt sweet in the nostrils of some popes as they fought to control their own anarchic territories in central Italy, the Papal States. They also saw a need to concentrate not on the religious

See page 2

life but on the new game of international diplomacy to guarantee their position, threatened as it was by the onset of the Italian Wars. It is this quest for security that helps us to understand why the popes dealt with the question of reform so gingerly for so long, and also why, given the threats to their authority at Constance and Basle, they were so reluctant to summon a General Council of the Church.

The attitude of the Renaissance popes to reform can be seen in the fate of Savonarola, a new-style reformer in Florence who wished to turn his native city into a city of God, with Renaissance vanities – books, priceless paintings – being cast into the fire. In 1498 Pope Alexander VI (1492–1503) applauded when the reforming Savonarola was cast into the fire instead. But Alexander was not just acting with the immorality typical of his family, the Borgias. Savonarola was an ally of the Pope's enemy, France, during this dangerous period of the Italian Wars. It was politics not religion that called the tune.

This was true for Pope Julius II (1503–13). He was more comfortable in armour than in priestly robes as he sought to drive the French out of Italy and to crush the petty tyrants who had carved up much of the Papal states between them. The French threatened Julius with deposition and summoned a 'reforming' Council at Pisa. The Pope responded in 1512 by calling the Fifth Lateran Council (in effect an advisory committee) to attract genuine reformers to his side. Much was decided about the need to improve Church law and to co-ordinate the work of bishops and of monks but little was done. The new Pope, Leo X (1513–21) was not inclined much to reform. ('Now God has given us the Papacy', he is reputed to have said, 'let us enjoy it.') He was also preoccupied with politics and with the shortage of money, which decreed the further sale of indulgences.

Cuts could be attempted to solve the financial problem. This was tried by the reformist Pope Adrian VI (1522–23), formerly Charles V's austere tutor. There were howls of protest from citizens of Rome now unemployed, and vested interests in the Curia (the papal civil service) resisted the Pope's every move. The epitaph on Adrian's tomb reads 'Woe! How even a most righteous man's power to act depends upon the times in which he happens to live.' But times were about to change.

See pages 246–9

Pope Clement VII (1523–34) was a surprisingly virtuous pope for a Medici, but he was still obsessed with politics. His hopelessly bad diplomacy prepared the way for the Sack of Rome in 1527. For weeks a motley band of Spaniards, Italians and German Lutherans murdered, stole and raped their way quite methodically across Rome. The Pope was a helpless prisoner inside his fortress of the Castel Sant'Angelo. Gone were those Renaissance visions of the glory of Man. Even when Rome had recovered physically from the sack, the atmosphere had changed drastically. The disaster was seen as a visitation of God upon the sins of Rome. Gian Matteo Giberti, already a member of the Oratory of Divine Love, exemplifies this new spirit. In 1528 he gave up his lucrative post as datary, in effect a broker for the sale of dispensations (permits for otherwise forbidden practices). He then remedied his years of absenteeism by moving to his bishopric of Verona where he became the first 'model bishop' of the Catholic Reformation, raising the standards of the clergy and giving more direction to the spiritual lives of the laity. Pope Clement himself did not respond fully to this new spirit. He played politics to the end of his reign, shadow boxing with the Emperor, Charles V. But it was clear to Clement's successor that political security would avail the Papacy nothing. The only way forward was to raise its moral status.

Pope Paul III (1534–49) clearly understood the need for reform to avert the ruin of the Church and saw the possibility of renewal through the work of the Oratory of Divine Love, raising five of its members to the cardinalate in the two years after becoming Pope. He then asked four of these Cardinals, along with five others, to take part in a reform Commission, rendering advice on the improvement of the Church – the *Consilium de Emendanda Ecclesia*.

POPE PAUL III (1534–49)

PROFILE

Born in 1468 into the high Roman nobility, the Farnese family, Paul first won promotion through his sister Giulia who was one of the mistresses of Pope Alexander VI. Made a Cardinal in 1493, he acted as a Renaissance prince of the Church, lavishing money on buildings and art, and fathering a number of illegitimate children. Elected Pope in 1534 at the age of sixty-six, he was not expected to be responsible for many innovations, but although he pursued dynastic ambitions on behalf of his children in the traditional way, he did see the urgent need for peace among Christian princes to allow for reform of the Church. He tried to end the conflict between Charles V and Francis I. He established the *Consilium* in 1536 and promoted reformers to the College of Cardinals. He recognised the Jesuits as a new order and summoned the Council of Trent in co-operation with the Emperor. That co-operation was no doubt made easier by Charles's willingness to help Paul's son, Pier Luigi, establish himself as ruler of Parma and Piacenza in northern Italy. However, in line with Paul's wishes but against those of Charles, the Council of Trent dealt with doctrinal issues first. Relations deteriorated because of this, and the Pope feared Charles's increasing power following his victory over the Protestants in 1547. Paul III died in 1549 at the age of eighty-one. He had been a relentless **nepotist** and yet also the first pope to back reform with any determination: his reign was a turning point in the Counter-Reformation.

nepotism giving posts to one's own family

Here is an abstract from the *Consilium*, the report presented to the Pope in 1536:

Q

1. *What evidence is there here of a new sense of urgency in the higher councils of the Church?*
2. *What did the consilium identify as having been the main obstacles to effective reform?*
3. *Doctrine was not dealt with by the consilium. Given that, how would convinced Lutherans react to these proposals? Why might some of the cardinals on the commission have been reluctant to broach matters of doctrine?*

> Most blessed father, we are very far from able to express in words what thanks Christendom ought to give to Almighty God for making you pope at this time and shepherd of His flock, and has given you the mind you have ... For the Spirit of God, by which the heavens are held up [as says the prophet], has decreed that Christ's Church, falling and indeed almost collapsed, should be restored by you and that your hand should save it from ruin; and that you should re-erect it in its earlier glory and return it to its pristine splendour ... And Your Holiness ... knows well that the origin of all these evils arose from the fact that several popes, your predecessors ... collected expert [opinions] according to their desires, not in order to learn from them what they should do, but to find by their zeal and craft a reason to justify their wills ...
> Concerning the institution of ministers by means of whom, as by instruments, the worship of God is to be well administered and Christ's people are to be well instructed and guided in the Christian life, the first abuse here is the ordination of the clergy, and especially of priests, in which no care is taken or diligence displayed. Whoever they might be – totally unlearned, of the vilest origins and appalling morals, or under age – they are regularly admitted to holy orders, and particularly to the priesthood, that condition which most notably expresses Christ ...
> Concerning the Bishop of Rome. This city and church of Rome are the mother and teacher of other churches. Therefore the worship of God and honesty of manners should flourish here above all ...

congregation a senior Church committee, such as a royal council

Curia the papal civil service in Rome

The *Consilium* was indicative of a new attitude in the Church and a reform '**congregation**' (committee) did follow it up with reforms in the Curia reducing the favours and dispensations from Church law that could be bought for cash. Nonetheless its effect was very limited.

Paul III was sympathetic to the Commission's report but he was not the man to overcome the dead weight of the **Curia**. He had what he saw as the greater matter of Catholic peace to establish – he was in Nice in 1538 arranging a truce between Charles V and Francis I. It soon became clear that the *Consilium* had only just touched on what threatened the ruin of the Church.

KEY ISSUE

Why had the popes been so reluctant to embark on reform?

5 ⟿ THE CRISIS OF THE CATHOLIC REFORMATION, 1541–42

Charles V had been distracted by wars against the Turks and the French for most of his reign. By the late 1530s he urgently required a negotiated settlement with the Protestants before the structure of the

Catholic Church in Germany collapsed completely. A conference of Protestant and Catholic representatives, planned in 1539, finally took place in 1541 in the form of the **Colloquy** of Regensburg. The leader of the Catholics at the conference was Cardinal Contarini, prominent among the *spirituali*, those churchmen with leanings towards Lutheranism. At the head of the Protestants was Philip Melanchthon, a close colleague of Luther but placing a much higher value than he did upon Church unity.

Within a few weeks the two delegations had managed to agree on the first five articles of the draft agreement, *The Book of Regensburg*. The atmosphere of optimism was tremendous. It seemed as though the end of the schism was at hand. Thorny questions about the nature of original sin had been sorted out. The even thornier question of justification by faith alone or by faith and works was resolved in the doctrine of 'double justification'. It was agreed that faith was fundamental to salvation and that while the value of good works depended entirely on the faith underlying them (that satisfied the moderate Protestants), they were vital all the same (sufficiently traditional for the moderate Catholics). The problem was that, while the moderates were at Regensburg, the dogmatists at Wittenberg and Rome were to have the final say.

Luther and the Pope were swift to condemn 'double justification'. For them such a compromise would be a betrayal of the cause. It would also have been very difficult to persuade their embattled followers to accept the subtle theological formulae involved. The collapse of negotiation, however, was not due just to the dogmatism of Luther and the Pope but also to the impossibility of finding a compromise to cover every doctrinal issue.

Five articles of *The Book of Regensburg* had been agreed upon by the moderates, but there were eighteen other articles under consideration. Of these, the issue of **transubstantiation**, the starkest symbol of the difference between Catholics and Protestants, seemed to defy all attempts at compromise. While it may be wrong to say that the failure of conciliation was inevitable, the day of the moderate was certainly passing.

The failure of the Colloquy of Regensburg convinced many Catholics that a definitive, uncompromising statement of Catholic doctrine was long overdue. Machinery was immediately set in motion to preserve the purity of the faith even before such a statement could be issued. In July 1542 the Papal Inquisition was reorganised after years of ineffectiveness. Cardinal Carafa, that leading representative of the *zelanti*, obsessed with the need to stamp out heresy, was put in charge of it. No doubt its model was in part the successful Spanish Inquisition. But Carafa was not concerned mainly with those who lent towards Judaism or Islam, as in Spain. He was obsessed with the Lutheran heresy spreading like a disease in Italy. The Papal Inquisition had been revived as a direct response to the fear that two Italian cities, Modena and Lucca, were about to turn Protestant. Those cities actually remained Catholic but there was evidence enough that the crisis of the Catholic

colloquy conference, usually religious

transubstantiation the Catholic belief that in the Eucharist the bread and the wine are physically transformed into the Body and Blood of Christ

Church was not confined to northern Europe but was spreading to the heart of the Church in Italy itself. In August 1542 Bernardino Ochino, General of the Capuchins and a renowned preacher, fled soon after another great preacher Peter Martyr Vermigli, across the Alps into Protestant Switzerland.

They had fled, at the height of their preaching careers, because they felt that the logic of their *spirituali* ideas, drawn like Luther's to a great extent from St Augustine, led inescapably towards Protestantism. Their decision, though, had more than personal consequences. The responsibility for stemming heresy in Italian cities had lain largely with *spirituali* bishops – at least, that was so until the flight of the two preachers who had been so eagerly employed by the same bishops to keep the Italian people within the embrace of the Catholic Church. In the same month as the flight to Switzerland, Contarini died. It was symbolic of a change in the direction of reform. With the reformers in disarray and the *spirituali* suspected of heresy, the resolution of the crisis was found in a new emphasis on defence against Protestantism. Carafa and the *zelanti* set the tone, and amidst fears of an independent national settlement in Germany, as well as fear of heresy at home in Italy, a General Council was at last summoned to Trent to put the Church to rights.

KEY ISSUE

What eventually caused the Council of Trent to be summoned?

PROFILE

CARDINAL POLE (1500–58)

One of the three papal legates appointed to open the proceedings of the Council of Trent was Cardinal Reginald Pole. His loyalty to the Church of Rome never wavered, but he was one of the *spirituali* who felt that Luther's views on justification by faith alone should be carefully considered rather than condemned out of hand. He was born an English nobleman with royal connections, the great-nephew of Edward IV. Unwilling to support Henry VIII's divorce he left England in 1532 to resume his studies in Italy where he won great respect as a scholar and moved in the reformist circles of the *spirituali* such as Contarini and Morone. In 1536 Paul III staffed his *Consilium* with members of this circle, including Pole, and appointed him a cardinal. In 1537 the Pope wanted to use Pole to persuade Francis I and Charles V to invade England and depose Henry VIII. The king's fury could not be vented against Pole, although there were threats of assassination, but Pole's cousin, his brother and finally in 1541 his mother were executed. Pole was greatly relieved when in 1541 he was given the much less political post of governor of the territory surrounding Viterbo, just north of Rome.

Under his guidance the Viterbo circle flourished, where theologians and reformers would meet to discuss, cautiously and privately, ideas similar to Luther's. Unlike Luther, however, they would not risk further schism or the destruction of the tradition of the Church. Pole advised Vittoria Colonna, for instance, that she should believe as though she could be saved by faith alone and act as though it were by works alone. The crisis of 1542, however, with the threat of open heresy in Italian cities and the defection of leading reformists to Calvinism, threatened the tranquillity at Viterbo. In particular, the zealous Cardinal Carafa nursed suspicions of Pole which were to turn into implacable hatred. Because of his known discretion, however, Pole was appointed one of the legates at the opening of Trent in 1545. He had to withdraw after a year because of illness but accepted the decisions of the Council, despite the unequivocal condemnation of justification by faith alone – he placed obedience before his own beliefs. Charles V felt that Pole held out the best hope of reconciliation with the Protestants and backed him for pope following Paul III's death in 1549. Pole lost the vote of the cardinals by the narrowest of margins, which must be seen as one of the points where the Church might have turned but didn't.

Instead he was to find his last role in working alongside Mary Tudor from 1554 to reclaim England for Catholicism. Ironically, despite his main efforts being to reform the abuses of the Church and renew its spirituality, he became identified with the persecution and burnings of 'Bloody Mary's' reign. In 1555, however, Carafa had become Pope and pursued his vendetta, summoning Pole back to Rome where he would undoubtedly have been put on trial for heresy as had been Cardinal Morone. Mary would not let Pole go, but neither survived much longer, dying on the same day, 17 November 1558. Carnesecchi commented that 'in the eyes of the world' he had died unhappily 'being regarded in Rome as a Lutheran and in Germany as a Papist'. Within the framework of obedience to the Church, Pole had explored creatively the grey areas of theology, but as the Counter-Reformation gathered force and the world around him changed, the issues seemed to many to be inevitably black and white.

6 ↽ THE COUNCIL OF TRENT – THE MEETINGS

Paul III summoned a General Council to meet in 1542. Yet again, that was forestalled by war when in that year Francis I invaded Charles V's territory in the Netherlands. In 1544 the Peace of Crèpy established the peace for which Paul III had been waiting. The Council opened on 13 December 1545 in the small town of Trent, a compromise location in that it was on the Italian side of the Alps which pleased the Pope, while it was a free city of the Empire which pleased Charles V. There were to be three meetings of the Council: 1545–47, 1551–52, and 1562–63.

The remote, cramped town with its poor climate did not seem to please many bishops. Only thirty-one turned up for the opening session. The numbers, however, did grow and in later sessions there were 237 voting members of the Council. But even that number does not indicate a truly 'general' Council. The Protestants were not included, despite a brief and redundant appearance by their representatives at the second meeting of Trent in 1551, and there were only very few Catholic bishops from north of the Alps. On 15 July 1563, during the third meeting, a complete list of those present was taken. Out of 235 there were 135 Italians. This did not guarantee papal control, however, as has sometimes been suggested. Of the 135 Italians, eighty-nine were from Spanish-controlled or independent territories.

While the debates were quite free and wide-ranging this does not imply a democratic approach. Whereas at the Council of Basle (1431–49) the joke had been that anyone turning up could vote, at Trent only the fathers (bishops and monastic leaders) took part in the final decisions. They in turn were not merely subject to the **papal legates**, but were under pressure all the time from secular princes.

papal legates the special representatives of the Pope

Ambassadors were present at all the meetings at Trent and played a relentless diplomatic game on behalf of their princely masters, often diverting the Council from its decision making. Considering the political turmoil of the time it is more surprising that the Council ever completed its business at all than that it took so long.

The first meeting at Trent (1545–47) ended when an epidemic of plague broke out. But it would have ended anyway given that Charles V was seeking to impose an independent settlement on the German Protestants by use of force, beating the Schmalkaldic League at the Battle of Mühlberg in 1547. The Emperor had planned force for some time, but he was also disappointed that the Council had concentrated so much on the reform of doctrine, a papal priority given the threat of heresy in Italy. Charles first wanted the reform of abuses, which he felt held the key to recovering Germany.

See page 237

Pope Julius III (1550–55) recalled the Council to Trent for its second meeting in 1551–52. It made little headway given the presence of hostile Protestants and was again overtaken by war. In 1552 Charles V's policy of force and reform of abuses was in ruins. The Peace of Augsburg in 1555, engineered by his brother Ferdinand, acknowledged the permanent religious division of Germany.

The Peace of Augsburg might have been the immediate cause of a third meeting of Trent to try and pick up the pieces. However, there was a new pope in Rome – Carafa had become Paul IV (1555–59). Obsessed not just with the purity of doctrine but also with the undivided authority of the Papacy, he decided that he would direct reform on his own. His action was fast and furious. He attacked the extravagance of Church leaders, he suppressed simony (the sale of Church offices) and in 1559 established the *Index of Prohibited Books*, banning any publication that was remotely deviant from loyalty to Rome and its orthodoxy.

The immediate problem was that even a vigorous pope like Paul could be no substitute for a General Council. His authority, in reality, extended little beyond the Papal states. Frustrated by this, even driven near to madness, Paul declared war on Philip II, that most zealous of Catholic princes. He then went on to accuse Cardinal Pole of heresy at the very time when Pole had abandoned his earlier suspect views, those of the *spirituali*, and under Mary Tudor was faithfully seeking to reclaim England to the Catholic fold. It was clear to the cardinals after Pole's death that this divisive approach had to be terminated, especially after the Counter-Reformation had come to an abrupt halt in England upon the death of Mary Tudor. (This aborted Pole's reform decrees of 1556, which were almost a model of what the Fathers of Trent were trying to achieve.)

On his election, Pius IV (1559–65) was made to promise that the Council would be recalled to continue the spiritual regeneration of Christendom. Pius, much influenced by his holy nephew Archbishop Carlo Borromeo of Milan, kept his word, but it was due more to his diplomatic skill than to his spiritual dedication that the Council actually met. The Emperor, now Ferdinand I, wanted no continuation of dogmatic Trent, as he feared to provoke the Protestants in recently settled Germany. The Cardinal of Lorraine, the dominant ecclesiastic in France at this time, wanted conciliation with the French Protestants, the Huguenots, and so he sided with Emperor Ferdinand. Philip II of Spain, a more dogmatic Catholic, wanted to continue Trent if anything, but preferred to delay as he made his bid to woo the new Queen of England, Elizabeth.

These political obstacles were finally overcome with some papal sleight of hand. The Cardinal of Lorraine conveniently panicked Ferdinand and Philip on to the Pope's side by proposing a separate national Council in France. The Pope then followed this up by fooling the Cardinal of Lorraine into thinking that the new meeting at Trent would start afresh and not be a continuation of the previous two meetings. With these clear indications that reform depended on political manoeuvre as well as on spiritual renewal, the third meeting (1562–63) of the General Council opened at Trent.

This time the meeting was to end not because of the outbreak of war, but because the work of the Council was complete. However, it was not achieved easily. The papal legate Cardinal Morone had had to fight off an attack on papal authority led by the Spanish Archbishop of Granada, Guerrero. The independent-minded Spaniard had used the issue of bishops being made to reside in their sees in order to raise the further issue of whether bishops received their authority direct from God by divine right or from the Pope. Morone undermined Guerrero's position, promising papal favours to Ferdinand, the Cardinal of Lorraine and, most importantly, Guerrero's own prince, Philip II. He finally clinched agreement with a compromise formula. That formula guaranteed the dignity of bishops with a promise that papal interference would be restricted, but it firmly established the principle of the papal monarchy over the Church.

TIMELINE

1512	Fifth Lateran Council
1527	The Sack of Rome
1536	The *consilium*
1540	Papal recognition of the Jesuits
1541	Failure of the Colloquy of Regensburg
1542	Papal Inquisition reorganised
	Ochino and Peter Martyr flee to Switzerland
	Contarini died
1545 –47	First session of the Council of Trent
1551 –52	Second session
1555 –59	Pontificate of Paul IV, who refused to reconvene the council
1559	*Index of Prohibited Books*
1562 –63	Third and final session of the Council of Trent

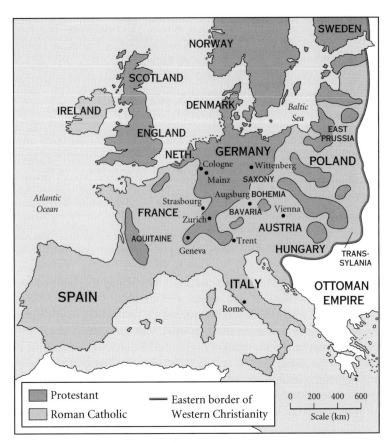

MAP 16
Religious divisions at the time of the Council of Trent

Protestant
Roman Catholic
—— Eastern border of Western Christianity

0   200   400   600
Scale (km)

KEY ISSUE

What were the political obstacles at Trent that almost prevented the council achieving anything?

The decrees of the Council could now be formally 'promulgated' (issued). There were still obstacles in the way of reform but, as we shall see in the next section, at last the Church had a clear statement of what ought to be believed by all Catholics, and of how the Church hierarchy from Pope to parish priest, should organise and behave itself. The Council had also empowered the Pope to continue reform, to encourage the greater growth of Catholic renewal and to prevent any further inroads of Protestantism into Catholic territory.

7 ⌐ THE COUNCIL OF TRENT – THE DECREES

The Decrees of the Council of Trent (the 'Tridentine' Decrees) fall into two categories: doctrine and discipline. Doctrine was decided upon first, largely during the first two meetings of the Council. The Pope and the fathers of the Council, unlike Charles V, recognised that the strength of the Lutheran offensive was in its doctrinal certainty and that many more Catholics, unless guided by clear authoritative beliefs, would follow Ochino and become **apostates**.

apostates religious 'deserters'

The Council affirmed the basis of all its doctrine. That was to be scripture, but tradition as well, not 'Scripture alone'. Where direction was sought from scripture, the Vulgate, the official text of the Church, was to be used. This was not to be publicly vetted, as Erasmus had done, but issued in an amended version by the Pope.

These are some extracts from the major doctrinal decrees:

(i) If anyone says that nothing is commanded in the Gospel apart from faith, that everything else, whether commandment or prohibition, is indifferent and up to the individual, and that the ten commandments have nothing to do with Christianity, let him be **anathema**.

anathema excluded from the Church; damned

(ii) If anyone says that the grace of justification is granted only to those predestined to life, and not to the others who are definitely called but do not receive grace, because they are predestined to evil by God's power, let him be anathema.

(iii) If anyone says that the sacraments of the new law were not all established by Jesus Christ, Our Lord; or that they are more or less than seven, that is, baptism, confirmation, the Eucharist, penance, **extreme unction**, **orders** and matrimony; or even that any one of these seven is not truly and properly a sacrament; let him be anathema.

extreme unction the last rites before death

orders ordination to the priesthood

(iv) If anyone says that in the most holy sacrament of the Eucharist there remains the substance of the bread and wine together with the Body and Blood of our Lord Jesus Christ, and denies that marvellous total conversion of the substance of the bread into the Body and of the wine into the Blood, even though the appearance of the bread and wine remain, which the Catholic Church most appropriately calls transubstantiation, let him be anathema.

(v) If anyone says that in the Catholic Church there is not a hierarchy established by divine ordination, consisting of bishops, priests and ministers; let him be anathema.

Q

1. *Draw up two lists side by side from the decrees. One should be the name of the Catholic doctrine being re-asserted; the other should be the implied Protestant doctrine being condemned.*
2. *How might such statements of doctrine help the Catholic Church?*

In their urgent attention to doctrine the Fathers of the Council did not want to neglect discipline, even if the main bulk of that legislation had to wait for the third meeting (1562–63). They recognised that it was the essential counterpart to a clearer doctrine. It was not just that abuses were morally objectionable in themselves, it was that they weakened the central activities of the Church. A seven-year-old archbishop could scarcely oversee his province effectively, a bishop who has never visited his diocese could hardly check up on his clergy and an ignorant priest could not set the Mass in its proper context or preach correct doctrine to the people. The following are some of the major disciplinary reforms.

KEY ISSUE

What was the main aim behind the Council of Trent's doctrinal decrees?

With regard to bishops:

(*i*)   Preaching was established as a bishop's chief duty. Severe penalties were threatened for neglect of this duty to instruct the faithful.
(*ii*)   Pluralism was condemned.
(*iii*)   Absenteeism was condemned. Absence without permission was to last no more than three months unless on state service, which was not unusual. If the bishop failed in his attendance, his revenue was to be used to repair churches or given to the poor rather than to him.
(*iv*)   A bishop had to attend a provincial synod (church conference) every three years and hold one in his own diocese every year.
(*v*)   Visitation was to occur regularly, meaning that the bishop had to go on tours of inspection in his own diocese.
(*vi*)   The authority of the bishop to do all this was reinforced as he was to be the delegate of the 'Apostolic See', i.e. of the Pope himself, empowered to overrule other clerics in his diocese. So the Pope's reinforced authority actually enhanced rather than competed with that of the bishop with the aim of Catholic renewal.

With regard to parish priests:

(*i*)   Preaching was, of course, as much the duty of the parish priest as of the bishop, and it was to be 'in conformity with the capabilities of its hearers'. For too long, Protestants, with their emphasis on preaching and aptitude for it, had had the ear of the people.
(*ii*)   In dress and in speech, priests were to show themselves to be a distinct and worthy group of men. Concubinage would result in dismissal. Housekeepers were to be respectable older women.
(*iii*)   Wandering priests and relic pedlars were to be banned, as were the *quaestors* – indulgence sellers – just forty-six years too late!
(*iv*)   Admission to the priesthood was to depend upon a knowledge of Latin and the Bible as well as an upright life. Candidates for ordination had to be at least twenty-three years old.

All the above, however, would be merely airy idealism unless action was taken to produce men of the right quality for the priesthood. The Council's action was to decree that a seminary, i.e. a training college, should be set up in every diocese where there was no university. Boys were taken in at secondary school age and then given a decade or so of training, concentrating heavily on theology, before they became priests. Despite all the educational difficulties of this project, and despite it being more than a century before the Council's decree was effective throughout Catholic territories, the seminaries, more than anything, guaranteed that priests remained a distinct caste, doing their jobs properly and maintaining their status in whichever society they found themselves.

This does not exhaust the list of disciplinary decrees. Amongst other things the Council continued the reform of monastic orders which had long been such a notable feature of the Catholic Reformation. But however much reforming zeal the Council fathers had shown and whatever their joy when the work of the Council seemed complete in 1563, the fate of the **Tridentine decrees** were still uncertain. Now, the

KEY ISSUE

What were the disciplinary decrees of the Council of Trent designed to achieve?

Tridentine decrees
decrees of the Council of Trent

application of the decrees of the Council depended on the popes and on princes as well as on the bishops and priests.

8 ⌐ POWER AND REFORM AFTER TRENT – THE POPES

The popes of the later sixteenth century did not fail the Council of Trent. Pius IV's successors, Pius V (1566–72), Gregory XIII (1572–85) and Sixtus V (1585–90), were all dedicated to building on the work of the Council and could rely on reformist bishops, led by Carlo Borromeo, Archbishop of Milan, to help them.

The most immediate task for these popes was the restoration of the liturgy, that is, the form of Church services which had to express the doctrines newly clarified at Trent. In 1568 the Pope issued a breviary, the order of service to be recited by a priest each day. In 1570 this was followed up by the missal, which specified the procedures followed during Mass. These, with the authorisation of a new catechism, an instruction manual for the faithful, gave a new direction to what went on inside Catholic churches day by day.

The popes did not just address themselves to the work left over by Trent. There were plenty of longstanding problems in Rome itself. The Curia, although not purged completely of its abuses, was at last cut down to size. Pius IV dismissed 400 excess officials, while Pius V, when dismissing more, reassured them with the words: 'Better starve yourselves than lose your souls.' The Curia was, anyway, being starved of corrupt business. With the only recently halted shrinkage of the Church in Europe and with the disciplinary legislation at Trent, there was simply not as much trade in dispensations from Church laws or the sale of Church offices. Also, the money that was coming into the Curia came from the better administration of more legitimate revenue such as taxation of the Papal states and the papal monopoly of alum, a valuable chemical.

Curial administration of the Church as a whole was improved. The twenty new cardinals created by Pius V included not just pious men but efficient ones as well. More and more administration was entrusted to specialist committees. These were known as 'congregations'. In 1588 Sixtus V confirmed fifteen permanent congregations, able to overcome the uncertainty in earlier, more chaotic, papal decision-making. Eventually a congregation was set up in 1622 to take charge of spreading the faith – *Congregatio de Propaganda Fide*. The new dynamism and efficiency of the Counter-Reformation had given a name to 'propaganda'.

The whole tone of life in Rome changed after the Sack of Rome and more so after Trent. There was a new austerity. Moral fashion as much as papal decrees had changed. The glorious nudes of Renaissance art were suddenly seen as little more than pornography. Many courtesans, high-class prostitutes, had been reformed or had left the city. Church leaders could work without the secular distractions of an earlier generation. What was suitable for the Papacy in its earlier quest for security had given way to the new power of morality and efficiency that was fitting to a much more genuinely self-confident and renewed Papacy.

The cardinals of the *Consilium* would have been pleased to see this. But that only serves to remind us that any reform of Rome would be insignificant if it were to stop there. After Trent, the popes and the reformed bishops could attend to renewal in Italy but, for the rest of Europe, so much depended on the princes and their reaction to the Tridentine decrees.

KEY ISSUE

How did the popes after Trent further the work of the council?

9 ↩ POWER AND REFORM AFTER TRENT – THE PRINCES

In January 1564 the Pope issued a bull declaring the decrees of Trent obligatory in all Catholic lands. That in itself was one cause of the reluctance of Catholic princes to accept the decrees. While they might be genuinely enthusiastic for the reform decrees themselves, they were deeply suspicious of the assertion of papal authority they involved. The zealous Philip II was to complain that he had sent bishops to Trent and they had come back parish priests.

Philip nevertheless agreed to the publication of the decrees in Spain in 1564, although he inserted a 'catch all' clause that his royal rights were not thereby to be infringed. Too much has been made of that clause. It did lead to some jurisdictional wrangles – as to whether the Pope or the royally-controlled Spanish Inquisition should try a bishop for heresy , for instance – but this did not prevent the implementation of the important reforming decrees.

See pages 404–6

These decrees were to have greater consequence in the Netherlands, where they were also published, than they had in Philip II's Spanish dominions where the Reconquista tradition made them easy to adopt without much change or turmoil. In the Netherlands Philip was carrying out a policy of religious and political centralisation in which the Tridentine decrees had a major role. The problem was that this policy offended noble and urban liberties to the extent that it stimulated what was to become the Dutch Revolt. This had two effects on the Counter-Reformation. In one way it was a disaster in that the largely moderate Catholic population of the northern Netherlands was to come under the sway of a minority of Calvinists in the new United Provinces. It was a success, however, in that from 1590 onwards the southern Netherlands was thoroughly reclaimed for Catholicism. Calvinists fled north or submitted to the combined efforts of papal ***nuncios***, bishops conscientious in their visitations and 3000 Jesuits and Capuchins. By the time of the long postponed peace settlement between the Spanish and the Dutch in 1648, once great centres of Protestantism like Antwerp and Brussels in the Spanish Netherlands again looked to

See pages 424–5

nuncios papal ambassadors

Rome for guidance. The foundations of a Catholic Belgium had been laid.

By 1648 the religious lines of Germany were also more clearly drawn than they had been at the Peace of Augsburg in 1555. Many supposedly Catholic territories in the mid-sixteenth century, such as the Habsburg lands themselves, were full of Protestants. In 1556 the Catholic princes accepted the Tridentine decrees, with just a few modifications. The dukes of Bavaria were among the first to back the setting up of that most effective of Jesuit seminaries at Ingolstadt in 1556, co-operating with Peter Canisius, the Jesuit who masterminded the Counter-Reformation in southern Germany. The dukes had already done much towards undermining those protectors of Protestantism, the local Estates, and when they accepted the Tridentine decrees the grateful Pope made over ten per cent of clergy income in Bavaria for princely use. It is clear that princes could expect to make nearly as much out of the Counter-Reformation as the princely followers of Luther had made out of Protestantism.

Of all the Catholic princes, Ferdinand, Charles V's brother, seemed the most reluctant to support the Tridentine decrees actively. He was fearful of strife with the Protestants and even touchier than his nephew Philip about his prerogatives with regard to the Church. He had summoned the Jesuits to Vienna in 1551, but resisted the confrontation they urged on him – he did not want to disturb the consensus of Catholics and Protestants working effectively together in the administration and often related to one another. (This shows that members of rival religions were not necessarily always at each other's throats.) The Jesuits played a long game. In Loyola's words, they aimed to win the confidence of 'men who count for most in the common weal' and especially those in the ruler's entourage and family. It was not until Ferdinand's Jesuit-trained great-grandson became the Emperor Ferdinand II in 1619 that there was a concerted effort to purge the Habsburg lands of Protestantism. In the process, the Emperor increased his secular authority in his hereditary lands greatly, having humbled the Estates and extended his administration. This was confessionalisation, practised by Lutheran and Calvinist princes alike, whereby the much greater use of state power was justified by the need for the prince to intrude into his subjects' lives to impose his religion.

Ferdinand II's religious and political ambitions set off the Thirty Years' War (1618–48) during which, in the Edict of Restitution (1629), he tried to take back all Church lands in the Empire which had been illegally taken over by Protestants. This would have been the high point of the Counter-Reformation – if it had worked. However, the Habsburg failure on a European scale should not obscure the fact that, at home in the Bohemian and Austrian lands, Protestants had finally lost their liberties and Jesuit education had provided the basis for a triumphant Catholicism.

The character of southern Germany was changed by the Counter-Reformation, but even more affected was the character of Poland. With much power in the hands of noblemen, the elected kings of Poland could only exert their authority if they were men of a remarkable personality. While the papal *nuncio* persuaded the King of Poland to accept the Tridentine decrees almost immediately in 1564, it was not until the reigns of the vigorous Stephen Bathory (1576–86) and then Sigismund III (1587–1632) that energetic reform began. There was little concerted opposition to the Catholics as Poland was as anarchic religiously as it was politically, with at least six different religious affiliations vying with each other. The kings enjoyed the legacy of reform in Poland conducted by Cardinal Hosius (d. 1579) and the continuing support of Jesuits teaching in colleges and preaching on missions. This activity gave Poland a Catholic identity that has been a mainstay of its national tradition up to the present day.

While Poland was the scene of an undoubted triumph of the Counter-Reformation, in the later part of the sixteenth century France looked as though it would be the scene of its most signal failure. No Tridentine decrees were accepted there in the 1560s. Instead the country was plunged into the Wars of Religion which were to last over thirty-five years.

See Chapter 14

In 1598 peace was made when Henry IV, having converted to Catholicism five years earlier as a political expedient, came to a compromise settlement with his former supporters the Huguenots (French Protestants) in the Edict of Nantes. This looked like a major Catholic defeat in that it guaranteed the security and near independence of large Protestant areas in the south and west of France. In fact, it effectively quarantined Protestantism in those areas and paved the way for a triumphant Catholic renewal in the seventeenth century. The early seventeenth century in France saw a whole gallery of saints, St Vincent de Paul, St Jean Eudes, St Francis de Sales and many others, who were to revitalise the Catholic priesthood and Catholic devotion in France, with the aid of aristocratic patronage. The kings of seventeenth-century France gave their tacit approval even though they continued to foster some abuses, such as pluralism. (Henry IV even gave two abbeys to the Protestant Duc de Sully.) While the Tridentine decrees were never officially registered in France, an assembly of the clergy in 1615 did acknowledge their acceptance of them, without opposition from the king. Men of power might be diverted from spiritual matters – the reformist Bishop of Luçon became that scheming politician Cardinal Richelieu – but their whole way of thinking was coloured by Catholic reform.

By the end of the seventeenth century reformist vitality had ebbed, although the Counter-Reformation reached its climax in a dubious way in the reign of Louis XIV. Where saints had failed Louis seemed to think troops would succeed; he tried to convert the Huguenots by force, finally revoking the Edict of Nantes in 1685, which merely deprived Protestants of their civil liberties rather than enhancing Catholic renewal. There had also emerged in France a brand of reform Catholics called the Jansenists, whose views on predestination made them dangerously like the Calvinists for Louis and the Jesuits. The king's unsuccessful attempt to rout the Jansenists by destroying their

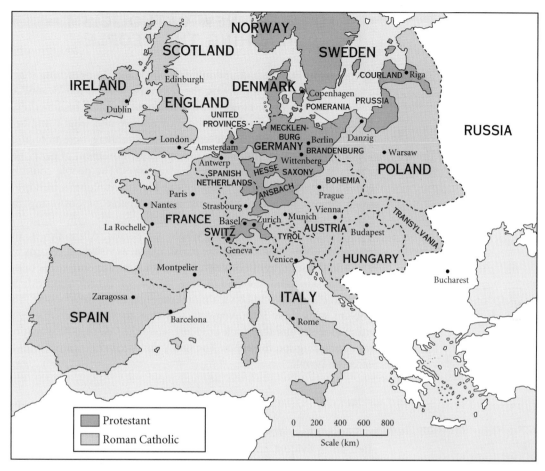

MAP 17
Religious divisions by 1600

convents and by calling on the Pope for help shows us how sterile the Counter-Reformation could become. It also shows how resilient diverse brands of Catholic reform could be, with the Jansenists maintaining their influence into the eighteenth century.

Catholic reformers were confined to certain areas – they were excluded from England, northern Germany and Scandinavia after 1558 – but it is clear that we cannot confine Catholic reform or Counter-Reformation to the sixteenth century. Varieties of political circumstances determined where and when the reformers could do their work, spreading it out over at least a century-and-a-half. However, historians writing recently have begun to realise that the exact nature of its impact upon the people must also be taken into account, and this forces us to take up an even broader perspective.

KEY ISSUE

How significant were princes to Catholic Renewal after the Council of Trent?

10 ↶ THE NEW CATHOLICISM – REACHING THE PEOPLE

The people of Europe had undoubtedly witnessed the preaching friars, the pious brethren of the towns, the reformist writers, the 'devout' of the later Middle Ages. However, the impression could be superficial, particularly as the 'devout' tended not to venture into what could be a semi-pagan countryside, and even in the towns there were numerous parishes not remotely touched by this sporadic movement of piety. The Fathers at Trent thought that they had answers. The people could be reached through an invigoration of the hierarchy: Pope – bishops – parish priests, with the last being newly capable of answering the religious needs of the people.

The Council fathers were not wholly unrealistic. Albeit slowly, the Tridentine decrees did change the parish priest, as visitation records for France in the seventeenth century, for instance, clearly show. The priest knew his Latin and the liturgy (the 'script' of church services), he preached effectively and he set a moral example to his parishioners. The problem with these improvements was that they were variable even within dioceses and they took time just when the Counter-Reformation was demanding speedy results. The new priest needed new auxiliaries to reach the people.

A *Saints*

Sociologists have noted that the starting point of popular movements is often an individual possessing 'charisma', that capacity to express in personality, action and words the profound aspirations of a whole group of followers. (One historian has more prosaically described it as star quality.) In the late sixteenth and early seventeenth centuries there were large numbers of men and women with marked charisma and the Church recognised their value. Nearly all have since been made saints. Some of these saints found their strength in preaching. St Philip Neri in Rome provides a most extraordinary example. He would make his mark by joking and dancing even during church services and his preaching became enormously popular. St Philip did not just reach the people direct. He passed on his skills by gathering together his followers in a new **Oratory**, the Roman Oratory. This in turn inspired Pierre Bérulle to found a French Oratory in 1611. Preaching was to be conducted not just by old-style friars or workaday priests, but by newly trained professionals.

oratory association for prayer

St Philip was not just a preacher; he was also something of a mystic – someone blessed with ecstatic visions of the workings of God. The classic mystic of the later sixteenth century was St Teresa of Avila. In her autobiography, she told of her ecstasy when a most beautiful angel thrust his great arrow into her three times, consuming her soul with the love of God. But Teresa was not by any means obsessed by visions; her success also lies in the fact that she was an intensely practical person. In

PICTURE 30
Ecstasy of St Teresa *by Giovanni Bernini*

her opinion, true religion found its origin in common sense, and common sense told her to reform her own order of nuns, the Carmelites. She did that with great success. Many in Castile were suspicious of that success. Mysticism smacked of bypassing the Church on the route to paradise and there were interests vested in the old ways of the Carmelites. But Teresa was unstoppable. She was too valuable in bringing Catholicism to the people.

Similarly suspect earlier in Rome had been St Ignatius Loyola, founder of the Jesuits. He too was a mystic and yet an intensely practical man. His 6000 letters show how well he kept his finger on the pulse of reform all round the world. His 'charisma' was to find its way into his *Spiritual Exercises*, methodical prayers to enhance spiritual fitness, and into the *Constitutions*, the rules of the Jesuit order. We shall be looking at those at the end of the chapter.

While St Ignatius attended to missionary work in Europe as a whole and far round the globe, St Carlo Borromeo worked on a smaller scale and with minute attention to the detail of the Christian life. Active as Archbishop of Milan between 1566 and 1584, he copied and expanded upon Giberti's work in Verona as a model bishop. His was to be the model execution of the Tridentine decrees. He held frequent synods and set up six **seminaries** in his archdiocese. To ensure that his detailed reforms were carried out, he founded the Oblates of St Ambrose, a local version of the Jesuits, their oaths of loyalty being to the archbishop. Borromeo saw the need to control the laity as well as the priests. He used police to arrest those who obstructed his policies, as well as employing sophisticated techniques of social control.

This sounds like the sort of repression which might stimulate reaction rather than reform, but Borromeo's charisma carried it through. The people saw the archbishop threaten to excommunicate the hated Spanish governor, who quailed at his moral authority. The people saw him give away all his possessions and set an example of self-denial hitherto unknown in Milan. In 1576 the people saw their saintly archbishop follow the example of the lowly Capuchins, tending plague victims in person. It was moral authority that gave Borromeo his hold over people, and this hold was not confined to northern Italy. In 1582 the *Acts of the Church of Milan* were published and became the textbook for every would-be reforming bishop in Europe. Again 'charisma' had carried reform to the people and had not perished with the person of the saint.

seminary training college for priests

See pages 380–2

B *Teachers*

It was realised by the saints described above, as by other reformers, that efficient preaching, organisation and charity were not enough by themselves. The new Catholicism required a full understanding as well as outward compliance, and that could only be achieved through education.

This had been perceived, of course, in the early days of the Catholic Reformation. Erasmus saw the need for efficient education. In France, Jean Standonck had made Montaigu College an exemplary academy of learning from 1499 onwards and Loyola was one of its former pupils – but so was Calvin. Clearly a more systematic 'Counter-Reformation' approach was needed. In the realm of secondary schooling, as in missionary training, this was largely at the initiative of the Jesuits. At first Loyola had thought of training only his own Jesuit priests. But, flexibility being the mark of his character and his order, he saw the education of ordinary children as the invaluable tool it was. In 1552 the first Jesuit non-clerical school was opened at Billom in France. Thereafter the number of Jesuit colleges, combining Jesuit training with secondary schooling for ordinary children, grew to around 200 by 1650, and the Jesuits, renowned for their learning, were frequently to be found on the staff of non-Jesuit universities.

To ensure that their educational investment was earning a maximum return, the Jesuits were highly selective as to ability in their admissions policy. As with so much effective education, the Jesuits indoctrinated their pupils with basic principles but also gave them the capacity to apply them independently. This may be contrasted with the failures of Lutheran schooling where indoctrination pure and simple was tried and largely failed. Parents, even if lukewarm in religious terms, sent their children to the Jesuits for the best education available. Good Catholics were produced, often more pious than their parents, and with a sense of mission.

See page 179

Not all pupils were as high-born as Ferdinand of Styria, later to be Emperor Ferdinand II, but most were aristocratic and many were destined to be men of influence. They remained loyal to their schools, organised in later life into **sodalities**. The Duke of Bavaria was enrolled in 1584 and the nobility were eagerly recruited, but membership spanned the whole social scale from the Emperor to Neapolitan fishermen. Magistrates who were members made it their business to impose discipline on their communities, banning carnival celebrations and 'immoral' dancing. Towns were divided into areas, and sodality members appointed for each to supervise morals and to recruit. Although not constituted in the same way, they bore some resemblance to Calvinist lay elders. They were active in rural missions – a Jesuit would preach on the village green while sodality members would mingle in the crowd in support. In 1640 there were 11 300 members of Jesuit sodalities in the Franco-Belgian province alone.

Jesuit sodalities Jesuit 'old boys' associations

Coupled with their activities as confessors to kings and the high-born, the Jesuits' role as teachers consolidated more than anything else the Catholic renewal among the upper classes of Catholic Europe. But, along with other reforming orders, they were not content with that. There was a missionary impetus to take a re-invigorated Catholicism beyond the bounds of the elite of Catholic Europe.

C *Missioners*

The Jesuits provide the most dramatic examples of missionary work across the globe. They were received by suspicious Samurai in Japan, executed by Protestants in England and eaten by Huron Indians in North America. At the Jesuits' English college founded in 1568 at Douai in Flanders, Fathers Campion and Parsons were trained for what proved to be their fatal mission to England in 1580. Their execution has been made much of in English history but despite the hue and cry surrounding their capture, their work did not go beyond succouring a few of the faithful and must, quantitatively, be put into perspective beside the immense task of converting the pagans of Asia and America and the semi-pagans of rural Europe. It is the latter whom we shall look at next.

See pages 382–4

'Missions being necessary everywhere, we shall preach everywhere, but with preference in the country' (St Jean Eudes, one of the leading French missioners of the seventeenth century). Here the missioners could often find garbled combinations of Protestantism and Catholicism. The people of the remote Alpine valley of Defereggental, for instance, travelled to Salzburg as peddlars and had picked up some Lutheran ideas there, which they had simply tacked on to their usual Catholic devotions. The Capuchins were sent in (with troops) but failed to reconvert these mountain people. The Capuchins and, of course, the Jesuits had seen the need to make religion a country matter, but all manner of missioners and orders were also employed to do so. Many who answered St Vincent de Paul's call to preach to the 'poor people of the fields' came from that saint's establishment at St Lazare founded in 1632. It offered priests fortnight 'refresher courses', as well as basic training for missioners. Some priests needed refreshment when they had found themselves on the front line. A German priest, Nithard Schmidt, found it hard to cope in his parish in 1619 when the villagers, both Catholic and Protestant, refused to stop work for feast days, mocked him during Mass and threw stones at him.

As might be expected from newly efficient Catholics, the rural missions were characteristically methodical. Preaching took place when it would interfere least with agricultural work. To start with, the people were taught simple basic prayers and learned to sing hymns set to popular tunes. Success was judged to be when all the parishioners had recognised their sins. As St Vincent de Paul put it in 1639 'Our maxim is not to leave a village until everybody has made his general confession; and there aren't many in the places we visit who don't.' The approach could be inspirational; alternatively it could be repressive. In 1597 the Jesuits descended upon the people of Aschau-Wildenwart in Bavaria where they found widespread ignorance of Catholic teaching and the influence of Protestant ideas. They interrogated parishioners, holding out the incentive of 'confession certificates' if they would submit, and they would then be left alone, or there was the threat of exile if they chose not to co-operate. Of course, it could not simply end with a round of confessions. Missioners had to leave behind them the signs of greater devotion in attention to the sacraments and feast days and the machinery of instruction in the form of catechism classes, where the essentials of the faith would be recited, and of primary schools. The missioner also had to return every few years to check up on everything.

This sounds quite straightforward. The Tridentine priest, supplemented by saints and missioners, would bring the Catholic renewal to rural Europe. But perhaps 'renewal' is an important word. While one must be wary of exaggerating the point, Jean Delumeau has shown, in *Catholicism between Luther and Voltaire*, that there were many ways in which people of the Middle Ages had scarcely ever been Christianised at all. With regard to them, it was not so much renewal as starting from scratch.

> **KEY ISSUE**
>
> *In what ways were saints, teachers and missioners important to the cause of reform?*

11 ∽ POPULAR CULTURE AND 'CHRISTIANISATION'

'The Age of the Cathedral Builders' – this cliché is too often used to imply that the Middle Ages was an era of simple, constructive faith in comparison to our own secular age. In fact, recent historians, acquainted with the methods of anthropology, have revealed a faith that is far from simple. A primitive rural society grapples with forces – storm, flood, disease – which are not naturally controllable and which require a religion to provide remedies in this world as much as redemption in the next. Delumeau claims that animism – the belief that spirits inhabit all material objects – was prevalent in Europe at least until the Industrial Revolution. Festivals, processions, relics all helped to ward off those evil spirits. Protestants and, up until recently, historians, wrote this off as superstition. It now seems necessary to take it more seriously.

See pages 15–16

Quite consciously, the Church itself had taken these superstitions seriously in its early missionary days. In 601 AD Pope Gregory the Great had recommended that churches be erected on the sites of ancient temples. There is debate about how far the Church went in compromising itself in order to Christianise pagans, but there is firm evidence that the Church was alarmed about the capacity of the people to turn the tables and paganise the Christian religion. Even as late as 1674, the peasants at Autun in France sacrificed a heifer to the Virgin Mary to win protection for cattle against the plague. But the Church was fearful of worse paganism than this – witchcraft.

See pages 202–11

Although the witch hunts started before this period, it is no coincidence that they intensified during this time of Protestant and Catholic reform, although there were other factors involved. Delumeau's argument is that both Protestantism and Catholic reform, for all their differences, were part of a more general movement of 'Christianisation'. There was a demand for a distinctively Christian commitment and no tolerance for folk magic. There was to be no tolerance for the sort of custom in Brittany where women threw dust from the floor of their chapel into the air in order to charm a good wind for their men folk at sea. There was to be no tolerance for the healing at St Dié where the cure for a peasant's dislocated hip was to hang up his breeches, full of ritually gathered horse dung, in the church.

Not only magical charms and folk healing were to be censured by the reforming Church; communal rituals and celebrations were to be condemned where they were too much akin to paganism. May Day fertility rites were banned by Borromeo. He also condemned carnival as a period of gross self-indulgence. In doing so he was reiterating the opinion of so many Catholic reformers starting with Savonarola and Erasmus, and duplicating the attitude to be found amongst the Calvinists of Geneva or the Puritans of seventeenth-century England.

However, while it is true that Protestants and Catholics shared a common aim in Christianisation involving an onslaught on witchcraft and the lesser evils of popular custom, it was the Catholics who were more willing to accommodate the old ways. Semi-pagan customs might be transformed. The Fires of St John, with accompanying rituals the night before the Feast of St John the Baptist, could be made acceptable.

In Catholic Germany the main ritual was the burning on the bonfire of an image of Luther.

Alternatively, the Church might find substitutes for popular customs. Veneration of saints was encouraged. In the bishopric of Passau there had been fifty-six pilgrimage sites before the Reformation, and there were 132 new ones as the Catholic revival progressed. There was no need for a traveller to appeal to a pagan god for protection when St Christopher could do the job. Saints could be popularised by being portrayed in art. St Joseph, often a figure of fun in the Middle Ages, had his reputation enhanced by many a pious painting of the Holy Family.

The great age of baroque art thus derived in part from the need to give the Catholic Church visual appeal and to provide a 'book for the unlearned'. Great artists like van Dyck and Rubens belonged to Jesuit sodalities, and owed much to the Counter-Reformation in the form of patronage and subject matter. Baroque art resided in ornate baroque churches, dramatic buildings designed to impress the people. The Jesuits amongst others were great builders in this style.

Where passive contemplation of art was insufficient, the people could be organised in processions winding their way around the new churches. A wake, a boisterous celebration in the church the night before a Saint's feast day, could be replaced by a vigil, a night spent in religious contemplation under the guidance of a priest. It was seen that popular activity was useful to the Church if only it could be channelled properly.

The guidance of a priest was deemed essential to combat paganism and to reform popular culture and the renewal of Catholicism in the sixteenth century and beyond ensured that guidance was available. However, simple guidance alone did not guarantee success.

KEY ISSUE

How did the Catholic reformers react to popular beliefs and culture?

12 ⌒ SOCIAL CONTROL AND THE NEW CATHOLICISM

In a sense the Church was fighting on two fronts – to stop the people from becoming Protestant and to prevent them clinging to a virtually pagan tradition. To pre-empt both of these, priests could not just guide people or, as a last resort, hand them over to the authorities to burn them when they proved stubborn. They had to learn subtle methods of social control.

Some of these methods have already been touched upon. Education was of great importance. Primary education was virtually invented in the Early Modern period to catch the individual young and bring him or her up with a basic knowledge of Church doctrine and, of course, the authority of the Church.

That authority was reinforced when the priest sat in one side of the Confessional box, brought into use by Carlo Borromeo, while the individual sinner, alone and in the dark, sat in the other side. At a psychological advantage, the priest could then try to ensure inner repentance rather than just a ritual show of 'satisfaction' for sins committed. The Church, through the confessional, learned how to manipulate guilt in an individual rather than relying on society in general to inspire shame in him for his sins.

In fact, the Church relied on society in general as little as possible. Parish registers were introduced to ensure that the major events of life were recorded and controlled. After the Council of Trent, marriage, for instance, was no longer regarded as purely a matter of family alliances; it had no validity unless carried out in the proper sacramental manner before a priest with the free consent of bride and groom. Ordinary people were no longer allowed to organise themselves into free religious associations. These confraternities either died out or were taken over by the Church and placed under the bishop's control, following the example of Borromeo in Milan. Ironically, the Brethren of the Common Life, a confraternity and a fount of Catholic renewal, could not have flourished under this new regime.

John Bossy has emphasised how this destructive side of social control by the Church could be self-defeating. Social structure in the Middle Ages depended very much on kinship – real as in marriage alliance, or artificial as in a confraternity. The Church's new controls hit that structure hard. In addition, the basic social unit remained the family and the Church failed to use that to further its cause. Protestants in contrast did use it successfully in family prayer and domestic Bible reading. Bossy suggests that it was for that very reason, the Protestant example, that the Counter-Reformation Church was afraid of working through the family, domestic religion being seen as 'a seedbed of subversion'. Owing to the Church's reluctance to use the family, 'its educative programme misfired' and its whole impact was brought into question.

Much more research needs to be done before the success of the Church's control of the people in the Early Modern age can be assessed. There was much regional variation and that has yet to be mapped. But the story of one extraordinary character, a miller called Menocchio from Friuli in Italy, pinpoints something of the success and the failure of the Church.

Menocchio drew on wide reading, much conversation and some original thinking to come to the conclusion that the universe had existed before God and it could best be compared to cheese. The cheese had putrefied and out of it had emerged worms, which were God and His angels. The Inquisition could not tolerate these views, especially as Menocchio would preach them to anyone who would listen, and forced him to recant in 1584. The miller, however, was irrepressible. He appeared before the Inquisition again in 1599 and this time he was handed over to the secular authorities to be burned.

In one sense, the case of Menocchio shows the Church's failure. He could not be psychologically controlled. Also, Carlo Ginzburg, who has written his life story entitled *The Cheese and the Worms*, suspects that in Menocchio's talk 'we see emerging, as if out of a crevice in the earth, a deep-rooted cultural stratum'. There were certainly others like him – another miller called Pighino living near Modena, for instance. There may have been many more still who were afraid to talk. The Church could force a show of devotion, boosting the numbers taking Holy Communion at Easter for instance, but it could never be quite certain that those communicants were really devout.

In another sense, however, the Church could face up to Menocchio and his kind as a success. It had kept him under physical control for a time and then kept track of him when his behaviour lapsed. There was an efficiency in that, albeit a cruel one, and Menocchio was at least out of date when he claimed that 'the law and commandments of the Church' were 'all a business'. Even if it was not entirely successful, even if it had to resort to terror tactics sometimes, the Church was more than a business. It had a renewed spiritual mission by the end of the sixteenth century. This meant that the Catholic Church did advance into enemy territory on both fronts, against Protestantism and against independent popular traditions, even if the forces of Catholicism did not entirely win the war.

> **KEY ISSUE**
>
> *How effectively did the Church impose social control on its congregations?*

13 ⌐ THE MISSIONS OVERSEAS

The clearest indication that the Catholic Church of the sixteenth century was not merely responding to the Protestant threat is the extraordinary dynamism with which it undertook missions to the newly discovered lands around the globe. By 1500 Franciscan and Dominican friars had started to cross the Atlantic to use their skills in popular preaching to convert the pagans. Before Ignatius Loyola thought of combating Protestantism, he was all set to convert the Infidel. Jesuits went on to show as much dedication in China or South America as they did in Europe. Some contemporaries saw this activity abroad as compensation for the souls lost to Protestantism at home. But this compensation may be more of an effect than a cause. A vision of Christendom embracing a whole New World certainly pre-dated Luther's protest.

There was as complex a relationship between power and conversion across the world as between power and reform at home. This was especially true in central and southern America, where the Spanish *conquistadores* brought Christianity as part of their imperial baggage. For these crusaders the notion of a just war involved the *requerimento*: a notice could be read to the Indians instructing them to convert. If they ignored it, which would hardly be surprising, that was the justification for the glorious slaughter to begin. The *conquistadores*, however, did not get it all their own way. Bartolomé de las Casas was just one of the leading missionaries to contest this soulless approach. The Pope was persuaded to issue the bull *Sublimis Deus* (1537) which stressed the humanity of Indians and even their willingness to be converted if only a chance was given.

The rate of conversion was enormous. For instance, moving on from South America, the Spaniards had started to colonise the Philippines in the middle of the sixteenth century. By 1620 there were two million Christian converts. Mass baptisms took place, which could admit thousands each day to the Catholic faith, but this raises the question of just how far these converts were actually Christianised.

It is likely that many went through the motions of Christianity because they were scared, at least where the missionaries came with *conquistadores*. Prestige was also a great incentive for conversion. Lower caste Hindus were tempted by the offer of joining that superior caste, the Portuguese. In some cases the simple novelty of a strangely dressed missionary appearing from nowhere would convince indigenous peoples that here was a visitation from a superior god. There is no certain method of assessing or counting faith or its superficiality across the sixteenth-century world. There is one acid test though – the incidence of martyrdom.

In 1549–51 there took place the first Jesuit mission to Japan. St Francis Xavier was the missionary. He had already helped to confirm Goa, a Portuguese settlement on the west coast of India, as a 'little Rome'. During his lifetime he was responsible for about 30 000 baptisms. He was clearly a saint of the charismatic type and Loyola did right to entrust him with the mission to the East. Xavier was to leave a solid base of about 1000 Christians in Japan. By the 1590s there were 300 000 responding strongly to the Christian message during a period of religious and political decadence in their own land. But a national reaction led to the persecution of Christians in 1613, in which many thousands of Japanese Christians died. Their loyalty to their faith to the point of martyrdom suggests something more deep-rooted than a faith founded on fear of Europeans, power, prestige or novelty value.

Even with martyrdom as a test, the nature of the faith could be disputed. The problem of the Church accommodating itself to a pagan culture was raised in the global mission as much as it was in Europe. A fierce debate known as the Rites Controversy beset Matteo Ricci, a missionary in China from 1582 to 1610. His Chinese philosophical writings were thought by some to be adulterating rather than transmitting the Christian message. There was the fear that anything deviating from the culture of the Christian elite was a threat to Christianity; and that was a feature of the Catholic renewal in Europe as it was in the missions abroad.

The unique capacity of the Jesuits to operate successfully in the political sphere showed itself in the overseas missions, as well as in Europe. The Jesuits in China, the Peking Fathers, kept the favour of changing emperors by acting as advisers, even showing their intellectual breadth in running the royal observatory. At the other end of the social scale, the Jesuits of South America organised the territories of the Guaraní along the Parana and neighbouring rivers. The territory was granted to them by Philip III of Spain in 1608 and it accommodated about 100 000 Indians in what evolved into an almost classic utopia – a peaceful population living in well-planned towns, serving the commu-

KEY ISSUE

What were the achievements of Catholic missionaries beyond Europe?

nity and holding goods in common. The Jesuits were in fact creating a secular version of themselves, the Indians living elements of a monastic life while outside the usual monastic discipline. These 'reductions', as the Guaraní autonomous territories were known, lasted until the aggression of slave traders, and the waning of Jesuit fortunes, spelt their end in the eighteenth century.

The example of the Guaraní shows how the Catholic renewal of the sixteenth century could find the fullest expression beyond the confines of Europe. In that remote part of South America, there had been no political obstacles, the dead weight of tradition in that sense being absent. There were also no Protestants to combat – this was something more than just Counter-Reformation.

14 ✍ BIBLIOGRAPHY

**K. Randell, *The Catholic and Counter Reformations* (Hodder and Stoughton, 1990), M. Mullett, *The Counter Reformation* (Lancaster Pamphlets, 1984) and *N.S. Davidson, *The Counter Reformation* (Historical Association, 1987) all outline Catholic renewal well and clarify the main lines of debate. M. Jones, *The Counter Reformation* (CUP, 1995) is an up-to-date survey. While both *M.R. O'Connell, *The Counter Reformation* (Harper Torchbooks, 1973) and *A.G. Dickens, *The Counter Reformation* (Thames and Hudson, 1968) are less recent, they are still full of insight. R. Po-Chia Hsia, *Social Discipline in the Reformation: Central Europe 1550–1750* (Routledge, 1989) shows how Catholicism – or Lutheranism or Calvinism – could be imposed by force by rulers consolidating their power through 'confessionalisation', and his *The World of Catholic Renewal 1540–1770* (CUP, 1998) is the best survey of the consequences of the Counter-Reformation.

15 ✍ STRUCTURED AND ESSAY QUESTIONS

A *Structured questions.*
1. (a) What was achieved at the Council of Trent?
    (b) How effectively did popes and princes apply the Tridentine decrees?
2. (a) What were the main activities of the Jesuits?
    (b) How important were the new orders to the recovery of Catholicism in the sixteenth century?

B *Essay questions.*
1. How adequately does the term 'Counter-Reformation' describe the Catholic renewal of the Early Modern period?
2. What was the role of the popes in the Counter-Reformation?

3.   'It was the work of the new orders rather than the Council of Trent which was most important to the Catholic renewal of the sixteenth century.' Discuss.

4.   Assess the significance of the Jesuits in the Counter-Reformation.

5.   'The Catholic princes of Europe did more to hold back than to advance the cause of Catholic renewal in the sixteenth century.' Do you agree?

6.   What impact did the Counter-Reformation have on the people of Early Modern Europe?

Advice

In a structured essay, it is important not to waste time on irrelevant material because the time for answering such questions is comparatively limited.

See below two sample answers to question 1 (a), *What was achieved at the Council of Trent?* The first would get fewer marks than the second. It is making valid points, and it is putting the Council of Trent in context, but it does not give a direct answer to the question. The second example answers the question quite economically and highlights aspects of the Council's decisions which were most important.

A The Council of Trent was called at the insistence of Charles V. He had wanted a Council to deal with the Protestant question ever since the 1520s but one did not actually meet until 1545. The first session lasted for two years and did not deal with the abuses of the Church as Charles had hoped; instead it defined Catholic doctrine. The second session from 1551–52 was not very successful because Protestants were present and no compromise could be found. The third session was not until 1562–63 because Paul IV (1555–59) was not prepared to risk losing any of his power. At this session the abuses of the Church were finally tackled and many useful decrees were passed.

B The Council of Trent helped to revitalise the Catholic Church in two ways, first by stating what it actually meant to be a Catholic and secondly, by tackling the abuses of the Church which had helped to promote Protestantism. The definition of Catholic doctrine explicitly rejected the major beliefs of the Protestants. The importance of Church tradition and its hierarchy was affirmed, the Bible was still to be the Vulgate although the Pope was to issue an amended version, the seven sacraments and transubstantiation were confirmed and predestination was rejected. The decrees of the third session concentrated on discipline. The responsibilities of bishops and priests were clearly stated and abuses such as pluralism and non-residence were attacked. Seminaries were to be set up to improve the quality of the clergy. Taken together, although the decrees were implemented at a variable pace in different parts of Europe, they were the starting point for a major improvement in the commitment and quality of the priesthood.

16 ⤳ DOCUMENTARY EXERCISE ON THE JESUITS

The purpose of this exercise is to establish what made the Jesuits unique and what made them successful.

See pages 355, 375, 376–7, 383–4

1 The Jesuits have been mentioned in this chapter in relation to various aspects of the renewal of Catholicism. Gather the relevant information together in note form as the starting point of your investigation. As you do so, give emphasis to what made the Jesuits most important to the Church.

2 Ignatius Loyola (1491–1556) was the founder of the Jesuits. His life story was important as his *Autobiography* was to be an inspiration to his followers. Consider the following information and extracts drawn from the *Autobiography*.

PICTURE 31
St Ignatius of Loyola, *attr.*
Juan de Roelas

(i) Loyola was a professional soldier until injured at Pamplona in 1521. While convalescing he read religious works including *Lives of the Saints*, from which he drew his heroes. Thereafter he decided to dedicate his life to the service of God.

(ii) In 1522–23 he lived the life of a holy beggar at Manresa near Barcelona. There in his own words:

> often and for a long time while at prayer, I saw with interior eyes the humanity of Christ. The form that appeared to me was like a white body, neither very large nor very small...I have also seen our Lady in a similar form...if there were no Scriptures to teach us these matters of the faith, I would be resolved to die for them, only because of what I had seen.

(iii) In 1527 Loyola's unusual appearance and preaching landed him in prison in Salamanca where he was investigated by the Inquisition, albeit only for a short time. To a lady who sympathised with him he replied,

> Does imprisonment seem to be such a great evil to you? Well, I will tell you that there are not so many grills and chains in Salamanca that I would not wish for more for the love of God.

(iv) Loyola moved to Paris where he furthered his education from 1528 to 1535. There, with eight friends, he took the three monastic vows and a special one of obedience to the Pope.

(v) At first the aim was to serve as missionaries in Palestine, but war made this impossible. By 1537 Loyola and his followers, now going by the name of the Society of Jesus, were in Rome, but being Spaniards and without a clearly defined role, they were not well received by everyone they encountered there. Loyola reported that some accusers said of him and his companions that they

> were fugitives from Spain, from Paris, from Venice...The legate ordered silence to be imposed on the whole affair, but I did not accept that, saying that I wanted a definite sentence...I went to speak to the Pope at Frascati...he ordered sentence to be given and it was in my favour...

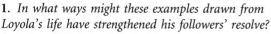

1. *In what ways might these examples drawn from Loyola's life have strengthened his followers' resolve?*
2. *What difficulties does the historian face in using the autobiography as evidence of Loyola's life?*

3 While at Manresa in 1522–23 Loyola was developing his 'spiritual exercises'. They were to be a distinguishing feature of Jesuit practice, but the exercises were often used by non-Jesuits, even including that leader of the *spirituali*, Cardinal Contarini. Here are some extracts from the day-to-day programme of meditation intended to last about a month under the guidance of a spiritual director:

(i) First preliminary. The picture. In this case it is a vivid portrayal in the imagination of the length, breadth and depth of hell.   1

'Second preliminary. Asking for what I want. Here it will be to obtain a deepfelt consciousness of the sufferings of those who are damned, so that, should my faults cause me to forget my love for   5
the eternal Lord, at least the fear of these sufferings will help to keep me out of sin.

First Heading. To see in imagination those enormous fires, and the souls as it were with bodies of fire.

To hear in imagination the shrieks and groans...   10

To smell in imagination the fumes of sulphur...

To taste in imagination all the bitterness of tears...

To feel in imagination the heat of the flames...

(ii) I will try to be ashamed of all my sins, using illustrations; for   14
example, I may think of a knight, standing before his king and the whole court, utterly ashamed at having greatly offended one from whom he had received many gifts and acts of kindness.

(iii) Another picture. A great plain, comprising the entire Jerusalem district, where is the supreme commander-in-chief of the forces of good, Christ our Lord: another plain near Babylon, where Lucifer   20
is, at the head of the enemy.

(iv) 'To arrive at complete certainty, this is the attitude of mind we should maintain: I will believe that the white object I see is black if that should be the decision of the hierarchical Church, for I believe that linking Christ our Lord the Bridegroom and his Church, there   25
is one and the same Spirit, ruling and guiding us for our souls' good.

(v) 'Whilst it is absolutely true that no man can be saved without being predestined and without faith and grace, great care is called for in the way in which we talk and argue about all these matters.   29

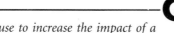

1. *What technique did Loyola use to increase the impact of a religious idea (lines 1–13)?*
2. *Why does Loyola refer to a knight (line 15) and to armies (lines 18–21)? What response was he trying to stimulate?*
3. *Why was it necessary to give entire obedience to the 'hierarchical Church' (line 24)? Is there a connection with Loyola's caution over discussing predestination (lines 27–29)?*

4 In 1539 Loyola put forward a draft charter for the Society of Jesus. It was difficult to get it accepted as there was much suspicion of these monks who did not spend most of their time in prayer and monastic rituals but were free to do other work and to travel wherever they were needed.

Here is an extract:

> All members shall be aware…that this entire Society and its members serve as soldiers in faithful obedience to the most holy lord Paul III and his successors…We are bound to carry out instantly, as far as in us lies, without any evasion or excuse his orders: whether he sends us to the Turks, or into the New World, or to the Lutherans, or into any other realms of infidels or believers…

The Pope accepted the charter in 1540. In 1547–50 Loyola perfected the organisation of the society in his *Constitutions* which included:

> One who is sent to an extensive region such as the Indies or other provinces and for whom no particular district is marked out, may remain in one place for a longer or shorter period. Or, after considering the reasons on one side or the other, while praying and keeping his will indifferent, he may travel about wherever he judges this to be more expedient for the glory of God our Lord.

And as to qualifications the *Constitutions* laid down:

> The profession [to join the society] should be made only by persons who are selected for their spirit and learning, thoroughly and lengthily tested, and known with edification and satisfaction to all after various proofs of virtue and self-denial.

1. *Why did Loyola place such emphasis on the so-called fourth vow 'of obedience to the Pope'?*
2. *What prevented the Jesuits from being mere automatons in the service of the Pope?*

5 Clear evidence of the society of Jesus in action comes from the letters written to and by Jesuits.

Margaret of Parma, later Regent of the Netherlands (1559–67), wrote the following to Father Polanco, a leading Jesuit, in 1556:

> ...I can only tell you, therefore, that you can depend upon my assistance in everything as far as lies in my power, and that you will always find me ready to further your interests and do whatever I can for you in all things.
>
> Accordingly I beg you not to hesitate to address yourself to me on any question which may arise and to remember me in your holy prayers. This will always give me the greatest satisfaction and this we ask in the conviction that it will also be acceptable to God our Father.

A keen follower of Loyola in 1554 was Joanna of Austria, sister of Philip II and shortly Regent of Spain (1555–59). She applied to become a Jesuit, but the Society of Jesus was an all-male order, and it was also necessary that Joanna should remain available for a marriage arranged to suit Habsburg diplomacy.

Much correspondence passed between Castile and Rome, Joanna being referred to under the pseudonym 'Matteo Sanchez' in an attempt to keep the delicate matter secret. It was decided to admit Joanna, ignoring her sex. She was also allowed to take her vows in the knowledge that although she could not break them, the general of the order could release her from them as was the case with any novice. On this basis Joanna became the only Jesuitess in history. In connection with this, Loyola wrote in 1554 to the leading Jesuit in Spain, Father Borgia (the Duke of Gandia):

> ....As to the rest, this person shall not have to change their dress, or residence, nor to give any demonstration whatever of what it is sufficient should be kept between themselves and God our Lord. The Society, or someone from it, shall have the obligation of the care of this person's soul, in so far as it is demanded by God's service and the comfort of that soul, to the glory of God our Lord.

1. *What do these letters tell us about how the Jesuits worked?*
2. *The Jesuits have been accused of casuistry – tortuous moral argument or the assumption that the ends justify the means. How far does the case of Joanna of Austria support the accusation?*

6 To summarise, make a list of the important ways in which the Jesuits were distinctive, identifying their special strengths.

13 Philip II: The Mediterranean

OVERVIEW

Philip II inherited a collection of states that formed a Mediterranean empire comprising Spain, Milan, Naples and Sicily and some outposts in North Africa. Then there were his Atlantic possessions consisting of the Netherlands and the New World. To this was added, in 1580, Portugal and its immense Empire. The Atlantic states had the potential to become a powerful empire to match that of the Mediterranean but Philip failed to forge any links between them, preferring to treat them as distinct entities connected only through Madrid. Like his father Charles V, Philip was beset by problems that made conflicting demands on his resources. He had to face a serious revolt in Granada in 1568 and another in Aragon in 1590. There was also a long-running struggle with the Turks for domination of the Mediterranean and, from 1565, revolt in the Netherlands, which proved impossible to crush.

The reign of Philip II saw a decisive shift in Spanish orientation. For the first twenty years, Philip pursued a defensive policy, seeking to minimise conflict. Spain was a Mediterranean power, concerned above all with the menace of Islam and the Ottoman Turks, but the conquest and annexation of Portugal brought a dramatic change. The focus of attention swung away from the Mediterranean to the Atlantic and Philip became much more aggressive in his foreign policy, waging war not only on the Netherlands but also against England and France. Nonetheless he became ever more dependent on Castile – this is hardly surprising since it was not only his home but also the major supplier of revenue and soldiers for the Empire. In theory each part of the Empire was self-supporting but in many instances Spain had to subsidise the rest. Only Italy and the New World provided a net gain to the treasury. As Kamen has pointed out, Spain was forced into new commitments by being given the Netherlands that it was ill-equipped to bear. Communications with the Netherlands required the maintenance of a precarious supply route through northern Italy and along the eastern border of France, known as the 'Spanish Road'. Creating a sense of unity in the Empire would always have been very difficult. As Braudel wrote, 'The Spanish Empire . . . expended the better part of its energy in struggles against distance.' The burden of empire simultaneously made Spain a great power and promoted a 'golden age' of cultural achievement, while sowing the seeds of decline as the economy struggled to meet the enormous demands placed upon it. The price of pre-eminence was to be very high.

1 ↫ THE NEW KING

Philip II was born in 1527, the much-loved son of Charles V, whose influence had a profound and lasting effect on his son. Philip was the effective ruler of Spain from 1543 when he became regent at the age of sixteen. His father took the opportunity to give him detailed advice which Philip was to follow for the rest of his life. Charles exhorted Philip not to trust anyone and to take advice from as many as possible. He was to rely on God, conceal his feelings and be just to all men. These became the hallmarks of Philip's rule. His piety was unquestioned, he attended Mass daily and religion pervaded all aspects of his life. He endeavoured always to be just in his dealings although at times he justified involvement in assassination, as we shall see. He kept his feelings under strict control, greeting both the triumph of Lepanto and the disaster of the Armada with the same lack of emotion. Philip also disliked ostentatious display, preferring to wear simple clothes and to be addressed as 'Sir' rather than the traditional 'Sacred Catholic Majesty'. Contemporaries, and sometimes historians, found this hard to understand and saw him as cold and uninterested, but Philip could display very warm emotions, as his letters to his daughters reveal.

PICTURE 32
Philip II of Spain, *attr. Sofonisba Anguisciola*

Most of the above characteristics could be seen as strengths but the same is not true of Philip's obsessive lack of trust, which poisoned the atmosphere at court. It also made him reluctant to delegate responsibility and this slowed the workings of his empire to the speed at which he alone could transact business. Although Philip was extremely hard-working, spending some eight or nine hours a day at his desk, he could not hope to deal with all the business of empire unaided and maintain an efficient administration. The problem was compounded by Philip's inability to distinguish the important from the trivial. When the Armada was in preparation, he was engaged in correspondence with Rome about clerical vestments.

Philip was aware of the delays in sending and receiving instructions and it made him determined to make the right decision first time. Unfortunately this slowed the process still further as he sought to consult as widely as possible before making up his mind. His own lack of incisive thought can be seen in this margin note on a suggestion by the Duke of Alva that councillors be given correspondence early enough to make an informed judgement about it: 'Of the zeal of the Duke I am very sure; about the rest, although he is often right about many things, still in some instances perhaps not, and therefore I do not expect to look into all [he says] in order to arrange matters suitably, unless there is more time for it, but for now I will go on thinking about it. In order to take care of this it is necessary to look into other matters, but as I said, all will be studied in order to do what I believe is suitable.'

While Philip deliberated, his empire suffered. Pius V wrote sternly, 'Your Majesty spends so long considering your undertakings that, when the time to perform comes, the occasion has passed.' Philip was not entirely to blame for the slowness of communication but he exacerbated the problem by his hesitancy and his refusal to delegate responsibility so that everything had to go through the centre.

Philip's family life was dominated by death: he lost all four wives, seven of his children and all his siblings. There were also other tragedies. The only surviving son of his first three marriages was Don Carlos, born in 1545, the son of Philip's first wife Maria. His parents were closely related, both grandchildren of Joanna the Mad, and Don Carlos revealed an unstable character from an early age. He could be unpleasantly violent and sadistic. In 1562, Philip made him president of the Council of State hoping that this would produce a sense of responsibility, but in fact Don Carlos became more erratic and began to criticise his father openly. In the mid-1560s he began plotting to escape to the Netherlands and he was also in contact with the rebels. Philip decided that something must be done and in January 1568 Don Carlos was arrested. In July he died in prison. Many blamed Philip for his death and there was considerable speculation that Philip had ordered his murder. In fact this is highly unlikely; Don Carlos indulged in a hunger strike and then excessive eating and it is far more likely that his constitution could not take the strain. It was also perfectly reasonable that Philip should imprison his son who was obviously a menace to society and not fit to rule.

Don Carlos's death left Philip with a problem over the succession that was further magnified when his much-loved third wife, Elizabeth of Valois, died later in 1568 leaving two daughters. As his fourth wife Philip chose his own niece, Anna of Austria, whom he married in 1570. She bore him a succession of sons but only one, the future Philip III, survived beyond infancy. The succession was safe-guarded but only by a hair's breadth.

> **KEY ISSUE**
>
> *How did Philip's style of working affect the government?*

2 ↜ THE ADMINISTRATION

Philip ruled his empire through a series of councils, which had responsibility either for territory, such as the Council of Italy and the Council of the Indies, or for some aspect of government, for example the Council of War. These councils would receive reports, which they would consider and then send with their recommendations to the king. He would annotate these and send them back for further consideration by the council, which would comment before the king made a final decision. (This process was capable of being repeated.) The procedure was painstaking and extremely cumbersome. Philip disliked transacting business directly and therefore everything had to be written down. Not surprisingly, the king often complained that the volume of work was becoming excessive: 'We will see to all this tomorrow, for now I have neither the time nor the head for it.'

The Council of State was nominally the most important council but its function was purely advisory and Philip frequently ignored its suggestions. In practice, all the councils reported directly to the king and functioned independently of one another. I.A.A. Thompson has detailed the ways in which the authority and function of councils clashed, even allowing petitioners to play off one council against another. This led to conflicting orders and disagreements over each council's legitimate sphere of activity. In 1581, for instance, the Council of War protested against the issue of exemptions from billeting obligations by the Council of Castile and the Council of the Indies. Such conflicts were bound to limit the effectiveness of conciliar government, especially as Philip himself often reversed council decisions without bothering to inform them. In these circumstances it is hardly surprising that the councils failed to develop policies of their own. During the sixteenth century the Spanish Empire was unrivalled for its depth of knowledge about its territories and the attention that was given to detail, but since the entire system rested on the speed at which Philip could work, the almost daily flow of information from the provinces was not utilised effectively and the councils were unable to develop their potential administrative efficiency.

It became apparent that some changes would have to be made because the whole system was liable to break down in a crisis; the last years of the reign were a time of even greater stress as the king's capacity to deal with it was declining. Thus, in the 1570s as the financial crisis worsened, Philip turned to the Council of Finance and an assortment of other advisers for a solution. By 1574 a course of action had been agreed upon but nothing was done and a decree of bankruptcy was forced on the king the following year. Ten years later it became physically impossible to transact all business with the old informality, and with Spain taking the offensive in the north a change in the structure of government became essential.

From 1586 the Grand *Junta* acquired an important role in government. This was an informal committee of Philip's chief ministers and it supervised the overall direction of policy. Philip often disregarded its advice at first, but increasingly came to rely on its recommendations. The Grand Junta had a number of sub-committees that dealt with specific problems and were convened for as long as was necessary. The real power in the Grand Junta was exercised by an inner ring, known as the Junta of the Night. As Philip's reign drew to a close, this inner ring was formulating overall strategy and taking decisions that were referred to the king for his approval. This relieved much of the burden on Philip and enabled Spain to prosecute her wars against the Atlantic powers. A key figure in the conciliar system was the secretary of state, who acted as an intermediary with the king and had an important role in directing the business of the councils. Philip's secretary from 1543 to 1566 was Gonzalo Pérez, who enjoyed enormous influence. On his death the secretaryship of state was divided into two roles, one dealing with northern Europe and the other with the Mediterranean. This division may have been due to the volume of work but it is equally likely to have been dictated by Philip's excessively suspicious nature – he disliked anyone but himself having a total knowledge of events. Gabriel de Zayas became secretary of the north

Junta a committee for running the country

and Gonzalo's illegitimate son, Antonio Pérez, became secretary of the south and came to wield great influence over the king.

The secretaries all came from the class of university-educated lawyers. This was the group that Philip preferred to employ because, unlike the *grandees*, they owed their position entirely to him. Diego de Espinosa (1502–72) is an example. He was a priest who had trained in law and became president of the Council of the Inquisition in 1564 and additionally president of the Council of Castile in 1565. He was described a year later as 'the one man in all Spain in whom the King places most confidence and with whom he discusses most business'. No one else was allowed to even approach the position of trust which Espinosa had enjoyed.

Philip could not, however, ignore the *grandees* and they were given positions of the highest status, but Philip did not allow them much influence. Koenisberger has pointed out that Philip, like Charles V, tried to rule his empire through his personal control of patronage and all official appointments. Unfortunately, as Philip did not follow his father's practice of constant travelling, the non-Castilian parts of the Empire felt excluded from the king's favour. It also made Philip more reliant on his secretaries since he needed advice, and the nature of his government excluded a free flow of information. This gave the secretaries enormous power because all petitioners had to work through them and it is hardly surprising that the system was open to abuse. Philip wished to choose only good ministers but because he insisted on rigid personal control, he actually promoted corruption and secrecy.

KEY ISSUE

What were the strengths and weaknesses of the conciliar system?

3 ↠ FACTION AND THE PÉREZ AFFAIR: A CASE STUDY

'Transact business with many and do not bind yourself to or become dependent upon any individual.' Philip took these words of his father's to heart and encouraged subordinates to spy on their masters and report back to him. He also encouraged quarrels between ministers and institutions in the vain hope that he would have a clearer idea of what each was doing and be in a position to control them more easily. In fact the results were wholly negative. Mediocrity and conservatism were encouraged as no one wished to draw unfavourable attention to himself. Paradoxically, even Philip disliked the results of this system despite promoting it in the first place. He hated the tension between opposing camps and wanted above all 'holy harmony and good government'.

Faction was most serious at court, where career advancement was impossible without allegiance and even the greatest would seek allies. So 'when Ruy Gomez de Silva sought military office for his brother in Italy, he did not rely solely on his personal request to the king; he urged secretary Gonzalo Perez to help him persuade the council to recommend his brother. The request was successful' (M.J. Rodriguez-Salgado). It could also be very difficult if one's patron was in disgrace. Between 1560 and 1564, Cardinal Granvelle dominated the government of the Netherlands but his views carried little weight in Spain because his patron the Duke of Alva was out of favour.

Koenigsberger has shown how this damaging faction spread throughout Spanish society. 'Everywhere, provincial estates, city councils, cathedral chapters, law courts, even universities, tended to manoeuvre against each other, to dispute rights of jurisdiction, to claim financial and administrative autonomy.' These struggles transferred themselves to the court through the patronage system, 'everything depended on who had the king's ear. Given the unreliability of the king's favour … political and corporate manoeuvres turned into deadly power struggles.'

The factions were not fixed in their personnel or ideology. They were loose groupings with broad policy aims, which altered according to the perceived advantage of maintaining or transferring allegiance. There were two main factions, one led by the Duke of Alva (which argued for repression of rebels in the Netherlands as a priority) and the other by Ruy Gómez de Silva, Prince of Eboli, who had married into the powerful Mendoza family (which backed a more conciliatory approach in the Netherlands and a more assertive foreign policy elsewhere). Gabriel de Zayas was linked to Alva's faction and Antonio Pérez to Eboli's, and on the latter's death in 1573, Pérez became leader of his faction. In the same year Alva was disgraced because of his unsuccessful policy of repression in the Netherlands.

PICTURE 33
Antonio Pérez, *artist unknown*

Philip already relied heavily on Pérez and he exploited this dependence. In the Netherlands, Don John of Austria, the king's illegitimate half-brother, was made governor in 1576. Don John was a good soldier and one of Philip's most trusted commanders, but he was ambitious and sought a kingdom for himself. He had hoped to carve one out in North Africa and only tolerated being sent to the Netherlands because of the possibility of invading England and marrying Mary Queen of Scots. Don John's secretary, Juan de Escobedo, had been a protégé of Pérez who expected to be kept informed of Don John's plans. Conflict between these and the wishes of Philip, who suspected the ambitions of his brother, was to lead to trouble.

Escobedo was sent to Madrid in 1577 to try and obtain more money. To further his cause Escobedo apparently threatened to reveal to Philip that Pérez had been selling state secrets and that he was involved in a liaison with the Princess of Eboli, which might have involved negotiations with the Dutch rebels. Pérez decided that Escobedo must be eliminated and he persuaded Philip that Escobedo was a danger to the state. Three assassins murdered Escobedo in March 1578. Popular rumour immediately blamed Pérez and Escobedo's family demanded vengeance, which Philip was not prepared to take since he was implicated himself. His suspicions about Pérez were, however, aroused and these deepened during the negotiations about the Portuguese succession in 1578. Pérez was working with the Princess of Eboli to secure the throne (which Philip wanted himself) for the Duchess of Braganza, in the hopes that a marriage could be arranged between Eboli's daughter and Braganza's son.

These suspicions were confirmed when Don John's private correspondence arrived in Madrid in 1579 and showed that Pérez had been lying when he persuaded Philip that Escobedo was a danger to the state. All that Philip needed before he could take action was an alternative adviser. The Duke of Alva had been banished to his estates for allowing his son to make an unauthorised marriage, so with both factions discredited, Philip turned to Cardinal Granvelle, who had been in Italy since 1564. The night he arrived in Madrid, Pérez was arrested and the two factions disappeared from court. No real action was taken against Pérez until 1589, in the soul searching which followed the defeat of the Armada. He was tortured, made to confess to murder and sentenced to death, whereupon he escaped and fled to Aragon where he was instrumental in provoking revolt in 1590. The factions might have been overthrown by 1580 but their effects were to dog Philip into the last decade of his reign.

> **KEY ISSUE**
>
> *How far can Philip be blamed for the unhealthy results of faction?*

4 ⌐ CHECKS TO ROYAL AUTHORITY

It was once fashionable to assert that Philip II was an 'absolute' king, in other words that he had no effective checks to his power. This is a misleading view. Philip may have appeared to be free from constraints but there were many features of his rule that prevented it from being absolute. These checks included physical factors such as distance and the lack of sufficient royal officials to keep a firm hand on administration.

Philip's attempts to exert a centralised control over every aspect of government were seen in the army. Under Charles V, much of the permanent military establishment had been farmed out to contractors. By 1580 the entire military establishment had been restored to the Crown and was run by royal ministers. The demands of war placed great strains on the administration, especially after 1580 when Spain took on a more aggressive role and had to create a high seas fleet. The Council of War was in control of military organisation but it did not function entirely satisfactorily; in February 1586 there were only three members left in the council and the secretaryship was vacant, yet this was the moment when it was decided to send an Armada against England. This caused a breakdown in the system of centralisation and private contractors and the localities gradually assumed responsibility for military matters again.

corregidores royal officials who administered the localities

Taxes were farmed out with a corresponding lack of control. Inefficiency was rife at all levels, from the king down, and it was only in co-operation with local oligarchies of nobility or clergy that the Crown could enforce its wishes. There were sixty-six *corregidores* in Castile who acted as the king's representatives but they were powerless on their own and could only hope to be effective working with local élites. The *Cortes* of Castile, although reduced to little more than a tax-voting machine, did retain some hold on the king because it voiced popular feeling about government policy and, if the *Cortes* became too insistent, the king was unwise to ignore it. Thus, in the 1590s the *Cortes* refused to grant more money for nearly four years because of the exhaustion of the country.

Cortes the Castilian or Aragonese equivalent of a parliament

Outside Castile, Philip respected the traditional liberties, which put considerable restraints on royal power, especially in Aragon. But the biggest restriction to his power was the large part of the country that was outside his jurisdiction. For example, as Kamen shows, in the province of Salamanca sixty-three per cent of the territory was under noble jurisdiction and six per cent under Church control. Some of the nobles ran their holdings as virtually independent states and this gave the *grandees* great power. The Duke of Medina Sidonia was able to raise 10 000 militia from his estates; like many nobles he increased the size of his holdings under Philip II because the king sold the lands of the three military orders. Eighty towns were transferred from royal to seigneurial jurisdiction between 1516 and 1575. The motive behind this

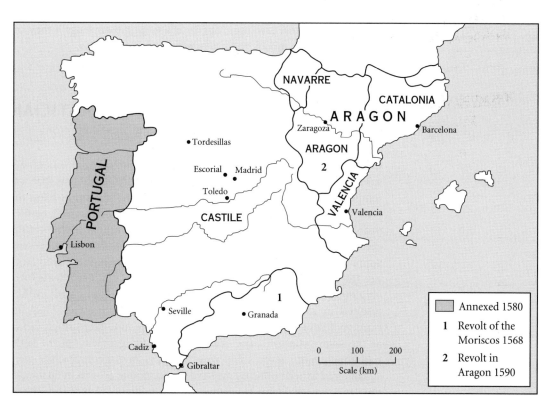

MAP 18
The Spanish possessions of Philip II

diminution of royal authority was finance. Lack of sufficient resources was the biggest constraint on Philip as absolute ruler.

Michele Suriano, a Venetian ambassador, commented on the limits to Philip's authority in 1559:

KEY ISSUE

Is it true that 'Philip II had absolute jurisdiction over national affairs but could intervene little in the localities'?

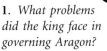

1. *What problems did the king face in governing Aragon?*
2. *Summarise in your own words the king's position in Castile.*

The Aragonese claim to be independent and to govern themselves as a republic of which the king is head. He may not succeed to the government unless they have elected him. They are so zealous to preserve their independence that they contest every little thing to prevent the king from having greater authority over them. They make difficulties even where they have no right, so that Queen Isabella used to say that her husband, King Ferdinand, would have been pleased if the Crown of Aragon had actually rebelled, since he would then have been able to reconquer it and impose his own laws. The kingdom of Castile, on the other hand, is governed by councillors and ministers whom the king appoints, because he is the supreme arbiter of laws, finances, grants, justice and matters of life and death. All the nobles, however, are so privileged that they have no other obligation than to serve the king in time of war, at his expense and then only for the protection of Spain. When Charles wished to abolish their privileges, he was opposed by all the grandees ... So the Aragonese maintain their liberty, and the nobles of Castile their privileges, openly challenging their kings if they try to abolish or modify their privileges and jurisdictions.

5 ↝ ROYAL FINANCE AND THE CASTILIAN ECONOMY

Like most monarchs, but more acutely than many, Philip was always short of money. He was in a state of perpetual financial crisis that was temporarily alleviated, but not solved, by bullion shipments from the New World because the underlying problems were not tackled. Spain's problem above all was that her resources were insufficient to meet the demands of empire that were placed on them. The Castilian economy simply could not cope with the constant warfare which resulted from her imperial commitments and therefore short-term expedients were employed in order to maintain the next season's campaigns, which resulted in mortgaging the future to pay for the present. Thus the burden of debt and consequent repayments became increasingly heavy as the reign progressed and made the financial problems of the latter part much more severe. The windfall gains of American silver were squandered instead of being invested for economic growth in Spain and they encouraged Philip to change from a policy of defence to one of aggression, which was to have disastrous results for Spain in the seventeenth century.

Philip more than trebled his income but the debt, which he had inherited from his father, rose even faster and his commitments continued to increase so that the gap between income and debt yawned ever wider. What made matters worse was that Crown expenditure was much heavier at the end of the reign, largely because of the enormous increase in the cost of war. The Lepanto campaign of 1571 cost 1 100 000 ducats, of which 400 000 came from the Italian kingdoms. Seventeen years later the Armada cost about 10 000 000 ducats, of which Castile contributed around seventy per cent. These appalling costs destroyed the financial viability of the state. The only way for Philip to resolve his financial problems and establish a firm foundation for future expenditure was to have a prolonged period of peace during which the exchequer could be reformed and the country's economy built up again. He never achieved this and so his financial plight worsened, not helped by such projects as the building of the Escorial.

The king relied principally on two sources of revenue – the Indies and Castile. His other dominions were self-supporting in theory and in the case of Italy this was largely true. Although Castile bore the bulk of the cost of campaigns against the Turks, the Italian kingdoms contributed according to their means. They were not prepared to be as generous for hostilities in the Atlantic. The Netherlands, which had made an important contribution to Charles V's imperialism, became the most serious drain on the treasury. Between 1567 and 1600 about 80 000 000 ducats was sent to the Netherlands. The eastern kingdoms of Spain were too poor to yield much and too hedged about by liberties to make it worth pressing them. Only Castile and the Indies were left.

The amounts received from the New World showed a steady increase throughout the reign, from about 500 000 ducats a year to 2 000 000 ducats in the 1590s. Even in the best years it never amounted to more than one-fifth of government revenue but its great value lay in the fact that it was hard currency, it could be relied upon and financiers were willing to make loans on the basis of repayment from the treasure fleets. It thus enabled Philip to continue with his grandiose projects for longer than would otherwise have been possible.

Castile provided almost all of the rest of Philip's income and there were three different sources. There was the king's own revenue, church dues and votes by the *Cortes*. The king's own revenue included Crown lands, feudal dues, salt taxes and mineral rights and the lands of the Castilian military orders. Together, all these brought in about 600 000 ducats a year but this tended to diminish over time as the king sold land for immediate profit.

The Church revenues were much more significant. They included the 'Royal Third' which was a third of all tithes. This yielded 400 000 ducats a year rising to 800 000 ducats by the end of the reign. There were also the 'three graces', Church taxes such as the *cruzada* (originally intended to finance the *Reconquista*) which depended on periodic renewal by the Pope, an important political issue. All three brought in 1 400 000 ducats by the 1590s when the Church was providing more than one-fifth of government income. It seems likely that one bishop who complained in

1574 that the Crown was taking more than half of the wealth of the Church was speaking the truth.

The final and most important source of all was taxation voted by the *Cortes*. Existing taxes were tripled between 1559 and 1577 (compared with overall inflation at twenty-five per cent). This was a turning point: many towns were unable to pay and the *alcabala*, the main sales tax, had to be reduced by 1 000 000 ducats to 1 900 000 ducats a year. The limit had been reached in Castile's taxable potential but even so, faced with the financial crisis caused by the Armada, the *Cortes* reluctantly agreed to a new subsidy, the *millones* of 8 000 000 ducats to be collected over six years. The municipalities raised this money by excise taxes on basic foodstuffs, meat, wine, oil and vinegar, so that the poor were hardest hit. In 1592–93 Philip received nearly 10 000 000 ducats from Castile but this was the peak; the Castilian economy could no longer tolerate such heavy exactions and its decline was hastened.

Even these levels of support were insufficient for Philip's needs and he resorted to the sale of lands, titles and offices with a corresponding diminution in his future revenues and an additional burden of salaries, as well as the inevitable increase in corruption and inefficiency of inferior officials. The worst expedient in terms of its long-term effect was the sale of *juros* or state bonds, which brought in immediate cash at the price of mortgaging future income. By 1600 interest payments to *juro* holders took forty per cent of total income. With all his efforts, Philip was unable to prevent himself going bankrupt in 1575 and 1596. (This meant that he had to reschedule his debts and arrange a lower rate of interest over a longer period. It is not the same as the modern cancellation of debts.) Many textbooks also claim that he went bankrupt in 1557 as well. Rodríguez-Salgado has shown that, although effectively insolvent, the order for bankruptcy was never actually carried out. The reign ended as it had begun, in financial chaos.

Philip II's warfare did not bring the benefits to the Spanish economy that might have been expected. Spanish industry was unable to provide the necessary munitions so that four-fifths of the firearms used to suppress the revolt of the **Moriscos** were imported. Much of the bullion was immediately re-exported to foreign financiers in payment of debts and most of the soldiers were overseas so that those countries received the benefit of their wages. Thus there was a lack of capital investment in Spanish industry which was coupled with crippling taxation to create industrial stagnation. Spain became vulnerable to imports of manufactured goods, especially as she was unable to supply the expanding American market and this further depressed local industrial initiative. Seville boomed because of the activities of foreign merchants but it was a false prosperity relying on external investment. It created a temporary illusion of economic activity but there was no solid base for long-term growth. A series of epidemics made matters worse, with a dramatic effect on the population in some areas; for example, Segovia, a city of 28 000, lost 12 000 in the plague of 1598–99. Deserted villages and the decay of agriculture became increasingly common phenomena

TABLE 11

Finance in Castile

National debt (in millions of ducats)

1560	25.5
1575	40.0
1598	85.5

from 1570 onwards. It would seem that the imperialism of Philip II brought little benefit to his native land.

6 ⤳ THE REVOLT OF THE *MORISCOS*

1568 was a black year for Philip; not only did he have the personal tragedy of the deaths of his wife and son but there were also major political upheavals including strained relations with both England and France. The worst of these was a major rebellion by the **Moriscos** of Granada which broke out on Christmas Eve 1568, and took two years to suppress, laying the heart of Spain open to an attack by the Turks.

The causes of the *Morisco* dissatisfaction were deep-rooted. They were brought to breaking point by the ill-considered policies of the government and the insidious effects of faction. The *Moriscos* were dangerously concentrated in a few areas of Spain; in Granada they comprised over fifty per cent of the population. Here they formed a race apart, with their own language, customs and lifestyle. These had been prohibited under Charles V but the edicts had not been strictly enforced and the Captain General of Granada, the Marquis of Mondejar, acted as their protector, keeping in check the hostility of the Christian population.

At the time of Philip II's accession, a number of factors, which were not entirely planned, combined to bring about a drastic decline in *Morisco* fortunes. The *Moriscos* derived much of their income from silk cultivation and weaving; this industry suffered when export restrictions were imposed in the 1550s and the tax on silk was more than doubled between 1560 and 1565. A further threat to *Morisco* livelihood came after 1559 when agents of the Crown checked all title deeds in order to reclaim Crown lands. Those who had no legal evidence of ownership were fined or lost their land. Those who suffered were almost all *Moriscos*: 100 000 hectares was transferred to Christian hands in the period 1559–68 alone.

These difficulties for the *Moriscos* coincided with a weakening of the position of Mondejar, exposing them to further attacks. Mondejar was in dispute with the Church, the *audiencia* (the supreme court in the south of Spain), the municipal council and the Inquisition. These feuds brought local administration in Granada to a virtual standstill. The enemies of the captain-general found a spokesman at court in the Marquis de Los Vélez, so the protests and warnings of Mondejar about new measures against the *Moriscos* went unheeded. After the siege of Malta in 1565, there was much greater fear about the existence of the Moorish community and in 1567 new restrictions were issued prohibiting the use of Arabic, native costumes, Moorish surnames, customs and ceremonies. Philip showed no awareness of the likely backlash to such cultural oppression.

Petitions by the *Moriscos* and Mondejar for the suspension of the edicts were ignored. There was a complete harvest failure in the south in 1567 and this, together with the failure of the judges of the *audiencia* to protect the *Morisco* farmers from bandits, led to a breakdown in public order and the plotting of rebellion which erupted at the end of 1568. The revolt of the *Moriscos* broke out partly because they knew there was no militia, the guards were undermanned, the towns had no military supplies and the coasts were incapable of resisting enemy attack.

The rebellion involved about 30 000 *Moriscos* at its height. The two years before it was suppressed were the most dangerous of the reign for Philip. Spain had been stripped of troops to send with Alva to the Netherlands and the internal defences were pitiful. Philip was saved because the Turks and the Algerians contented themselves with sending messages of support while seizing the opportunity to take Cyprus and Tunis. Eventually, Don John, Philip's illegitimate half-brother, re-established royal control at the end of 1570 after a campaign marked by atrocities on both sides.

It was decided to settle the *Morisco* problem by breaking up their communities and relocating them throughout the peninsula. Long processions of chained and fettered *Moriscos* were led away, at least twenty per cent dying on the way. Granada lost about 120 000 people and the Christians sent to replace them lacked their skill in agriculture. This did not solve the *Morisco* problem but merely extended it. They remained an unassimilated minority and a final solution was adopted in 1609 when the *Moriscos* were expelled.

KEY ISSUE

How far was it Philip's fault that the Moriscos *rebelled?*

7 ⌐ THE CHURCH

A *Relations with the Papacy*

'The King of Spain, as a temporal sovereign, is anxious above all to safeguard and to increase his dominions..The preservation of the Catholic religion which is the principal aim of the Pope is only a pretext for His Majesty whose principal aim is the security and aggrandisement of his dominions.' Thus wrote Pope Sixtus V in 1589, illustrating that, far from the Pope and Philip II working in harmony as the two halves of the Counter-Reformation, there was considerable friction between them. Philip's relations with Sixtus were particularly bad but there were conflicts with virtually every pope on two main issues: foreign policy and ecclesiastical jurisdiction.

Men said there was no pope in Spain and Lynch has stated that the Crown's domination of the Church was 'probably more complete in Spain than in any other part of Europe including Protestant countries'. The king made all the major ecclesiastical appointments, he controlled the Council of the Inquisition and he enjoyed the revenues of vacant sees. In 1572, appeals by Spaniards to Rome were forbidden and the king insisted on his right to scrutinise papal bulls and, if necessary, forbid their publication in his dominions.

In foreign policy, religious considerations were secondary to political and economic ones. Philip would not be rushed into war against England, nor was he prepared to follow up the Battle of Lepanto in the eastern Mediterranean. It was the question of France after the accession of the Protestant Henry of Navarre as Henry IV that caused most friction.

Philip wrote stiffly to Sixtus V:

> Nothing has surprised me more than to see Your Holiness, after an act inspired by God [the bull against Henry IV] leaving time to the heretics to take root in France, without even ordering that the Catholic partisans of 'the Béarnais' [Henry] should separate from his cause. The Church is on the eve of losing one of its members; Christendom is on the point of being set on fire by the united heretics; Italy runs the greatest danger, and in the presence of the enemy we look on and we delay! And the blame is put upon me because, looking at those interests as if they were mine, I hasten to Your Holiness as to a father whom I love and respect, and as a good son remind him of the duties of the Holy See!... God and the whole world know my love for the Holy See, and nothing will ever make me deviate from it, not even Your Holiness by the great injustice you do me...But the greater my devotions the less I shall consent to your failing in your duty towards God and towards the Church, who have given you the means of acting, and, at risk of pressing Your Holiness and displeasing you, I shall insist on your setting to the task.

Q

1. *How would you characterise the tone of this letter? What effect would such a letter be likely to have upon the Pope?*
2. *'Looking at those interests as if they were mine...' Why would Philip and the Pope have divergent views on what were properly Philip's interests?*

Philip was greatly relieved when Sixtus died in 1590 and made great efforts to secure Spanish nominees for the next two popes, but both died within months and eventually the cardinals rebelled and chose Clement VIII who was reluctant to serve Spanish policy and recognised Henry IV as King of France.

Although relations with the Papacy were often strained, neither side wished to push them to breaking point. This had been illustrated at the beginning of the reign by the case of Carranza, Archbishop of Toledo, who was arrested in 1559 on a charge of heresy, although it was more a matter of his having clashed with the inquisitor-general. The Pope claimed the right to try such an important archbishop, rather than the Inquisition, but Philip was determined to keep the case within Spanish jurisdiction. As a result, the unfortunate Carranza was kept in jail without trial for seventeen years. He was moved to Rome in 1566 because Philip needed his ecclesiastical revenues and the *cruzada* and *excusado* relied on periodic renewal by the Pope. He was then detained in Rome until 1576, being released just before he died. The Pope had not released him earlier because he, for his part, needed Philip to lead the struggle against the Turks and to promote the Counter-Reformation, which both sides valued. Carranza had been the victim of jurisdictional conflict in which neither side would give up or push the other too far.

B *Counter-Reformation and orthodoxy*

The Spanish Church of the mid-sixteenth century was badly in need of reform in spite of Cisneros' work under Ferdinand and Isabella. Absenteeism was widespread – in the diocese of Barcelona in 1549 only six out of sixty-seven parish priests were resident – the clergy were uneducated and ignorant and there were extremes of wealth and poverty. Philip was anxious to reform the Church but only if his existing rights were not infringed, which conflicted with the Pope's desire for universal reform of the church directed by himself. The Jesuits were welcomed by Philip and they undertook important missionary work. Six new bishoprics were created in Aragon and religious houses were revitalised by the suppression of some and the merging of others. The decrees of the Council of Trent were promoted to improve the standard of the clergy and to impose uniform services. The effects must not be exaggerated, but gradually a new spirit of religious fervour became apparent. All theatres were closed in 1597, church buildings became completely dedicated to sacred use and parish priests were instructed to record the attendance of their parishioners.

This new spirit was encouraged by the Inquisition; as long as it retained the authority to determine what constituted orthodoxy, it saw lay religion as a passive affair which was mainly concerned with avoiding error. The Inquisition concentrated less on the discovery of heretics, since there were very few, and more on the moral education of the people. Nearly two-thirds of those arrested in this period were ordinary Catholics unconnected with heresy, and the emphasis was on re-education rather than mere punishment. There was much fear of Protestant heresy in Spain, even though there was so little of it.

Throughout Europe, the middle years of the century saw an end to reconciliation and the growth of militant theology of which both the Jesuits and the Calvinists were examples. Spain was already sensitive to the presence of large numbers of barely assimilated *Moriscos* who might at any time link up with the Turks, and of *conversos* (converted Jews) whose allegiance to Christianity could justifiably be doubted. The discovery in 1557–58 of a number of supposed Protestants in Valladolid and Seville was sufficient to unleash repression against anyone who seemed to deviate in any way from the established orthodoxy. In fact the 'heretics' were not all Protestants – some were mystics who sought direct communion of the soul with God, continuing a tradition begun decades before. It was a sign of the new nervousness that such a harmless deviation should lead not only to severe measures against those involved, but also to a ban on the import of foreign books and to the licensing of all books by the Council of Castile.

From mid-century onwards, the Inquisition, firmly backed by Philip, gradually cut Spain off from external ideas. In 1559 all study in foreign universities was forbidden. The index of censorship was extended until it included over 2500 books, many of them by Spaniards of unquestionable orthodoxy. Spain, which had previously been one of the most open of societies culturally, became virtually isolated.

Philip was determined to eliminate all traces of heresy. He also saw that the Inquisition was a useful instrument to do this and that it simultaneously increased his control. King and *La Suprema*, the Council of the Inquisition, were in complete harmony.

KEY ISSUE

What was the main role of the Inquisition?

8 ↜ FOREIGN POLICY

A *The Turks and the struggle for the Mediterranean*

The *Moriscos* represented one part of the struggle against Islam. The greater part of Spanish effort was directed to the continuing war in the Mediterranean against the Ottoman Turks and their North African clients. Spain was open to attacks by corsairs and **Barbary pirates** but it was Italy that was in real danger from the Ottoman offensive. With some exceptions, the major sea battles concentrated on the narrows between Sicily and Tunis. This was to prove the decisive line between east and west, Turk and Christian.

See Chapter 10

Barbary pirates Muslim pirates who operated out of ports on the north African coast

Philip did not entertain the grandiose dreams of Charles V; he had no desire to lead a crusade to Constantinople. After a brief and disastrous expedition to Djerba in 1560 described below, his policy was strictly defensive, with the aim of containing the Ottoman advance as much as possible. In this he was relatively successful. The 1550s were a bad decade for the Christians; the knights of St John were expelled from Tripoli, the Spanish fortress of Bougie was lost, a Turkish force penetrated to Minorca and Corsairs severely disrupted trade from Spain to Italy. It is no wonder that the defence of the Mediterranean was considered to be of primary importance by Castilians, and it was in this area that the resources of the monarchy were concentrated until 1567, when the Netherlands came to the fore.

It was the Peace of Câteau-Cambrésis which freed Philip from his northern commitments and enabled him to attempt the recapture of Tripoli, lost in 1551, and so restore the barrier across the central Mediterranean, leaving Algiers isolated. The original idea of a swift raid was abandoned, against Philip's better judgement, for a more ambitious project which took six months to prepare. The element of surprise was lost and the island of Djerba was taken as an advanced base in 1560. This was an exposed position and the Turks attacked. Twenty-eight galleys were lost and 10 000 troops were stranded and forced to surrender. This was a great blow to Spanish power and prestige and the loss of twenty-five or more galleys with 4000 crew in a freak storm in

1562 meant that the fleet was almost halved in size. Spanish resources had to be diverted to carry out a costly programme of reconstruction and all operations in the future were designed to safeguard the fleet. In the meantime, Italy and Spain had to endure attacks by squadrons of Barbary pirates, which they were powerless to prevent. So, in 1561, Naples was blockaded by thirty-five vessels and there was a raid into the interior of Granada which carried off 4000 prisoners. Every summer the Christian powers braced themselves for the next attack and it was not until the end of September that the tension relaxed as the campaigning season drew to its close.

By 1564 Spain had nearly a hundred galleys, which were soon to be needed, as in May 1565 the Turks attacked Malta. Twenty-five thousand troops confined the knights of St John to a few forts but they continued to resist stoutly until September when a relief force eventually arrived. Philip has been criticised for the time taken to relieve the island but he did not want to risk losing by sending an inferior force. The successful relief of Malta raised Christian morale and they were given a respite over the next four years as Suleiman I died in September 1566 and it took some time for Selim II to establish himself as sultan. Philip was thus able to send Alva to the Netherlands with the best troops from Italy and he also turned his attention to the revolt of the *Moriscos*. These problems meant that Spain was less prepared than

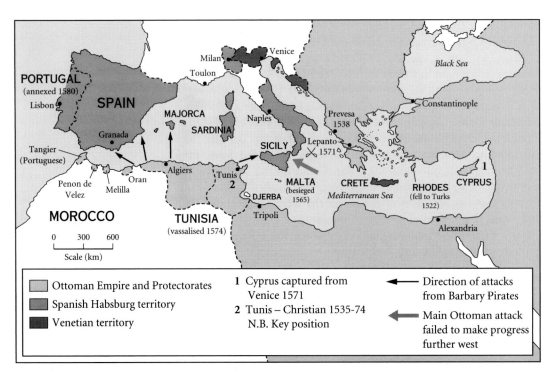

MAP 19
The struggle for the Mediterranean

she might have been for the new Turkish offensive when it came in 1570.

The Turks returned in force, seized Tunis and then invaded the valuable Venetian possession of Cyprus. This new threat caused the Christians to overlook their differences and to form a Holy League of Spain, Venice and the papal states in 1571. In return for appointing the commander, Spain contributed half of the money and forces, but in practice it was an Italian campaign with major contributions from Naples and Sicily. The Pope also granted a special tax, a *subsidio*, for the maintenance of sixty galleys. The commander-in-chief was Don John. On 7 October 1571 he led his forces in the last great galley battle off the coast of Greece at Lepanto. The Christians' victory was absolute. Only thirty-five out of 230 Turkish galleys escaped, 30 000 were killed or wounded while the allies lost only twelve galleys. The whole of Christendom rejoiced at the humiliation of their apparently invincible foe.

In fact the victory solved nothing. It gave a boost to morale but did not change the unfavourable military situation. The Turks completed their conquest of Cyprus thus driving the Christians out of the east Mediterranean. A massive rebuilding programme was undertaken so that the Turkish fleet in 1574 was larger than it had been in 1571. However, it was a severe blow to the prestige of a Muslim leader who depended for support on his success in the Holy War and it paved the way to eventual disengagement by both sides.

In the short term, there was no follow-up to the victory because Philip was not prepared to risk his fleet in the eastern Mediterranean, especially when there was the possibility of an attack by France. He also told his ambassador in Rome in June 1572 that he wanted 'to gain some benefit for my own subjects and states from this league and all its expenses, rather than employ them in so risky an undertaking as a distant expedition in the Levant'. This illustrates that the differences between the allies were surfacing once more. Don John remained in Sicily, firmly in the western half, while the interests of Venice lay in the eastern Mediterranean. It was only the persuasiveness of the Pope, Pius V, which had brought them together and it came as no surprise to Philip when Venice abandoned the League and made a separate peace with the Sultan in March 1573. Reverting to a Spanish policy, Don John took Tunis in 1573, providing an obvious target for the rebuilt Turkish fleet in 1574. The Sultan tried to link up with the rebels in the Netherlands and the *Moriscos* in Spain but the effort of co-ordinating attacks over such great distances proved too difficult. However, Philip was aware of the diplomatic activity and, as he was also on the verge of his 1575 bankruptcy, Tunis was abandoned to the Turks once more in 1574.

In 1576, Morocco was captured by a Turkish vassal and turned into an **Ottoman protectorate**, completing Turkish control of North Africa. Then the Persian Shah died, which opened possibilities for the Ottomans to the east, while those in the Mediterranean were becoming increasingly difficult to exploit as the frontier of Ottoman power grew

KEY ISSUE

What was the significance of the Battle of Lepanto?

Ottoman protectorate a state which was under the protection of the sultan but which was nominally independent

ANALYSIS

Braudel and the history of the Mediterranean

The modern view of Philip II and his empire has been shaped to a great extent by the work of one historian – Fernand Braudel. His *The Mediterranean and the Mediterranean World in the Age of Philip II*, first published in 1949, has coloured later historians' perceptions of that period and also challenged many to reassess the study of history as a whole. Braudel belonged to the Annales school of historians which sought to reverse the traditional way of looking at history through a political narrative, by concentrating on the underlying structure of geographical, social and economic conditions which governed events. As he put it, 'statesmen were, despite their illusions, more acted upon than actors'; 'even in the investigation of short-term causes, we are often obliged to look to structural history for an answer'. History for him was in three layers – on the surface, the least important, the play of events; beneath them the *conjonctures*, that is the material, economic or social conditions which might change over several generations; finally, the history of the *longue durée*, the bedrock of mostly geographical constraints which change imperceptibly if at all.

Even something like a shortage of fish could be a *conjoncture* with far-reaching consequences. There was a scarcity of fish in the Mediterranean, so there were not enough fishermen and therefore not enough sailors. The Basque fishermen discovered seemingly inexhaustible supplies of cod off the coast of North America and this helped to transform the Atlantic into a region of vast economic potential while the Levant and Venice, once the major source of riches in Europe, was condemned to a slow decline. The annexation of Portugal becomes just one part of a more complex picture, which explains why Spain turned its orientation away from the Mediterranean and towards the Atlantic.

Braudel's subject was the Mediterranean – its climate and currents, the mountains, rivers and plains of the lands that bordered it. They constituted the history of the *longue durée* within which Philip II and the Ottoman sultans fought their battles. Most historians concentrate on these conflicts. Braudel was concerned with the environmental conditions that all rulers had to face, underlying all that happened.

further from Constantinople. (The Ottoman sultans were subject to distractions on other fronts, as much as Charles V or Philip II.) For his part, Philip was very anxious to have a respite in the Mediterranean because of the collapse of royal authority in the Netherlands. He held secret talks about peace, leading to a truce in 1578, which became a formal armistice in 1580. Two generations of conflict ended favourably for the Turks who had greatly extended their territory and power. The Mediterranean became a historical backwater as the centre of conflict shifted to the Atlantic. Philip's policy had not defeated the Ottoman menace but it had contained it and peace was eventually secured.

B *The annexation of Portugal*

While Philip was recognising the futility of further conflict against the Turks, his nephew King Sebastian of Portugal was planning a crusade against the new puppet ruler of Morocco. In 1578, Sebastian and the greater part of the Portuguese nobility were killed at the battle of Alcazar. The childless king was succeeded by his elderly uncle, Cardinal Henry. Philip immediately saw his chance as the next legitimate heir, especially as the destruction of the army had left the country undefended.

Philip adopted a two-pronged policy with considerable skill. He sent one of his chief ministers to Portugal to build up a party in his favour and ransomed the Portuguese nobles captured by the Moroccans. The towns and lower clergy remained violently anti-Castilian but the nobility and rich merchants backed Philip's claim against his two main rivals, the Duchess of Braganza and Dom Antonio, prior of Crato, who was illegitimate. Philip also assembled a large army, ready to press home his claim as soon as the moment came. It was at this time that Philip began to suspect the ambitions of Antonio Pérez and removed him in favour of Cardinal Granvelle who in effect became chief minister until about a year before his death in 1586. Granvelle favoured a more active, imperialist policy and fully supported the king's actions in Portugal. He persuaded Philip to restore the disgraced Alva to favour and to appoint him commander of the army.

Cardinal Henry died in January 1580 having failed to designate his successor. The supporters of Dom Antonio seized Lisbon, the royal arsenals and the Crown treasury, and the commons proclaimed him king. On the expiry of an ultimatum, Philip ordered his troops across the border in June. They encountered little determined resistance. Dom Antonio fled abroad after the fall of Lisbon and by September the conquest was complete. Over the next few years Dom Antonio made a number of attempts to win back the country, helped by England and France, but none of these posed a real threat.

Philip made a triumphal entry into Lisbon in December 1580. He then had to decide what policy to adopt for his new country. Granvelle favoured major changes of law and government, which would closely identify Portugal with Castile. He suggested making Lisbon, with its much more strategic position, the capital of the Empire. It is not coincidental that Granvelle was the only non-Castilian to achieve high office and he was the one with the most imperial vision. Philip ignored these suggestions, the capital remained at Madrid, near the great palace of the Escorial that Philip had built, and Portuguese traditions and institutions were left virtually intact. In part this may have been out of a desire to minimise opposition, but it also reflected his conviction that preserving local government was the best way to rule his kingdoms. Thus, he announced that the Portuguese alone would administer their country and its overseas possessions and their commercial and colonising monopolies would be respected. In effect, Portugal remained an autonomous country under a foreign king.

The annexation of Portugal coincided with other events to bring about a decisive shift in Spanish orientation and policy. It had already become clear that the Atlantic was becoming the battleground of the future, leaving the Mediterranean in comparative obscurity, and the acquisition of Portugal with its huge empire, its large fleet and its long Atlantic seaboard completed the change in orientation. Together Spain and Portugal had a combined fleet of 250–300 000 tons (compared with 232 000 tons in the Netherlands and only 42 000 tons in England). Their empires complemented each other. Portuguese possessions stretched from Africa to Brazil, India and the Moluccas, and the Empire was essentially commercial. The Spanish Empire was concentrated largely in the New World and provided the bullion necessary for trade with the Far East for pepper, spices and silks. Already Lisbon had been dependent on Seville for the gold and silver that only the Spanish American mines could produce.

The 1580s saw dramatic increases in the amount of bullion arriving from America because of the introduction of amalgam of mercury into the refining of silver. Two to three million ducats began to arrive annually on the treasure fleets and this gave Philip a freedom of manoeuvre he had hitherto not enjoyed. His foreign policy, which had been defensive for the first two decades of the reign, changed to aggressive imperialism. England and France were alarmed at the increase in Spanish power and the stage was set for a major confrontation. If Granvelle's advice about moving the capital to Lisbon had been followed, it would have signified a crucial reorientation for the monarchy. Granvelle hoped that from Lisbon Philip might have been much better placed to meet the challenge of the maritime powers, the English and the Dutch. But Philip preferred to return to Madrid in 1583. It was to be a symbolic withdrawal into the heart of Castile. Before the end of the reign it had become apparent that the battle for the Atlantic had been lost; Portugal was not effectively absorbed into the Empire and Castile was to remain the centre and chief support of an increasingly unwieldy monarchy.

KEY ISSUE

In what way did the annexation of Portugal bring a change in Spanish foreign policy or government?

9 ⤇ THE CRISIS OF THE 1590S — THE REVOLT OF ARAGON

1580 was the high point of Philip's reign. Spain dominated Europe and the last outposts of resistance in the Netherlands did not appear to have much chance against the brilliant tactics of Philip's nephew, Alexander

Farnese, Duke of Parma. Ten years later, the position was very different. Spain was at war with England and had failed in the most costly military endeavour of the reign, the Armada. There was a real possibility that a heretic would be accepted as king of France, and Spanish intervention there allowed the Dutch rebels to counter-attack. These additional commitments involved heavy extra expenditure and therefore demands for tax increased. Discontent within Spain was widespread. The *Cortes* complained vociferously against new taxes and said that if the rebels in Flanders and France 'wanted to earn damnation, let them'. Inflation was high in the 1590s: the price of grain increased by more than fifty per cent in Castile between 1595 and 1599. By the end of the reign, Philip's popularity had been considerably diminished and the high cost of his imperialist policies was openly questioned. The 1590s also saw the most serious constitutional crisis of the reign, which broke out not in over-taxed Castile but in the neglected eastern kingdom of Aragon.

Philip had paid little attention to Aragon because of its poverty and its concern with its liberties, the ***fueros***, which made extracting either money or troops extremely difficult. He visited his eastern kingdoms in 1563 and then not again until 1588. These long absences were resented. There was more concern over Catalonia, given its proximity to France and the danger of Huguenot infiltration, but this concern took the form of harsher censorship and the arrest of some nobles. Aragon itself became an increasing worry for the government as the reign progressed because the growth of lawlessness made it virtually ungovernable and Philip could not ignore his duty to protect his weaker subjects. The nobility in Aragon enjoyed absolute rights over their vassals but when they began to shelter bandits, a large proportion of whom were *Moriscos*, Philip could no longer ignore this threat to security.

> *fueros* the liberties enjoyed particularly in Aragon, e.g. the right to a public trial

Violence and disorder surfaced in Aragon when Philip tried to take a firmer grip on the country. In 1588 a Castilian, the Count of Almenara, was appointed viceroy. The Aragonese protested that this was infringing their liberties but Philip insisted that the choice was his and the ***Justicia***, who was the guardian of Aragon's *fueros*, accepted his argument.

There was thus already a tense atmosphere when Antonio Pérez escaped from prison in 1590 and fled to Aragon, claiming the privilege, as an Aragonese, of being tried in the open court of the ***Justicia*** rather than a closed court in Castile. He thereby effectively removed himself from royal justice and began making sensational allegations, using secret state papers, implicating Philip in the murder of Escobedo and claiming that the appointment of Almenara was the start of a campaign to undermine the *fueros*.

> *justicia* an Aragonese appointed to ensure that Aragon's liberties were not infringed

The only way for Philip to silence Pérez was to accuse him of heresy because the Inquisition was not subject to the *Justicia's* court. (Here we see the importance to the Crown of the Inquisition, the only institution to operate throughout Spain.) But as an attempt was made to move Pérez to the Inquisition's prison in May 1591, riots broke out and Almenara was fatally wounded. A second attempt in September also ended in failure and a group of young nobles seized Zaragoza's armouries. Philip was uncertain what to do. He was heavily committed against England, France and the Dutch and there were fears for Portugal. On the other hand he knew that, 'If there is no action at once, with a strong hand and a rapid punishment, Aragon will be like the Netherlands.' Such arguments won the day and in October an army of 14 000 was sent into Aragon while Philip announced that only the leaders of the troubles would be punished and 'my wish has always been that the *fueros* be maintained'. There was no resistance and the rebellion was over in four days. Most of the supporters of Pérez had come from the minor nobility who were fighting to preserve their feudal rights. The mass of the people stood to gain nothing from the revolt or from defence of the *fueros* and trouble was confined to Zaragoza. The new young *Justicia* who had supported the revolt was executed; otherwise there was a general pardon. Pérez fled to France where he spent the rest of his life writing a vicious attack on Philip.

With Aragon at his mercy, the king could have destroyed *the fueros* if he had so wished. In fact, his policy mirrored that in Portugal eleven years previously. With minor amendments, he scrupulously observed the traditional liberties and, learning from his experience in the Netherlands, he went in person to ensure that order was restored. In 1592 he presided over the *Cortes* which approved the changes that were made. The *Justicia* was to serve at the king's pleasure; majority votes, not unanimity, would suffice in the *Cortes*; nobles younger than twenty-two were not to sit in the *Cortes*; and the king had the right to choose non-Aragonese as viceroys.

> **KEY ISSUE**
>
> *How wisely did Philip act in his dealings with Aragon at the time of the revolt there?*

10 ↪ PHILIP II'S LEGACY TO SPAIN

Philip successfully surmounted the problem of Aragon and annexed Portugal with great skill. When he died in 1598 he left a united peninsula with Castile at the head of the first empire on which the sun never set. However, there would be trouble in the future: the burden on Castile was enormous and the Dutch revolt, as we shall see, was not yet over. The *Moriscos* were still a problem, there was no effective machinery of government to take over if the king was deficient, the financial predicament of the monarchy was well nigh insoluble, and the Empire had no coherence to make it a manageable unit. Nonetheless Philip had inherited many of these problems himself and by unstinting application and a heavy sense of responsibility he had maintained a functioning empire that struck fear into the rest of Europe. His failure to resolve the contradictions and weaknesses within his empire was not entirely his fault, owing to the burdens of office which allowed no respite for the resolution of problems, although his manner of working – his failure to delegate and his encouragement of faction – made the problems far worse than they need have been. This meant that his less capable successors faced an impossible task, which they increasingly proved themselves unable to manage. Koenigsberger relates a story illustrating how Philip's system of government tended to produce paralysis and inaction when the opposite was called for. At a memorial service for Philip to be held in Seville Cathedral a dispute arose over who was allowed to sit on cushions. This quickly developed into a major row involving most of the dignitaries who were there. Insults and threats were exchanged and then the servants started fighting. In the end the service had to be abandoned.

11 ⮌ BIBLIOGRAPHY

**G. Woodward, *Philip II* (Longman Seminar Studies, 1992) and **J. Kilsby, *Spain, Rise and Decline* (Hodder and Stoughton, 1989) are fine introductions, Kilsby the more manageable. Henry Kamen, *Philip II* (Yale University Press, 1997), *P. Pierson, *Philip II of Spain* (Thames and Hudson, 1975) and **G. Parker, *Philip II* (Hutchinson, 1979) are the standard biographies. *J. Lynch, *Spain Under the Habsburgs, Vol. I* (3rd ed., Blackwell, 1991) and J.H. Elliott *Imperial Spain 1469–1716* (Edward Arnold, 1963) comprehensively discuss Philip's government of Spain. H. Kamen, *Spain 1469–1714: A Society of Conflict* (Longman, 1983) offers more provocative interpretation. **G. Parker, *The Grand Strategy of Philip II* (Yale, 1998) shows how many of Philip's problems inter-locked. F. Braudel, *The Mediterranean and the Mediterranean World in the Age of Philip II* (2nd ed., Fontana, 1975) is a classic well worth sampling.

12 ⮌ STRUCTURED AND ESSAY QUESTIONS

A *Structured questions.*
1. (a) What problems did Philip II face in ruling Spain?
   (b) How far were these caused by his system of government?
2. (a) What were Philip II's relations with the Papacy?
   (b) Does Philip deserve the title of 'the champion of the Counter-Reformation'?

B *Essay questions.*
1. Was the reign of Philip II a disaster for Spain?
2. How far were Philip II's problems in Spain of his own making?
3. 'Rebellions within Spain posed a serious threat to the authority of Charles V and Philip II.' Discuss.
4. How successful was Philip II as a Mediterranean monarch?
5. Compare Charles V and Philip II as rulers of Spain.

Advice: *Comparative essays*

It is always a good idea to compare rulers or countries in order to sharpen up your arguments but some essay questions require you to do so systematically. Consider question 5 above: 'Compare Charles V and Philip II as rulers of Spain.'

One approach would be to write one half of the essay on Charles and the other half on Philip. However, even if it were a good assessment of the ways they governed Spain, such an essay would really be two short essays rather than one comparison.

The best approach would be to compare the two monarchs issue by issue.

(i)   Make a list of the main issues concerning Spain and its government in the sixteenth century. This would certainly include:

- administration;
- the nobility;
- patronage;
- rebellion;
- finance;
- the *fueros* of Aragon;
- the economy;
- the Church.

(ii)   Then, under each of the above headings summarise the main relevant policy of each of the monarchs in a couple of sentences, with a comment on the degree of their success.

(iii)   Next, review what you have written and decide where the two monarchs' policies were alike and where they differed. This should help you to structure your essay – you could start with the similar policies and then move on to the differing ones.

(iv)   Finally frame your overall argument. In your 'Introduction' you could comment on how far Philip did follow his father's example as he intended to. In your 'Conclusion' you could compare their respective legacies to Spain.

13 ⌐ DOCUMENTARY EXERCISE ON THE CHARACTER OF PHILIP II

Philip II has aroused extraordinary passions among historians. He has been vilified and praised in ways that are almost impossible to reconcile. Many historians have not displayed objective judgement in the case of Philip and have allowed their own strong prejudices to colour their accounts. For this reason it is important to identify the preconceptions of a historian before one can fully assess the accuracy of his or her portrayal.

Unfavourable views of Philip II and the Spanish, 'heretics, schismatics, accursed of God, the offspring of Jews and *Marranos*, the very scum of the earth' (Pope Paul IV), originated in Italy. This so called 'black legend' was given greater strength by Dutch propaganda during the Revolt of the Netherlands. In order to further their own cause, it was in the interests of the Dutch to blacken the name of Philip II as much as possible. Their pamphleteers therefore exaggerated the actions of the Spanish and even resorted to outright forgery, which was to be a fruitful source for later Protestant historians.

The most notorious forgery of the Dutch, which was not exposed until early this century was 'The Advice of the Inquisition'. This was supposedly a sentence passed in February 1568 and confirmed by royal decree by which the entire population of the Netherlands, with very few exceptions, was declared guilty of high treason and therefore lost any right to either life or property.

The 'black legend' was given a particular boost by the 'apology' of Philip's arch-opponent, William of Orange.

Having just claimed that Philip murdered his own wife Elizabeth in order to form an incestuous union with his niece, Anna of Austria, Orange went on to write:

It was not a single murder that was perpetrated for the sake of this extraordinary marriage. His son too, his only son, was sacrificed, in order to furnish the Pope with a pretext for so unusual a dispensation; which was granted, in order to prevent the Spanish monarchy from being left without a male heir. This was the true cause of the death of Don Carlos, against whom some misdemeanours were alleged; but not a single crime sufficient to justify his condemnation, much less to vindicate a father for imbruing his hands in the blood of his son...

In response to Philip's orders to have Orange assassinated, the latter continued:

For there is not, I am persuaded, a nation or prince in Europe, by whom it will not be thought dishonourable and barbarous, thus publicly to authorise and encourage murder; except the Spaniards, and their King, who have been long estranged from every sentiment of honour and humanity. In having recourse to private assassinations against a declared and open enemy, does not this mighty monarch confess his despair of being able to subdue me by force of arms?

SOURCE A
William of Orange.

Philip II possessed, in an eminent degree, penetration, vigilance, and a capacity for government. His eyes were continually open upon every part of his extensive dominions. He entered into every branch of administration; watched over the conduct of his ministers with unwearied attention; and in his choice both of them and of his generals, discovered a considerable share of wisdom. He had at all times a composed and settled countenance, and never appeared to be either elated or depressed. His temper was the most imperious, and his looks and demeanour were haughty and severe; yet among his Spanish subjects, he was of easy access; listened patiently to their representations and complaints; and where his ambition and bigotry did not interfere, was generally willing to redress their grievances. When we have said this much in his praise, we have said all that justice requires, or truth permits. It is indeed impossible to suppose that he was insincere in his zeal for religion. But as his religion was of the most corrupt kind, it served to increase the natural depravity of his disposition; and not only allowed but even prompted him to commit the most odious and shocking crimes. Although a prince in the bigoted age of Philip might be persuaded that the interest of religion would be advanced by falsehood and persecution; yet it might be expected, that, in a virtuous prince, the sentiments of honour and humanity would on some occasions, triumph over the dictates of superstition: but of this triumph there occurs not one single instance in the reign of Philip; who, without hesitation, violated his most sacred obligations as often as religion afforded him a pretence; and under that pretence exercised for many years the most unrelenting cruelty, without reluctance or remorse. His ambition, which was exorbitant; his resentment, which was implacable; his arbitrary temper, which would submit to no control, concurred with his bigoted zeal for the Catholic religion, and carried the sanguinary spirit, which that religion was calculated to inspire to a greater height in Philip, than it ever attained in any other prince of that, or of any former or succeeding age.

SOURCE B

A later historian, Robert Watson, commenting on Philip in 1794.

His power was absolute. With this single phrase one might as well dismiss any attempt at specification. He made war or peace at will with foreign nations. He had power of life and death over all his subjects. He had unlimited control of their worldly goods. And he claimed supreme jurisdiction over their religious opinions... The whole machinery of society, political, ecclesiastical, military, was in his single hand... If Philip possessed a single virtue, it has eluded the conscientious research of the writer of these pages. If there are vices – as possibly there are – from which he was exempt, it is because it is not permitted to human nature to attain perfection even in evil. The only plausible explanation... of his infamous career is that the man really believed himself, not a king, but a god...

Homicide such as was hardly ever compassed before by one human being was committed by Philip when in the famous edict of 1568 he sentenced every man, woman and child in the Netherlands to death. That the whole of this population, three millions or more, were not positively destroyed was because no human energy could suffice to execute the diabolical decree.

SOURCE C
J.L. Motley, the great nineteenth-century historian of the Revolt of the Netherlands, writing on Philip II.

He was an exceptionally dutiful son, a devoted husband, and a singularly understanding and affectionate father. His letters written to his daughters Isabella and Catherine during his journey in Portugal (1581–83), show a mixture of kindly interest in their childish doings together with a homely humour that is altogether charming. His love for his children is important in view of the accusations brought against him in connection with the death of Don Carlos... Duplicity and even crime are possibly, though by no means certainly, to be found as incidents in his diplomatic and political life; but such things were no part of his normal behaviour. Philip set out in life to train himself for the duties of a king. He gradually acquired an iron self-control expressed in immobile features that would register no sign of emotion... Every decision, great or small, rested with the king. This was the strength and the weakness of the system. Its strength, in that no favouritism and no undermining of royal power was possible... the weakness of the system was the inevitable and intolerable delay that resulted from it... This failure to distinguish between the great and the small was the most glaring fault of his system... The papers fought an inevitably winning battle against the king. As time went on, the piles of them awaiting attention grew ever larger, and the king, though working almost all the hours of the day and much of the night, was falling ever more and more behind with his decisions, so that the Spanish Government achieved world-wide notoriety for its delays. 'If death came from Spain', said Philip's Viceroy of Naples, 'we should live to a very great age.'

SOURCE D
A more recent historian, R. Trevor Davies, writing on Philip II in 1937.

The first extract refers to Don Diego who died in childhood.

I think he will have managed to fill in the coloured letters: this is why I am sending you others... and I've got some more. Make sure he occupies himself in filling them in, but little by little, so as not to tire himself.

Let me know how much you have grown since I last saw you, and send them to me taken very exactly with ribbons. Add your brother's to them. I will be delighted to see them, though I would be happier still to see you all. I trust in God it will be soon.

SOURCE F
Extract from Philip's letters to his daughters in 1581–83.

SOURCE E

(Picture 34) Philip II with his children, *artist unknown*

Q

1. (a) *Compare Sources A and F. What different impressions of Philip are given and is it possible to reconcile them?*
    (b) *What justification can you offer for William making such outrageous accusations?*
2. *Robert Watson (Source B) uses a familiar technique to make one believe he is being impartial. What is it?*
3. *Re-read Source B and identify where it has drawn on Source A.*
4. *Source C contains major errors of fact (as opposed to interpretation). What are they?*
5. *Is Source D more believable than the others and, if so, why?*
6. *Does Portrait E have any value for a historian studying Philip II?*
7. *In your own words write a summary of the character of Philip II, giving specific examples where possible to support your case.*

Philip II: Northern Europe – the Revolt of The Netherlands

14

OVERVIEW

The Revolt of the Netherlands was in fact not one revolt but several, motivated by different causes and involving different groups of people. They led ultimately to the creation of a new nation – the modern Netherlands, often incorrectly called Holland. It must be remembered, however, that the aims of those involved in the revolts were much more modest than the end result might suggest. Certainly, they did not set out with the intention of creating a republic; this was forced upon them by circumstance. The pressures leading to rebellion were political, religious, economic and local and each was present to a different degree in all the revolts. The multiplicity of the revolt cannot be overstressed. While it is not unreasonable to regard William of Orange (known sometimes as William the Silent), the main opponent of Philip II between 1567 and 1584, as the father of the Dutch nation, it is important to recognise how accidental was the final shape of the country and that, if William had had his way, there would have been no division between north and south nor would religion have driven men apart.

The causes of the first two revolts in 1566 and 1572 were fairly traditional – a combination of political ambition, religion and insensitive handling by the government. The third revolt in 1576 was rather different as it was caused by revulsion at the behaviour of undisciplined, mutinying Spanish troops. A real sense of nationalism began to become apparent and the nobility in general began to question their allegiance to the Habsburgs. The Spanish were driven from the Netherlands and had to begin the slow process of winning back the entire country. It was their inability to achieve this that led to stalemate and the eventual success of the Dutch.

The northern Netherlands were not to be finally recognised as an independent state by Spain until 1648, after eighty years of nearly continuous warfare. However, effective independence was conceded in 1609 when a twelve-year truce was agreed by each side. It seems incredible that such a small territory should have been able to withstand the might of the most powerful state in Europe. The answer lies in Spanish commitments elsewhere. As the rebels themselves realised, events in the Mediterranean were crucial to their progress. Up to 1578, events in southern Europe took precedence over the north.

Also to be considered were Dutch control of the sea, the boost that Dutch trade gave to the rebel war effort, the distance from Spain to the Netherlands and the consequent difficulty of transporting men and money between them along the 'Spanish Road', and the intervention of foreign powers, especially France and England, which at some points gave a vital boost to rebel morale.

1 ↬ THE NETHERLANDS IN 1555

The Netherlands was not a 'nation' in the mid-sixteenth century. The seventeen provinces were geographically compact, but they enjoyed a common link only through the person of their ruler. All but the north-eastern provinces sent delegates to a parliament, the States General, but its decision-making powers were severely limited as on every issue delegates had to refer back to the home province. The titles held by Philip II indicate that his position in each province was subtly different. For example he was Duke of Brabant, Count of Flanders and Lord of Friesland; in each province he had to swear to uphold their liberties at the same time as he was recognised as ruler. These entrenched local privileges were a source of annoyance to the government since they made any centralisation extremely difficult and the simple voting of taxes was a cumbersome affair. It was the duty of the provincial states to resist any breach of their privileges, and they carried out their role with energy so that government edicts would only be published after they had been examined and found to comply with local privileges. Inevitably this **particularism** was a source of tension with the government.

particularism putting the interests of the locality first

Particularism was a powerful force and overrode any feeling for a wider community. It was a problem that was seriously to hinder William of Orange's later efforts for a united opposition. There were enormous differences between the provinces. The south was French-speaking with a powerful landed nobility. The north was Dutch-speaking and had very few noble families; the rich merchants of the towns were more influential. In the centre was Antwerp, a town of 80 000, the greatest commercial centre in Europe. These all sought to promote their own interests, at the expense of others if necessary.

While there was not much fellow feeling between the provinces, there was a definite identification of the Low Countries as a unit distinct from foreigners. This sense of identity was reinforced by the accession of a foreign Spanish king in the form of Philip II, who had little understanding of the traditions of his new possession. Under Charles V, the Netherlands had enjoyed the reflected glory of his imperial title. In the reign of Philip II they were relegated to the northern outpost of a Spanish empire. No longer would the high nobility cluster around the king as trusted advisers and the prestigious Order of the Golden Fleece was allowed to decline in status. Even before Philip left the Netherlands

MAP 20

The Netherlands in 1559

for Spain in 1559, never to return, there were fears amongst the nobility about their position.

2 ⁓ PRELUDE TO REVOLT, 1559–65

These fears were soon to be justified. Outwardly Philip acted correctly, made the great nobles members of the Council of State and stadholders of the provinces and appointed his half-sister, Margaret of Parma, as regent. However, he left secret instructions that she was to consult only with an inner ring of three ministers, known as the *consulta*, of whom the most important was Cardinal Granvelle, who had served Charles V. As a cardinal, Granvelle took precedence over the nobility and it was rapidly apparent to them that they were excluded from all real power, a position in which Margaret of Parma also found herself since Philip

KEY ISSUE

What legacy did Philip II inherit in the Netherlands?

insisted on retaining all executive power himself and ordered that no decision was to be made without first consulting him. This would have been an unwieldy process at the best of times but when uncertain communications were added to Philip's notorious inability to make up his mind, the prospect of anarchy in government became a real possibility.

The alienation of the high nobility from the government unleashed forces that neither it nor they were able to control. The nobility were in no sense revolutionary; they merely wanted to improve their own position. They were suffering from a fall in their effective income because of inflation and with the French wars at an end, military service and plunder was no longer a way to a quick fortune. This left them dependent on government posts to increase their income and they disliked the influence of the Spanish. The French ambassador wrote that Margaret was 'surrounded by Spanish minds which are hated here to the death... nothing here is well said, well done or well considered unless it comes in Spanish and from a Spaniard'. In order to put pressure on the government to wring concessions from it, the nobility therefore resisted attempts to put down the growing Protestant movement because this was the issue that would most gravely embarrass the king. In doing so they encouraged the spread of a revolutionary movement which soon developed a momentum of its own.

There had been severe persecution of heresy under Charles V but this had evoked little sympathy because most of the victims were Anabaptists. In 1559 a new element was added by the opening of the border with France. This enabled increasing numbers of Protestant preachers to penetrate the Netherlands. (These Protestants were not yet fully organised as Calvinists but they held very similar views.) The Netherlands was a tolerant country placed as it was at the centre of European trade. This meant that the courts, charged with enforcing the severe anti-heresy laws, were reluctant to do so. Unusually, in the Netherlands the vast majority of alleged heretics were tried by civil courts because the ecclesiastical courts might seek to persuade the accused to renounce his beliefs, which delayed the process. While Philip was pressing for harsher measures against heretics, Protestants were taking over England, Scotland and, to some extent, France. Margaret of Parma complained that the strict orthodoxy which might be suitable for Spain 'closed by sea and by mountains' was impracticable for a trading country ringed by heretical neighbours.

Philip had left behind 3000 Spanish troops to guard the French frontiers. This most visible evidence of Spanish power was resented by the provinces, who felt that their status was being undermined, and they refused to release any money through the States General until the garrisons left. Reluctantly the king was forced to give way in 1561, to the jubilation of the Netherlanders. As Granvelle forecast, 'There will be trouble here sooner or later on some other pretext.'

This pretext was the 'new bishoprics' scheme, which appeared to be an admirable and long overdue reform of the structure of the Church. There were only four bishoprics in the Netherlands with its population of 3 000 000 and Philip proposed to create fourteen new bishoprics under the new Archbishopric of Mechlin. Ten of the new bishoprics were to unite with wealthy abbeys and receive the abbot's revenue. When the reorganisation became known in 1562 there was immediate and widespread opposition. Antwerp, one of the proposed new sees, protested so strongly against the arrival of a bishop, fearing for its trade with heretic states, that Philip agreed to suspend the appointment. The scheme was (wrongly) seen as the first step towards the introduction of the Spanish Inquisition; there were fears about the growing power of the Crown because the new bishops would sit in the states. The Archbishop of Mechlin would have the first voice in the States of Brabant and the new Archbishop was the hated Granvelle. William of Orange, one of the greatest noblemen of the Netherlands and nicknamed 'the Silent' because of his alleged deviousness, saw that the plan would dangerously strengthen royal power. It would not only increase religious persecution but also render unnecessary the co-operation of nobles and towns. The scheme was also disliked by the nobility because it was intended that the bishoprics would go to senior churchmen and this would exclude their younger sons who had often seen the church as a useful career.

For the first time, there was a point of focus for different groups of opposition. Over the next forty years religion was often to be the unifying feature of the revolt, not provoking rebellion on its own but acting as a powerful secondary motive to compel people to action. Philip was heavily committed in the Mediterranean and could give little attention to the Netherlands, whose government rapidly lost authority. There was a continuing financial crisis caused by the debts from the French wars and Margaret had to appeal to the states for financial help. Granvelle was seen as the source of the trouble and every occasion was taken to attack him and the government's religious policy. When Orange and Counts Egmont and Hoorn withdrew from the Council of State and the states of Brabant withheld their taxes, Philip bowed before the storm and in 1564, Granvelle was transferred to Italy.

The high nobility on the Council of State began to assume a more active role in government, working closely with Margaret of Parma. The greatest problem facing them was a marked spread of Protestantism. Many exiles had returned when Granvelle left and in several provinces persecution had virtually ended. In Holland, no one had been executed for his beliefs since 1553. The Brussels government therefore moderated the anti-heresy laws to make them more acceptable and sent Count Egmont to Madrid in 1565 to explain their actions and seek approval of the new position of the Council of State in government. Egmont arrived at a bad time for Philip, as he had just heard that the Ottomans were planning a great expedition in the Mediterranean. It may be that the king was accordingly very conciliatory in attitude and Egmont returned to the Netherlands convinced that Philip approved of all they were doing, although there is a suspicion that Egmont deliberately misunderstood in order to take advantage of the government in Brussels.

In any case, it came as a tremendous blow to the Netherlands nobility when Philip was finally able to state his case clearly and unambiguously after the relief of Malta in September in the notorious 'letters from the Segovia Woods' which he wrote to Margaret of Parma, the regent, on 17 October 1565:

> Madame, my dear sister... You say that I did not make it clear in the aforementioned instruction that it was not my intention to ask you or the seigneurs of the State Council in the Netherlands for more advice in this matter but in fact you were made to understand my definitive intention. As to whether I would wish to ask the advice of the private and great councils and of the governors and provincial councils, this would be a considerable waste of time since my mind is made up...
>
> As to the resentment you have noticed at some of the things which the Prince of Gavre [Count Egmont] says I told him and which don't seem to correspond with my letters from Valladolid and with the negotiations in progress over the matter of religion, I don't see or understand that I wrote anything different in these letters from what was entrusted to the Prince of Gavre. For as to the Inquisition, my intention is that it should be carried out by the inquisitors, as they have done up till now...
>
> If one fears disturbances there is no reason to think that they are more imminent and will be greater when one does allow the inquisitors to perform their proper duties and when one does assist them. You know the importance of this and I command you urgently to do in this matter all that is so necessary and not to agree to any different policy. You know how much I have these things at heart and what pleasure and satisfaction this will give me...

Q

1. *What religious policy did Philip instruct his sister to pursue?*
2. *What does the extract reveal about Philip's understanding of the situation in the Netherlands?*

KEY ISSUE

What was Philip's response to the idea that the Council of State should have a greater say in government?

Philip believed that religious repression was necessary in the Netherlands and acceptable to the majority, given that about 1300 heretics had been executed there between 1523 and 1566. But, as Bonney has pointed out, under Philip II executions moved higher up the social scale from lowly Anabaptists to prosperous Calvinists and were therefore seen by provincial leaders as more of a threat. Heresy was also equated with treason so victims lost not only their lives but their relatives lost their property. This was seen as a general attack upon property.

3 ↪ THE FIRST REVOLT AND THE SENDING OF ALVA

The nobility were appalled at the complete disregard of their views. About 400 of the lesser nobles drew up a 'compromise' in December 1565 which opposed the Inquisition and forced Margaret to suspend the anti-heresy laws. The high nobility held aloof from the 'beggars', as those who signed the compromise became known, but they sympathised with its aims. This challenge to the government coincided with a period of great hardship in the Netherlands, caused by harvest failure in 1565 linked with the closure of the Baltic, which drove prices to famine levels. In addition, England had placed an embargo on the cloth trade with the Netherlands, which had caused widespread unemployment. All the ingredients of an explosive situation merely needed a spark to set them off.

It is now disputed whether the spark was provided by Protestant 'hedge-preachers' who had been addressing crowds of thousands in fields outside the towns throughout the summer of 1566. However in August, after a rise in prices, mob violence broke out, which became directed against churches and images (i.e. religious paintings and statues) in an orgy of destruction known as the iconoclastic fury. The nobility were appalled and, with the exception of Orange who seemed uncertain in his allegiance, allied themselves with the government. Slowly, order was restored but not before Margaret had written to Philip in the most lurid terms about the desperate plight she was in. There was little opposition to the activities of the iconoclasts, which pointed to a strong anti-clericalism and a corresponding readiness to listen to the message of the Protestants, even if the 'hedge-preachers' were not responsible for the riots. The revolt was over and open Protestant worship at an end by May 1567, but by then Philip had decided that force was the only course of action.

In July 1566, Philip had been preparing to make some concessions but the outbreak of the iconoclastic fury hardened his attitude. His decision to use force in the Netherlands changed the history of his reign and has been hotly disputed. Philip has been blamed for sending the Duke of Alva with a large army to crush a revolt that was already over, although he was merely following the conventional wisdom of the day, which said that rebellions must be crushed in their infancy. The Spanish Council of State unanimously supported this view: 'If the Netherlands situation is not remedied, it will bring about the loss of Spain and all the rest.'

What was not agreed upon was the degree of force necessary. This division reflected, and was a part of, faction struggles within the Spanish court, with each side vying for the king's confidence – a situation Philip encouraged. The Prince of Eboli favoured limited use of force and a personal visit by the king to settle matters. The Duke of Alva argued that firm measures taken immediately would end the problem, but he too thought that it was essential for Philip to go to the Netherlands. The king, profoundly shocked at the presence of open Protestantism in his dominions, supported Alva's view. Conditions were favourable. The Ottoman emperor, Suleiman I, had just died, so a Turkish attack was unlikely in the near future. France and England were preoccupied with internal divisions and, for once, financial constraints were less pressing because a treasure fleet had just arrived.

KEY ISSUE

What was the role of religion in the outbreak of the first revolt?

However good the omens seemed in 1566 for Spanish policy, in retrospect it can be seen as a grave mistake, probably the worst of Philip's reign, because Alva was sent to administer punishment but Philip never arrived to heal the wounds. The conflict in the Netherlands was to become a terrible burden which crippled Philip's other enterprises. As Arias Montano wrote in 1573, 'I see clearly an unending problem, unbearable expense and the loss of innumerable lives, both theirs and ours.' A more conciliatory policy, seeking to win back the favour of the nobility might well have produced a quick resolution to the problem, especially as the general population returned to political apathy once the economic crisis of 1565–66 had passed. There would have remained only the Protestants. It is impossible to guess whether they would have been easy to deal with. Certainly Philip would have been most unlikely to tolerate the pragmatic co-existence that the Crown was trying to achieve in France. In 1566 he wrote to the Pope, 'Before suffering the slightest damage to religion and the service of God, I would lose all my estates, and a hundred lives if I had them, because I do not propose, nor do I desire, to be the ruler of heretics.'

> **KEY ISSUE**
>
> *How far can Philip II be blamed for the outbreak of the first revolt?*

4 ∽ ALVA'S RULE, 1567–72

> **PROFILE**

> See pages 397–8

PICTURE 35
The Duke of Alva *by Antonio Moro*

THE DUKE OF ALVA (1567–72)

Alva was born in 1507 and had been one of Charles V's chief ministers. Charles did not trust him, seeing him as too ambitious, but he did value his skills as a soldier. Alva had a forceful personality and, as one of the leading nobles in Spain, he was impossible to ignore. He was the leader of one of the main factions and enjoyed the king's support, although never his trust. Alva pressed for harsh treatment of the Dutch opposition and was despatched north to the Netherlands with an army of 10 000 men in 1567. His mere presence on the French border set off an attempted coup by the French Protestants, the Huguenots, fearful of a Catholic conspiracy between Catherine de Medici and Alva. Under his direction the 'Council of Blood' repressed all resistance in the Netherlands, even executing two of the most respected noblemen, Egmont and Hoorn.

But it was his attempt to impose new taxes that sparked off the Second Revolt in 1572. He had succeeded in turning constitutional resistance into a patriotic war against Spain. He was an able general, but Dutch resistance and terrain was too much for him. He was recalled to Spain in 1573 and dismissed. In 1580 he returned to favour to command the army which annexed Portugal. He died in 1582.

The despatch of the Duke of Alva with 10 000 Spanish and Italian troops not only transformed the situation in the Netherlands but also caused grave concern to England and, above all, France, along whose borders the troops marched. Philip assured the French government of his peaceful intentions, but not until Alva had safely arrived in the Netherlands in August 1567 were the French towns on the borders able to relax.

Alva had not been the king's first choice of commander, but those preferred had excused themselves. His instructions went only so far as the restoration of royal authority. He was to work with the regent, Margaret of Parma, and prepare the way for a visit by Philip either at the end of 1567 or in 1568. Unfortunately for Spain and the Netherlands, events made these orders meaningless. Margaret found the duke difficult to work with and resented her loss of power. She therefore resigned within a few weeks of Alva's arrival. In the absence of any other candidate, Alva himself took over her position by becoming the governor-general. Then Philip found it impossible to come to the Netherlands, first because Alva informed him that it would be dangerous to do so, and then because of the disasters of 1568 beginning with the arrest and subsequent death of Don Carlos and ending with the revolt of the *Moriscos*. A visit to the Netherlands in such troubled times had to be postponed indefinitely. In the event it was never to occur, a serious deficiency in this age when kings were respected in person so much more than their deputies.

Alva was left in control of the Netherlands even though he was ill-fitted and unprepared for such a role. It is typical of Philip's haphazard way of providing for his northern provinces that he was happy to let such a state of affairs continue, even though he was aware of the unpopularity of the duke's rule. In 1572, he went so far as to send the Duke of Medina Celi to spy on Alva's activities.

It is not difficult to understand why Alva's rule was unpopular. The duke had come to crush any sign of rebellion and he was determined to show no mercy. A 'Council of Troubles' was set up which soon became known as the 'Council of Blood'. It tried over 12 000 people, of whom between 1000 and 2000 were executed and about 9000 lost all or part of their lands. Counts Egmont and Hoorn were arrested and executed in 1568, a fate that would certainly have been shared by Orange if he had not prudently remained in Germany. In Spain, Baron Montigny, who was putting the nobles' case to Philip, was secretly garrotted in prison. These punishments had the desired effect and when William of Orange mounted an invasion in 1568 not a single town rose in his support. It seemed as if the policy of force was vindicated.

As a military commander, Alva had shown his effectiveness; as governor-general, he proved unable to contain the discontent his policies aroused. Philip was anxious to make the Netherlands easier to govern and administer. He instructed Alva 'to make all the states into one kingdom with Brussels its capital'. This would involve attacking local liberties and Alva's attempts to do so met with immediate hostility even from staunch Catholics. In beheading Egmont and Hoorn, he had executed two members of the Order of the Golden Fleece, the great chivalric order of knights, and that was an attack on all noble privilege. He surrounded himself with Spanish and Italian advisers and left posts vacant rather than fill them with Netherlanders. Thus, the class upon which the administration of the country had always depended became alienated from government.

This alienation was turned into outright opposition by Alva's response to Philip's insistence that the Netherlands must become financially self-sufficient. Alva decided to impose new taxes known as the 'Hundredth' and 'Tenth Pennies'. The former, to which the States General agreed in 1569, was a one-off tax of one per cent on all capital; the latter, which provoked an outcry, was to be a permanent sales tax of ten per cent. If it came into effect, the Tenth Penny would remove the need to call the states again since it would apply to everyone, and it would hit the wealthiest most – usually they passed the burden of taxes on to the lower classes. A temporary grant by the states postponed the conflict but in 1571 Alva proposed to collect the Tenth Penny by force, although he was not in a position to do so. Philip was totally occupied by a new offensive against the Turks and could spare neither money nor attention for the Netherlands. With discontent mounting rapidly, William of Orange saw his chance and the Second Revolt of the Netherlands began.

> **KEY ISSUE**
>
> *What mistakes did Alva make in governing the Netherlands?*

5 ↩ THE SECOND REVOLT, 1572–76

Initially, everything went wrong. A four-pronged simultaneous invasion had been planned for 1572 by sea, from France, and two invasions from Germany. In the event, the **sea beggars**, refugees from Alva's rule in the Netherlands who had been operating as pirates from English ports, were expelled by Elizabeth I and this led them to capture the little port of Brill in Holland in April 1572. William's brother, Louis of Nassau, led a Huguenot (French Protestant) invasion which took Mons in May, but the main invasion force under Orange himself was not ready until August and the massacre of St Bartholomew's Day in that month put an end to French help. Alva was able to recapture Mons and then turn against the heart of the revolt in Holland and Zeeland. The loss of French help was a severe blow to Orange. When Philip heard the news of the massacre he laughed out loud and danced around the room. It seemed that it would be only a matter of time before the revolt was utterly crushed.

> **sea beggars** Calvinists who had turned to piracy after fleeing from the Netherlands

> See pages 477–9

Alva marched north and sacked Mechlin, whereupon the rest of Brabant surrendered. Orange retreated in despair to Holland. In November 1572, Zutphen was sacked and the rest of the north east returned to obedience; only Holland and Zeeland were left in defiance. Alva moved in to complete his work and found he had gone too far. After a seven-month siege, Haarlem surrendered in July 1573 on condition that no one in the town would be harmed. In fact, the garrison of 2000 was massacred. This seemed to be a warning to other towns and all preferred to fight on to the death since they could not trust any surrender proposals. The loss of Haarlem cut the rebel provinces in two but, more important, it gave them the will to resist, turning the revolt into a nightmare for Philip.

The survival of the second revolt was due to the reaction to Alva's repressive regime but also to the ceaseless efforts of William of Orange to regain his place in the Netherlands. He was a sovereign prince in his own right (along with his great estates in the Netherlands, he had inherited Orange, a tiny independent principality in the south of France) and he used his status to cultivate international contacts. He had spent his years in exile negotiating with the German princes, Elizabeth I and the Huguenots. He had most success with the latter: in 1568 they signed a treaty promising mutual assistance, and he and Louis of Nassau had served with the Huguenots later that year. This campaigning bore only limited fruit in 1572 but was to be of much greater significance later.

The opposition to the Tenth Penny and the widespread hardship that had resulted from efforts to avoid it, which had created unemployment, provided fertile ground for the spread of the revolt but the importance of religion cannot be ignored. The sea beggars were Calvinists and anxious to spread their creed. William of Orange had become a Protestant in exile and in 1573 was to become a Calvinist to harness the support of this determined group. There could be compromise over taxes but Philip II would never consent to toleration on religious matters and this kept the revolt alive.

The sea beggars followed a clear strategy in their seizure of towns. The town councils were overwhelmingly loyal Catholics, but they hated Alva and his centralisation and taxation and were therefore unwilling to accept Spanish garrisons. In each town, the sea beggars could usually rely on a small number of fanatical Calvinists who would open the gates to them. In most cases the town militias, the *schutters*, thoroughly alienated from Alva's regime, were quite prepared to let this happen. Once the sea beggars were inside, they ignored any agreements that might have been made with the authorities and purged them of any over-enthusiastic Catholics; churches and monasteries were plundered and priests murdered. The behaviour of the sea beggars was so extreme that Orange was forced to dismiss their leader in order to retain the support of the **regents** in the towns.

The geography and traditions of Holland and Zeeland were in large part responsible for the survival of the revolt in its crucial years when only a small area maintained its resistance (a mere thirty towns by December 1572). The terrain was extremely inhospitable to an invading army, composed as it was of a network of rivers, dykes and islands which made the movement of large numbers of men and their supplies difficult. In addition, much of the country was below sea level so that the dykes could be broken to flood the fields around towns and prevent their capture, as happened at Alkmaar in 1573 and Leiden in 1574. The

TIMELINE

1566 First revolt
Religious unrest and opposition to governor-general
1567 Alva embarks on repression
1572 Second revolt
1573 Alva replaced by Requesens

regents the ruling class in the towns

MAP 21
Rebel-controlled areas in late 1572

advantages of Holland as a centre for revolt had been recognised in 1571 by one of William's advisers:

> Once you have got a foothold in the maritime provinces, it will be easy to resist all attempts at expulsion. Next time, therefore, Holland should be the objective. There is to be found the converging point of trade routes which he who obtains a firm footing there will be able to command. It will be unnecessary to occupy more than a few towns... that will at once give to our privateers a safe retreat and a market. The enemy, hampered by the rivers and lakes, will not easily surprise us there.

For the revolt to be successful, it was necessary to have an alternative government to replace that of the king. The long tradition of particularism meant that the institutions of administration were already there. In 1572 the states of Holland agreed to recognise Orange as (technically) the king's ***stadholder*** (governor) for Holland, Zeeland and Utrecht and to fight against Alva to recover their lost rights and liberties. In effect they merely transferred allegiance from Brussels to the Prince of Orange. They also agreed to pay for the army and navy fighting for the province and to grant freedom of worship for all. This freedom did not last long. In 1573 Catholic worship was forbidden in Holland in the interests of public order. From very small beginnings (in Delft, a town of 14 000, there were 200 communicant Calvinists and three pastors), Calvinism became the official religion. The active Calvinists remained in a small minority but they were the most dedicated, organised and powerful religious group.

> ***stadholder*** the king's official representative or governor in the provinces

To assist Orange in governing the country, a number of committees were set up, the most important of which was the Standing Committee of the States. Much power was retained at local level by the town councils and it was a constant complaint of Orange that he was hampered in the war effort by the unwillingness of each locality to consider the needs of the whole. Where Alva had used repression, Orange was to use all his gifts of diplomacy to overcome such particularism.

The early 1570s were a financial nightmare for Spain – Philip was spending almost twice as much of his revenue and it was essential for him to find relief from somewhere. In these circumstances it is hardly surprising that he decided that the Duke of Alva must be replaced. The duke was slowly overcoming the rebels but Philip could not afford a siege of several months at every town. Realising that Alva's harsh measures had provoked the revolt, Philip decided on a change of policy and, in December 1573, appointed the moderate Don Luis de Requeséns, then in Milan, as the new governor-general.

The new governor faced an unenviable task. The Spanish troops had mutinied in July 1573 over their lack of pay and had refused to attack Alkmaar in the autumn. No money was likely to be forthcoming in the near future and Requesens's own position was unclear. He was still officially governor of Milan and his status in the Netherlands was not settled until Alva seized the opportunity to return to Spain as soon as Requesens arrived. The greatest difficulty, however, lay in the lack of instructions from Madrid, coupled with a refusal to delegate any power.

A few quotations from Philip's letters will illustrate the problem. Requeséns was:

> 'to effect the said pacification and settlement in accordance with my future commands'. 'As I do not know the truth of the matter I cannot suggest a remedy. The safest thing is to distrust both sides equally ... You should try to adopt a middle course using the

maximum circumspection.' 'I want you in all things to appear as if you place great confidence in the local officials and that you are gaining their strong support. At the same time you must not allow anything detrimental to our interests.'

Requeséns was unhappy about his appointment but he made determined efforts to be successful. In March and November the army mutinied, allowing the Orangists to consolidate their hold on the north-west. Philip doubled his remittances to the Netherlands but it was still not enough. The cost of the army was estimated at 1.2 million florins a month (2 florins = 1 ducat) which was more than Philip's combined revenue from Castile and the Indies. At the same time, the war in the Mediterranean was going badly with the loss of Tunis. Philip was in despair. In June 1574 he wrote, 'I believe that everything is a waste of time, judging by what is happening in the Low Countries, and if they are lost the rest [of the monarchy] will not last long, even if we have enough money.'

KEY ISSUE

What problems did successive governors face in their relations with the king?

Requeséns decided that direct peace talks with the rebels was the only answer. These were held at Breda in 1575 but the governor was pessimistic from the start because of differences over religion. He complained bitterly to his brother about the government's silence during the talks: 'They have not made a single remark with reference to my suggestions about the talks and negotiations which have been held with the rebels.' 'They do not reply to my requests because they wish to make me responsible for what is done or not done at the peace talks.'

When, predictably, the talks failed, Requeséns launched a successful attack to divide the rebel provinces. However, Philip's decree of bankruptcy in September 1575 spelt ruin for his efforts, as he realised: 'I know full well that those who arranged and advised the Decree have lost these states for the Catholic Church.' Requesens died in March 1576 and before his successor could be appointed, the situation was transformed by a mutiny of the army in July. It turned into the 'Spanish Fury' when the mutineers invaded Brabant in search of plunder.

ANALYSIS

Factors enabling the Dutch revolt to survive

Geography

The inhospitable nature of Holland and Zeeland which made conquering the towns so difficult provided the rebels with a crucial breathing space in which to build up support for the revolt. Geyl has stressed the importance of the great river barriers in obstructing the Spaniards, along with the fortresses built by Charles V which the rebels now took over. In Geyl's view, it was strategic and geographic factors, rather than any pre-determined linguistic or cultural boundaries, which were ultimately to settle the boundary between an independent north and a Spanish south. This view has recently been challenged by Jonathan Israel who considers that there were significant political and cultural differences between north and south before the revolt, which were merely intensified by the conflict. The religious division between a Protestant north and a Catholic south, however, was to follow the revolt rather than precede it.

Control of the sea

Control of the sea was essential for possession of Holland and Zeeland. This was obtained by the sea beggars in 1572 and the war fleet of the Brussels government was destroyed by them between 1572 and 1574 and never allowed to regain its strength.

Political traditions

The political traditions of the Netherlands enabled the rebel provinces to set up a government to challenge that of Brussels. Without such a government the revolt could not have succeeded in establishing a new nation because there would have been no alternative to Philip II's rule, except annexation by a foreign power. The support of the urban ruling class (known as the 'regents') for the revolt and their consequent retention of power was another important reason for the successful avoidance of anarchy and chaos. William of Orange recognised how vital the support of the regents was for the success of the revolt and he took few decisions without assuring himself of their consent first.

Philip II's distractions

Philip II was beset by other problems. In 1572 he was concentrating on the Mediterranean because he knew the Turks would be seeking revenge after the victory of Lepanto in 1571. From 1578–80, his first concern was Portugal and from 1585, he decided that the Netherlands would never be settled until he had dealt with England. Then in 1589 Philip wrote to Parma, 'The affairs of France are at this moment the principal thing,' and this remained his view until 1598. It is no coincidence that 1580–85 was the period without distractions and that was when the Spanish were able to make the greatest advances.

Spanish shortage of money

The scale of Philip's commitments meant that he was perpetually short of money. The second revolt had been precipitated by the Tenth Penny and the third was caused by Philip's bankruptcy in 1575 which meant that he was unable to pay his troops. After 1585, Philip's spending reached new heights: the Armada cost ten million ducats and then he was engaged in simultaneous wars against both England and France. From 1590, the Spanish army in the Netherlands was virtually paralysed by continual mutinies because the troops were paid so rarely.

Distance from Spain

The thousand or so miles which separates Spain from the Netherlands presented serious problems to the Spanish. There were the logistical problems of transporting large numbers of men and supplies, which involved a trip across the Mediterranean to Genoa, and then the march up the 'Spanish Road' along the borders of France through Habsburg or friendly territory. Worse than this, however, was the time taken in communication, especially as Philip was reluctant to delegate any real power and frequently left his governors uncertain about the policies he favoured.

The economies of Spain and the Netherlands

As the revolt progressed, one factor which enabled seven small provinces to withstand the Spanish Empire was the relative performance of their economies. The Dutch continued to prosper and with their control of the sea, their trade was unaffected. They even began to supply the war needs of the Spanish! Spain had to bear the greater costs of an army of occupation and its economy stagnated under the pressure of excessive taxation.

Military advances

The war in the Netherlands was primarily one of sieges, which were very slow as towns were so well defended by complex series of embankments that they they had to be starved into submission. In the 1590s William's successor, Maurice of Nassau, developed new tactics: he moved away from big squares of pikemen with musketeers at the corners to a more flexible system of long thin lines of separate units of pike and shot backed up by cavalry. He also introduced a new, smaller unit – the battalion of about 550 men – which was easier to deploy. In the event there were few field battles for Maurice to demonstrate the effectiveness of these new tactics, but his formidable reputation was a deterrent to the Spaniards and his innovations were copied in much of Europe during the seventeenth century.

6 ～ THE THIRD REVOLT, 1576–81

The death of the governor-general left the Council of State, composed largely of southern Catholic nobility, in control of the government. The council proved unable to cope with the menace of the mutineers and so it was replaced by the States General which began negotiations with William of Orange to end the war and expel the Spanish. Agreement was reached five days before the Spanish mutineers attacked Antwerp on 4 November and in the 'Spanish Fury', an orgy of looting and destruction, laid waste to the greatest city in northern Europe. Eight thousand people died in one of the worst outrages of the century. The entire Netherlands, horrified and revolted by the actions of the troops, united to expel the hated foreigner. All internal differences were temporarily forgotten and it would not be an exaggeration to say that the mutineers had lost the revolt for Philip. On 8 November the Pacification of Ghent proclaimed the existence of a united Netherlands led by the States General.

The Pacification of Ghent ended what had been a state of civil war between the loyal provinces and the rebels of Holland and Zeeland. Now it was agreed jointly to drive out the Spaniards and then submit all differences to the States General. Religion was a worrying issue for the future but the heresy edicts were suspended on condition that 'those of Holland, Zeeland or others shall not be allowed to disturb the common peace and quiet outside the provinces of Holland, Zeeland and associated places, or in particular to attack the Roman Catholic religion'. Orange was recognised as Stadholder of Holland and Zeeland, although his authority was restricted to those territories he already had under his command.

1576 represented the high point of the revolt. Philip was faced with the reconquest of the entire Netherlands and the new governor-general

PICTURE 36
'The Spanish Fury' from
Tortures at Antroff in 1576,
artist unknown

Don John, appointed because he would have greater authority as the son of Charles V, was forced into humiliating concessions. Philip recognised that compromise was necessary to allow Don John to establish his position but he included the important proviso: 'safeguarding religion and my authority as much as may be'. In other words, there would be no movement on the real issues in dispute.

The government of the Low Countries was now in the hands of the States General. This was an unwieldy body as all agreements had to be referred back to the provincial states and achieving agreement, except on the expulsion of foreign troops, was difficult. William of Orange persuaded them to sign the Union of Brussels in January 1577 which restated the Pacification of Ghent, but he was unable to prevent a separate agreement, known as the Perpetual Edict, being made between the States General and Don John in February. In return for the maintenance of Catholicism in all areas and their recognition of Don John as governor-general, all Spanish troops were removed. Holland and Zeeland, firmly opposed to the religious clauses, withdrew their delegates from the States General. The first signs of the division of the Netherlands had already appeared, but fortunately for Orange and the northern provinces, the impatient Don John destroyed his own political position by attacking Namur, which had the effect of reuniting the whole Netherlands in opposition to the Spanish.

Meanwhile the states themselves appointed a new governor-general – the Archduke Matthias, the nephew of Philip II. This was designed to restrict Orange's power and the conditions imposed on Matthias made him totally dependent on the states. In fact, Orange became Matthias's deputy and the latter had little real power during his three years in the Netherlands.

By the end of 1577 Don John had withdrawn from the Netherlands and Spanish power had again almost collapsed. However, a dramatic change was already under way. In March a truce had been arranged with the Turks, freeing Philip from war in the Mediterranean. In August a shipment of 2 000 000 ducats arrived from the Indies, the largest yet received. Philip was able to reschedule his debts and the Spanish army of Flanders was ordered to return. On their arrival in January 1578, they inflicted a crushing defeat on the army of the States at Gembloux. The reconquest of the Low Countries had begun.

The progress of the royal troops was made more rapid by the internal disagreements of their opponents. It was soon apparent that the aims of the Catholic *Walloon* (southern) nobility were almost irreconcilable with those of the Calvinists. This became obvious as Calvinists began to take control of towns in the south (where their numerical strength lay at this stage) and to impose their will by force, contravening the pacification. A notable example of this was Ghent where the Calvinists took power and in 1577 went so far as to arrest the Duke of Aerschot, a leading Walloon nobleman and committed opponent of Orange. Unlike the north, the Calvinists of the south, as in Ghent, were often artisans and social revolution was threatened by their ousting of the Catholic magistrates. In these circumstances, continued allegiance to

Walloon the southernmost French-speaking provinces

the revolt began to appear more dangerous to the nobility than loyalty to the king and this combined with the traditional particularism of the provinces to produce serious rifts in the States General.

The States were already experiencing problems in financing the war and maintaining an army of 50 000. In 1578, Don John died. His successor was Alexander Farnese, later Duke of Parma. In January 1579 the three southern provinces of Hainault, Artois and Walloon Flanders formed the Union of Arras to preserve the Catholic religion. In May the union signed a treaty with Parma in which he agreed to the removal of foreign troops from its provinces and the restoration of all old provincial and aristocratic privileges in return for renewed allegiance to the king. Parma now had a strong territorial base from which to attack the north.

The reconciliation of the Walloon provinces prompted those in the north into their own union, signed at Utrecht in January 1579. This union was opposed for some months by William of Orange because he realised that it formalised the separation that had already begun between north and south. It would be much harder to unite the two sides after the unions had been signed. But strive as William might to avoid it, the final division of the Netherlands had begun.

ALESSANDRO FARNESE, DUKE OF PARMA (1586–92)

Alexander Farnese, Prince of Parma and Duke from 1586, was Philip II's nephew and the son of Margaret of Parma. On the death of Don John in 1578 he had become governor of the Netherlands at the age of thirty-three, and he served Philip loyally until his death from disease caused by a wound in 1592. He knew the Netherlands well, and being a master of diplomacy, sought to divide the more conservative nobility of the Walloon south from the rebels in the north, which he succeeded in doing in 1579. He was also an excellent soldier and strategist, and under his leadership the Spanish cause prospered as never before; he had retaken the southern and much of the central Netherlands by 1585.

His preparations of bridgeheads across the great rivers protecting the northern rebels came to nothing, however, when his troops were diverted in support of the Armada in 1588. He knew the foolhardiness of this scheme, as there was no deep-water port in Spanish hands from which the troops could be safely embarked, but he still shared the blame for its failure. In 1590, against his protests that the opportunity to defeat the Dutch would be lost, Philip then ordered him to intervene in the French Wars of Religion. He died in 1592 during his third campaigning season in France. Philip had already issued the order to dismiss him.

PICTURE 37
Alessandro Farnese, Duke of Parma *by Sofonisba Anguisciola*

KEY ISSUE

Why were the seventeen provinces unable to maintain their united opposition to the king for long?

TIMELINE

1575 The Spanish Fury: sack of Antwerp
1576 Pacification of Ghent: Netherlands unite against the Spanish
1577 Perpetual Edict: Don John accepts the Pacification
1578 Don John dies; succeeded by Parma
1579 Union of Arras: three Walloon provinces make peace with Spain
Union of Utrecht: six northern provinces unite to fight on
1585 Treaty of Nonsuch: England promises assistance to Dutch rebels
1588 The Armada

The Union of Utrecht was formed by Holland, Zeeland, Utrecht, Friesland, Gelderland and the Ommelanden of Groningen. It was a formal alliance of provinces that acted as if they were independent states. They agreed to act as a single province in matters of peace and war; otherwise each province would retain its independence, including the question of religion.

The Netherlands was now divided into three. In the south, the rule of the king had been restored and with it Catholic worship. In the centre, the States General were increasingly unable to cope with the strains of war and unresolved religious differences. In the north, the Union of Utrecht had effectively thrown off all allegiance to the king and Calvinist worship was imposed. The States General had little option but to seek negotiations with Spain and they were ready to attend a peace conference at Cologne.

At the same time Parma continued his steady progress north, following the strategy of isolating each centre of resistance, and then starving it out. In June 1579 he captured Maastricht and Mechlin surrendered soon after. Parma's generous terms to the defeated towns encouraged others to return to the royalist fold, for example Groningen in March 1580.

As the area covered by the revolt slowly diminished it became clear that the peace negotiations would not bring a settlement. Complete surrender or outright rejection of the king were the only options. In July 1581 Philip was deposed as head of state in the northern provinces by the Act of Abjuration. This made explicit a situation that had long existed, but it did nothing to solve the problem of whom to put in Philip's place. The search for foreign allies, which had been conducted ever since the revolt began, took on a new urgency.

7 ⌐ THE INTERNATIONAL CONTEXT OF THE DUTCH REVOLT

The Revolt of the Netherlands was more than an internal Spanish matter from the start. Because of its position in northern Europe neither England nor France could ignore events there. If the Spanish army were to be victorious, where would it turn next? To the English, especially after Elizabeth's excommunication in 1570, the answer seemed obvious. Consequently Elizabeth was ready to listen to the rebels' pleas for aid, although she rarely assisted them until after 1585. In fact Philip was so concerned at the prospect of French control of England through Mary, Queen of Scots, that he was prepared to overlook a number of English provocations including the seizure of a treasure fleet that was blown into English ports in 1568, and he actually opposed the excommunication of the English Queen in 1570.

Relations with the French were complicated by the position of the Huguenots to whom many of the Netherlands nobility were related; for example, the leading Huguenot nobleman, Admiral Coligny, was a relative of the brothers Hoorn and Montigny. Philip was a supporter of the Guise faction, which meant that their enemies tended to support the Netherlands rebels. Thus there was the curious spectacle of the French king's brother, the Catholic Duke of Anjou, in alliance with Calvinist opponents of the King of Spain. Initial assistance was given to the rebels by Anjou in 1578 when he assembled an army, but more importantly in 1581 he agreed to become the new sovereign of the Netherlands. William of Orange was behind this move in order to harness permanent French support for the rebel cause.

See page 467

This alliance across the religious divide indicates French dislike of Spanish power, which reached new heights after the annexation of Portugal and her empire in 1580. Neither France nor England could tolerate the increased power this gave to Spain, and the Netherlands became the focal point of resistance. There had been a 'cold war' operating for decades in the Channel, partly in response to the Spanish monopoly in the New World, but in the 1580s this broadened into open intervention in the Netherlands themselves. The tireless efforts of William of Orange to procure foreign involvement in the revolt led to him being branded as an outlaw by Philip II in 1580, with a price on his head. William was seen as the main obstacle to the suppression of the revolt, which was a necessary precondition for the subjection of England. Assistance for the Netherlands rebels was therefore a matter of state security for England. Ironically it was not to be forthcoming until after the assassination of Orange in 1584 when the apparently unstoppable progress of the Spanish army finally decided Elizabeth I that open intervention could no longer be delayed.

In August 1585 she signed the Treaty of Nonsuch with the rebels. Elizabeth agreed to send a force of 4400 (later increased to 8000) and to pay the states 600 000 florins. The Earl of Leicester was to become the lieutenant-general, advised by a Council of State. In return the Dutch were to surrender Flushing, Rammekens and Brill to the English until all the Queen's expenses were repaid after the war.

English intervention was the major turning point in the revolt because it finally pushed Philip into the decision that England must be defeated before the Netherlands could be dealt with. For a few years the Netherlands had been Philip's major concern. At the end of the reign they were pushed into second place again, not by the Mediterranean conflict this time but by war, first against England and then also against France.

8 ∽ THE SPANISH RECONQUEST, 1581–85

The States General had not sought a revolution and did not want supreme power themselves, but merely a different sovereign. They proved incapable of holding the provinces together given the strength of local particularism. The Duke of Anjou was accepted as the new head of state with reluctance – and by Holland and Zeeland not at all – and severe restrictions were placed on the duke's authority. He found this galling and made an abortive attempt in January 1583 to seize the principal towns of Flanders, including Antwerp. The United Provinces turned against Anjou after this 'French Fury' and he left for good in June 1583 but there now seemed no alternative to submitting to Spain. Anarchy was rapidly developing and only Holland and Zeeland provided determined resistance to Spain under the leadership of William of Orange. It seemed that the revolt must inevitably fail when Orange was killed in July 1584 by an assassin paid by the Spanish. He had seemed the only man capable of holding the factions of the revolt together.

The tensions in the north had been made more acute by the steady success of Parma. His strategy was to capture the coastline and block the River Scheldt above Antwerp because this would fatally weaken all the great towns of Flanders and Brabant, which were heavily dependent on water transport. In 1583 he captured the major Flemish ports, except Ostend, and the towns along the Scheldt estuary. In 1584 Parma continued his attack on towns on the Scheldt, capturing Aalst, Bruges and Ghent amongst others. In March 1585, Brussels was taken and then Antwerp was cut off from the sea by the construction of a bridge across the Scheldt. In August the great city fell without a shot being fired. In three years Parma had doubled the area under royal control.

Parma had less money than his predecessors but at least remittances were regular and this enabled him to make plans and to avoid the mutinies which crippled the Spanish war effort on many occasions. This was all to change from 1585 onwards.

Enormous sums were sent after 1585 but these were mainly spent on foreign enterprises. For example, between August 1590 and May 1591 nearly four million was received by the treasury. Three million was spent on the war with France, leaving less than one million for the Netherlands. This explains why, despite the vast sums received, there were few real gains after 1585 and mutinies again began to paralyse the army.

There were five mutinies between 1572 and 1576 and thirty-seven between 1589 and 1607. The major ones involved up to 4000 men and could take a year to settle. The mutineers were highly disciplined and made reasonable demands – their arrears of pay often ran into years – but they presented a grave problem to the government who could not continue the war effectively until the mutiny was settled. Consequently they nearly always ended successfully with each mutineer paid in full and in cash. Despite this, mutinies destroyed the offensives of 1589, 1593 and 1600 and led to the loss of Groningen in 1594. Philip's inability to pay his troops promptly is one of the main reasons for Dutch success in the campaigns of the 1590s under Maurice of Nassau.

KEY ISSUE

Why was Parma so successful up to 1585?

TABLE 12

Money received from Spain by the Military Treasury of The Netherlands (millions of florins)

1572–77	22.4
1580–85	15
1585–90	44.7
1590–95	37.8
1595–99	52.9

9 ∽ THE ENTERPRISE OF ENGLAND

For both Spain and England, the traditional enemy was France and the two countries had pursued a fairly consistent policy of friendship since the end of the fifteenth century. Philip had begun his reign as husband to Mary Tudor and he even offered to marry Elizabeth after her accession. England had been an important ally. It therefore took a considerable time before Philip would seriously consider attacking England, even though their differences and rivalries might have made such an attack seem highly justified and even prudent. Religion was not the main factor in Philip's decision, although it was obviously a secondary consideration and the one that Philip chose to emphasise. More important were political and economic factors.

For many years, English privateers had been preying on Spanish shipping, especially in the New World. France and England disputed Spain's exclusive claim but attempts to break the monopoly led to violent clashes – three expeditions led by Sir John Hawkins ended in pitched battles in the 1560s and two colonies of French Protestants in Florida were massacred by Spanish forces in 1566. The activities of Drake, which culminated most spectacularly in his circumnavigation of the world in 1577–80 and his capture of Spanish treasure in the Pacific, were a serious irritant to the Spanish, although his practical effect was small. English piracy was in fact a tribute to the superior power of Spain, as was the assistance given to Dom Antonio of Portugal and even to the Dutch. This did not make them more acceptable to the Spanish and from about 1585 onwards Philip became convinced that he would have no success until England had been taught a lesson. When Drake raided Vigo on the Spanish mainland in 1585 and Elizabeth signed the Treaty of Nonsuch with the rebels, Philip's intentions were confirmed and plans were made for an invasion of England in 1587. In fact English help for the Dutch had little effect. Unlike the States General, Elizabeth wanted to retain weak Spanish control of the Netherlands, and Leicester behaved insensitively, imposing new taxes while two of his commanders actually betrayed their positions to the Spanish.

It would have been impossible to mount a full-scale invasion from Spain; therefore it was decided to send a strong fleet which would join up with Parma's army and escort it across the Channel. This plan ignored the vital point, repeatedly made by Parma, that there was no deep-water port in Spanish hands where such a junction could occur. Nevertheless the plans went ahead, to be delayed for a year by a daring raid by Drake on Cadiz which sank a number of ships and, importantly, destroyed the barrels in which stores were to be carried – a deficiency that was never remedied, so much food and water was spoiled before it was used. The death of the Armada's commander, the Marquis of Santa Cruz, in February 1588 was another set back which was not allowed to halt proceedings. His replacement, the Duke of Medina Sidonia, was no sailor, but he was a powerful *grandee* who could exercise authority over the captains of the fleet. By May the fleet was as ready as it ever would

See case study on pages 454–6

KEY ISSUE

Why did Philip decide to invade England?

TIMELINE

The Armada

May 1588	Armada sets sail, delayed by storms
July	Armada arrives off English coast
	Week long dog-fight in Channel; English unable to break Spanish crescent formation
	Spanish anchor off Calais
	English send in fire-ships; crescent formation broken
	Spanish nearly driven onto Dutch sandbanks by harrying English ships
August	Winds blow Armada north around Scotland and Ireland; many losses
Sept	Fleet struggle home

be and it set out on its fateful mission. The flaws in the planning are discussed more fully in a documentary exercise at the end of the chapter. The great fleet advanced up the Channel as intended, although there was no real chance of picking up Parma's troops without a deep-water port for embarkation and barges suitable for shallow water would have been picked off easily enough by the Dutch navy. In any case, the Armada's formation was broken by fire-ships, and the storms which followed prevented the Spanish ships from re-grouping. The surviving vessels limped home round the north of Scotland.

The failure of the Armada dealt a fatal blow to Philip's prestige in both France and the Netherlands, but as far as England was concerned, it was not the end of the war but only the beginning. Fears of Spanish invasion continued throughout the 1590s and there were two more Armadas in 1596 and 1597, both scattered by gales, and a further fleet in 1599 was diverted to the defence of the Canaries and the Azores. The Armada was the start of an Atlantic fleet for Spain; priority was given to

PICTURE 38

Engraving No. 4 of House of Lords Tapestries, 'The English Pursue the Spanish Fleet East of Plymouth' *by John Pine*

making good the losses suffered. The English found that their spectacular raids on shipping were harder in the 1590s than before. More bullion reached Spain between 1588 and 1603 than in any other fifteen-year period. However, the costs of defence were very heavy. The Earl of Essex led a dramatic raid on Cadiz in 1595 but otherwise the English had little success and the war became a costly stalemate. Philip became increasingly anxious for peace as the financial burdens mounted, especially as from 1589 he had started to intervene in France.

10 ⌐ INTERVENTION IN FRANCE

For the first thirty years of the reign, Philip's policy in France had been to aid the enemies of the Huguenots, usually by verbal encouragement but occasionally by financial assistance. This position was changed in 1584 with the new heir becoming the Huguenot Henry of Navarre. Philip was faced with the prospect of his greatest national enemy and near neighbour becoming Protestant. To avert such a catastrophe he signed the secret Treaty of Joinville in December 1584 with the Guises, the leaders of the Catholic League in France. In August 1589, Philip's fear of a Huguenot succession was realised when Henry III was murdered. He decided that he must intervene in the French wars himself.

See pages 485–6

It was a disastrous decision for the reconquest of the Netherlands. Under their new leader, Maurice of Nassau, the United Provinces were able to win back some of the territory conquered by Parma and so consolidate their position. The Dutch were also well served by their chief diplomat, Johannes Oldenbarnevelt, who did much to maintain the international alliance against Spain. Spanish victory became impossible, especially as intervention in France meant that Philip was fighting three opponents.

The early 1590s was the first and last time that the lines of political and religious division were exactly the same. It seemed that at last a decisive clash between the two faiths was to take place, which would settle the religious question for good. Of course, it was not that simple: relations between the Dutch and the English were bad and the Pope was furious at Philip's claims to be the protector of the Catholics in France.

It was necessary to have an alternative monarch to Henry IV. Philip put forward the claim of his daughter Isabella, the granddaughter of Henry II of France, although the French parliament, the Estates General, rejected it. The prospect of Habsburgs in control of almost the whole of western Europe was not an appealing one to any but the most fanatical of Catholics, and was always unlikely to succeed. Ignoring this, Philip turned away from his legitimate interests in the Netherlands, where the war became purely defensive, and used it merely as a base for the operations against France. As money was diverted away from the Netherlands, the mutinies which destroyed the Spanish war effort began. Parma suggested a peace plan which would grant private

TIMELINE

1590	Parma diverted to France Maurice of Nassau starts to retake Spanish bridgeheads in the north
1591	Parma again diverted to France
1592	Parma dies

KEY ISSUE

What was the effect for the Netherlands of Spanish intervention in France in the 1590s?

Calvinist worship in specific towns but Philip was only interested in victory, not compromise, ignoring the fact that he was denying Parma the means to make victory possible.

Henry of Navarre besieged Paris in 1590. Parma was ordered to raise the siege, which he did successfully, but meanwhile the States General won their first military success for twelve years, capturing Breda. The Dutch then mounted a major campaign in 1591 in which they captured Zutphen, Deventer and Nijmegen. Disobeying Philip's order, Parma marched north to meet the new threat and it was five months before he obeyed the king's express instruction to return to France and relieve the siege of Catholic Rouen. Parma was disillusioned by his new role and its inevitable failures and he had already begun to lose Philip's confidence, typically but quite unjustifiably. This act of insubordination led Philip to decide on his dismissal but before his replacement arrived, Parma died in December 1592 and so Philip lost his best general.

In the confusion which followed Parma's death, Maurice of Nassau was able to capture all the Spanish outposts north of the Maas. Two men claimed to succeed Parma – the Count of Fuentes who was sent from Spain as commander-in-chief, and Count Mansfelt who had been Parma's deputy in Brussels. Neither would recognise the other and two parallel governments were set up with a combined result of anarchy. Spanish authority ebbed dangerously and there were riots when new taxes to pay for the French war were announced. In July 1593 the Brussels government was forced to conclude a truce with Henry of Navarre. In 1593 he became a Catholic and captured Paris in 1594. Gradually the whole of France rallied to his cause. Further fighting was profitless to Philip but nevertheless the war continued. In January 1595 Henry IV formally declared war and in 1596 formed the Triple Alliance with England and the Dutch. The United Provinces were now recognised as a sovereign state by two of the major powers of Europe.

Philip was in a desperate position. The Spanish war effort continued and Calais was captured in April 1596 but the cost was immense. Eighty-eight million florins was sent to the Netherlands in the 1590s and by 1598 Spanish government debts were estimated at 100 000 000 ducats, while interest payments amounted to two-thirds of revenue. The strain on the treasury could not be continued and in 1596 Philip had gone bankrupt again. It was essential to make peace.

The Treaty of Vervins was signed with France in May 1598. Spain gave up Calais and other conquests and in other respects the Treaty of Câteau-Cambrésis was reaffirmed. Elizabeth I was not interested in negotiations and war continued until after her death, the Treaty of London (1604) being one of the first acts of James I. Philip was not prepared to relinquish the northern Netherlands so the conflict dragged on there until 1609.

The war had gained little for Spain. Although Henry IV had become a Catholic he was still Spain's committed enemy. The legacy of this war, and that against the English, would be felt in Spain for decades to come in a crippled economy and a treasury that staggered from one crisis to another.

11 ⤚ THE REVOLT OF THE NETHERLANDS: THE FINAL PHASE, 1598–1609

The independence of the United Provinces was not officially recognised by Spain until 1648 but in practice the conclusion of a twelve-year truce in 1609 marked the end of the revolt and the emergence of a new nation. The death of Philip II in 1598 made no difference to Spanish determination to continue the war but it was recognised that some new system of running the country was necessary. In 1596 Philip's nephew, the Archduke Albert, was made governor-general. Two years later he married the Infanta Isabella and, known as the archdukes, they became joint sovereigns of a partially independent Netherlands. Spain still provided the army and decided foreign policy and so retained overall control but other matters were left to the discretion of the archdukes, who therefore had more freedom than their predecessors. With some restoration of order and prosperity, they soon became popular in the south but the north was not impressed by the apparent new independence.

The war became a stalemate. 'The net result of nine summer campaigns (1598–1606) was a few towns gained and a few towns lost' (P. Geyl). Marice of Nassau launched an invasion of the south in 1600 but not a single town in Flanders rose to support him. It was clear that the south was not prepared to endure further protracted warfare in order to be reunited with the northern provinces. The Spanish then began to recover lost territory under the leadership of Ambrogio di Spinola of Genoa who became commander-in-chief in 1605. Both sides became anxious for peace. The war had cost the United Provinces 10 000 000 florins a year in 1604–06 and Spain needed a respite from the continuous warfare she had endured.

It proved too difficult to negotiate a permanent peace. Instead a twelve-year truce was concluded in 1609 which was a great victory for the seven northern provinces. Their independence was implied, if not openly stated, trade with the Indies and the position of Catholics in the north were not mentioned, and the Scheldt remained closed so that Antwerp in the south of the Netherlands would not revive as a trading competitor to the booming Dutch city of Amsterdam. All that the south obtained was twelve years' rest. The tiny United Provinces of the northern Netherlands had defeated the greatest power in Europe.

TIMELINE

1599 Peace negotiations – unsuccessful
1600 United Provinces attack Flanders
1601 Spanish begin siege of Ostend
1602 –03 Some gains by Dutch
1604 Ostend falls
 Peace made with England; Dutch now have no allies
1606 Spanish win back recent losses; stalemate
1607 Cease-fire agreed
1609 Twelve-year truce

12 ⤚ THE DIVISION OF THE NETHERLANDS

Particularism had always been a potent force in the Netherlands but there had also been a strong sense of common ties. By the time hostilities ceased, however, clear differences were beginning to emerge between the two new countries. In the north, Catholics were probably

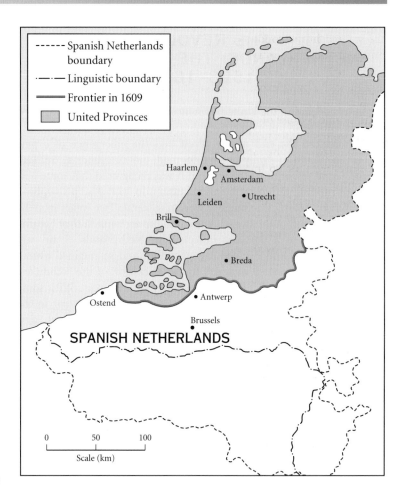

MAP 22
The division of The Netherlands

still in the majority, partly because the lack of ministers meant that priests who appeared at least to accept the reformed religion remained in their posts. Open Catholic worship was, however, forbidden and Calvinism made rapid progress so that outwardly the United Provinces was a completely Protestant country.

Equally significantly, the north had prospered while the south stagnated. Holland and Zeeland were no longer a battlefield after 1576 and a burgomaster of Amsterdam was able to write, 'It is known to all the world that whereas it is generally the nature of war to ruin land and people, these countries on the contrary have been noticeably improved thereby.' The merchants of Holland had grown rich supplying the war needs of their enemies which the Spanish lacked the capacity to obtain for themselves. The Dutch dominated trade from the Baltic. In 1590 the first Dutch ships entered the Mediterranean and this led to an enormous expansion in their overseas trade. They also exploited the routes to the Indies – both East and West – much to the annoyance of Spain. In 1596 the states of Holland acknowledged, 'In the command of the sea and in the conduct of the war on the water resides the entire prosperity of the country.'

Not only trade flourished in the United Provinces. Industry too experienced a great expansion, helped mainly by the 100 000 refugees from the south. Many were Calvinists seeking sanctuary in the north. Others came because of the disruption from endless fighting; thus linen production at Oudenarde and textile production at Hondschoote were severely damaged by army activity in the 1580s and profitable industries were set up in the United Provinces.

As time passed, the difference became increasingly marked between the States General of the north, which wielded sovereign power, and their sister body in the south, which lost even the power to refuse new taxes. The United Provinces only wanted re-unification on the basis of complete surrender by the south. Although there was a war party, led by Maurice of Nassau, which was willing to attempt that, the regents, the Dutch merchants who ran the towns and held the purse strings, wanted neither the expense nor the disruption to their trade.

The conquest of the south was in any case impractical. Not only were the Spanish capable of defending the south, if not re-taking the north, but the population of the south would give no support to Dutch invaders, as had been shown in 1600. They saw the Dutch not as liberators but as a threat. The Spanish Netherlands had emerged as a distinct entity.

Under the ordered rule of the archdukes, the population began to increase and a reorganised local economy developed. The fruits of that can be seen in the fine houses built for merchants in Antwerp in the early seventeenth century, in spite of the closure of the Scheldt and the loss of artisans to the north.

Many of those artisans had been Calvinists and their departure helped to settle the religious problems of the south, which became firmly Catholic. This renewal of Catholicism was not just a matter of inquisitions and heresy trials – there were 3000 Jesuits and Capuchins at work in the south to restore the faith of the people.

The differences between the north and south have continued to the present day. The United Provinces retained the name of the Netherlands and has been shaped by the Calvinist Dutch Reformed Church. The southern provinces eventually became Belgium with its own very different identity.

13 ∽ BIBLIOGRAPHY

**Martyn Rady, *The Netherlands: Revolt and Independence 1550–1650* (Hodder and Stoughton, 1987), *R. Bonney, *The European Dynastic States 1494–1660*, pp. 145–63, (OUP, 1991), or *P. Limm, *The Dutch Revolt* (Longman Seminar Studies, 1989) are the best starting points. **G. Parker, *The Dutch Revolt* (Allen Lane, 1977) is essential reading and not difficult. **G. Parker, *The Grand Strategy of Philip II* (Yale,

1998) shows how many of Philip's problems inter-locked, in particular the Dutch Revolt, relations with England and the Armada. G. Parker, *Spain and the Netherlands 1599–1659* (Collins, 1977) contains useful essays on aspects of the revolt. *P. Geyl, *The Revolt of the Netherlands* (2nd ed., Ernest Benn, 1958) is a classic study, although his conclusions have been much debated. *K.W. Swart, *William the Silent and the Revolt of the Netherlands* (Historical Association Pamphlet, 1978) is a general analysis as well as a biography. G. Mattingly, *The Defeat of the Spanish Armada* (2nd ed., Jonathan Cape, 1983) shows how events in England, France and the Netherlands were all connected, although in some respects it has been superseded by C. Martin and G. Parker, *The Spanish Armada* (1988). *Alastair Duke, *Reformation and Revolt in the Low Countries* (Hambledon, 1990) shows the infuence of religion on politics. Jonathan I. Israel, *The Dutch Republic. Its Rise, Greatness and Fall 1477–1806* (Clarendon Press, Oxford 1995) is a provocative recent study with incisive comment on the revolt.

14 ꞈ STRUCTURED AND ESSAY QUESTIONS

A *Structured questions.*

1. (a) In what ways were the nobility of the Netherlands dissatisfied with the rule of Philip II in the 1560s?
   (b) Why was Alva unable to crush the Dutch revolt of 1572?
2. (a) What forced William of Orange into revolt?
   (b) How far do you agree that the United Provinces only came into being because of the House of Orange?

B *Essay questions.*

1. What was the role of religion in the revolts in the Netherlands up to 1609?
2. How did the United Provinces succeed in their struggle for independence against the might of the Spanish Empire?
3. Why did only seven provinces in the Netherlands succeed in breaking away from Spanish rule?
4. 'Spanish commitments elsewhere'. How far do these explain the failure to crush the Revolt of the Netherlands?
5. When and why did resistance to Spanish rule in the Netherlands become a movement for independence?

15 ꞈ BIOGRAPHICAL STUDY ON WILLIAM OF ORANGE

At the age of thirty-four, William of Nassau, Prince of Orange (1533–1584), better known as William the Silent, became the leader of the people of the Dutch Netherlands in their revolt

TIMELINE

William of Orange: Early career and opposition

1533 Born, son of Lutheran German count
1544 Cousin leaves him vast estates in France and the Netherlands, including principality of Orange
Moves to court of Charles V and becomes a Catholic
1556 Member of the Council of State and of the Order of the Golden Fleece
1559 *Stadholder* of Holland, Zeeland and Utrecht
Most important noble in the Netherlands
1561 Marries Anne of Saxony, Lutheran niece of the Elector
Begins campaign against Granvelle
Moves into opposition
1564 Announces opposition to the heresy laws
1566 Ambivalent role in the revolt; will neither lead rebels nor swear new oath of obedience to the king
1567 Goes into exile

In rebellion

1568 Fails in attempt to invade the Netherlands to win back his lands
1568 –72 Develops contacts with French Huguenots and the English
1572 Four-pronged invasion
Orange driven onto defensive in Holland
Alone against Spain
1573 Becomes Calvinist to keep control of sea beggars
1572 –76 Orange almost single-handedly keeps revolt alive

Skilful handling of the states
Use of propaganda keeps opposition to Philip steady
Controls radicals so as not to lose the support of the ruling class
Looks for foreign allies and particularly a new sovereign

Triumph and division

1576 Pacification of Ghent: highpoint for Orange
Unable to prevent subsequent divisions
1579 Opposes the Union of Utrecht, which makes re-unification more difficult
1581 Offers the sovereignty of the United Provinces to the Duke of Anjou
1584 Assassinated

PICTURE 39
William of Orange (the Silent), *by Adriaen Thomasz*

against Philip II. William has been called by some 'the wisest, gentlest, and bravest man who ever led a nation' and by others a 'deceitful, self-seeking politician, and traitor'. The Dutch referred to him as 'the Father of his people', but to the Spanish he incarnated the evils of the Reformation, the cunning of the Flemings and the ingratitude of an upstart. William's character represents a blending of both virtues and vices, making him, like Philip II, the subject of heated discussion to this day.

SOURCE A
From The Character of Philip II, *J.C. Rule and J.J. Te Paska (eds.), 1963.*

SOURCE B
From William the Silent and the Revolt of the Netherlands, *K.W. Swart, 1978.*

Convinced that necessity breaks any law, Orange was not too particular either in the choice of his new allies or in that of his methods of warfare. It is very likely that Orange was a party to plans to assassinate the Duke of Alva, and during his abortive invasion of the Netherlands in 1568 his mercenary troops surpassed the Spanish army in maltreating the civilian population. At the same time, the numerous pamphlets issued under Orange's authorisation not only exaggerated the atrocities committed by the enemy out of all proportion to their actual misdeeds but also accused the Spaniards of many devious designs of which they were entirely innocent. In the time-honoured art of vilifying the enemy, the advantage clearly rested with Orange.

SOURCE C
William of Orange to the states and people, 1572.

Attack that monster, [Alva] hated by Spaniards, Italians and Germans alike, see that this rogue of rogues...does not escape you, this prototype of utter cruelty, who littered the gates, harbours, and streets of your fine towns with the corpses of your citizens, who spared neither sex, age nor rank, who slaughtered free-born men like cattle, who made children into orphans and accused innocent men, who plunged all your homes into mourning, who either laid out the slaughtered bodies on the wheel or would not allow them to be fetched for burial or at least made it impossible for you to give them a decent funeral; I, on my part, will never desert you.

SOURCE D
From Princes, Politics and Religion 1547–89, *N.M. Sutherland, 1984.*

Historians tend to confine William narrowly within the affairs of the Netherlands. While it is not to be contested that the Low Countries were, and remained, his principal concern, it is because they became the political hub of western Europe that William's life and role should be placed in a broader European context...Besides his involvement in the variegated elements of the Netherlands – of close concern to all their neighbours – William steadfastly opposed the international Catholic movement whose guiding purpose was, necessarily, the extermination of Protestantism everywhere...William was publicly proscribed by King Philip...as the supreme enemy of Spain. As such, William obstructed the subjection of the Netherlands, whose resistance depended, if not uniquely, upon Calvinist fervour. He also obstructed an enterprise of England for her restoration to Rome, without which it was alleged, and Philip fitfully believed, there could be no settlement of the Netherlands. This supreme enemy of Spain was also the supreme enemy of the Roman Catholic crusade...the Papacy, the Queen of Scots, English exiles and Catholics everywhere all cast him in that role and periodically induced him to assume it.

In practice, it was the prince's skill in handling the estates which overcame the inherent difficulties of the system. Thomas Wilkes, Leicester's representative in The Hague in 1587, has left us an account of William's methods:

'He always entertained some five or six of the most credit; the needy ones with pensions, the rest with presents, and all with calling them to his table and society. Through these he wrought upon the rest, and there was nothing handled in their assemblies but he knew of it beforehand.' When he had anything to propose, he always consulted with these persons 'whether the matter would pass or be impugned [discredited].' He knew the arguments that would be brought against his proposition and came 'armed with all the answers and counter-reasons to the wonderful admiration of all, and so prevailed.'

SOURCE E
From Estates and Revolutions, *H.G. Koenigsberger, 1971.*

The provinces may want to choose a prince as their protector. All things considered His Excellency thinks that in that case no lord or prince could be found whose authority and means are of greater importance and consequence than those of the kingdom of England or the Duke of Anjou ... But if the provinces think it more advisable not to elect a prince as their protector, His Excellency will comply with their discretion and counsel. In that case too he promises to serve and assist them as much as he can in all matters that they may consider advisable for the benefit and prosperity of these countries.

SOURCE F
William of Orange to the deputies of the union, September 1579.

Your first and foremost mistake is that as yet neither you nor your masters, the provincial States, have established any assembly or council on behalf of the States which has the power to take decisions beneficial to the whole of the country. Everyone in his own province or town acts as he thinks is beneficial to himself and his particular affairs without realising that when some town or province is under attack, it may be useful not to help it for the time being so that in the end the whole country, including these towns and provinces, may be saved.

...As a result we are always compelled to stay on the defensive without daring to attack because each time it is difficult for us to use more than the army of a single province. This of course is not sufficient to resist the forces which the enemy can easily concentrate while our army is scattered ... We meet often enough and deliberate long enough, but are as negligent in implementing our decisions as we are diligent in deliberating at length.

SOURCE G
William of Orange to the States General, January 1580.

William liked to put forward the idea that he was the father of his people, who had sacrificed his own interests and those of his family in order to liberate the Netherlands from Spain.

SOURCE H

William of Orange's 'apology' presented to the States General, December 1580.

It is this head they have destined for death, putting upon it so high a price [25 000 crowns]...and saying that as long as I remain among you this war will not come to an end. I wish it were God's will, gentlemen, that either my eternal exile or even my death could indeed deliver you from all the evil and misery the Spaniards have in store for you...how delightful a death for such purpose! For why did I leave all my goods at the mercy of the enemy? Was it to get rich? Why did I lose my own brothers, who were dearer to me than life? Was it to find others? Why have I left my son so long under arrest, my son whom, did I correctly call myself a father, I should long for? Does it lie within your power to give me another or to give him back to me? Why have I risked my life often? What price or reward could I expect for my long trouble and toil in your service, in which I have grown old and lost all my goods, other than to win and buy your freedom even; if necessary, with my blood? If, gentlemen, you therefore believe that my absence or even death may be of use to you, I am willing to obey. Bid me go to the end of the world, and I shall willingly do so. Here is my head over which no prince or potentate but you alone have power.

Q

1. *In your own words, sum up William's attitude to the following and then find a quotation from him to support your view:*
(i) *religion,* (ii) *the states,* (iii) *particularism,* (iv) *foreign assistance,* (v) *the intentions of the Spanish,* (vi) *his own role in the revolt.*
2. *How did William manage the states (see Sources E, F, G and H)?*
3. *In what ways could William be seen as an idealist? (Take care not to accept his words at their face value.)*
4. *Could the Revolt of the Netherlands have succeeded without William of Orange?*

See pages 443–5

16 ∽ CASE STUDY ON THE ARMADA

SOURCE A

The Duke of Medina Sidonia.

The principal reason which has moved his Majesty to undertake this enterprise is his desire to serve God, and to convert to His Church many peoples and souls who are now oppressed by the heretical enemies of our holy Catholic faith, and are subjected to their sects and errors.

Philip's overriding objective was not to conquer England but to stop English interference in his affairs. The first task of the Armada was to parade, to sail up the Channel and beat its chest before England's gates. What mattered most was that it should look imposing, hence the inflation of its size by including as many ships as possible, however unserviceable, and the exaggeration of the number of troops by issuing false muster rolls.

SOURCE B
I.A.A. Thompson, 1988.

The wiser wonder what can induce the King to insist quite against his natural temper, that the Armada shall give battle to the English, who are known to be awaiting the attack with eager courage, and so they surmise that, over and above the belief that God will be on his side, two motives urge the King to this course; first, that he has secret understandings which will fail if there is any delay; secondly, that these expenses of a million of gold a month cannot be supported for long, and so he has resolved to try his fortune, believing that if the enemy win a battle it will have been so bloody that they will immediately be compelled to make peace, whereas if they lose a battle they lose all at one blow.

SOURCE C
Girolamo Lippomano,
Venetian Ambassador in
Spain.

We found the enemy with a great advantage in ships, better than ours for battle, better designed, with better artillery, gunners and sailors, and so rigged they could handle them and do with them what they wanted. The strength of our Armada was some twenty vessels, and they fought very well, better even than they needed, but the rest fled whenever they saw the enemy attack. Of that I will say nothing in my account to save the reputation of our nation. Furthermore, we brought so few cannon balls that I hardly had a fighting ship that had anything to fire. Thus the San Mateo, having run out of powder and shot, was caught and destroyed, and if the enemy had attacked us one day more after we made to the north, the same would have happened to the rest of the ships.

SOURCE D
Don Francisco de Bobadilla.

The risk of the Armada had always been that failure would strengthen the resolve of the parties Philip was seeking to destroy. The Dutch recognised that they had little to fear from a sea-borne invasion, and their primary objective henceforth was to strengthen their landward defences to the south and east. The English were encouraged to attack the Spanish Empire: between 1589 and 1591, 235 English ships raided the Spanish colonies in America (although as a result of improved defences the raids gradually became

SOURCE E
Richard Bonney, 1990.

unprofitable). Spanish inability to assist the Irish Rebellion in the last four years of Philip II's reign was an accurate reflection of the shift in fortunes that had occurred since the ill-fated Armada of 1588.

SOURCE F
I.A.A. Thompson, 1988.

In one way the Armada succeeded . . . by contemporary lights it was a fearfully impressive looking force, and despite everything, it reached its objective off Calais almost unscathed. That long-running fight up the Channel with its four battles, each one far exceeding what those who had been in both campaigns had experienced at Lepanto, did not destroy the reputation of Spanish naval power, it made it. Lord Howard of Effingham said: 'Some made but little account of the Spanish force by sea; but I do warrant you, all the world never saw such a force as theirs was.' Within two years, Spain again had a fleet of a hundred ships and 43 000 tons, and with the memory of that week in August 1588 behind them, no Englishman could feel confident that there would not be other Armadas and that the next one might not succeed.

1. *What reasons are given in Sources A–C for the Armada? How can the differences between them be reconciled?*
2. *What deficiencies in the Armada are revealed by Source D?*
3. *Compare the assessments of the Armada in Sources E and F. Which do you find more convincing? Give reasons for your answer.*

The French Wars of Religion

15

OVERVIEW

The death of Henry II in 1559 precipitated the French Wars of Religion which were not to be brought to an end until 1598. Henry left behind him sons who were too young to meet the challenges facing them, and too weak once they had grown to adulthood. They were Francis II (1559–60), Charles IX (1560–74) and Henry III (1574–89). The Queen Mother, Catherine de Medici, worked with tireless devotion in her sons' interests, but found that neither conciliation nor ruthlessness worked when the king could not command respect. The challenges the young kings faced were immense. There was faction: the great families of France – the Guises, the Bourbons and the Montmorencys – jockeying for power. There were the bands of soldiers returning from the Italian Wars which had ended at last in 1559, still eager to make their living from war. There were **Huguenots** who, once royal control weakened in 1559, mushroomed in numbers and challenged Catholic control of communities across France and particularly in the south and west. Huguenots and Catholics started to fight it out in the town squares and on the streets, and such riots could escalate into war when noble factions intervened.

There were three stages in the conflict. From 1562 to 1572 the wars were fought within towns and communities as much as between noble-led armies; the Huguenots maintained their challenge across much of France but never won enough concessions from the Crown to satisfy them, while always too many for their hard-line Catholic opponents to accept. 1572 saw the turning point – the Massacre of St Bartholomew – when thousands of Huguenots were slaughtered in Paris and provincial towns, and hundreds of thousands terrified into returning to the Catholic faith.

During the second stage from 1572 to 1584 the remaining Huguenot communities in the west and the south formed what was almost a state within a state, running their own affairs independently of the rest of France and declaring their right to resist the king. The political situation at court went from bad to worse as noble ambition and foreign intervention sparked off further wars, despite the emergence of the *politiques*, a loosely organised group of moderate Catholics.

The final phase of the war began in 1584 when the Protestant Henry of Navarre, a distant cousin of the Valois kings, became heir to the throne on the death of Henry III's last brother. Another state within a state grew up in reaction, a Catholic League of towns and nobility determined to prevent Henry of Navarre from taking the throne. King Henry III at first

Huguenots French Calvinists

gave in to the League and then tried to destroy it by murdering its leaders in 1588, the Duke and the Cardinal of Guise; he succeeded only in enraging it and was himself, the last Valois king, assassinated in 1589. Henry of Navarre, now Henry IV of France, had to fight off Spanish armies which invaded in support of the League as well as the League itself. But in the end there was no alternative to a legitimate king of the male line. War-weariness, social protest, the growing radicalism of the League, all took their toll. In 1593 Henry declared his conversion to Catholicism and the one war aim which had given the League unity disappeared. With protection promised to the Huguenots in the Edict of Nantes of 1598, he was to bring peace to France at last.

1 ᑐ PROBLEMS OF ROYAL AUTHORITY

See pages 465–7

In an age of personal monarchy, as has been seen in the reign of Francis I, the success of a king in France depended to a large extent on the strength of his character; he had to be able to dominate and weld together the large and unruly noble class and control the diverse institutions on which France's past greatness had depended. Unfortunately, the children of Henry II and Catherine de Medici lacked their parents' strength, in both personality and health.

Despite possessing the power to tax at will and the introduction of fiscal reform under Francis I, money was a major problem for the French monarchy by the mid-sixteenth century. The reasons for this were twofold: first, the burden of the Habsburg–Valois wars and second, the inflation which had accelerated in the last phases of the war between France and Spain. Financial stability is essential for the well-being of any state and France was now about to be overtaken by one of the most turbulent periods of its history with its credit in ruins. The debt at the death of Henry II has been estimated at about 40 000 000 livres whilst royal income then averaged about 12 000 000 per year and a great part of this never reached the treasury. When it came to war there was simply not enough money to keep royal armies in the field for any length of time. Time was needed, as royal troops were garrisoned in the frontier provinces so that it could take months to get them across France, the largest country in Europe, to the scene of conflict, and the mercenaries needed to supplement them equally took time to raise. These were reasons why, once the Wars of Religion had broken out, the Crown found it so difficult to bring them to an end.

During the crisis to come there was no alternative to the use of force in the form of an effective royal bureaucracy. We have spoken about the growing centralisation of French government under Francis I, but this must be put into perspective. Compared to medieval government, France now had something that could be called a bureaucracy, but it was still in its embryonic state. The need for ready cash had led to increasing venality, the sale of government offices, under Francis I and

Henry II. These posts were then regarded as private property and there was little ethos of government service. In times of crisis office-holders were as likely to ignore the government or give their allegiance to the leaders of noble factions as they were to obey the king.

There were still no uniform laws or taxes; the provincial **Parlements** and **Estates** ensured this. The provincial governors were therefore key to the exercise of royal authority in the provinces, but they were equally well placed to undermine the monarchy in the event of rebellion. They had troops at their disposal, and were essential links in the chain of **patronage** extending from the king across all of France. Here lies the paradox: kings of France had recognised the difficulties of moulding the different provinces into one state and had chosen to work through provincial governors, but these were powerful noblemen and their intricate network of officials and followers could be used in support of the king or turned against him. More than ever before, an effective king was required.

2 ⇝ THE ARISTOCRACY AND FACTION

The relationship between king and aristocracy depended on mutual respect and recognition of landed interests and honour. To maintain the political loyalty of the nobility, kings had exempted them from personal taxation and showered them with royal pensions and gifts. But this never seemed enough, given a general belief at the time that noble income was declining owing to inflation. Historians now believe that this was perception rather than reality, and that there was no general economic decline of the nobility in the sixteenth century because they did manage to increase rents and exploit their privileges as *seigneurs*. However, as Le Roy Ladurie points out, the nobles could see the profits of merchants and leading townsmen out-stripping them amidst the economic growth of the sixteenth century, and that this threatened them with relative decline in terms of their wealth and status. Also, many government offices were being filled by those newly ennobled. The old military nobility – the *noblesse d'epée*, or nobility of the sword – resented these bureaucratic noblemen – the *noblesse de robe* – as upstarts, even though they inter-married with them to tap new sources of wealth. As the perceived threat to their status grew in the sixteenth century the great nobility became ever more concerned with taking control of the government to protect what they saw as their rights.

The lesser nobility were also resentful. They had been compelled to contribute to forced loans and had been lured into lending the Crown money at enticing but unpaid rates of interest. To make matters worse, a ban was placed on the entry of French noblemen and their children into trade. Unlike their English counterparts, younger sons found themselves bearing an empty dignity of nobility with many large families carving up the family estates in the absence of primogeniture, and with war their only permissible occupation. When peace broke out

parlement the equivalent of a supreme court; the jurisdiction of the Paris *parlement* covered central France, but there were also six provincial *parlements* in outlying regions

Estates the Provincial Estates were local parliaments

patronage benefits given by a superior in return for support, often professional advancement or gifts of money

KEY ISSUE

What were the main flaws in the authority of the Crown in 1559?

in 1559 even that was snatched away from them. It was hardly surprising that many nobles became Huguenots (the name for Calvinists in France) not merely as a spiritual comfort, but in an attempt to maintain their prestige and as a way of attacking the government. By 1562 it is estimated that one-third of the provincial nobility had become Huguenots.

In this highly inflammatory atmosphere there hovered three most important families, all wishing to assume control of the young Francis II. The leading protagonists were the Guise family who had profited enormously from the favour of Francis I and Henry II at a time when it was royal policy to favour noble families rather than princes of the blood. So the Guises as royal favourites and provincial governors had acquired vast territory in the northern and eastern regions of France; they had also built up diverse ecclesiastical holdings and international influence. In return they had served their kings well, particularly in Italy in the Habsburg–Valois conflict. Head of the family was Francis, Duke of Guise, defender of Metz and winner of Calais in 1558. His brother, Charles, Cardinal of Lorraine was an experienced diplomat and played an influential role at the Council of Trent. Staunchly Roman Catholic, their great advantage in 1559 was that Francis II was married to their niece, Mary Stuart, which automatically gave them a head start in the fight for control over the young king.

The family most closely related to the Valois (and thus princes of the blood), and great rivals of the Guises, were the Bourbons. They were

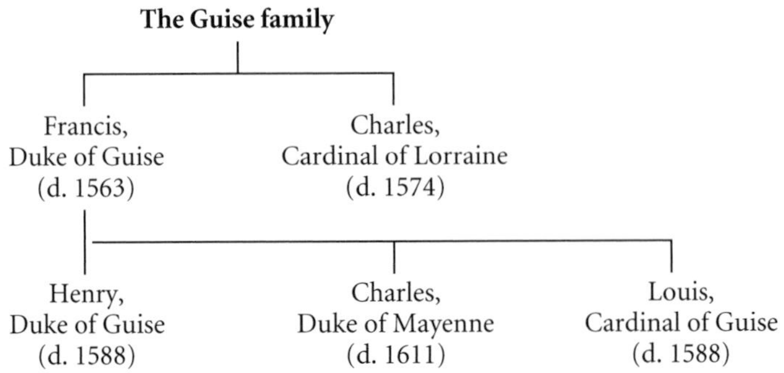

See page 277

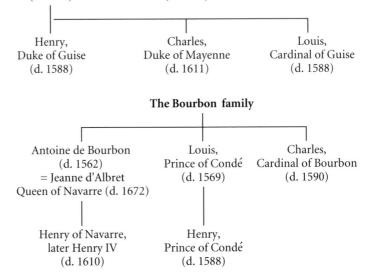

The Guise family

Francis,
Duke of Guise
(d. 1563)

Charles,
Cardinal of Lorraine
(d. 1574)

Henry,
Duke of Guise
(d. 1588)

Charles,
Duke of Mayenne
(d. 1611)

Louis,
Cardinal of Guise
(d. 1588)

DIAGRAM 5

The Guise family

The Bourbon family

Antoine de Bourbon
(d. 1562)
= Jeanne d'Albret
Queen of Navarre (d. 1672)

Louis,
Prince of Condé
(d. 1569)

Charles,
Cardinal of Bourbon
(d. 1590)

Henry of Navarre,
later Henry IV
(d. 1610)

Henry,
Prince of Condé
(d. 1588)

DIAGRAM 6

The Bourbon family

also kings of Navarre through the marriage of the head of the family, Antoine, to Jeanne d'Albret, Queen of Navarre. Antoine, an occasional Huguenot, was rather spineless and not quite as independent in attitude as was usual in the Bourbon family; he was preoccupied with the Spanish threat to Navarre and with keeping safe his estates in south-west France and Picardy. His brother Louis, Prince of Condé, was a Huguenot, but though brave, lacked the qualities of reliability and leadership. In many ways the strongest character in the family was Antoine's wife, Jeanne d'Albret, a devout Huguenot.

The Montmorencys were the oldest noble family in France, with a tremendous record of loyalty to the Crown. Their head was Anne de Montmorency, Constable of France, the most important military officer in the realm. He had been raised to high favour by Francis I until 1540 and returned to prominence under Henry II as his chief minister. But the Guises tried to compete with him for influence over the king, and whilst the Duke of Guise was hailed as saviour of the country for his triumphs at Metz and Calais, Montmorency was defeated and captured at the disastrous battle of St Quentin in 1557. Montmorency was unswervingly Catholic, but his nephews were Huguenots and his sons at any rate sympathetic to Protestantism. The nephews from the Châtillon branch were led by Gaspard de Coligny, Admiral of France,

---

KEY ISSUE

In what ways could rivalries among aristocratic families be dangerous?

MAP 23
France in 1559

The Montmorency family

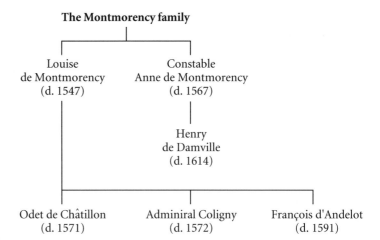

DIAGRAM 7
The Montmorency family

Louise
de Montmorency
(d. 1547)

Constable
Anne de Montmorency
(d. 1567)

Henry
de Damville
(d. 1614)

Odet de Châtillon
(d. 1571)

Adminiral Coligny
(d. 1572)

François d'Andelot
(d. 1591)

---

clientage system
patronage by leading
noblemen secured the
dependence and loyalty
of a network of
followers called clients

See biographical
exercise on page 491

PICTURE 40
*Catherine de Medici by
François Clouet*

who was to be one of the most staunch leaders of the Huguenot forces
in the Wars of Religion. The Montmorency lands were in the centre of
France and to the south, the Île de France and the Midi.

The regional power bases of these three great families were important
but to divide control of France in 1559 geographically into three
portions, Bourbons in the south-west, Montmorencys in the centre and
Guises in the east, is to simplify what was in fact a complex situation.
Many noble families did not belong to the *clientage* system of these
three and, even in their own territories, they still faced opponents. This
made them all the more determined to gain control of the royal
council. However, they all faced a fourth rival, a personality much
closer to the young king than anyone else, his mother Catherine de
Medici.

The widowed queen mother represented the one consistent element
in French government during the religious wars and her life spanned
those of three of her sons. In 1559 she was pitied as the neglected wife
of Henry II, driven into the wings by his powerful and beautiful
mistress, Diane de Poitiers. Catherine was also scorned for the
commercial associations of her family and viewed with suspicion
because of her foreign background, although on her father's side she
was descended from a Florentine family of popes and on her mother's
she was related to the highest French nobility. Without any deep
religious conviction, Catherine's main aim was to restore peace and
preserve the French monarchy intact for her sons.

3 ∽ RELIGION

J. Garrisson-Estèbe estimates that around 1560 there were 2 000 000
Calvinists in France, making up ten per cent of the population. The
amazing growth of Calvinism at this time can be attributed mainly to
the missionary zeal of John Calvin and his Geneva Company of Pastors.

From 1555 these missionaries, carefully vetted and trained, were sent into France in utmost secrecy to previously planned locations. The French Catholic Church was in no state to resist, wracked as it was with abuses. The provinces of south and south-western France, particularly the cities, soon numbered many Huguenots among their inhabitants, as did Normandy and much of central France. In the north and east the missionaries were ultimately less successful, as they were in Paris and several other big cities such as Toulouse and Bordeaux. The reaction of particular areas to Calvinism had much to do with social and economic factors. For example, the missionaries did well in Normandy where the tax burden was heavy; in Lyon, a great commercial centre and open to influence from Switzerland, one of the earliest Huguenot churches was founded in 1546. Also, much depended on the effectiveness of the local church authorities. A quarter of French bishops were absentee Italians (a consequence of the Concordat of Bologna) and their dioceses were concentrated in the south, where Calvinism was able to spread more readily. In contrast, Bishop Mayeuc of Rennes had been so thorough in nipping any sign of heresy in the bud that Calvinism had no more than a foothold in Brittany, in Nantes and on some noble estates.

From a diplomatic point of view – the need to ally with Protestants against the Habsburgs – it might have been advantageous for the French monarchy itself to embrace the new faith, but the king's control over appointments to the Church ensured that there was no constitutional incentive to breaking with Rome and in any case elaborate Catholic rites, including the *sacre*, the anointing of the king at his coronation, were essential to the status of the king. So persecution continued but the sporadic anti-Protestant campaign of the government only succeeded in promoting Calvin's cause as his doctrine and organisational skills were those best suited to a situation of extreme danger to the Protestants.

See pages 279–81 and Chapter 11

The greatest Calvinist success in conversions was amongst the urban classes, the artisans and small tradesmen. Heller sees this as disadvantaged groups rebelling against their Catholic superiors, and very often against domination of towns by church officials, although as these groups had no coherent aims this social rebellion then dissolved into religious civil war. In contrast with this view, Natalie Zemon Davis, taking Lyon as a case study, found little evidence of Catholic 'haves' versus Huguenot 'have-nots' but rather a preponderance of Huguenots amongst trades which were new in some way and so more receptive to the new religion. Either they had only just been established in the city, for example the silk industry, or they used new technology, such as printers, or were rising in social status, such as artists.

Social conflict, as emphasised by Heller, may however have been more prevalent in the countryside where, for instance, peasants of both religions in Agen in south-west France came together to take advantage of the general chaos to seize their hated noble landlord, the Catholic Fumel, and then behead him in front of his wife. Nonetheless, this was labelled a Huguenot uprising by the courts and public opinion –

religious conflict was the way in which any disturbance was interpreted at the time.

The turning point for the Huguenots was winning the support of so many of the lower nobility and later the great magnates and princes of the blood. During 1560 and 1561 most of the Huguenot churches placed themselves under the guard of a noble captain, the colloquys appointed a colonel and synods took on a general. The Huguenot church structure, already a source of great religious solidarity, had transformed itself into a military organisation well placed to threaten not only the Roman Catholic Church in France, but also the Roman Catholic monarchy. Furthermore, the nobility had taken over the position of leadership from the generally more conservative pastors. (It used to be thought also that peasants only converted on the orders of their noble landlords because deference, fear, and the very low literacy rates in the countryside impeded any independent religious thinking. However, Le Roy Ladurie has demonstrated that the strength of rural Calvinism correlates more neatly with the presence of large numbers of rural craftsmen with links to the towns, rather than with domination by Huguenot landlords.)

The motivation behind aristocratic conversions has been the subject of much debate. At the commencement of the wars, the chancellor, L'Hôpital remarked of the Protestant nobility, 'Several take shelter beneath the cloak of religion even though they have no God, and are more atheist than religious; among them there are lost souls who have consumed and wasted their all, and can only survive in the troubles of the realm and the possessions of other men.' Lucien Romier has spoken of 'a dissident nobility under the cloak of religion'. Mack Holt criticises this view as unduly cynical, and even in a description of Louis, Prince of Condé (a member of the Bourbon family), whose conversion Calvin himself always found suspect, he writes of his 'ardour for the new faith'. Admiral Coligny seems to be the clearest case of genuine Protestant zeal; having long agonised over whether or not to embrace the Huguenot cause, he became a source of inspiration to all his followers.

Blaise de Monluc was a Catholic who reacted strongly to the religious changes. From the start he loathed the Huguenots as anti-monarchist as well as heretics – in 1562 he overheard one call Charles IX 'that kinglet of shit'. In his memoirs he tells us of the situation he discovered when he returned home to Gascony as the wars were about to begin:

KEY ISSUE

Why was Calvinism particularly able to gain support in France?

> Some months after my return home, I had news brought me from all sides of the strange language and most audacious speeches the ministers of the new faith impudently uttered, even against the royal authority. I was moreover told that they imposed taxes upon the people, made captains and listed soldiers, keeping their assemblies in the houses of several lords of the country who were of this new religion ... I saw the evil daily to increase but saw no one who appeared on the King's behalf to oppose it. I heard also that the greatest part of the officers of the treasury were of this

religion (the nature of man being greedy of novelty) and the worst of all and from whence proceeded all the mischief, was that the men of justice in the Parlements...and other judges, abandoned the ancient religion and that of the king to embrace the new one.

When Monluc went to Guienne as royal lieutenant in 1562 he found this situation:

The ministers publicly preached that if they would come over to their religion, they should neither pay duty to the gentry nor taxes to the king, but what should be appointed by them. Others preached that kings could have no power but what stood with the liking and consent of the people.

Monluc supervised the first execution of Huguenots at St Mézard in Guienne, February 1562:

The other two I caused to be hanged upon an elm that was close by, and being the deacon was but eighteen years old I would not put him to death, as also that he might carry the news to his brethren; but caused him nevertheless to be so well whipped by the hangman that, as I was told, he died within ten or twelve days after. This was the first execution I did at my coming from my own house without sentence or writing; for in such matters, I have heard, men must begin with execution, and if everyone that had the charge of provinces had done the same, they had put out the fire that has since consumed all.

Q

1. *Why was Monluc so outraged by judges adopting Calvinism?*
2. *What other reasons had he for fearing the spread of the new religion?*
3. *What was his remedy for the dangerous religious situation? Why might that remedy have been counterproductive?*

THE LAST VALOIS (1559–84)

Francis II (b. 1544, King 1559–60)

PROFILES

Francis II was married to Mary Queen of Scots at the age of fourteen and was fifteen when he came to the throne. Technically he had come of age and his mother Catherine de Medici did not have the influence over him she was to wield over his two younger brothers. But he was still too young and unsure of himself to assert his authority, and decisions were taken by his wife's uncles, the Guise brothers. Under Francis I and Henry II the political game had been all about winning the king's favour. Under Francis II it became a violent contest, with the enemies of the Guises trying to dislodge them from power, by any means. The sickly Francis died in December 1560.

PICTURE 41
King Charles XI of France
by François Clouet

See page 199

Charles IX (b. 1550, King 1560–74)

On accession to the throne, Charles IX was too young to rule, and his mother Catherine de Medici became regent. Her regency technically ended in 1563 when Charles came of age at thirteen, but physically weak and unimpressive as a personality, he was regarded as a cipher, and attention remained fixed on the political maneouvrings of his mother. He seemed to be about to assert himself in 1572 and adopt the policy of war with Spain proposed by the Huguenot Admiral Coligny. However, he reversed his position, and on 22 August 1572 there was a botched attempt to assassinate the admiral, most probably by the Guises. Fearing a violent backlash over this, Charles almost certainly authorised the Massacre of St Bartholomew, the mass murder of Huguenots, which followed. Charles won the praises of extreme Catholics but he also earned the undying hatred of the Huguenots and only succeeded in setting off another round of wars. He died in 1574, leaving his mother once again as regent.

Henry III (b. 1551, King 1574–89)

Henry III as the Duke of Anjou, aged eighteen, had won famous victories against the Huguenots in 1569 and when war broke out after the Massacre of St Bartholomew he was sent to besiege La Rochelle (1573). It looked as though the Valois dynasty had again produced a military hero, but then he was offered the throne of Poland and accepted it even though he was hedged about by such conditions that he had virtually no power. He was pleased to return home, slipping away furtively one night from his Polish court, when he heard of his brother's death in 1574. A first sign that he might not be so much the hero was that he chose to take months on his journey home via Italian cities and all the entertainments they had to offer, leaving the government of France to his mother. As king he showed little resolution and was unable to control his ambitious younger brother Alençon (who was given Henry's former title of Anjou in 1576) or his tempestuous sister Marguerite. He lavished his patronage on a group of rowdy young companions such as Joyeuse and Epernon, known as *les mignons*. This was much resented, and since Henry's affections for them seemed intense he has been labelled as homosexual, although there is no direct evidence (and the term may be anachronistic in any case). He certainly engaged in bouts of over-indulgence and wore the most flamboyant jewels and clothes, although this may have gone down better than his fits of piety when he would withdraw from the court, even at politically critical moments, and join processions as a common penitent, an action seen as humiliating rather than admirable.

In 1584 Henry's last brother, Anjou, died, leaving Henry of Navarre as heir. This sparked off a renewal of the Catholic League and a revival of the power of the Guises, which caused Henry finally to murder the duke and his brother the Cardinal of Guise. 'I do want to be a king', he told his mother, 'and no longer a prisoner and a slave...' His violence from a position of weakness merely alienated most of his remaining support and, commanding territory only in the region of the Loire, he had to turn to Henry of Navarre and the Huguenots for support. Together they prepared to besiege Paris, but on 1 August 1589 Jacques Clément, a fanatical young friar, gained access to the royal presence by claiming to be a messenger. He found the king sitting on his latrine, and Clément, convinced he was acting as the hand of God, stabbed the king fatally in the abdomen.

The Duke of Alençon, Duke of Anjou from 1576 (1555–84)

The Duke of Alençon was the youngest of the royal brothers, and irresponsible to the last. At the age of sixteen his mother planned to marry him off to Elizabeth I of England, but the English queen was only playing a waiting political game and in any case does not seem to have found the prospect of this pock-marked, unreliable youth attractive. A year later Alençon was sulking that he had not been given military command at the siege of La Rochelle and began to draw closer to the enemies of the Guises. This has given him the reputation of being a *politique*, that is, a Catholic who refused to support those waging religious war, but pure ambition motivated him rather than any desire to restore the state. In 1575 he fled the Court and, allying himself to the Huguenots and *politiques* in the south of France, he fought his brother the king. Henry III bought him and his allies off and Alençon was granted lands and his brother's former title, Duke of Anjou. He then turned his attention to the Netherlands and offered his support to the Dutch, rebelling against Philip II. They welcomed him, hoping substantial French support would follow, and he was made 'prince and lord of the Netherlands' in 1581 in place of Philip II. Rather than establish his sovereignty he left for England to continue wooing Elizabeth. She played him along, but without the slightest intention of marrying him. He returned to the Netherlands in 1582 but found that he could exercise almost no authority there despite his new titles. He grew desperate at the Dutch reluctance to fund his army and stormed Antwerp in 1583 – this 'French Fury' was not a diplomatic master stroke. He was negotiating to restore his position with the Dutch in March 1584 when he began to vomit blood. He died of tuberculosis in June.

4 ↶ PRELUDE TO THE WARS OF RELIGION – THE REIGN OF FRANCIS II

There was no one to offer an effective challenge to the Duke of Guise and the Cardinal of Lorraine when they assumed dominance of the council for Francis II, the husband of their niece Mary, Queen of Scots. Although he was the first prince of the blood, Antoine de Bourbon was handicapped by his Protestantism and was not the man to make so decisive a move; meanwhile, Catherine de Medici was too stunned by the sudden and unexpected death of her husband.

Two problems confronted the Guises: a debt of over 40 000 000 livres, the legacy of Francis I and Henry II's wars, and the growing strength of the Huguenots. In an effort to deal with the former, the Guises sensibly, but rather too energetically, cut back on pensions which particularly hit the nobles returning from the Italian wars, creating an incentive for them to join the anti-Guise faction. Regarding the Huguenots, the Guises began a fresh wave of persecutions. The most notable victim was Anne du Bourg, councillor of the Paris *Parlement,* who was executed for heresy in December 1559. This inflamed violent passions and the Huguenots quickly retaliated by openly defying the government; open-air services were held outside many towns including Paris, and in May the first national synod (a Huguenot parliament) met.

Once the Huguenot nobility took up their role as 'protectors' the Huguenot movement was transformed into an active party of resistance both at court and in the provinces. This was first apparent in the attack on the Guises known as the Tumult of Amboise. The conspiracy was the work of a number of Huguenot nobles, mainly La Renaudie and Condé, who plotted to seize the young king, assassinate Guise and the Cardinal of Lorraine and elevate Antoine of Navarre as chief adviser to the Crown. Its aim was purely political; to remove the Guises from power and replace them with the princes of the blood, the Bourbons. In the event it failed, and La Renaudie was killed in the skirmish. Once the existence of armed insurrection against the king had been established, the government retaliated severely. Fifty-seven leading Huguenots were found guilty, although Condé escaped blame. On Catherine's orders the executions were staged for public display and windows for viewing procured at the exorbitant price of ten livres! The royal family and court watched as the victims mounted the scaffold in the square beneath the walls of the Château of Amboise.

However, the significance of the event goes much deeper, for it drew together diverse elements of the Huguenot movement and gave it a common purpose. Religion now became entwined with high politics. For the first time, the passive resistance advocated by Calvin was thrown aside and the Huguenots began to project an organised political front.

Although the Tumult of Amboise had demonstrated the potential threat of the Huguenots, their leaders had shown that they were not yet

ready for open opposition. The attack on Guise rule gave Catherine de
Medici the excuse she needed to intervene. Her desire for appeasement
was shared by the new Chancellor, Michel de L'Hôpital, a lawyer and
Christian humanist. Together, they persuaded the Guises to permit the
calling of a great council, composed of the leading men in the kingdom,
in the hope of gaining some toleration for Huguenots and so to appease
them. The assembly met at Fontainebleau in August 1560 with Gaspard
de Coligny representing the Huguenots. It was agreed that, due to
the unprecedented financial crisis, the Estates General should be
summoned, plus an assembly of Church leaders to review the religious
situation.

5 ↫ CATHERINE AND CONCILIATION

Francis II's sudden, though not altogether unexpected, demise in
December 1560 spelt the end of Guise supremacy, at least temporarily.
Their final desperate attempt to oust the Bourbons was outmanoeuvred
by the machinations of the queen mother, who this time was
determined to win control of the regency for the new king, her ten-
year-old son, Charles IX. Catherine's political deviousness is well
illustrated in her treatment of her closest rival, Antoine de Bourbon.
Three nights before Francis' death she summoned Bourbon to her
apartments and, playing on his cowardice, pressurised him to renounce
his possible rights as regent, in return for the title of 'lieutenant-
general', an empty title.

In private she was capable of breaking down in tears, and wrote to
her daughter, Elizabeth, Queen of Spain: 'God...has deprived me of
your brother, leaving me with three small children and a kingdom
divided among itself, in which there is not a single person whom I can
trust, as each has some compelling interest.' In public she presented
a commanding and capable presence. Determined to keep the
Crown intact for her son, she skilfully negotiated with the various
factions by short-term diplomacy, retaining the dubious allegiance of
Navarre, whilst persuading the Guises not to undertake acts of
repression.

At the meeting of the Estates General in Orleans in December 1560,
Catherine hoped to win support for a period of compromise in which
to re-unite Christians. She also wanted assistance in solving the
Crown's financial problems. The Estates General ignored Catherine's
requests and simply demanded immediate reforms in Church and state.
A problem throughout for Catherine was that when the Crown's
authority was at its weakest there was no other institution in France
which could or would give it any support.

Catherine began to lose her grip on the situation, as she wrote in
December 1560, 'This farce has so many different actors that one of
them is bound to spoil things.' She was right; the following spring three
of the leading Catholics, Montmorency, Guise and the Marshal de Saint

André, worried about the apparent favour shown to the Huguenots, put aside their personal rivalries and formed the Triumvirate. Catherine had been foolish to concentrate on keeping Guise and Bourbon satisfied and neglecting the middle party on whose independence the monarchy ought to have been based in a crisis. It was important in the history of the wars of religion in France for, as Sir John Neale says, 'a party existed, menacing in its power, whose object was to defend the Catholic faith, apart from the king and if need be against him'. This became more dangerous when an international flavour was added with the Pope, Philip of Spain and the Duke of Savoy all offering help to the Guises. The royal edict of July 1561 condemning Protestant assemblies came too late to have any effect.

In a desperate attempt to reach some settlement in the religious controversy, Catherine daringly called an assembly of the French clergy to meet with Huguenot leaders in September 1561 at Poissy. She hoped that the **colloquy** would act as a national council of the French Church, working out a much-needed programme of reform that would also reconcile Protestants and Catholics. Notorious Protestants, such as Theodore Beza from Geneva and Peter Martyr of Zurich, were received at court and faced the leading Catholics across the assembly hall.

colloquy conference, usually religious

Despite this auspicious beginning, the Colloquy was a catastrophe and no agreement was reached. Catherine may have had good intentions but she failed to understand that this was not just a political debate but a fundamental disagreement over religious doctrine. Whereas both sides could agree about the necessity of reform of abuses, unity over doctrine, especially concerning the Eucharist, was an impossible dream. If anything, it imbued Huguenot ranks with increased daring. Beza was allowed to preach at court, and he wrote to Calvin, 'Thanks to God I have won permission for our brethren to meet in complete safety.' The seizing of churches by Huguenots spread, along with iconoclasm – the destruction of Catholic images, paintings and statues. On the other side, the colloquy enraged the Catholics to such an extent that they vented their frustrations on the Huguenots.

The failure of the colloquy plus the alliance of Guise and Montmorency meant that there now existed a party apart from the Crown which was determined to defend the Catholic faith if necessary. 1561 was a turning point because it heralded the beginning of the wars of religion proper. Until this point the struggle had been primarily political, a fight for power at the top. After 1561 two organised parties, Catholic and Huguenot, existed, both intent on self-preservation and the extinction of the opposition. Providing the moderate force between them was the Crown, under Catherine de Medici.

6 ∾ ARISTOCRATIC RIVALRY AND THE FIRST DECADE OF WAR, 1562–72

The Colloquy of Poissy having failed, Catherine decided to revert to a policy of limited toleration to appease the Huguenots. The January Edict of 1562 gave legal status to the Protestant religion in France, granted the Huguenots places of worship in the city suburbs, authorised their assemblies of synods and consistories and forbade the involuntary imposition of additional taxes upon them. The significance of the edict was that the Huguenots had at last achieved legal recognition; they would not win as favourable a settlement until the Peace of Monsieur in 1576. The edict was extremely unpopular and the queen mother had difficulty in persuading the *Parlement* of Paris to register it.

Its immediate results were to increase religious tensions: Catholics feared that Catherine de Medici was aiming to Protestantise France. The Triumvirate was in touch with the Papacy and Spain. The final blow for Catherine was the defection of Antoine of Navarre in December, lured by the Guise faction with the promise of the regency after the queen mother had been deposed. It was the prospect of a Catholic rising supported from abroad that made Catherine appeal to the Huguenots for armed support. Coligny replied that there were 2150 churches at her disposal. But Catherine had unleashed a force as yet unknown. Her action provided the Huguenots with the invaluable argument that they were really fighting for their king and so direction of their policy passed from the more cautious leaders to those girding themselves for war. Both sides were ready for war and any spark would be enough to cause an explosion.

This came in the Massacre of Vassy. On 1 March 1562 the Duke of Guise came across a Huguenot assembly worshipping in the town of Vassy, in a place not authorised by the January edict. In the ensuing slaughter his men killed about thirty of the congregation and wounded another 120. Guise had not planned the incident; in fact earlier he had avoided Vitry where he knew that there were Huguenots breaking the law, and he had just returned from a meeting with his old friend the German Protestant Duke of Württemberg, who had been trying to convert him. However, as it had occurred, he took advantage of the situation and, determined to break Catherine's alliance with the Huguenots, marched to Paris to seize the royal family. The Huguenots immediately looked to Condé for leadership, but seeing that they were greatly outnumbered, he fled to the Midi. This left the royal family defenceless and Paris, which at times had seemed ready to embrace Protestantism, now permanently in the hands of the Catholics. The monarchy was stranded; Catherine's policies were in shreds and she had no choice but to join with the Catholic forces. After Vassy, war was inevitable.

Both sides appealed for outside help, the Catholics and Catherine to Spain and Savoy, and the Huguenots to the German Protestants and

TIMELINE

1559	Death of Henry II
1560	Tumult of Amboise
	Death of Francis I;
	Catherine as regent
1561	Estates General at
	Pontoise
	Colloquy of Poissy
1562	January Edict

KEY ISSUE

How did Catherine try to provide France with good government and why did it prove disastrous?

KEY ISSUE

What was the significance of the Massacre of Vassy?

Elizabeth of England. The latter offered her support in exchange for Le Havre and at the end of the war she would exchange it for Calais; Condé's promises to Elizabeth revealed the desperate situation in which he found himself. This international dimension of the conflict raised the stakes from the beginning of the wars and it was to become even more important in later decades when larger numbers of troops invaded France from abroad, German Protestants in support of the Huguenots and the Spanish in support of the Guises and their Catholic allies.

In the ensuing fighting Montmorency and Condé were captured by the opposing sides, and both Antoine de Bourbon and the Duke of Guise were killed. (The Huguenot assassin of Guise, Poltrot, claimed under torture that Coligny had authorised the murder. This was the origin of a blood feud that was to perpetuate the wars and was evident in the Massacre of St Bartholomew nearly ten years later.) The two rival armies disintegrated and Catherine de Medici was able to negotiate a peace with the exchange of captives.

This Peace of Amboise in March 1563 allowed the Huguenots freedom of private belief, but freedom of worship was severely restricted for those other than the nobility, who had been prepared to settle on the basis that their own privileges were intact. When Calvin heard the terms he accused Condé of having 'betrayed God by his vanity in his desire for a settlement and freedom'. Certainly one result of the peace was that Protestantism began to lose its mass appeal and became more of a religion for the nobility. The peace had brought the fighting to an end, but only temporarily. Coligny, alone of the Huguenot leaders, opposed the settlement, but he was voicing the opinion of the Calvinist pastors who thought it a betrayal and prepared for further conflict. It was still felt to have gone too far by Catholics, and the *Parlement* of Paris was very reluctant to register the peace. The extent to which it was enforced depended greatly on whether the local officials responsible were Catholic or Huguenot. This pattern was to be repeated again and again. There were eight wars followed by equally inconclusive peace settlements. Not until 1598 and the Edict of Nantes was the Crown able to make such a settlement stick.

Following the Peace of Amboise Catherine tried to bolster the authority of the government and rally public opinion behind the Crown. Throughout 1564 and 1565 she and the king, Charles IX, progressed around France. In each of the great towns they were solemnly received and lavishly entertained. Catherine's energy was inexhaustible. In 1565 she wrote, 'All things are as peaceful here as we may hope; the further we go, the more is obedience established.' She ensured that the nobility enjoyed diversions aplenty, for instance with the eighty or so beautiful noblewomen she gathered together at court, since known as her 'flying squadron' and much appreciated by Condé in particular.

When Catherine reached Moulins she summoned an assembly of notables, that is the leading nobles and government officials, to meet there in January 1566. She stage-managed the exoneration of Admiral

Coligny as the alleged assassin of Guise and even persuaded the admiral and the Cardinal of Lorraine to embrace. Chancellor L'Hôpital introduced what was to become the Ordinance of Moulins, intended to restore royal government by ending venality, curbing corruption in the courts, and insisting that the nobility obeyed the courts on pain of having their fortresses confiscated. It streamlined the number of *généralités* (tax districts) from seventeen to seven, and made provision for royal commissioners to be sent on tours of inspection in the provinces. The ordinance would have been a more systematic reform than anything achieved under Francis I or Henry II, but it was never enforced as once again war intervened. N.M. Sutherland, however, credits Catherine and L'Hôpital with establishing a blueprint for the absolutism of French kings that was to come in the seventeenth century.

KEY ISSUE

How did Catherine try to conciliate the opposition in 1564–66?

The peace had been shattered by the Huguenots' fear that Philip II's determination to repress his own Protestant subjects in the Netherlands would spill over into France – again the international dimension was crucial. Catherine had arranged to meet her daughter, the Queen of Spain, in Bayonne in 1565 and to have an interview with the Duke of Alva in the hope of arranging several marriage alliances for her offspring and reducing the tension between France and Spain. This destroyed the positive effects gained by the royal progress, as Alva had been ordered to demand that the queen mother take the threat of heresy seriously. But the importance of this meeting lay not so much in what was said, but in what the French Huguenots thought was said. They believed that the interview was to seek Spanish help against them and it seemed to them to be proven when Alva led his army from Milan along the eastern frontier of France to the Netherlands in 1567.

Alarmed by Alva's march, the Huguenots attempted to seize the king, who was with his court at Meaux, a town to the north-east of Paris. Their failure was the signal for a fresh outburst of civil war. The second round of fighting which ended in March 1568 changed nothing, although the aged Montmorency had been killed.

The central regions of the country remained in turmoil, whilst the Catholics began to organise themselves into 'holy leagues', which foreshadowed the nationally organised Catholic League of the latter stages of the conflict. Catherine de Medici, enraged by the surprise attack at Meaux, now had no sympathy for the Huguenots; she became convinced that her earlier policies had been misguided and that the Huguenots planned a political revolution. The moderate L'Hôpital was dismissed and edicts were issued withdrawing previous grants of freedom of worship to the Huguenots and ordering Protestant ministers to leave the country. Fearing the queen mother, Condé and Coligny fled to La Rochelle. Their retreat symbolised the end of any hope of Huguenot victory in France as a whole: the Huguenot headquarters was no longer Orléans, in the centre of France, but on the western coast with outposts in the south, around which future conflict would be based. After a lull lasting scarcely six months, the third war began in September 1568, possibly engineered more by the Cardinal of

Lorraine than by Catherine, as he had become a dominant voice on the king's council.

Condé was captured and killed in 1569, and it seemed that the Guises' triumph at court was secure, but the Cardinal of Lorraine's overbearing nature turned the queen mother against him. (The cardinal was finally exiled from the court in disgrace as a result of encouraging a flirtation by his nephew, Henry, the new Duke of Guise, with Marguerite, Catherine's daughter. This had interfered with Catherine's core concern, marriage alliances with her children.) Desperately short of money in any case, Catherine opened negotiations with the Huguenots. The Peace of Saint Germain, agreed in August 1570, was yet another version of the 1563 Peace of Amboise, although with some additions. The Huguenots were granted civil rights (e.g. proper protection by the courts) for the first time, and as a guarantee of Catherine's good faith, they were also given the right to hold four towns, La Rochelle, La Charité, Montauban and Cognac, for two years. The Pope called this 'the most deadly blow the faith has received since the beginning of the religious troubles'. His reason was that the Huguenots now had political security as well as religious toleration. For her part, Catherine, seeing complete defeat of the Huguenots to be impossible, was returning to her former policy of moderation.

Since 1559 the Crown had faced one of the most traumatic periods in its history. The policies of Catherine de Medici are often criticised, but she had at least brought the monarchy through intact. There were growing demands for peace, and the Huguenot leaders even returned to court. It was at this point in 1571 that the king took over the reins of government for himself. Conflict intensified and continued over the next twenty years, mainly because of the lack of ability of Charles IX and his two younger brothers. Ineffective and incompetent, their rivalries helped to deepen the divisions in the realm and without firm direction from the centre, the factions took power into their own hands.

ANALYSIS

The Wars of Religion in the towns

The narrative of the Wars of Religion generally concentrates on high politics, the rivalries and struggles for power at court and on the battlefield. However, one reason why the wars were so ferocious and difficult to stop was the escalating riots between Catholics and Huguenots in most of the towns of France, street battles which embittered the religious divisions within communities. Noble faction leaders drew support from those who had been radicalised by this urban violence, and in turn the nobles stirred up their supporters to seize control of their towns and exterminate the opposition. The political uncertainty following the death of Henry II in 1559 gave space for the numbers of Huguenots to multiply. Although their pastors urged restraint on them, they lashed out at the outward signs of Catholicism, engaging in iconoclasm (destroying images – pictures and statues – which they regarded as idolatrous), or disrupting services and processions. The Catholics fought back and, unable to vent their fury on material objects, took it out more often in bloody attacks on the Huguenots themselves. Those who today regard religion as a matter of personal decision and conscience find it hard to understand these passions of 400 years ago (or similar passions more recently in Northern Ireland). Religion was fundamental to the identity of the community. In a time of alarming change it seemed to each religious group that it was fighting for its life, with as much aggression and fear as a community fighting a foreign invasion.

The ritual character of these urban battles has been analysed by Natalie Zemon Davis – the 'rites of violence' as she has called them. For instance, funeral processions were prone to spark off conflict, as any procession served to mark out territory; the religious opposition might attempt to seize the corpse to claim the dead soul as one of its own. Drowning your enemies was not just a way of killing them but a ritual purification of the town, as in the symbolic use of water in baptism. People were not behaving pathologically, Davis argues, but taking action when they thought the regular authorities had failed, in order to purify the city of the heresy which polluted it.

In contrast, Mark Greengrass took Toulouse as a case study, where there was an attempted coup by the Hugeunots in 1562. He claims that it was politics and practical decision making rather than ritual actions which shaped the violence. Condé called on the Huguenot minority in Toulouse to seize the city, but the Catholics moved swiftly and, with authorisation by the local *parlement*, burned the Huguenot quarter. When the jails were overflowing with Huguenot prisoners, they began drowning them. Finally, many of those Huguenots who successfully ran the gauntlet of the Catholic mob and escaped the city were murdered by peasants who had heard that it was lawful to pillage them. (On one stretch of road fifty-three Huguenot corpses were found, half eaten by wild animals.) Greengrass does not believe that the Catholics were more violent because they were reacting to Huguenot iconoclasm, but because they were a majority in a confined space using whichever methods to destroy their opponents came to hand. Much of the violence was directed by the local *parlement*, which thought it was doing its duty by taking over the government of the city, and purging the local elected officials, known as the *capitouls*, for being lax on Protestantism. These were, in Greengrass's view, the 'rights of violence'.

A similar Huguenot coup was staged in Rouen in 1562, studied by Philip Benedict. In contrast, though, it was successful for a time: key points such as the city gates were seized in April, and in May the local *parlement* was driven from the city. However, Catholic forces won the city back. Following the Peace of Amboise in 1563 the Huguenot community nonetheless not only survived but even grew slightly. However, it was now introverted and defensive, and the events of 1562 had confirmed the majority of Catholics in their belief that they would never be secure until the Huguenots were destroyed. When the Massacre of St Bartholomew occurred in Paris it was copied enthusiastically in Rouen, and its strongest support came from the older members of the *parlement* who had lived through the coup of 1562. The number of Huguenots in Rouen shrank from 16 500 to 3000.

The massacre in Paris itself was a classic example of urban religious violence. The city had been a powder keg waiting to blow for at least three years. In 1569 the Huguenot Gastine brothers had been arrested and in the ensuing riot fifty people were thought to have been killed. The Gastines' house was demolished and a cross erected in its place as a symbol of Catholic triumph. The royal authorities later removed the cross in 1571 in accordance with the peace settlement the previous year which had banned such monuments; but the cross was too important a symbol to be destroyed and it was placed in a nearby cemetery. In the following year, it became the focus for barely subdued Catholic hatred of the Huguenots, which was given vent in the massacre once the murder of Coligny and the Huguenot nobility had signalled the end of any government restraint. Sometimes Huguenots were protected by Catholic friends – even the Duke of Guise did this – and sometimes a Huguenot attacked by Catholics was saved by reciting the rosary or agreeing to go to Mass. However, appalling atrocities were committed. For instance, the wife of the Huguenot Philippe Le Doux begged to be allowed to complete the birth of her twenty-first child. She was stabbed in the stomach and the half-born baby thrown into the gutter. This was not just religious violence – the assailant was a neighbour paying off old scores. It is hard to ascertain how many such reports were influenced by later Huguenot propaganda, but the slaughter was undoubtedly great. It is estimated that 2000 Huguenots were killed in Paris – remaining members of the Gastine family were early victims – and 3000 more in a dozen other major cities such as Rouen. Countless others in terror converted to the Catholic faith. So the Massacre of St Bartholomew was the last as well as the greatest example of urban religious violence – most cities thereafter were finally purged one way or another and were therefore no longer divided communities. 'The golden age of the religious riot', as Benedict calls it, had begun in 1562 and ended in 1572. Religious passions all but disappeared from the wars after that, until revived by the Catholic League in the years following 1584.

KEY ISSUE

Why was religious violence so savage in the towns?

7 ∽ HIGH POLITICS AND THE MASSACRE OF ST BARTHOLOMEW, 1572

The events that led to the Massacre of St Bartholomew were directly connected with French foreign policy. Having abandoned the ultra-Catholic side, Charles IX and his mother were now influenced by the Huguenot leaders and the king began to consider intervention in the Netherlands on behalf of the Dutch rebels. The traditional view, that the king favoured this policy owing to the insistence of Coligny who had become one of his closest advisers, has been disproved. In fact it seems to have been the younger Huguenot nobles who wished to involve themselves in the Netherlands and forced Coligny to join them.

There were positive reasons for intervention in the Netherlands – the traditional anti-Spanish foreign policy, particularly with Spain's dominant position in Europe since her victory in Italy, and the new threat to France in the north with Alva's occupation of the Netherlands. Also, Charles was following the long-standing idea of uniting his subjects by directing their attention towards foreign war.

If French intervention in the Netherlands was to succeed, English co-operation had to be agreed. It was to this end that a marriage between Elizabeth I and Henry, Duke of Anjou, the king's younger brother, was proposed. Although major religious differences ensured that nothing came of this, a defensive treaty between England and France was signed at Blois in April 1570. The French did manage semi-official raids into the southern Netherlands during the early summer of 1572 and this successfully diverted Alva's attention from the sea beggars' invasion of Holland, thereby ensuring their success. However, the queen mother, although initially agreeing to this policy, became fearful that it would provoke all-out war with Spain, as well as antagonising the Catholics at home. Charles dithered, but allowed plans for a full-scale invasion of the Netherlands to go ahead.

So tensions were already rife when, on 18 August 1572, both Huguenots and Catholics were in Paris for the marriage of Charles's sister, Marguerite, to the young Huguenot king Henry of Navarre, outside Notre Dame since Henry could not attend Mass inside. This was yet another part of Catherine's earlier policy of compromise, but the situation was far from conciliatory. The Guises obviously found it intolerable that Coligny, the presumed murderer of Francis of Guise, should have so much influence over royal policy and Catherine de Medici had her own reasons for destroying Coligny: not only had he alienated the affections of her son, but he was connected with what now seemed to her as disastrous policy abroad.

On 22 August a Catholic assassin shot and wounded Coligny, it is thought on the orders of the Guise family, although whether the queen mother was implicated as well is difficult to ascertain. Some Huguenots rashly threatened to attack the royal family and this was more ominous with the closeness of Huguenot forces to Paris, preparing to march to the Netherlands.

PICTURE 42
The Massacre of St Bartholomew, 1572 *by Caspar Luyren*

It is impossible to establish exactly how the decision to authorise the massacre was taken on 23 August. One can only assume that, in the ensuing panic, Catherine and the king decided that they must strike first. But their intended victims seem to have been confined to a small group of Huguenot leaders, primarily Coligny, sparing princes of the blood.

The murder of the admiral on the streets of Paris in the early hours of 24 August set off an orgy of killing as the Paris mob ran wild, hunting down and killing between 2000 and 3000 Huguenots in the next few days. The queen mother's adviser, Tavannes, wrote, 'there was no alley in Paris, however small, in which they did not assassinate someone'. The streets of the capital ran with 'torrents of blood as if it had rained heavily', and this was replicated in a dozen other cities, where a similar number died.

Earlier generations of historians have seen the chief instigator of the massacre as Catherine. This view has now been much criticised, and Salmon attributes most blame to the king himself, seeing one of the few occasions when Charles took control of foreign policy as prompting the domestic crisis. We can only make calculated guesses, but whoever was the culprit, the Crown had to pay the price of its mistake for the next thirty years. Catholic Europe reacted with jubilation – a solemn Te Deum

See page 476

was sung in Rome in celebration – and this encouraged the king and the Guises to claim more premeditated responsibility than they had actually assumed. Protestant countries, horrified, saw it as a premeditated plan revealing the duplicity of Catherine and her son. The immediate consequences of the massacre were to end any danger of a war with Spain and to force the Crown into an alliance with the Guises.

See biographical exercise on pages 491–5

KEY ISSUE

What brought about the Massacre of St Bartholomew?

8 ↪ STATES WITHIN A STATE – THE REPUBLIC OF THE MIDI

To the Huguenot movement it must have seemed to be the greatest crisis they had ever faced, but in fact this ruthless act pulled them even closer together. Previously divided amongst themselves over politics, war and religion, these differences mattered little now and their bitterness became centred on the monarchy. The numbers of Huguenots declined after 1572, but they concentrated the strength left to them, defending their provincial strongholds with great determination. This exclusiveness was to their advantage and they abandoned all hopes of national toleration. Initially the Huguenots had not set out to be rebels. They acted as faithful followers of Calvin who deplored resistance to the lawful ruler. As Coligny had said, 'They claimed to be fighting not against the King, but against those who have tyrannically forced those of the reformed religion to take up arms in order to defend their lives.'

In the 1560s their aims and arguments were conservative, wanting freedom of worship for their sect with political safeguards guaranteed by the Crown. In the post-massacre period, Huguenot propaganda began to defend the right of rebellion by subjects for the first time and the idea of kingship itself was critically questioned. Protestants beforehand believed that even a tyrannical monarch should be obeyed, as anarchy would otherwise be the result of human sinfulness. After 1572 some Huguenot thinkers introduced the novel concept that liberty was natural and that therefore rulers were accountable to those they governed. This new basis for resistance is apparent in the work of Francis Hotman, a Huguenot lawyer who appealed for a limited monarchy controlled by the Estates General and aristocratic magistrates. In 1574 Beza, Calvin's successor in Geneva, opened a new phase of controversial religious literature against the government in his *The Right of Magistrates over Subjects* which emphasised that a king's power rested on the fulfilment of his religious and political duties. But Huguenot ideology did retain a conservative core. Beza had stressed that resistance could only be through 'lesser magistrates'. Likewise, Philippe du Plessis-Mornay's *Vindiciae Contra Tyrannos* did not allow ordinary people to initiate resistance; they could only act through their superiors. Therefore, to the Huguenots, popular sovereignty was the privilege of the people to follow their aristocratic or ecclesiastical leaders in opposition to a government that those leaders had pronounced to be in violation of divine law. (This change in Huguenot theory only survived until the Protestant Henry of Navarre became heir to the throne in 1584, whereupon Huguenot political thinkers became royalist once more.) The importance of the printing press in spreading these ideas, and so hardening the lines of conflict, cannot be overestimated. As Zagorin says, 'The press became for the first time an important means of combat and propaganda by both rebels and their opponents.'

In 1573 representatives of the Huguenot churches in the Midi met at Milhaud and produced a plan of government that was the blueprint for a militant republic independent of the Crown in military and civil affairs. (Compare this with the similar move by Holland and Zealand against Philip II, which was to develop into the independent Dutch Republic.) Power was to lie with political assemblies, which were to meet every three months and choose a general to command the militia. On a day-to-day basis, the general would be accountable to an executive council of the assembly. There was to be no pluralism or venality of office and officials were to be appointed on the basis of merit rather than rank. Above all, this plan's commitment to representative government instead of the hereditary principle embodied some of the revolutionary political thought discussed above. But within a year the plan was compromised when the Huguenots allied with the *politiques*, those Catholics opposed to the Guises.

KEY ISSUE

What effect did the Massacre of St Bartholomew have on the surviving Huguenots?

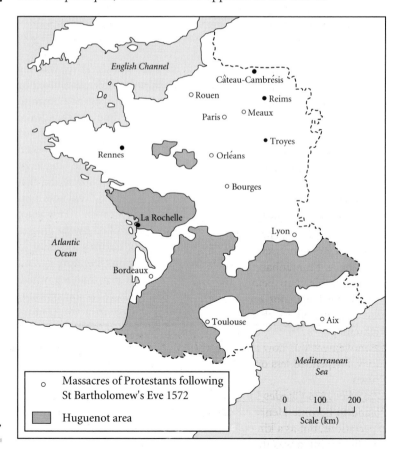

English Channel

Câteau-Cambrésis

Do

o Rouen

● Reims

Paris o

o Meaux

● Troyes

Rennes

o Orléans

o Bourges

La Rochelle

Lyon o

Atlantic
Ocean

Bordeaux
o

Toulouse

o Aix

Mediterranean
Sea

o   Massacres of Protestants following St Bartholomew's Eve 1572

Huguenot area

0   100   200

Scale (km)

MAP 24

France following the Massacre of St Bartholomew

9 ↬ THE *POLITIQUES* AND THE DEFENCE OF THE PROTESTANT REPUBLIC

The **politiques** were not an organised party but shared a common hostility towards the Guises and the more extreme Catholics. They also generally believed that the unity of the state was the most important problem and this they felt could best be remedied by the restoration of strong monarchical power. Desire for peace and national unity compelled the *politiques* to advocate religious tolerance. They included leading members of the nobility such as Montmorency's younger son, Damville, governor of the important province of Languedoc. Francis, Duke of Alençon, Catherine's unscrupulous youngest son allied himself to them. Many lawyers and administrative officials were drawn to the *politiques* because of their desire for a return to strong government, and merchants and financiers because their businesses had suffered from civil war. The varied composition of the *politiques* is shown by the identification of some pacifist Huguenots with the party.

> **politiques** moderate Catholics

Jean Bodin in his *Six Books of the Republic (1576)* states the theoretical position of the *politiques*. His theory, that ideal order was the result of men obeying a prince who governed according to the laws of God, was something to which all parties could subscribe. But as for the rights claimed by the Huguenots to revolt against an unjust ruler, Bodin concluded that 'a subject is never justified under any circumstances in attempting to do anything against his sovereign prince, however evil and tyrannical he may be'. This was the theory but it was not always to be the practice of the *politiques* – they recognised that the Protestants might need to be supported and the policies of the king resisted in order to save the Crown as an institution from further decline.

The Protestant cause was saved at this vital stage by the struggle for survival of its urban followers, led by their preachers. La Rochelle withstood a seven-month siege, saved finally in June 1573 by the departure of Anjou, the king's younger brother in command of the royal army, to take up his new position as the elected King of Poland. The Peace of La Rochelle then granted freedom of worship all over France for noble households but only in a limited number of towns – La Rochelle, Montauban, Nîmes – and none in the north. These terms, less favourable than before, showed that the massacre had failed to destroy the Huguenot movement but had narrowed its geographical basis and altered its character by killing so many of its leaders and frightening away noble support. The Huguenot numbers were reduced, the movement was now confined mainly to the south of France and its survival depended less on its own strength than on the weakness of the Crown.

In May 1574 Charles IX died and the Duke of Anjou returned from Poland to become Henry III. His reputation as a general aroused high expectations, but as a king his talents as a leader deserted him. One who was disappointed was the *politique* Damville, one of the Montmorency

KEY ISSUE

Under what circumstances did the politiques *emerge and what was the significance of their alliance with the Huguenots?*

family and governor of Languedoc. He had been loath to bring the rebellious Huguenots to heel there, and one of Charles IX's last acts had been to dismiss him. However, the extent of his lands and networks of supporters in the region made it impossible to remove him. With the accession of Henry III, he entered a military alliance with the Huguenots in July 1574 for the common defence and, they said, for the good of the realm, in what was an extension to the Huguenot state within a state. The southern provinces of Languedoc, Provence, Dauphiné and Guienne levied their own taxes and customs duties and Damville negotiated as an equal with the royal council. The realm of France seemed to be disintegrating and such separatism was to prolong the wars.

The following year Damville gained the support of Condé (son of the one killed in 1569) and Francis, formerly Duke of Alençon and now Duke of Anjou. The rivalry and antagonism between the ambitious and unprincipled Anjou and his brother the king intensified, despite Catherine's attempts to reconcile them. In 1576, having escaped from court where he had been held captive since the Massacre of St Bartholomew, Henry, King of Navarre, the head of the Bourbon family, joined Damville and Anjou and declared himself protector of this 'state'. So, in spite of the *politique* claims of loyalty to the Crown, Damville and his associates pursued a very independent course for many years. Policy was dictated by circumstances; sometimes they allied with the Huguenots and at other times with the government or the Catholics.

10 ⤳ STATES WITHIN A STATE – THE CATHOLIC LEAGUE

Terrified by the advance on Paris by Henry of Navarre, Damville and Anjou, the king sued for peace in 1576. Once again the international dimension had transformed the situation – the Huguenot-*politiques* alliance commanded 10 000 troops of their own, but in addition the German Protestant, John Casimir of the Palatinate, brought 20 000 troops, so outnumbering the royal forces decisively. The Peace of Monsieur (named in honour of Monsieur, le duc d'Anjou) was the most favourable settlement the Huguenots were ever to obtain. In short, they were granted full religious liberty, except in Paris, and eight fortified towns as security. The weakness of the king's position was shown in another clause, which made Henry of Navarre Governor of Guienne, Condé Governor of Picardy and left Damville supreme in the Midi.

In the long run, the treaty was worthless, as it proved as impossible to enforce as its predecessors. It was soon clear that Protestants would never be able to convert the whole of France; that opportunity had been missed before 1572. The issue at stake now was how much toleration the minority would receive. Catholic zealots were horrified by the Peace of Monsieur and this led to the organisation of the Catholic League. While technically loyal to the king, it almost formed another 'state within a state' under the leadership of Henry, Duke of Guise. The League at this stage lasted only a year, but it was an indication that the Catholics could threaten the authority of the Crown as much as the Huguenots. Meanwhile a realignment of forces in the south (Anjou and Damville deserted the Huguenots) led to the Peace of Bergerac in 1577, by which the Huguenots lost some of the privileges they had gained at the Peace of Monsieur.

An eight-year truce followed, with only a brief renewal of 'official' war in 1580, an assertion of strength by Henry of Navarre. However, by this stage a general anarchy prevailed, with small bands of soldiers living off the land and surprise assaults on villages or small towns, irrespective of religion. Captain Merle, for instance, was technically a Huguenot partisan in the Auvergne, but kept on fighting for profit whatever peace treaties had been agreed with the government. Taxation and pillage by uncontrolled troops ruined the rural economy in parts of France, and during 1578–80 the first major peasant risings occurred, such as the so-called *Razats* in Provence, peasants of both faiths who joined forces with local nobility to fight the hated Comte de Carcès, the local Catholic League commander. For eighteen months Catherine de Medici toured the provinces in the south to hear grievances and restore order. The Venetian ambassador observed that the French 'now recognize her merits...and are sorry not to have appreciated her sooner', but he knew she had only temporarily calmed, not resolved, the conflicts in the south. Meanwhile Henry III announced another series of government reforms, which achieved nothing. Distracted by the antics of his brother Anjou and his concern for his own favourites, the *mignons*, he wasted these years of comparative peace.

> **KEY ISSUE**
>
> *Did the personality and policies of Henry III prolong the conflict?*

11 ↪ THE WARS OF SUCCESSION

The death of Anjou in June 1584 led to the last phase of conflict in France, and this time it centred on the succession. Henry III was childless, so the heir to the throne was now Henry of Navarre. Faced with the prospect of a Huguenot king, the Catholic League reappeared in a different but more dangerous form. This time it was no longer merely an association of noblemen. The revitalised League began in Paris among the clerics, spread to the guilds, the artisans and municipal officials and then to the lower orders of the other towns. The urban classes flocked to it, their religious zeal fuelled by the hardship resulting from years of conflict. The nobility, led by the Guises, took up a position of leadership, but much power lay in the hands of the League's urban representatives.

The administrative nucleus of this revitalised League was established in Paris on the initiative of a group of lawyers and officials. Its organisation was in the hands of a Council of Sixteen, named after the

TIMELINE

1585 Treaty of Joinville
1587 War 8: the War of the Three Henries
1588 Day of Barricades Assassination of the Guise brothers
1589 Death of Catherine de Medici Assassination of Henry III Henry of Navarre becomes Henry IV War 9

sixteen political divisions of Paris. The council was made up mainly from lawyers with some clergy and only two from the artisan class, 'Poccart, a tin-worker and professional assassin and Gilbert, a butcher'. They had social as well as religious reasons for overthrowing the established authorities in Paris, as by and large their careers had previously ground to a halt owing to the chaos and faction fighting of the wars. In contrast other League towns, such as Rouen, tended to be led by a much less socially radical group of established Catholic leaders.

The League also received the support of Spain by the secret Treaty of Joinville (1584) negotiated by the Duke of Guise, that recognised Henry of Navarre's aged Catholic uncle, the Cardinal of Bourbon, as heir to the throne. The danger presented to the Crown by the existence of the League was tremendous for it separated Catholicism from the monarchy and was as threatening to the king as to the Huguenots. It created a third party, which only complicated and prolonged the struggle.

Faced by overwhelming force Henry III had little choice but to submit to the League, and in 1585 he made the Treaty of Nemours with the Duke of Guise. This withdrew all religious concessions, condemned heresy and offered the choice of conversion or exile. Henry of Navarre claimed that half his moustache turned white on hearing these terms!

For three years there was inconclusive jockeying for power. Finally, the Duke of Guise was infuriated by Henry's continuing patronage of the *mignons*, especially by Epernon becoming Governor of Normandy, when the duke felt his military success merited the job. Then, invited to Paris by the radical Catholics of the Council of Sixteen, Guise defied a royal command and entered the capital on 9 May 1588. Catherine attempted to mediate between the duke and her son, but Henry, blaming her policies and ministers for allowing the crisis to develop, attempted a counter-attack that failed. This was on 12 May, the famous Day of the Barricades, when the Parisians drove out the king's Swiss Guards, and he himself fled. To try and retrieve the situation, Catherine de Medici negotiated the Edict of Union, whereby Henry agreed to eradicate heresy and recognise the Cardinal of Bourbon as Lieutenant-General of France. In what was to be her final intervention in affairs of state, the queen mother had restored Henry to his place as King of France even if it involved compromising his views. Henry also summoned an Estates General which met at Blois in the autumn of 1588 and was dominated by Leaguers, as the south sent no representatives.

With only hostility from the Estates General and spurred on by the setback to Guise's ally, Philip II, with the defeat of the Spanish Armada, Henry decided on the elimination of his rivals once and for all. On December 23, the Duke of Guise was summoned from the council chamber to a meeting with the king, but in a preconceived plan he was murdered in the royal antechamber by the king's guard. The duke's brother, the Cardinal of Guise, suffered the same fate the next day. The king might have rejoiced at the removal of his main enemies at one stroke, but his mother exclaimed 'What has he done?...I see him rushing towards his ruin.' She said to Henry, 'You have killed two men who have left a lot of friends.' A few days later she too died on 5 January 1589, worn out by the continuing conflict she had striven to end. Catherine de Medici was proved right for, when news of the Guises' murders spread, the alliance between the League and the towns tightened. Paris erupted and, unlike the Day of the Barricades, this rebellion radiated out to the provinces. The youngest Guise brother, Charles, Duke of Mayenne, assumed control of a League region stretching from Burgundy across northern France to Brittany. There was less support south of the Loire but the League did control Marseilles and Toulouse. Of the most important towns, only Blois, Tours, Saumur and Bordeaux remained loyal to the king. As in 1563, assassination had not resolved matters, but only intensified conflict.

With Paris in uproar, the Council of Sixteen began a formal trial of the king in his absence. The Sorbonne proclaimed that the king's subjects were released from any allegiance to him and Catholic publicists, such as Boucher, declared Frenchmen were free to defend themselves against a tyrant, as the Huguenots had earlier advocated. Printers in Paris were printing almost one pamphlet a day, carrying the message that Catholics must defend themselves against the king as well as the Huguenots. Whatever the social aspects of the uprising, it was religion that provided the language of protest, and religion which was the single element common to the disparate forces of the League.

In this political climate Henry had little choice but to seek reconciliation with Navarre. Negotiation proved difficult but eventually the two kings mustered their armies to march on Paris and began the siege of the capital. Just before the final assault was accomplished, on I July 1589 Jacques Clément, a fanatical young friar, assassinated the king at Saint-Cloud. The death of Henry III saw the extinction of the House of Valois, for Henry of Navarre was a Bourbon.

KEY ISSUE

How did the Catholic League come to be so powerful from 1584 onwards?

HENRY IV (1589–1610)

PROFILE

Henry of Navarre, later to be Henry IV, was born in 1553. Through his father, Antoine de Bourbon, he was a prince of the blood, i.e. in line for succession to the throne. Through his mother, Jeanne d'Albret, he was heir to the kingdom of Navarre, an enclave in the south-west of France. Although born a Catholic, Henry was converted to Protestantism by his mother, who had become one of the leading Huguenots. Henry was fighting in the Wars of Religion by the end of the 1560s, but when it appeared that Admiral Coligny had found favour for the Huguenot cause at court, it was agreed that Henry should marry Charles's sister Marguerite. This seemed to be the triumph of Catherine de Medici's policy of marriage alliances, intended to bring peace at home and abroad, but it immediately went sour following the

Massacre of St Bartholomew. Henry survived the Massacre, owing to his status as a prince of the blood, by sensibly finding sanctuary in his wife's apartments, and by a speedy conversion to Catholicism. He was in effect under house arrest at court, but having managed to escape in 1576 with Alençon, he re-converted to Protestantism and became leader of the Huguenots in the continuing Wars of Religion, which became an even keener struggle when Henry became next in line to the throne in 1584.

Henry was an effective military leader, although the heroic charge was more his way than a carefully thought through execution of strategy. He won a great victory over Henry III's forces at Coutras in 1587, but rather than follow it up he rode as fast as he could to lay the enemy's battle standards at the feet of his then mistress. (His marriage to Marguerite was not happy – she was a firebrand and had a string of lovers of her own, but Henry's reputed tally of fifty-six mistresses seems more than adequate compensation.) A more calculating general would have taken greater military advantage than Henry, but his impulsive, romantic temperament and his generous nature won him much support.

He became king in 1589, but could not secure the throne, facing the greatest military challenges of his career as Parma intervened from the Netherlands to relieve his sieges of Paris and Rouen. The Catholic League tried to find an alternative heir, but once Henry's uncle the Cardinal of Bourbon died in 1590 there was no one in the legitimate line of succession. (The Salic Law in France meant that the Crown could only pass through the male line.) In 1593 Henry realised that he needed to convert once again to Catholicism in order to be accepted as king by all in France. (He probably never said 'Paris is well worth a Mass', however characteristic that seems.) Henry's Huguenot followers had little choice but to accept his conversion, although they were threatening war once again, before being bought off by the Edict of Nantes in 1598. Mack Holt argues that Henry's conversion was sincere, although as it was his fourth change of religion, it does look more like political than divine inspiration. With adroit diplomacy Henry conciliated his remaining opponents and brought peace to France. Under the supervision of his immensely capable first minister, Sully, the royal finances were restored, along with ordered government in the provinces. The early 1600s were a time of peace and prosperity, and Henry IV's reign came to be looked upon as a golden age. In 1610, however, when about to renew war against the Habsburgs, a fanatical Catholic, François Ravaillac, gained access to the royal coach while it was stuck in a traffic jam, and stabbed Henry to death.

12 ↩ THE TRIUMPH OF HENRY IV

As in 1561–62, 1572 and 1585, the role of other European countries had a significant part to play in the outcome and the prolonged nature of events. Elizabeth I rallied to the cause of Henry on his accession, sending him generous supplies of money and munitions that were to play an important role in his early victories. The Dutch and German princes also contributed to what they saw as the fight against the forces of international Catholicism. Now Philip II, who had pledged his support of the Catholic League in 1584, ordered the reluctant Duke of Parma to abandon his campaign against the Dutch rebels and take support to Mayenne, the Guise brother now in command of the League. Philip was desperate to prevent the largest country in Europe from becoming Protestant.

Parma drove the king away from besieging Paris in 1590 and Rouen in 1592, but he was unable to inflict a resounding defeat on the small royal forces which Henry commanded with daring and ability. Meanwhile divisions amongst different sections of the League were becoming more marked, in particular those between the aristocratic and popular elements. The Council of Sixteen still governed Paris and faced hostility from the higher ranks of urban society. Matters reached a climax in November 1591 when these popular, radical leaders vented their hatred on the conservative *Parlement* of Paris by executing the president and two councillors for alleged treason. Even Leaguers were stunned and the Duke of Mayenne was forced to intervene and put to death four of the instigators. This left Paris in turmoil. The radicals of the Council of Sixteen had been enraged but not defeated. So the *Parlement* and the upper ranks of urban society were still prey to the radicals and they felt betrayed rather than protected by Mayenne.

Disillusionment with the Leaguers was not unique to the capital. After the initial enthusiasm of a League victory had waned, towns found themselves ever deeper in economic distress. The presence of Spanish troops on French soil, war exhaustion, rampaging soldiers, a series of poor harvests and consequent rise in prices, all led to a desire for peace, a return to strong government and a move away from extremism.

In 1590 Cardinal Bourbon, the League's claimant to the throne, had died. This put the League in a dilemma for there was no other obvious Catholic candidate. Philip II proposed his daughter, fortuitously the granddaughter of Henry II. Apart from being contrary to Salic law, which barred women from succession to the throne, the thought of a Spanish queen created a deeper rift within the League and alienated yet more of their supporters. This revival of national feeling was only enhanced by Parma's arrival in France after Henry IV's defeat of Mayenne's forces at Arques in 1589 and Ivry in 1590.

In 1593 Mayenne summoned an Estates General to resolve the question of the succession and to find an alternative to the Spanish suggestion. To this end, Mayenne invited some of the Catholic

TIMELINE

1590 Siege of Paris
1592 Siege of Rouen
1593 League's Estates General
Henry IV's conversion
1595 War against Spain
Pope recognises Henry IV
1598 Edict of Nantes

royalists, hoping to lure them over to his side by the election of a Catholic prince.

At this point, in July 1593, Henry IV conveniently chose to announce his return to the Catholic Church. Ever since 1589 in order to maintain the loyalty of royalist Catholics and in the knowledge that he would have to become a Catholic eventually to secure the loyalty of the greater part of France, Henry had promised to take Catholic instruction, with the proviso that the League must surrender first. However, his adviser Sully, although a Protestant, argued that he should convert before he was forced into it by the growing pressure from his own Catholic supporters, as that would damage his authority. Henry agreed that conversion, with appropriate guarantees to reassure the Huguenots, would be 'a course of action by which I will easily achieve all I have fought for, without upsetting anyone'. Finally, Henry calculated that in 1593 the time was ripe to capitalise on the rifts in the League. He was right. The League preachers protested that the king's conversion was insincere but their influence was diminishing. Henry was crowned with all the solemn ritual of the Catholic kings of France at Chartres in February 1594, and in March he entered the gates of his capital, Paris. The newly acclaimed king showed his diplomacy by allowing the small Spanish garrison to depart in peace and granting a pardon to his opponents and generous bribes to their leaders. The League collapsed as it had lost its one reason for existence – opposition to a Protestant king – and its members took advantage of the clemency of the king. By the summer of 1594 most areas around Paris were royalist; resistance remained on the borders of the kingdom, around Champagne under the Guises, Brittany under Mercoeur and Languedoc under Joyeuse, but their surrender began in November 1594 with that of Guise. In 1595 the Pope set the seal of approval on Henry by recognising him as king.

13 ⌒ WAR WITH SPAIN AND THE EDICT OF NANTES

What finally brought about the unity of France was war with Spain in 1595; many rallied to their king to drive out the Spanish, and Henry continued to pick off the leaders of the League one by one with bribes, honours and royal offices. He was shrewd enough not to have attempted a negotiated settlement with Mayenne, which would have left the duke's authority over the League intact. Finally, Mayenne himself (also suitably bribed with royal office and cash) made his peace with the king in October 1595.

By 1598 Philip was close to death and suffering the effects of bankruptcy. He sued for peace, formalised by the Treaty of Vervins. Similar in terms to the earlier Treaty of Câteau-Cambrésis, all Spanish troops were removed from French soil. France had thrown off the last fetter of foreign involvement. This phase of the old Franco–Spanish rivalry, which had been rekindled by France's internal conflict but also prolonged her agony, now ended and this time it ushered in domestic peace. Without Spanish support the last area of resistance, Brittany, could no longer hold out and the Leaguer nobleman Mercoeur surrendered.

Social protest was also beginning to scare war-weary noble combatants. France had descended into chaos in the 1590s. At Vitré a peasant band had almost annihilated a Huguenot army. In Brittany an aristocratic wedding party had been broken up by rebels, and sixty of the guests had been lynched. From 1593 to 1595 Guyenne was convulsed by the peasant rebels, known as the *croquants*. Such incidents and risings spread across much of the country, and clearly the only alternative to such anarchy was the restoration of royal authority.

As royalist support reached a peak, Henry put in place a settlement with his erstwhile Huguenot supporters as the last element in domestic peace. At the same time (April 1598) as he was making peace with Spain, Henry IV signed the Edict of Nantes for the 'union, concord and tranquillity' of both his Huguenot and Catholic subjects.

This was really a repetition of previous edicts of pacification in its granting of freedom of worship in a number of designated areas except for Paris. It was only slightly extended in that two further towns in every *bailliage* (district) were added to those specified in 1577, while the Catholics were guaranteed freedom of worship everywhere. However, the Huguenots were allowed to hold colloquys and synods which could clearly double as political assemblies (which were technically forbidden). The Huguenots' civil rights were also affirmed, to be protected by special chambers in the *Parlements* – the *chambres mi-parties* – which were staffed by Huguenot as well as Catholic judges. The most controversial aspects of the settlement were contained in two additional brevets, i.e. articles dependent solely on the king's authority and not registered by the *Parlements*. The king agreed to pay the salaries of Huguenot pastors and permitted the Huguenots to maintain garrisons in 200 towns, which he also subsidised. In doing this it has been suggested that Henry sacrificed some of the Crown's authority by sanctioning a 'state within a state'. However, this was a confinement of the Huguenots to limited areas, almost a religious quarantine, and by no means amounted to toleration for their religion in France as a whole. Also the Huguenots, now shrinking in numbers and influence, knew that their best hope of defence for their freedoms was the Crown – in any case, the additional brevets were only valid in the first instance for eight years and, as paymaster of the Huguenot garrisons, the king still held a measure of control.

Essential to the settlement was the king's determination that this time it would endure, despite the opposition from the *Parlement* of Paris and initial dissatisfaction in Catholic and Huguenot ranks with the terms. In many ways it was just another in a long line of religious truces, and the king had had little choice as the Huguenots were preparing for another war. This time, however, given that it preceded a restoration of royal authority, this religious truce was indeed to last.

Peace with Spain and the end of the religious wars meant that Henry IV was now able to begin the restoration of France in the consolidation

KEY ISSUE
How did Henry IV become the undisputed king of France?

of the administration at home and in her role on the European stage. His record so far boded well for a new era of French politics as the first Bourbon king led France into the seventeenth century.

14 ⤳ BIBLIOGRAPHY

**Mack P. Holt, *The French Wars of Religion, 1562–1629* (CUP, 1995) is the most up-to-date and readable general account. *R.J. Knecht, *The French Wars of Religion 1559–1598* (2nd ed., Longman Seminar Studies, 1996) and **M. Rady, *Access to History: France 1494–1610 Renaissance, Religion and Recovery* (Hodder and Stoughton, 1988) both provide excellent introductions. R. Briggs, *Early Modern France 1560–1715* (OUP, 1977) is useful and concise while *P. Zagorin, *Rebels and Rulers, Vol. 2* (CUP, 1982) both summarises the wars of religion and compares them with other similar conflicts. *J.H.M. Salmon, *Society in Crisis: France in the Sixteenth Century* (Ernest Benn, 1975) is particularly good on the wars in the provinces and on the Edict of Nantes. R.J. Knecht, *Catherine de' Medici* (Longman, 1998) offers a balanced judgement of the queen mother and clarifies the political circumstances with which she had to deal and *N.M. Sutherland, *Catherine de Medici and the Ancien Regime* (Historical Association Pamphlet, 1966) is a good alternative.

15 ⤳ STRUCTURED AND ESSAY QUESTIONS

A *Structured questions.*
1. (a) What led to the outbreak of the French Wars of Religion in the three years after the death of Henry II?
   (b) Why did the policies of Catherine de Medici and her sons fail to bring them to an end?
2. (a) How did Henry IV bring the French Wars of Religion to an end?
   (b) 'The most important cause of the French Wars of Religion was the lack of an effective monarch.' Discuss.

B *Essay questions.*
1. What problems faced the French monarchy on the death of Henry II?
2. Who or what was responsible for the weakening of the French Crown from 1547 to 1589, during the reigns of Henry II and his sons?
3. 'To dismiss Catherine de Medici as a failure is to misunderstand her aims and to underestimate her achievements.' Discuss this comment.
4. Why did the French Wars of Religion last so long?
5. Discuss the view that the French Wars of Religion were fought over issues that were only indirectly religious.

6. Why did the Edict of Nantes succeed in terminating the French Wars of Religion when earlier attempts had failed?

Advice: *Essays covering a long period*

Some questions cover a much longer time span than others. In such questions it is not necessary to go into as much detail – these questions are principally testing your ability to make connections and to see trends over a period of time. An example of this type of question is:

2. Who or what was responsible for the weakening of the French Crown from 1547 to 1589, during the reigns of Henry II and his sons?

An attempt to answer this question in a narrative way would be disastrous. It would be too long and would not pick out the crucial factors. Such a question must be answered thematically. The best way to ensure that you do this is to break the main question down into a series of sub-questions. To start with, two might be:

A. What effect did the personalities of the kings have?
B. Did Catherine de Medici make matters better or worse?

Add another six to eight questions to this list. Then review your notes to check that you have covered all the main themes.

Put the questions in a logical order – the role of Catherine de Medici, for instance, follows naturally on from the personalities of the kings.

Write a paragraph in answer to each sub-question, drawing together the most significant examples in support of your argument. With an appropriate introduction and conclusion, your essay will be complete.

16 ∽ BIOGRAPHICAL STUDY ON CATHERINE DE MEDICI

Few historical figures have received such a bad press as Catherine de Medici. The legend of the 'wicked Italian Queen' began at the hands of extreme Protestant pamphleteers and reached its climax in the nineteenth century. This stigma is only just being lifted. It is, however, interesting to discover that during her lifetime Catherine attracted not only hostility but also admiration, from Catholic and Protestant alike.

Catherine's influence was felt as much in Europe as in France. She is important as one of several women active in top-level sixteenth-century politics. Her career, which spanned nearly half a century, revealed at its height a subtle diplomat capable of restoring peace to Catholic Europe, and at its depth a schemer unable to control France's two warring factions.

In order to assess Catherine, first summarise what you have read about her. A convenient way to do that would be a date chart set out as follows:

Date	Event	Aim of Catherine	Extent of her influence	Result

Now consider Catherine's personality and try to work out the reasons that lay behind her actions. You will need to expand on the information you have gathered from the chapter and do some personal research. Consult the bibliography at the end of the chapter. Then read the extracts below and answer the questions that follow them.

SOURCE A
From Sir John Neale, The Age of Catherine de Medici *(1943).*

She was undoubtedly a woman of great qualities, if not a great woman. Her vitality was boundless: she was always ready, with tireless energy, to tackle every difficulty that arose. But she lacked any grasp of principles and was apt to see political problems in terms of a Palace intrigue which could be solved by getting folk together and making them shake hands. She was, in fact, a very able politician, not a statesman; and her charm coupled with her vitality made her most successful at the game.

Modern psychologists would shake their heads over her possessive maternalism. She loved her children and dominated them with her affection and personality that was ruinous to them...

SOURCE B
From R.J. Knecht, Catherine de Medici *(1998).*

Catherine, it seems, could not understand religious fanaticism. Having been born and brought up as a Catholic, she practised her faith out of habit...But religion did not enter her soul...The Reformation only began to interest her once it had become politicized, and even then its doctrine passed her by. She was not hostile to Protestant thought, merely indifferent, which explains why she underestimated the strength of religious conviction, imagining that all would be well if she could only get the party leaders to agree.

On August 24, 1572, Paris proved to Catherine that she had made a mistake...The battle on which Catherine had insisted had ended in disaster. Indomitable fighter that she was, she first of all covered her retreat. She had gambled and lost; now she paid up, without arguing. She went over to the victors. Machiavellism had failed her because she was a woman and a mother before she was a politician. Faced with the domestic tragedy of her sons' mutual hatred and the submission of the elder to Coligny, the Queen had given way to the woman. Yet Machiavellism was an instrument that should not be discarded. Since violence adopted for the reasons of State had only made the situation worse it was better to resort to treachery. Catherine pulled herself together with her usual willpower. She would lie to everyone and she would not be believed – that she knew. Nevertheless, behind this smoke-screen of lies that she would spread over the battlefield on which she had been beaten, the Florentine Queen would be able to retreat in order to prepare her rehabilitation...Her genius for dissimulation and deceit was now to be given full rein.

SOURCE C
From J. Heritier, Catherine de Medici *(1963).*

Catherine has been accused by many historians of instigating Coligny's murder. [Knecht outlines the view of Catherine's recent biographer, Cloulas, that she was indeed guilty, being determined to save Charles IX from Coligny's 'mad adventure' in the Netherlands. He then presents N.M. Sutherland's arguments that the plot was not Catherine's but an international, ultra-Catholic conspiracy involving Spain, the Papacy and others working through the Guises, and that the 'maternal jealousy theory', whereby Catherine was motivated by hatred of Coligny's influence over her son, is 'fatuous'.] The truth is unlikely ever to be known. What is evident is that many people, including Catherine, had strong reasons for wishing to be rid of Coligny. She has perhaps received more than her fair share of the blame. Catherine has been the target of Huguenot propagandists angered by the Massacre of St Bartholomew and powerfully influenced by misogyny and xenophobia...A notable example is the *Discours merveilleux de la vie, actions et déportements de Catherine de Médicis, Royne-mère,* which purports to be a factual account of her life. We find in it most of the stories, notably the poisonings, which eventually became part of the so-called Black Legend...The *Discours* was used as a rich quarry by historical novelists in the nineteenth century [such as Alexandre Dumas who wrote *La reine Margot,* in which Catherine is portrayed as a malevolent spirit presiding over a debauched court. In 1993 it was turned into an extremely gory film by Patrice Chéreau and Danièle Thompson, which will doubtless serve to extend the life of the Black Legend].
[But] whitewashing Catherine can be taken too far. She was no saint and had certainly dabbled in political assassination...There are grounds for thinking that her policy was less consistently pacific than her defenders have claimed...In 1567 she seems to have favoured the suppression of the Huguenots or at least the extermination of their leaders after they had betrayed her trust at Meaux and defied the king's authority. The only consistent principle to which she adhered was a touching faith in the matrimonial solution to all political problems.

SOURCE D
From R.J. Knecht, Catherine de Medici *(1998).*

Charles had not governed for himself...but it is clear...that Catherine expected Henry to do so. Far from resenting any consequent change in her own position, she had always wanted France to possess an effective king. No other authority could ever restore the realms of Francis I and Henry II...Her attitude is clearly illustrated in a long letter of advice to the king; it also disposes of the traditional allegation that her judgement was impaired by her maternal affections.

This long and remarkable memoir, dated 8 August 1574, began with an expression of her love for Henry and her hopes for his future greatness...She exhorted him to take magisterial possession of his kingdom, and to restore order with firmness and benevolence...The memoir urged him to stand alone, as master in his realm, and to avoid provoking opposition by the entertainment of favourites. To obtain the support of the provinces...Similarly, Henry was to maintain a well-ordered court, himself providing the example...[he] must personally assume all control and direction...thus all policy and advancement would proceed from him, and all allegiance and gratitude return to him...

She affirmed her belief in his opportunity and her fear of his insufficiency...Catherine's fears were indeed, well-founded, and nothing reveals more clearly the extent of her moral courage than her love for Henry and her considered opinion of the king.

SOURCE E

From N.M. Sutherland, Princes, Politics and Religion 1547–89 *(1984).*

The following year (1577) Catherine set out on her last great undertaking – a journey of pacification in the south, which lasted for sixteen months, though she had hoped to accomplish it in three. She visited Guienne and Languedoc, Provence and Dauphiné, even Navarre itself. Frequently she found the towns and chateaux of the lesser nobility had shut their gates against her but she pitched her camp wherever she could find a suitable site, set up a portrait of the king, summoned the important men of the district and addressed and argued with them. Hostility and suspicion, bad roads and brigandage, plague, her gout and her age – nothing deterred her. The Huguenots who came at her summons were impressed in spite of themselves. Nowhere was she attacked or insulted.

SOURCE F

From H. R. Williamson, Catherine de Medici *(1973).*

Q

1. *How far was Catherine working, in the short term, for the survival of her sons or, in the long term, for the interests of France?*

2. *How far did religious considerations affect Catherine's policies?*

3. *Do you detect a shift in the direction of her policy at any time? If so, why?*

4. *How would you describe the 'style' of the queen mother's involvement in government? How was it Machiavellian? How was it moderate?*

5. *How successful were her policies?*

16 Ivan the Terrible

OVERVIEW

'I surpassed in iniquities all of the transgressors from Adam to this day...I have desecrated my very head with unseemly desires and thought; my mouth with murderous and lustful words; my tongue with obscenity and profanity, with uttering words of anger and wrath; my hands for reaching for what I should not, with insatiable robbery.'

This extract from the will of Ivan IV of Russia, which he wrote in 1572 and which is translated in George Vernadsky's history of Russia, provides a justification for the traditional view of Ivan the Terrible. His lengthy reign was an odd combination of sensible reform at home in the 1550s followed by the horror and barbarism of the 1560s and 1570s. In foreign policy, a neat parallel can be seen; there were early triumphs in the 1550s against the **Tatars**, but these were followed by the costly and ultimately fruitless Livonian War from 1558 onwards.

Interest in Ivan lies both in an examination of his own personality and motivation and of his role in Russian history. Wielding unchecked power, he strangely combined sensible and progressive ideas with outbursts of irrational and sadistic brutality. He can also be seen as ruling the country at a vital time in its history, when it was beginning to emerge as a major power in the region and also to develop internally in a very different fashion to its western neighbours.

Tatars Turkic tribesmen whose power extended across Asia to the border lands of Europe

1 ✑ BACKGROUND: RUSSIA BEFORE THE ACCESSION OF IVAN

All states are deeply influenced by their geography and the emergence of Muscovy, the territory surrounding Moscow, which was the core of the Russian state, illustrates this clearly. In his book, *Russia under the Old Regime*, the historian Richard Pipes wrote, 'In the case of Russia the geographic element is particularly important because the country is inherently so poor that it affords at best a precarious existence.'

In the north lies the tundra, which can only support very limited plant life and is incapable of supporting organised human life. The tundra merges into the forest zone, which lies between approximately 45 and 50 degrees latitude. South of this is found the flat lands known as the **steppe**. These features combine with a harsh climate of long, cold winters and short, hot summers, which leads to a short growing season and a constant degree of crop failure. Equally important is the lack of easily defensible natural frontiers. Most of Russia consists of a flat plain. Indeed, no point in European Russia is more than 1400 feet above sea

steppe the enormous grassy and treeless plain of great fertility which covers much of southern Russia

level and even the Urals, which are usually taken as the boundary between Europe and Asia, present no great geographical obstacle. Although the forest regions presented a formidable barrier to movement before the modern age, there is a unique network of navigable rivers, which flow mostly from north to south. These have made transportation significantly easier than might be expected. The result of all this was to create an environment where the struggle for survival was especially harsh and the fear of invasion and conquest ever present.

The history of Kiev, which was the earlier Russian state, illustrates many of these problems. Kiev was probably founded by Vikings, who used the Russian rivers to trade with Constantinople. In the thirteenth century, Mongol invaders from the east destroyed the Kievan state and drove the Russians from the steppe lands to isolated settlements in the north east, such as Moscow, where the forest afforded some protection from the invincible *Tatar* cavalry of the **Golden Horde**. For 200 years, there was no strong Russian state. The small principalities, such as Moscow, which emerged in north-eastern Russia were cut off by the *Tatars* from any significant contact with western Europe. Kiev and the western Ukraine were, on the other hand, eventually absorbed into **Poland–Lithuania**.

> **KEY ISSUE**
>
> *Why has geography been particularly important in Russian history?*

> **The Golden Horde** the Tatar tribesmen who dominated much of what is now Russia in the later Middle Ages

> **Poland–Lithuania** the strongest state in eastern Europe at this time

PICTURE 43
Ivan the Terrible

ANALYSIS

Did Asiatic or European influence predominate in Russia's early development?

Many historians of Russia are concerned to play down the Asiatic element in Russian history. Riasanovsky argues that the nomadic and unstable state of the Asiatic tribesmen, the *Tatars*, barely influenced Russian history and government, which was far more affected by the traditions of the Byzantine Empire, from which the Russians derived their orthodox religion. George Vernadsky, on the other hand, belongs to the Eurasian school of historians, who argue that the *Tatars* deprived the Russians of the best land and also cut them off from any contact with the Renaissance and the Reformation in western Europe. Richard Pipes further developed Vernadsky's arguments. Pipes argues that the early princes of Muscovy were notorious for their subservience to the *Tatars*, and keener to compete with other Christian city states, such as Novgorod and Vladimir. Ivan I, who was the first prominent Muscovite prince, made his name by crushing a revolt against the *Tatars* in the city of Tver in 1327. In gratitude, the *Tatars* appointed him to collect tribute. Karl Marx described him as 'possessing the characters of the *Tatars'* hangman, sycophant and slave in chief'.

autocracy a state in which there are virtually no limitations placed on the power of the ruler

Khan title of the rulers of Tatar and other tribes of Mongol origin

Pipes suggests that the tradition of Russian **autocracy** derived from the regular contact with the Golden Horde, whose capital, Sarai, on the lower Volga was regularly visited by Ivan I and his successors, where they were treated in a humiliating fashion by the **Khans**. Constantinople, on the other hand, was distant and inaccessible. He notes that key words of government in Russia, such as *kazna*, which means treasury, are of Mongol origin, and argues that the princes of Moscow learned from the *Tatars* a view of politics in which the ruler was responsible for the collection of tribute, the maintenance of order and the preservation of security, but not for the well-being of the public. What is clear is that between the fourteenth and sixteenth centuries, a strong principality was established in Muscovy, in which the absolute power of the ruler gradually increased to a level matched only by the Turkish Sultan.

However, it was not simply subservience to the Golden Horde which caused the rise of Muscovy to its dominant position within Russia. The princes of Muscovy were shrewd and surprisingly healthy and long-lived, which gave a stability to the state. Great prestige came to the principality at the beginning of the fourteenth century, when the centre of the Russian Orthodox Church became Moscow. After 1439, the Greek Orthodox Patriarch at Constantinople lost all control over the Russian Church and the princes of Muscovy emerged as the protectors of Orthodoxy. By tradition the Orthodox Churches subordinated themselves to the rule of the state. After 1448 the Church in

Moscow had its own Metropolitan (next in rank to a Patriarch) who was seen as the equal of all others in the Orthodox Churches, although these men were appointed by the ruler of the state and rarely challenged his authority.

However, it was not simply subservience to the Golden Horde that caused the rise of Muscovy to its dominant position within Russia. The princes of Muscovy were shrewd and surprisingly healthy and long-lived, which gave stability to the state. Great prestige came to the principality at the beginning of the fourteenth century, when the centre of the Russian **Orthodox Church** became Moscow. After 1439, the Greek Orthodox Patriarch at Constantinople lost all control over the Russian Church and the princes of Muscovy emerged as the protectors of Orthodoxy. By tradition the Orthodox Churches subordinated themselves to the rule of the state. After 1448, the Church in Moscow had its own Metropolitan (next in rank to a patriarch), who was seen as the equal of all others in the Orthodox Churches, although these men were appointed by the ruler of the state and rarely challenged his authority.

Orthodox Church The Russian Orthodox Church was one of the eastern churches and did not recognise the authority of the pope

2 ↝ THE REIGNS OF IVAN III (1462–1505) AND BASIL III (1505–33)

Ivan III was the shrewdest and most successful of the early Russian princes and Ivan the Terrible based much of what he did on the achievements of Ivan III's reign. It was during his reign that the 'gathering of the Russian land' – the conquest of Russia by Moscow – accelerated. Ivan III annexed various smaller principalities, such as Tver, but most important was his conquest of Novgorod, which was the most prosperous trading city of north-western Russia. He followed this by the suppression of the traditional liberties of the city and the annexation of its land after a campaign in 1478. Ivan III's reign coincided with the disintegration of the Golden Horde into the khanates of Crimea, Kazan and Astrakhan. Effective *Tatar* influence over Moscow had probably ended by 1452, but in 1480 Ivan III formally renounced *Tatar* control and kept for himself the tribute that had previously been sent to the Golden Horde.

Ivan III's reign also saw a growing ideological justification of the power of Moscow and its princes. In 1472, he married Zoe Paleologos, the niece of the last Byzantine Emperor. The marriage was the idea of the pope in an unsuccessful attempt to create an anti-Turkish coalition, but through it the Muscovites began to develop a view of themselves as the heirs to the traditions of Constantinople and Rome. Ivan III added the Byzantine doubled-headed eagle to his standards and over the next century elaborate genealogies were developed, which were supposed to prove the descent of the princes of Moscow from the Emperor Augustus.

At the same time, the doctrine of the 'third Rome' emerged. This was developed after 1500 by Filofei of the Eleazer monastery in Pskov. He argued that, when the Church of Rome under the pope broke with the doctrines of the eastern Orthodox Churches in the Middle Ages, Constantinople became the 'second Rome'. However, the Greeks had lost their position as the 'second Rome' when they betrayed the tradition of Orthodoxy in their attempted reunification with the Church of Rome in Florence in 1439. Their punishment had been the fall of Constantinople to the Turks in 1453. Now, only Moscow preserved the true traditions of the Orthodox Church. In 1512, Filofei wrote, 'Two Romes fell down, the third is standing, and there will be no fourth.' He also argued that it was the ruler's task to protect and encourage Orthodoxy, since Russia was the only truly Orthodox state. He advocated a close unity, a 'symphony' of Church and state. In practice, these ideas greatly increased the prestige of the rulers of Moscow. Ivan III and Basil III occasionally started to use the title 'Tsar' (Caesar), with its assertion of imperial power.

Basil III, in particular, built monasteries and churches, while at the same time strictly subordinating the Church to his authority. He continued the expansion of Muscovy with the annexation of Pskov in 1511 and Riazan in 1517. Three campaigns were fought against Lithuania, which was the other major state with a significant Russian population. As a result of these, Smolensk was captured in 1514 and its acquisition was confirmed by treaty in 1522.

By 1533, Muscovy had established itself as the strongest Russian state. Various factors had contributed to this. The location was favourable; Moscow lay at the crossing of three roads, one of which was the major route from Kiev to the north east, and close to four major rivers, the Oka, the Volga, the Don and the Dnieper. There were no geographical barriers to expansion and the forest brought relative freedom from invasion. Muscovy's rulers were shrewd in their policy towards the Golden Horde. Also, they were healthy and produced male children to maintain the family line, while the establishment of the Metropolitan See had brought power and prestige to the state and favoured the development of strong monarchy. But inevitably a reaction was always likely against the system of government that had emerged in Muscovy.

By tradition, Russian princes had divided their realms equally between their sons. This was one reason for the emergence of so many small principalities in Russia, which were constantly subdivided between sons – the *appanage* princes. It was common, before the sixteenth century, for the *appanage* princes and the *boyars* to choose the great prince whom they would serve. The right of 'free departure' might even involve going to serve the ruler of another country altogether. Gradually the division of lands into *appanages* was restricted.

Ivan III went further and used the land that had been seized after the conquest of Novgorod to foster the development of a different system of landholding by the nobility, known as *pomestia*. It could not be sold, or divided among their heirs. By this method, a 'service aristocracy'

KEY ISSUE

Why did the Russians stress their historic links with Constantinople?

appanage a large estate where the owner also had the right to levy taxes and administer justice

boyar the Russian term for great aristocrat

pomestia land was given by the ruler in return for military or government service

began to emerge in the sixteenth century, which was dependent for its status on service to the ruler rather than inherited rights, as with the *appanage* princes. Many *boyars* obviously resented their decline in status. They would have favoured the development of a state in which the aristocracy held the real power, such as did in fact emerge in the neighbouring state of Poland–Lithuania. Naturally, the aristocracy would attempt to take advantage of any weakness in royal authority. The early death of Basil III brought such an opportunity. Although the nominal power of the ruler was very great, like all European rulers he depended on the aristocracy to enforce his authority and lacked the military force and bureaucracy of the modern state.

Sigmund von Herberstein travelled to Muscovy in 1517–18 and again in 1526–27 as an ambassador of the Holy Roman Empire. He produced the first substantial first-hand account of life in Muscovy in the time of Basil III and commented interestingly on the way in which the Russians viewed their rulers:

1   All in the land call themselves Kholopi, or sold slaves.

The Grand Duke exercises his power over both clergy and laymen, both property and life. None of his councillors has ever dared to gainsay his Lord's opinion. One and all agree that their Lord's will is

5   the will of God, hence what the prince does is divinely inspired. Thus, they call their prince God's Klyuchnik or key bearer, in the sense of chamberlain, and only regard him as the fulfiller of God's purpose. So when someone pleads for a prisoner he will say, 'What God orders will take place without your plea.' And when one asks

10   about something to which there is no proper answer they say, 'God knows and the Grand Duke.' It is debatable whether such a people must have such oppressive rulers or whether the oppressive rulers have made the people so stupid.

Albeit he [Basil III] has been unfortunate in war, yet his people call

15   him successful. And when there remained not half of his troops they dared to say they had not lost a man. He surpasses all other kings and princes in the power that he has and uses over his own people; what his father began he completed. That is, he turned out the princes and others from all the fortresses neither leaving nor

20   entrusting any fortress to his brothers. He holds one and all in the same subjection.

Q

1. *Why is it significant that the people called themselves 'sold slaves' (lines 1–13)?*
2. *Why do you think that Basil entrusted no fortress to his brothers (line 20)?*
3. *What are the advantages and disadvantages in relying on the evidence of a foreign ambassador?*

In 1533 Basil died and was succeeded by his three-year-old son, Ivan.

3 ↜ IVAN IV'S EARLY YEARS, 1530–47

Ivan IV was born in August 1530 and was the first son of Basil III and his second wife, Elena Glinskaya, a member of the Glinsky family who

PROFILE

IVAN THE 'TERRIBLE'
(1547–84)

Few men are as little known, but as widely remembered, as Ivan the Terrible. In the popular mind his name is on the list of noted historical villains, such as Attila the Hun or Vlad the Impaler, all of them exotic figures associated with unimaginable evil. This makes it very hard to disentangle myth from reality. In Russian, he is Ivan '*Grozny*'. '*Grozny*' means 'stern' or 'awe-inspiring'. Russian history is littered with tyrannical figures whose actions seem to veer from the rational to the wildly excessive. Ivan belongs to a tradition that produced Peter the Great and Joseph Stalin, both of whom also embarked on policies of dramatic and violent change.

There is no doubt that Ivan was in many ways a gifted man. He was educated and widely read, with a genuine interest in theology. From the start of his life, he was also prone to outbursts of violence and cruelty. In some ways, he was inspired by an utterly rational view of what Russian society needed. Ivan was an autocrat and he envisaged a society in which personal rights and freedom were limited in favour of strict obedience to the needs of the state and the Tsar. In this way, the Tsar would stand above every social class and hold the balance, and there is a case for arguing that a strong Tsar would have protected the peasantry from the exploitation of the nobility, as was the case with the Ottoman sultans in the sixteenth century. Ivan, however, lacked the personality to establish an enlightened autocracy. As the years passed, so the violent and arbitrary side to his character became more pronounced. The second part of his reign, after 1564, can be explained as a sustained campaign to weaken the aristocracy and strengthen the Tsar. In practice, it became a reign of terror, strangely anticipating the methods of Joseph Stalin in the 1930s. Ivan treated Russia as if he had won it through conquest; his legacy was economic ruin and the political instabilty of the 'Time of Troubles' of the early seventeeth century.

PICTURE 44
Woodcut of Procession of Boyars at the Court of Maximilian, c. *1573*

were great landowners on the Lithuanian border and had recently transferred their allegiance to Basil III.

In any European state at this time, the accession of a child brought fear of social and political discontent. In December 1533, Basil III died and in accordance with Muscovite law and custom, Ivan's mother, Elena, became regent during his minority. Elena was not popular with the *boyars*; she was seen as heavily influenced by her Lithuanian connections and western ideas. After two strong rulers, who had consciously sought to advance their power at the expense of the great aristocrats, it was inevitable that there should be an attempt to reverse the growth in royal power.

In fact, Ivan's childhood was a time of almost continuous violence and civil strife, the effects of which were never to leave him. Until her death in April 1538, Elena maintained some semblance of royal authority. Princes Ivan and Andrei Shuisky, who had been imprisoned by Basil III and belonged to one of the great princely families, were released from prison and began a conspiracy with Yuri, Ivan's uncle, to seize power.

Naturally, neighbouring states attempted to capitalise on these problems. The aristocratic conspirators turned to Sigismund I of Lithuania and to the Crimean *Tatars*, whose close links with Suleiman the Magnificent made them especially dangerous enemies. Elena maintained some control, but after her death, possibly from poisoning, royal authority virtually collapsed.

From 1538 to 1543, the great aristocratic families ruthlessly struggled for power. The struggle centred around the rival Belsky and Shuisky clans. Ivan suffered various traumas and humiliations, such as the dismissal of his nurse, Agrafena, to a nunnery, and these experiences helped to foster the violent and autocratic streak in his character. Suddenly, on 9 December 1543, Ivan ordered the arrest of Andrei Shuisky and had him thrown to a pack of hounds, which tore him to pieces. This decisive and ruthless action broke the hold of the *boyars* on the government of the country and gave a clear indication of Ivan's temperament and approach. For the rest of his life he often showed himself to be unpredictable and violent. He never lost his suspicion of the *boyars* and consistently sought to advance his power at their expense.

The next four years showed no clear direction in policy. Generally, Ivan left direction of the affairs of state to his unpopular Glinsky relatives.

KEY ISSUE

What might have been the effect on Ivan of his early life?

4 ↪ IVAN'S CORONATION, 1547

On 16 January, 1547, Ivan was crowned Tsar of all Russia. Although Ivan III and Basil III had used this title on occasions, Ivan IV was the first Muscovite ruler actually to be crowned Tsar. His title was approved by the patriarchs of the Greek Orthodox Church and he now used the title regularly at home and in his dealings with foreign countries. In the coronation ceremonies, which were conducted by the Metropolitan *Makary*, a cross and regalia were used which it was claimed had been sent by the Byzantine Emperor Constantine to Prince Vladimir of Kiev in the early twelfth century. This claim was false, but it illustrates the lofty view that Ivan held of his role. He intended to be a great Tsar and to continue the expansion of the Muscovite state which had grown dramatically over the previous century and which was to double in size during Ivan's reign.

Ivan saw his task as being the completion of the 'gathering of the Russian land' and bringing together under his rule all those of the Russian Orthodox faith. Obvious targets for expansion were Lithuania, whose population was predominantly Orthodox and Russian, the *Tatar* states of Kazan and Astrakhan, which blocked access to the fertile steppe of the south and east, and Livonia, possession of which would bring access to the Baltic Sea and western Europe.

Ivan's coronation was followed by his marriage to Anastasia, a member of the Zakharin family, who were Muscovite *boyars,* but not of princely blood. He did not yet, however, seem to have shown the qualities required in a Tsar of such lofty ambition. But in April 1547 there was a serious fire in Moscow, which was a city mainly built of wood. This was followed by an uprising in Moscow in the summer, during which the Tsar's uncle, Yuri Glinsky, was murdered.

These events seem to have shocked Ivan, who was prone to sudden personal and spiritual crises and constantly tormented by a view of himself as a sinner, which was not wholly unjustified. For a time he became far more responsible as a ruler, and the next twelve years were the most successful of his reign. At home, a policy of reform was followed with many positive results; in foreign policy, Ivan continued the expansion of Muscovy with great success. From around 1560, however, inconsistent and brutal policies were introduced within Muscovy and an inconclusive and ultimately unsuccessful war gradually drained the resources of the state. Undoubtedly, Ivan instigated and directed most of the dramatic changes in direction. Some historians, such as Ian Grey, while not defending his violent excesses, argue nonetheless that many of his policies were justified and in the interests of the Russian state and people, who clearly preferred his rule to that of the *boyars.* Certainly expansionism and autocracy, two major themes in Russian history, were Ivan's central preoccupations. At the same time, like any sixteenth-century European monarch, practical obstacles and the need to keep the support of the ruling classes greatly restricted Ivan's autocratic ambitions. When he did try to challenge his opponents in Muscovy, the result, as we shall see, was to be the greatest crisis of his reign.

5 ↪ THE FOREIGN POLICY OF MUSCOVY, 1547–83

A *The conquest of Kazan*

Although the Golden Horde had broken up and the Khanates of Kazan, Astrakhan and Crimea could not match its strength, they still provided formidable obstacles to the expansion of Muscovy. The strength of these nomadic tribesmen lay in their skill as horsemen. They excelled at mobile warfare, to which the steppe was particularly suited. Muscovites had suffered at the hands of the *Tatars* for centuries and there was undoubtedly a widespread sense of military inferiority. *Tatar* raids from Kazan constantly devastated the villages to the south and east of Moscow and the villagers were killed or taken as slaves. In 1551 alone, it is estimated that 100 000 prisoners were taken. If Muscovy was to expand to the east and south, the conquest of Kazan was essential. The defeat of Kazan would open up the fertile steppe to Muscovite farmers, to whose way of life the nomadic *Tatars* were particularly hostile. It would ease the problem of defending Muscovy's enormous land frontier, along which there were few natural barriers to *Tatar* raids except the forest. Finally, the conquest of Kazan could be presented as a crusade against the Infidel, which could bring Ivan much credit in the Christian world and unite his people behind him.

As early as 1545, Ivan launched an unsuccessful campaign against Kazan. A winter campaign in January 1548 failed when the frost and snow, which often made movement in winter easier than at any other time by hardening the ground, did not materialise. But in March 1549 Safa Girey, the Khan of Kazan, died. His successor, Utemish, was a child of two, which encouraged further invasion plans.

In 1550, after another unsuccessful campaign, Ivan began to reorganise his forces. A particular problem was that military appointments were based on social rank, or **mestnichestvo**. Although this system clearly showed how highly regarded service to the Tsar was among the aristocrats, it prevented Ivan from selecting by merit alone. The system was too deeply entrenched to be abolished, but a decree of 1550 modified it by strengthening the power of the commanding officer over the *boyars* who served him. In the same year, the **streltsi** were created as a professional core to the army.

In the spring of 1551, the campaign was launched. The fortress of Sviyazhsk was built as a stronghold near Kazan and many of the nomadic *Tatar* tribesmen gave their allegiance to Ivan. In August, the siege of Kazan began. Ivan had 150 000 troops against 30 000 defenders and in October the city fell. Despite opposition by some *Tatars*, supported by the Crimeans, further expeditions in 1552 and 1556 consolidated Russian control.

The conquest of Kazan was followed by a successful expedition to Astrakhan in 1554, which led to its annexation in 1556. The only Tatar khanate not in Muscovite hands now was the Crimea. The Crimean

mestnichestvo literally 'place order', meaning that no one would serve under a superior army officer or government official who was of lower social rank

streltsi a force of around 3000 men, who became the nucleus of the regular army

MAP 25
Russia and the annexations of Tatar lands

khan, Devlet Girey, presented a constant threat and could rely on the backing of the Turkish Sultan. He supported Kazan and Astrakhan and raided Muscovy. In response, in the summer of 1556, an expedition reached as far as Ochakov, which was over 700 miles from Moscow.

The impact of the conquest of Kazan and Astrakhan was enormous. Ivan was given the title '*Grozny*' which is commonly translated into English as 'terrible', but should more accurately be rendered as 'awe-inspiring' It was a great victory for Christendom and to mark this, St Basil's Cathedral was built in Moscow. For the Russian people, great opportunities appeared. Much of the black earth belt, which was land of outstanding fertility, was now available for settlement. The peasants saw this opportunity and mass settlement of these regions, which had formerly been too dangerous, began. Russian agriculture was no longer restricted to the relatively unproductive forest region. Moreover, the Nogay Tatars east of the Volga soon recognised Ivan as overlord and the whole of the Volga was now in Russian hands. This secure eastern frontier gave Muscovy access to the Caspian Sea and the trade routes to central Asia, Persia and the Caucasus, which had previously been in enemy hands. Moreover, there was now no obstacle to expansion into Siberia, into which Russian settlers advanced with astonishing rapidity over the next century.

> **KEY ISSUE**
>
> *What benefits did the campaigns against the Tatars bring to Ivan?*

B *The Livonian War (1558–83) and the debate over foreign policy*

After the great triumphs against the *Tatars*, there was no doubt that the expansion of the Muscovite state should continue, but much disagreement as to the direction. Three possible courses were open to Ivan: he could attack the Crimean *Tatars*; he could attack the parts of Poland–Lithuania in the west largely inhabited by Orthodox Russians; or he could expand north-west towards Livonia and the Baltic Sea.

Many of Ivan's advisers strongly favoured a campaign against the Crimean *Tatars*. It was argued that they had actively opposed Ivan in Kazan and Astrakhan and that their constant raiding for slaves posed a threat to the security of the state. It was also true that this campaign could be presented as a crusade. Ivan rejected this idea. He believed that it would be impossible to cross 700 miles of steppe with 100 000 men and feared the possibility of a war with the Ottoman Turks. Despite the successful raids against the Crimea, in 1560 Ivan adopted a defensive policy on his southern frontier. Defences, which mainly consisted of trenches and ramparts and fortified stockades, were constructed along the southern frontier and eventually a frontier guard was established.

A campaign against the Polish–Lithuanian state was considered. At this time Poland and Lithuania were two separate states which shared the same ruler. Lithuania contained the heartland of the state of Kiev, to which the Muscovites had a rather spurious claim. But Poland–Lithuania was a strong state, in which there was a growing mood of unity. This was to lead to the Union of Lublin in 1569, which joined the two countries with a single constitution, as well as sharing a ruler. Moreover, in case of war, it would not be difficult for Poland–Lithuania to make a tactical alliance with the Crimean *Tatars* and the Turks.

Livonia was certainly the weakest of Muscovy's neighbours. Originally Livonia had formed part of the territories of a group of crusaders, the Order of **Teutonic Knights**. Most had now become Lutheran and they were divided into pro-Polish and pro-Russian

Teutonic Knights a military order of mostly German crusaders originally formed to convert the Lithuanians to Christianity

ANALYSIS

Comparison of Russia and Poland–Lithuania

The histories of Russia and Poland–Lithuania present a fascinating contrast. While in Russia, Ivan was determined to strengthen the power of the Crown at the expense of the aristocracy, Polish history moved in the opposite direction. In the sixteenth century, Poland should more properly be called Poland–Lithuania. After 1385, the two states were ruled by the same family; in other words, the King of Poland was also Grand Duke of Lithuania. The population of Poland–Lithuania was exceptionally diverse. The Poles were Catholic and strongly influenced by the Renaissance and Christian humanism. The Reformation also put down strong roots in Poland. Lutherans predominated in the German-speaking northern towns, while Calvinism enjoyed a strong following amongst the Polish-speaking nobility. Amongst many other diverse groups, the Jewish community was the largest in Europe. Lithuania had been the last pagan state in Europe and was never as deeply Catholic; within Lithuania, there was also a substantial Orthodox population. To the Russian Tsars, this provided an excuse for expansion into Lithuania. They claimed that the Orthodox population required protection and should be absorbed as part of the 'gathering of Russia'.

The Union of Lublin of 1569 created a permanent constitution to replace the fragile dynastic link between Poland and Lithuania. Although both states were to keep their own laws and administration, they were to be ruled by an elected king and to have one parliament (the *Sejm*). Not only this, but in the *Rzeczpospolita* (Republic) of Poland–Lithuania, future monarchs were to be elected by the entire *szlachta* (nobility). Once elected they had to promise to uphold the principle of toleration, to summon the *Sejm* on a regular basis, and to maintain the system of elective monarchy. Poland–Lithuania became an aristocratic republic, whose king was legally bound to consult with the aristocrats who had elected him. The contrast with Tsarist Russia was extraordinary. While Ivan IV consciously sought to break the power of the *boyars*, his neighbouring state moved in precisely the opposite direction.

factions. There is no doubt that the capture of Livonia and access to the Baltic Sea would have given Muscovy what Vernadsky describes as a 'corridor to Europe'. Ivan's western neighbours constantly blocked contact with the west and the Baltic states allowed trade with Muscovy only in goods that were of no military or industrial value. In 1547, Ivan had sent a German named Schlitte to the Baltic States to recruit skilled men to serve Muscovy. One hundred-and-twenty-three men assembled at Lubeck, but the Livonians protested to Charles V and the men were prevented from sailing. One of the Germans, who tried to make his own way to Moscow, was executed on the border by the Livonians. There was similar opposition to the English expeditions of Willoughby and Chancellor, who travelled to Muscovy in the 1550s via the White Sea and Archangel and made contacts which continued for the remainder of Ivan's reign. Poland–Lithuania, Sweden, Denmark and the Holy Roman Emperor all protested against the alleged English sale of arms to Muscovy.

Ivan's decision to invade Livonia was to be unsuccessful and to have terrible consequences for the Russian people. Historians are divided as to the wisdom of his move. George Vernadsky argues that the war was not necessary. He feels that the true enemies of the Russians were the Crimean *Tatars*, who constantly menaced the Russian peasantry, and that Ivan imposed upon himself a war on two fronts, since in only three of the twenty-four years of the Livonian War was there no *Tatar* raid. For Vernadsky, the war was a disastrous mistake. Ian Grey and J.L.A. Fennell, on the other hand, stress the enormous advantages that the capture of Livonia would have brought. The economic and strategic benefits of an outlet to the Baltic would be vast; not only would trade benefit, but Poland–Lithuania would have been threatened from the north and the east and Muscovy would never again have been blockaded. They also point out the practical difficulties and dangers of a campaign in the Crimea. Ivan's policy – and the Livonian War was certainly his decision – must be regarded as a mistake as it turned out, but not necessarily as irrational or foolish.

> ## KEY ISSUE
>
> *What do the debates over Ivan's foreign policy illustrate about the strengths and weaknesses of sixteenth-century Russia?*

C *The outbreak of the Livonian War*

The war itself was a lengthy struggle of great diplomatic and military complexity. Apart from the Livonians, Sweden, Denmark and Poland–Lithuania were all deeply concerned in its action and outcome. Ivan also constantly suffered from the lack of a fleet, which made it very difficult to hold any bases on the coastline. A lengthy and complex war was, therefore, to be expected.

Initially, the war brought great success. A huge invading army captured Dorpat and Narva in 1558. Control of Narva gave Ivan an invaluable port on the left bank of the River Narva, which was only ten miles from the Gulf of Finland. In 1559, there was a further Muscovite invasion; an army of 130 000 men conquered the northern territories of the Livonian Order.

The inevitable result of this was to frighten all the other powers, especially after a further Russian campaign in 1560 led to the virtual collapse of the Livonian Order. In a treaty of 28 November 1561 all the possessions of the order were ceded to Poland–Lithuania. The Swedes occupied northern Estonia and the important port of Reval, while the Danes occupied the island of Osel. Livonia had effectively ceased to exist and was now a battleground for the major powers of the region.

It was important for Ivan not to fight all his opponents at the same time. Eric XIV of Sweden was at war with Denmark (1563–70), and was strongly anti-Polish, so Ivan chose to maintain good relations with Sweden and concentrate his efforts against Poland–Lithuania. The 1560s were a time of domestic upheaval and diplomatic confusion. The major success for Ivan was the seizure of Polotsk in 1563. This gave him control of the western Dvina, the major waterway to the Baltic. This war was followed by a lengthy period of diplomatic bargaining, which brought little change to the situation.

D *The strengthening of the opposition to Muscovy*

See page 507

In the late 1560s, the international position of Muscovy began to deteriorate rapidly. In Sweden the mad, pro-Russian Eric XIV was overthrown by John III, the brother-in-law of King Sigismund Augustus of Poland–Lithuania, who followed a pro-Polish policy. In June 1569, the Poles and Lithuanians concluded the Union of Lublin. The aristocracy of these states would now elect a king jointly. Each country was to remain independent internally, but in foreign affairs and war the two countries now formed a single state, which was a formidable threat to Muscovy. Nor could the threat of the Ottoman Empire be ignored. Sultan Selim II wished to control Astrakhan. Ivan's only allies were the Danes, but they assisted him little.

Within Muscovy, many *boyars* still argued that the greater threat came from the Crimean *Tatars*. This opposition increased the violence and brutality of Ivan's policies. In 1571, Devlet Girey, the Crimean leader invaded Muscovy and on 23 May, Moscow was set on fire. The city recovered with remarkable speed, but the increasing burden being placed on the people of Muscovy is clear. Except for the palace of the Kremlin, the whole city with its wooden buildings was destroyed and 150 000 Russians were captured. Although a further *Tatar* invasion was defeated in 1572, these problems prevented Ivan from taking any initiatives in the west.

This was unfortunate, because Polish–Lithuanian affairs were in some confusion at this time. After the death of Sigismund in 1572, Ivan advanced himself as a candidate for the throne in this elective monarchy. Some Orthodox Lithuanians did favour Ivan, but his chances of election were never serious. It is clear that after the short and disastrous interlude of Henry of Anjou, who fled back to France in 1574, Ivan's main aim was to block the claims of Stephen Báthory, Prince of Transylvania. The election of Báthory would be a disaster for Ivan. He was a close ally to the sultan, and was his vassal. He clearly intended to maintain good relations with the Ottoman Empire and the Crimean *Tatars* and to fight Muscovy. In addition, he was an energetic leader and a capable soldier.

See page 466

Báthory's successful election and assumption of the throne in early 1576 demonstrated the failure of Ivan's diplomacy. In late 1576, Ivan attempted to take advantage of a rebellion against Báthory in Danzig and launched one final attempt to conquer Livonia. He met with initial success but the siege of Reval, which was still held by the Swedes, was unsuccessful and abandoned in March 1577. Ivan was now without allies and faced the forces of Poland–Lithuania and Sweden, combined with a constant threat of *Tatar* raids on his southern frontier. In 1578, the counter-attack began and the Swedes defeated a Russian army at Wenden. In the following year Báthory, with the help of the Danish prince Magnus, attacked and seized Polotsk, which gave him control of a vital river route. His capture of Velikie Luki in the following year cut off Ivan's troops in Livonia and provided a base for a possible invasion of Muscovy. Báthory's further plans were limited by the lack of enthusiasm of the Polish parliament, the *sejm*, and his own financial problems saved Ivan from complete humiliation. Nonetheless, Ivan's armies had now been driven from Livonia, and the war had devastated his country. It was essential that he should make peace.

KEY ISSUE

Why did Ivan's Livonian campaign fail?

E *The Treaty of Yam Zapolsky*

Papal mediation led to the Treaty of Yam Zapolsky with Poland–Lithuania in January 1582. Ivan renounced all claims to Livonia and the districts of Polotsk and Velizh; the only concession was the return of Velikie Luki. In the following year the whole of Estonia, including Narva, which the Swedes had captured in 1581, as well as the districts of Ivangorod and Yam, were ceded to Sweden. Only the extreme eastern

PROFILE

STEPHEN BÁTHORY, PRINCE OF TRANSYLVANIA (1571–75) AND KING OF POLAND (1575–86)

Stephen Báthory succeeded to the Polish throne in what were potentially very difficult circumstances. The reign of Henry of Valois had lasted 118 days before he fled the country. The election of Stephen in 1575 was a complex affair with six serious candidates including Ivan the Terrible, whose troops happened to be invading Poland at the time.

Báthory, the Prince of Transylvania, on the borders of the Ottoman Empire, was a gifted and experienced man. He was a devout Catholic – who was already ruling a country with four different religions – and a capable soldier. Báthory reformed the Polish army and disciplined the nobility. He identified Ivan the Terrible as his major foe, while maintaining close and peaceful relations with the Ottoman Empire. In return, Ivan described Báthory as a 'Turkish employee'. Báthory's success was personal. After his death, the weaknesses of the constitution of the Republic of Poland–Lithuania were again revealed.

end of the Gulf of Finland around the mouth of the River Neva was left to Muscovy – even less of the Baltic seaboard than before the war. It is worth noting that one reason for the weakening Russian resistance in the last years of the war was the raids by the Nogay *Tatars* on the Lower Volga, further emphasising the problem of fighting a war on two fronts.

F *England and Siberia*

It is not strictly true that the capture of Kazan and Astrakhan were the only gains of Ivan's foreign policy. Although the discovery by the English of the White Sea route to Russia was quite accidental, this opened up an important trade route to England and the Low Countries, which came into regular use. Ivan genuinely, if somewhat inconsistently, encouraged and saw the importance of this. Ivan's interest in close contact with England never waned. At the very end of his reign, it was revived in his rather eccentric proposal of marriage to Elizabeth I's cousin, Lady Mary Hastings.

Even more significant were the Russian advances into Siberia. As early as the fifteenth century, the powerful Stroganov family had begun to develop the east and they always took great care to maintain good relations with Muscovy. The capture of Kazan and Astrakhan opened the way to the colonisation of Siberia. The peoples of Siberia, many of whom were *Tatars*, were few in number and constantly feuding with each other. The extensive river systems made communications far easier than might initially be imagined. In 1558, the Stroganovs were given a charter for twenty years to develop territories to the east of Kazan. In 1573, settlers crossed the Urals into Siberia and were authorised by Ivan to pursue aggressive tactics against the Siberian khan. The Stroganovs raised a private army of *Cossacks*. Tribesmen raided the Russian settlements in 1581 and in September, the **Cossack** leader Ermak mounted a retaliatory attack. His tiny force defeated the Siberian khan in October 1581. Ivan received representatives from the *Cossacks* and was officially proclaimed Tsar of Siberia. Although Siberia was thinly populated, its resources, especially furs, were considerable. Ivan's appreciation of the value of his acquisition, in which he was keenly interested, serves to emphasise the breadth of his vision.

Cossacks nomadic peoples from a variety of backgrounds who inhabited the steppe and were renowned for their skill as horsemen

G *The significance of the Livonian War*

Ivan's early victories over the *Tatars* had been of great long-term importance for the development of Russia, but the Livonian War was an unmitigated disaster for Muscovy and completely over-shadowed later achievements, such as the expansion into Siberia. Ivan lacked reliable allies and found himself constantly threatened to the south as well as to the west. It is true that a Crimean expedition would have posed enormous difficulties and that Ivan was almost certainly right to reject that policy. The choice of Livonia was based on sound reasoning and its capture would have brought enormous economic and strategic benefits. It is not without significance that a century later Peter the Great chose to concentrate his own efforts there, while the Crimea was not acquired for nearly two centuries. Despite this, the actual result of the Livonian War was economic devastation and it also had a direct bearing on the political upheavals of the second part of Ivan's reign.

6 ᔕ IVAN'S DOMESTIC REFORMS, 1547–60

A *The 'Chosen Council'*

There is a close parallel between domestic and foreign affairs in Ivan's reign. In both cases, the early years saw a rational and coherent policy, which was quite successfully sustained. This was followed in domestic affairs by a growth in violent and autocratic behaviour, much of which casts doubt on Ivan's mental state.

It does seem that the great fire in Moscow in 1547 was seen by Ivan as a punishment for his sins and encouraged him to pursue a policy of reform. He was strongly influenced by a group of advisers, who have commonly been described as the 'Chosen Council'. The 'Chosen Council' should not be seen as a formal political institution, but simply as an influential group. These saw the *boyars,* who were strongly represented on the official state council, as obstructive to a policy of reform. There were three men who seem to have had most influence on Ivan. Sylvester was a scholarly and devout priest, who had been the young Ivan's personal confessor. He hoped to reform Ivan's character and to reform the administration of the country. The Metropolitan *Makary* also encouraged Ivan to reform. *Makary* favoured an autocratic tsar, who would enhance the position and prestige of the Orthodox Church. But Sylvester's closest ally was Alexei Adashev. Adashev's origins lay in the minor gentry. He became a court official and by June 1547 had become keeper of the Tsar's bedchamber, which gave him daily contact with Ivan and the management of his personal treasury. Adashev was an attractive and popular character who was regarded as possessing almost saintly qualities.

It is not realistic to ascribe an absolutely rigid political outlook to the 'Chosen Council'. But it does seem that these men feared a return to the princely strife and feuding of earlier years and particularly sought to diminish the power of the *appanage* princes. They believed that Muscovy had to be a strong centralised state with an autocratic tsar, or there would be constant danger of civil strife. If a general theme can be discerned in the reign of Ivan, it is the weakening of the power of the great aristocracy and the strengthening of that of the service gentry, who were granted land in return for service to the state.

Zemsky Sobor literally 'assembly of land', which brought together representatives of the clergy, aristocracy and gentry summoned by the tsar

KEY ISSUE

Why was the policy of autocracy attractive to many Russian people?

kormlenie literally 'feeding', whereby governors were paid by taking goods from the people in their province, an arbitrary and unpopular practice

B *The Zemsky Sobor, 1549*

In 1549, the **Zemsky Sobor** (Assembly of Land) was summoned. This contained representatives of the clergy, the aristocracy and the service gentry. There were no representatives of the towns or the peasantry and its members were probably appointed, rather than elected. There is no doubt that the administration of the state needed to be overhauled to cope with the phenomenal growth of Muscovy over the previous centuries. Typical proposals came from a man called Peresvetov, who had served in various countries before settling in Muscovy. In a petition, he urged the need for strong autocratic rule, the centralisation of finance and justice, and the creation of a standing army. He urged the Tsar to consider the example of the Turkish sultan, who ruled without fear of his great aristocrats. These general principles were attractive to many Muscovites and Ivan's reforms of the 1550s made some attempt to satisfy them.

In February 1549, the service gentry were granted almost complete freedom from the legal control of the provincial governors, who were widely regarded as corrupt and incompetent. The governors were paid for their services, usually by the system of **kormlenie**. The more important an aristocrat was, the larger his *kormlenie* would be. They held these appointments as governors for a short time and were expected to accumulate enough to provide for themselves when they were out of office.

C *The Sudebnik of 1550*

A further attempt to control the provincial governors was made in 1550 with the S*udebnik*, a new legal code. This was an impressive and wide-ranging reform of the legal system, which revised and extended the earlier law code of 1497. If there was a general aim of the *Sudebnik*, it was to protect the people from aristocratic abuses. The presence of locally elected representatives of the people at the courts of the provincial governors was made compulsory. Special clerks were appointed to advise the people on the amount of taxation that could legally be levied by the provincial governor. Finally, in 1555, each district was permitted by law to replace their governors by elected authorities, which would be responsible for local administration, justice and the collection of taxation. Taxes were now to be paid to the treasury and not to the governor. This measure increased the control of the state and weakened the system of *kormlenie*; it was not compulsory, but offered the population of the provinces the opportunity to free themselves from the arbitrary control of their governors.

D *The aristocracy*

A clear trend in the history of Muscovy at this time was the growing control of the Tsar over the *boyars* and the attempt to create a ruling class to act as the Tsar's servants. The development of the service gentry (the *pomestia*) has already been mentioned and Ivan's dislike of the hereditary *appanage* princes who owed him no service was clear. Equally, it was never easy for any sixteenth-century monarch to rule without the cooperation of the great aristocrats and many of Ivan's reforms were undoubtedly more impressive in theory than in practice, since they relied on the cooperation of the nobility for their enactment. Land was needed for the service gentry, however. In 1550, Ivan granted estates close to Moscow to many members of the service gentry. This was to provide land for about half the members of the court and central government close to the capital and increase the speed and efficiency of mobilisation in war. It was also intended to be a massive extension of the system of *pomestia,* although there was clearly the practical problem of insufficient land being available for this policy to work.

See pages 500–2

The connection between serving the state and ownership of land was further stressed by the statute on military service of 1556. Each owner of land was now required by law to serve the Tsar personally. He was also, according to the size of his land, expected to provide armed men and supplies, or make a financial payment. In return, it was permitted for sons to inherit their father's land, provided that they continued to provide service to the Tsar. Again, a policy of this nature would have been very difficult to enforce.

E *The peasantry*

The growing demands that were placed on the nobility were bound to lead to growing demands on the peasantry by the nobility. One of the odder developments of Russian history is that **serfdom** developed in the sixteenth and seventeenth centuries at a time when it was in decline in western Europe. A key element of serfdom is that the peasant may not freely leave the estate on which he works. The *Sudebnik* (law code) of 1497 had restricted the date when a peasant could leave his master to the period around 26 November, which was St George's Day. St George was considered by Orthodox Russia to be in charge of the whole growing season, which came between his two holidays, 23 April and 26 November. The time chosen for movement was, therefore, the end of the agricultural season. The *Sudebnik* of 1550 confirmed the peasant's right to move freely at this time and this quite clearly shows that the Russian peasants were by no means completely enserfed in the reign of Ivan. These years were a time of growing population and relative prosperity and there was little need to control the peasants.

serfs similar to slaves in that they were legally owned and forced to work on their lord's estate for part of the week; unlike slaves in that during the rest of the week they could grow produce and earn income from a plot of land granted by the lord

But the conquest of Kazan and Astrakhan opened up the fertile black earth lands of the central and lower Volga to the Russian peasantry and a great shift of population to the south east began, in particular during the chaos of the second half of Ivan's reign. In late 1580 or early 1581, the government did begin to restrict the right of the peasants to move on St George's Day, probably initially on an annual basis. Ivan's reign therefore saw the beginning of a process of enserfment, which was to last into the nineteenth century and distinguish developments in Russian society so dramatically from those in western Europe.

F *The Church*

The spiritual, political and economic power of the Church in Russia was as great as anywhere else in sixteenth-century Europe. In a country with no universities, education was effectively a monopoly of the Church and monasteries were great landowners in their own right. It was therefore inevitable that the summoning of the *Zemsky Sobor* should be followed by that of a *Stoglav Sobor* (Council of the Church) in 1551.

First of all, Ivan submitted to this council the new law code, the *Sudebnik*, and the local government reforms, which were approved. But the Church itself contained divisions and factions that needed to be reconciled. The two major factions were the Josephans and the Trans Volga Hermits. The Josephans, who were named after the Abbot of Volokolamsk, maintained that the Church must retain all its wealth and land and the protection of the state if it was to fulfil its religious tasks effectively. Members of the movement known as the Trans Volga Hermits argued that the Church must reject luxury and the ownership of land and dedicate itself purely to prayer and spiritual activity. At the beginning of the century, the Josephans had emerged as the stronger faction, but clearly some of the ideas of the Trans Volga Hermits appealed to a tsar who constantly needed land to provide estates for his serving gentry. In particular, it seems probable that the plan to settle many serving gentry near Moscow, which was advanced in 1550, never came into effect because of a shortage of land. Acquisition of Church lands would solve many of Ivan's problems.

Of Ivan's close advisers, Sylvester and Adashev were both attracted to the ideas of the Trans Volga Hermits and favoured the **secularisation** of Church lands. The Metropolitan *Makary* and most of his bishops were Josephans but were anxious to reform the Church, in part to protect its land from critics. Two major proposals were submitted to the Stoglav Sobor: first that the clergy should no longer be exempt from the Tsar's laws, and second that the Church should not obtain land as a result of special privileges. But although it was agreed that the laws of the Church should be more strictly enforced, the Stoglav Sobor defended the jurisdiction of the Church and rejected the suggestion that any priests and monks who had committed crimes should be tried in the court of the Tsar, rather than Church courts. Also, it was totally opposed to the loss of any Church lands. Ivan was not prepared to confiscate Church lands and risk a dangerous conflict. But the position of the Trans Volga Hermits was strengthened, and in May 1551 the Church's purchase of further lands without the Tsar's permission was forbidden. Despite this, it appears that the Josephans remained dominant and were able to press successful charges of heresy in 1553 against leading supporters of the ideas of the Trans Volga Hermits.

secularisation seizure by the state of land belonging to the Church

G *The fall of the 'Chosen Council'*

There may be reservations about the overall success of the work of the 'Chosen Council'. Despite the curbing of *kormlenie*, it is likely that corruption continued in the countryside. The *Sudebnik* did provide the basis for a just legal system, but a just legal system needs just administration, and many judges were probably corrupt and came from those very aristocratic classes whose powers Ivan was anxious to curb. Nonetheless, as J.L.A. Fennell has written, the reforms of the 'Chosen Council' were 'far sighted and shrewdly conceived'. The major aims were increased centralisation and administrative efficiency. This was necessary in a state whose frontiers had rapidly expanded. Moreover, the constant strengthening of the *pomestia* and service gentry as opposed to the over-mighty *boyars* was a natural and legitimate reaction to the anarchy of Ivan's childhood. It is not at all clear how far Ivan instigated, or approved of, all these policies. What is clear, however, is that he gradually became disillusioned with this group of advisers and was to adopt dramatically different policies after 1560, having cast them aside.

As early as 1553, there were signs of tension. In March 1553, Ivan fell ill and there were inevitable fears of another succession crisis. Ivan wanted his leading *boyars* and advisers to swear loyalty to his son, Dmitri. Leading members of the 'Chosen Council' showed great reluctance to do this, preferring to support Ivan's cousin, Vladimir, as heir to the throne. Their main reason was distrust of the family of Ivan's wife, Anastasia. It was feared that they would be the true rulers of the state if Ivan were to die. Despite the fact that there was clearly no military conspiracy, Ivan's paranoia, never far below the surface, was aroused. He was always intensely suspicious of any hint of a conspiracy and a return to the aristocratic feuds of his childhood.

On 7 August 1560, Anastasia died. It was a sign of Ivan's growing instability that he held his opponents on the 'Chosen Council' responsible. But Ivan's mental instability is by no means the only explanation of his change of policy. Indeed, although his behaviour could be exceedingly brutal and acutely suspicious, there was usually an underlying rational purpose. On this occasion it is clear that most of the members of the 'Chosen Council', especially Adashev, opposed the Livonian War and strongly favoured a campaign against the Crimea, which Adashev had himself raided daringly and successfully. Above all, it was differences of policy and questions of loyalty that destroyed the 'Chosen Council' and ended the period of reform.

Ivan's treatment of Adashev and Sylvester illustrated his growing violence and disregard of the law. They were tried in their absence, which was against the principles of Russian law. In 1560, Adashev was imprisoned and died, possibly after poisoning. Sylvester was exiled to a monastery near the White Sea, where he also soon died. This was followed by a series of executions of aristocrats, especially after the loss of the restraining influence of the Metropolitan *Makary*, who died in 1563. Sigismund Augustus of Poland–Lithuania, Stephen Báthory's predecessor but one, took advantage of the fears of the *boyars* and received many exiles, the most notable of whom was Prince Andrei Kurbsky in 1564. Those who remained loyal to Ivan joined with the new Metropolitan, Afanasi, in urging him to stop the executions and concentrate on the Crimea. To do this would have been to admit that Adashev had been right and Ivan wrong. As Vernadsky has written, 'The alternative facing him was either to resign or to enforce his dictatorship by extraordinary measures.'

7 ⌁ THE *OPRICHNINA*

Fear of conspiracy by the *boyars* and the difficulties resulting from the Livonian War brought about the most infamous and controversial events of Ivan's reign. In December 1564, Ivan suddenly deserted Moscow for the village of Alexandrovsk, about sixty miles away. A month later, the Metropolitan Afanasi received two letters from Ivan. The first letter contained a denunciation of the *boyars* and the clergy. He accused them of treachery and wrote, 'Consequently, not wishing to endure your treachery, we, with great pity in our heart, have quitted the Tsardom and have gone where God may lead us.'

He commanded that the second letter be read to the people. In this he stated that he was not angry with them and assured them of his goodwill. The letters caused panic, especially among the ordinary people, for whom the Tsar was the pivot of society and their protector against the *boyars*. After a deputation had visited him, Ivan agreed to return, but only after certain conditions had been met.

When his conditions had been met, Ivan returned to Moscow, having aged almost beyond recognition. He had clearly suffered a mental and physical breakdown. The conditions of his return suggested that he was now determined to suppress all opposition to his will. First, he was given full power to punish and execute traitors and confiscate their possessions, where he saw fit. The second and extraordinary demand was that Muscovy should be divided in two and that a subdivision, called the *Oprichnina* be created. Here, Ivan would rule entirely as he wished.

Oprichnina derives from the word *oprich*, which means apart, and it was to be entirely separate from the rest of the nation, the *Zemshchina*, where traditional methods of government would be maintained. A force was recruited, initially of about 1000 men, to serve as the *Oprichniki*, who would be Ivan's personal servants. They came from a variety of backgrounds. Many were from the minor gentry, but there were some great *boyars* and a few foreigners. Their numbers eventually rose to about 6000, all of whom had sworn personal loyalty to the Tsar. They wore a black uniform and rode black horses, which carried a dog's head and a broom on the saddle to symbolise the idea of sweeping traitors from the country. Alexandrovsk was used by Ivan as his chief base. It was strongly fortified and Ivan's life there represented a

TIMELINE

1530	Birth of Ivan
1547	Coronation as Tsar of All Russia
1549	Summoning of the *Zemsky Sobor*
1550	The *Sudebnik* (law code)
1551	Conquest of Kazan
1558	Outbreak of the Livonian War
1560	Fall of the 'chosen council'
1564	Establishment of the *Oprichnina*
1571	Attack on Moscow by Crimean Tatars
1572	Abolition of the *Oprichnina*
1578	Swedish victory at Wenden
1579	Stephen Bathory captures Polotsk
1582	Treaty of Yam Zapolsky
1584	Death of Ivan

conscious parody of that of a monastic order, in which bouts of riotous self-indulgence were followed by guilt and self-denial.

Many areas were put under the direct control of the *Oprichnina*, although Alexandrovsk remained the great stronghold. A part of Moscow was included and other groups, such as the English Muscovy Company and the Stroganov family in the east, with their great commercial and industrial interests, petitioned to be included. In this way, they hoped to be protected and not subjected to harassment from the *Oprichniki*. In central Muscovy, the estates of many *boyars* were confiscated and they were settled in the middle Volga around Kazan.

The establishment of the *Oprichnina* and the debate as to its nature and purpose bring into focus all the major arguments about Ivan's character and motivation. There is a case for arguing, as do historians like Platonov, that the 'Chosen Council' had seized power from the Tsar and that it was the tool of the *boyars*. According to this view, therefore, in creating the *Oprichnina*, Ivan was making his own significant contribution to the establishment of the strong and autocratic monarchy so necessary in Russia and which, in the seventeenth century, proved so much stronger than Poland–Lithuania, where the aristocracy retained great power. A counter-argument is that autocracy subjected the state to the Tsar's whim, and Ivan's radical changes in policy left no sustained improvement in government.

There is no doubt that one of the main reasons for the creation of the *Oprichnina* was the opposition to the Livonian War. Equally, it is quite possible that this opposition came mainly from the *boyar* class and that the people as a whole generally supported Ivan. In 1566, Ivan summoned a *Zemsky Sobor* (National Assembly). This mainly included representatives of the gentry class, but about one-fifth of those present were merchants and it supported Ivan's opposition to concessions in the Livonian War. It is, of course, futile to speculate on the opinions of the ordinary people, but the reaction of the people of Muscovy to Ivan's departure to Alexandrovsk in 1564 does suggest that he did retain much popular support and that Tsarist rule was preferred to that of the aristocracy.

Moreover, those people who see a rational purpose in the creation of the *Oprichnina* point out that most of the land that was seized and taken into the *Oprichnina* was in central Muscovy and of great economic importance. It also included the vital trade route from Archangel to central Muscovy. Many *appanage* princes were driven from their hereditary estates where they had great prestige and authority over the peasantry and had kept the rights to act as judges and collect taxes. In their new estates, their power and prestige were dramatically reduced and they were replaced by reliable new men, who saw themselves as servants of the Tsar. In this way, Ivan was able to ignore the system of *mestnichestvo* and create a nobility whose prestige was based on service to him rather than hereditary succession. This service nobility was to be the cornerstone of Tsarist authority in the following centuries.

This view of Ivan IV as a far-sighted and rational ruler does merit serious consideration. It is equally possible, however, to see in the creation of the *Oprichnina* the fantasies of a paranoid and unpredictable ruler, who saw conspiracy all around him. The *Oprichniki* themselves may have been intended to be unselfish servants of the Tsar, committed to the purification of the administration of the state, but they usually behaved as a bunch of sadistic thugs who encouraged Ivan's tendency to violence.

It is certainly hard to see any constructive success resulting from the creation of the *Oprichnina*. It may have weakened the control of many *appanage* princes by driving them from their estates, but these estates were then often ruined economically by exploitation and mismanagement, so that for many years central Muscovy suffered from dreadful economic difficulties and many peasants fled to the south and east.

The local *boyars* had been responsible for military mobilisation within their regions and this system was severely disrupted, which may help to explain the dramatic success of the *Tatar* raid which led to the burning of Muscovy in 1571 and the capture of 150 000 Russian slaves. It is surely significant that the defeat of the Tatar invasion of 1572, which brought such relief to the Tsar, was the work of *boyars* under the leadership of Prince Mikhail Vorotynsky who was a member of the *Zemshchina* and not the *Oprichnina*.

Executions had always been common in Muscovy, where the loyalty of the aristocracy could not be guaranteed any more than elsewhere in Europe, but the *Oprichniki* undoubtedly employed cruel and sadistic methods which suggested that, for many of them, violence was an end in itself.

The Metropolitan Philip, who had succeeded Afanasi in 1566, was a pious and worthy man. His criticism of random executions and terror led to his deposition in 1568, after which he was tried and sentenced to life imprisonment. In December 1569 Malyuta Shuratov, one of Ivan's favourites, strangled him in his cell.

The greatest atrocity of this period was that inflicted on the city of Novgorod. Novgorod had a long tradition of independence and trading contacts with the west. In 1569, documents were produced which suggested that Novgorod was about to defect to Sigismund Augustus of Poland–Lithuania. It seems likely that these documents were forgeries. A Pskovian chronicle states, 'Wicked men slanderously informed Tsallvan that both Novgorod the Great and Pskov wanted to go over to the Lithuanian side.' These rumours coincided with the death of Ivan's unpopular second wife, Maria. Ivan assumed that she had been poisoned and blamed his own cousin Prince Vladimir Staritsky, who had been advanced as a possible successor to Ivan in 1553. Vladimir's lands had been confiscated already and exchanged for new land where he had no traditional authority, but Ivan believed that he had supporters in Novgorod. In October, Vladimir was forced to take poison and in December Ivan set out for Novgorod.

Ivan's force consisted almost entirely of *Oprichniki*. There were atrocities in Tver, where about 9000 were killed, but Ivan's attention was mainly concentrated on Novgorod. His forces arrived there in early January under his personal command. Estimates vary as to how many were killed in the five weeks of unrestrained violence that followed, but it may have been as many as 60 000. Archbishop Pimen of Novgorod was taken to Moscow, put on trial and sent to a monastery. His escape from execution suggests the flimsy nature of the evidence against him. But in the trials for conspiracy, leading *Oprichniki* were also implicated. About 200 were executed in all and this included close advisers of the Tsar, such as Alexei Basmanov and his son Feodor, who had been trusted members of the *Oprichnina*.

KEY ISSUE

Why was the Oprichnina created? How far can its work be justified?

8 ↝ THE ABOLITION OF THE *OPRICHNINA*

It does seem that the discovery of treachery in these men contributed to Ivan's decision to abolish the *Oprichnina* in 1572, although the divisions in the state persisted until 1575. A further factor was the failure of the *Oprichniki* to organise effective defence against the Tatars in 1571.

The next decade did see a decline in violence, but Ivan's behaviour continued to show irrational and unpredictable elements. For example, in 1575–76 a converted *Tatar* prince was given the name Simeon and the title Grand Prince of All Russia, while Ivan used the lesser title of Prince of Muscovy. Ivan's motives in taking this action remain obscure. It may have been superstition, since he had been told to beware of this year, or to make his position less exposed. Suddenly, on 31 August 1576, he resumed the title of Tsar and reasserted his supreme power. Against the laws of the Church, Ivan took six further wives, although none played a significant role in the government of the state. Perhaps, however, the most significant evidence of the uncontrolled violence of one part of Ivan's character is to be found in the unintentional killing of his son in a fit of anger in 1581, an act which further increased Ivan's sense of guilt.

9 ↝ CONCLUSION

Despite his outbursts of violence and lapses into insanity, Ivan's overall aims seem quite clear. He wished to expand the frontiers of the state and to increase his power within the state. The conquest of Kazan and expansion into the steppe country were great triumphs, as was the move into Siberia. But his most ambitious project, the Livonian War, although a reasonable policy at the outset, proved to be a complete disaster.

At home Ivan wished to control the aristocracy he feared, and create a strong autocratic monarchy. But the most successful period of his reign, the time of the 'Chosen Council' in the 1550s, came when he co-operated closely with at least a section of the aristocracy. Ivan did prevent the development of an aristocratic state, such as Poland–Lithuania, in Russia, but the failure of the *Oprichnina* demonstrates that he could not rule without the co-operation of at least a large portion of his most powerful subjects.

It is surely not insignificant that Ivan's death was followed by a lengthy period of turmoil and crisis, the so-called 'Time of Troubles', an immensely complex period of civil war, during which Poland–Lithuania and Sweden almost brought about the collapse of the Russian state. But Tsarism did survive under the Romanov dynasty and the policies of powerful successors, such as Peter the Great in the late seventeenth century, echo those of Ivan.

Peter the Great acknowledged the influence of Ivan and Ivan has remained a potent and controversial figure in Russian life ever since. It is surely no coincidence that, in the time of another great autocrat, Stalin, the famous Russian film maker Sergei Eisenstein produced an unforgettable portrait of Ivan the Terrible which caused enormous controversy within the Soviet Union. It is fair to say that Ivan the Terrible left a permanent imprint on the Russian state.

> **KEY ISSUE**
>
> *What were the major successes and failures of Ivan's reign?*

10 ⇦ BIBLIOGRAPHY

Many books on eastern Europe assume specialist knowledge. All the books on this list can be highly recommended. The books by Rady, Hingley and Hoetzsch provide the most straightforward introduction. **J. Blum, *Lord and Peasant in Russia from the Ninth to the Nineteenth Century* (Princeton, 1961). **N. Davies, *God's Playground* (Oxford, 1983). **M. Rady, *Access to History: The Tsars, Russia, Poland and the Ukraine 1462–1725* (Hodder and Stoughton, 1990). *J.L. Fennell, *Ivan the Great of Moscow* (Macmillan, 1961). **R. Pipes, *Russia under the Old Regime* (Penguin, 1977). *N.V. Riasonovsky, *History of Russia* (OUP, 2nd ed., 1969). *G. Vernadsky, *The Mongols and Russia* (Yale, 1953). *G. Vernadsky, *Russia at the Dawn of the Modern Age* (Yale, 1959). **R. Hingley, *A Concise History of Russia* (Thames and Hudson, 1972). *Otto Hoetzsch, *The Evolution of Russia* (Thames and Hudson, 1966).

11 ⇦ STRUCTURED AND ESSAY QUESTIONS

A *Structured questions.*

1. (a) What were the challenges Ivan the Terrible faced in domestic affairs when he came to the throne?
   (b) How and why did his domestic policies change during his reign?
   (c) Can Ivan be credited with any enduring achievements in his government of Russia?

2. (a) What were the main characteristics of Ivan the Terrible's foreign policy?

(b) 'With regard to foreign policy, the reign of Ivan the Terrible was a disaster for Russia.' Do you agree?

B *Essay questions.*
1. What did Ivan IV contribute to the development of Russia?
2. How important was the domestic opposition to Ivan IV and his policies?
3. To what extent can the *Oprichnina* of Ivan IV be regarded as a rational policy?
4. Can Ivan IV fairly be considered an 'oriental despot'?
5. Do you agree with the view that the Livonian War was the greatest error of Ivan IV?

12 ⤙ DOCUMENTARY EXERCISE ON THE KURBSKY LETTERS

One of the oddest features of Ivan's reign is that he did try to justify his actions in correspondence with Prince Andrei Kurbsky. Andrei Kurbsky was a member of an ancient princely family and had been a prominent adviser of Ivan. After the fall of the 'Chosen Council', he became disillusioned and crossed to Lithuania in 1564. His wife, son and mother were put to death by Ivan. Kurbsky became a leading critic of Ivan and entered into a lengthy correspondence with him, in which the major issues of dispute in Ivan's reign are discussed. Although Professor Keenan has suggested that these letters are forgeries, their authenticity seems almost certain and they provide a fascinating insight into the political dispute about the 'Chosen Council' and the *Oprichnina*. Here are some selected extracts from the correspondence:

Ivan:
And so the priest Sylvester joined Alexei too in friendship and they began to hold counsel in secret and without our knowledge, believing us to be incapable of judgement; and they began to give worldly counsel in the place of spiritual and little by little to lead all the boyars into resistance to authority taking the splendour of our power from us and leading you into opposition...

.... And so neither in external affairs nor in internal affairs, nor in the small and pettiest things (and I refer to such things as footwear and sleeping) was anything according to my will; but everything was done according to their desire, while we remained, as it were, a child...

Is it then light or sweetness for servants to rule? And is it darkness or bitterness for a divinely ordained sovereign to rule?... Yet concerning the German towns how can I but recall the opposition of the priest Sylvester and Alexei and all of you [who said] on every occasion that we should not wage war.

Kurbsky's reply:

You might also have remembered how, thanks to the Grace of God, in the time of your days of piety, things prospered according to your will, owing to the prayers of the saints and the Chosen Council of your eminent advisers; and how, afterwards, when the most wicked and cunning flatterers seduced you, the destroyers of you and of their fatherland, events turned out and what plagues were sent by God; hunger, I say, and the arrows of pestilence, and afterwards the sword of the barbarian, the avenger of the law of God, and the sudden burning of the most renowned city of Moscow, at the laying waste of all the land of Russia.

Q

1. *What justification does Ivan advance for his behaviour? How does this illustrate the view that he took of the role of the Tsar.*
2. *Why would Kurbsky have chosen Poland–Lithuania as his place of refuge?*
3. *What reservations might a modern historian have about using the writings of Kurbsky as a source?*
4. *How effectively do these extracts summarise the conflicts of Ivan's reign?*

---

13 ↩ COMPARISON EXERCISE ON EAST AND WEST

It is clear that the history of Russia differs from that of western Europe but how much and in what ways?

1 As a case study compare the powers of Ivan and Francis I. Write a paragraph on each of the following issues, drawing attention to what was most alike and what differed most in the experience of the two rulers:
 (i) the relationship of the aristocracy with the Crown;
 (ii) faction;
 (iii) religious conflict;
 (iv) representative assemblies;
 (v) trade;
 (vi) absolutism.

2 Compare the Russian Orthodox Church and the Roman Catholic Church.
 (i) Which was most powerful and why?
 (ii) How did the structure and attitudes of those Churches affect the development of the state?

3 Compare the status of the peasantry in Russia with that of western Europe (see pages 21–2).
 (i) In which part did the peasantry have greater freedom?

(ii) How, if at all, was the status of the peasantry changing in western Europe in the sixteenth century in comparison with Russia?

Glossary

Purgatory, *see page 87*
reaya, see page 297
Reconquest, *see page 88*
Red whore, *see page 247*
redress of grievances, *see page 226*
regents, *see page 431*
regular orders, *see page 156*
relief, *see page 118*
rentes, see page 260
rentier, see page 25
sacramentarians, *see page 320*
safavids, see page 291
schism, *see page 2*
scholasticism, *see page 18*
sea beggars, *see page 430*
sectarian, *see page 327*
secular, *see page 4*
secular priests, *see page 158*

secularisation, *see page 516*
secularism, *see page 114*
seigneurial, *see page 20*
seminary, *see page 376*
serfs, *see page 515*
servicio, see page 216
Shari'a, see page 290
simony, *see page 191*
sipahi, see page 295
sola fide, see page 147
sola scriptura, see page 151
sovereign, *see page 7*
spirituali, see page 353
stadholder, see page 433
steppe, *see page 496*
streltsi, see page 505
Sultan, *see page 287*
syndic, see page 338
taille, see page 259

Tatars, see page 496
Teutonic Knights, *see page 507*
The Golden Horde, *see page 497*
timar, see page 295
transubstantiation, *see page 17*
Tridentine decrees, *see page 368*
Unitarians, *see page 329*
vassal, *see page 8*
veillée, see page 190
venality, *see page 9*
virtù, see page 127
Walloon, *see page 438*
woodcut, *see page 7*
work ethic, *see page 347*
yeomen, *see page 192*
zelanti, see page 353
Zemsky Sobor, see page 514

Index